The Unknown Monet

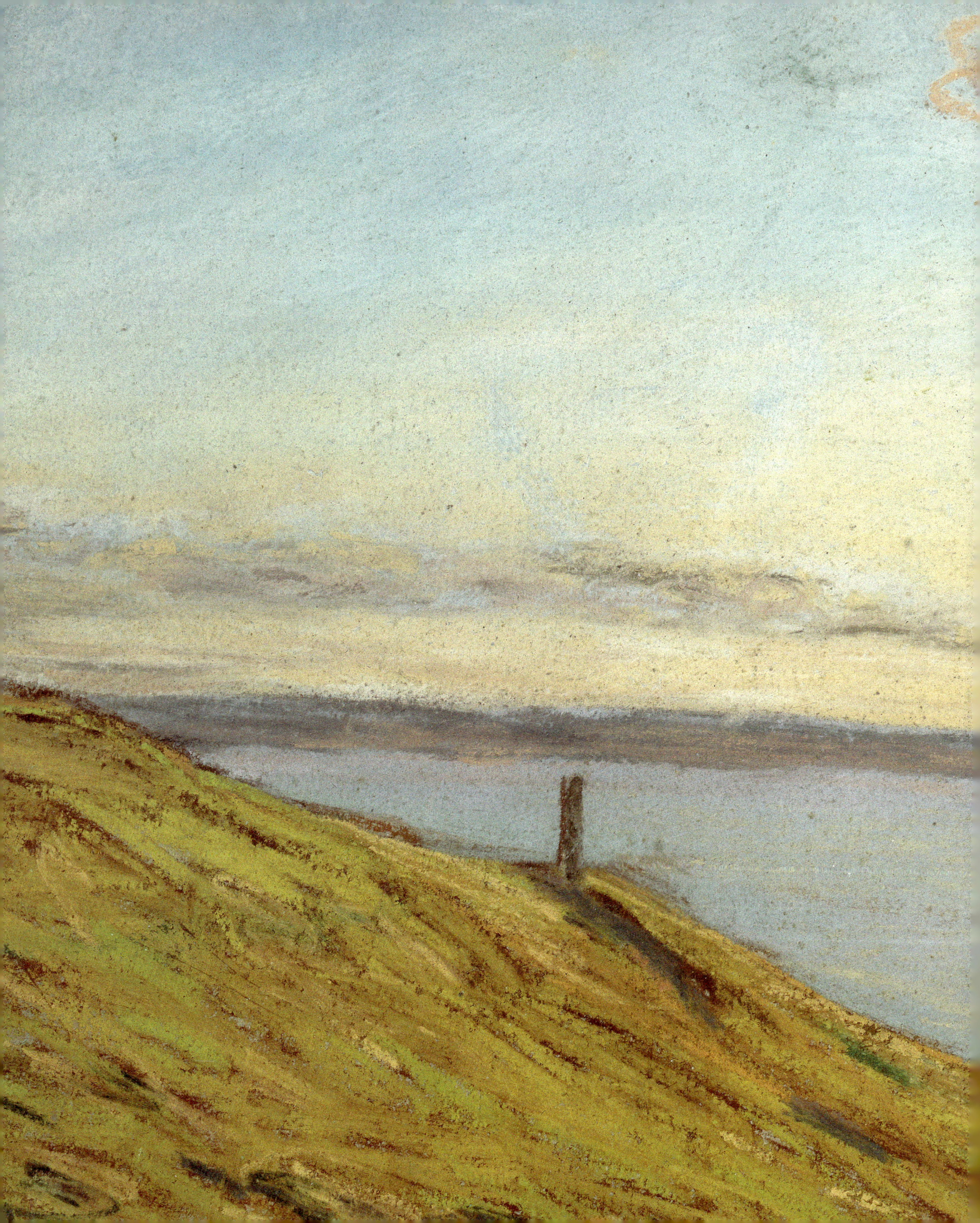

The Unknown Monet

PASTELS AND DRAWINGS

JAMES A. GANZ AND RICHARD KENDALL

STERLING AND FRANCINE CLARK ART INSTITUTE *Williamstown, Massachusetts*

DISTRIBUTED BY YALE UNIVERSITY PRESS *New Haven and London*

This book is published on the occasion of the exhibition *The Unknown Monet: Pastels and Drawings*

Royal Academy of Arts
London
17 March–10 June 2007

Sterling and Francine Clark Art Institute
Williamstown, Massachusetts
24 June–16 September 2007

The Unknown Monet: Pastels and Drawings was organized by the Sterling and Francine Clark Art Institute, in association with the Royal Academy of Arts, London. This exhibition is supported by an indemnity from the Federal Council on the Arts and the Humanities. The project is supported in part by the National Endowment for the Arts.

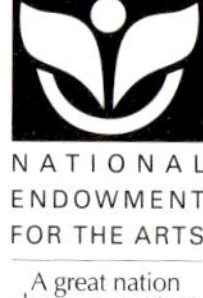

Produced by the Publications Department of the Sterling and Francine Clark Art Institute
225 South Street, Williamstown, Massachusetts 01267

Curtis R. Scott, *Director of Publications*
Katherine Pasco, *Production Editor*
Mari Yoko Hara, *Publications and Curatorial Assistant*

Copyedited by Martin Fox
Designed by Susan Marsh
Composed in Adobe Garamond Pro
and Futura by Matt Mayerchak
Index by Kathleen M. Friello
Map adapted by Mary Reilly
Production by The Working Dog Press,
Whately, Massachusetts, and New York City
Color separations and printing by Trifolio, Verona

COVER ILLUSTRATIONS: (Front) Detail of *Étretat, the Needle Rock and Porte d'Aval* (fig. 138); (Back) *Cliffs and Sea, Sainte-Adresse* (fig. 78)

TITLE PAGE: Detail of *Sainte-Adresse, View across the Estuary* (fig. 119)

PAGE VI: Detail of *The Côte Sauvage* (fig. 198)

DETAILS USED AS CHAPTER OPENERS:
Chapter 1, *Alley of Trees, Gournay* (fig. 14); Chapter 2, *Little Theatrical Pantheon* (fig. 34); Chapter 3, *Yport and the Falaise d'Aval* (fig. 59); Chapter 4, *The Port at Touques* (fig. 83); Chapter 5, *Broad Landscape* (fig. 113); Chapter 6, *The Seine Estuary* (fig. 116); Chapter 7, *Jean-Pierre Hoschedé and Michel Monet Drawing* (fig. 157); Chapter 8, *Mouth of the Seine at Honfleur* (fig. 180); Chapter 9, *Grainstacks, Last Sunrays* (fig. 229); Chapter 10, *Water Lilies* (fig. 268)

Distributed by Yale University Press
New Haven and London
www.yalebooks.com

PRINTED AND BOUND IN ITALY
10 9 8 7 6 5 4 3 2 1

Library of Congress Cataloging-in-Publication Data
Ganz, James A.
The unknown Monet : pastels and drawings / James A. Ganz and Richard Kendall.
p. cm.
Catalog of an exhibition at the Royal Academy of Arts, London, Mar. 17–June 10, 2007; and at the Sterling and Francine Clark Art Institute, Williamstown, Mass., June 24–Sept. 16, 2007.
Includes bibliographical references and index.
ISBN-13: 978-0-300-11862-9 (cloth : alk. paper)
ISBN-13: 978-0-931102-72-1 (pbk. : alk. paper)
1. Monet, Claude, 1840–1926—Exhibitions.
I. Kendall, Richard. II. Monet, Claude, 1840–1926.
III. Royal Academy of Arts (Great Britain). IV. Sterling and Francine Clark Art Institute. V. Title.

NC248.M64A4 2007
759.4–dc22

2006039600

Contents

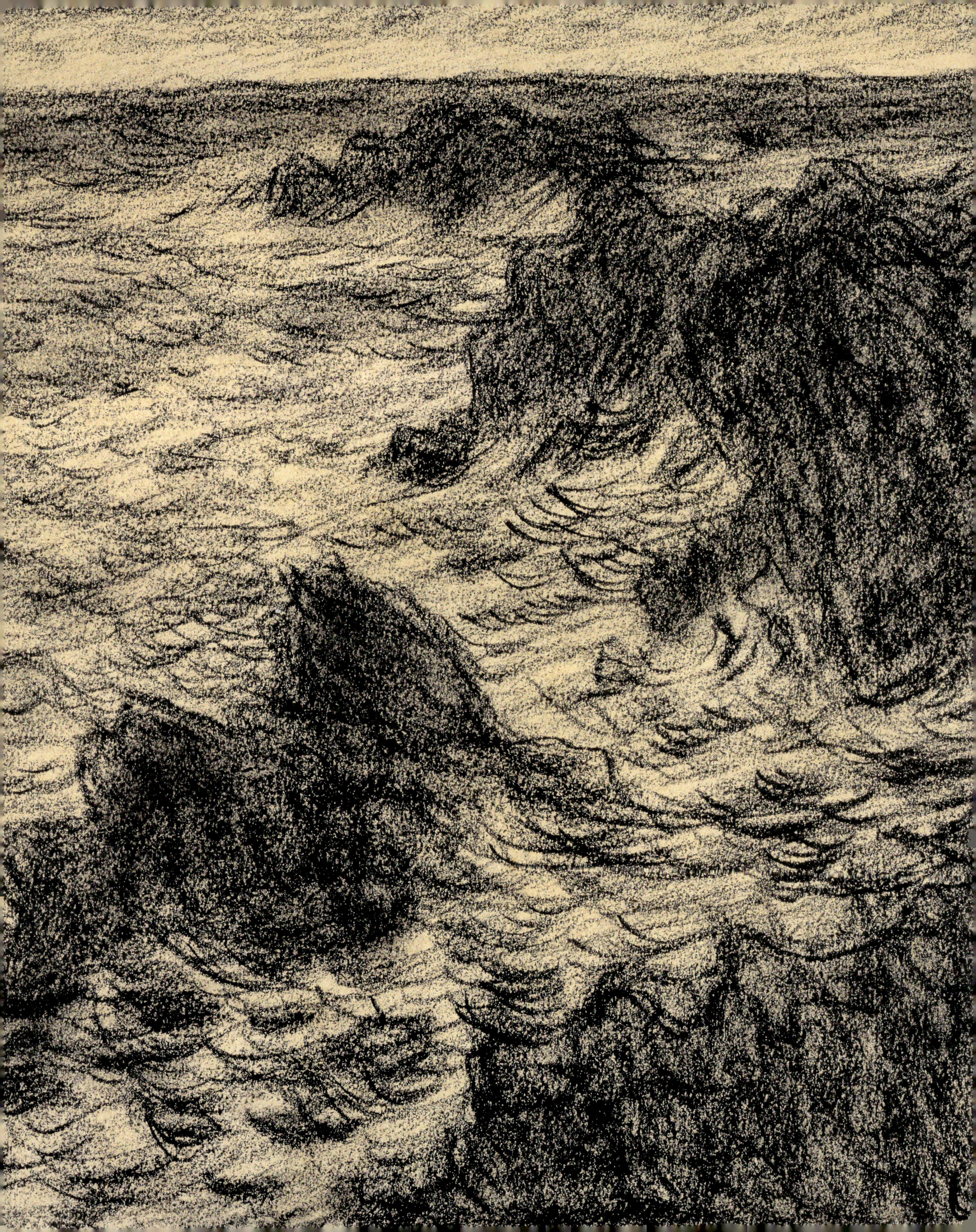

Directors' Foreword

Claude Monet made three visits to London between 1899 and 1901, during which time he worked on a series of highly acclaimed paintings. Upon arriving for his third sojourn there, Monet realized that his canvases and oils had been delayed, and he decided to bide his time by working with pastels — a preparatory exercise, he thought, for the paintings that he hoped to begin when his equipment arrived. He had not worked with pastel for many years, and at first he struggled with the medium. Nonetheless, within a few days, Monet produced over two dozen pastels: all nuanced visions of the Thames and the Waterloo and Charing Cross bridges that reflect, in their subtle variations in tone, a remarkable sense of the shifting weather and light of London in winter.

Monet's later acknowledgment that his work in pastel played an instrumental role in his working process was a rare admission. To advance his public image as an Impressionist, he had long denied the importance of drawing in his artistic practice. While he succeeded in persuading his critics, and indeed, to a great extent convincing himself that isolating line from color was foreign to his working method, this exhibition reveals for the first time that Monet repeatedly used pencil, chalk, and pastel not only to develop ideas for paintings but also to create independent works of art.

The seed for *The Unknown Monet: Pastels and Drawings* was planted in 1939, when Sterling and Francine Clark made a prescient purchase of an expressive black-crayon drawing of Rouen. That work joined a group of oils by the Impressionist painter and an impressive collection of works on paper by his contemporaries. Many years later the crayon drawing piqued the curiosity of Clark curators James A. Ganz and Richard Kendall, who found a shared excitement with MaryAnne Stevens at the Royal Academy of Arts in London.

We are delighted at the outcome of the project: a richer understanding of the artist through a host of unexpected and exciting revelations unearthed by the curators in their long search for the "unknown" Monet. In assembling the more than one hundred pastels, drawings, and paintings — many of which have never before been seen in public — we are afforded a more complete view of one of the most renowned artists of our time. We are grateful to the staffs of both the Clark and the Royal Academy for the hard work that made this possible.

Of course, assembling such disparate works, many of which are still in private hands, required not only the strong sleuthing skills of the curators but also the generosity of numerous collectors, dealers, and Monet experts who either loaned works to this exhibition or led us to those who could do so. We are also grateful to our colleagues at the Musée Marmottan Monet in Paris for their assistance with the project, as well as the National Endowment for the Arts, which supported the exhibition with a generous grant. In London, the exhibition has been generously sponsored by the Bank of America.

It is our hope that this transatlantic exhibition and its accompanying publication will make a lasting contribution to scholarship and to the public understanding of Monet's art. Though far from the last word on this complex subject, *The Unknown Monet* offers a rare new look at a pivotal artistic career and opens the door for further discoveries.

MICHAEL CONFORTI
Director, Sterling and Francine Clark Art Institute

SIR NICHOLAS GRIMSHAW CBE
President, Royal Academy of Arts

Lenders to the Exhibition

Faruk A. Alatan
The Art Institute of Chicago
Prince Xavier Beguin Billecocq, Paris
Bibliothèque de l'Institut National de l'Histoire de l'Art, Paris
Family of Richard S. Davis
Des Moines Art Center
Fine Arts Museums of San Francisco
The Fogg Art Museum, Harvard University Art Museums, Cambridge, Massachusetts
Fondation Beyeler, Riehen/Basel
Indianapolis Museum of Art
The Israel Museum, Jerusalem
Memorial Art Gallery of the University of Rochester
The Metropolitan Museum of Art, New York
Dr. Morton and Tobia Mower
Musée Carnavalet–Histoire de Paris
Musée des Beaux-Arts de Nantes
Musée d'Orsay, Paris
Musée Eugène Boudin, Honfleur
Musée Marmottan Monet, Paris
Museum Boijmans Van Beuningen, Rotterdam
Museum of Fine Arts, Boston
The Museum of Modern Art, New York
National Gallery of Art, Washington, D.C.
National Museum of Western Art, Tokyo
Philadelphia Museum of Art
San Diego Museum of Art
Sterling and Francine Clark Art Institute, Williamstown, Massachusetts
Szépművészeti Múzeum, Budapest (Museum of Fine Arts, Budapest)
Triton Foundation, The Netherlands
Villa Flora, Winterthur, Switzerland
W.E.B. Du Bois Library, University of Massachusetts Amherst
The World Children's Art Museum, Okazaki, Japan
Private collections

Special thanks to the following galleries and dealers for their assistance with loans from private collections: Brame & Lorenceau, Paris; Christie's, New York; Elrick-Manley Fine Art, Inc., New York; Richard L. Feigen & Co., New York; The Fine Arts Gallery of New Orleans; Galerie Jan Krugier & Cie., Geneva; Lefevre Fine Art Ltd., London; Christian Neffe, London; Jill Newhouse and Neffe de-Gandt Fine Art, London; Pyms Gallery, London; Sotheby's, New York; and Stiebel, Ltd., New York

Acknowledgments

From its earliest conceptual stages through its realization in the form of this book and accompanying exhibition, *The Unknown Monet: Pastels and Drawings* has been prepared by the curators and staff at both the Sterling and Francine Clark Art Institute and the Royal Academy of Arts. We are grateful to the Clark's director Michael Conforti and senior curator Richard Rand for supporting this ambitious effort from the outset, and to Kathleen M. Morris for bringing it to fruition so effectively. We have also benefited from our collaboration with MaryAnne Stevens, who brought to this project her great expertise and sensitivity to its subject matter. At the Clark, with the support of Gwendolyn Smith, Mattie Kelley orchestrated the loans from across the United States, Europe, and Japan. At the Royal Academy, Hillary Taylor has worked tirelessly and patiently to arrange initial shipping. Production of the catalogue was overseen by Curtis Scott and accomplished by his dedicated staff in the Clark's publications department. It has been a pleasure to work closely with our patient editor Katherine Pasco and publications intern Mari Yoko Hara. For all their outstanding efforts in producing this beautiful volume, we also wish to thank Michael Agee, Merry Armata, Martin Fox, Susan Marsh, Matt Mayerchak, Susan Medlicott, Nerissa Dominguez Vales, Kathleen M. Friello, Massimo Tonolli, and Suzanne Warren. In the exhibition, the digital presentation of Monet's complete sketchbooks from the Musée Marmottan Monet was accomplished by the brilliant teamwork of David Keiser-Clark, Jacob Lewis, Jake Koprowski, and Melissa Dean. This historic effort could not have been undertaken without the generous cooperation of Marianne Delafond, Adrian Gibbs, Ed Whitley, and Didier Lenart.

Many other staff members and interns contributed their energy and expertise to this project at both the Clark and the Royal Academy. We wish to recognize Brian Allen, Esther Bell, Harry Blake, David Breuer, Andreja Brulc, Karen Bucky, Michael Cassin, Cayetana Castillo, Julie Chase, Sharon Clark, Daniel Cohen-McFall, Molly Coogan, Anouk Dey, Paul Dion, Jay Dubé, David Edge, Arthur Evans, Andrew Fox, Jennifer Francis, Bryan Frank, Lindsay Garratt, Laurie Glover, Diane Gottardi, Sue Graves, Lisa Green, Frank Gregory, Sarah Hammond, Darci Hannah, Michael Heslip, Christine Hoek, Sarah Hoffman, Becca Johnston, Tim Johnson, Tony King, Valerie Krall, John Ladd, Barbara Lampron, Monique LeBlanc, Sarah Lees, Mary Leitch, Jacob Lewis, Jennifer Lindsey, Bonghee Lis, Kori Yee Litt, Keelan Loftin, Julie Mackaman, Sally Morse Majewski, Jane Marriott, Tom Merrill, Phyllis Michaelson, Jim Moran, Joshua O'Driscoll, Leslie Paisley, Katia Pisvin, Bill Powers, Susan Roeper, Norman Rosenthal, Andrew Schaer, Jennifer Schreck, Jae Shannon, John Skavlem, Danielle Steinmann, Alexandra Suda, Colleen Terry, Heather Thomas, Ronna Tulgan-Ostheimer, Viktoria Villanyi, Sandra Webber, Emeline Winston, and Diane Wortis.

During the course of our research, we consulted with a number of specialists in the field and benefited tremendously from their words of encouragement and advice. We are especially indebted to Richard Brettell, John House, George Shackelford, Paul Tucker, and John Zarobell for sharing their insights with us. To Prince Xavier Beguin Billecocq we are most grateful for his generosity in providing access to his great-grandfather's unpublished Grand Journal, a major source of new insights into Monet's life as a draftsman. Among the other individuals who were forthcoming with information, access to works, and illustrations, it is our pleasure to acknowledge Susanna Allen, Sylvie Aubenas, Joseph Baillio, Frederic M. Bancroft, Frances Beatty, Emmanuel Benador, Guy Bennett, Jacques de la Béraudière, Sylvie Brame, Mark Brock, Christa Carroll, Jacquie Cartwright, Phillipe Cazeau, Marjorie B. Cohn, Alexander Corcoran, Desmond Corcoran, Marie-Christine Decroocq, Lucy Dew, Simon Dickinson, Annette Dixon, Ann Dumas, Dorothy Braude Edinburg, Alice Egbert, Ali Elai, Marianne Elrick-Manley, Hilarie Faberman, Richard Feigen, Gail Feigenbaum, Evelyne Ferlay, Hester Finch, Peter Findlay, John Fong, Jamie Franklin, Aprile Gallant, Marie-Rose Gréca, David Hanson, Catherine Herbert, Alan Hobart, Waring Hopkins, Ken Jacobson, Jan Krugier, Catherine Lampert, Shelley Langdale, Bruce Livie, Katharine Lochnan, Denis Lorenceau, François Lorenceau, Nicholas Maclean, Paul Martineau, Robert McHarg, Lilah Mittelstaedt, Charles Moffett, Bona Montagu, Nathalie Muller, Christian Neffe, Jill Newhouse, Martha Parrish, Roy Perkinson, Jill Quasha, Pierre-Lin Renié, Ikkan Sanada, Margo Schab, Marjorie Shelley, Matt Sikora, André-Déconchat Simon, Samantha Sizemore, John Steinert, Gerald Stiebel, Harriet K. Stratis, Carla Trinidad, William Weston, Guy Wildenstein, and Aaron Young.

We are also profoundly indebted to the many individual and institutional lenders to the exhibition, and wish to recognize the curators, directors, and registrars who facilitated our requests: Clifford S. Ackley, Masanori Aoyagi, Scott Atkinson, Tammie Bennett, Anne-Marie Bergeret, Sandra Bos, John Buchanan, Chase Carter, Derrick Cartwright, Judy Cline, Philip Conisbee, Dr. Willem Cordia, James Cuno, Kathy Curry, Marianne Delafond, Corinne Diserens, Henk Van Doornik, Douglas Druick, Albert Elen, Sjarel Ex, Evelyne Ferlay, Jeff Fleming, Jean-Marie Granier, Margaret Morgan Grasselli, Darrell Green, Gloria Groom, Anne d'Harnoncourt, Grant Holcomb, Erin Hyde, Colta Ives, Robert Flynn Johnson, Yasuhisa Kanaguchi, Ellen Lee, Serge Lemoine, Thomas W. Lentz, Jean-Marc Léri, Glenn D. Lowry, Rebekah Marshall, Caroline Mathieu, Suzanne Folds McCullagh, Nadège Monneger, Philippe de Montebello, Miklós Mojzer, Hiroya Murakami, Takaaki Naito, Mark Pascale, Kim Pashko, Sylvie Patry, Meira Perry-Lehmann, Martine Poulain, Michelle Povilaitis, Earl A. Powell III, Sue Welsh Reed, Maria Reilly, Kathryn Ridenour, Joseph Rishel, William W. Robinson, Andrew Robison, Malcolm Rogers, Vincent Rousseau, Nicole Rüegsegger, Shannon Schuler, Monica Simpson, James S. Snyder, Whitney Snyder, Miriam Stewart, Sandra Tatsakis, Martha Tedeschi, Gary Tinterow, Joseph Tursellino, Christophe Vitali, Margreet Wafelbakker, and Yigal Zalmona.

For their help in critical organizational issues, we owe a debt of thanks to Ben Adams, Walter Sulzynsky, Brian Waldron, and Alice Whelihan.

Finally, James Ganz offers his deepest thanks to his personal support team of Sherrill Ingalls, Molly Ganz, and Sally Ganz, and Richard Kendall expresses his gratitude, as always, for the unparalleled encouragement and editorial perspicacity of Jill DeVonyar.

JAMES A. GANZ
Curator of Prints, Drawings, and Photographs
Sterling and Francine Clark Art Institute

RICHARD KENDALL
Curator at Large
Sterling and Francine Clark Art Institute

Note to the Reader

All works by Claude Monet include reference numbers from the catalogue raisonné by Daniel Wildenstein. The first four volumes (Vol. 1: *1840–81, paintings*; Vol. 2: *1882–86, paintings*; Vol. 3: *1887–98, paintings*; and Vol. 4.: *1899–1926, paintings*) were published in 1974. Vol. 5, a supplement including additional paintings, as well as drawings and pastels, was published in 1991.

References to the catalogue raisonné are abbreviated as follows:

W	PAINTINGS
D	DRAWINGS
P	PASTELS
L	LETTERS

In 1996, Taschen released a revised edition of Wildenstein's original catalogue raisonné, with entries in French, English, and German. However, this edition does not include Monet's pastels or drawings, nor does it include any of the letters or footnotes from the original edition. As a result, the original 1974–91 edition proves to be the most valuable resource for scholars of Monet's works on paper, and therefore the vast majority of citations in *The Unknown Monet* draw from the original edition.

The Unknown Monet often cites the Grand Journal, a two-volume unpublished manuscript completed by Comte Théophile Beguin Billecocq in 1906. While the original manuscript is now in the collection of Prince Xavier Beguin Billecocq in Paris, the citations here are from a typed transcription completed by Pierre-Olivier Caperan in 2005 and available in the library of the Sterling and Francine Clark Art Institute in Williamstown, Massachusetts (Beguin Billecocq 2005).

Dimensions provided for prints correspond to image size, not sheet size.

Translations from original or secondary sources in French are by the authors unless otherwise indicated. Chapters 1–2 and 7–9 were authored by James A. Ganz. Chapters 3–6 and 10 were authored by Richard Kendall.

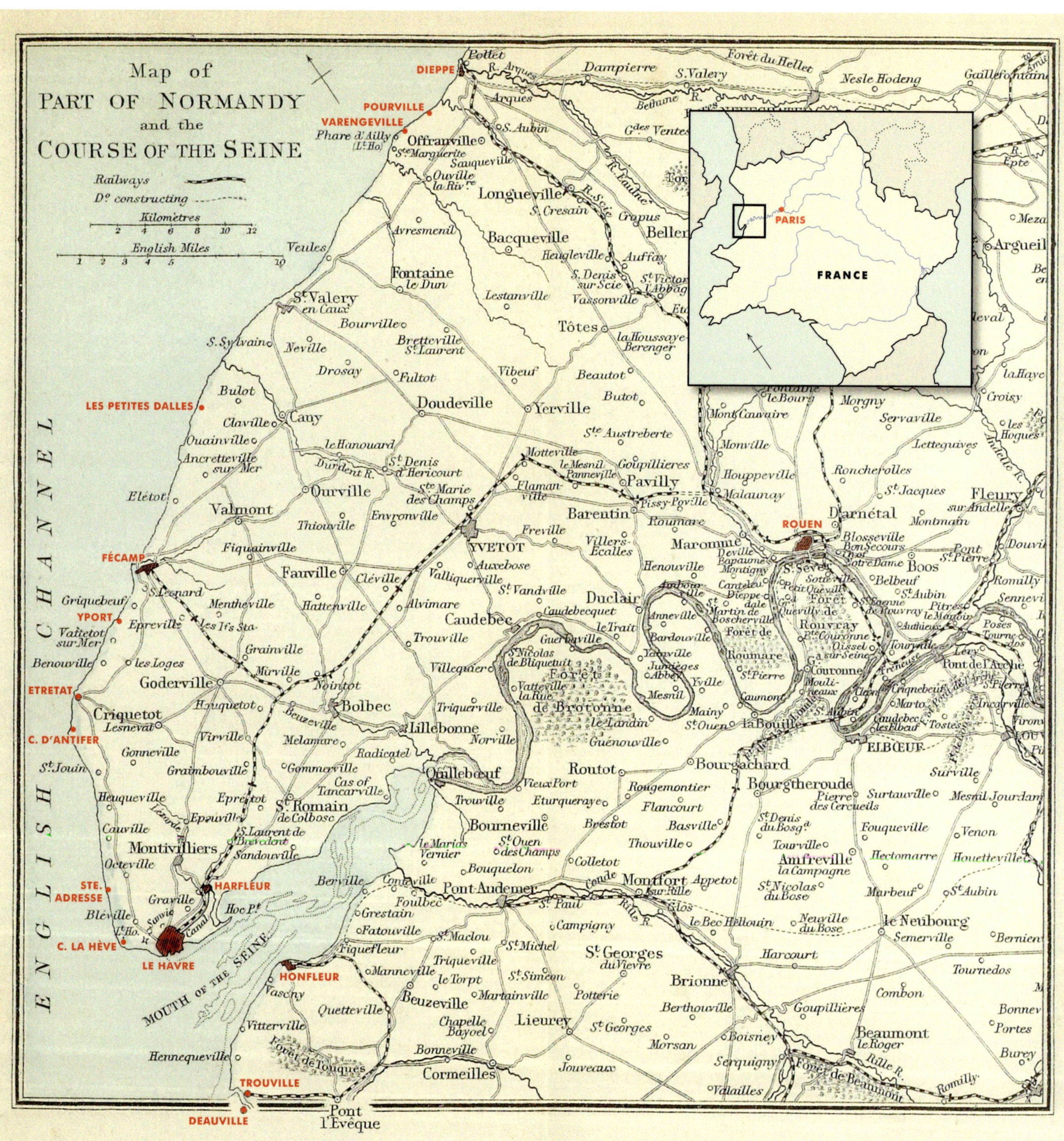

Map of
PART OF NORMANDY
and the
COURSE OF THE SEINE
Railways
D° constructing
Kilometres
2 4 6 8 10 12
English Miles
1 2 3 4 5 10
ENGLISH CHANNEL
MOUTH OF THE SEINE
DIEPPE
POURVILLE
VARENGEVILLE
LES PETITES DALLES
FÉCAMP
YPORT
ETRETAT
C. D'ANTIFER
STE. ADRESSE
C. LA HÈVE
LE HAVRE
HARFLEUR
HONFLEUR
TROUVILLE
DEAUVILLE
ROUEN
PARIS
FRANCE
Offranville
Longueville
Bacqueville
Fontaine le Dun
St. Valery en Caux
Tôtes
Doudeville
Yerville
Cany
Pavilly
Valmont
Ourville
Barentin
Maromme
Darnétal
YVETOT
Fauville
Duclair
Caudebec
Goderville
Criquetot
Bolbec
Lillebonne
Quillebœuf
Montivilliers
St. Romain
Bourneville
Pont Audemer
Montfort
Routot
Bourgachard
Bourgtheroude
Amfreville
Elbœuf
Boos
Fleury
St. Georges
Brionne
le Neubourg
Beuzeville
Lieurey
Cormeilles
Beaumont le Roger
Pont l'Evêque
Forêt de Brotonne
Forêt de Rouvray
Forêt de Beaumont

The Unknown Monet

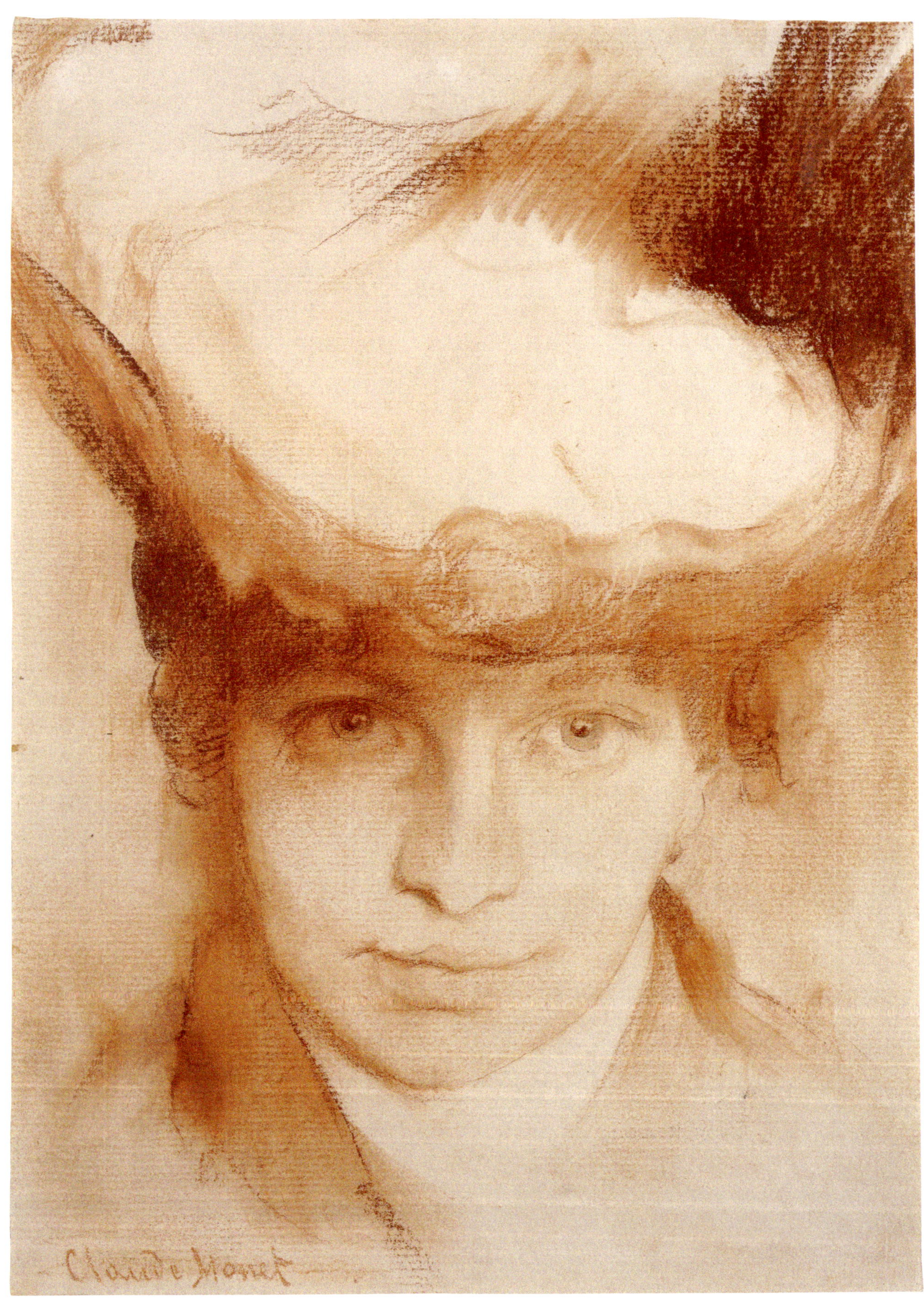
Claude Monet

Introduction

Her eyes bright and her sensuous mouth close to a smile, the subject of Oscar Claude Monet's *Portrait of a Woman* (fig. 1) is both arresting and enigmatic. The remarkable qualities of this drawing have been recognized for more than half a century, yet almost every aspect of the work — as with so many examples of Monet's draftsmanship — has remained elusive. It was once thought to represent the artist's first wife, Camille Doncieux, who posed for several paintings in the 1860s but died after the birth of their second son. A subsequent writer associated the portrait with Monet's companion of later years, Alice Hoschedé, and yet another authority has suggested a link with "the prettiest of the Hoschedé girls," Alice's daughter Suzanne. Monet's favorite model in the late 1880s, Suzanne appeared in nearly twenty canvases as a notably poised, mature young woman, though none show her facial features clearly. The author of the Monet catalogue raisonné, Daniel Wildenstein, had no doubts that Suzanne was the sitter for *Portrait of a Woman*, noting that her "hat of a rather unusual style" belonged to the period "around 1890 to 1895."[1]

With three proposed models and as many implied meanings, and a range of dates over thirty years, *Portrait of a Woman* is emblematic of the uncertainty that has long surrounded Monet's graphic oeuvre. As with the majority of his known drawings, this portrait has not previously been included in an exhibition of the artist's work and has an unclear place in his technical development. Executed in "charcoal" according to one commentator and in "red chalk" for many others, it is quite distinct from the hundreds of drawings found in Monet's sketchbooks, the scores of pastels, and the few surviving preparatory studies from his early maturity.[2] Not previously noticed is its kinship with certain sheets — one of which represents Suzanne — that are related to Monet's collaboration with printmakers in mid-career, where black chalk was used with comparable subtlety.[3] As a subject it is also exceptional: hardly celebrated as a portraitist, Monet made a few informal pencil sketches of the Hoschedé children in the early 1880s, including some in pastel on canvas, though none approached the sophistication of *Portrait of a Woman*. Such drafts were not used as the basis for oil paintings, and their role in Monet's larger creative project is unmentioned in his voluminous letters and in contemporary accounts of his art. Whatever its origin and purpose, however, this intimate, stylish image

1
Portrait of a Woman, c. 1890–95. Red chalks with stumping, 285 x 210 mm. Private collection [D447]

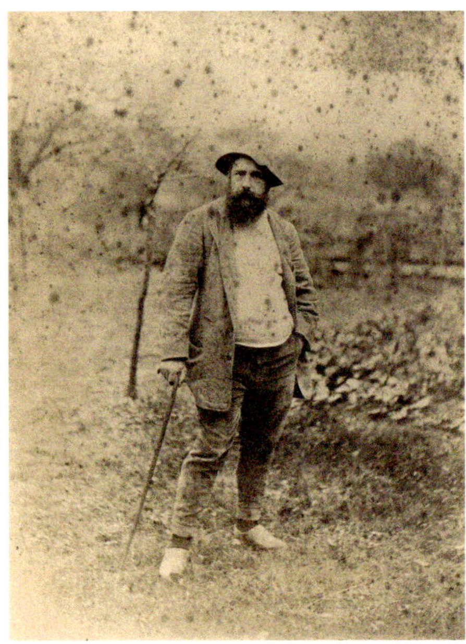

2
Claude Monet in his garden, c. 1888–90 (photo by Theodore Robinson)

was signed with a flourish and must surely count among Monet's finest achievements.

The Unknown Monet: Pastels and Drawings is the first critical study dedicated to the artist's varied and challenging works on paper. Surveying his entire career—an extraordinary period of seven decades—it engages with every aspect of Monet's graphic output, from the sketchbooks of his teenage years to the drawings made in the 1920s for his final water-lily paintings. Between these extremes we encounter Monet the young caricaturist and the truculent art student, analyzing naked models in Paris and experimenting with watercolor under the African sun, during military service in Algeria. After returning to France, Monet soon executed drawings and pastels in preparation for his first major canvases, alongside future colleagues such as Bazille, Renoir, and Pissarro. By the time of the inaugural Impressionist exhibition in 1874, he had become the leading pastellist of this circle, showing seven works in the medium alongside his notorious painting *Impression, Sunrise*. As his reputation grew, Monet continued to use sketchbooks to tackle and initially define new motifs, summarizing a railway station or a Normandy cliff in brisk, expressive lines. In his forties and fifties, he worked closely with several print processes, heralding the age of the illustrated magazine article and inspiring William Thornley to produce an almost forgotten sequence of lithographs that offered a virtual retrospective of Monet's art. Some of his most celebrated accomplishments, such as the *Grainstacks* and *Rouen Cathedral* paintings, seem to have been stimulated by pocket-size drawings, and even his turn-of-the-century views of London had their counterparts in a suite of color-saturated pastels.

Unlike his distinguished peers Degas and Cézanne, Monet's evolution as a draftsman was neither consistent in its own terms nor continuous in its relationship with his painted oeuvre. Even when lost works—which may have been numerous—are taken into account, Monet's use of drawing appears to have been sporadic. Many of the outstanding studies on paper represented in this volume were contingent on the demands of a particular creative project or responsive to circumstances, as when he needed to improvise with materials at hand or to promote his career. Strikingly, occasions like these would often prompt his involvement with a new technique, such as pen and ink or gillotage, which Monet typically applied with flair and ingenuity, then abandoned. Innovative departures like the series pastels made in the late 1860s might also be pursued briefly, only to be transposed into another medium as time passed. Unquestionably skilled in the manipulation of line, Monet could be ill at ease with his own mastery. The artist's perception of himself as a draftsman offers a further narrative throughout *The Unknown Monet: Pastels and Drawings*. Thanks to new documentary material, it is now clear that the young Oscar Monet was a proud and obsessive maker of drawings of all kinds. It was not until he reached his twenties and mixed with radical artists ranging from Jongkind and Courbet to Bazille and Pissarro, that Monet stepped back from his linear drafts to explore the liberating possibilities of direct, open-air painting. Drawing retreated into the shadows, especially when he described his novel working practice to the journalists who increasingly courted him and explained his originality to the public. Behind Monet's rhetoric, however, we find him repeatedly turning to pencil, pastel, and crayon, making isolated studies—such as *Portrait of a Woman*—or more sustained graphic records of Étretat, Giverny, and Fresselines, and later Norway and London. Such drawings were never exhibited, maintaining his image as the Impressionist painter *par excellence*, even as he gave away or sold individual works on paper to visitors, dealers, and friends (such as the American painter Theodore Robinson, who photographed him around 1888–90 [fig. 2]).

There was certainly no decade in Monet's career prior to 1900—perhaps no single year—when he failed to make drawings or was involved with graphic procedures of some kind. On this basis alone, the draftsmanship of this internationally admired painter demands our careful attention and a greater understanding of its complex, multifaceted, and sometimes contradictory purposes. When we discover how central the act of drawing was to Monet's thinking at certain periods, this challenge becomes imperative. It was arguably his use of black chalk to encapsulate the rocky shore at Sainte-Adresse in the mid-1860s, for example, that propelled him toward a more rugged, dynamic matrix for his early paintings. Monet's experiments with pastel similarly helped to bridge the historic divide between line and color, bringing graphic energy to some of his finest canvases and forging a new, rhythmically brushed language that stayed with him until the end.

Of Monet's more than 2,500 works catalogued by Daniel Wildenstein, nearly 500 are sketchbook pages, independent drawings, and pastels. Despite the relatively high proportion of works on paper within his complete oeuvre, the previous art-historical literature has focused almost exclusively on his oils, thus perpetuating a myth that Monet was a painter who did not—and perhaps could not—draw. Exceptionally, in his important monograph *Monet: Nature into Art* (Yale University Press, 1986), John House devoted a compact but erudite four-page appendix to the artist's drawings. Beyond this concise overview, only a single book has been devoted to the subject of Monet's graphic oeuvre, the fifth and final volume of Wildenstein's catalogue raisonné that was published in an edition of 2,500 copies in 1991. The appearance of this volume marked the completion of a monumental scholarly task to locate, document, and reproduce every known work of art by Claude Monet in public and private collections alike. Given its revelatory nature, it is remarkable that volume five was greeted with relatively little fanfare. When Taschen published a reprint of the catalogue raisonné in 1996, with updated entries, color reproductions, and text in French, English, and German, a decision was made to drop the fifth volume from the set, thereby excluding Monet's graphic oeuvre from the new edition.

Buried within the pages of Wildenstein's original catalogue is one explanation as to why this aspect of Monet's work has been given so little attention. An analysis of the provenances of the individual drawings and pastels reveals that the majority of his works on paper have remained scattered among private collections all over the world, that many of the objects are currently of unknown location, and that with the possible exception of the Musée Marmottan Monet, no single collection, either public or private, holds a significant number of Monet's drawings. His paintings, conversely, have always been well represented on museum walls, and their abundance and availability, combined with the relative inaccessibility of the pastels and drawings, has had an undeniable influence on how the artist has been presented in exhibitions and publications. *The Unknown Monet: Pastels and Drawings* tips the balance in the opposite direction by bringing together a large number of his works on paper and exhibiting them with a small, closely related group of oils in an effort to challenge an accepted view, directly traceable to Monet himself, that his drawings were of little or no significance to his artistic project.

The Grand Journal of Comte Théophile Beguin Billecocq

It was only during the final stages of organizing *The Unknown Monet: Pastels and Drawings* that the curators gained access to the archive of Comte Théophile Beguin Billecocq (1825–1906). Handed down among his descendents over the last century, this fascinating collection includes a two-volume unpublished manuscript entitled the Grand Journal, a memoir compiled by Théophile at the end of his life, as well as miscellaneous ephemera, several albums of photographs, and an assortment of drawings.[4] Carrying out a thorough scholarly analysis of this substantial material so late in the course of this project has proven challenging, but the discovery of the unique consequences of Monet's relationship with the Billecocq family, particularly in light of his early artistic development, has made it imperative to integrate as much of this new information as possible into this study of Monet's draftsmanship.

Several important provisos must be emphasized concerning the Beguin Billecocq archive. The first, and most significant, is that the Grand

Journal is a memoir compiled many years after the experiences it describes, rather than a daily diary concomitant with those experiences. Consequently, every incident recalled in Beguin Billecocq's account has been subjected to a double-filter of time and distance, from the writer's original observations of current events to their reiteration in his Grand Journal. In recounting Monet's early years, the writer was fully aware of his future success; therefore, he made certain observations with the benefit of hindsight. For example, in discussing Monet's manner of drawing at the age of seventeen, he noted that his rapid sketching technique was "Impressionistic," using a deliberate anachronism that presages later developments in Monet's art.[5]

In his *avant-propos* to the Grand Journal, Beguin Billecocq explained that the text was based on his own personal archive of documents, including a detailed diary kept over a thirty-year period (roughly 1854 to 1884) as well as his vast original correspondence. Unfortunately, none of these primary sources survive, making it difficult to independently verify many elements of the text. It is noteworthy that the content relating to Claude Monet represents only a small portion of a long and elaborate story, one that touches on numerous historical personages and events. After making an extended appearance in entries dating from the 1850s, Monet reverts to a cameo role in later parts of Beguin Billecocq's autobiography. Still, many new and illuminating facts emerge about the artist's life and career over the course of his fifty-year friendship with the writer, some of profound significance for our understanding of Monet's formation as an artist.

On the question of the text's reliability, it should be noted that its author, a distinguished and decorated member of a noble family, held in the greatest respect his family's heritage of absolute honorability. "On the paternal side, as on the maternal side, in all of the lines of my ancestors, I have discovered only examples of virtue," he affirmed in his foreword.[6] Further, it should be observed that the writer was clearly in full possession of his faculties at the end of his life. He had spent much of his professional career deciphering coded messages for the ministry of foreign affairs, and these mental exercises seem to have had a lasting benefit as he entered old age. "I had the felicity of being provided with an excellent memory," Théophile boasted.[7]

Indeed, efforts to fact-check Beguin Billecocq's text have upheld the Grand Journal to a high level of veracity. Just two examples will be cited here: first, on 29 April 1881 Théophile noted that Monet was in Paris from Vétheuil and stopped by the ministry of foreign affairs to pay him a visit.[8] The artist, he stated, was in a rush because he was running around Paris showing his latest work to several dealers, including Durand-Ruel. The timing of this visit is confirmed by a letter written by Monet to Paul Durand-Ruel from Vétheuil on 28 April 1881 in which he stated that he would be arriving in Paris the next day, and requests an appointment with the dealer. The letter was first published in Lionello Venturi's *Les archives de l'impressionisme* in 1939.[9]

A second episode reported in the Grand Journal that is corroborated in sources that were unpublished as of 1906 concerns another of Monet's business trips to Paris, this one from Giverny in mid-November 1884. Théophile reported on 17 November 1884 that Monet had a number of important appointments in Paris and was staying with him.[10] He mentioned Octave Mirbeau and Georges Petit as among the individuals the artist was meeting. This visit is confirmed in several letters from Monet to Paul Durand-Ruel and Camille Pissarro, including one dated 10 November 1884 in which he promised the dealer that he would be in Paris in eight days' time and suggested a rendezvous with Mirbeau,[11] and another dated 17 November 1884 from his home indicating that he was leaving immediately for Paris but would return quickly, so any correspondence should be sent to Giverny.[12]

The few mistakes that have been discovered in the Grand Journal are of the inadvertent and inconsequential variety, mainly the result of clerical errors. One of the few consistent inaccuracies perpetrated by Théophile in the text was to miscalculate Monet's age. Because he was apparently unaware that Monet's birthday occurred late in the year — 14 November, to be precise — the writer usually misrepresented his age when describing events that took place during the summer months. So, for instance, Beguin Billecocq stated that Monet was thirteen when he first met him in the summer of 1853, when he was in fact still twelve years old.[13]

In this catalogue's first chapter, the implications of Monet's suppression of his relationship with the Billecocq family will be discussed in detail. Among the artist's surviving correspondence, there is but a single reference that confirms his association with the Billecocqs, and there may be some significance in the fact that it does not relate to his acceptance of their largesse, but is an attempt to render assistance. On 16 December 1883 Monet wrote to another of his patrons, Dr. Georges de Bellio, concerning the plight of his old friend Théodore Billecocq (1837–1915), the cousin of the author of the Grand Journal, whom he had befriended during his teenage years. Théodore had lately fallen on hard times, having lost his fortune in the 1882 stock market crash.[14] As Théodore was experiencing health problems, Monet asked his physician friend to intervene:

My dear Bellio,

I come to ask you a service. First of all, please excuse me for not coming in person, but Renoir and I are leaving this evening for Genoa and I need to go hug my children before departing.

In short, this is the situation. I have often spoken with you of a good friend of mine, M. Théodore Billecocq, whose uncle [Adolphe Billecocq (1800–1875)] you have known since he was made consul to Bucharest. He has come to experience all manner of hardships. He lost his wife and he nearly died himself. Alone and without fortune, he is on the verge of being forced into the hospital for the removal of an abscess from his thigh. I thought that as a favor to his uncle and to me since he is a friend, you could give him advice concerning his illness. I would be most grateful. He is a charming lad and very intelligent. I hope thus that you will receive him well and that he presents himself to you on my behalf.[15]

There is no record of the immediate outcome of his illness, but Théodore Billecocq is known to have lived until 1915.

Beyond the 1883 letter, there are a few additional pieces of evidence linking Monet and the Billecocqs. Théodore Billecocq's older brother Ernest (1830–1912), who became Consul Générale de France, developed a close friendship with the artist's brother, Léon Monet. Ernest's daughter Jeanne Billecocq (1870–1956) was the godmother to Léon's only daughter, Louise Monet (1901–1979). Ernest's son, André Billecocq (1902–1992), an architect by profession, left a brief unpublished memoir of his own entitled "Les Relations entre les familles Monet et Billecocq" ["The Relationship Between the Monet and Billecocq Families"] (1981). It was André Billecocq who in 1982 gave to the Académie des Beaux-Arts/Musée Marmottan Monet a collection of nine caricatures by Monet dating from the 1850s that he had inherited from his uncles Théodore and/or Ernest.[16] These will also be discussed in chapter 2.

Supplementing the Grand Journal is a large collection of ephemeral items comprising photographs, postcards, printed documents, and drawings, some mounted in albums and others loose, many dating from the late nineteenth century and directly linked to Théophile Beguin Billecocq. Like the Grand Journal itself, most of these materials bear no relationship to Claude Monet, but touch on other historical personages and family members. The Monet-related items include an assortment of studio photographs of the artist, invitations to his exhibitions at Durand-Ruel (1895) and Georges Petit (1898), and to the weddings of his stepdaughters Suzanne Hoschedé (1892) and Marthe Hoschedé (1900). Of the original drawings and watercolors, a large number are inscribed with Monet's name or initials but their attributions remain problematic, as several family members were amateur artists and great admirers of his work. The archive awaits systematic study and cataloguing; it is hoped that the Grand Journal will be published in its entirety in the wake of the current exhibition and publication.

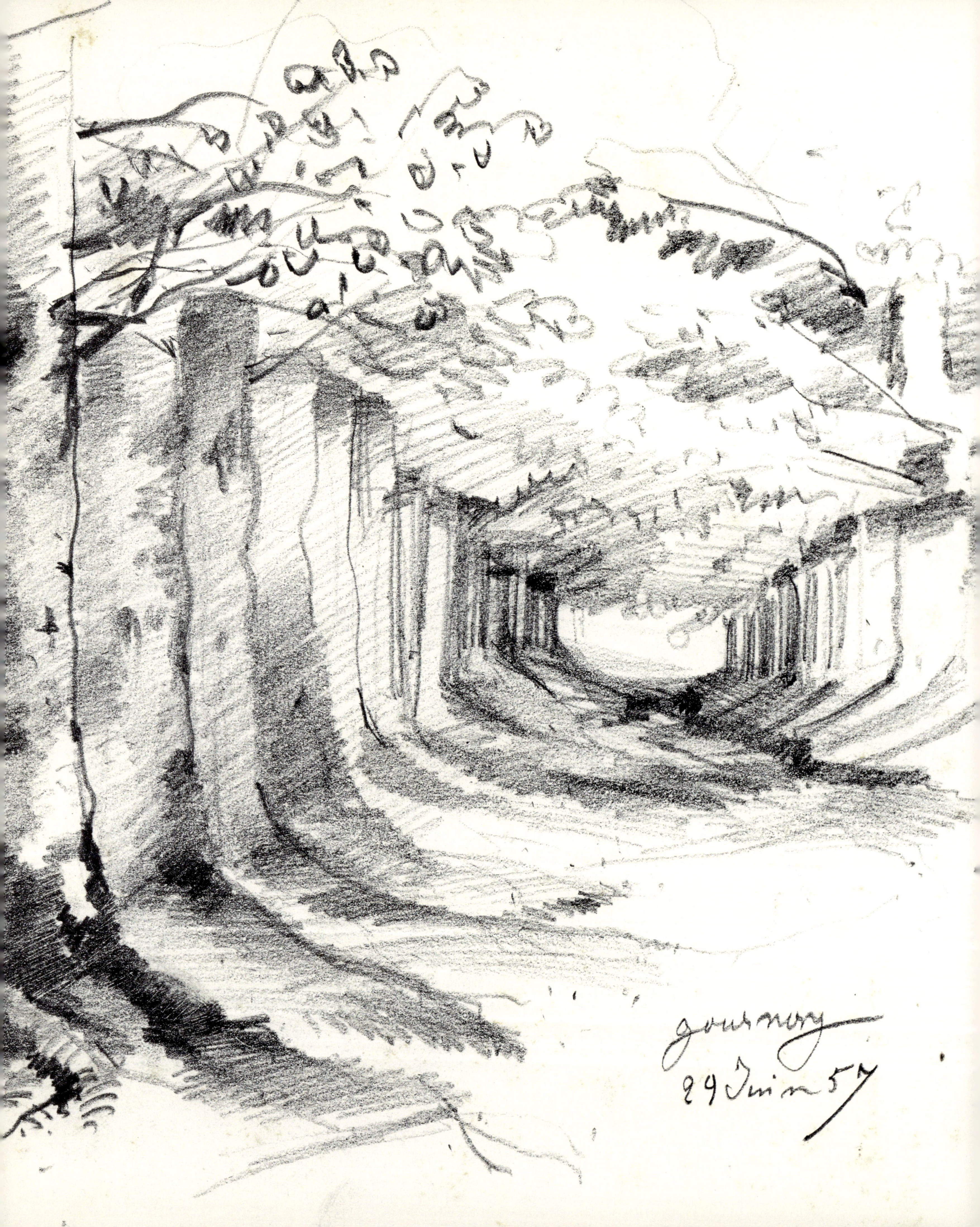
gournay
29 Juin 57

CHAPTER ONE Portrait of the Artist as a Young Draftsman

It is generally acknowledged that Oscar Claude Monet was the master of at least two art forms: painting and self-promotion. Scholars of Impressionism have long recognized Monet's significant role in the construction of his own public image. He was ultimately as entrepreneurial in his relationships with journalists as he was with dealers and collectors: Monet knew how to work both systems to his advantage. Had his father lived into the 1890s, when Monet's annual income exceeded 100,000 francs, he would have been as proud of his son's business acumen as of his artistic accomplishments.

With Monet's rising celebrity from the mid-1860s onward, journalists, critics, and the public began to take an interest in his personal history. The style and subject matter of his earliest drawings and paintings offered visual clues to the artist's geographic and aesthetic heritage. Documentary evidence, such as basic biographical data, did not begin to appear in print until the 1880s. The exclusive source for this information was the firsthand testimony of the artist. In his later years, the venerated Old Master admitted a stream of interviewers to his home in Giverny and authorized the publication of several biographies.

Monet could hardly have been expected to provide an objective account of his own life story. His recollections of his early years were first recorded when he was in middle age. Like the sea cliffs that became his obsession, these childhood memories were naturally eroded by the passage of time. And like his paintings of these same motifs, they were vigilantly selected and shaped, iterated and reiterated. In the end, Monet's personal reminiscences were constructed from an admixture of historical events and his own artistic ideology.

The goal of this chapter is to reexamine both the history and historiography of Monet's formative years in the light of an important new source, the unpublished memoirs of a family friend who first came to know young Oscar when he was twelve years old. This fascinating testimony fills in gaps in the story of his artistic upbringing with a particular emphasis on the major theme of this exhibition: uncovering Monet's hidden talents as a draftsman, the third but no less important art form, besides painting and public relations, in which he excelled.

The Unfolding Biography

"Monet (Claude-Oscar), born in Paris, the fourteenth of November 1840. Has exhibited at the Salons of 1865, 1866, and 1868. Has been rejected at the Salons of 1867, 1869, and 1870. Has exhibited at the three impressionist exhibitions on the boulevard des Capucines in 1874, at the gallery of M. Durand-Ruel in 1876, rue le Peletier in 1877."[1] So reads one of the first passages ever published on Monet the man, in Théodore Duret's *Les Peintres Impressionnistes* of 1878. In his introduction to the catalogue of Monet's first one-man exhibition, held at the gallery of *La vie moderne* in 1880, Duret filled in a few additional biographical details relating to the artist's travels over the previous decade: "Monet has devoted the larger part of his career to painting the area around Paris. He has lived, successively, in Argenteuil and Vétheuil, where the Seine provided him with the capricious, changeable waterscape of which he is especially fond. He has also made frequent trips to the Channel coast and has painted in England and Holland."[2]

The earliest published references to Monet's upbringing in Le Havre are found in an interview with Émile Taboureux that also coincided with the 1880 exhibition. "Monet is a true freshwater sailor," Taboureux revealed. "He might easily have been one on saltwater too, because a large part of his childhood was spent at Le Havre. It was there that he did his first two paintings, if I'm not mistaken, which won awards at the Salon of 1865 to the most enthusiastic critical acclaim."[3] Taboureux was only partially mistaken: Monet's seascapes were well received in the press but did not garner a medal.

The first descriptive account of Monet's Le Havre years appeared in Philippe Burty's article "The Landscapes of Claude Monet," in the 27 March 1883 issue of the newspaper *La République française*:

Claude Monet is a Parisian, brought to Le Havre as a very young child. His father was in the business of selling supplies to outward-bound ships. As soon as he was strong enough, he had to help his father. But commerce, with its physical fatigue and offer of only limited horizons, inspired only repugnance in this sensual and independent spirit. At the age of fifteen, hardly out of school, to have a bit of money that he could spend as he pleased, Monet drew caricatures with huge heads (like those made fashionable by Daumier's Representatives Represented*) of the regulars at the harbor cafes, the brokers and captains of the coastal trade. He would supply himself with vellum, pencils, and penknives at Boudin's stationery store. The owner, whose kindness and reserve we outlined recently, even framed these caricatures, appreciating their allure while finding the drawing technique somewhat insufficient.*[4]

In this brief passage, several basic elements of the story were set down that would be repeated and elaborated upon in subsequent articles and interviews with the artist: the teenager's rebellion against his father's trade; his "sensual" and "independent" spirit; and his prodigious—indeed, professional—talent as a caricaturist.

François Thiébault-Sisson conducted one of the most frequently cited interviews with Monet on the subject of his childhood for *Le Temps* in November 1900. There is little doubt that the views and opinions represented those of the artist, even if the quotes were likely embellished and perhaps even fabricated by the journalist. At the beginning of his account, the sixty-year-old Monet was quoted on his lonely pursuit of art and nature in romantic isolation: "I was born . . . in a circle entirely given over to commerce, and where all professed a contemptuous disdain for the arts." He went on to spin a tale of youthful rebellion:

[My] youth was essentially that of a vagabond. I was undisciplined by birth; never would I bend, even in my most tender youth, to a rule. It was at home that I learned the little I know. School always appeared to me like a prison, and I never could make up my mind to stay there, not even for four hours a day, when the sunshine was inviting, the sea smooth, and when it was such a joy to run about on the cliffs, in the free air, or to paddle around in the water. Until I was fourteen or

fifteen years old, I led this irregular but thoroughly wholesome life, to the despair of my good father.[5]

It is at this point in the narrative that his knack for drawing caricatures emerged:

I made wreaths on the margins of my books; I decorated the blue paper of my copybooks with ultra-fantastical ornaments, and I represented thereon, in the most irreverent fashion, deforming them as much as I could, the face or the profile of my masters. I soon acquired much skill at this game.[6]

Monet gave a similar account of his childhood obsession with drawing to Marc Elder:

Throughout my boyhood I was really gifted in drawing. I instinctively scribbled all the time, sketching silhouettes and types at the theatre, in the street, everywhere. At the same time, I was inclined toward caricature, and at around age sixteen, I had mastered the portrait-charge *so well, in the eyes of the locals of Le Havre, that my patrons began to flow. I didn't do bad selling* portraits-charges *for a louis apiece. This income, carefully set aside, would help me much later to make it to Paris.*[7]

The role of Monet's mother in nurturing his interest in drawing came out in a conversation with René Gimpel, which the dealer recorded in his diary in October 1920. "I questioned Monet on his past," Gimpel reported. "At twelve [*sic*; he was actually sixteen] he lost his mother, but already she had urged him to draw and had praised his [drawings after] plaster models. 'I was expelled,' he said, 'from all the schools in Le Havre. I covered my books with sketches—worse, all of my friends' books. Later my father was opposed to my vocation."[8]

Much the same sequence of events was rehashed by nearly all of Monet's early biographers.[9] Modern scholars have done their best to reexamine this account, but they have been stymied by the scarcity of information beyond Monet's recorded statements. As Paul Tucker conceded in the opening of his groundbreaking biography *Claude Monet: Life and Art* (1995), "The facts about his early upbringing in particular are surprisingly few given his renown. They are also unrevealing, which makes them frustrating but simple to rehearse."[10] After briefly recounting Monet's birth, his parents' move to Le Havre, and his early schooling, Tucker concluded, "beyond these modest facts, we know little about Monet's activities as a child or what kind of experiences he had as an adolescent."[11] In painting the backdrop to Monet's childhood, Marianne Alphant quoted Stendhal on the "profound obscurity" of the Le Havre air that was caused by pollution from the busy marine traffic.[12] Writing "*cette profonde obscurité*," she could have been just as easily referring to the fog enshrouding these lost years.

A few significant documents had been unearthed during Monet's own lifetime by the early biographers of Eugène Boudin (1824–1898), the Le Havre artist sixteen years his senior who played a critical role in encouraging him to take up pastels and oil painting. In 1900 Gustave Cahen published Monet's first letters to Boudin, written shortly after his arrival in Paris in 1859.[13] In 1922 Georges Jean-Aubry published one of two letters from Monet's father to the municipal council of Le Havre dated August 1858 and March 1859.[14] This letter related to Adolphe Monet's unsuccessful grant application for his son to study art in Paris. Daniel Wildenstein later quoted relevant passages from the registers of the city council relating to their deliberations over this matter in his multivolume biography and catalogue raisonné, the foundation for all modern studies on the artist.[15]

Wildenstein's text contains two fleeting references to another little-known source, the memoirs of Théophile Beguin Billecocq (1825–1906), the nephew of one of Adolphe Monet's boarders who first visited during the summer of 1853.[16] Portions of this unpublished manuscript had privately circulated during the 1950s in the form of a barely legible copy and had come to Wildenstein's attention, but he apparently did not have access to the full text. Although subsequent scholars have seized on these brief references, the complete original document has been unavailable for study until now.[17] When it

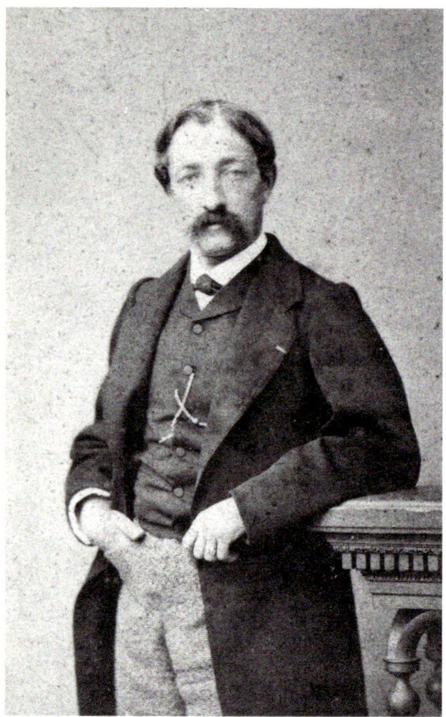

3
Comte Théophile Beguin Billecocq, c. 1865

is finally published, this memoir will be recognized as the single most important resource on Monet's early years.

Oscar Monet and the Beguin Billecocq Family, 1853–55

In 1905 the former head of diplomatic codes and ciphers within the French ministry of foreign affairs, Comte Théophile Beguin Billecocq (fig. 3), finished writing out his memoirs in the form of a substantial manuscript he entitled the Grand Journal (fig. 4). The text was based primarily on a daily journal maintained by Beguin Billecocq from the time of his marriage in 1854 (when he was nearly thirty) until his retirement in 1884. The Grand Journal provides a rich and fascinating overview of Parisian society during the Second Empire and Third Republic from the unique perspective of a well-connected professional diplomat. The journal touches on Beguin Billecocq's family life, his friendships with artists and writers, and vital matters of state. His position in the government involved considerable foreign travel, including visits to the United States, as well as receiving, decoding, and disseminating to high government officials news of current world affairs, including such breaking stories as the execution of the Emperor Maximilian in Mexico and the Battle of Gettysburg.

One of the most extraordinary aspects of this memoir is its documentation of the author's lifelong engagement with the arts. He makes repeated references to his family's contacts with painters such as Elisabeth Louise Vigée-Lebrun (1755–1842), Antoine-Jean Gros (1771–1835), and their generation, and his regular visits to the Salon and other exhibitions, including those of the Impressionists. Beguin Billecocq's Grand Journal is a major untapped resource on Monet's early career, filling in gaps on the artist's life where there was previously no information. As the writer was himself an amateur draftsman, he was well qualified to observe and comment on the main driving force behind young Oscar Monet's aspiration to become a professional artist: his overwhelming passion for drawing.

Théophile had joined the ministry of foreign affairs in 1848, an inauspicious year, perhaps, to enter the diplomatic service, given that it would be marked by revolutions in France and across Europe. He recalled that a few days after the fall of the July Monarchy and the declaration of the Second Republic, he found himself donning his National Guard uniform to stand sentry at the Palais-Royal. He took the opportunity to peek inside the ransacked royal apartments and noted the most beautiful paintings had been lanced by bayonets, the Sèvres porcelains had been smashed to pieces, and the draperies around the throne had been reduced to rags.[18] Shortly afterward, his uncle, Hippolyte Billecocq (1794–1859), announced his retirement from his post as head of ciphers and codes in the diplomatic

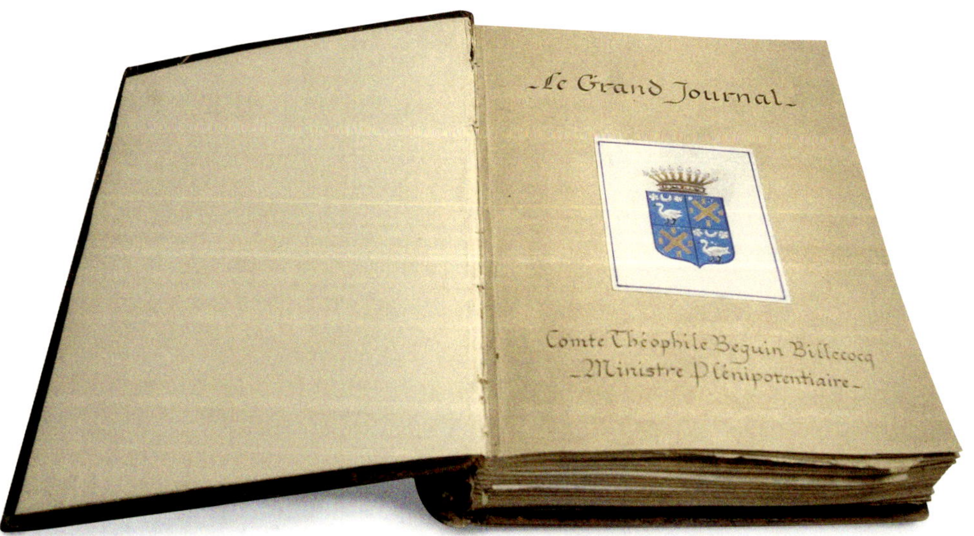

4
Cover and frontispiece of the Grand Journal by Comte Théophile Beguin Billecocq

5
Louise-Justine and Adolphe Monet, Claude Monet's parents, c. 1855

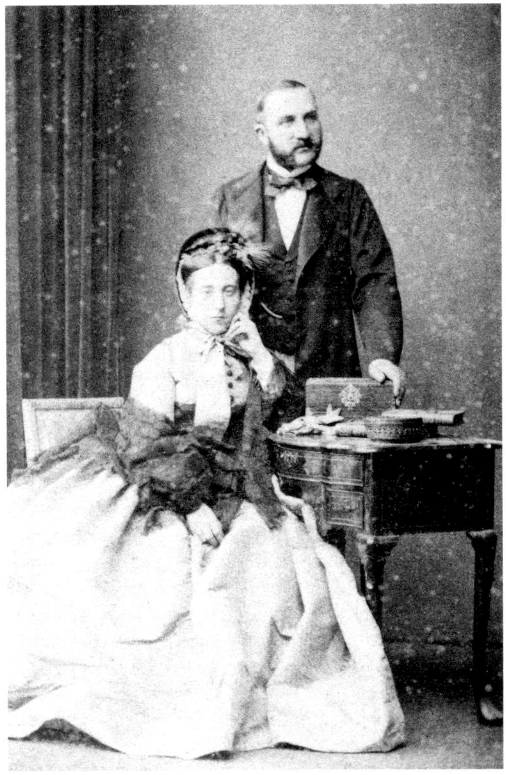

moved his family from Paris to settle permanently in Ingouville, a quarter of Le Havre, in 1845. Between the steady flow of seaport traffic and the seasonal influx of tourists, Le Havre had been transformed by the mid-nineteenth century from a sleepy fishing village to a dynamic seaside metropolis.

It was during his brief, though momentous, holiday at Ingouville in 1853 that Théophile made the acquaintance of the Monet family. His aunt Abdonne and cousin (and future wife) Amélie were enjoying an extended holiday as lodgers in the Monet household, which seems to have functioned as a bed-and-breakfast for Parisian tourists. Théophile lavished great attention on his description of Madame Louise-Justine Aubrée Monet (1805–1857; fig. 5), who comes across as a Madame Charpentier *avant la lettre*: "Intelligent and lively, she had the informed and amiable conversational skills of young women raised in Paris," Théophile wrote:

service, and encouraged his nephew to pursue a career in his former division within the ministry of foreign affairs.

Théophile's leisure activities involved the kind of cultural pursuits and travel that one would expect of a well-to-do young gentleman. He attended operas and art exhibitions, took voice lessons with a certain Monsieur Dupond, and studied drawing with the prominent Swiss-expatriate sculptor James Pradier (1790–1852), a professor at the École des Beaux-Arts.[19] During his summer holidays, Théophile embarked on a series of foreign excursions, with travel in Belgium and Rhenish Prussia (1849), Holland (1850), and Switzerland (1851, 1852). Because of an extended leave of absence taken by his supervisor, he had to curtail his travel plans in the summer of 1853, limiting himself to a week on the Normandy coast with the family of his uncle Hippolyte.

At the time of Théophile's visit, the Channel coast was well on its way to becoming a major holiday destination for Parisians, who could reach Dieppe via railway in a matter of a few hours. Drawn by the prospect of employment in the shipping industry, Monet's father had

She appreciated Romantic poetry and since her childhood had written Alexandrian verses, quatrains and sonnets, and what's more, they were reasonably good. She drew with talent and kept her works, drawings and watercolors, in little sketchbooks that she guarded assiduously and only showed her family. In addition, she played comedy with grace and loved to receive in her salons upper-Havre society, the consuls of powerful foreigners, the mayor and the under-sheriff, religious authorities, as well as members of elegant Parisian society who came to stay in the country during the summer, along the Channel coast. She also enjoyed reading, notably the prose of Balzac and the poetry of Lamartine.[20]

Théophile provides the only known description of the ornate living room of Monet's boyhood home:

Madame Monet had all of the traits of a woman of the world and received visitors with elegance in her grand salon at Ingouville, a room pleasantly furnished with mahogany, rosewood, and decorated with floral percalines that gave a certain sense of affluence. A piano, an instrument of

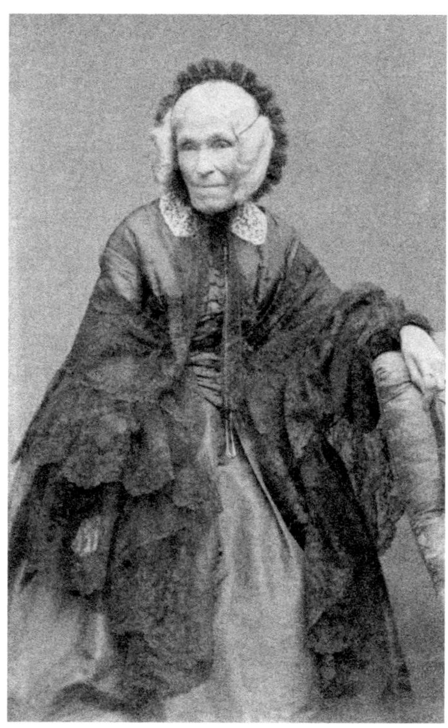

6
Marie-Jeanne Lecadre, Claude Monet's aunt, c. 1865

capital importance, formed part of the harmonious furnishings. Large pastoral landscapes of the eighteenth-century French school decorated the walls and, on the fireplace overmantel, a chased and gilded bronze clock was set between two candlesticks. A beautiful collection of Bayeux porcelain completed the decoration of this reception room.[21]

Above all, Madame Monet was remembered by Théophile as a music lover with a trained soprano voice. She organized informal after-dinner concerts in which she was accompanied on the piano or violin, or staged one-act comedies with her family in the living room.

Théophile's thumbnail sketches of the other members of the Monet family are equally informative. Monet's father, Claude-Adolphe (1800–1871), was characterized in more sympathetic terms than in the accounts left by the artist: "While he was not as smitten with art and literature as his wife, he appreciated her special talents and took part with interest . . . in the parties and the comedies that his charming wife organized in bringing together the notables of Le Havre and its environs."[22] Théophile described him as an honorable businessman and an admirer of the Empire, under which he had prospered, and reported that his office was decorated with two items: a large portrait of Napoleon III and an imposing map of the world. "His passions were for geography and foreign politics," Théophile observed, and he particularly enjoyed gossip of the grand Parisian balls hosted by the emperor and empress that some members of the Billecocq family attended.[23]

Adolphe Monet's business partner, his brother-in-law Jacques Lecadre (d. 1858), is portrayed in similar terms, as a driven entrepreneur with little time for art. His wife, and Adolphe's half-sister, Marie-Jeanne Lecadre (d. 1870; fig. 6), was, like Madame Monet, a cultured amateur. "She was an exquisite person who appreciated, like her sister-in-law, the arts and most particularly painting and drawing. She had a recognized teacher, and had applied herself, like a good schoolgirl, to watercolor and oil painting."[24] Théophile reported that she organized for her friends "séances de dessin" and doted on her nephew, Oscar, who shared her love of drawing. His older brother Léon-Pascal (1836–1917) was said to take more after his father and uncle.

Théophile described young Oscar as inheriting his mother's pronounced taste for the arts and possessing an independent and undisciplined spirit that exasperated his father. Adolphe dubbed him "an American savage," a good-for-nothing child who disrupted his classes by drawing grotesque caricatures in his schoolbooks. Théophile saw in him the fantasist, reminiscent of his own childhood friend Alexandre Dumas, *fils* (1824–1895). "He was a fair-haired child with a mischievous smile, cheerful, roguish, and greedy. Intelligent, lively, curious, a good boy of course."[25]

One of Monet's closest friends was Théodore Billecocq (1837–1915), a brother of Théophile's future wife, Amélie. Théodore was three years older than Oscar and apparently shared his friend's independent spirit and love of the sea. He had aspired to a career in the Admiralty and enrolled and dropped out of a number of academic programs in a failed effort to gain the appropriate qualifications.[26] Oscar and Théodore became inseparable during the long summer days in and around Le Havre.

Théophile's exposé of the Monet family in the year 1853 stands in marked contrast to Monet's later reminiscences of growing up amid a circle of philistines "where all professed a contemptuous disdain for the arts." On the contrary, Théophile describes a milieu that was a virtual oasis of culture at the seashore in which several adults—Monet's mother, his aunt, and now Théophile and his family—supported the boy's exceptional interest in drawing.

Until his conscription into the French military, Oscar Monet spent many of his holidays with his friend Théodore and the rest of the Beguin Billecocq clan, starting with Christmas and New Year's in Paris at the end of 1853.[27] From all indications, it appears that the Billecocqs (Hippolyte, Théodore) and the Beguin Billecocqs (Théophile, Paul [his father], Amélie) treated young Oscar as a member of the family, offering him a respite from his parents' household and a generous taste of the good life.

Early Sketchbooks and Excursions with the Beguin Billecocqs, 1855–56

Like all children, Oscar Monet led a double life. In the classroom of the *collège communal* of Le Havre, which he had attended as a day student from the age of ten, he saw himself as nothing less than a prisoner.[28] It is not known precisely when he left school, or even if he received his baccalauréat, though his departure from academics seems to have occurred by 1857. One of his teachers was the local artist Jacques-François Ochard (1800–1870), who had studied painting with Jacques-Louis David but ended his days as a drawing instructor and a curator of fine arts at the Le Havre Museum.[29] Ochard's teaching methods are undocumented but were likely to have been based on academic standards of instruction that emphasized the basic elements of geometry and copying motifs from plaster models and drawing manuals. None of Oscar's school exercises have survived.

Oscar's life outside the classroom was gloriously unstructured, allowing his inner life, that of the fantasist-draftsman, to have free reign. This aspect of Monet's youth is preserved in two primary sources: loose sheets torn and scattered from his earliest sketchbooks, and the memoirs of Théophile Beguin Billecocq, whose contacts with him during the free summer months and holidays provide the only known firsthand testimony regarding these lost years. Because he did not own a country house, Théophile spent his annual summer holidays in a variety of choice locations, usually within easy reach of Paris. As a frequent guest of the family, the boy from Le Havre gained exposure to diverse aspects of the French landscape before embarking on his professional career. He would revisit many of these locales as a mature artist.

Théophile's descriptions of his summer holidays with Oscar Monet contain a number of significant extended references to drawing. In 1855, he rented a house in Nemours, a village in Fontainebleau on the Paris-Lyon railway line. "Théodore and his friend Oscar Monet came to entertain our little world," he reported, "and spent two long months, making numerous excursions in the surrounding countryside."[30] The carefree duo took countless daytrips together on horseback, led by a riding master "through the immense and splendid alleys of the imperial forest of Fontainebleau." Théophile recalled how "they were gone for entire days, carrying with them a robust lunch composed of patés, bread, cheese, and wine. They sometimes returned late in the evening, exhausted by the tremendous excursions. Thus, they were able to

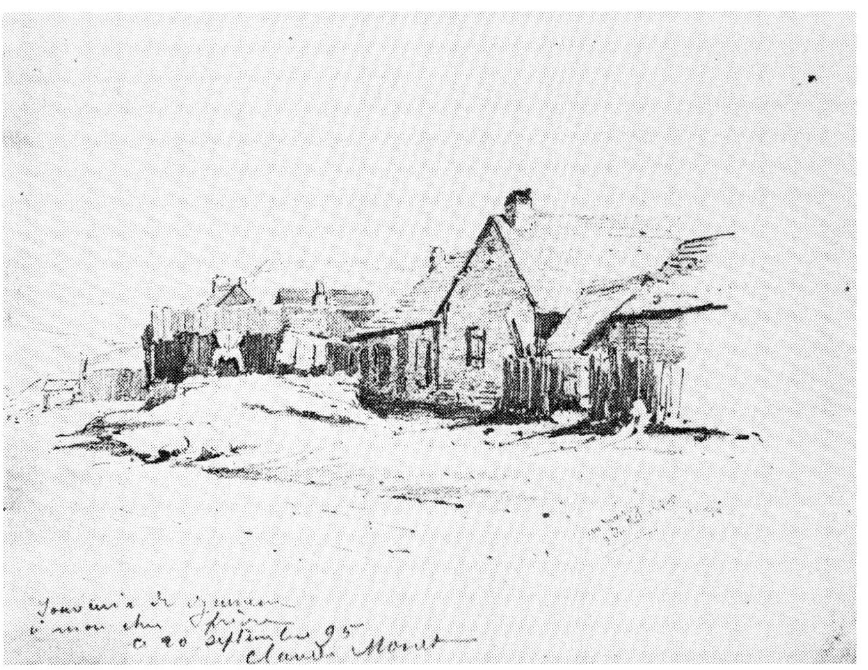

7

Perrey, a Neighborhood in Le Havre, 1856. Pencil, 205 x 270 mm. Location unknown [D1]

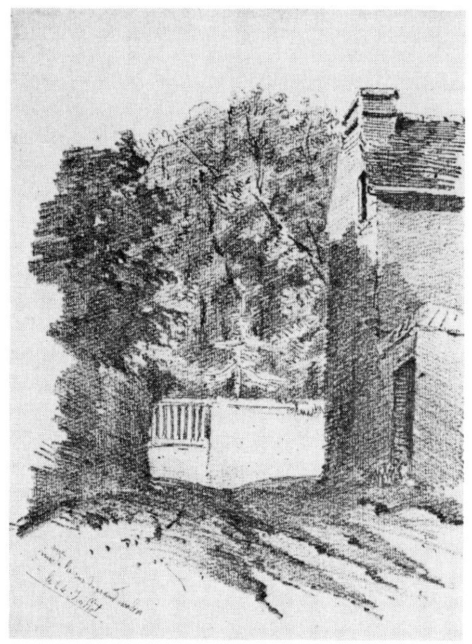

8
La rue du Grand-Escalier at Ingouville, 1856. Pencil, 270 x 205 mm. Location unknown [D14]

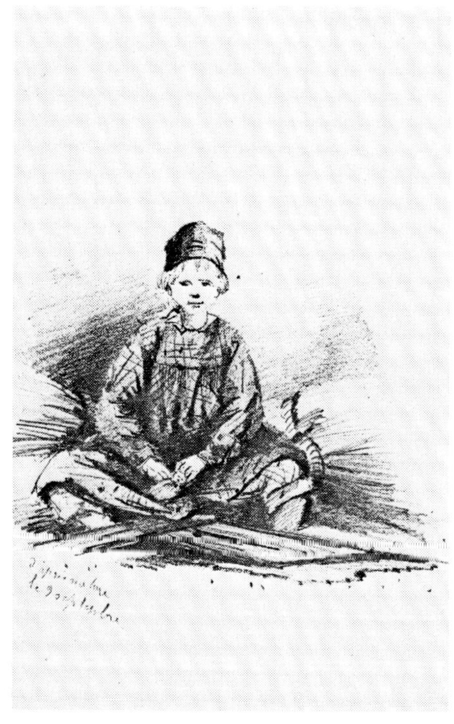

9
Seated Child with a Doll, 1856. Pencil, 290 x 190 mm. Location unknown [D44]

visit all of the forest of Fontainebleau . . . Oscar executed numerous drawings representing trees, groves, pastoral scenes, farms, and delightful manor houses that he signed 'Oscar Monet' and presented to us," Théophile stated, explaining that the young draftsman took pride in affixing his signature to his drawings.[31]

In these, his earliest-known excursions into the ancient forest of Fontainebleau, Monet was treading on what was already artistic hallowed ground. The woods were notorious as the site of the first great revolution in nineteenth-century art, a labyrinth of gnarled oaks and boulders, painters and photographers. In the absence of surviving drawings from his 1855 visit, one is left to imagine Monet's first quest for motifs in this art-historically charged setting; he would return with Frédéric Bazille in 1863 and make the forest the backdrop two years later for his painted *Déjeuner sur l'herbe*.

In late June or early July 1856, Oscar would rejoin his friend Théodore to spend two weeks with the vacationing Beguin Billecocqs, who that year were ensconced in a pavilion located on the grounds of a large estate at Les Mesnuls, in the southwestern suburbs of Paris. The group traveled together around the environs, including Montfort, Rambouillet, the valley of the Chevreuse, and Vaux de Cernay, with Oscar all the while carrying out rapid sketches of the landscape.[32]

The contents of two lost sketchbooks dating from just after this jaunt with the Beguin Billecocqs, 9 July to 22 September 1856, are recorded in Wildenstein's catalogue raisonné.[33] The first consisted of twenty-eight drawings measuring 205 by 270 millimeters, and the second held nineteen drawings measuring 190 by 290 millimeters. When they appeared together at auction in 1895, the albums were apparently authenticated by Monet himself; he wrote on one of the sheets a dedication to his brother that reads "Souvenir de jeunesse, à mon cher frère, ce 20 septembre 95" (fig. 7)[34] Although Wildenstein was able to secure and publish small black-and-white photographs of the individual drawings in the fifth volume of his catalogue raisonné, he was unable to identify their whereabouts, and to date none of these drawings has surfaced.

The subject matter of the two sketchbooks consists mainly of picturesque pencil studies of local architecture, trees, and sailboats. The landscapes are rendered in the form of vignettes, whereas the representations of sailing vessels are organized methodically across the page, with as many as eleven separate motifs sharing a single sheet of paper. Paul Tucker has made the insightful suggestion that Monet's choice of "quaint" subject matter in these albums demonstrates that at this early age, his preference was for timeless rustic subjects in the face of Le Havre's modernization.[35]

Given the sketchbooks' disappearance and the negligible quality of the photographic images published by Wildenstein, only a few additional observations may be offered. Setting aside technical concerns, which are virtually impossible to gauge from the photographic evidence, the most interesting features of the drawings are inscriptions on a number of the sheets indicating their dates of execution and the locations represented (transcribed in tables 1 and 2). Several identify specific roads (rue de la côte d'Ingouville, rue du Grand-Escalier; fig. 8), property owners (Mme Delaroche, Mlle Agasse), and in one instance, the name of an individual (Édouard Perdrieux, a young schoolboy). A sheet in sketchbook 2 representing another boy sitting with his legs crossed is dated and inscribed "d'après nature," the only caption to make such an assertion (fig. 9). Oscar's use of this designation seems, in this instance, a gratuitous affectation, an artistic convention that he may have seen on contemporary prints.

Each sheet offers a tantalizing glimpse of the young man at work: a half hour, perhaps, out of a morning, an afternoon, or a full day of exploring the rural landscape in search of motifs. The inscriptions tell a fragmentary story, for a single drawing surely could not have represented a day's activity. The 1856 albums were relatively bulky and probably supplemented by smaller pocket-sized sketchbooks. It is easy to imagine Monet reserving the larger books for his most ambitious "presentation" studies. He probably would have used smaller sketchbooks for less-

TABLE 1 Itinerary of sketchbook 1 (July 1856)

DATE	WILDENSTEIN NO.	LOCATION (NOTES)
4–5 JULY	D20	(boat studies)
9 JULY	D1	Perrey (neighborhood in Le Havre)
9 JULY	D2	Quartier des Briqueteries (neighborhood in Le Havre)
10 JULY	D4	Leure (portion of Graville, east of Le Havre)
10 JULY	D5	rue de la cote d'Ingouville, property of Mme Delaroche
11 JULY	D21	Sainte-Adresse, beach
12 JULY	D6	rue de la côte d'Ingouville
13 JULY	D7	rue de la côte d'Ingouville
17 JULY	D8	rue de la côte d'Ingouville, property of Mme Delaroche
17 JULY	D22	(boat studies)
18 JULY	D11	"sur les bords de la mer"
22 JULY	D12	Harfleur
22 JULY	D13	Harfleur (houses)
24 JULY	D14	rue du Grand-Escalier, Ingouville
29 JULY	D16	"à la côte"
29 JULY	D17	Le Havre or Ingouville (property of Mlle Agasse)
29 JULY	D26	"sur les bords de la mer"
5 AUG.	D18	"intérieur de ferme"
9 AUG.	D19	(tree and farmhouse)

TABLE 2 Itinerary of sketchbook 2 (Aug.–Sept. 1856)

DATE	WILDENSTEIN NO.	LOCATION (NOTES)
13 AUG.	D29	Bléville
16 AUG.	D31	(trees and buildings)
18 AUG.	D32	(valley)
21 AUG.	D33	(tempête)
22 AUG.	D36	"aux huileries"
28 AUG.	D37	(buildings near Le Havre)
29 AUG.	D38	Graville
29 AUG.	D39	Graville
3 SEPT.	D40	Between Le Havre and Cap de la Hève ("dans les basses falaises")
4 SEPT.	D41	(alley of trees)
4 SEPT.	D42	(tree and farmhouse)
5 SEPT.	D43	Graville
9 SEPT.	D44	"d'après nature" (seated child)
10 SEPT.	D45	"édouard perdrieux" (standing child)
10 SEPT.	D46	Cap de la Hève, "Les Phares"
12 SEPT.	D47	Graville

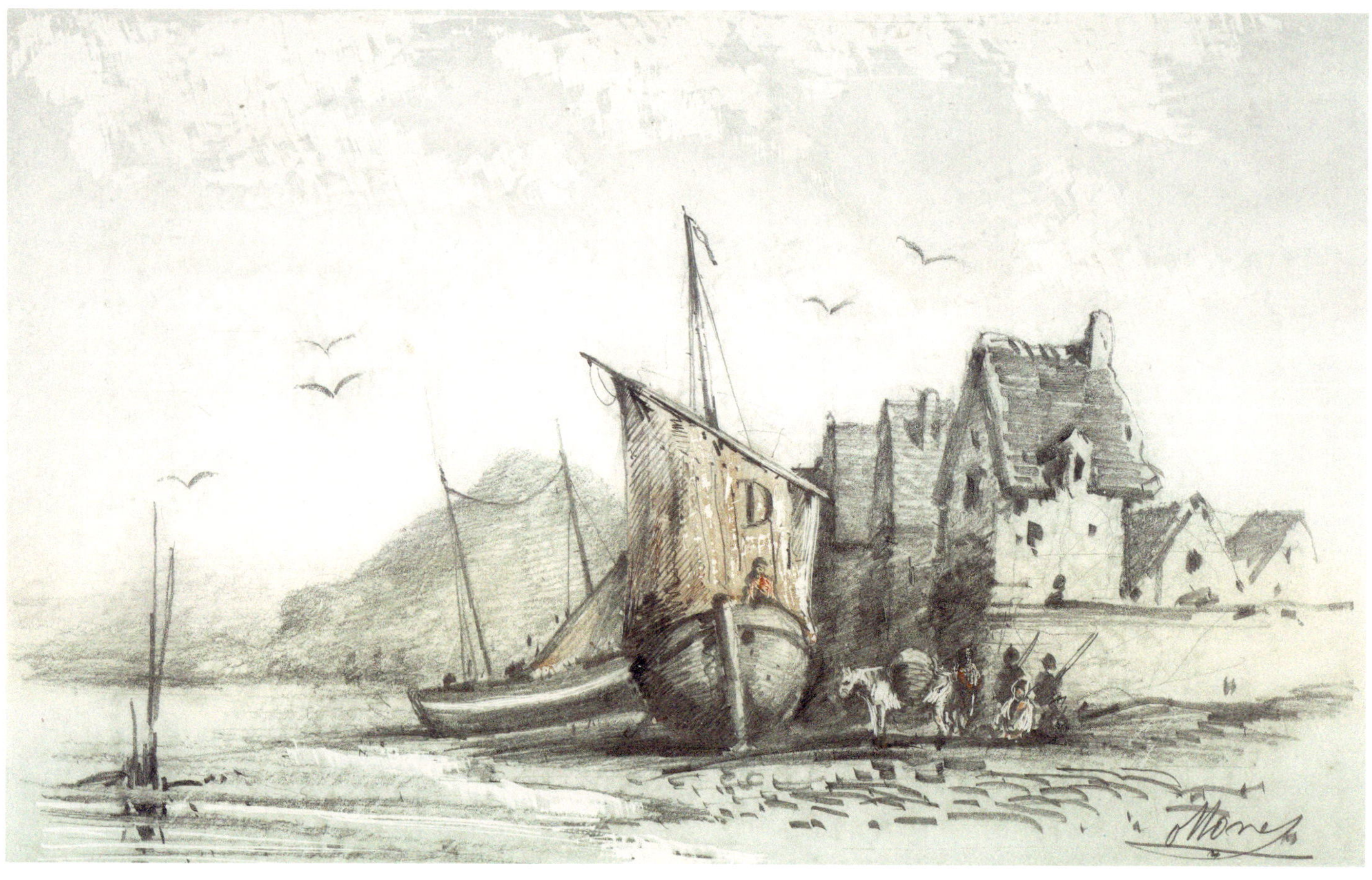

10
The Old "Le Pollet" Quarter of Dieppe, 1856–57. Graphite and watercolor on scratchboard, 134 x 219 mm. Museum of Fine Arts, Boston. Gift of Elizabeth K. Davis [D406]

finished drawings, perhaps preliminary studies for the larger compositions. One is quickly thrust into the realm of pure speculation, connecting the dots represented by these lost sheets to create routes, itineraries, and ultimately a picture, albeit an incomplete one, of Monet as a young draftsman in the summer of 1856.

Consistent with the subject matter of these early albums is a small pencil and watercolor view of *The Old "Le Pollet" Quarter of Dieppe* (fig. 10), which, if it were drawn from life, would represent one of the most distant sites visited by Monet in 1856–57. The locale, roughly fifty-two miles north of Le Havre along the Channel coast, was identified by Wildenstein by virtue of the letter "D" on the sail of the small fishing boat.[36] It seems more likely, however, that this modest drawing was inspired by a print, perhaps by or after the painter Eugène Isabey (1803–1886), who worked extensively around Dieppe and specialized in imagery of this sort. The unusual medium—graphite and watercolor on scratchboard—further suggests that the work was not executed out in the field. It may represent an early attempt by Monet to emulate commercial illustration using appropriate tools of the trade, which would have been available to him in the artist's supply shop in Le Havre formerly owned by Boudin. Also setting it apart from the sketchbook drawings is the fact that it is signed in the lower-right corner, indicating that Monet considered it a finished independent work.

In late December 1856, Monet joined the Beguin Billecocqs in Paris to celebrate the Christmas holidays and ring in the New Year. The family staged a number of amateur theatricals in the salons of Théophile Beguin Billecocq on the rue de Monceau and his brother-in-law Edmond de Beauregard on the rue du Bac. Among the pieces in which Oscar acted was Théodore Leclercq's *Le Sapho de Quimper-Corentin* and Eugène Scribe's *Mon étoile*. Théophile wrote that "the young Oscar appreciated the *théâtre de salon* although he was a little wild, and indeed, really shy."[37]

Oscar Monet's family life was about to be disrupted. At the end of January, his mother died unexpectedly at the age of forty-seven. Adolphe uprooted his sons to move in with the Lecadres at Le Havre. In March, perhaps in an effort to cheer Oscar, his wealthy Parisian friends invited him back to celebrate a more festive change of house: the inauguration of Hippolyte Billecocq's new apartment on the rue de Monceau with a theatrical soirée. In the elegantly adorned grand salon, beneath paintings by Hubert Robert, Oscar reportedly charmed the large assembled party with his impeccable playing of the comic roles.[38] Scenes like this one contribute to a vivid picture of the young man that stands at odds with the accepted view of the teenage Monet as a juvenile delinquent drifting around Le Havre, waiting to be discovered by Boudin.

The Sketchbook of 1857

Around this time, Oscar began making drawings in a large album of about fifty-five pages measuring approximately 220 by 310 millimeters.[39] This sketchbook, left to the artist's son Michel and subsequently dispersed, is one of the most important records of Monet's artistic activity during the 1850s, providing valuable insights into his development as a draftsman at this early stage of his career. Besides Daniel Wildenstein, the only scholar to give it any serious consideration was Joel Isaacson, who produced the first detailed analysis of the sketchbook in his 1967 doctoral dissertation "The Early Paintings of Claude Monet."[40] During the mid-1960s, he paid a visit to Michel Monet at his home in Sorel-Moussel and examined the sketchbook in its existing state: at the time thirty-nine pages were still bound together and accompanied by seven additional loose sheets. The covers were lost.[41] Table 3 records this pagination and itemizes the detached leaves, as well as additional sheets not seen by Isaacson.

The major scholarly divergence between Isaacson's and Wildenstein's accounts of this album concern its dating, an issue of real significance in the present attempt to thoroughly chronicle Monet's early draftsmanship. The artist inscribed four of the drawings with the day, month, and year (covering the period 15 February–29 June 1857), and annotated eight additional drawings with the day and month only (from 22 February to 3 October). Unaware of the album's original pagination as recorded in part by Isaacson, Wildenstein arranged his catalogue according to his own thematic classification, with representations of boats, bathers, and other caricatures and figure studies followed by a series of landscapes. He concluded based on the evidence of the inscriptions that Monet began using the sketchbook by February 1857 and abandoned it in early October of that year.

At first glance, the sequence of inscribed drawings in the original stitched binding suggests a different chronology. The first four sheets bore the dates "14 septembre," "17 septembre," "1er octobre," and "15 février 1857." The seventh sheet remaining in the album was dated "14 juin 57," the twenty-fourth sheet "29 juin," and the twenty-eighth "17 sept." While admitting that Monet probably did not follow a consistent progression from one page to the next, Isaacson deduced that he took up the album in September 1856, set it aside from early October until February 1857, and then made use of it periodically for the next eight months. This hypothesis is particularly intriguing, as it provides temporal continuity between the first and second sketchbooks of 1856, and thus a continuous record of Monet's drawing practice from July 1856 through October 1857.

The flaw in this proposed chronology is that Monet's approach to filling in a large empty sketchbook was anything but systematic. Folios two (fig. 11) and twenty-eight (fig. 12), are both dated 17 September, forcing the question: is it really possible, based solely on their placement in the album, that these two sheets were drawn exactly a year apart? In fact, the sites depicted were both located relatively near each other, north of Le Havre: folio two was carried out, according to its inscription, "dans les basses

TABLE 3 Sketchbook of 1857

FOLIO / ORIENTATION	WILDENSTEIN NO.	DATE	PAPER COLOR	TITLE / LAST KNOWN LOCATION
1 RECTO; V	D100	14 SEPT.	GRAY	Ancient Well of the Farm of Le Hêtraie, at La Mare au Clerc; *Michel Monet, Sorel-Moussel*
2 RECTO; H	D94	17 SEPT.	GRAY	Cliff with Rocks and Shrubs at Sainte-Adresse; *Michel Monet, Sorel-Moussel*
3 RECTO; H	D96	1 OCT.	GRAY	Cliff at Sainte-Adresse; *World Children's Art Museum, Okazaki*
4 RECTO; H	D78	15 FEB.	GRAY	Entrance to a Farm; *Michel Monet, Sorel-Moussel*
5 RECTO; V	D92		GRAY	Tree Foliage; *Michel Monet, Sorel-Moussel*
6 RECTO; H	D95		GRAY	Outcropping of Rocks; *Michel Monet, Sorel-Moussel*
7 RECTO; H	D83	14 JUNE	WARM GRAY	Water Mill on the Lézarde at Épouville; *World Children's Art Museum, Okazaki*
8 RECTO; H	D97?		WARM GRAY	Thatched Roof (Isaacson: "Hut or Arbor"); *Michel Monet, Sorel-Moussel*
9 RECTO; H	D59 OR 60		IVORY	Sailboats; *Christie's, London, 28 June 2001, lot 403*
10 RECTO; H	D50		IVORY	Sailboat (lightly sketched); *Michel Monet, Sorel-Moussel*
11 RECTO; H	D59 OR 60		IVORY	Sailboats; *Christie's, London, 28 June 2001, lot 403*
12 RECTO; V	D63		BUFF	Bather Wearing a Hat; *Private collection, Boston*
13 RECTO; H	D81		BUFF	Side of a Hill with a Wooden Gate; *Michel Monet, Sorel-Moussel*
14 RECTO; H	D60		IVORY	Four Sailboats; *Michel Monet, Sorel-Moussel*
15 RECTO; H	D53		IVORY	Six Sailboats; *Michel Monet, Sorel-Moussel*
16 RECTO; H	D74		IVORY	Kiln of a Tileworks; *Christie's, London, 23 June 2005, lot 350 (bought in)*
17 RECTO; H	D79		BUFF	Farmhouse; *Michel Monet, Sorel-Moussel*
18 RECTO/VERSO				(blank); *Michel Monet, Sorel-Moussel*
19 RECTO; H	D71		IVORY	Boy Reclining on His Stomach; *Michel Monet, Sorel-Moussel*
20 RECTO; V	D61 OR 69		IVORY	Boy Standing; *Michel Monet, Sorel-Moussel*
21 RECTO; H			IVORY	"Study of Sailboats (just begun)" (Isaacson); *Michel Monet, Sorel-Moussel*
22 RECTO; H	D98		BUFF	Caloges; *Michel Monet, Sorel-Moussel*
23 RECTO; H	D88		BUFF	Landscape with Fence; *Michel Monet, Sorel-Moussel*
24 RECTO; V	D84	29 JUNE	IVORY	Alley of Trees, Gournay; *World Children's Art Museum, Okazaki*
25 RECTO; H	D49		IVORY	Trawler; *Michel Monet, Sorel-Moussel*
26 RECTO; V	D91		BUFF	Landscape with Trees; *Michel Monet, Sorel-Moussel*
27 RECTO			IVORY	(blank); *Michel Monet, Sorel-Moussel*
27 VERSO; V	D68		IVORY	Profile Caricature of a Man with a Top Hat; *Michel Monet, Sorel-Moussel*
28 RECTO; V	D93	17 SEPT.	BUFF	Fir Trees, Sous-Bois; *Michel Monet, Sorel-Moussel*
29 RECTO /VERSO				(blank); *Michel Monet, Sorel-Moussel*
30 RECTO; H	D82		BUFF	Side of a Cliff with Wooden Footbridge; *Michel Monet, Sorel-Moussel*
31 RECTO; V	D67		IVORY	Caricatures of Three Men in Profile; *Michel Monet, Sorel-Moussel*

TABLE 3 (continued)

FOLIO / ORIENTATION	WILDENSTEIN NO.	DATE	PAPER COLOR	TITLE / LAST KNOWN LOCATION
32 RECTO; H	D48		IVORY	Tower of François I at the Entry of the Port of Le Havre; *Michel Monet, Sorel-Moussel*
33 RECTO; H	D66		IVORY	Caricature of Two Bathers; *Michel Monet, Sorel-Moussel*
33 VERSO; V	D64		IVORY	Caricature of a Man in Profile; *Michel Monet, Sorel-Moussel*
34 RECTO; H	D65		IVORY	Caricature of a Bather; *Michel Monet, Sorel-Moussel*
35 RECTO; H	D58		IVORY	Dinghys; *Michel Monet, Sorel-Moussel*
35 VERSO; V	D62		IVORY	Caricatured Head of Man in Profile; *Michel Monet, Sorel-Moussel*
36 RECTO; H	D54		IVORY	Two Sailboats; *Christie's, London, 28 June 2001, lot 403*
37 RECTO; H	D73		IVORY	Still Life with Fruit; *Michel Monet, Sorel-Moussel*
38 RECTO; H	NOT IN W.		IVORY	Letters "PL" blocked out; *Michel Monet, Sorel-Moussel*
38 VERSO; H	D57		IVORY	Two Caricatures of Zouaves; *Michel Monet, Sorel-Moussel*
39 RECTO; H	D56		IVORY	Sailboat; *Michel Monet, Sorel-Moussel*
LOOSE; V	D76	22 FEB.	IVORY	Portrait of a Boy; *Michel Monet, Sorel-Moussel*
LOOSE; H	D103	22 FEB.		Boy Seated by a Rowboat (not seen by Isaacson)
LOOSE; H	D80	1 MAR.	BUFF	Cottage at Guéneville (Gainneville); *Jacques Seligmann & Co., Inc., Galleries, New York*
LOOSE; V	D104	21 MAY		Houses on the Lézarde at Montivilliers; *Private collection, France* (acc. to Wildenstein)
LOOSE; V	D85	15 SEPT.		Two Studies of Houses at Graville; *Michel Monet, Sorel-Moussel*
LOOSE; V	D90	16 SEPT.		Tree Trunks at La Mare au Clerc; *Musée Eugène Boudin, Honfleur*
LOOSE; H	D99	3 OCT.		Two Houses at Graville; *Michel Monet, Sorel-Moussel*
LOOSE; V	D75			Portrait Bust of a Zouave (not seen by Isaacson)
LOOSE; H	D86			Unfinished Sketch of a Roof (not seen by Isaacson)
LOOSE; V	D101			Barren Tree (not seen by Isaacson)
LOOSE; H	D102			Boats and Jetty; *Private collection, France* (acc. to Wildenstein)
LOOSE; H	D77		IVORY	Two Boys, Seated and Standing; *Michel Monet, Sorel-Moussel*
LOOSE; V	D72		GRAY	An Artist Drawing (said to be Boudin); *Musée Eugène Boudin, Honfleur*
LOOSE; H	D52		IVORY	Sailboats; *Michel Monet, Sorel-Moussel*
LOOSE; H	D55		IVORY	Sailboats; *Michel Monet, Sorel-Moussel*
LOOSE; H	D89		IVORY	Man Seated by a Tree; *Private collection, France, c. 1980* (acc. to Wildenstein)
LOOSE; H	D87			Park with House in the Distance (not seen by Isaacson)
LOOSE; V	D70		IVORY	Boy in the Country; *Harry B. and Bessie K. Braude Memorial Collection, Chicago*
LOOSE; H	D51			Beach at Sainte-Adresse; *Katia Pissarro, Paris* (acc. to Wildenstein)

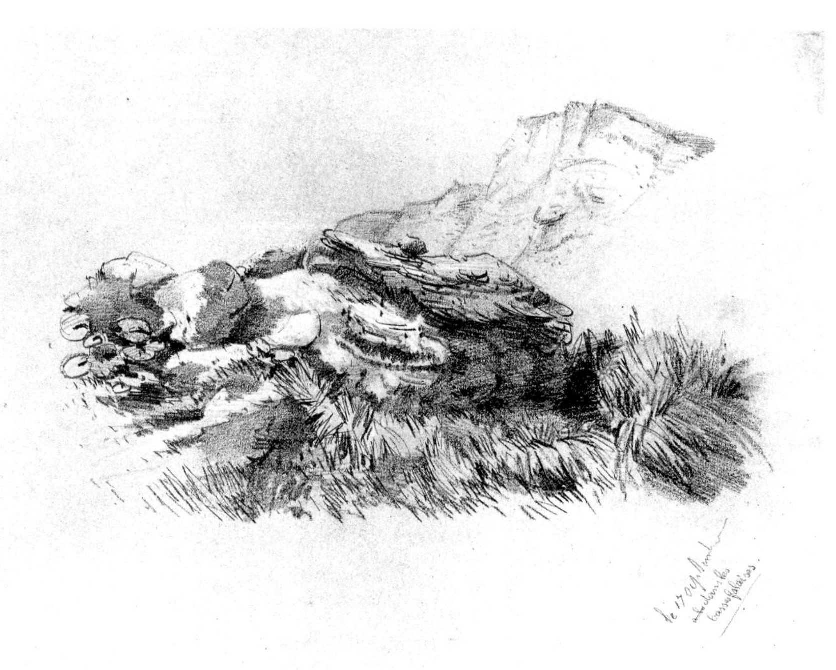

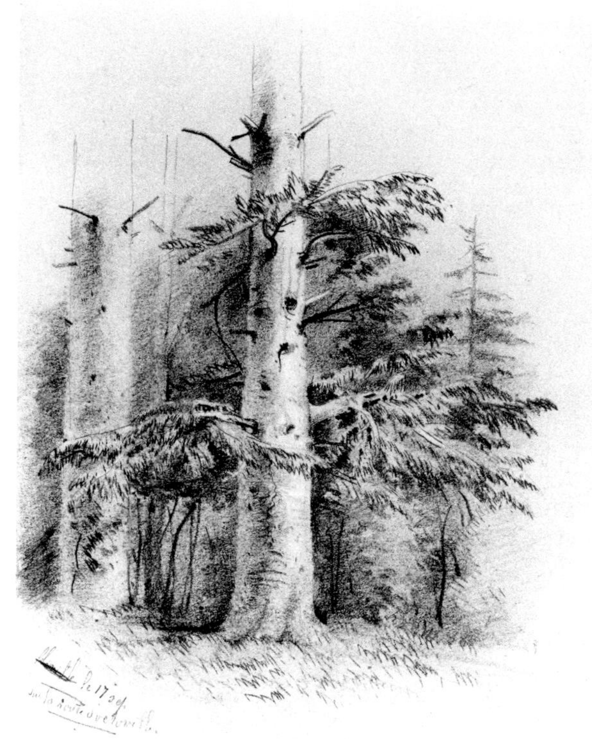

11
Cliff with Rocks and Shrubs at Sainte-Adresse, 1857. Pencil on gray paper, approx. 220 x 310 mm. Location unknown [D94]

12
Fir Trees, Sous-Bois, 1857. Pencil on buff paper, approx. 310 x 220 mm. Location unknown [D93]

falaises" ("in the lower cliffs," that is, halfway between Le Havre and the Cap de la Hève), while folio twenty-eight was drawn at "bléville . . . sur la route d'octoville [*sic*]" ("Bléville on the road to Octeville," approximately two miles north of Le Havre). Further, all of the sheets inscribed with dates in September and October exhibit clear stylistic and technical affinities and are among the most polished graphic performances in the album.

Thus, despite the sequence of dated drawings in the original album, it appears that this sketchbook was indeed used by the artist between February and October of 1857. Monet did not draw on the sheets consecutively from the front to the back of the album, but filled them in haphazardly, leaving blank at least two pages (folios eighteen and twenty-nine, recto and verso) and the recto of one other page (folio twenty-seven). As the album was nearing capacity in September, he returned to fill in two empty sections, starting with folio twenty-eight, which was bounded by at least two other unused sheets, and then folios one to three at the front of the album.[42] Paper color appears to have been the primary factor in influencing his choice of a particular page to make a drawing. Like many commercially sold sketchbooks of the period, this album contained multiple tints of paper—specifically, ivory, gray, warm gray, and buff. Wildenstein was unaware of this feature of the album, because he was working from old black-and-white photographs that did not clearly reveal the qualities of the paper. Isaacson observed Monet's penchant for applying certain tints to specific subjects, generally reserving the ivory sheets for his images of sailboats and caricatures, and the toned papers for his landscape studies.[43]

Viewed in its totality, the sketchbook of 1857 offers a comprehensive survey of the adolescent artist's dexterity in several distinct graphic modes, a flexibility that will characterize his mature draftsmanship. Three broad categories of drawing coexisted within its pages: rapidly executed sketches, precise linear studies, and conventional landscape vignettes. No evidence has been found to establish that any of the images in this sketchbook were copied from prints; rather, all were the products of Oscar's own direct encounters with elements of the world around him, selected and transcribed *d'après nature* according to his own vision. Yet as an aspiring graphic artist Oscar Monet was neither an autodidact nor a *tabula rasa*, so that his handling of each of these manners may be usefully probed for traces of his early training and his exposure to preexisting conventions and models.

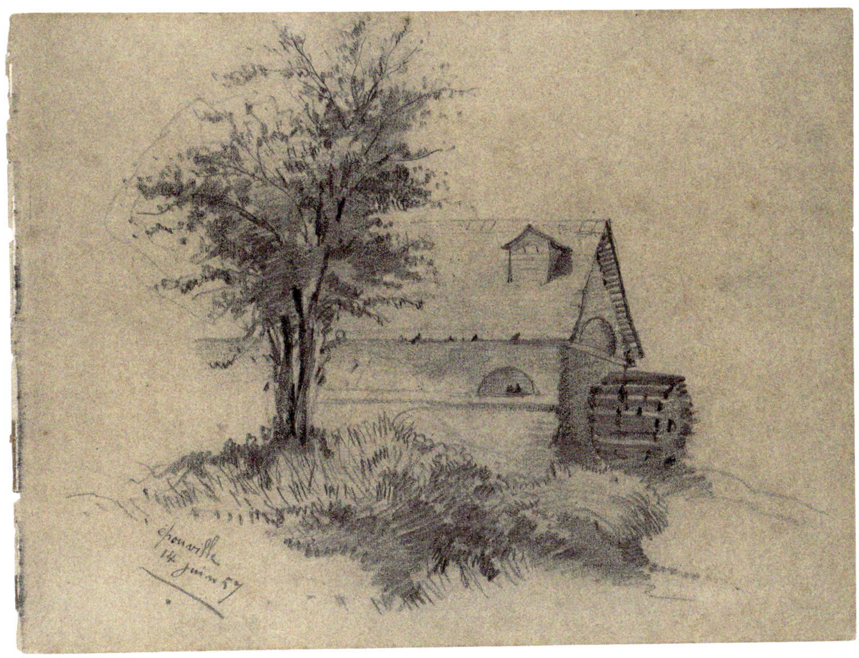

13

Water Mill on the Lézarde at Épouville, 1857. Pencil on warm gray paper, 228 x 307 mm. The World Children's Art Museum, Okazaki, Japan [D83]

Monet's active use of this sketchbook coincided, in part, with the annual summer holiday of his friends, the Beguin Billecocqs. In May Théophile rented the country house in the quaint fishing village of Sainte-Adresse that belonged to Jacques Lecadre, and there installed his wife Amélie, his young daughters Alice and Geneviève, his father Paul, and his cousin Théodore. He related the experiences shared that summer by Théodore and Oscar, whose devotion to drawing was more obsessive than ever:

They went vagabonding in the environs, swimming in the ocean, fishing, going out for lunch and staying out through dinner. Oscar drew a great deal and always carried with him little sketchbooks and pencils, with which he sketched pastoral landscapes and marines. In addition every scrap of paper, no matter how small, was drawn upon with country scenes, tiny seascapes, and fishermen. Every sheet of paper that came into his hands was destined for a drawing. He preferred old papers of the previous century, made from real rags. His sketches, whether in crayon or pencil, were always excellent, even if they were rapidly executed. He knew how to capture the essential characteristics of a scene.[44]

This passage reveals that the sketchbook of 1857 was among several albums of various sizes that Oscar had in his possession. Given its relative bulkiness, this album would have been impractical to transport on a daily basis. Indeed, the extended length of time he took to fill the album demonstrates the sporadic nature of its use. Smaller pocket-sized sketchbooks of the type favored by his mother were more likely to have been habitually carried around by the young artist. Unfortunately, none of his more portable albums from this period is known to have survived.

Nearly half of the large album was composed of landscapes. Many of these, if not all, were executed in the environs north and east of the city of Le Havre, within walking distance of his home in the Ingouville quarter. A drawing made prior to Théophile's arrival on 14 June depicts a water mill on the Lézarde at Épouville, located some six miles to the northeast (fig. 13). Like the majority of the landscapes, this view takes the conventional form of a vignette, with the principal elements—water mill, tree, patch of ground—finished in greatest detail near the center of the warm gray sheet, and the outer edges left blank. Sharp lines play a limited role in the drawing, primarily to demarcate the mill's roof; tone is achieved through soft parallel lines. Compared with the crisp definition of the architecture, the tall grasses in the foreground are conveyed by an abstract network of pencil strokes. In its humble, picturesque subject matter and traditional format, this drawing was an unpretentious attempt by the young artist to emulate what amounted to an international style of landscape illustration during the first half of the nineteenth century.

Fifteen days later, Oscar ventured into the forest at Gournay, north of Harfleur, and created an energetic *plein-air* study of an alley of trees that reveals a far less restrained style of draftsmanship (fig. 14). Opening his sketchbook to an ivory sheet of paper, he proceeded to select and transcribe a fragment of the scene with confident and freely drawn strokes of the pencil. Like the Épouville view, the *Alley of Trees, Gournay* floats in the center of the page, but the contrast of the dark graphite lines against the stark white sheet produces a less conventionally atmospheric

14

Alley of Trees, Gournay, 1857. Pencil, 307 x 228 mm. The World Children's Art Museum, Okazaki, Japan [D84]

15

Tree Trunks at La Mare au Clerc, 1857. Pencil, approx. 310 x 220 mm. Musée Eugène Boudin, Honfleur [D90]

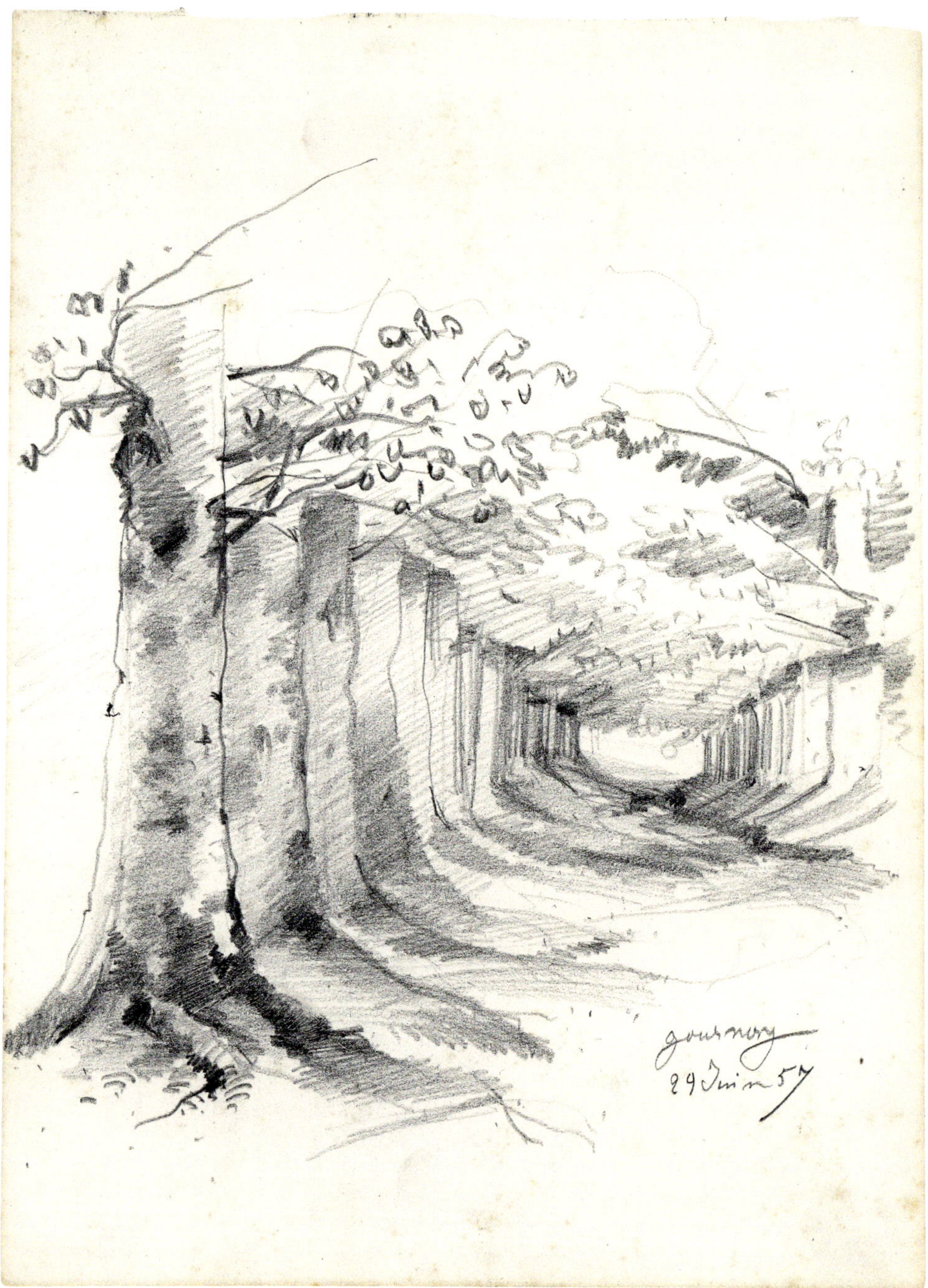

effect. Chiaroscuro is achieved through rapid diagonal shading put down with varying degrees of pressure. The drawing in the upper portion of the sheet, rendering the limits of the canopy of foliage, is remarkably emancipated. Leaves are suggested not by patches of tone but by a cursory tangle of notational marks.

In September, Oscar executed another tree study at La Mare au Clerc, a quarter east of Ingouville, in a similar bold manner (fig. 15). He focused his attention on a pair of knotty tree pollards, rendering them with particular attention to their texture and contour against the ivory sketchbook page. Picturesque horticultural specimens like these were favorites of the Barbizon painters, and long before them, the Old Masters of Dutch landscape painting. The widely circulating lithographs of the Swiss painter Alexandre Calame (1810–1864), from instructional portfolios marketed to drawing students and amateurs, have also been put forward by Monet scholars as typifying what had

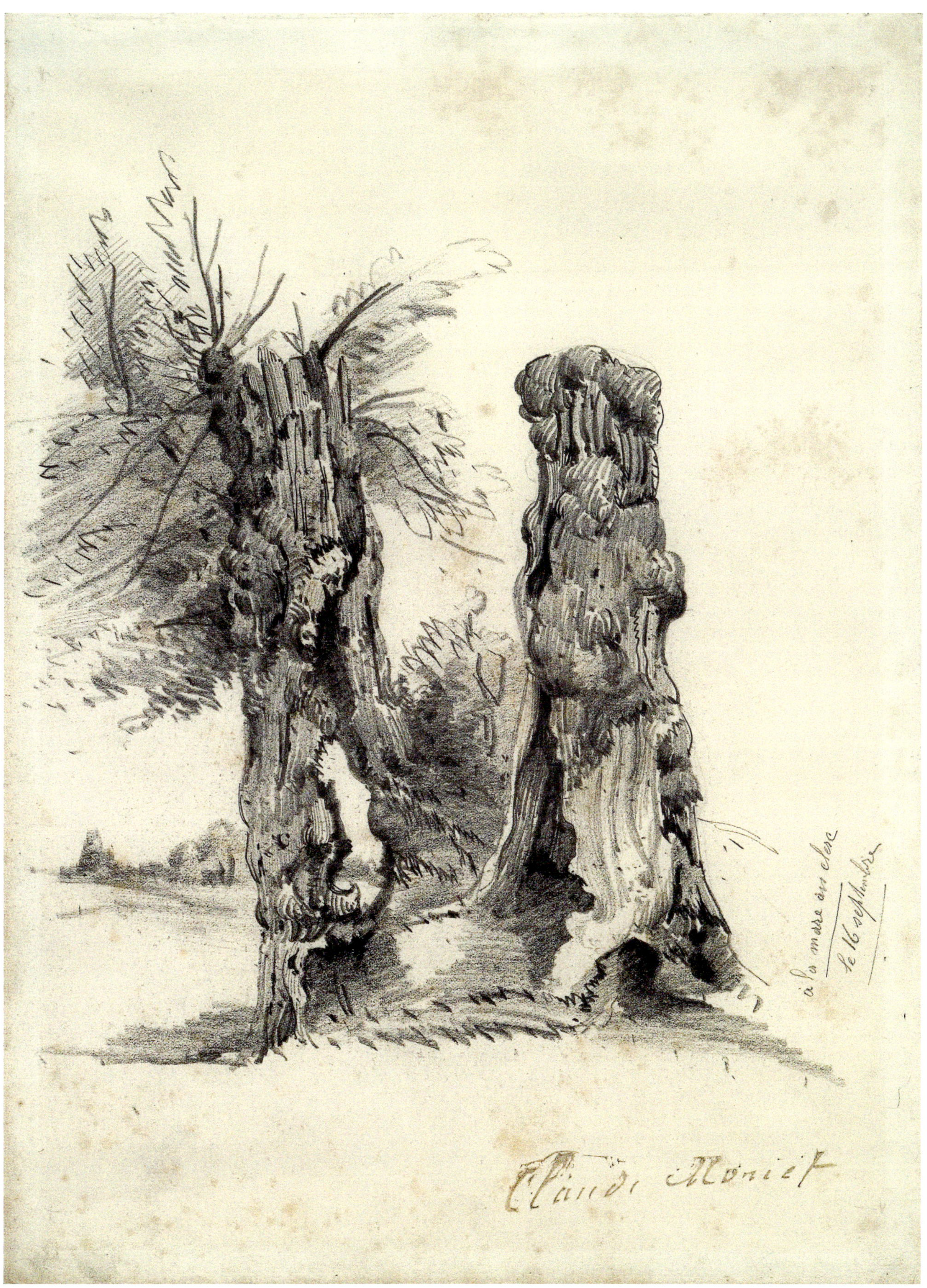
à la mare aux clerc
le 16 septembre
Claude Monet

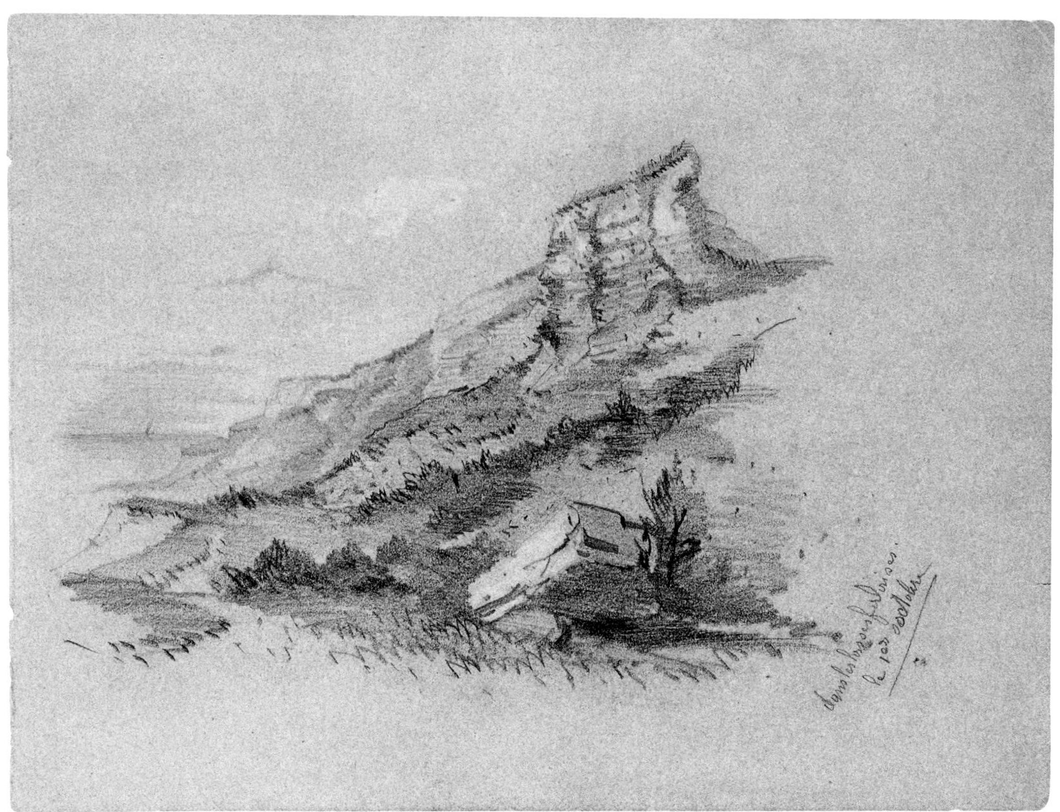

16
Cliff at Sainte-Adresse, 1857. Pencil and white chalk on gray paper, 228 x 307 mm. The World Children's Art Museum, Okazaki, Japan [D96]

already become a somewhat clichéd aesthetic.[45]

A drawing of a cliffside at Sainte-Adresse (fig. 16), dated the first of October, returns to the more formulaic manner of *Water Mill on the Lézarde at Épouville*. On this sheet, Oscar followed the traditional approach of simplifying the infinite tonal gradations of the natural world into three rudimentary shades: the gray middle-ground of the tinted paper, used to convey a sense of atmosphere; the dark lines in pencil, which record the principal forms; and highlights applied with white chalk. This approach to landscape draftsmanship was so widely practiced by the mid-nineteenth century that it is difficult to specify a particular source for Monet's knowledge of this manner.

Théophile would join his family at Sainte-Adresse for the month of July. "Since our stay in Ingouville in 1853, Oscar Monet had become an elegant young man with a dash of the bohemian," Théophile observed:

He was amiable, droll and knew how to laugh from word games and puns. A bon vivant, he liked good food, and his independent character had developed, so too his sense of curiosity and fantasy. But sometimes, he fell into a profound melancholy that would leave him just as suddenly as it overtook him. He had a pronounced taste for the theatre, developed when he became a habitué of our cultural and artistic soirées. Although his father said of him that he was a 'revolutionary anarchist and extravagant,' Oscar was down-to-earth, pleasant, a good citizen, generous, and always did his utmost to make our family's sojourns go as smoothly as possible. He knew the region perfectly well and offered to be our guide. I had the greatest affection for him because he maintained the youthfulness and spontaneity of his early childhood.[46]

During Théophile's stay, Oscar arranged the hire of a carriage and two horses to lead the Beguin Billecocqs on a two-day sightseeing tour to the south of Sainte-Adresse around Honfleur, Trouville, and down to Deauville; the group returned to Sainte-Adresse via steamer. Afterwards, he carried on his role as guide on an excursion up the coast to the spectacular rock cliffs of Étretat. The group visited the village's twelfth-century church, the port of Fécamp, the abbeys of

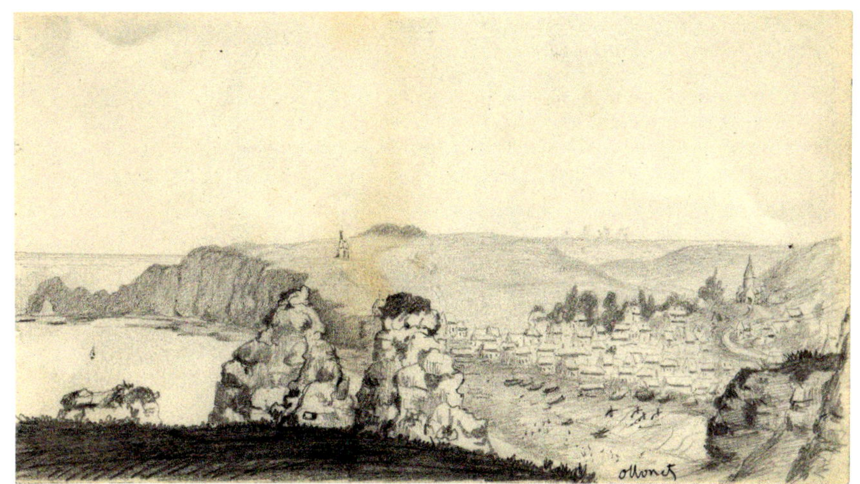

17
Circle of Théophile Beguin Billecocq (French, 1825–1906), *Falaise d'Amont (Étretat)*, c. 1857(?). Pencil, 80 x 142 mm. Collection of Prince Xavier Beguin Billecocq, Paris

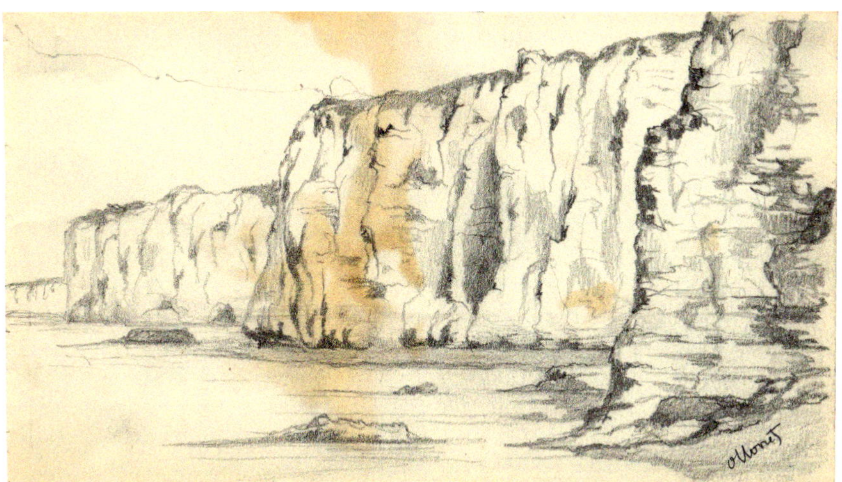

18
Circle of Théophile Beguin Billecocq, *Cliffs at Étretat*, c. 1857(?). Pencil, 80 x 142 mm. Collection of Prince Xavier Beguin Billecocq, Paris

Valmont and Bec-Crespin. As was their custom on these jaunts, they enjoyed a picnic lunch in the countryside, a proper *déjeuner sur l'herbe* prepared by the two boys.

Théophile's memoir contains a description of Monet making drawings at a location that by the 1850s had already become a mecca for professional artists:

Oscar did not neglect his drawing, realizing little refined sketches of the cliff, of Étretat, of the roads and the delightful small half-timbered farmhouses of Normandy with their thatched roofs. The drawings that he made were detailed, as precise as reality, and delicate, representing the houses, trees, people, etc., in the best possible manner.[47]

Two carefully rendered pencil drawings from Théophile's collection, removed from a small sketchbook and signed in ink "O Monet," may derive from this episode. One is a view from the top of the Falaise d'Aval looking toward the Falaise d'Amont, with the *Chambre des Demoiselles* rising in the foreground and the village off to the right (fig. 17). The other is an intensely observed segment of a limestone cliff face (fig. 18). The drawings are obviously the work of an amateur, albeit a promising one. Although their attribution to the sixteen year-old draftsman is uncertain — as they bear little resemblance to the landscapes in the large 1857 album — they have the intriguing potential to be the earliest known works executed by Monet at Étretat.

In early September 1857, Théophile Beguin Billecocq returned to Le Havre at the invitation of the mayor, Édouard Larue, to attend the regattas sponsored by Prince Jérôme Bonaparte. He invited his cousin Théodore and Oscar Monet to accompany him, and the three

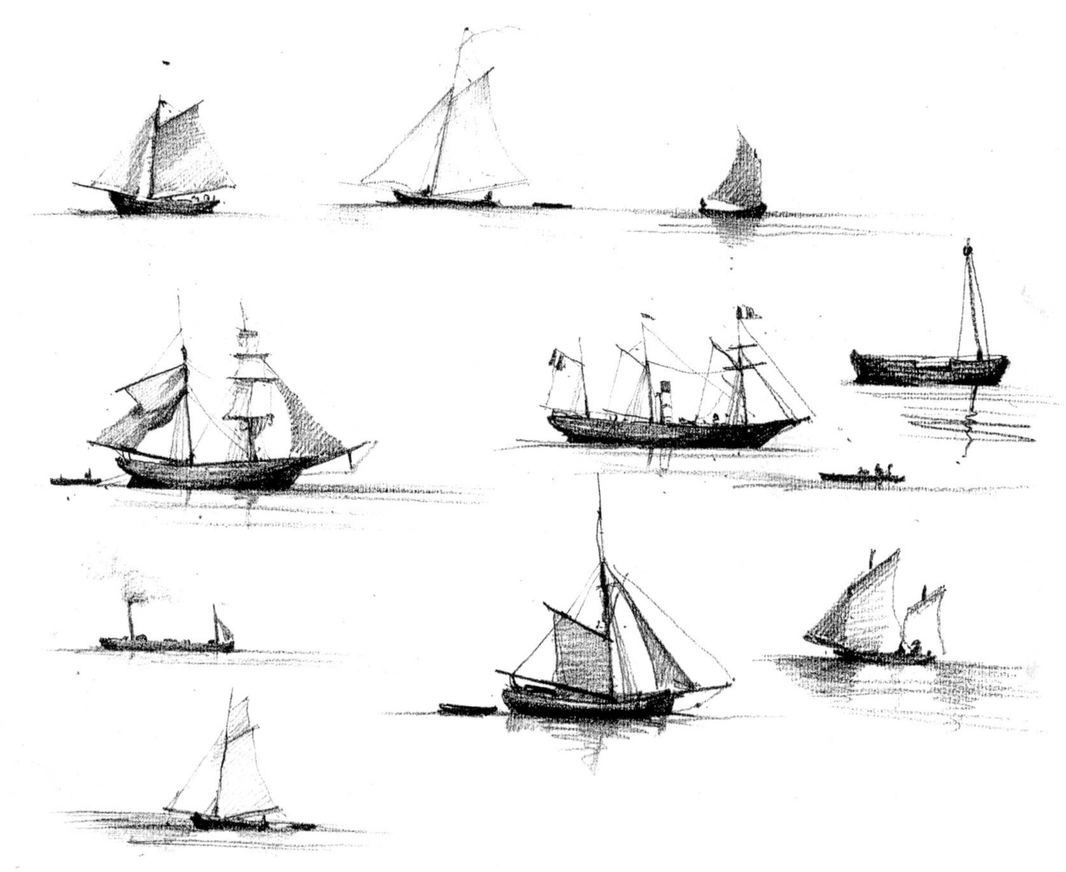

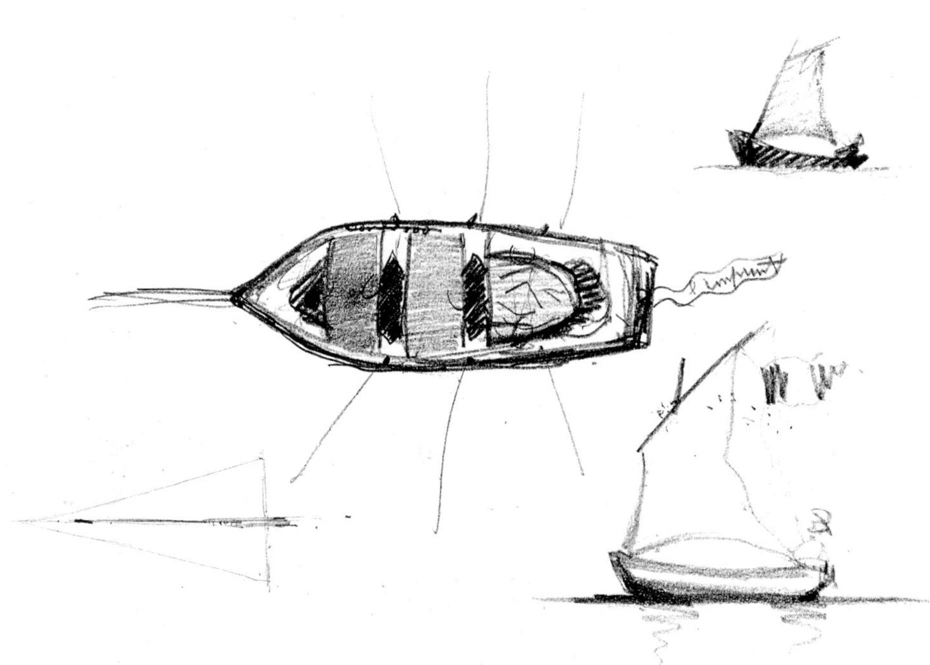

19

Sailboats, 1857. Pencil, approx. 220 x 310 mm. Location unknown [D52]

20

Dinghys, 1857. Pencil, approx. 220 x 310 mm. Location unknown [D58]

enjoyed seats among the notables in the tent of honor. On this occasion, Oscar made drawings of "all sorts of sailing ships and bathers," Théophile recalled.[48] These subjects — boat studies and portraits, including representations of bathers — make up the balance of the large 1857 sketchbook, and while the majority of these drawings are undated, it is possible that some were made during the course of this event. Compared with the rather more conventional landscapes in this album, the boat and figure studies represent significantly different aspects of his draftsmanship.

Oscar executed his diminutive renderings of watercraft, fifty-two boats of various types arrayed across twelve pages in the album, with such great attention to detail that the markings on some of the sails are legible, and in a few cases, specific historic vessels can be identified (fig. 19). All of the drawings were carried out in sharp pencil on off-white sheets of paper. The majority of the boats are shown in profile, strictly parallel to the picture plane; a few are depicted directly from the stern. He gave little attention to their settings, other than a few horizontal strokes of the pencil to suggest the water's surface. The somewhat monotonous studies attest not only to Oscar's mania for drawing but to his deep affection for the sea and his impressive expertise in the minutiae of watercraft.

In their clinical precision, these nautical studies have nothing in common with the picturesque tradition of amateur bourgeois draftsmanship as practiced by Oscar's mother, his aunt, or his friend Théophile Beguin Billecocq. On the contrary, they may reflect the exercises that Oscar was obligated to perform as a *collègien*. Draftsmanship was considered an essential part of the core curriculum at both the primary and secondary levels of the nineteenth-century French education system.[49] Teaching draftsmanship was regarded as an important step in ensuring the future preeminence of French art and industry. One sheet in particular, representing a schematic view of a small open boat seen from above with oars and mast (fig. 20), suggests his exposure to the practice of technical illustration as taught in school. Courses and manuals in linear drawing *(le dessin linéaire)* stressed the importance of representing objects, particularly products of industry, in a manner sufficiently precise that the drawing could serve as a design model.[50]

Representations of the human figure, undoubtedly another component of the drawing instruction Monet received in school, took up more than a quarter of the 1857 sketchbook. These range from serious efforts — naturalistic portraits of individuals and types — to more hastily executed caricatures, the self-confident scribbles of a boy drawing for sheer pleasure. All indications are that young Oscar was a gifted portraitist. At the time of his earlier summer visit, Théophile remarked on Oscar's special talent in this genre:

He executed numerous portraits, making one and all pose. My father was sketched sitting in his armchair, my little family and myself on a large sheet. Théodore was also the object of the stroke of his pencil as well as my sister Marie de Beauregard. The only one to escape Oscar's touch was my brother-in-law Edmond de Beauregard. As soon as he made a drawing, whatever its subject, he offered it to a member of the family. If the drawing was in a sketchbook, he removed the page and affixed his signature or his initials. We were all thrilled to receive these little drawings that we collected in albums. Oscar was generous and he was delighted to see that his work gave us pleasure. He felt useful and valued.[51]

Naturalistic figure studies such as his *Bather Wearing a Hat* (fig. 21) show that as a young man Monet was completely at ease rendering the human form. The drawing depicts not a plaster cast of a classical nude, nor a professional model, but an unidealized modern man, perhaps sketched surreptitiously as he stood on the beach. Images like this of bourgeois swimmers and bathers formed part of the repertoire of Daumier's lithographs (fig. 22). With the utmost economy of line, Monet succeeded in bringing to life the amusingly attired beachgoer, capturing his rugged likeness, his slightly pudgy

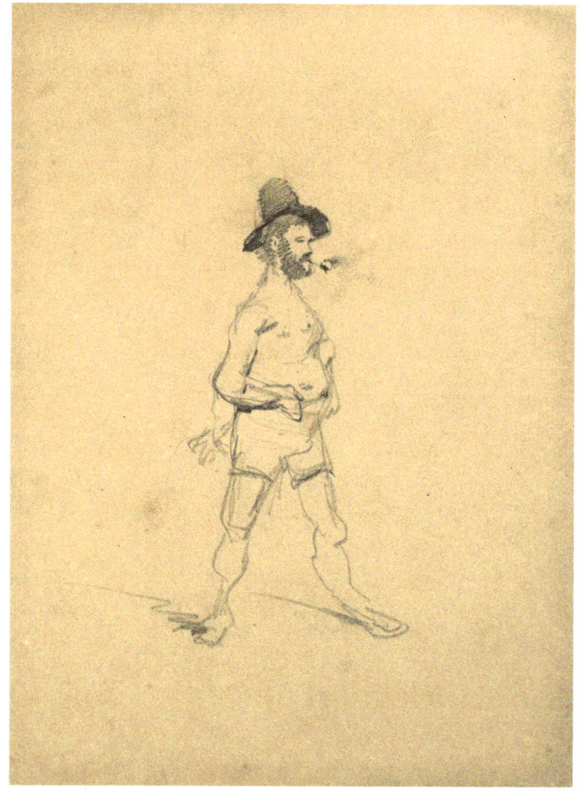

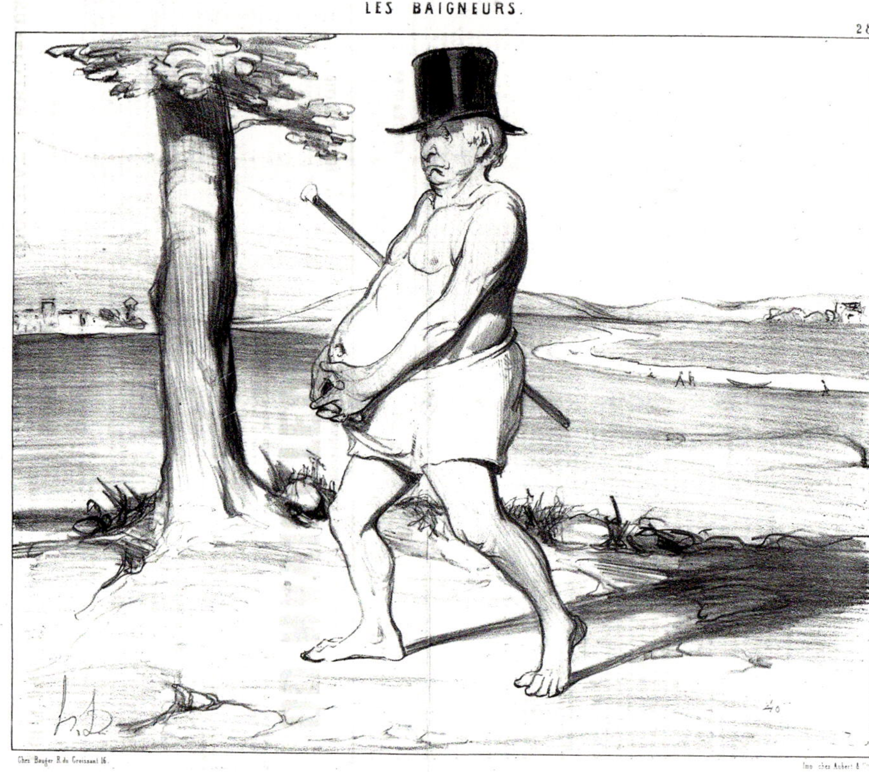

21
Bather Wearing a Hat, 1857. Pencil on buff paper, 309 x 230 mm. Private collection [D63]

22
Honoré Daumier (French, 1808–1879), *A Breach of Trust* (from the *Baigneurs* series), 1842. Lithograph, 257 x 208 mm. The National Gallery of Art, Washington, D.C. Ailsa Mellon Bruce Fund

anatomy, and even imparting a sense of personality through his jaunty pose. Here the spirited result transcends the simple graphic means.

Another figure study from the sketchbook of 1857 has attracted a disproportionate amount of scholarly attention in light of the sitter's presumed identity. Although it bears neither an identifying inscription nor a date, it has been traditionally recognized as a portrait of Eugène Boudin sitting outdoors at work on a drawing (fig. 23). Michel Monet apparently subscribed to this attractive view, and made a gift of the sheet in 1956 to the Musée municipal de Honfleur (co-founded in 1868 by Boudin and now called the Musée Eugène Boudin), which catalogued it as a portrait of Honfleur's most famous painter.

In fact, the date of the first meeting between Boudin and Monet—variously pinpointed to between 1855 and 1858—remains an unresolved preoccupation in the literature on both artists. In the end, it must be admitted that this drawing contributes nothing to a resolution of this issue. The fact that it depicts an older draftsman does not prove it to be a portrait of Boudin, who was not known to have been photographed until much later. It could just as easily show Théophile Beguin Billecocq, or any of a number of amateur and professional artists who were attracted to the Normandy coast during this era. And even if it could be established to represent Boudin, there is no proof that the drawing was carried out within the documented chronological confines of this sketchbook; indeed, it could have been inserted on a blank sheet in subsequent years. There is no doubt that Oscar Monet's encounter with Eugène Boudin was a fortuitous event that would influence the course of his career. There is no evidence, however, that this event had occurred prior to 1858, when the two artists exhibited paintings together in a show organized by the Société des amis des arts in Le Havre.

From May through September 1858, the Beguin Billecocqs rented the Château de Villiers in Poissy, a large neoclassical-style mansion with beautiful fruit and flower gardens that belonged to a family friend. Its relative proximity to Paris meant that Théophile could buy a first-class railroad pass so he could leave his job at the ministry and join his wife and daughters

23
An Artist Drawing (said to be Boudin), c. 1858. Crayon on gray paper, 300 x 220 mm. Musée Eugène Boudin, Honfleur [D72]

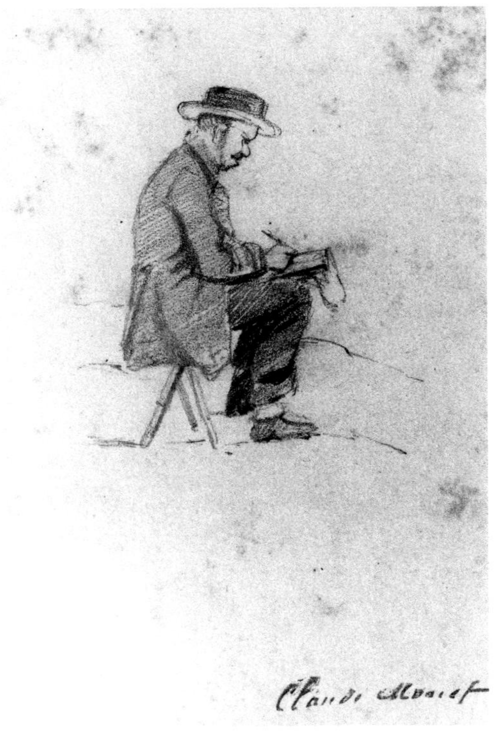

for dinner every evening. He took his vacation from the middle of June through the middle of July, and was joined once again by Théodore Billecocq and Oscar Monet, who came to stay at the château. "Oscar passed the long days drawing numerous varieties of fruit trees in the park, as well as landscapes in the environs."[52] He gathered flowers to make still-life arrangements, and in addition to pencil, used crayons and sanguine. Théophile hired a carriage and driver to transport the group on excursions to the forest of Saint-Germain, Marly, Saint-Nom-La-Bretèche, Retz, Aigremont, Chambourcy, and the group followed the Seine from Meulan through Villennes, Médan, Vernouillet, and Verneuil.

Besides sampling the gastronomic specialties of the region, the major pastime enjoyed by Oscar and his wealthy friends was drawing the landscape:

We drew charming scenes along the banks of the Seine. We all applied ourselves, and the drawings were quite successful. Those by Oscar were undoubtedly the best. This young man had a real talent because in a few strokes of the crayon he captured the principal lines of what he saw, then applied himself to draw in a precise manner and sketch the forms that appeared the most interesting to him. This manner of working was Impressionistic in the rapidity of its execution: neither a mark too many or too few.

During our promenades, we carried with us all of our sketchbooks and crayons and when we found a site that attracted our attention, we all set about to draw it. Everyone participated in these artistic séances in the open air directed by Oscar. In a few excellent strokes of the crayon, Oscar always finished first. Then, it was amusing to make the comparison with our efforts. This game was a great diversion.[53]

Scenes like this would be repeated in the summers of 1859 (at Nemours) and 1860 (in Honfleur), after Monet had come of age and moved on from Le Havre to Paris, and they would be recalled in some of his earliest and most ambitious figure paintings.

In revisiting episodes from Monet's adolescence through the eyes of Théophile Beguin Billecocq, and comparing his memoirs with the artist's own recollections, a basic question arises: what is to be made of Monet's reticence — in fact, his absolute silence — concerning his close relationship with this aristocratic family in interviews about his early years? Why did he erase them from the record? Perhaps he sensed that the story of his bold, even cocky pursuit of art in a provincial backwater might seem less heroic if it was revealed that he had been nurtured by a culturally literate coterie. Indeed, in these early years, Monet's supporters extended beyond the circle of his mother and his dear aunt, further even than the locals who bought his caricatures, to include several members of a wealthy Parisian family for whom Le Havre was a prime holiday destination. When Monet was a teenager, the Billecocqs lavished praise on his drawings; later, when he was a struggling professional artist, they would become patrons in his times of need. It was a privileged relationship that he seems to have kept from his colleagues and journalists at the risk of spoiling his cultural rags-to-riches story.

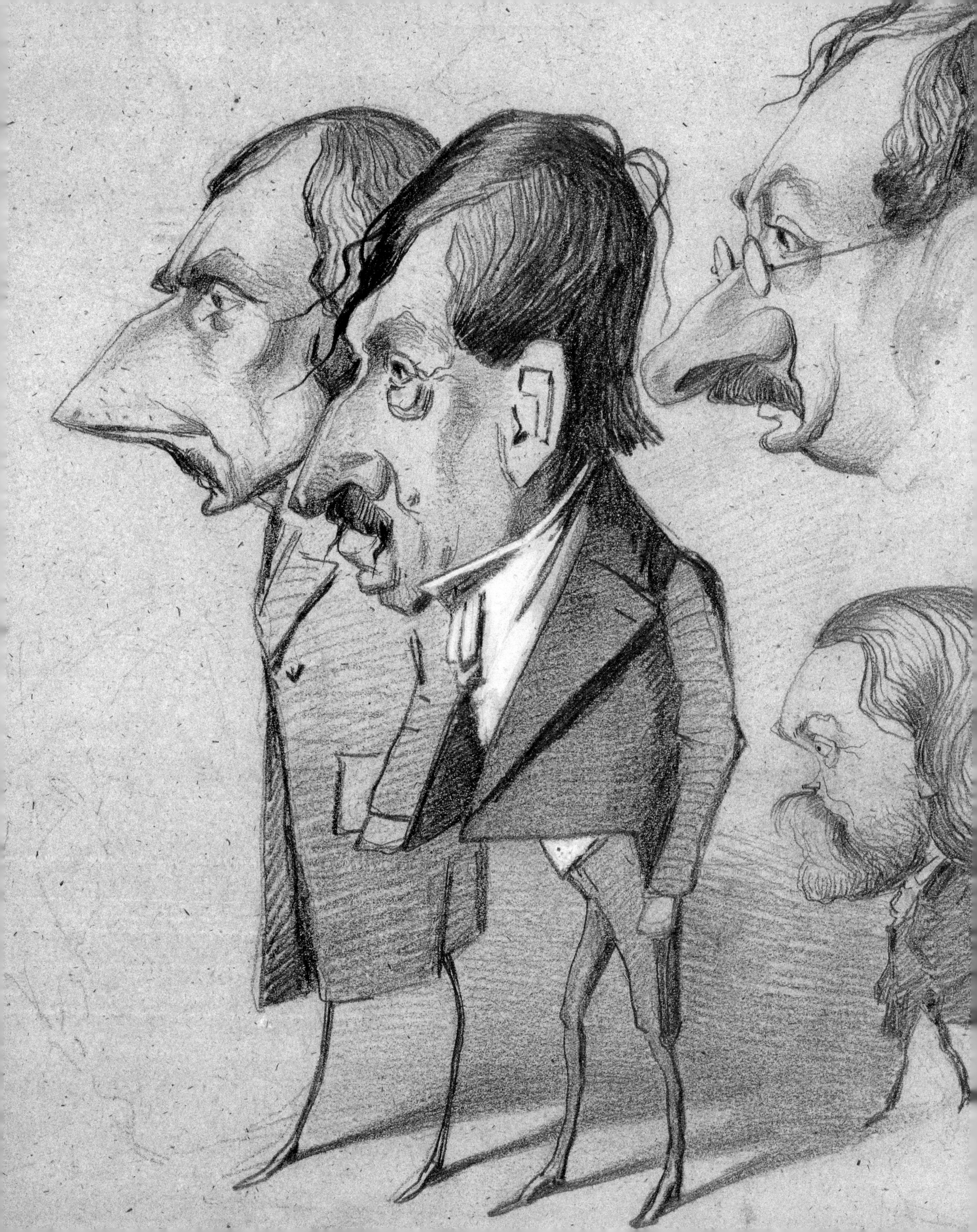

CHAPTER TWO Oscar Monet, Caricaturist

I went to see the Durand-Ruels. At one point the conversation touched on Monet, and I learned that at the age of sixteen, to earn a living, he did caricatures in Le Havre under the name of Oscar. These have in fact been brought in recently, but are of no interest; they didn't buy them."[1] So wrote René Gimpel upon a visit to Monet's primary dealer in September 1927, less than a year after the artist's death and some four months after the *Grand Décorations* were unveiled to the public. Although as an adult Monet was forthcoming about his youthful activity as a caricaturist, the perceived disconnect between this specialized segment of his juvenile oeuvre and his mature paintings contributed to the devaluation of these early drawings even when he had become world famous. Other than the works handed down within the Monet[2] and Billecocq[3] families, and those few sheets that were kept by descendents of the original sitters,[4] only a single cache of ten caricatures — the drawings turned away by the Durand-Ruel Gallery in 1927 — is known to have surfaced on the art market prior to the 1970s.[5]

In one sense, Monet's caricatures have retained a remarkable degree of their original power as *portraits-charges*, literally "charged portraits." Indeed, their shock value may be even greater now than when Monet first drew them, precisely because this strange assortment of enormous heads on miniature bodies seems a world apart from the paintings of seascapes, grainstacks, and water lilies so adored by the museum-going public. How are we to assimilate this substantial corpus of wayward drawings into the story of Monet's artistic development? Should the caricatures be dismissed as an eccentric footnote, a curious dead end in the trajectory of Monet's career, or do they constitute an essential chapter in his advancement as an artist?[6] Although he was not to become a professional caricaturist, and in this sense these works represent an iconographic blind alley within the catalogue raisonné, Monet's experience in this genre gives unique insight into his intellectual formation as he embarked on his career as a painter.

Monet's activity in this specialized genre coincided with the publication of Charles Baudelaire's three landmark essays on the art of caricature that first appeared between 1855 and 1857.[7] In much the same way that Monet's *portraits-charges* have been marginalized in the literature on his painted oeuvre, Baudelaire's three articles have been customarily dismissed as falling outside the mainstream of his literary corpus. More recently, Michele Hannoosh has argued persuasively for their centrality, claiming that "these seemingly inconsequential essays on so seemingly inconsequential an art form work out some of Baudelaire's most innovative ideas, specifically those concerning the modern aesthetic."[8] To Baudelaire, caricature was not a minor genre, but a serious art form, blended together in his thought process with the theory of modernity he would shortly put forth in "The Painter of Modern Life," his revolutionary examination of the work of Constantin Guys.[9]

Clearly, Baudelaire was just as unlikely to have encountered Monet's caricatures as the Le Havre teenager was to have read the critic's erudite essays in *Le Portefeuille*, *Le Présent*, and *L'Artiste*. Yet, the historical concurrence in the prominent writer's and aspiring draftsman's devotion to the same droll form of artistic expression helps to situate the young man's work in a larger and more cosmopolitan movement, one that was appreciated by critics of the vanguard. With the benefit of hindsight and Baudelaire's rhetoric, we might see in Oscar Monet more than just a provincial fantasist-draftsman, but a budding *artiste-flâneur*.

The sketching of humorous portraits of one's friends and family is a not uncommon extracurricular activity for young artists. Among Monet's generation, Courbet, Manet, Degas, and Pissarro are all known to have drawn caricatures in their youth. What set Monet's activity apart from his contemporaries was the sheer intensity with which he took to this genre, as reflected both in the quantity and the quality of his efforts. It was as a caricaturist that Monet first made his name and earned an income from his art, and through this occupation rubbed shoulders with the likes of Eugène Boudin. It was as a caricaturist that he made a decisive early leap from gifted amateur to skilled professional, from child prodigy to working artist. Monet's caricatures are his most technically accomplished productions dating from the 1850s, and they form the largest class among his surviving drawings outside the sketchbooks.[10]

Monet's Exposure to Caricature

Among the great revelations of Théophile Beguin Billecocq's Grand Journal are the character sketches it provides of the artist's mother and father, who had become effectively obscured by the shadows of time. In one passage, Beguin Billecocq related Adolphe Monet's interest in foreign politics, and his delight in gossip brought back from the French capital by his friends in the diplomatic service:

> *He loved to hear all about the many parties that we attended in Paris. Balls, dinners, receptions in the court of the Tuileries with the Emperor and Empress; with Baron Haussmann at the Hôtel de Ville, in the many embassies, legations, or general consulates. He appreciated the anecdotes, the eclecticism of the receptions, the ostentation of the Second Empire, the French personalities and the many European or exotic sovereigns who came to visit the imperial couple, which always gave the occasion for magnificent celebrations.*[11]

In considerations of Monet's early career, caricature has always been regarded as a form of youthful rebellion against the values of his teachers and his family. Given Adolphe's fascination with celebrity gossip, and Louise's passion for amateur theatricals, however, their son's cheeky caricatures might be reconsidered as a product of his early upbringing at the hands of relatively enlightened parents. Further, through his friendship with members of the Billecocq clan, he gained significant firsthand exposure to cultural activities in the French capital even before moving there.

Monet's childhood coincided with the waning years of what was arguably the golden age of French caricature, a graphic genre that had developed into a potent form of expression during the July Monarchy (1830–48). The popular press, in response to the ever-increasing demand for illustrations of current events and leading personalities of the day, put dozens of caricaturists to work and sent their images into wide circulation. Such daily and weekly newspapers of both the left and right as *Le Charivari*, *Le*

24
Honoré Daumier, *Caricature of Tocqueville* (from the *Representatives Represented* series), 1849. Lithograph, 357 x 273 mm. Sterling and Francine Clark Art Institute, Williamstown, Massachusetts

Journal Amusant, *Le Gaulois*, and *La Presse* published satirical illustrations by Honoré Daumier (1808–1879), Paul Gavarni (1804–1866), Nadar (1820–1910), Étienne Carjat (1828–1906), and others in the form of lithographs, gillotages, woodcuts, and wood engravings. Through the efforts of several contemporary writers (most notably Baudelaire, Champfleury, and the Goncourt brothers), the individual bodies of work produced by a select group of French caricaturists, whose latest prints were seen by hundreds of thousands of readers on a daily basis, were singled out for critical attention.

In his 1857 article "*Quelques caricaturistes français*" ["Some French Caricaturists"], Baudelaire turned the spotlight on both eighteenth-century and contemporary caricaturists, treating their works with the kind of seriousness of purpose normally reserved for high art. His comments are both stinging and laudatory. When discussing the modern school, he reserved his greatest praise for Daumier, whom he commended for his excellent draftsmanship, his sense of humor, and his deep insights into the modern condition, particularly of the middle-class. "No one better than he has known and loved (in the manner of artists) the bourgeois, that last vestige of the Middle Ages, that Gothic ruin that dies hard, that type at once banal and eccentric," Baudelaire extolled. "Daumier has lived intimately with him, he has spied on him day and night, he has learned the secrets of his bedroom, he has become acquainted with his wife and children, he knows the shape of his nose and the structure of his head, he knows the spirit that animates his household from top to bottom."[12]

Given their enthusiasms for art, politics, and current events, there is little question that the Monet family would have been regular consumers of Parisian caricature journals such as these. The suggestion that young Oscar's caricatures were informed, in part, by the work of Daumier was first made by Philippe Burty as early as 1883 in his article published in *La République française* (quoted in chapter one, p. 10). Burty observed that Monet's "big heads" were similar to those found in Daumier's series *Representatives*

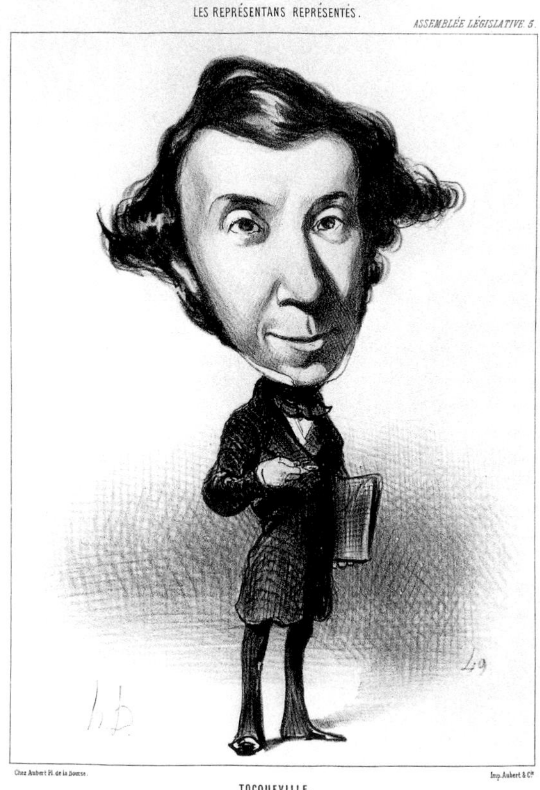

Represented [*Les représantans représentés*], which first appeared in *Le Charivari* between 1848–50 (fig. 24). From his direct copies made after published lithographs by Paul Hadol (1835–1875), Carjat, and Nadar, we know that he was at least exposed firsthand to *Le Gaulois*, the *Journal amusant*, and *Le Figaro*. Monet began as an artist in the age of mass media, and his caricatures demonstrate a remarkable degree of visual literacy with regard to the French illustrated press. A growing influx of printed images and Parisian tourists into the seaside community of Le Havre contributed to the young draftsman's cosmopolitan point of view.

Physiognomies of Le Havre

In addition to relatively naturalistic portraits, Monet's sketchbook of 1857 contained several figure drawings that seem to represent generic social types along the lines of Daumier's lithographs. In chapter one, a drawing of a bather in a top hat (see fig. 21) is reproduced alongside a

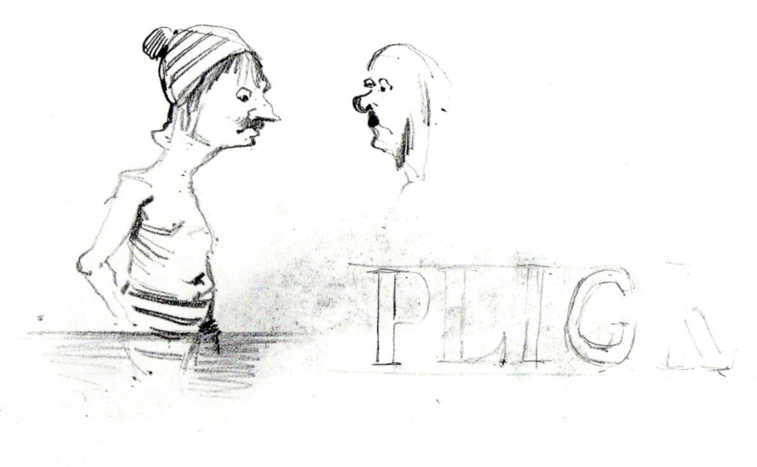

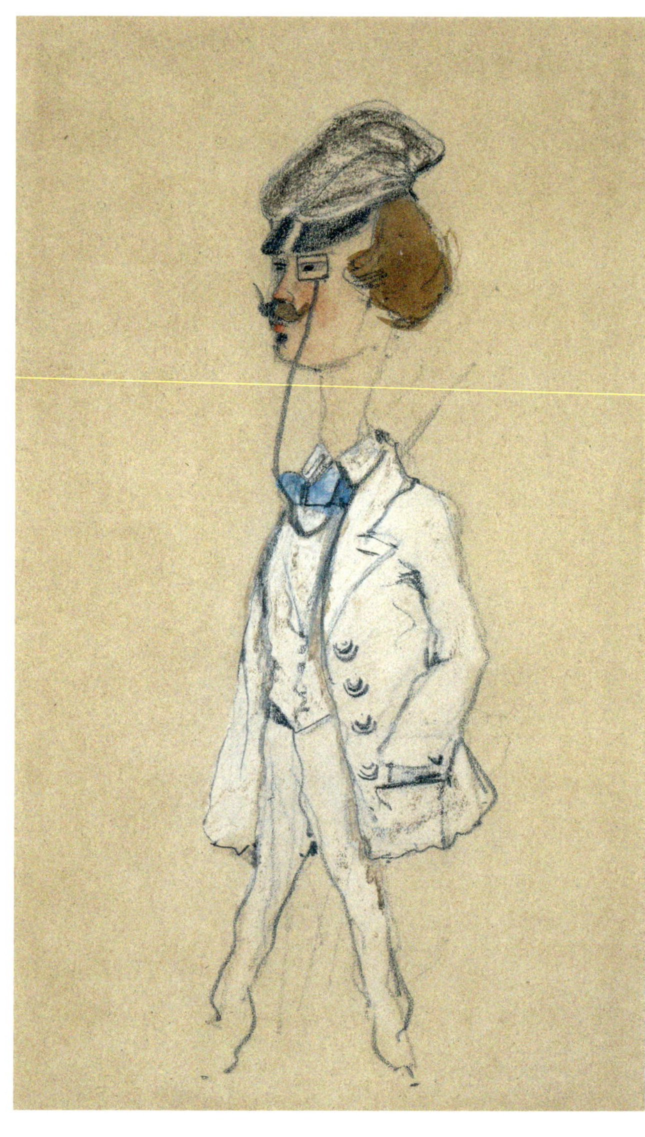

25
Caricature of Two Bathers, 1857. Pencil, approx. 220 x 310 mm. Location unknown [D66]

26
Young Man with a Monocle, c. 1857. Pencil heightened with gouache on beige paper, 240 x 160 mm. Musée Marmottan Monet, Paris [D451]

print from Daumier's 1839–42 series *The Swimmers* [*Les Baigneurs*] (see fig. 22), originally published in *Le Charivari* and subsequently issued in a separate album. To this pairing we might add another, more comic sketch of a skinny swimmer wearing a striped bathing cap and trunks (fig. 25) in conversation with a second disembodied head.[13] Also contained in Monet's early sketchbooks are studies of gamins, bare-footed little boys who must have been a common sight around Le Havre, as well as two sketches of Zouaves.[14]

Outside of these albums there appears a more homogenous and perhaps even systematic group of colored pencil drawings representing an assortment of humorous local types of which *Young Man with a Monocle* (fig. 26), *Dandy with a Cigar* (fig. 27), and *The Painter with a Pointed Hat* (fig. 28) are but three examples. The larger collection consisted of at least nineteen drawings catalogued by Daniel Wildenstein, of which sixteen originally belonged to the Billecocqs.[15] These works descended from Théophile Beguin Billecocq's cousins Ernest and Théodore down through the family to the architect André Billecocq (1902–1992), who placed them all on loan to the Musée Marmottan Monet in Paris for several years during the 1970s and ultimately presented nine as a gift to the museum in 1982.[16]

The Billecocq caricatures offer a lively survey of modern social types that Monet could have observed in the busy port city of Le Havre, with particular attention given to foreigners

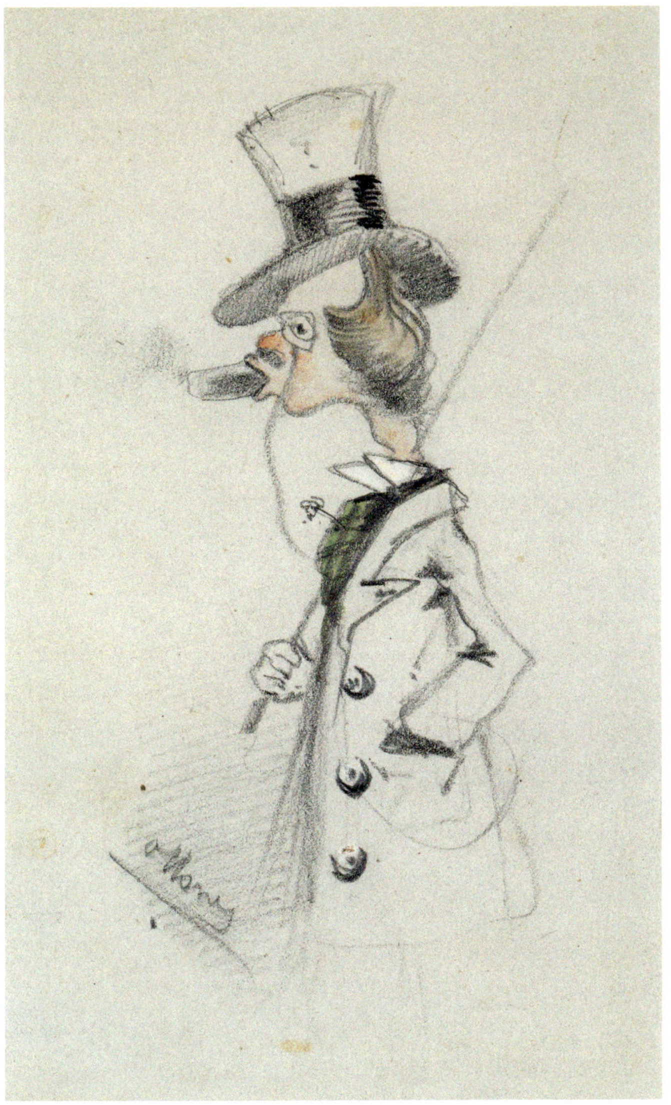

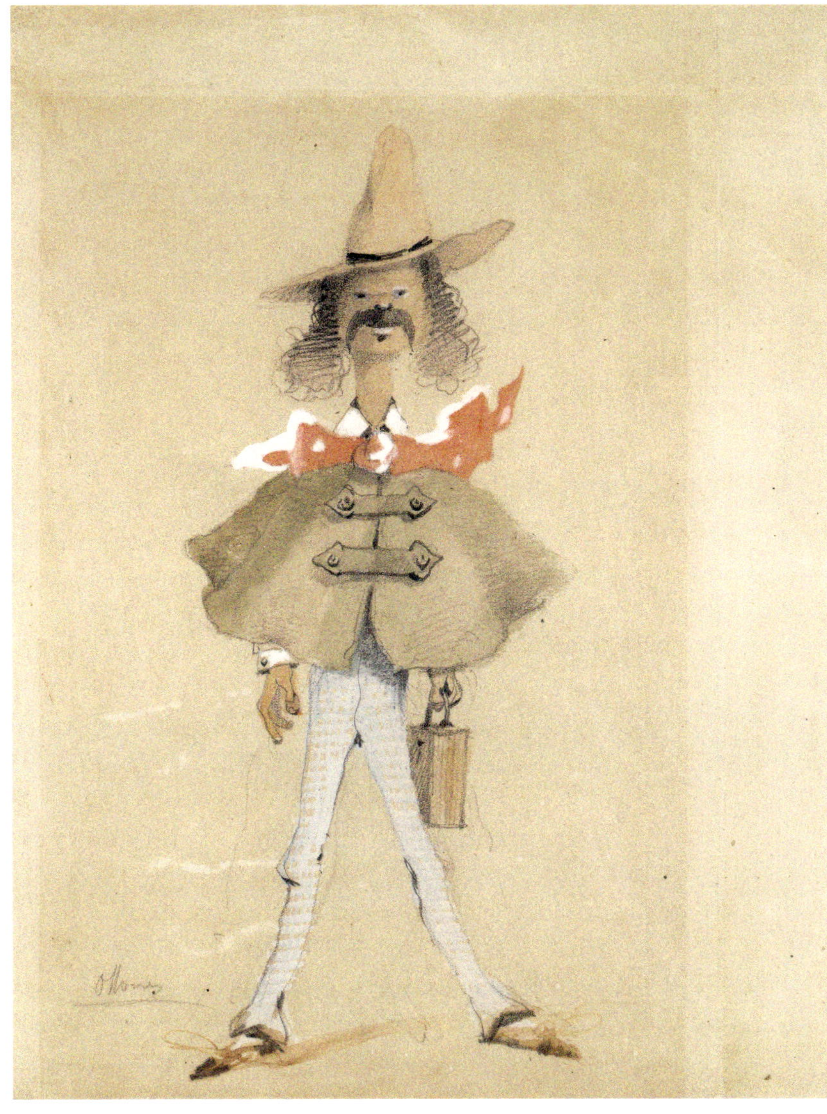

27
Dandy with a Cigar, c. 1857. Pencil heightened with gouache on gray paper, 240 x 160 mm. Musée Marmottan Monet, Paris [D457]

28
The Painter with a Pointed Hat, c. 1857. Watercolor and pencil with white gouache on beige paper, 312 x 242 mm. Private collection [D466]

(especially British tourists) and their peculiar modes of dress. Several strata of the social order are represented, including old and young women in traditional Norman attire, peasants, sailors, a black groomsman, a rosy-cheeked wine drinker (whose head emerges from a bottle of Bordeaux), and an artist carrying his paint box. Most take the form of single figures in three-quarters length, isolated in vignettes centrally placed on the page. The beige and gray-toned sheets are of roughly uniform dimensions, and probably originated in a small sketchbook; four have additional unfinished pencil caricatures on the verso.[17] The figures were first sketched in pencil, and several were subsequently heightened with watercolor and gouache, a few also with pastel. Most are signed in pencil, "O. Monet," and just one, a depiction of a foppish young person, is inscribed with a caption, "*progéniture anglaise*" ["English progeny"].[18]

There is a subtle element of physical exaggeration in Monet's types. The men, in particular, have elongated necks and a few have disproportionately large heads. They give the impression of being captured unaware, passersby glimpsed in the street rather than individuals posing for a portrait. The draftsman circulated among them as an observer, maintaining his distance, playing the role of *artiste-flâneur*. The only full-length figure in the group of drawings, the bemused *The Painter with a Pointed Hat* stands frontally and confidently on a sheet of paper roughly twice as large as the others. He is a comic figure, yet superior in stature and pose. With his dark handlebar mustache and long curly locks, he bears no physical resemblance to Monet, but it is difficult not to see him as an imaginary self-portrait, the young draftsman's comic alter ego staring out at his maker.

In their simple and direct format, Monet's drawings of assorted Le Havre types call to mind the published lithographs and watercolors of Parisian types by Paul Gavarni. During his long career, Gavarni excelled in a wide variety of popular genres but made a particular specialty of costume and fashion prints. Since we have to assume that the survival rate of Monet's 1850s body of drawings is relatively low, it is difficult to draw conclusions based on what can only be a partial sample. Nevertheless, it is intriguing to ponder whether this uniform group of signed drawings, the majority of which stayed together when they first left Monet's possession, was meant to be seen as a cohesive cycle in much the same way as Gavarni's various lithographic series. They might be seen as the Le Havre equivalent of Gavarni's *Physionomies parisiennes* that appeared in the journal *Paris* in 1857–58.

Copies from Caricature Journals

Before attempting to draw live models, young artists in the nineteenth century were advised to follow academic guidelines and make copies from classic works by the great masters, which were primarily available to them in the form of plaster casts or reproductive engravings. While Monet likely engaged in such activities, the evidence is lacking among his extant graphic oeuvre of the 1850s.[19] What do survive from this period are a number of drawings copied from *portraits-charges* by several contemporary masters of the genre, and a single drawing after a caricature figurine in plaster.[20] This body of work might be seen as the result of self-imposed didactic exercises, the evidence of a course of independent study pursued by the teenage draftsman. While Monet was, in effect, an autodidact in the art of caricature, it has been said that his copies from Nadar and company amounted to a "clandestine apprenticeship."[21]

Monet's selection of particular *portraits-charges* to replicate seems to have been based primarily on the subjects' identities. Ten of the eleven individuals represented in his copies were professional writers (including Champfleury), four of whom were primarily playwrights. Among the dramatists represented was Eugène Scribe (1791–1869), the author of a play in which Monet performed in an amateur production at the Billecocqs' Paris salon.[22] His favoring of such personages reinforces the picture painted by Beguin Billecocq of the teenage artist as a theater buff, an affinity handed down from his mother and further elaborated in the subjects of his original caricatures.

Monet based his *portrait-charge* of Mario Uchard (1824–1893) (fig. 29)[23] on a gillotage by Carjat that appeared in the 10 March 1858 issue of *Le Gaulois*, a right-wing newspaper that likely would have appealed to his father.[24] The drawing is carried out in crisp graphite, with darker lines reinforcing a light preliminary sketch. It is a carefully wrought work, produced in a slow and deliberate manner. The subject Uchard, a prominent dramatist whose plays were seen at the Comédie-Française, was briefly married to the actress Madeleine Brohan. His relatively genteel portrait belies an unsavory personal reputation; he was reportedly so enraged at his wife's decision to leave him that he threatened to disfigure her with acid, causing her to flee to St. Petersburg.[25] He penned *La Fiammina* (1857), an autobiographical comedy in which the title character based on Madame Brohan was portrayed in a malicious light. It was staged at the Comédie-Française during her Russian leave of absence.

Monet's *portrait-charge* of the playwright and novelist Adolphe Philippe Dennery (1811–1899; fig. 30) derived from a caricature by Nadar in the *Journal amusant* of 27 November 1858.[26] Dennery's long and lucrative career began in the 1830s. Among his recent credits was the libretto for Charles Gounod's *Faust* (1856). As with his portraits of Uchard and Scribe, Monet concentrated on copying the stylized facial features of his subject, leaving the diminutive body in rough outline. Thus, the drawing of

29
After Etienne Carjat (French, 1828–1906), *Caricature of Mario Uchard*, c. 1858. Graphite on tan wove paper, 320 x 243 mm. The Art Institute of Chicago. Mr. and Mrs. Carter H. Harrison Collection [D499]

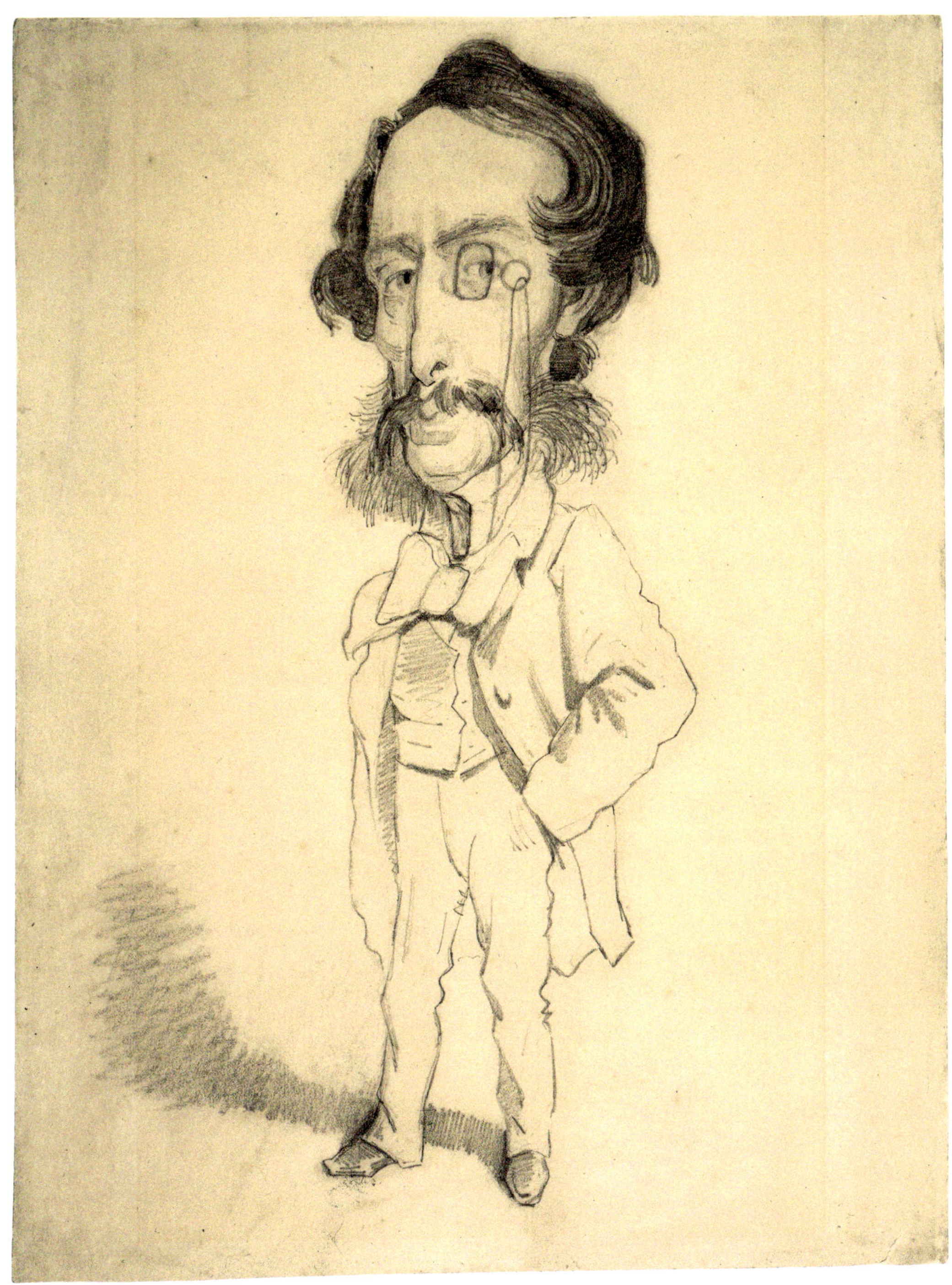

the head is immaculate in execution, while the body gives the appearance of being unfinished. Enough detail is retained, however, to see that Dennery is costumed as an archetypal "Alpine virgin," with a patterned kerchief around his bulbous head, playing a mandolin. His eyes are nearly closed, yet his mouth is open, giving the impression that he is performing a melancholy song, perhaps "*A la grâce de Dieu*" ("To the grace of God"), a popular ballad that was sung several times in the course of his 1841 play of the same title.[27]

Monet's *portrait-charge* of the playwright/poet/art critic Auguste Vacquerie (1819–1895; fig. 31) is one of five caricatures he lifted from the *Panthéon Nadar* (fig. 32). As a copy it is somewhat exaggerated from the original, the head larger and the body thinner than in

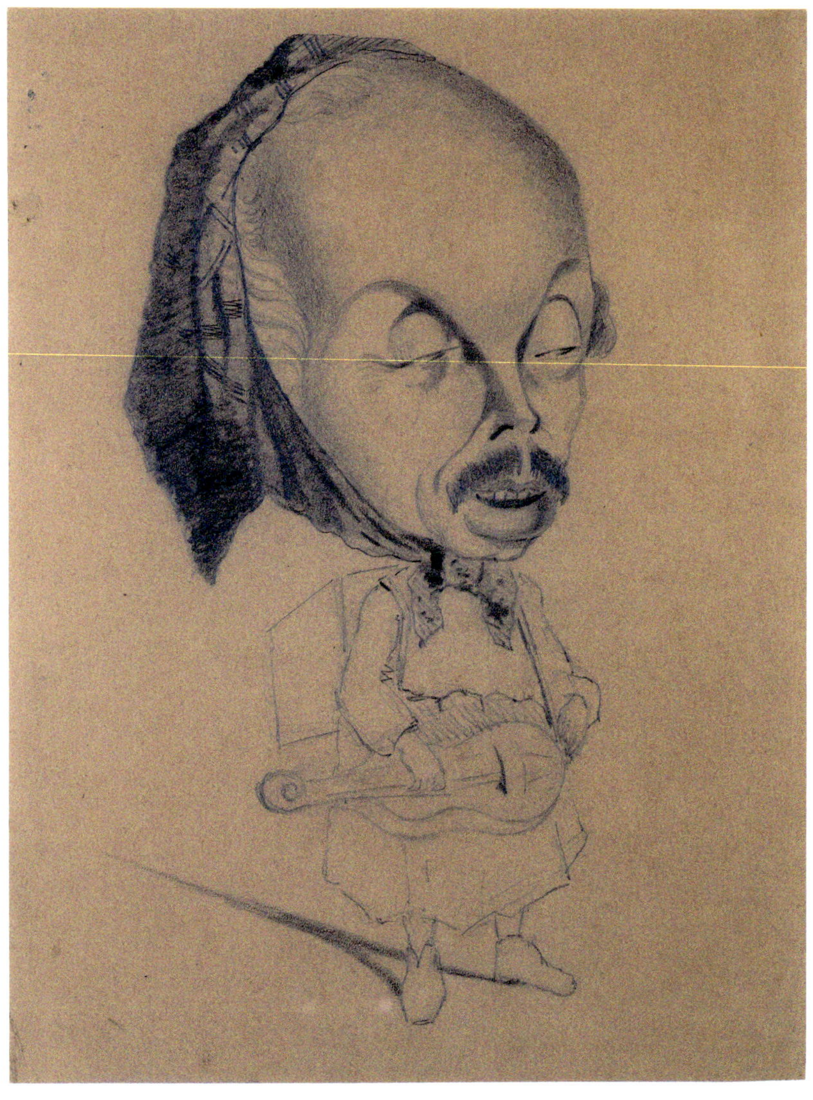

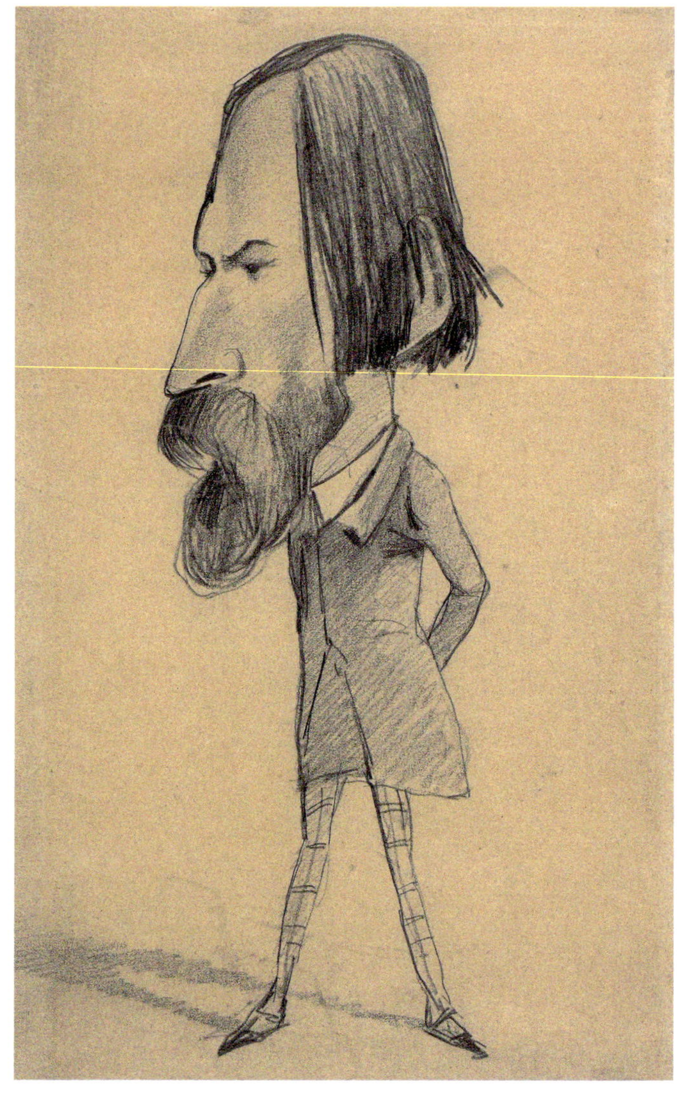

30
After Nadar (Félix Tournachon) (French, 1820–1910), *Caricature of Adolphe Dennery*, c. 1858. Black crayon, 320 x 240 mm. Musée Marmottan Monet, Paris [D503]

31
After Nadar, *Caricature of Auguste Vacquerie*, c. 1859. Graphite on tan wove paper, laid down on commercially prepared cream wove card, 283 x 175 mm. The Art Institute of Chicago. Mr. and Mrs. Carter H. Harrison Collection [D505]

Nadar's print. A simple and unpretentious pencil drawing, it is, in fact, a masterful graphic performance, combining several different manners of drawing, with firm, dark lines defining the figure's straight hair and principal outlines, light diagonal hatching on his clothing, and soft, sensitive modeling in his face. Monet successfully used the side of his pencil to create purely tonal effects of flesh tone.

The source for this drawing, the *Panthéon Nadar*, was a lithographic production monumental both in scale (at 740 by 1000 mm) and conception.[28] Nadar's original vision was to produce an enormous four-part pantheon of 1,000 figures divided between theatrical personalities, visual artists, musicians, and men of letters. The overly ambitious project was eventually abandoned, with only the latter section completed and published as a single sheet in 1854, to critical acclaim but disappointing sales. A larger edition with wider circulation appeared in December 1858 as a special supplement for subscribers to the journal *Figaro*; it is assumed that Monet based his copies on the *Figaro* edition. Out of the serpentine procession of 249 writers led by Victor Hugo, Monet plucked four other figures in addition to Vacquerie: Jules de Prémaray (1819–68; no. 55 in the key to the print), Xavier Aymon de Montépin (1824–1902; no. 126), Théodore Pelloquet (c. 1820–1867; no. 190), and Champfleury (1821–1889; no. 231).[29] He had to invent a body for Montépin, whose own figure is obscured by other members of the procession. Otherwise, the portraits he copied

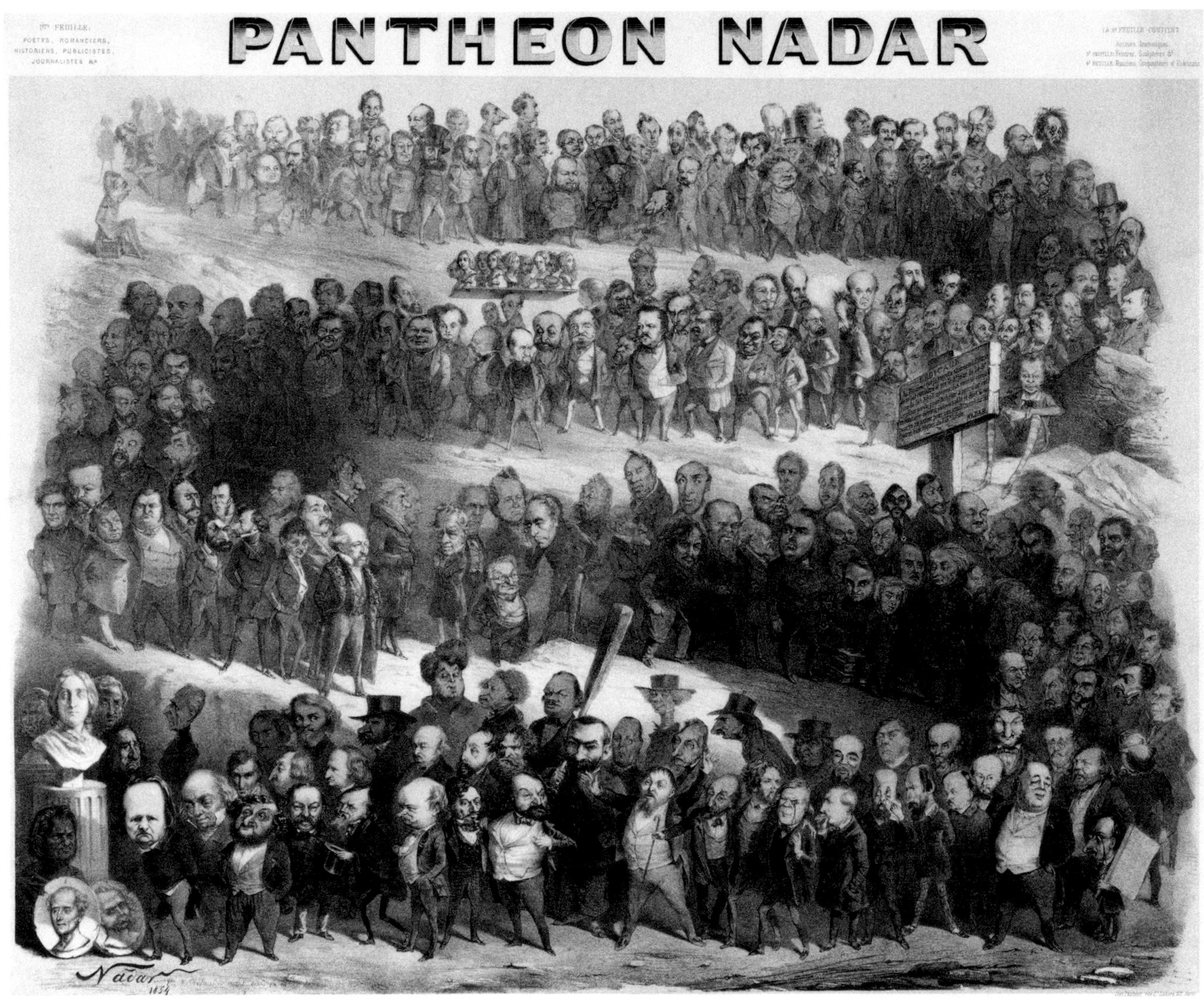

32

Nadar (Félix Tournachon), *Panthéon Nadar*, 1854. Lithograph, 819 x 1,149 mm. The Metropolitan Museum of Art, New York. A. Hyatt Mayor Purchase Fund. Marjorie Phelps Starr Bequest, 1993

were of individuals depicted fully from head to toe by Nadar.

Although the genre of caricature was customarily degraded as low art, it provided the mass readership of the newspapers with images of many of the most advanced and provocative thinkers of the era. In the absence of documentation regarding Monet's own reading habits as a young man, this group of copies provides valuable insight into his awareness of major literary personalities. It seems unlikely that he made his selections at random, or for purely formal reasons (as the cropped source image of Montépin demonstrates), but rather that he chose to copy the portraits of men whose writings, or at least whose reputations, he must have grasped. The authors Monet picked out of Nadar's *Panthéon* represented a sophisticated group of left-wing playwrights, novelists, and particularly art critics. It is noteworthy that one of the figures the eighteen-year-old had the intellectual consciousness to extract was Champfleury, the great theoretician of art whose *Le Réalisme* had only just appeared in 1857.

Monet's copies might be seen as more than just formal exercises, but as encounters, on paper, with leading figures whose cultural politics he shared. Pelloquet (see fig. 61), the art critic for *Le Siècle*, was one such personality, a champion of progressive painters who published a dictionary of contemporary artists in 1858. He was a bohemian type who frequented the Brasserie des Martyrs in the Latin Quarter. According to the reminiscences of Georges

33

Caricature of Félix (Alexandre Ursule Cellérier), c. 1858. Pencil, 310 x 237 mm. Musée Marmottan Monet, Paris [D513]

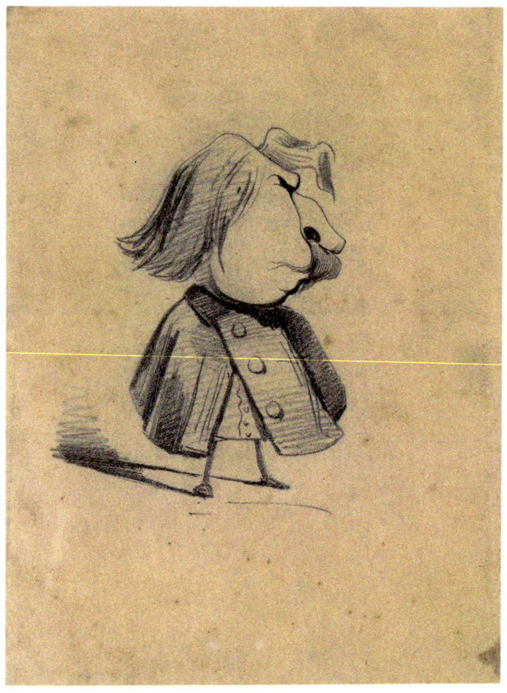

Clemenceau (as reported by François Thiébault-Sisson), Monet made Pelloquet's acquaintance during his early years in Paris: "When I met [Monet] for the first time, it was in the Latin Quarter . . . he was almost always accompanied by Pelloquet, an occasional journalist, bright but nonchalant, who made fun of everything and everyone, including himself, with a biting and delicious irreverence. In his spare time, Pelloquet dealt with art criticism, vigorously supporting the young, a fact that had endeared him to Claude Monet."[30] Thus, Monet's encounter with Pelloquet in the *Panthéon Nadar* prefigured by a few years their contact in person.

Monet's copies have several common features besides their consistency of subject matter. Although some of the sitters are identified in inscriptions (for instance, Scribe and de Prémaray), none of the copies are signed. Also, allowing for minor variations as a result of inaccurate measurements and cropping, Monet executed the majority of these drawings on paper of roughly the same dimensions, 320 by 240 millimeters. The sheets vary in color—some are tan or gray—but they appear to derive from the same drawing tablet. Besides the eleven works catalogued as copies by Wildenstein, six other *portraits-charges* thought to be original inventions conform to the same format and scale, and also lack a signature.[31] It is possible that several of these drawings identified as anonymous "*caricatures havraises*" (D471–74) are in fact copies from publications yet to be identified.

One of the drawings almost certainly misidentified by Wildenstein as an original *portrait-charge* rather than a copy is the portrait of the actor known as Félix (Alexandre Ursule Cellérier [1807–1870]; fig. 33). After playing in the provinces as a young man, Félix made his debut on the Paris stage in 1840, eventually joining the company of the Théatre du Vaudeville. In an 1847 theatrical guidebook, he was described as "noble and dignified in drama, well bred and witty in comedy, and irresistibly amusing in farce."[32] A caricature of Félix by Henry Fusino (active 1860–65) appeared in the 1 September 1860 issue *Diogène*, a journal to which Monet had contributed a *portrait-charge* several months earlier. Wildenstein proposed that Fusino's effort took the place of Monet's rejected caricature, even suggesting that this rebuff might have contributed to Monet's ultimate decision to abandon thoughts of pursuing a career as a caricaturist.[33]

There are several reasons to doubt this theory. Stylistically, the figure of Félix is inconsistent with Monet's own inventions. The abstract formation of the nose and eye in lost profile are unlike any other design by Monet. The drawing of the profile is clean and firm, a quality that it shares with the other copies but not with the original caricatures, which show more evidence of the artist's hand at work, building up and occasionally correcting his lines. It is on the same size and type of paper as the other copies, and like them lacks a signature. It is difficult to imagine Monet submitting an unsigned work to a publisher, and in fact, the drawing materials and support would have been entirely different if the caricature had been intended for publication. A greasy ink and special soluble paper would have been used in order to facilitate transferring the drawing to a relief plate for printing in gillotage, the reproductive method employed by the journal. Further, the subject of this drawing was a popular enough performer that caricatures of

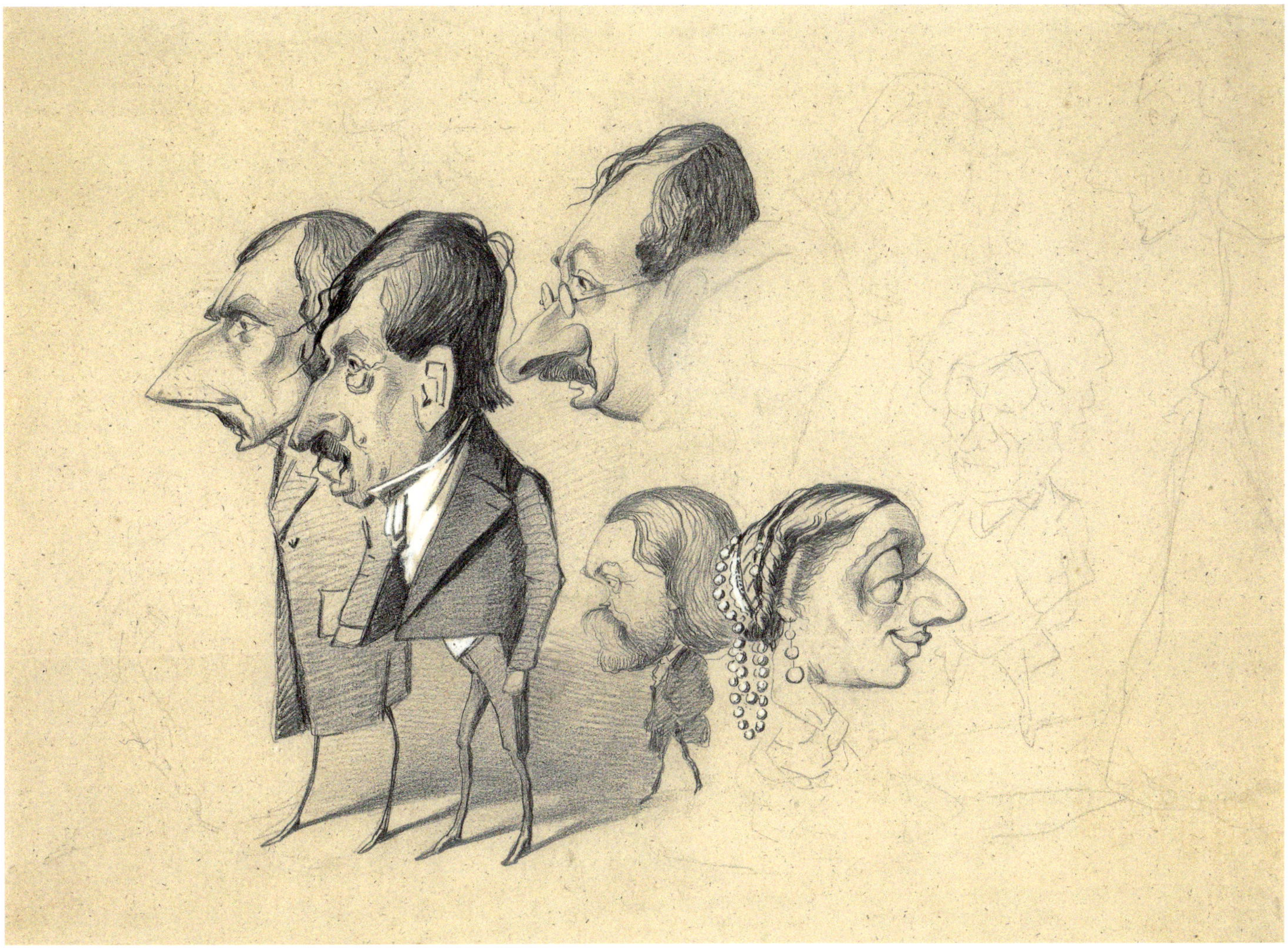

34

Little Theatrical Pantheon, c. 1859. Pencil heightened with gouache, 340 x 470 mm. Musée Marmottan Monet, Paris [D510]

35

Caricatures of Three Men in Profile, 1857. Pencil, approx. 310 x 220 mm. Location unknown [D67]

him are likely to have appeared in newspapers on more than one occasion. Monet's *portrait-charge* is probably a copy from one of these hitherto unidentified publications.

It is difficult to know where to place the so-called *Little Theatrical Pantheon* (fig. 34) in the chronology of Monet's caricatures. Despite the title assigned to it by Wildenstein, the drawing is one of the artist's largest extant graphic works. It is also the only unfinished composition among his *portraits-charges*, with three figures drawn and modeled in their entirety, two represented only by disembodied heads, and evidence of at least five additional figures visible in faint outline. One of these lightly sketched bodies, a man seen in profile at the extreme right edge of the sheet, is close in design to the leftmost figure in a hastily sketched *portrait-charge* of three men in the sketchbook of 1857 (fig. 35).

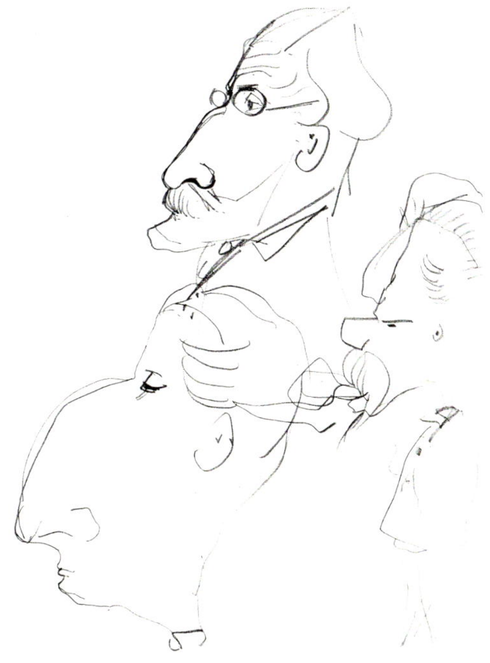

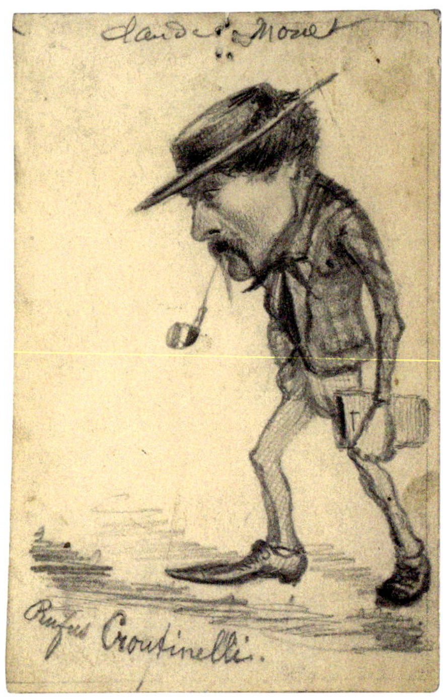

36

Caricature of Henri Cassinelli ("Rufus Croutinelli"), c. 1858. Graphite on tan wove paper, laid down on commercially prepared tan wove card, 130 x 84 mm. The Art Institute of Chicago. Mr. and Mrs. Carter H. Harrison Collection [D495]

With the aid of previously published caricatures by Nadar, Carjat, and Hadol, Wildenstein identified the famous theatrical personages assembled by Monet as the actors Paul-Louis Auguste Grassot (1800–1860), Jean-Baptiste Leclère (c. 1800–1861), Edmond Got (1822–1901), and Augustine Brohan (1824–1893), and the dramatist Louis Lurine (1816–1860).[34] He catalogued the drawing among Monet's "*caricatures parisiennes*," suggesting that it was loosely based on the aforementioned models, several of which appeared in print after his arrival in Paris. Unfortunately, given the proliferation of images of theatrical figures during this period, the identification of precise sources for Monet's *Panthéon* remains elusive. Thus, the dating of the drawing, and hence its place of germination (Le Havre versus Paris) are unresolved. There is no doubt, however, concerning Monet's source of inspiration: the unfinished *Panthéon Nadar*. Had Nadar carried on with his monumental project, one of its three remaining sections would have been devoted to men and women of the theater. In his *Little Theatrical Panthéon* Monet effectively took it upon himself to resume the impossible assignment and followed Nadar's precedent to the point of abandoning the task. It is easier to imagine this drawing as an experimental exercise by a teenage draftsman in Le Havre than a commissioned project intended for eventual publication.

Fame and Fortune in Le Havre

As a teenager in Le Havre, Monet applied his considerable skills in caricature to members of the local population, and in so doing, earned a reputation as well as a tidy income. To later interviewers he boasted of his entrepreneurship:

At fifteen I was known all over Hâvre as a caricaturist. My reputation was so well established that I was sought after from all sides and asked for caricature-portraits. The abundance of orders and the insufficiency of subsidies derived from maternal generosity inspired me with a bold resolve which naturally scandalized my family; I took money for my portraits. According to the appearance of my clients, I charged ten or twenty francs for each portrait, and the scheme worked beautifully. In a month my patrons had doubled in number. I was now able to charge twenty francs in all cases without lessening the number of orders. If I had kept on, I would today be a millionaire.[35]

A document dated 18 May 1859 in the municipal archives of Le Havre confirms Monet's account of his local celebrity status. Following a meeting of the city council, to which his father had submitted a grant application for his son to pursue the study of painting in Paris, the official minutes reported:

Monet (Oscar) born in 1841, having studied with Monsieurs Ochard, Wissant and Boudin, submitted with his application a still-life painting that would lead us to a poor assessment of his talent if it had not been so completely revealed by his witty sketches that we all know. Through caricature (since it is necessary to refer to it by this term) that has until now harnessed his remarkable natural abilities, Oscar Monet has already found the popularity that comes so slowly to serious works. But with his precocious success is there not a danger, that in following the facile path of his pencil that the young artist might be kept from the more serious and thankless studies that alone justify municipal liberality? Time will tell.[36]

With these words of advice, the council turned down his application.

Monet's original *portraits-charges* of the late 1850s, which survive in a variety of formats, sizes, and degrees of finish, exhibit considerable skill in drawing. They also demonstrate his self-taught fluency and creativity in the language of caricature, as well as the sharpness of his wit. One of the most mischievous of these works is a soft pencil drawing of "Rufus Croutinelli" (fig. 36) carried out on little more than a scrap of paper. Monet depicts the artist with his oversized head hunched down and sketchbook in hand, trudging forward on a pair of enormous feet. The delicate modeling of the facial features using the side of the pencil against the textured paper belies

37

Caricature of Young Woman at the Piano, c. 1858. Black crayon heightened with white chalk, 320 x 240 mm. Musée Marmottan Monet, Paris [D472]

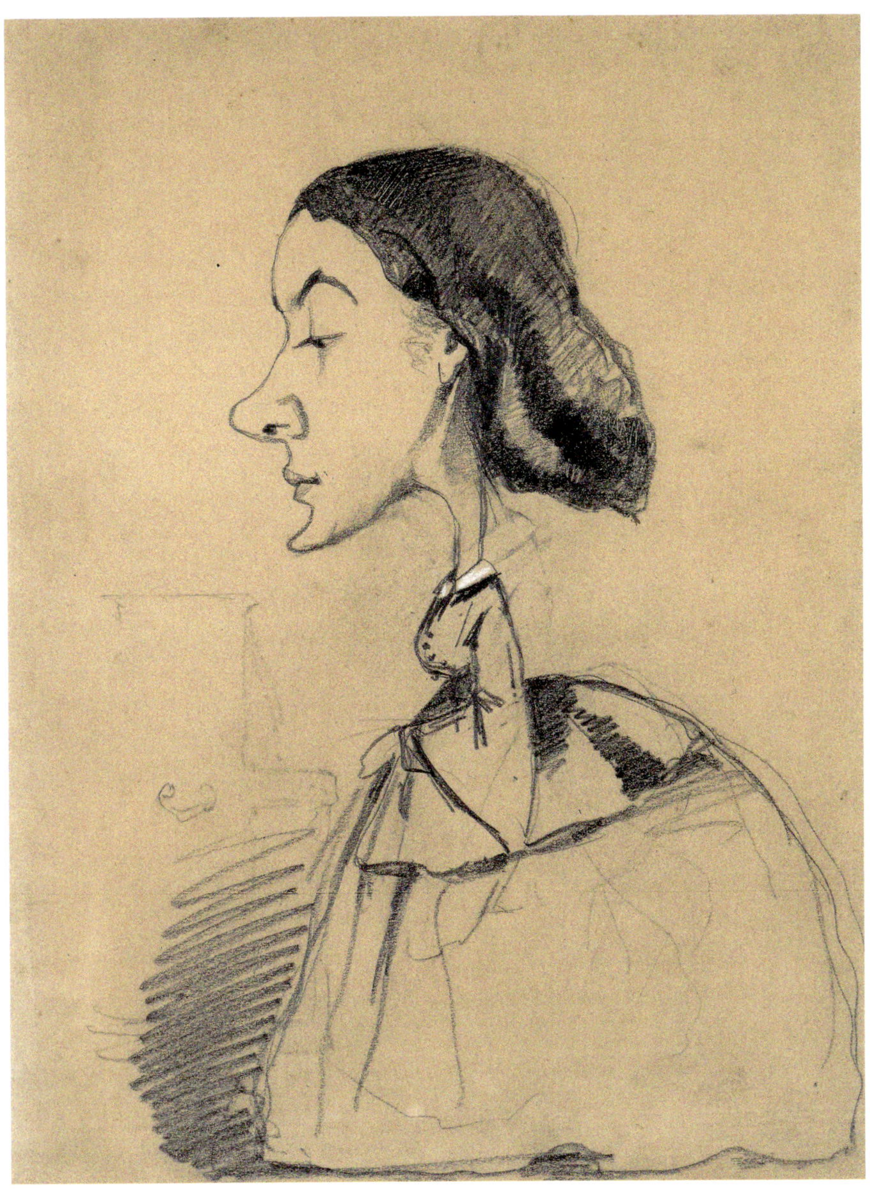

the draftsman's devious intent. Even more than the exaggeration of his anatomy, it is the legend, "Rufus Croutinelli," that adds a humorous twist to the image, for Monet has also distorted his subject's real name Henri Cassinelli to comic effect (the term "*croûte*" being a figure of speech for "daub," or bad painting).[37] It seems that Monet considered Cassinelli, the son of a print seller, as a potential rival in his pursuit of funding from the city council, in which case this little caricature was almost certainly a private joke. Interestingly, there is clear visual evidence that the inscription was originally placed immediately above its final location on the sheet, in an area that was subsequently effaced with irregular dark hatching. Perhaps Monet had second thoughts before committing himself to the provocative bit of wordplay.

Another *portrait-charge* identified with Monet's Le Havre years is the anonymous *Caricature of Young Woman at the Piano* (fig. 37). It conforms in format with the copies, and is likewise unsigned, but exhibits significant pentimenti that suggest it is an original composition. In his first partially erased attempt to draw this figure, he placed her neck and bodice slightly higher on the sheet, and at a more oblique angle to the head. Light pencil lines in the area of her large bustle appear to reflect a more compact preliminary design. The outline of a piano, faintly visible at the left, is

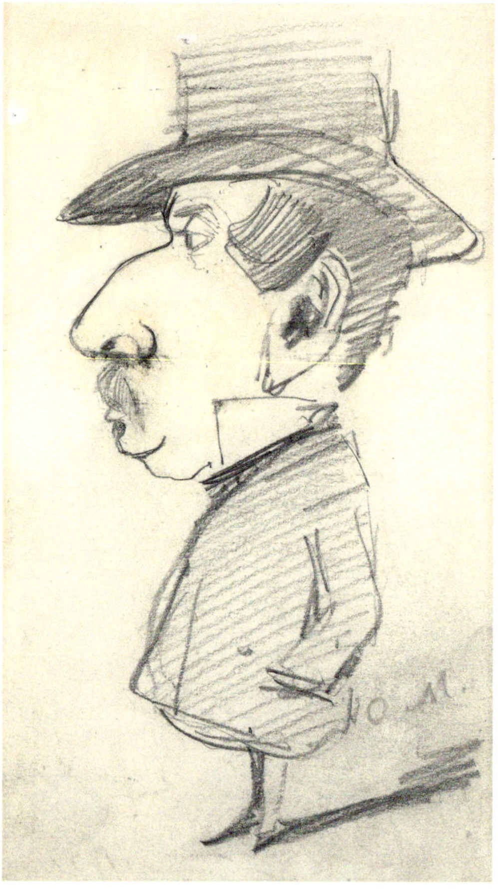

38
Caricature of Grandfather Lebas, c. 1858–59. Pencil, 241 x 146 mm. Private collection [D493]

partially obscured by a dense area of zigzag lines, yet the base of the keyboard clearly overlaps the front of her skirt. The title traditionally assigned to this work might be called into question, as the piano appears to be an unintentional vestige of Monet's first draft.

The majority of Monet's recognizable *portraits-charges* represent Le Havre businessmen of similar standing in the community as his father. Among the professionals that have been identified, either through inscriptions or early provenance, are local brokers, ship owners, notaries, and lawyers. One of the most rapidly executed is a pencil drawing of an older man in profile bearing an inscription on the back of its mount, "*caricature du grand-père Lebas, encadreur et marchand de tableaux*" ("caricature of grandfather Lebas, framer and picture-seller") (fig. 38). Wildenstein identified him as the "Lebas" listed in the Le Havre business directory of 1857–65 as a gilder and mirror-dealer.[38] One can imagine Monet executing a drawing like this one in a matter of minutes. The essential element is the man's profile, including a large hooked nose and double chin. He transcribed these features with the utmost economy of line, filling out the rest of the figure with a few deft outlines and zigzag hatching. Although the handling is somewhat lacking in assurance, the sketch must have been appreciated as a display of the speed with which Monet could capture the essence of his sitter with the simplest of materials, pencil and paper. It also may have served as a rough draft for a larger-scale *portrait-charge*, now lost.

Within the corpus of caricatures the most impressive works comprise a group of large-format drawings in which the heads of the sitters are represented at virtually life size. It is with this dramatic series of "big heads" that Monet demonstrated in the most spectacular fashion his full mastery of the *portrait-charge*. The fourteen known sheets in this category, ranging in scale from roughly 470 by 280 to 610 by 450 millimeters, are the largest drawings in Monet's graphic oeuvre.[39] They are carried out in charcoal with stumping and white heightening on relatively coarse-grained, heavy blue-gray paper (now generally faded to gray). All but one of the oversized caricatures are signed "O. Monet" or "O. M." and two are dated "1858": (D478) and "Havre 59" (D486), respectively. Clearly the artist considered these to be finished works, and several of those for which early provenance has been established may be traced to the original sitters. By commissioning their portraits from the teenage draftsman, Le Havre businessmen like Adolphe-Victor Coësme (fig. 39) and Léon Manchon unwittingly became the earliest known patron-collectors of one of the foremost artists of the nineteenth century.

Coësme, a broker ("*courtier de commerce*") listed at 10 rue Molière,[40] and an unidentified *Man with a Snuff Box* (fig. 40) are depicted in an analogous format, with their oversized heads perched atop miniature bodies. They occupy empty spaces defined on the page only by their cast shadows. The rather dashing figure of Coësme with his superabundant coiffure is shown in classic profile, while the big-nosed snuff-taker is rendered in a three-quarters view, allowing him to make eye contact with us. This

39
Caricature of Adolphe-Victor Coësme, 1858. Charcoal heightened with white chalk on blue laid paper (discolored to gray), 620 x 390 mm. Private collection [D478]

40
Caricature of a Man with a Snuff Box, c. 1858. Charcoal heightened with white chalk on blue laid paper (discolored to gray), 588 x 330 mm. Sterling and Francine Clark Institute, Williamstown, Massachusetts [D488]

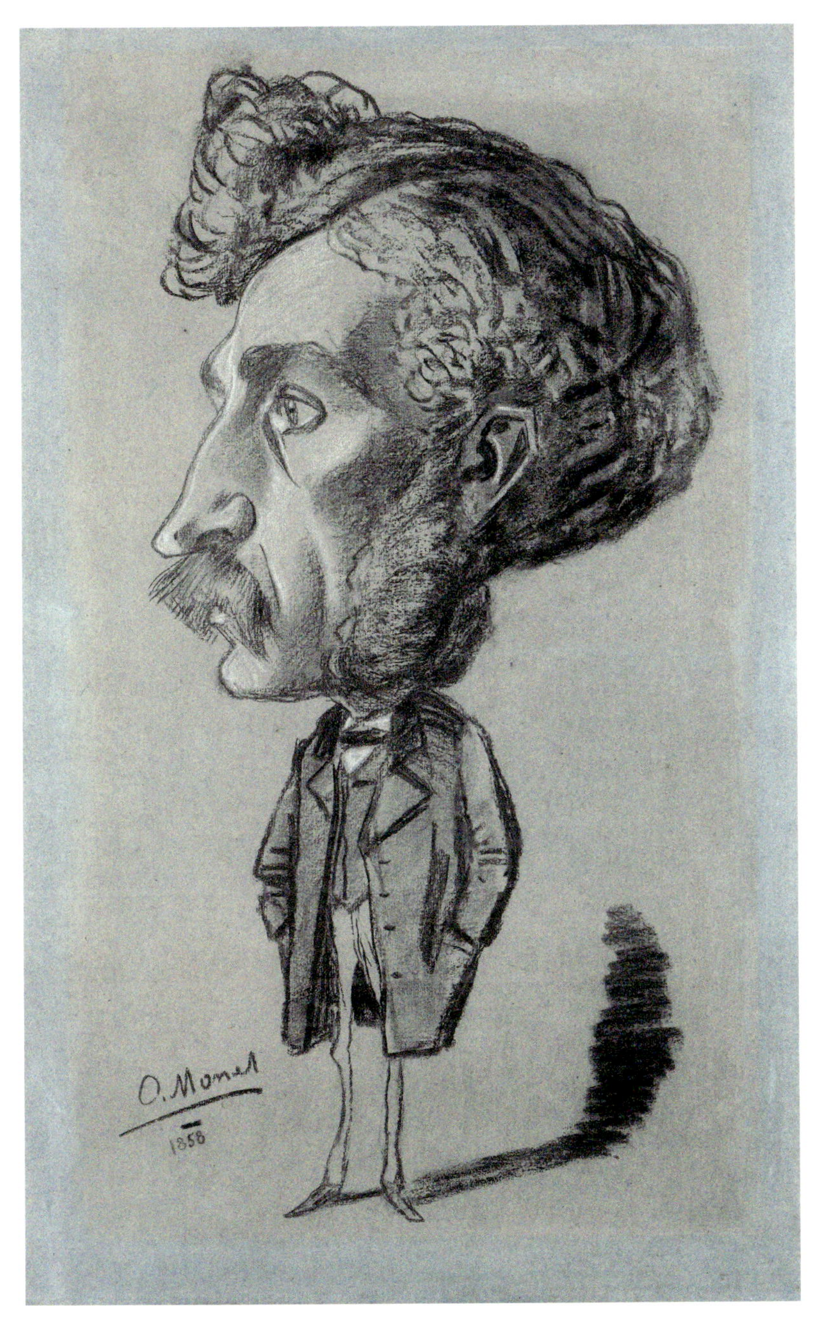
O. Monet
1858

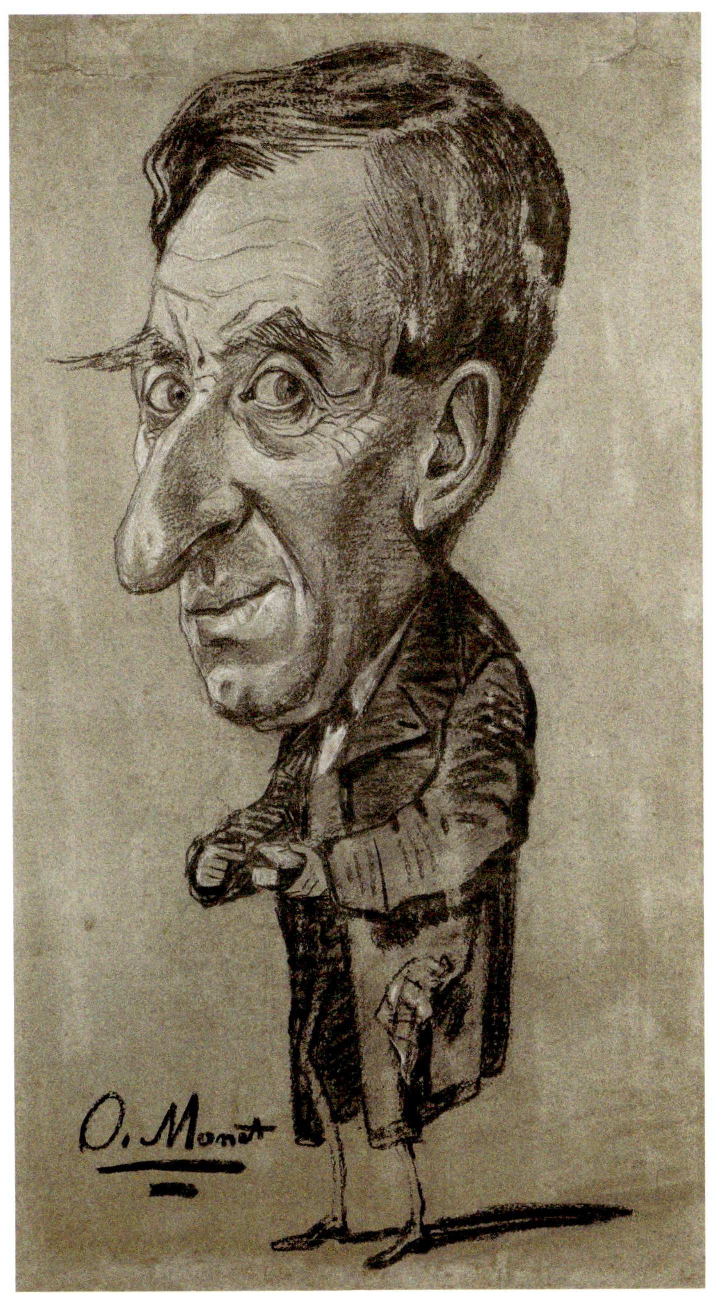
O. Monet

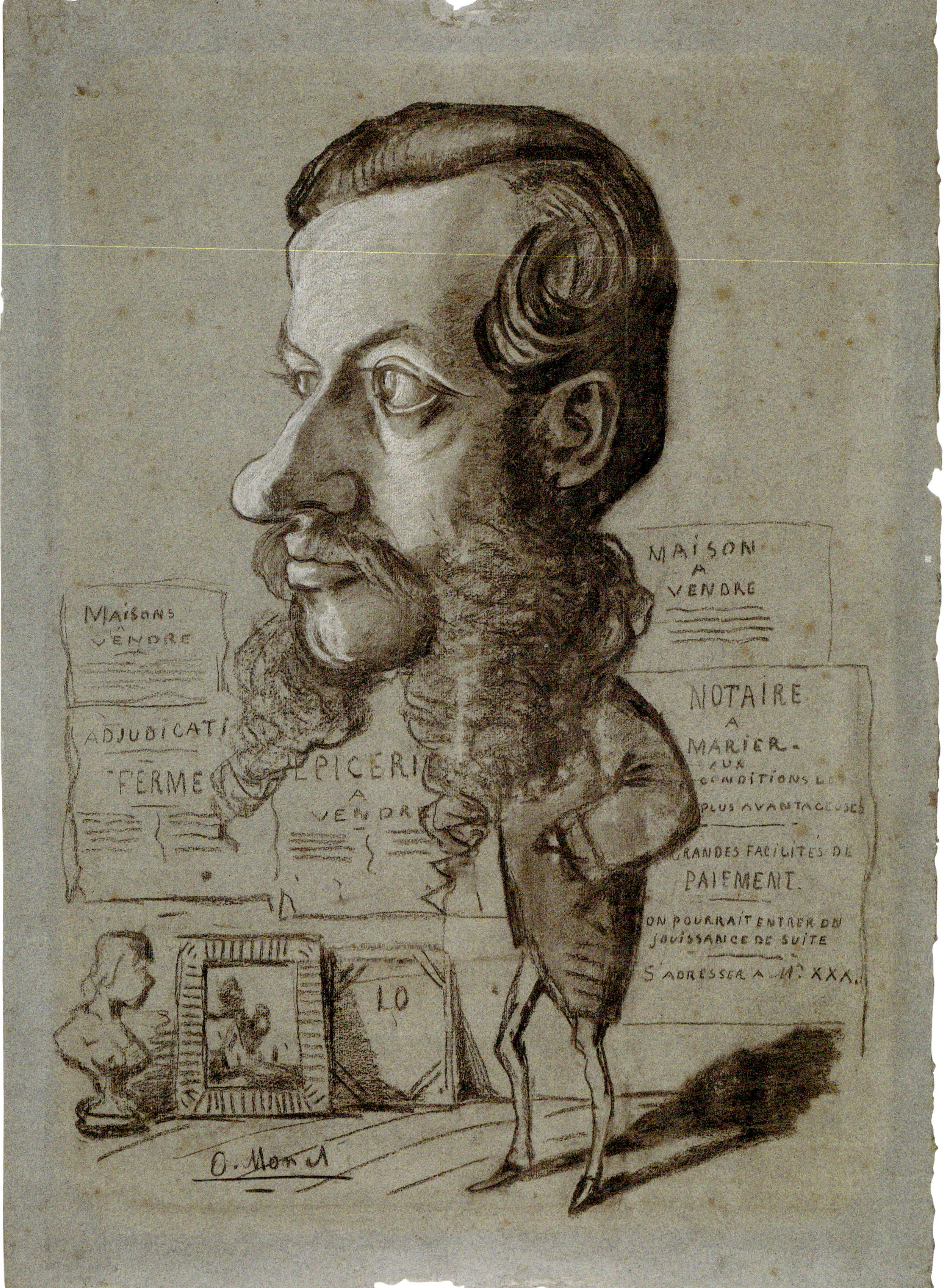
MAISONS A VENDRE
ADJUDICATI
FERME
EPICERI
A VENDR
MAISON A VENDRE
NOTAIRE A MARIER
AUX CONDITIONS LE
PLUS AVANTAGEUSES
RANDES FACILITES DE
PAIEMENT
ON POURRAIT ENTRER EN JOUISSANCE DE SUITE
S'ADRESSER A Mr XXX.
LO
O. Monet

41

Caricature of Léon Manchon, c. 1858. Charcoal with stumping heightened with white chalk on blue laid paper (discolored to gray), 612 x 452 mm. The Art Institute of Chicago. Mr. and Mrs. Carter H. Harrison Collection [D481]

42

Caricature of Léon Manchon, c. 1858. Charcoal and pastel on tan paper, 560 x 420 mm. Musée des Beaux-Arts, Rouen [D482]

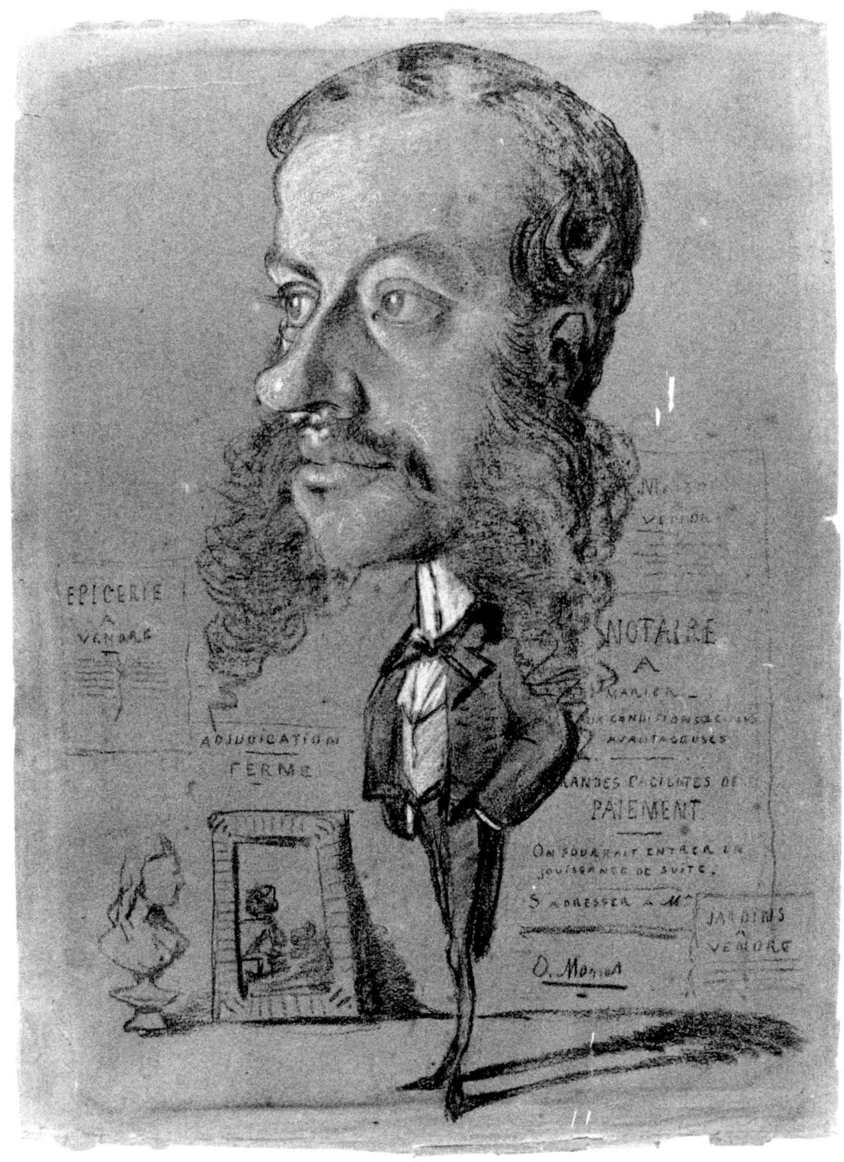

effect, combined with the verisimilitude of his large head, makes for an uncanny confrontation between charcoal personage and twenty-first-century viewer. The sheet includes a number of visible corrections in the outlines and position of the body. Given Monet's struggles with the human figure later in his career, the strength of personality with which these early portraits are charged is remarkable indeed.

Monet created an even larger and more elaborate *portrait-charge* of Léon Manchon, a notary public and treasurer of Le Havre's Société des amis des arts, which held an exhibition in the autumn of 1858 featuring the artist's first documented painting.[41] Manchon stands before a portrait bust and two frames leaning against a wall half-covered with printed placards, his huge head and exaggerated muttonchops almost dwarfing his tiny body. The posters are partially legible, including one directly behind him that reads *"Notaire a marier aux conditions [les] plus avantageuses / grandes facilités de paiement on pourrait entrer du jouissance de suite / s'adresser a Mr. XXX"* ["Notary for marriages offering the most advantageous terms / Range of easy terms for payment / you can pay with interest later / Apply to Monsieur XXX"].

An unusual feature of the portrait of Manchon is the existence of a variant drawing in the collection of the Musée des Beaux-Arts, Rouen, where it was left by a descendent of the sitter in 1952 (fig. 42).[42] The version in Rouen repeats the face and backdrop of the Chicago drawing but offers a variation on the sitter's attire, substituting a vest, formal frock coat, and high collar for the plain morning coat seen in the other sheet. The effect is altogether more flattering, as is the pose: straight and trim with feet together, rather than hunched over. As the early provenance of the Chicago drawing is unknown—it was one of the works acquired by Carter Harrison in Paris during the late 1920s—we have no way of knowing whether it stayed with the artist, perhaps having been rejected by the sitter and kept by Monet for a period of time as a sample sheet.

Monet's large *Caricature of Jules Didier, "Butterfly Man"* (fig. 45) is the most fanciful of his "big heads." It is similar in scale and drawing technique to the other Le Havre *portraits-charges* of the late 1850s but pushes the genre to a heightened level of bizarre fantasy. In constructing a hybrid creature from man and butterfly, Monet followed in the footsteps of popular illustrators like Benjamin Roubaud (1811–1847), who in his series *Panthéon Charivarique* combined the head of novelist Paul de Kock (1793–1871) with the body of a rooster (fig. 43). In Monet's drawing, another more traditional hybrid appears: an earthbound female centaur attempts to tether the airborne butterfly man. Above her head, a series of notices advertise an elaborate, if baffling spectacle, *"Guerre des Indes . . . / L'Homme Canon . . . / L'Homme Papillon . . . / Prix des places"* ["French and Indian War / Human Canonball / Butterfly

43
Benjamin Roubaud (French, 1811–1847), *Portrait of Paul de Kock* (from the *Pantheon Charivarique* series), 1842. Lithograph, 346 x 248 mm. Fine Arts Museums of San Francisco

44
Félix Bracquemond (French, 1833–1914), *Portrait of Jules Didier*, 1853. Etching, 345 x 263 mm. New York Public Library. Samuel Putnam Avery Collection, Miriam and Ira D. Wallach Division of Art, Prints, and Photographs. Astor, Lenox, and Tilden Foundations

45
Caricature of Jules Didier, "Butterfly Man," c. 1858. Charcoal heightened with white chalk on blue laid paper (discolored to gray), 616 x 436 mm. The Art Institute of Chicago. Mr. and Mrs. Carter H. Harrison Collection [D515]

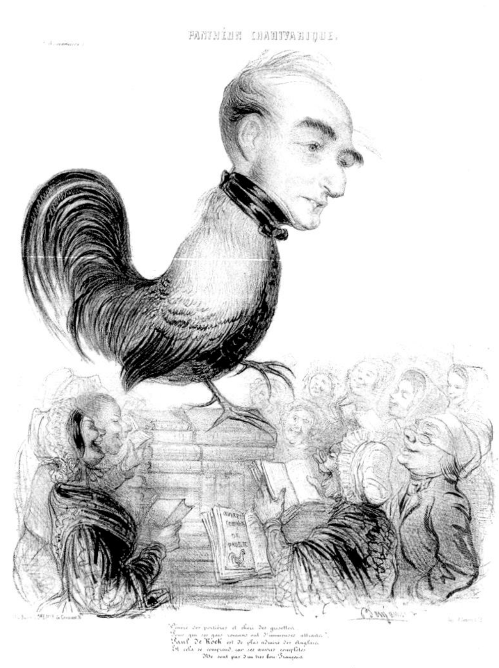

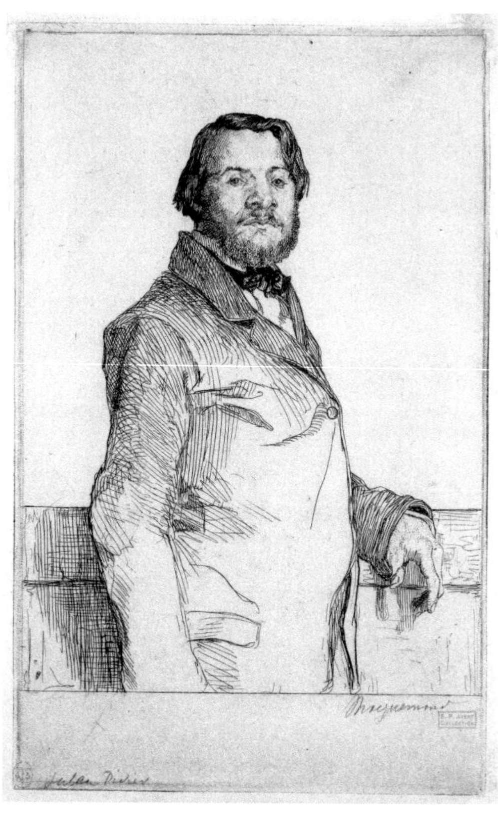

Man / Price of admission"]. Two pentimenti are visible in the drawing: the butterfly wings appear to have been enlarged after Monet first outlined them, and he erased and moved his signature into a slightly lower position on the sheet.

The identity of Monet's butterfly man has undergone its own mysterious metamorphosis since the drawing first surfaced. When it entered the collection of the Art Institute of Chicago in 1933, the work was described on the incoming receipt as a portrait of "Jules Dubois, banker," an identification consistent with the class of local businessmen represented in the other large caricatures, though strikingly at odds with its eccentric iconography. Early worksheets in the museum's object file equivocate on his surname, identifying him as "Jules Didier (or Dubois)." When the drawing was first published in the museum's *Bulletin* in 1943, it was titled *Caricature of Jules Didier, Banker.*[43]

Wildenstein recognized that Jules Didier was the name of a painter-lithographer (1831–1892) who won the Prix de Rome in 1857 for historical landscape, and suggested that he was the subject of the drawing rather than a banker from Le Havre.[44] Wildenstein noted a certain resemblance between Monet's butterfly man and a portrait of the artist Jules Didier at the Villa Medici. More convincing is a comparison between the drawing and the etched portrait of Didier by Félix Bracquemond that dates from 1853 (fig. 44).[45] The fact that the sitter was an animal painter, and had published a lithograph entitled *Le Papillon* in 1856,[46] further supports this identification. Yet the circumstances surrounding the drawing of the butterfly man — that is, precisely how, when, and where young Monet came into contact with Jules Didier — remain up in the air.

The identity of another anonymous *portrait-charge* linking Monet to a contemporary painter has been given no previous attention in the literature on the artist (fig. 46).[47] This large-scale black-and-white chalk drawing of a young man seated in profile is signed by Charles Lhuillier (1824–1898 or 99) and was among the works contained in Michel Monet's bequest to the Musée Marmottan Monet. Lhuillier was a slightly older painter from Le Havre who had also studied under Ochard, and seems to have

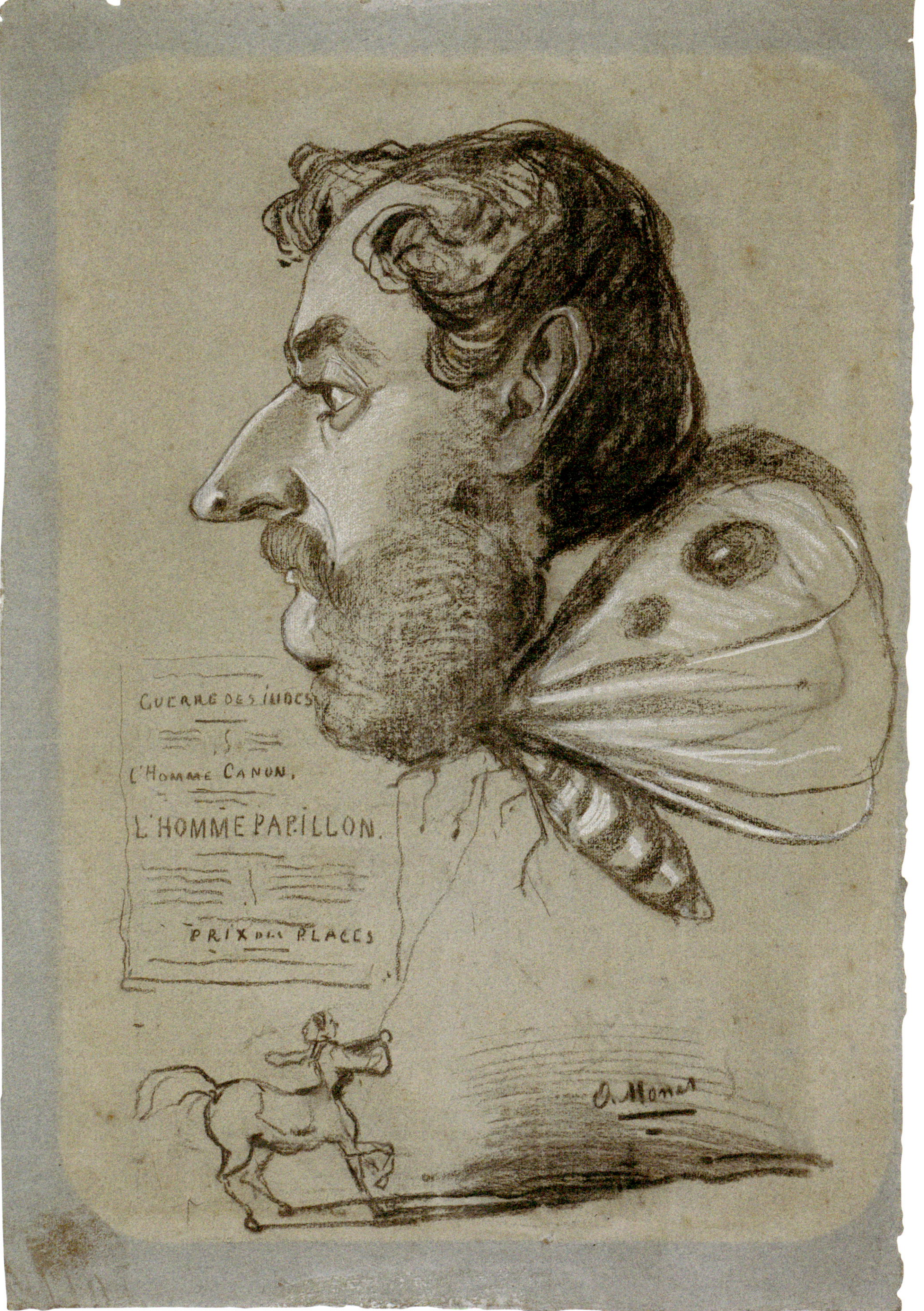
GUERRE DES INDES
L'Homme CANON.
L'HOMME PAPILLON.
PRIX DES PLACES
O. Monet

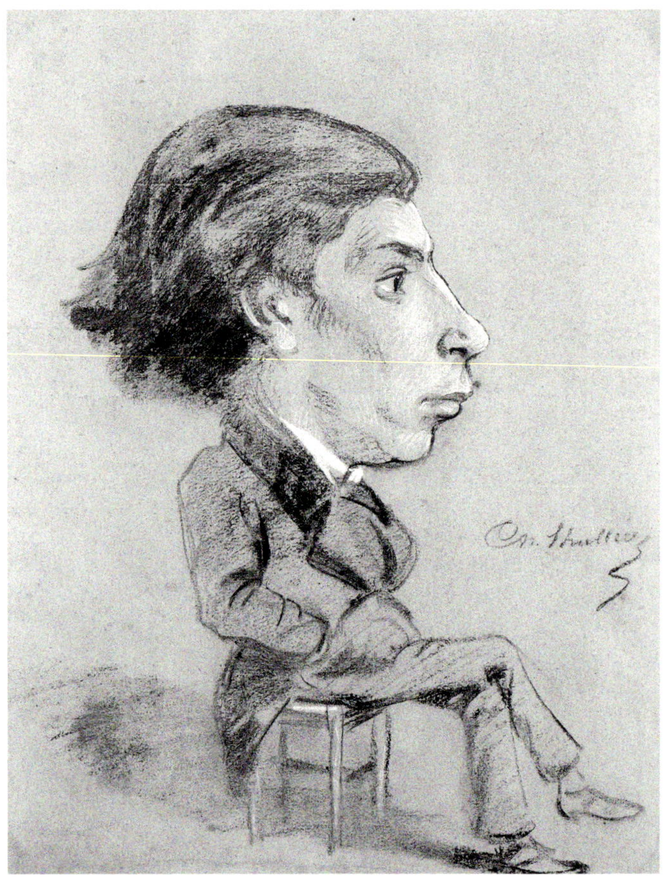

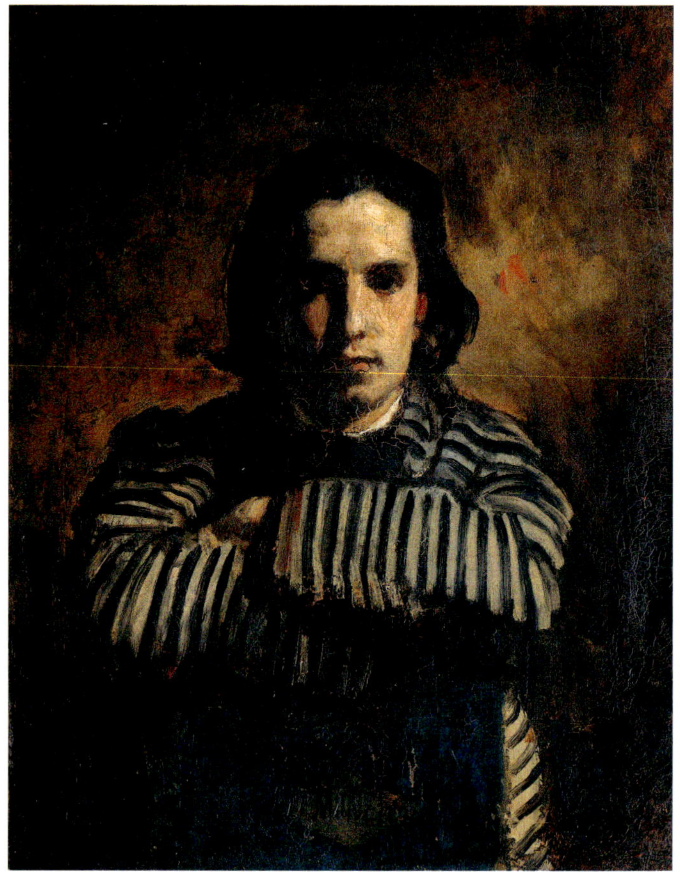

46
Charles Lhuillier (French, 1824–1898 or 99), *Portrait-charge*, c. 1858–60. Black and white chalk, 500 x 390 mm. Musée Marmottan Monet, Paris

47
Gilbert Alexandre de Severac (French, 1834–1897), *Portrait of Claude Monet*, 1865. Oil on canvas, 40 x 32 cm. Musée Marmottan Monet, Paris

made Monet's acquaintance by around 1860. In 1861 he painted a portrait of Monet in his Zouave uniform (see fig. 63). The seated figure in Lhuillier's *portrait-charge*, his only known foray into caricature, bears a striking resemblance to Monet in photographs and paintings from his early twenties (fig. 47): the swept-back shock of hair, prominent upper lip, and slight double-chin are all quite comparable. If it does represent Monet at the age of about eighteen or nineteen, the drawing may be a keepsake of the two artists' friendship, perhaps made in reciprocation for a similar portrait by Monet of Lhuillier.

There is some irony in that the young Monet's most technically advanced and finely wrought drawings were tainted by the vulgarity of their subject matter, a fact that was not lost on the city council of Le Havre. In a sense, his large-format *portraits-charges* might be regarded as taking the place of his lost *académies*. Representing the opposite of the academic ideals of classical beauty and proportion, and concentrating on the unique features of the modern face rather than the idealized anatomy of the nude body, they nevertheless display the draftsman's proficiency in modeling the tones of flesh in black and white.

The Road Not Taken

Having mastered the art of caricature through copying prints and perfecting his craft on the local population of Le Havre, Monet sought to follow in the footsteps of Daumier and Nadar and sell his work to the Parisian press. In March 1860 his first and only published caricature appeared in the pages of *Diogène*, a liberal weekly newspaper containing satirical portraits and biographies edited by Eugène Varner.[48] The print, a *portrait-charge* of the comedian Louis Fortuné Adolphe Laferrière (1806–1877; fig. 48), accompanied a biographical profile of the actor.[49] Laferrière was in the midst of a distinguished career at the Comédie-Française, where his contract apparently guaranteed him top billing, much to the chagrin

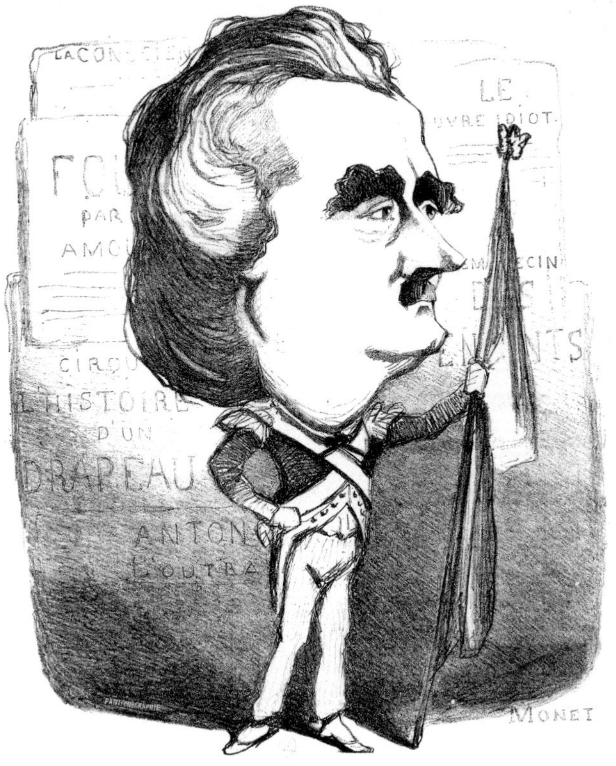

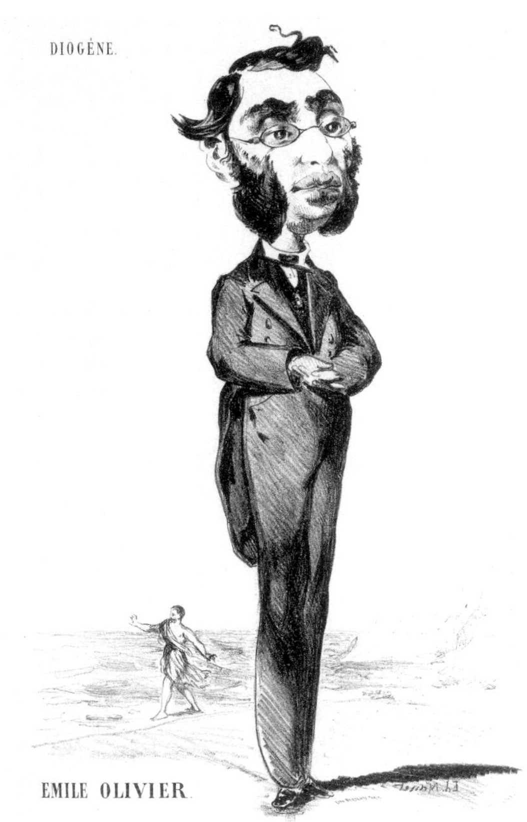

48

Caricature of Louis Fortuné Adolphe Laferrière, 1860. Gillotage, 385 x 280 mm. Musée Carnavalet-Histoire de Paris [D511]

49

Edouard Manet (French, 1832–83), *Caricature of Emile Olivier*, 1860. Lithograph, 374 x 267 mm. Bibiliothèque nationale de France, Paris

of his co-stars. A small pencil drawing by Monet of unknown location depicts Laferrière in the role of Saint-Mégrin in Alexandre Dumas *père's Henri III et sa coeur* (written in 1829) at the Théâtre de la Porte-Saint-Martin.[50] When Frédérick Lemaitre, who was to play the duc de Guise, learned of Laferrière's contractual stipulation, he reportedly shrugged his shoulders and uttered, "ladies first," a swipe at his colleague's notorious "feminine vanity."[51] Avoiding this aspect of the actor's reputation, Monet depicted him in military costume, his left hand gripping a flagstaff. The construction of the image is similar to the "big heads" of Manchon and *Butterfly Man*. On the wall behind him an array of placards are inscribed with the titles of his repertoire, including his latest play: Adolphe Dennery's *L'Histoire d'un drapeau* (1860) at the Cirque-Olympique.

The publication of Monet's *Laferrière* marked his official debut on the Paris art scene. It was as a draftsman that he had earned a reputation in Le Havre, and it was as a draftsman that he now appeared before the Parisian public. Interestingly, just three weeks after this print entered circulation, another debut took place in the pages of *Diogène*. In the 14 April issue, an article on the politician Emile Olivier (1825–1913) was illustrated with a *portrait-charge* by the twenty-eight year-old Edouard Manet (fig. 49), likewise his first (and only) published caricature.[52] It was not until the Salon of 1865, when some critics confused their surnames, that Monet and Manet appeared together again in the same venue.

Following the publication of *Laferrière*, Monet wrote to his painter-friend Amand Gautier (1825–1894) on 11 August 1860, indicating that he was at work on caricatures for *Le Gaulois* and *Le Charivari*, but these seem not to have come to fruition.[53] Although his *portraits-charges* helped him finance his move to the French capital in the spring of 1859, Monet was already in pursuit of a different career path. This new course would soon put a halt to his public activity as a draftsman and ultimately place him on the other end of the caricaturist's pencil.

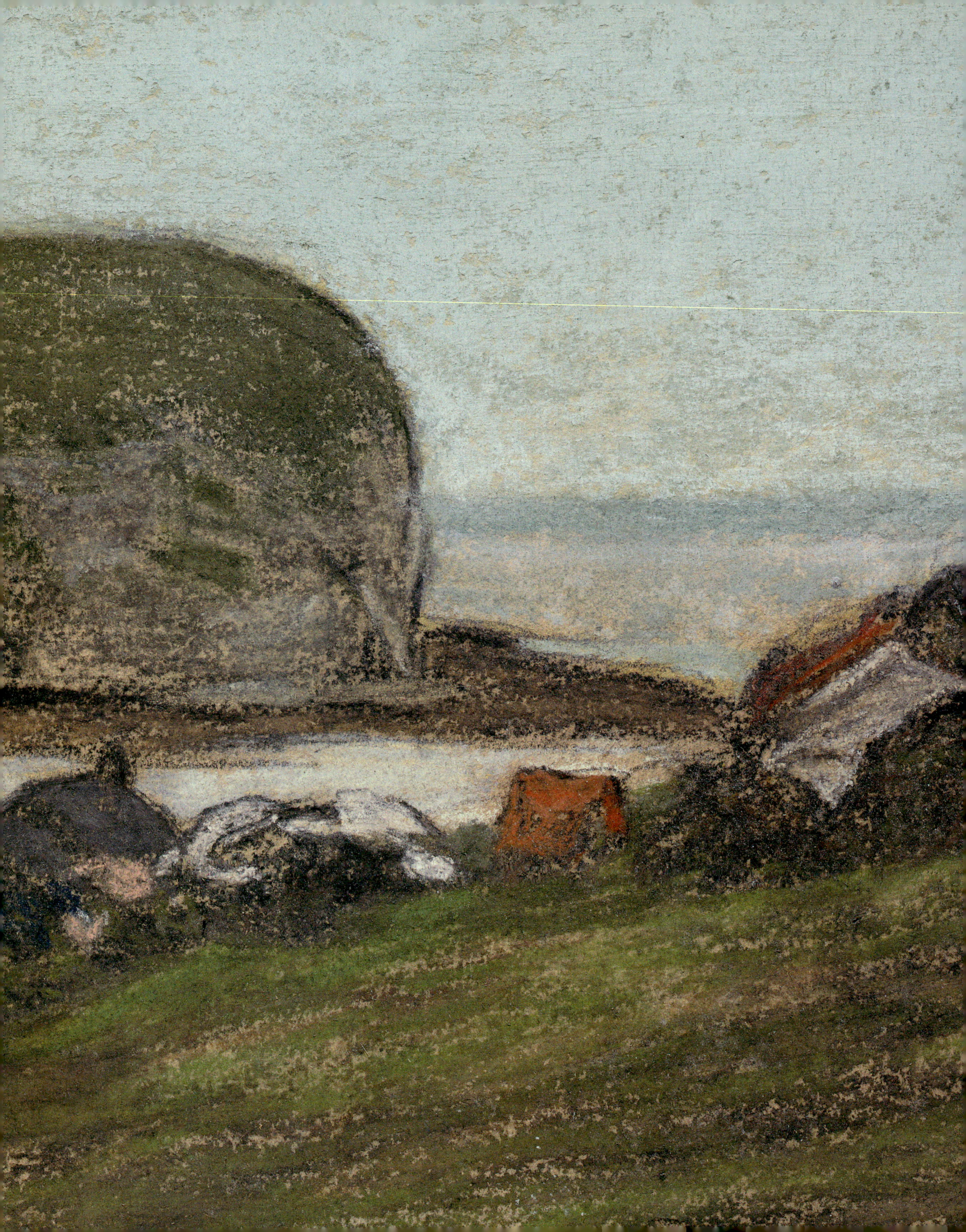

CHAPTER THREE Encounters with Draftsmen, 1859–63

"Learn to draw: that's what most of you lack today." In a letter written at the age of eighteen, Monet explained how he received this advice from Constant Troyon (1810–1865), the successful painter of rural and agricultural scenes such as *The Coming Storm* (fig. 50), a work completed shortly after their encounter.[1] Monet had traveled to Paris in May 1859 to seek guidance on his career from a number of established artists and study the latest pictures on view in the city. Shortly before the meeting with Troyon, he visited the annual Salon at the Palais de l'Industrie: "The landscape painters were in the majority," Monet wrote with obvious approval: "As for quality, the Troyons are superb and the Daubignys are, to my eyes at least, really beautiful." His mood persisted after he arrived at Troyon's studio; "I could not begin to describe all the lovely things I saw there," he continued, adding that Troyon "seems a really good man and he doesn't mince words." To demonstrate the standard he had already achieved, Monet brought with him from Le Havre two examples of his own still-life painting. Troyon was clearly impressed, recognizing in the teenager's work a certain command of color and a facility with paint, but directing him to "draw with all your might" and "get down to some serious study." "Begin by joining a studio where they only make studies of the figure, *académies*," Troyon urged, while reminding him not to neglect painting: "Go to the country from time to time and make studies and above all develop them. Do some copying in the Louvre."

As we now know from several sources, including Monet's early sketchbooks and the Beguin Billecocq Grand Journal, Troyon's counsel was dramatically ill informed. By this date, Monet had been drawing energetically for at least a decade, sketching scenery, buildings, boats, and portraits of friends, and achieving local fame as a caricaturist. His letter does not indicate whether these activities were revealed to Troyon, but we can assume that they would have been summarily dismissed by the older man. Troyon clearly had a quite different kind of drawing in mind, the making of an *académie*, a rigorously observed and meticulously delineated study of the human body that was the staple of all formal art education in France. Tracing its origin to the Renaissance and the classical world, this discipline was required of painters of all persuasions, including landscapists, as well as sculptors and printmakers. The young Monet was almost certainly aware of this

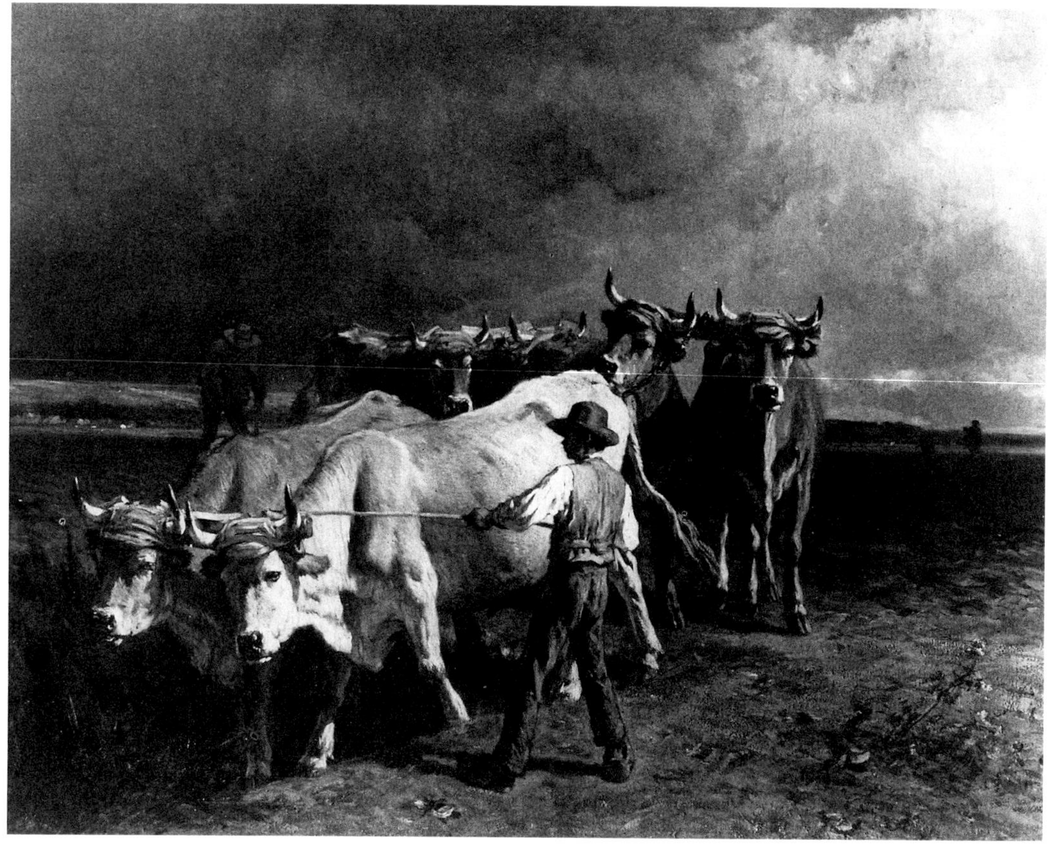

50
Constant Troyon (French, 1810–1865), *The Coming Storm*, 1860. Oil on canvas, 97.3 x 129.8 cm. Sterling and Francine Clark Art Institute, Williamstown, Massachusetts

tradition, perhaps from the teaching of his high-school drawing instructor in Le Havre, Jacques-François Ochard, a conventionally qualified artist who exhibited at the Salon until at least 1841.[2] Ochard had been a pupil of Jacques-Louis David, a legendary draftsman and a crucial influence on the formation of the modern academic system. Another of David's students, Jean-Auguste-Dominique Ingres, maintained the master's faith into the 1860s, telling his own acolytes that "drawing makes up three quarters of that which constitutes painting" and explaining "it is absolutely necessary to do nothing without the model . . . the masterpieces of antiquity were made with models like those we have at the moment before our eyes in Paris."[3]

Confronted by such solemnity in 1859, the eighteen-year-old from Le Havre may well have felt confused and perhaps provoked. Despite his remarkably accomplished caricatures and new evidence of his early involvement with portraiture, there is little doubt that Monet was already committed to becoming a landscapist.[4] His comments at the 1859 Salon make this preference explicit, as do remarks from his maturity about the obscure marine painters he revered in his youth, before coming to Paris.[5] One of these was Théodore Gudin (1802–1880), a specialist in stormy seas, naval engagements, and ships at anchor in French harbors and more exotic locations, to whom Monet's youthful eyes had become "accustomed," in his own words (fig. 51).[6] Monet's decision to seek out Troyon, an artist known almost exclusively for his rustic vocabulary and one who had worked in the Normandy countryside, is telling in this context.[7] Also significant were Troyon's own beginnings, which were almost the opposite of those he outlined for his young visitor. Learning his trade as an obscure porcelain decorator in the provinces, Troyon himself had never worked "in a studio where they only make studies of the figure," and even his biographer acknowledged that the rare human presences in Troyon's pictures were "painted mechanically."[8] Though he certainly went "to the country" to paint and draw, and was a proficient draftsman in his chosen domain, there is little evidence that Troyon

51
Théodore Gudin (French, 1802–1880), *Entry to the Port of Le Havre*. Oil on canvas, 54 x 46 cm. Musée Magnin, Dijon

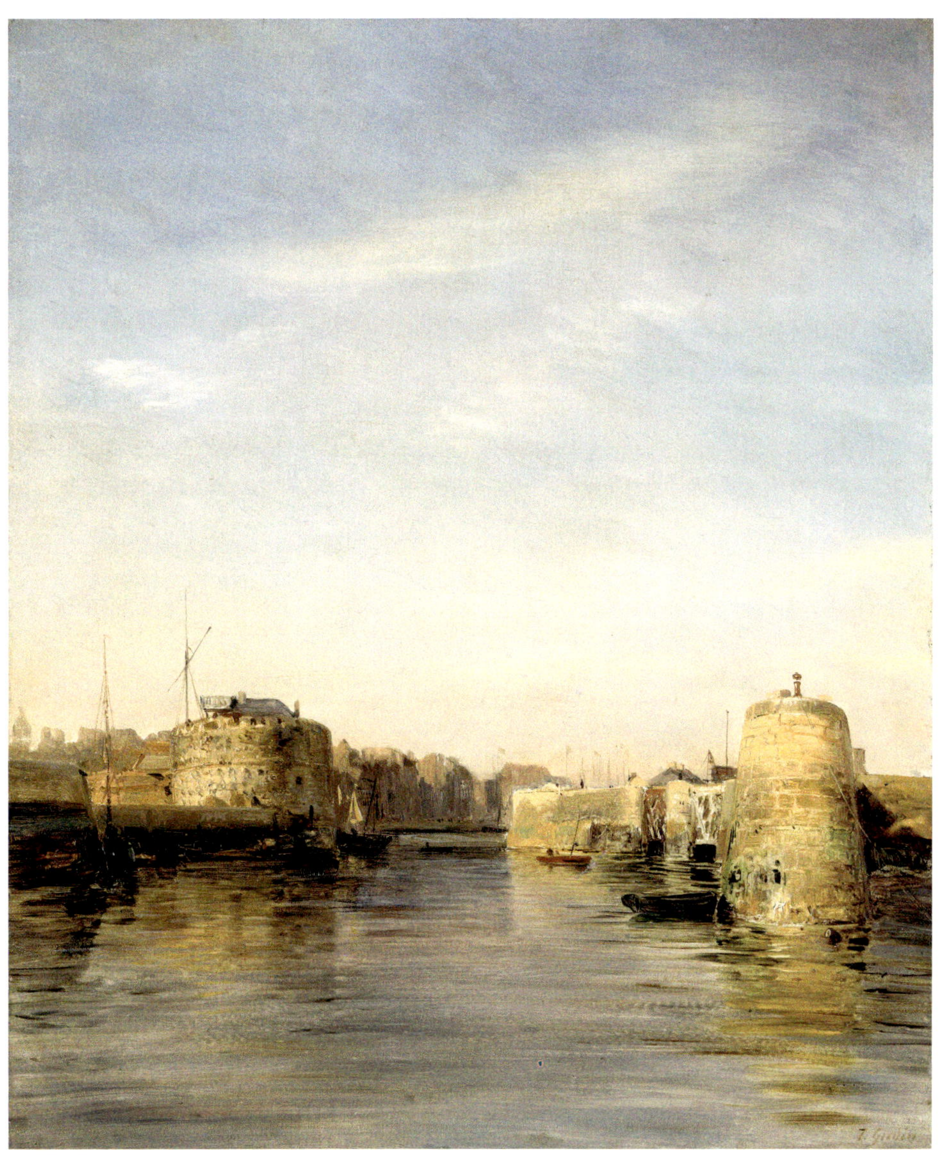

spent time "copying in the Louvre." Perhaps hoping to find a kindred spirit, Monet must have been doubly disappointed.

Troyon's directives to the young artist were thus more pious than practical, reiterating the established wisdom of the day and doing little to clarify Monet's career path. Underlying Troyon's attitude was the problematic status of landscape painting in general and its claims to attention at this moment. Landscape was traditionally regarded as a minor branch of art and was subject to periodic attempts to elevate its seriousness and stress its grounding in time-honored skills and sensibilities. As Monet embarked on his career, the subject was again under challenge from a number of directions. When the poet and critic Charles Baudelaire wrote his celebrated review of the 1859 Salon—where Monet had found the Troyons "superb" and the Daubignys "really beautiful"—he was decidedly skeptical. Announcing that "any landscape painter who does not know how to convey a *feeling* by means of an assemblage of vegetable and mineral matter, is not an artist," Baudelaire proceeded, "Like everyone else, I admit that our modern school of landscape painters is singularly strong and skillful; but in this triumph and predominance of an inferior genre, in this silly cult of a nature neither purged nor explained by the imagination, I see an obvious symptom of general degradation."[9] Later in his essay, Baudelaire found elements to praise in the submissions of several leading artists, but spared almost no one entirely: he identified "flabbiness" in Daubigny, "monotonous ugliness" in Millet, and an "absence of construction" in Rousseau, while associating Troyon with the "second-rate talents."[10] The adult Monet was to develop a great admiration for Baudelaire's writing, but there is no way of knowing if he read this text when it appeared. As we shall see, one of its later sections would have been of particular interest to him, since it contained the first public eulogy of Monet's first painting teacher, Eugène Boudin.

Encouraged by Troyon to make *académies* and to copy in the Louvre, and perhaps tempted by Baudelaire to "convey a feeling" through landscape painting, Monet seems to have attempted none of these things in the short term. He was still dependent on the good will of his family and on income from the sale of caricatures, but lingered in Paris until the summer of 1859 and met other artists such as Charles Lhuillier and Amand Gautier, who presumably offered their own advice. From the pages of the Grand Journal, further adventures can now be traced to these months. On 4 April 1859, prior to his talk with Troyon, Monet accompanied Théophile Beguin Billecocq and his younger brother-in-law Théodore to the *Opéra-comique* for the premiere of Meyerbeer's *Pardon de Ploërmel*, a light-hearted opera set in Brittany.[11] In July, all three were again united at Nemours, south of Paris, when the Beguin Billecocq family and their guest enjoyed a summer vacation near the forest of Fontainebleau. Making regular excursions into an area dense with recent artistic history, they were directed by Monet in a succession of "drawing parties," as at Poissy the previous year. "We carried with us pencils and crayons, watercolors, little drawing books," wrote Théophile, recounting their tours to such picturesque sites as Moret-sur-Loing, Barbizon, and Chailly-en-Bière. This was territory that Rousseau, Troyon, Daubigny, Millet, and many others had already made their own and to which Monet would soon return to paint, but for the moment it was works on paper that occupied them.

"Oscar had not lost his touch, quite the contrary." Théophile recalled: "His drawings, above all his landscapes, showed a great liveliness and an unequalled facility for this kind of art. The line was precise, but also expressive. He handled the watercolor brush just as well as wash, making drawings of trees, houses, and landscapes with great feeling." Describing him as "slightly bohemian," Théophile contrasted the Oscar "who was vilified by his father" with the "pleasant, good-humored young man" he now met, adding, "I have become truly fond of him. He enthusiastically revealed to us his great plans to succeed in drawing and painting, and repeatedly evoked the talent of one of his friends from Le Havre who needed help, a certain Eugène Boudin." Théophile concluded his account by noting a gift to Oscar of 500 francs and his help in acquiring materials for watercolor and gouache painting, with which the young prodigy made pictures of "delicious landscapes, trees and flowers," to be distributed to the party.[12]

Most, if not all, of the studies given by Monet to his hosts on this occasion seem to have disappeared, though some may survive among the varied sheets preserved from these family parties. While Théophile was a sincere admirer of the arts, he could also be imprecise about the character of Monet's drawings of "trees and houses" and "delicious landscapes." Our attempt to chart Monet's progress as a draftsman during this time is further exacerbated by a break in the succession of his sketchbooks between 1857 and the mid-1860s, and the uncertain fate of several groups of documented works. Critical though they were to his formation as a graphic artist, Monet's early years in Paris are defined by absences as often as presences. Some of the gaps in this record can be partly bridged, however, by descriptions in the artist's letters and in his later reminiscences, and by further episodes recorded in the Grand Journal. References to drawings associated with his army service in North Africa have added significantly to this story, while certain of his little-studied early pastels can now be more securely dated within this period. Seen as a whole, this fragmentary evidence allows us to piece together Monet's transition to the world of professional

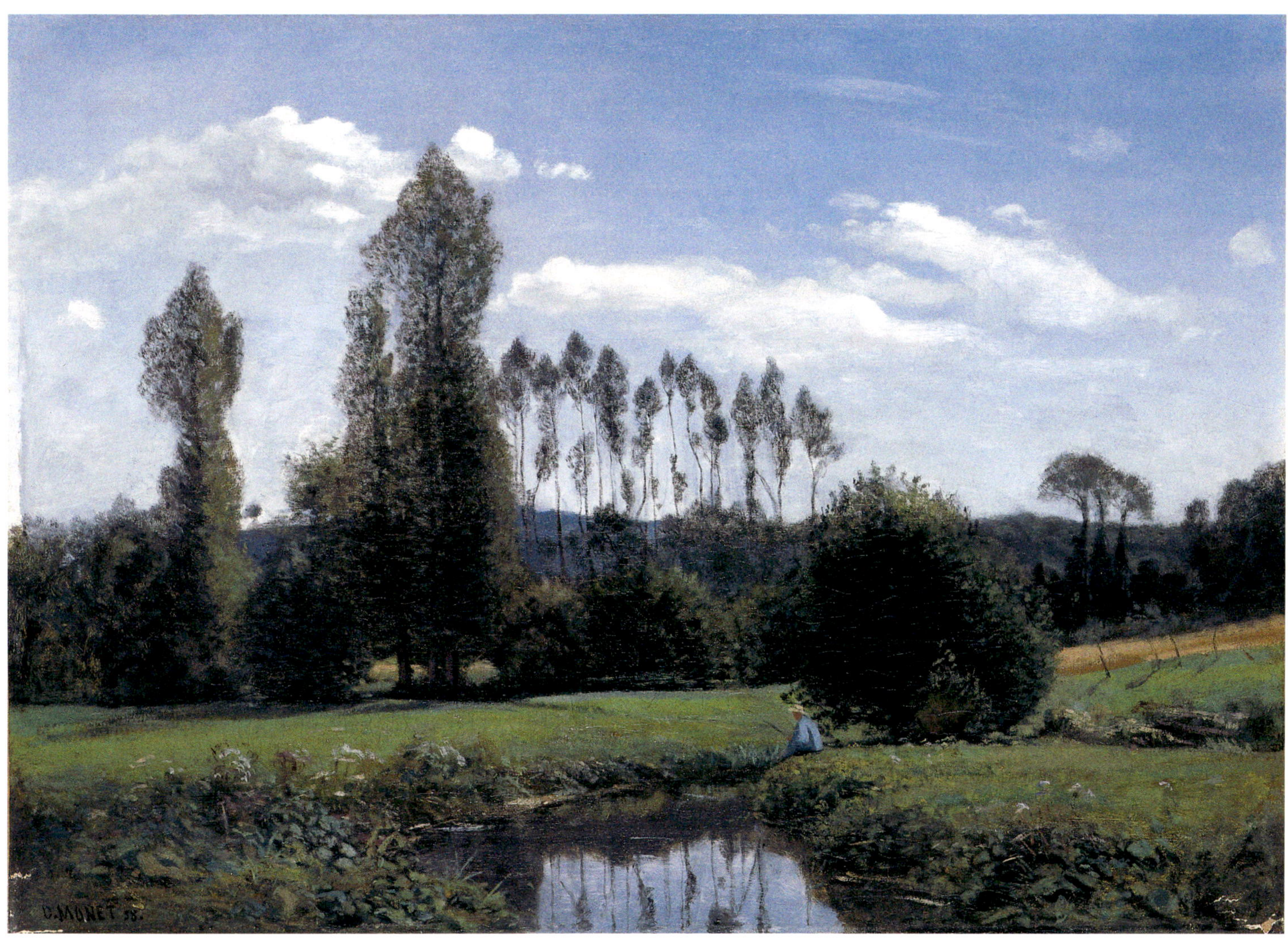

52
View from Ruelles, 1858. Oil on canvas, 46 x 65 cm. Private collection. On deposit, Museum of Modern Art, Saitama, Japan [W1]

draftsmanship, as represented by the teaching studios of Paris, occasional glimpses of his elders' drawings, and the complex values that lay behind them. Drawing, as Monet had soon discovered, was rarely an innocent activity. At its simplest, it could be a practical process that was accessible to children, amateurs, and students; at the opposite extreme, drawing represented a link with historically loaded systems of meanings that had pervaded the arts for centuries.

Boudin and Draftsmanship

In order to understand Monet's encounter with this world, we need to look back to a formative event that took place before his arrival in the city in 1859. Recounted by Monet himself in later life and echoed in other sources, it begins with his initiation into the practice of oil painting, which appears to have taken place the previous year near Le Havre, under the auspices of Boudin. The elderly Boudin himself recalled his first outdoor expeditions with Monet, when he went "drawing with him in the open fields" and soon afterward invited the youth to accompany him again.[13] This time, according to Monet, Boudin began work on a new canvas in front of his amazed pupil. "What a revelation!" Monet remembered, adding that he returned the following day with his own fresh canvas and began to paint with Boudin's help: "my eyes, finally, were opened, and I really understood nature," he claimed in 1900.[14] The picture in question may have been *View from Ruelles* (fig. 52), which bears the date 1858 and represents an area where

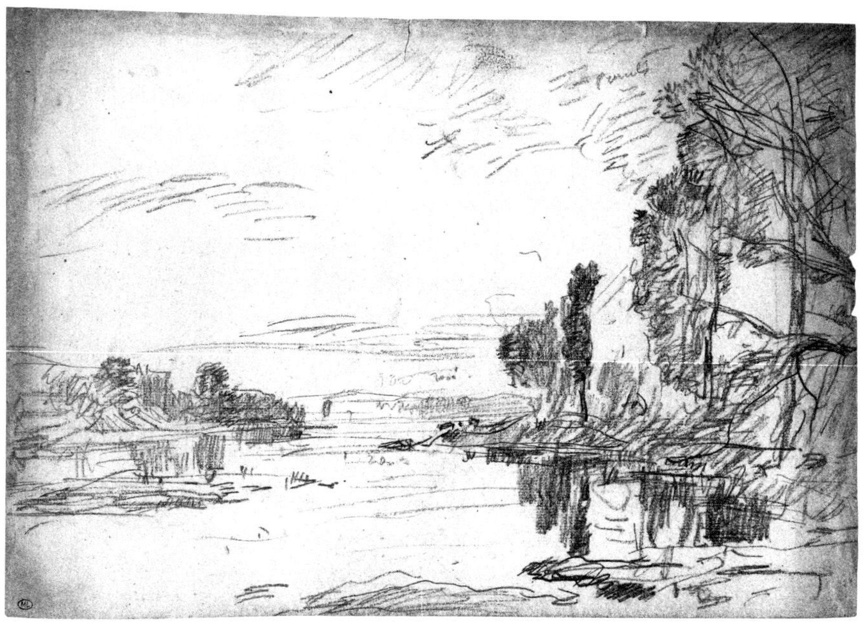

53
Eugène Boudin (French, 1824–1898), *View of a River Bordered by Trees*, n.d. Pencil, 230 x 337 mm. Musée du Louvre, Paris

Boudin had previously painted.[15] Much cited in the subsequent literature, this account is rarely accompanied by the next sentence with its more challenging implications. Still speaking of the natural scene in front of him, Monet continued: "I analyzed it in its forms with a pencil, I studied it in its colorations."

Following the custom of the day, Boudin's instruction involved a preliminary phase of drawing, made either on paper or directly on the canvas itself. Though no such study for Monet's Ruelles picture has come down to us, his initial response to the trees and reflections may have been close to the graphic manner of the 1856 or 1857 sketchbooks, or to the informal drafts described by Théophile Beguin Billecocq. Equally, he might have adopted the relaxed pencil technique used by Boudin in similar circumstances, as in *View of a River Bordered by Trees* (fig. 53). Despite its novelty for Monet, therefore, this lesson conformed in at least one respect to the daily labors of many thousands of landscape painters working across Europe at the time. Popular instruction manuals in oil painting, watercolor, and pastel invariably stressed the importance of this initial stage, when "a profound understanding of drawing" was considered "the most indispensable" accomplishment by writers such as Jean-Pierre Thénot in 1856.[16] Without overburdening the Ruelles anecdote, we should also note that such a practice connected Monet to a grander artistic principle that—like the notion of the *académie*—he had probably encountered in the teaching of Ochard. Drawing, in this sense, was seen to be literally fundamental to the creation of all works of art, determining the training of hand and eye, the forms of depicted figures and landscape elements, and the entire composition of a picture prior to the application of color.

Though such claims may seem bizarrely exaggerated in retrospect, the foundational roles of drawing also carried a symbolic and implicitly moral significance within academic ideology. The making of lines, in other words, represented not only skill but also discipline and mental rigor; "Drawing is the probity of art," Ingres had claimed.[17] From here it was a natural step to associate fine draftsmanship with rectitude and high principle, and thus with the loftiest virtues of civilized life. By contrast, the other dominant element of the fine arts, color, was easily regarded as a mere "ornament to painting," in Ingres's words, and thus seductive and treacherous.[18] Such views were clearly spelled out in a range of publications that were current during Monet's early years, among them the writings of the eminent theorist and historian of art Charles Blanc. Though highly distinguished in his profession, Blanc was also a popularizer of sorts, founding the *Gazette des beaux-arts* in 1859 and directing a series of studies of national painting schools for the general reader that were published between 1850 and 1876.[19] Many of Blanc's ideals came together in his monumental study of the arts, pointedly based on the principles of drawing and entitled *Grammaire des arts du dessin*, a work that first appeared in 1867 but whose influence persisted into the late nineteenth century. Explaining that "form is absolute," whereas color is "relative," Blanc declared that "the superiority of drawing over color is written even in the laws of nature," while conceding that "the union of drawing and color is necessary to give birth to painting, just as the union of man and woman is necessary to give birth to humanity."[20]

Creating a work such as *View from Ruelles* in

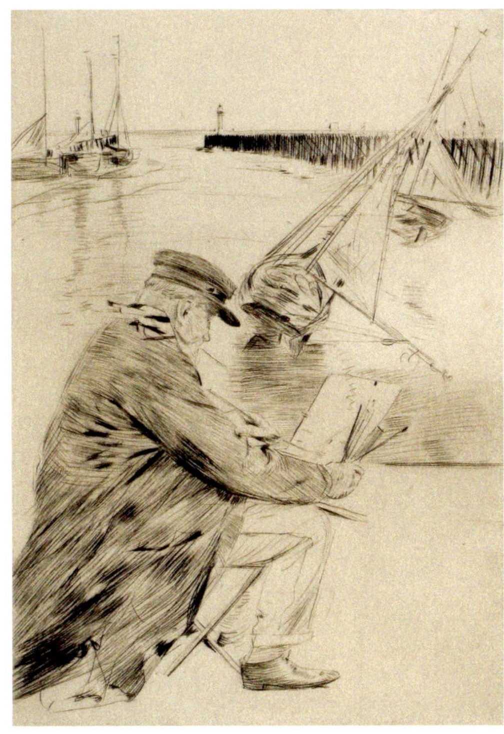

54
Paul César Helleu (French, 1859–1927), *Boudin Painting on the Jetty at Trouville*, 1897. Drypoint printed in black on laid paper, 281 x 200 mm. The Detroit Institute of Arts. Gift of Mr. and Mrs. Bernard F. Walker

a Normandy pasture, and presumably oblivious to most of these theoretical concerns, Boudin's student was nevertheless stepping into contested territory. As he scrutinized his modest group of poplars and picturesque river, Monet tells us that he "analyzed it in its forms with a pencil," before studying it in terms of color. With obvious technical advantages for a beginner, this procedure was one he would soon begin to question and ultimately abandon in his mature craft, by then fully conscious of its emblematic weight. Straightforward though the experiment at Ruelles appeared to be, it remains important as a rare, firsthand account of Monet's early picture-making and a crucial benchmark against which to articulate his subsequent development as a draftsman and painter. Unbeknownst to himself, the apprentice had briefly experienced a method whose larger significance would haunt many of his generation. In Blanc's understanding, Monet had defined a linear structure that would remain "absolute," even as it began to support and articulate the "relative" qualities of the paint he would gradually superimpose. Monet explored a number of variations on this sequence over successive years, including some that bypassed or even inverted the conventional pattern of operations and its ancient apparatus of morality. Eventually he took a public stand against draftsmanship itself, arguing through his painterly practice that color could be self-sufficient at every stage in the creation of a picture. Despite his repeated recourse to drawing and to works on paper of various kinds, Monet would challenge the beliefs of Blanc and his colleagues as no other contemporary had done.

After this revelation at Ruelles, Boudin continued to provide an inspirational, if somewhat contradictory model for Monet's "great plans to succeed in drawing and painting." Seventeen years older than his protégé, Boudin was still an obscure painter who lived meagerly outside the mainstream of his profession at the time they met, neither selling to wealthy clients nor exhibiting regularly.[21] Largely self-taught, he had learned his craft in part from artists visiting the area, such as Millet, Corot, Isabey, and Troyon. In the late 1840s, Boudin also copied extensively in the Louvre, though never submitting himself to the rigors of academic drawing or to mastering the *académie*.[22] In many technical respects, therefore, his example must have offered an appealing alternative to the career patterns envisaged by others for the young Monet. The son of a ship's officer who had briefly worked at sea himself, Boudin created an art that was grounded in close, palpable experience of the boats, harbors, and beaches on the coast of Normandy and Brittany, and in the towns and villages nearby. Central to this relationship was his immediate contact with the motif: "Everything painted directly on the spot always has a strength, a power, a vividness of touch that one doesn't find again in the studio," he famously claimed.[23] More than thirty years after his first meetings with Monet in Le Havre, Boudin was still working outdoors, as an evocative drypoint by Paul Helleu of 1897 attests (fig. 54).

The young Monet would soon have discovered that Boudin was also a prolific, unselfconscious, and highly resourceful draftsman. Several thousands of his pencil and chalk drawings still exist, many of them in the collections of the Louvre, ranging from small, hasty

55

Eugène Boudin, *Setting Sun*, c. 1860. Pastel on beige paper, 215 x 286 mm. Musée du Louvre, Paris

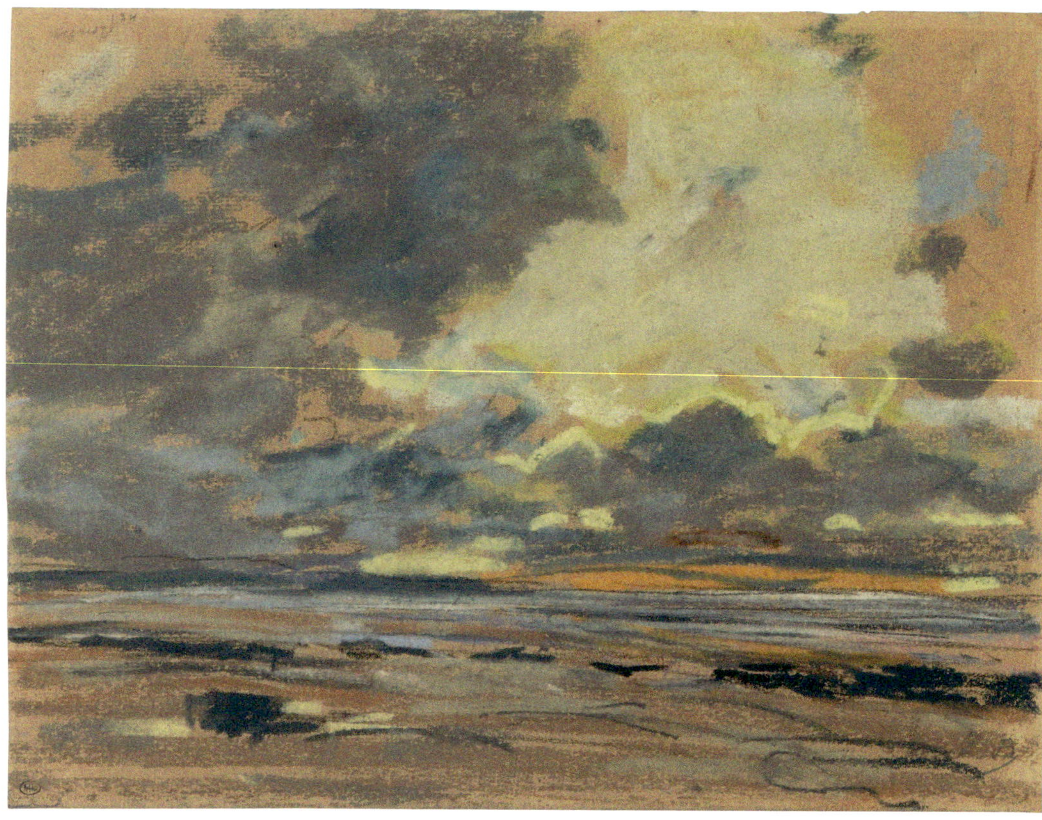

annotations of the landscape and patient studies of ships and their rigging, to sketches of women washing their laundry and of farm animals at market. Few have a precise relationship to his completed canvases, though Boudin appears to have consulted them when working on grander oil compositions and learned to handle other media, such as watercolor and pastel, that had a clearer intermediary function in his studio. For Boudin, drawing was a comfortable and unforced part of his working routine, the antithesis of the dutiful *académie* recommended by Constant Troyon and held in reverence by Charles Blanc. His energetic career as a pastellist extended this habit, contributing pale tints to numerous sketchbook pages and energizing finished pictures that rivaled his most audacious oils. It was in the years immediately prior to his meeting with Monet that Boudin's use of the brittle, chalky freshness of pastel reached a new level of gestural inventiveness. An imprecisely dated study such as *Setting Sun* (fig. 55), thought to have been made in the late 1850s, exemplifies this departure, in which streaks, ribbons, and flurries of dense color are woven into a radically new kind of image. Executed on a modest-size sheet of tinted paper, like scores of similar works from this time, Boudin's vibrant scene was clearly executed with speed and with a minimum of preparation. Crucially, there are only minimal signs of linear drafting in pencil or crayon beneath this effusion of light and water, effectively relegating it to a minor category of contemporary draftsmanship in the terms of the day. In Blanc's brief references to the medium in his 1867 volume, he conceded that pastel was useful for seizing "fugitive effects" in studies that required "no preparation," before dismissing pastel along with other kinds of "improvisation."[24]

Boudin's pastels and the discussions that accompanied them inevitably formed part of Monet's education as he began to embrace life in Paris. The same pastels achieved brief notoriety during young Oscar's first sojourn in the city, when they were eulogized by Baudelaire in his extended response to the Salon, published in *La Revue française* during June 1859.[25] Fascinated but somewhat cautious, Baudelaire explained how a recent visit to Boudin's studio

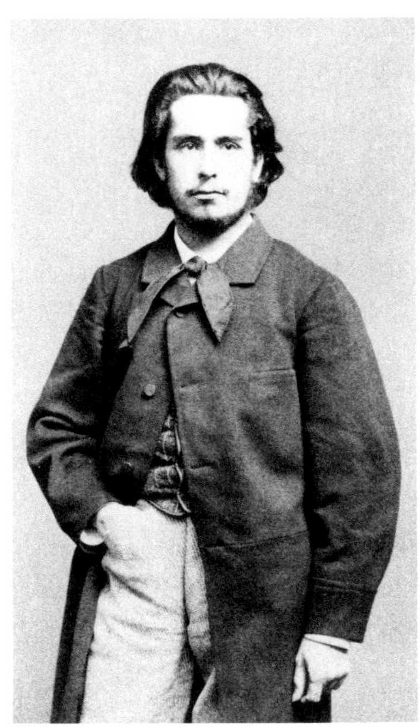

56
Claude Monet, c. 1865

in Honfleur had revealed "several hundred pastel studies, improvised in front of the sea and sky," which he likened to "prodigious enchantments of air and water." "All these clouds, with their fantastic and luminous forms," Baudelaire went on, "these ferments of gloom; these immensities of green and pink, suspended and added one upon another; these gaping furnaces; these firmaments of black and purple satin, crumpled and torn; these horizons in mourning, or streaming with molten metal; in short, all these depths and all these splendors rose to my brain like a heady drink or like the eloquence of opium."[26] Observing that some had the date, time of day, and weather conditions inscribed on them, Baudelaire also noted their accuracy as records of meteorological effects, but had reservations about their status as finished works of art.[27] Boudin's pastels, he argued, were "notes" that would "have to be turned into a picture, by means of the poetic impression recalled at will."

After returning to Le Havre later in the year, it was formerly believed that Monet settled again in Paris in early 1860, but the Grand Journal reveals that he was already there by Christmas 1859. Joining the Beguin Billecocq Christmas celebrations, we are told that Monet helped to organize "a spectacle of songs and poetry," to which he contributed "his tenor voice."[28] As on his previous visit to the capital, Monet sent Boudin an account of the paintings he saw, specifically mentioning an exhibition of "modern pictures" from the "School of 1830."[29] Itemizing works by Dupré and Rousseau, and telling Boudin that Courbet, Corot, and Millet "shone" at the exhibition, Monet also admired a sea subject by Delacroix, his *Barque of Don Juan* (1840). Of particular interest for his forthcoming career, however, though he could hardly have suspected it, was the presence in the same display at Martinet's gallery of nine Delacroix paintings with exotic or specifically North African subjects. These included *Arab Chieftain Signaling to his Companions* (1851) and *Fanatics of Tangier* (1837), as well as *View of Tangier from the Seashore* (1858).[30] Monet made no reference to these pictures in his letter and was more critical in his judgments generally, proclaiming that the Troyons were poor and adding that "the only good marine painter we have, Jongkind, is dead to art: he's completely mad."[31]

Drawing in Paris and Normandy

Undoubtedly the most significant step Monet took in January or February of 1860, however, was to begin attending the Académie Suisse, as a gesture toward his father and the earlier counsel of Troyon (fig. 56). Charles Suisse's establishment was famously informal and it appears that Monet may have needed the support of Théophile Beguin Billecocq to placate his relatives in Le Havre. We learn that it was Théophile who was instrumental in setting up the arrangement, when he notes, "I spoke about it with Camille Corot, whom I knew a little from meeting him on several occasions."[32] According to Théophile, it was Corot himself who suggested the Académie Suisse as suitable for the freedom-loving Oscar and appropriate to his limited means. The previous year, Troyon had recommended a stricter regime: "I'd go to Couture, if I had my time round again. . . . There's always Picot or Cogniet, but I've always hated their way of doing things," he told Monet.[33] By contrast, the Académie Suisse would have attracted Monet for several reasons, not the least being the presence there of many young, equally disaffected painters. There were neither professors nor rules of conduct, and those who paid the modest fees were free to draw and paint from the model, or work in any way they chose. Monet told Boudin little of his daily routine, though in the early months of 1860 he made a crucial confession: "I feel really happy here: I'm steadily drawing figures."[34]

How many figures Monet actually drew at the Académie Suisse and what became of them remains uncertain, though other insights into his experience appear in subsequent letters: "At the academy, there are only landscapists," Monet observed to Boudin, indicating that he was not alone in his compromised position and had already discovered the company of some sympathetic individuals. Camille Pissarro (1831–1903)

57
Paul Cézanne (French, 1839–1906), *Male Nude*, c. 1863. Black chalk, 493 x 310 mm. The Fitzwilliam Museum, University of Cambridge, UK

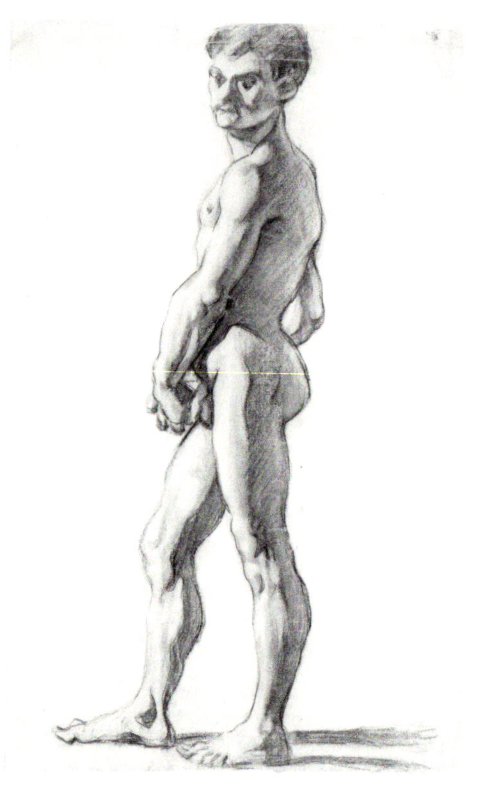

58
Paul Cézanne, *The Negro Scipio*, c. 1867. Oil on canvas, 107 x 83 cm. Museu de Arte de São Paulo, Brazil

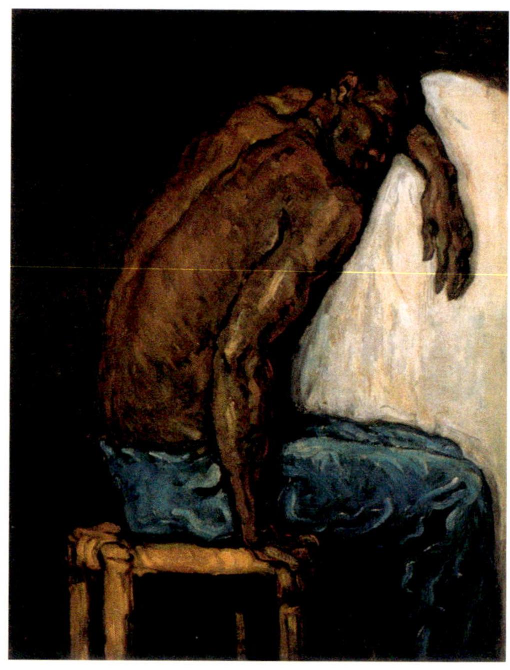

seems to have been there in the late 1850s and probably met Monet for the first time on these premises.[35] From 1861 onward, Paul Cézanne (1839–1906) interrupted his paintings of rural and urban motifs several times to work from the model at the Académie Suisse, where he found that "his figure drawings were ridiculed."[36] Cézanne's *Male Nude* of this period (fig. 57) helps us to imagine the more vigorous, personal styles of draftsmanship that were tolerated at the *Académie*, while his flagrantly unorthodox canvas of a regular model, *The Negro Scipio* (fig. 58), was later acquired by Monet for his own collection, perhaps in memory of these oppositional years.[37] Now part of a like-minded group, in April 1860 Monet announced to Boudin his plan to spend two or three weeks "in a charming little area, at Champigny-sur-Marne," in order to tackle some landscapes "in the company of friends."[38] Again, neither paintings nor drawings have been identified from this planned expedition, which conceivably failed to materialize. John Rewald suggested that one of Monet's companions on the trip may have been Camille Pissarro, who was certainly producing studies on paper in the open air at this time, using combinations of pencil, pen and ink, charcoal, chalk, and tinted wash, and revealing his awareness of several senior draftsmen, among them Corot and Daubigny.[39]

Monet's loyalties were still divided, however, and in the summer of 1860 we find him back in Honfleur, once more enjoying the company of Eugène Boudin. We also discover that Monet personally introduced Boudin to the Beguin Billecocqs, who were vacationing near the town and lodging on a track "that rose toward Notre-Dame de Grâce." They were therefore close to the Toutain farm at Saint-Siméon, where the party had stayed in 1857, and now enjoyed a view that "embraced part of the course of the Seine, its estuary, and the roadstead of Le Havre." In a remarkable extended passage that seems to reflect some of the vocabulary and the still unformed aspirations of Monet and his colleagues, Théophile went on to summarize his reaction to Boudin's art. "He executed small paintings that represented the everyday activity of beaches and country vacations: beach scenes, seascapes, bathers and walkers, and astonishing steamers, delicate sailing ships and simple boats. It was a very cheerful kind of painting

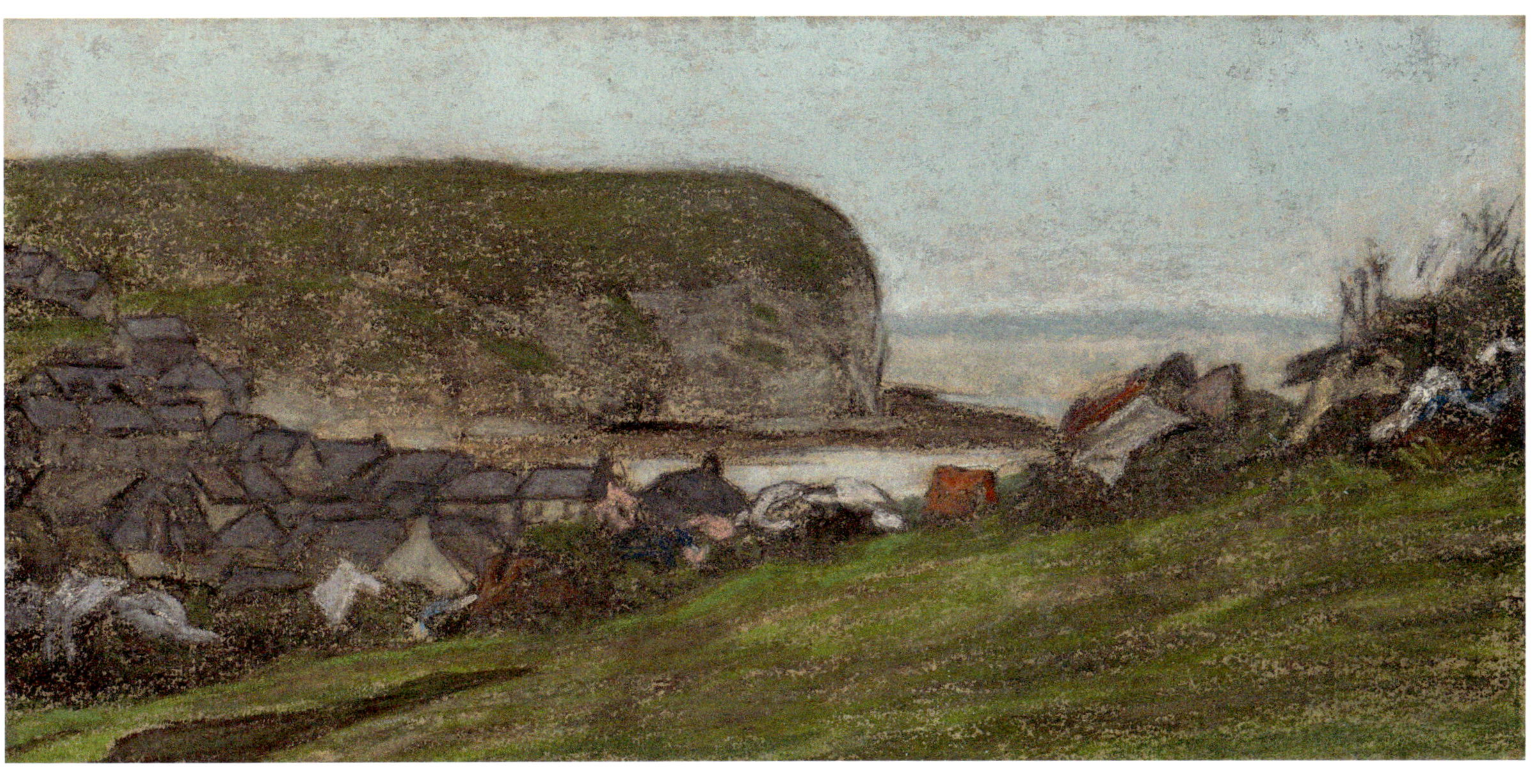

59
Yport and the Falaise d'Aval, c. 1861. Pastel, 185 x 395 mm. Private collection [P4]

that had an indefinable charm in its lightness and fresh colors. What a subtle means of suggesting, imparting impressions. This painting had nothing of the academic about it, quite the contrary." Showing considerable open-mindedness, Beguin Billecocq added that "the majority of people think of this technique as incomprehensible ineptitude, because it respects none of the rules of traditional painting, those so valued by the members of the Salon jury. Many consider that the artist does not know how to draw or paint, because for them the canvas remains unfinished, even an inept daub."[40]

Such reflections may have been informed by Théophile's conversations with Boudin and with Monet himself, and certainly help to explain the growing sympathy between the young artist and his diplomat friend. Boudin would continue to suffer from the prejudices of juries and public, but his quiet determination must have set a powerful example for the teenage Monet as he began to position himself for the fray ahead. The links between this unlikely trio of individuals were further enhanced in early 1861, when Boudin himself decided to move to Paris and took lodgings on the rue Pigalle, the street where Monet was then living. Monet told François Thiébault-Sisson that he "frequently saw him" in the city, and it is clear that the pupil soon became a partisan for his master's cause, urging Boudin to promote himself in the capital.[41] By now modeling some of his activities directly on those of Boudin, Monet appears to have dated his first pastels in these same months, including one of a pair of works that depict the Normandy village of Yport (fig.59).[42] Another early exercise in the medium shows a cluster of casually posed children (see fig. 108), a motif that comes directly from Boudin's graphic repertoire, while other precocious pastels take us to sites that Boudin had already painted, such as those around Sainte-Adresse.[43] In certain drawings made over the next two or three years, Monet explored techniques and compositions that can be traced back to Boudin, notably in small study of boats and cliffs at Étretat (see figs. 85 and 122).[44] As their intimacy developed, Monet again chose to spend the summer of 1864 at Honfleur, in the area close to Notre-Dame de Grâce that Théophile had described in 1861. This time Monet was joined there by both Boudin and Jongkind, when the young novice

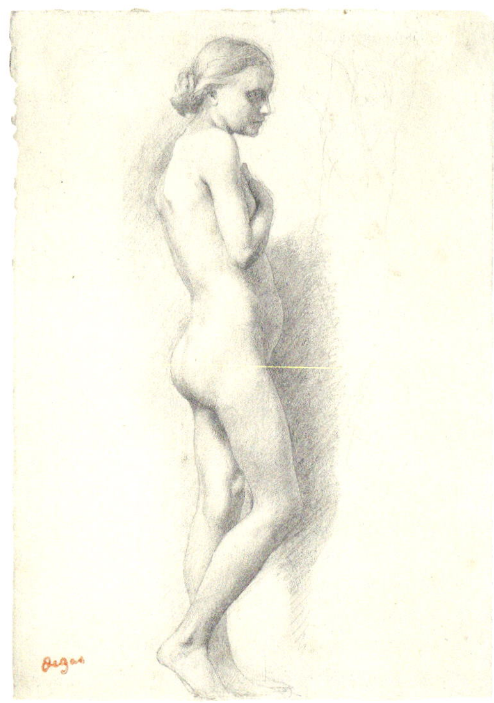

60
Edgar Degas (French, 1834–1917), *Standing Nude*, 1860–65. Pencil, 292 x 217 mm. Sterling and Francine Clark Art Institute, Williamstown, Massachusetts

seized his own opportunity to improvise pastels of "the sea and the sky" (see figs. 111 and 112).

Moving between country and city, Monet also found himself in the company of other young painters who shared his predicament. Like him, they were often engaged in negotiating parental support and disapproval, and some were under similar pressure to develop their graphic skills. By March 1863, he had met Bazille and almost certainly Pissarro, Cézanne, Renoir, and Sisley, who variously complemented and diverged from his chosen course. Though their paths would not cross for some years, one of the most instructive parallels is with Edgar Degas (1834–1917), another promising pastellist who was asserting his independence in Paris at precisely this time. Degas was his polar opposite in many respects, but would emerge alongside Monet as an initiator of the first Impressionist exhibitions, when commentators soon contrasted their sensibilities. Using language that echoed Blanc and his peers, they typically identified Degas as the prominent draftsman of the group and Monet as the leading colorist. Despite their differences and later professional rivalry, the two men's early careers overlapped in surprising ways in these years. Degas made numerous sensitive records of the landscape as he wandered in Italy in the late 1850s and similarly sought advice from the older generation. In 1855, four years before Monet's meeting with Troyon, the twenty-two-year-old Degas paid a call on the aging Ingres at his Paris studio and received almost identical direction: "Study line . . . draw lots of lines," Ingres told him, a sentiment Degas would later repeat to his own followers.[45] Already proficient in formal drawing, Degas—unlike Monet—found himself encouraged by Ingres and others in the route he had chosen and soon volunteered for the making of *académies* in both Rome and Paris. In a masterly study such as *Standing Nude* (fig. 60), made in the early 1860s, Degas contrived to follow Ingres's precepts and cautiously move beyond them. Working from a model he found "before our eyes in Paris," Degas laid the foundation for his own imagery of bathers and dancers, while Monet later admitted that he "detested" most of Ingres's art.[46]

An acquaintance in Paris who may have encouraged Monet's development in yet another direction was the painter and printmaker Amand Gautier, an "atheist fascinated by religious ritual" who was a close friend of Courbet's and exhibited with him in 1861.[47] When Monet first met Gautier, he found him planning "a large lithograph" and a year later announced that Gautier was "about to make an etching from my Daubigny," a reference to a small canvas that Monet had acquired from his aunt.[48] Monet's own print of Louis Laferrière (see fig. 48) had appeared in March of 1860, and a fragmentary letter to Gautier in August of 1860 revealed his hope of publishing more caricatures in the periodicals *Le Gaulois* and *Le Charivari*.[49] While these efforts seem to have come to nothing, there is further evidence of Monet's willingness to maintain this youthful graphic manner alongside his other studio activities.[50] Monet's new colleagues had introduced him to the delights of the Brasserie des Martyrs, a bohemian drinking hall in lower Montmartre where he was briefly renowned for drawing likenesses of the company, made in just "two pencil strokes."[51] Here he might also have encountered such Brasserie regulars as Courbet, Manet, and

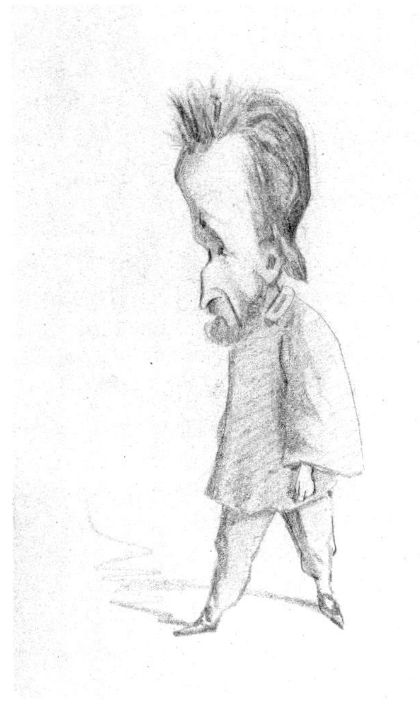

61
After Nadar, *Caricature of the Journalist Théodore Pelloquet*, c. 1859. Charcoal, 320 x 240 mm. Musée Marmottan Monet, Paris [D508]

Baudelaire, and is known to have enjoyed the company of Théodore Pelloquet, the subject of one of Monet's caricatures (fig. 61).[52] A writer and occasional critic, Pelloquet may well have earned his respect as a supporter of the "School of 1830" and of Millet in particular.[53] When such caricatures are taken into account, Monet had produced a formidable range of works on paper during his short spell in the capital: life drawings and satirical portraits, pastels of Normandy and plein-air sketches at sites like Champigny-sur-Marne, as well as the "delicious landscapes" described by Théophile. Even as he entered his twenties, it seems, Monet already understood that drawing could be a contingent activity, to be taken up and transformed at will, turned into cash or abandoned as necessary.

The Algerian Episode

Early in 1861, the newly urbanized Monet received news that was potentially disastrous for his career. Like all young Frenchmen of his age, he was required to enter a nationwide lottery that determined candidates for military service, unless their families elected to pay for a substitute. Monet learned in March that his number had been chosen and now faced a seven-year period of conscription. According to one story, his father offered the money required for a replacement on condition that Monet joined his business, but was met with a proud refusal.[54] There exist several such retrospective accounts of the events that followed, though in more than one case Monet insists that he was glad to seize this opportunity, which appealed to his "sense of adventure."[55] "I succeeded, by personal persistence, in being drafted into an African regiment," he told Thiébault-Sisson in 1900 and explained to André Arnyvelde, "I chose Algeria because of the sky."[56]

Unmentioned but perhaps equally influential were signs of a fascination with the Arab world from Monet's youth onward. In several early sketchbook drawings, he noted the uniforms and equipment of soldiers from the Algerian regiment known as the Zouaves, perhaps seen on the local quays.[57] Another reason for Monet's choice may have been his professed admiration at this date for the marine painter Théodore Gudin, whose oeuvre extended from views of Le Havre and the Normandy coast to scenes of the "Orient" and Algeria itself (fig. 62).[58] Gudin was highly successful and much honored, formerly patronized by the court and known for works with titles such as *The Coast of Africa*, *The Bombardment of Algiers in 1863* and *View of Algiers*. Inspired from several quarters, Monet himself had decided to join the Zouaves, the historic *Chasseurs d'Afrique*, and was painted by his friend Charles Lhuillier in his flamboyant new uniform before setting out (fig. 63). Arriving in Algiers in June, this improbable young soldier was attached to the barracks in the Mustapha quarter, to the east of the city, where he underwent training in horsemanship, finding it "tiresome."[59] A number of escapades then unfolded against the tedium of military routine, to be variously edited and embroidered in conversations at the end of Monet's life, as he gently shaped his own biography.

The published accounts of Monet's artistic activity in Algeria are frankly contradictory. In one, he claimed after returning home, "I had not even thought of painting for an instant,"

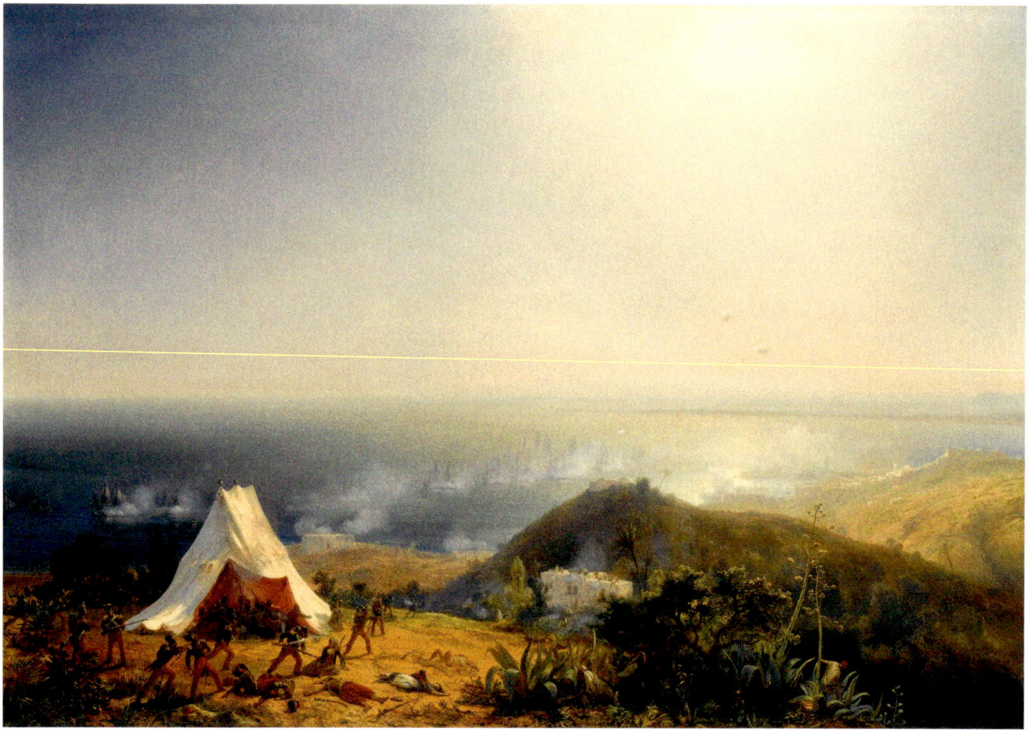

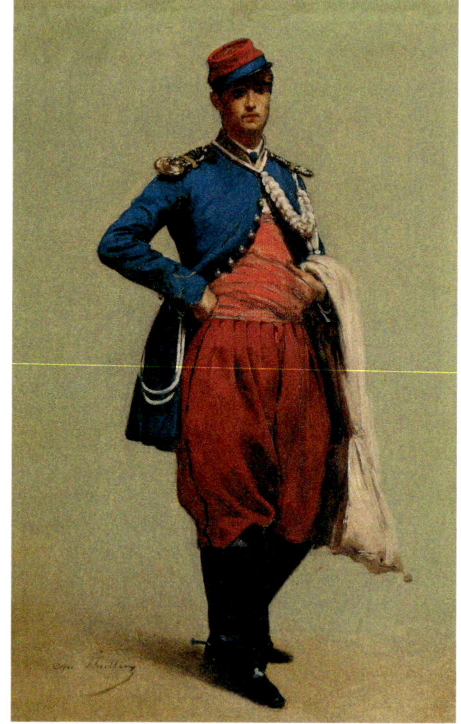

62

Théodore Gudin, *The Attack on Algiers by Sea*, 29 June 1830. Oil on canvas, 129 x 193 cm. Musée National du Château de Versailles

63

Charles Lhuillier, *Portrait of Claude Monet in Uniform*, 1861. Oil on canvas, 37 x 24 cm. Musée Marmottan Monet, Paris

but to the same interviewer more than two decades earlier Monet confided, "I incessantly saw something new: in my moments of leisure I attempted to render what I saw. You cannot imagine to what extent I increased my knowledge, and how much my vision gained thereby. I did not quite realize it at first. The impressions of light and color that I received there were not to classify themselves until later; but they contained the germ of my future researches."[60] On a third occasion, he told André Arnyvelde that "the officers took advantage of my talents a great deal, and that was good for some favors."[61] Yet another variant of this narrative comes from the diary of the dealer René Gimpel, who noted that Paul Durand-Ruel, Monet's principal dealer, was once offered "a canvas signed 'Monet,' an Algerian scene with camels, very much like Fromentin as to composition and execution."[62] Monet initially disowned it, saying, "I've never done any camels," then relented and proposed keeping it in exchange for another picture. Late in life, in 1920, the artist sent an effusive letter to his first biographer, Gustave Geffroy, recalling the pleasures of his Algerian sojourn and referring to "canvases" he had made there and "drawings and watercolors from 1862."[63] One of these, then owned by Georges Clemenceau, was vividly described as a watercolor of "the old Spanish gate of the Casbah at Oran" and details were also given of further works in the possession of a former comrade, Pierre-Benoit Delpech.

Several new perspectives on Monet's Algerian experience are opened up by the Beguin Billecocq Grand Journal. "He wrote to us often and detailed the harshness of the soldier's life," Théophile recalled, listing the "endless guard duties" and the "fierce instructors" he endured, and the "veritable nags" that Monet was required to ride.[64] But the artist also conjured up an Algeria that was "a splendid country with constant sunshine, with hot, seductive colors, an eternally blue sky accentuated by the greens of palms and exotic plants, Arabs and their veiled wives, the Arab language, guttural but beautiful, camels, donkeys, and horses."[65] More crucially still, a few sentences by Théophile transform our awareness of Monet's creativity at this moment:

We also received from Oscar a succession of delicious small drawings, very minutely executed, which represented picturesque little scenes of Algeria [depicting] . . . fauna and flora, various landscapes, countryside views, inhabitants, riders, camel-drivers, veiled women and young girls, buildings and mosques, scenes of the market and everyday life. I brought together these orientalist drawings, large vignettes, signed O. M., in a little album covered in pale linen. The young man gave the impression of being very happy and seemingly in good spirits. In any case, drawing was one of his principal occupations during his periods of freedom. He distracted his companions in the garrison by making caricatures of their seniors and of his friends.[66]

Another of these acquaintances was presumably a certain "J. Massé," with whom Monet appears to have kept in touch over the years, even dedicating a pastel of *Charing Cross Bridge* to him in the early twentieth century.[67] Regrettably, none of the caricatures, watercolors, or "vignettes" from the Algerian period itself have yet been identified, and the Fromentin-like painting of camels has left no trace.

Monet's time in Algiers was cut short by a period of severe fever, obliging him to return to France in the summer of 1862. The "Parisian brought up in Normandy, used to fresh air and the mists of the Channel," as Geffroy described him, "suffered from this overheated atmosphere . . . the Chasseur d'Afrique had exhausted his reserves, to the point where his relatives . . . bought a substitute for him." We are left to speculate about the longer-term significance of Monet's art-making in North Africa, apart from his claim that the experience of "light and color" had increased his "knowledge." References to a painting of camels, drawings of "veiled women and young girls," and a watercolor of "the Casbah at Oran," however, invite us to consider Monet as a previously unimagined orientalist-in-the-making. Extending his youthful fascination with the Zouaves at Le Havre and his awestruck admiration for the paintings of Gudin, these predilections would have been encouraged by Monet's previous contact in Paris with the exotic subject matter of Delacroix and his contemporaries, both at the 1860 Martinet exhibition and the Salon. But there were no signs in Monet's subsequent drawings of the graphic verve found in Delacroix's North African sketchbooks, nor the animation and dense palettes of the latter's widely admired paintings of horsemen, harems, and genre scenes. In later years, Monet would claim that Delacroix's *Journal* was his favorite book and the painter himself "one of my idols," and acquire two watercolors by his predecessor for his own collection: but in his early twenties, it seems, Monet was no more than distantly curious about the great Romantic himself.[68]

The pictures Monet made in Algeria cannot have been uppermost in his mind when he returned to France in the summer of 1862, "quite seriously" stricken with typhoid. Recuperating in Le Havre, he was visited by his childhood friend, Théodore Billecocq, who reported back to his uncle Théophile in Paris.[69] As he reflected on the African adventure, Théophile observed that Monet had experienced difficulties in accepting the rigors of the military life; "he who had acquired the habit of living as a free man, without constraint, appreciating nature and an untamed life."[70] When Théophile finally saw him, he found that the youth had lost weight, but "had become a man, excitedly affirming that he wished to become a painter acknowledged and recognized by everyone."[71] According to Geffroy, the artist accepted that the Algerian experience had concentrated his mind, doing him "a great deal of good" and putting some "sense into his head."[72] More determined than ever, he was soon back at work: in a telling phrase, Monet later recalled that his "six months of convalescence were spent in drawing and painting with redoubled energy."[73]

New Acquaintances in Gleyre's Studio

Apparently impressed by his industry, but still baffled by his career choice, Monet's family agreed to subsidize another period of study in Paris.[74] He was again directed to consult an artist of some reputation: this time, he approached Auguste Toulmouche (1829–1890), a distant relative who enjoyed considerable success at the Salon with his polished genre and conversation

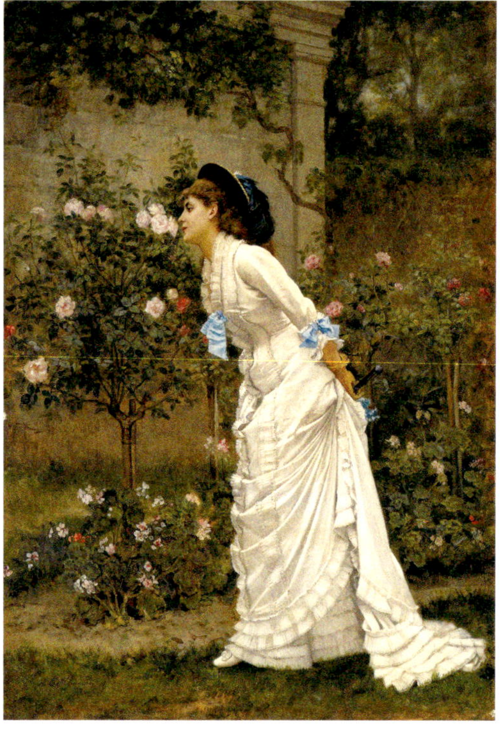

64
Auguste Toulmouche (French, 1829–1890), *A Girl and Roses*, 1879. Oil on canvas, 62.2 x 45 cm. Sterling and Francine Clark Art Institute, Williamstown, Massachusetts

pieces (fig. 64).[75] The counsel Monet received is less precisely recorded than that of Troyon, but Toulmouche could at least claim to have followed the path he was recommending.[76] Toulmouche proposed another variant of the academic regime, arranging a place for Monet with Charles Gleyre (1806–1874), his own former teacher. Offering instruction that was "founded on drawing," Gleyre's studio had been recognized in its earlier days as "the most desirable and progressive in Paris."[77] Submitting to its routines, Monet resigned himself to painting a "study of a nude from the living model," as he described it in old age, but was soon admonished for insisting on the "ugly" facts before his eyes: "When one draws a figure, one must think of the antique," Gleyre told him.[78] While Gleyre was considered sympathetic to "individuality" and to "the widest range of subjects," also countenancing such motifs as "landscapes, flowers, and animals," he urged his pupils to persist with their grounding in draftsmanship.[79] As with Troyon, Monet may well have felt that this advice was inappropriate to his own calling as a landscapist and to his long experience with a pencil. Monet once claimed that he lasted just "two weeks" with Gleyre, but no less an authority than Georges Clemenceau, the future premier of France who befriended him during these years, remembered that Monet was occupied at this time with "drawings from the model."[80]

As before, a broader picture of these months is provided by the Grand Journal. Théophile relates that Gleyre's studio on the rue du Bac was next to the house occupied by his own sister and father, who often invited Monet to dinner and supported him in other ways: "My father acquired many excellent drawings from Oscar, partly because he was pleased by the latter (country scenes, farm characters, Étretat and its environs, landscapes of Normandy), but equally to aid the young artist financially."[81] Théophile also observed, "Oscar rarely signed his works," adding that "my father henceforth asked him for signed works. A painting or a drawing without an author is the same as an individual who has no name."[82] For the first time, Théophile sheds light on the artist's formerly unexplained decision to change the name by which he had always been known. Finding himself mocked by his regiment in Algiers for "the ridiculous Christian name Oscar," with its unfortunate sound and "a pejorative connotation," he had decided to reinvent himself: "Goodbye Oscar, long live Claude!" Théophile noted.[83]

Application to a more severe variety of drawing can be found in a sheet executed in 1863 by Frédéric Bazille (1841–1870), who first met Monet in Gleyre's classes (fig. 65).[84] Alongside his sessions with Gleyre, Bazille was struggling to follow a course of medical studies that was financed by his parents, despite his growing desire to become a painter. Bazille's skillful drawing of a naked model combines something of his recently acquired knowledge of anatomy with close attention to a specific male physique, while acknowledging the example of Greek sculpture in the approved manner. Writing to his father in November of that year, Bazille explained that he had earned praise from Gleyre himself and had recently conceived "the idea of drawing the model life-size on an immense sheet of paper."[85] For Monet, however, the artificiality of such labors proved unendurable, and it was reportedly he who led the flight of

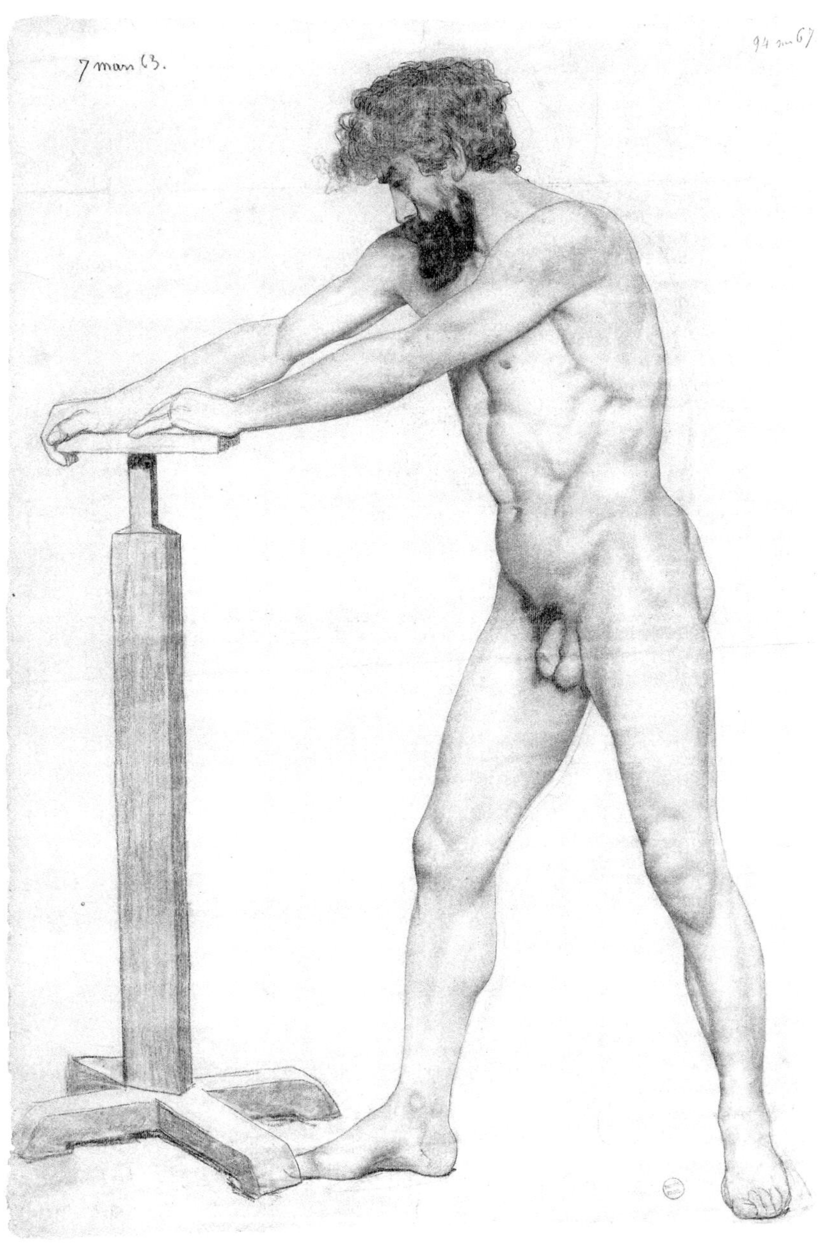

65
Frédéric Bazille (French, 1841–70), *Male Nude*, 1863. Conté crayon and charcoal, 620 x 470 mm. Musée Fabre, Montpellier

Bazille, Renoir, and Sisley from Gleyre's studio. Much cited in the prehistory of Impressionism, this final break with the perceived tyranny of academicism is not securely dated and may have happened over a period of months in 1863 and 1864.[86] When he reflected on the story in 1900, Monet summarized his moment of revelation in the presence of Gleyre: "I saw it all. Truth, life, nature, all that which moved me, all that which constituted in my eyes the very essence, the only *raison d'être* of art, did not exist for this man."[87]

While hardly amounting to a manifesto, this retrospective response to Gleyre's teaching is the nearest we have to a clear statement of Monet's artistic belief after his return from North Africa. The insistence on responding to "that which moved me" was probably a common ambition among certain young painters, but it also echoed Baudelaire's proposition in the Salon of 1859 that "a natural view has no value beyond the immediate feeling that an artist can put into it."[88] As we have seen, Baudelaire specifically criticized the work of Monet's seniors for failing in this respect and—knowingly or otherwise—the new generation appeared to have picked up the baton. Beyond Gleyre's reach, Monet and his companions had for some time been using their excursions around Paris to explore "truth, life, nature," and engage with the "*raison d'être* of art" as they experienced it. The studies they made have largely disappeared, along with so much of their energetic output from this time, but the earnestness of the group and the progress they made are hardly in doubt.

Within a year or two of leaving Gleyre, Monet and his circle had all become confident enough to submit canvases to the Salon jury, often presenting topical or personally resonant subjects that seem intended to "convey a feeling." The result of these initiatives, despite some setbacks, was distinctly impressive. After a solitary success by Renoir in 1864, both he and Monet had pictures accepted at the Salon of 1865, the latter showing his vigorous and overtly Boudinesque *Mouth of the Seine at Honfleur* (see fig. 179).[89] Encouragingly, Monet was also commissioned to make a summary drawing of this work, to be reproduced in a commercial publication accompanying the Salon (see fig. 181). The closing of Gleyre's studio in 1864, due to the artist's ill health, was another sign that the lives of young artists in Paris were changing. From this date, Monet and his companions were no longer students or apprentices, but aspiring painters, who now regarded drawing as a means to that end.

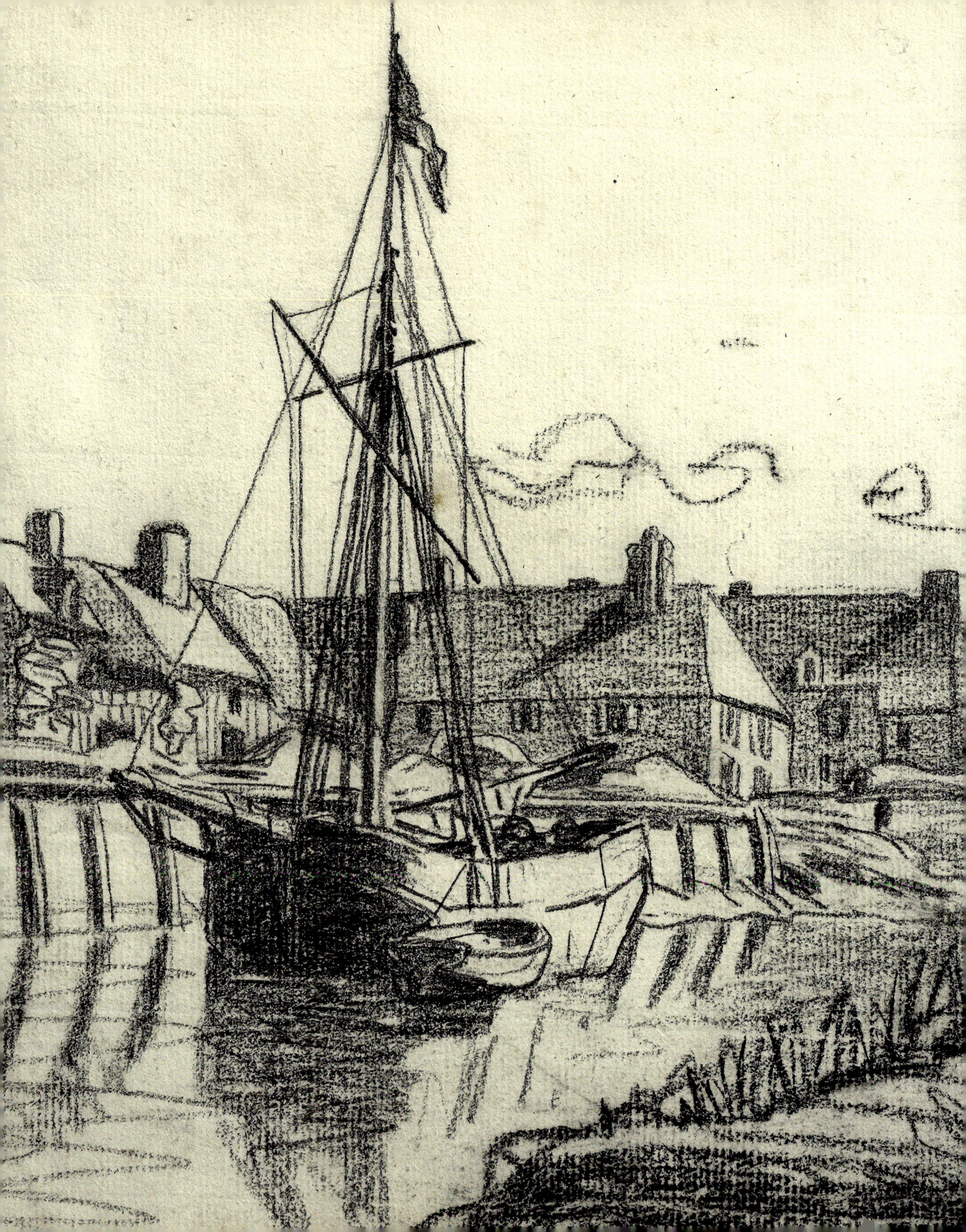

CHAPTER FOUR Drawing and Painting, 1863–66

It is now clear that, between his childhood and his early twenties, Monet produced a substantial body of drawings that reveals much about his approach to creativity. If many of these works were recreational in character, there were also significant clusters — the 1856 and 1857 sketchbooks, and the caricatures of 1857–59, for example — that represented a more focused and sophisticated achievement. In such cases, Monet tended to engage with a distinctive graphic manner and rapidly master its language, only to abandon both subject matter and syntax almost as quickly. Other categories, among them the figure drawings executed under Suisse and Gleyre, the sketches made on the Normandy coast with the Beguin Billecocq family, and his planned studies of Champigny-sur-Marne, remain inscrutable but may well have followed a similar pattern. Versatile and responsive to the task at hand, Monet showed a precocious grasp of the opportunism involved in draftsmanship and an ability to adapt style to circumstance. In 1863, as Monet turned his back on the teaching studios of Paris, his command of drawing would face yet another challenge. Now preparing to launch himself as a professional artist, he had to apply his skills to the creation of oil paintings, both large enough to attract attention and sufficiently distinctive to make his reputation.

At a practical level, Monet and his friends from the Gleyre establishment confronted a crisis; put simply, they had never been taught how to paint. Their formal art education in the city was brief — in Monet's case, almost nonexistent — and largely confined to drawing from a nude model. Had they stayed the course, such students would have graduated to larger and more sustained exercises in painting the human body, and to a closer acquaintance with the studio techniques of their teachers. Alongside this process, they might have painted copies in the Louvre and ultimately worked on individually conceived canvases of their own, under the eye of the master. For Gleyre and his colleagues, it was still axiomatic that each of the stages in the creation of such pictures was grounded in draftsmanship, which provided the structure of the composition and the necessary drawings for its figures and landscape elements. By leaving Gleyre, Monet forfeited the chance to acquire these accomplishments and the benefits of their association with the past. Though he claimed to have acted impulsively, Monet appears to have taken this step in full consciousness of its significance, which was summarized in his memory of Gleyre's drawing class. When the feeling for "truth, life, and nature" could be destroyed by the surgically exact delineation of a human model, it seemed that drawing itself was in need of reevaluation, or should perhaps be abandoned altogether.

When Monet arrived in Paris in 1859, he came with some basic experience of painting on a small scale and even signs of a facility that was noted by Troyon; "all this is very fine," Troyon told him, "but it comes very easily to you."[1] Like many beginners, Monet had tried his hand at still life, tackling some surprisingly complex arrangements of flowers, meat, and objects linked with the hunt, and completing at least two canvases over three feet in height.[2] No drawings for these works have come down to us, but Monet's brief training under Boudin suggests that he would have followed a conventional approach to his subjects, which were "analyzed" with a pencil on paper or canvas at a preliminary stage. He also tried another amateur's favorite, the landscape sketch in oils, presumably developing his experience at Ruelles and working in the open air.[3] As several writers have pointed out, such oil sketches may have had a longer-term significance for Monet's painting technique, offering an approach that minimized and sometimes bypassed the drawing process. Richard Brettell has called the plein-air oil sketch "one of the most important forms of direct painting" at this period, a practice that "developed in seventeenth century Europe and reached its apogee in the first half of the nineteenth century."[4] The oil sketch was advocated in both academic and popular treatises on painting, in which spontaneity of execution and effect were considered to be central to its appeal: still recommended in the 1880s, these works represented for one widely read author the "first burst of inspiration, which summarizes the feeling and the visual impression of the painter."[5]

When Troyon advised Monet to "go into the country from time to time and make studies," he presumably had such improvised works in mind. Pointedly, however, he added that the aspiring young painter should "above all develop them" when he returned with his sketches to the studio. A similar message was contained in Baudelaire's injunction to Boudin, whose pastel studies he had admired as "notes" that must later be "turned into a picture." It was this step from the first "impression" to the appropriately developed "picture" that now confronted Monet, and for which he was seriously unprepared. Drawing had been used for centuries to assist in this transition, helping artists to enlarge their earlier drafts and cope with the forbidding demands of scale that were associated with major exhibition pictures. Now well versed in the competitiveness and the chaotic conditions of the Salon, Monet knew that the largest canvases tended to attract crowds and the representatives of the press who reported on such occasions. Yet neither Monet nor any of his colleagues had ever attempted anything of this kind and were fully aware that their smaller paintings, however sincere or original, would pass unnoticed even if they were accepted. Monet, especially, seems to have understood that a grander vision was required, along with new pictorial strategies that would seize the world's attention and promote his paintings of "all that which moved" him.

Developed against this background of technical inexperience, the half-dozen canvases that Monet exhibited between 1864 and 1866 are almost breathtaking in their youthful mastery. Embracing not only landscape but still life, the full-length figure, and the suburban garden gathering, these works were also remarkable for their sheer size. The smallest, *Le Pavé de Chailly*, is more than four feet across, and the two largest, *Camille, or The Woman in the Green Dress* and *Women in the Garden*, are both around seven feet in height, while the unexhibited and now dismembered *Luncheon on the Grass* once measured at least fifteen by twenty feet.[6] Monet's procedures when tackling these formidable works are only partially documented, though they included direct labor in the open air and *alla prima* painting, where color is applied to the canvas directly, without initial preparation. In none of the contemporary accounts of the exhibited pictures are drawings mentioned, whether in the form of sketches for the figures in the composition or other kinds of linear preparation. A scattering of sheets of this kind does survive, however, for *Luncheon on the Grass*, an image that Monet seems to have prepared in broad drafts for the overall design as well as in detailed observations of costume.

How did Monet set about making such elaborate paintings, and what role did drawing have in this process? No sketchbooks from this decade are known prior to 1865, and references to technique in his sporadic letters are infrequent and oblique. Scrutiny of picture surfaces with the naked eye has yielded some information, but much laboratory analysis of their sometimes-encrusted paint layers remains to be done.[7] More directly illuminating are a number of smaller canvases from 1863 to 1865 with intriguing links to existing studies on paper. Cumulatively, the evidence for this interrelationship is compelling, pointing to a varied use of pencil, pen and ink, crayon, and pastel in supportive roles, as Monet used both conventional approaches and a range of maneuvers adopted from his artist acquaintances. At some unknown point in 1863, for example, he tackled a rustic motif in *Farmyard in Normandy* (fig. 66) that shows his awareness of the work of older figures such as Troyon, Daubigny, Boudin, and Millet.[8] Like these artists, Monet apparently made direct studies from certain of the subject's salient features and perhaps exploited his sketchbooks for more generic items. The project itself could almost be a textbook exercise, like those that had inspired some of his sketchbook drawings of the mid-1850s. Pencil studies from those years show modest rural cottages and traditional farmhouses in the Normandy countryside, often with adjacent trees that almost engulf the buildings.[9] In the Musée d'Orsay picture, he effectively transposed this kind of linear image into a new medium, presenting it on a larger scale and with all the attributes — including date and signature — of a public painting.

For *Farmyard in Normandy*, Monet chose a twenty-inch-high canvas that required a formidable breadth of competence from a relative beginner. It was certainly not large enough to stand out at the Salon but was otherwise ambitious for someone of his experience. In terms of drawing alone, he needed a rudimentary command of perspective and the ability to render trees and figures, cows and ducks, while as a painter he faced light and shadow, reflections in water, and the enveloping atmosphere. Conventional wisdom recommended the making of several preliminary sketches for such a scene, and perhaps a small-scale oil or pastel study; most unusually for Monet, there are several contenders from his hand that may have fulfilled such preparatory functions. The most immediately persuasive is *Study of Cows* (fig. 67), a confidently executed sheet in black crayon that remained in the artist's collection until his death.[10] The position of the cow at right is close to that of the foreground animal in *Farmyard in Normandy*, suggesting that Monet made his study with the painting in mind. Not coincidentally, Boudin himself was fascinated by these creatures, drawing many hundreds of individual cows and small herds in pencil, pastel, and watercolor, among them *Studies of Sheep and Cattle* (fig. 68). Boudin himself would often draw tethered animals when bad weather forced him to find shelter, sometimes using these sheets to make later paintings. Perhaps Monet's study originated in this way, along with other little-noted drawings and pastels of cows and horses from his hand that survive from this period.[11] Similar sketches by his forbears and contemporaries remind us that the accumulation of everyday visual materials was still part of the practicing artist's routine, as it had been for centuries.[12] In making *Study of Cows*, in other words, Monet the draftsman was at his most conventional.

Several additional studies on paper can be variously linked to *Farmyard in Normandy* and take us into more nuanced territory. Returning to a motif that was deeply characteristic of the region where he grew up, which is still renowned for its agricultural produce and orchards, Monet looked back to his teenage years in other ways. The small man and boy in the foreground of the painting have an awkwardness that is almost caricatural, but are directly prefigured in a series of coarse drawings in Monet's early sketchbooks.[13] The closest

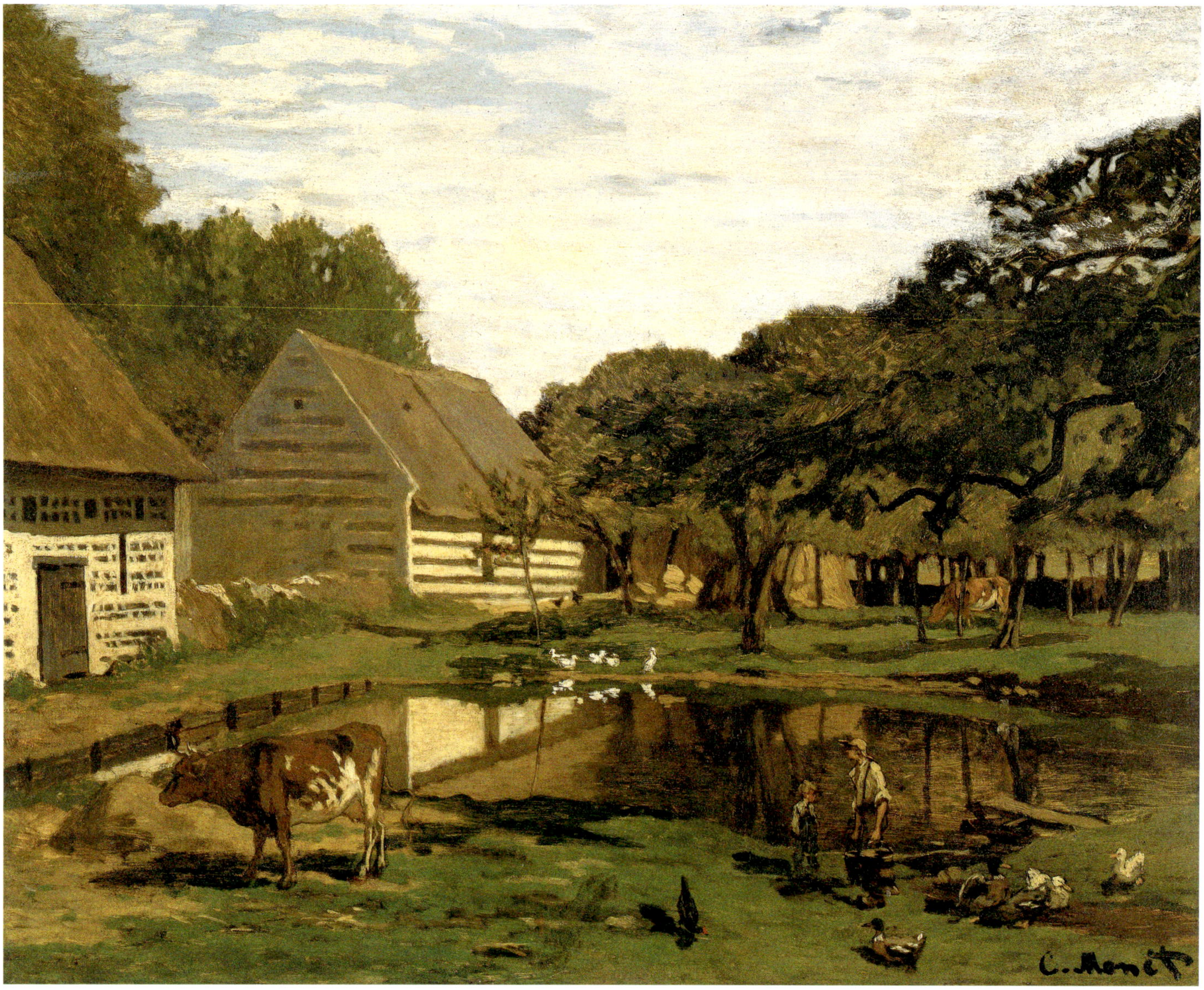

66

Farmyard in Normandy, 1863. Oil on canvas, 65 x 80 cm. Musée d'Orsay, Paris. Bequest of M. and Mme Raymon Koechlin, 1931 [W16]

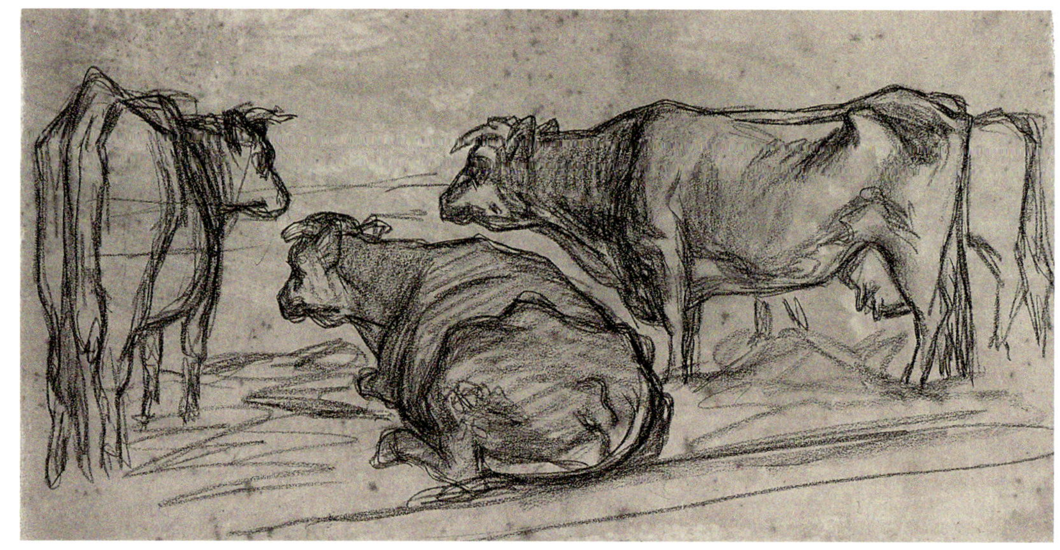

67

Study of Cows, c. 1863. Black crayon, 240 x 470 mm. Collection of Faruk A. Alatan [D413]

68

Eugène Boudin, *Studies of Sheep and Cattle*, n.d. Pencil, 188 x 278 mm. Musée du Louvre, Paris

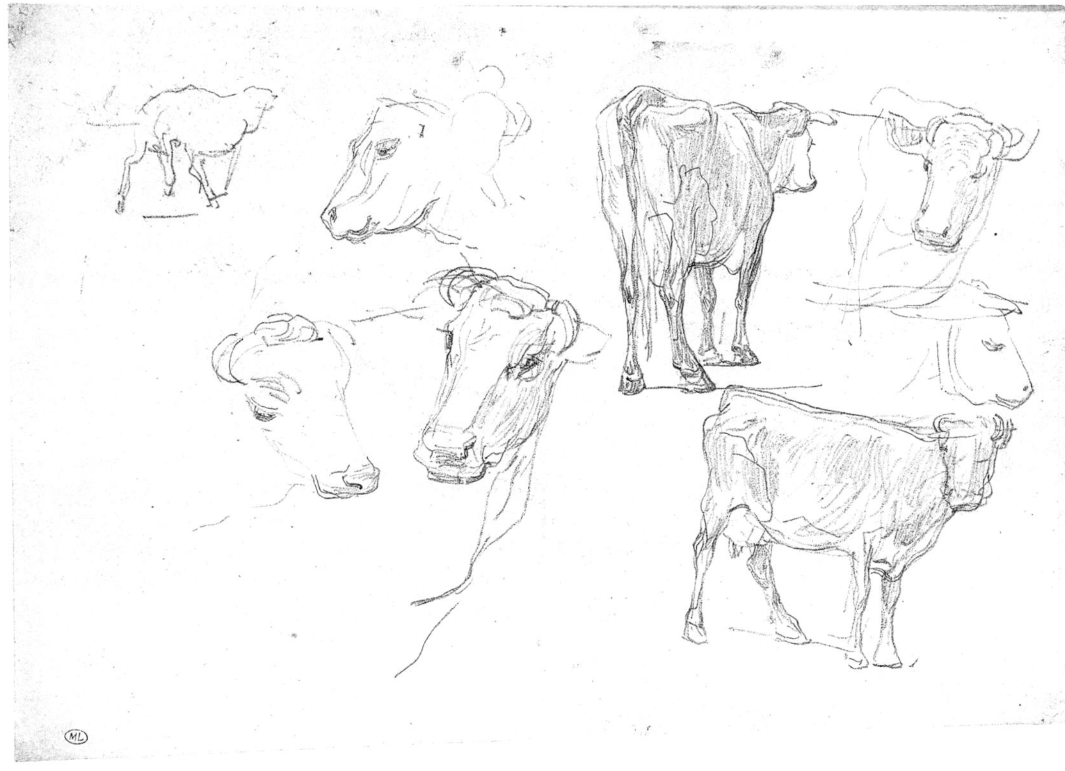

analogy with these two figures, however, may be found in a pair of pastels that were placed by Wildenstein among the artist's first exercises in the medium. In one, *Study of Five Boys* (see fig. 108), randomly grouped youths stare at the artist, hands in pockets, and in the companion work a younger boy adopts the precise pose of his counterpart in *Farmyard in Normandy*.[14] A contrary relationship may be indicated by the tangle of branches and foliage beside the principal building in this painting, which has a notable kinship with one of Monet's most adventurous pastels of the period, *Fruit Trees* (see fig. 73). Ablaze with color, this sensuous celebration of leaf greens and apple reds represents a strikingly similar motif and was conceivably made alongside the canvas. The freer handling of *Fruit Trees* may reflect the liberating experience of working with this new medium, though it could equally record a somewhat later return by Monet to the same pictorial territory.

Do these varied studies for *Farmyard in Normandy* indicate that comparable, but now lost, drawings and pastels lay behind most of Monet's early canvases? The confident execution of *Study of Cows*, while far from exceptional for artists at this date, suggests that Monet had continued his informal drawing habit from the previous decade into the 1860s, while becoming a little more refined. Further examples of this kind, such as the sheets made for *Luncheon on the Grass* around 1865, allow us to envisage an evolving—though possibly sporadic—graphic practice and a gradual extension of Monet's inventive application of line. But the general scarcity of such autograph works from these years must also be addressed. One of the few authors to confront this issue, Nicholas Wadley, has argued that "the low survival rate of early drawings by Monet probably reflects the relatively careless attitude to drawing that he displayed throughout his life. From all this evidence, there must have been a large corpus of early drawn work."[15] The discovery of Beguin Billecocq's Grand Journal, with its accounts of youthful drawing excursions, has done much to vindicate Wadley's view. It should be emphasized, however, that similar observations can also be made about most of Monet's colleagues at this date, among whom specimens of youthful draftsmanship are scarce and in some cases entirely absent.

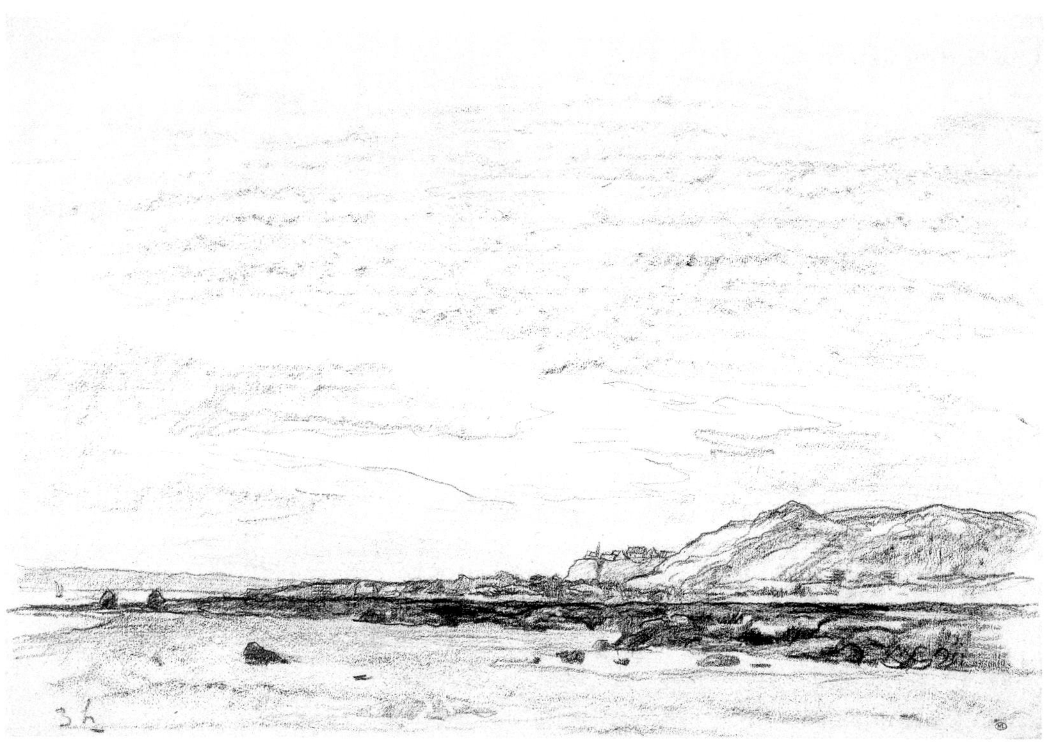

69
Charles François Daubigny (French, 1817–1878), *Low Tide at the Coast*, n.d. Black chalk, 351 x 508 mm. Musée du Louvre, Paris

Draftsmen Contemporaries and Precursors

Before the mid–1860s, the graphic oeuvres of Pissarro, Cézanne, and Bazille are represented by little more than scattered sheets, fortuitously preserved sketchbook pages, and occasional clusters of related works on paper, while formative drafts by Sisley and Renoir are even rarer. Only Degas, retentive in art as in life, appears to have hoarded every figure study, drawn copy, and compositional design from his adolescence onward, as well as dozens of sketchbooks that were compiled alongside them. Given that most of these artists would become overt and sometimes profligate draftsmen in their maturity, the general absence of works of this kind appears to indicate historical losses on an extensive scale. Leading impecunious lives and moving their lodgings frequently, these young men were heedless about many aspects of their output and perhaps uncertain about the status and wider significance of their drawings. There was virtually no current market for such objects and the chance of exhibiting even the best of them was remote. Technology for reproducing and promoting linear studies, though first encountered by Monet in a crude form during this decade and exploited to great effect in the more sophisticated 1890s, was still largely beyond the means of this wider group. Added to all these factors is the possibility that some of these individuals, including Monet himself, may have chosen to cover their artistic tracks by destroying quantities of youthful drawings.

Similar considerations dictated the availability to the Impressionist generation of drawings by their elders. The example of Charles-François Daubigny (1817–1878), an artist with considerable importance for Monet's practice during these years, summarizes the predicament. Echoes of Daubigny's graphic style can be found in a number of drawn sheets by Monet, yet it is far from clear how the younger artist became acquainted with Daubigny's own drawings. In the case of Boudin and Troyon, and figures with less significance in his development, such as Monginot, Gautier, and Toulemouche, we know that Monet visited their studios and was therefore exposed to a range of finished works of various kinds. In his 1859 letter to Boudin, Monet mentioned "the lovely things" he had seen at Troyon's, where another visitor described

70

Wood Gatherers at the Edge of the Forest, c. 1863. Oil on panel, 59.7 x 90.2 cm. Museum of Fine Arts, Boston. Henry H. and Zoe Oliver Sherman Fund, 1974 [W18]

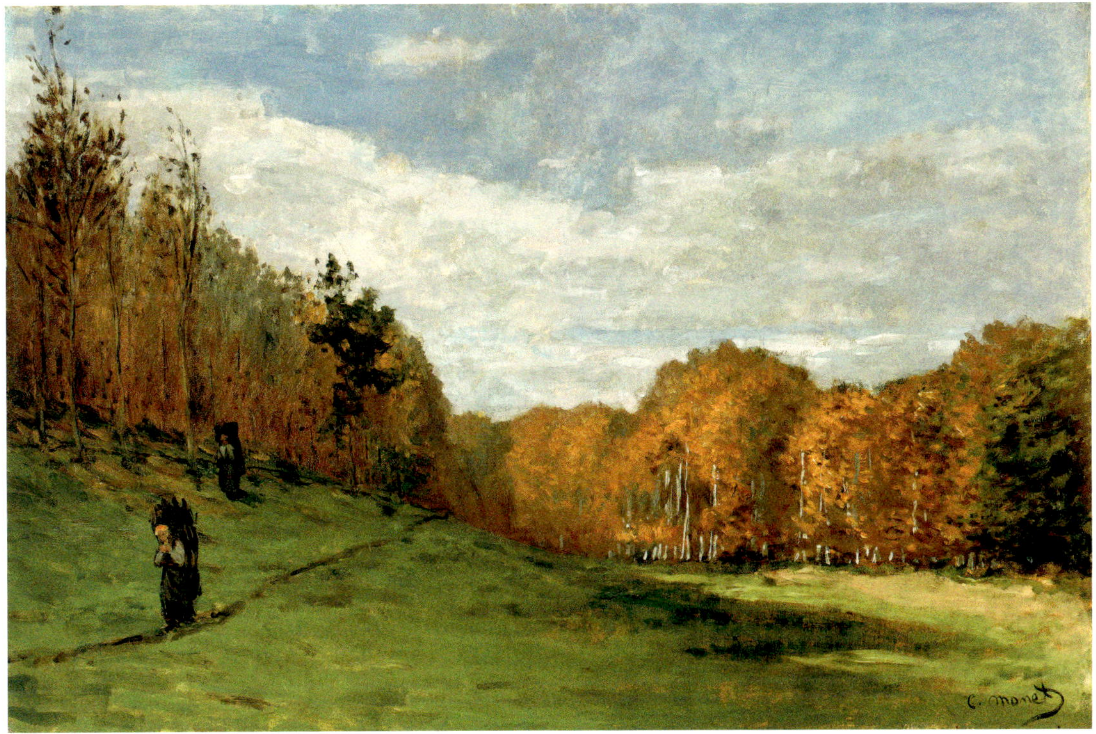

the astonishing sight of his "vast atelier" that revealed "more than four hundred oil paintings, pastels, portfolios full of drawings of every kind."[16] Though Monet's response to the 1859 Salon marked him as a precocious admirer of Daubigny, the two artists do not seem to have met until later in the following decade, when the older man reciprocated by actively endorsing the younger's pictures. Monet would have been attracted to Daubigny for a number of reasons, among them the latter's fondness for Normandy. Daubigny made several visits to the region during these years, including an 1863 sojourn at Villerville, close to Honfleur, which resulted in a painting exhibited at the following year's Salon.[17] Apart from such occasional public sightings and the intimate acquaintance with a small canvas owned by his Aunt Marie-Jeanne, Monet may well have come across Daubigny's prints, such as the 1862 series entitled *Voyage en bateau*. Resembling pen sketches as much as etchings, these small, vivacious scenes were nonetheless at a considerable remove from Daubigny's more pondered black-chalk drawings of rural vistas. Works such as his undated *Low Tide at the Coast* (fig. 69) might be made as reference material, as a relatively finished sheet in its own right, or as the basis for a later oil painting, and offered many of the qualities of expansiveness and clarity that appealed to Monet at this date.[18]

In the spring of 1863, and again in 1864, Monet worked at his painting in the countryside near Paris, choosing a location closely linked to several of his artist-predecessors. On each occasion he stayed at Chailly-en-Bière, some forty miles south of the city, situated near Barbizon and the forest of Fontainebleau in an area where Daubigny, among many others, had painted in the 1830s and 1840s. Monet's decision may also have been swayed by an earlier outing with the Beguin Billecocq entourage, who had vacationed at Nemours in 1859 and taken him on their trips to nearby Barbizon and Chailly.[19] On that occasion, a cascade of drawings and watercolors of "trees, houses, landscapes" fell from the teenager's hands, but it is significant that Monet's energies were directed elsewhere in the 1860s. Now concentrating on oil painting, Monet produced three grandly conceived, vigorously brushed canvases of the forest during the 1864 expedition, the largest of which he would show at the 1866 Salon.[20] Considered together, these pictures represent another bold step in Monet's assertion of his feeling for nature, but with quite different implications from *Farmyard in Normandy* of the previous year. Free of buildings and virtually unpopulated, a Chailly composition such as *Wood Gatherers at the Edge of the Forest* (fig. 70) is dominated by the visual drama of massed blocks of foliage, swathes of shadow, and a towering wall of sky. Begun by Monet on the spot and at least partially completed at Chailly, works of this kind required an imaginative approach to the logic of his craft and a flexible attitude to draftsmanship. Bold forms like these needed little or no conventional drawing, other than the division of the picture rectangle in its early stages, after which details of branches and occasional figures could be noted firsthand. In such situations, drawn lines on paper or canvas had begun to lose their centrality, a neglect hinted at by Monet in a letter sent to Gautier during his Chailly sojourn of May 1863: "It's so beautiful in spring, everything turned green, the fine weather came, and I couldn't resist the temptation of staying," he wrote, before reassuring his friend, "I'm going to get down to drawing once again. I'm not giving it up in any way."[21]

The emphasis in the Chailly paintings was on direct experience and raw sensation, largely unmediated by the traditional labors of the studio or lifeless instruction from the likes of Gleyre. Remarkable as works by an unknown twenty-three-year-old, the canvases brought back to Paris also spoke of Monet's wider appreciation of his immediate predecessors. The panoramic sweep of *Wood Gatherers at the Edge of the Forest* owes something to Daubigny, but perhaps more to recent pictures by Gustave Courbet (1819–1877), who had a lifelong fascination with dense woodland and looming natural forms. In 1862, Courbet had produced a succession of canvases on such themes, including a number in which the only sign of human presence was a deserted track that faded into forest shadows.[22] While Monet may have encountered Courbet at the Brasserie des Martyrs in Paris and certainly got to know him within a few years, we can only speculate about his contact with the canvases in question, though a huge landscape dominated by massive trees, *The Spring Rut*, was shown at the Salon of 1861.[23] As with Daubigny, Monet probably knew of Courbet's frequent residences in Normandy from 1859 onward, where he depicted its beaches, rocks, and stormy seas in a muscular, improvised manner. But it remains impossible to assess Monet's awareness of the use or otherwise of drawing in Courbet's execution of such works. Courbet, too, was effectively a self-taught draftsman who made powerful, crepuscular studies in charcoal, pencil, chalk, and crayon, more often as independent exercises than as preparations for paintings.[24] Taking pride in his direct attack with brushes and paint, Courbet offered a charismatic model of engagement with the landscape to those who felt burdened by convention and the rituals of draftsmanship.

A Crucial Summer in Normandy

In May 1864, after his second stay at Chailly, Monet set off for Honfleur and remained in and around the small harbor town until November. This extended summer at the coast was to have a defining impact on his technical procedures, exposing him to the working practices of several established artists and leading to a new maturity in his drawing, painting, and use of pastel. Monet was initially accompanied by Bazille, who had yet to sever the link with Gleyre: recalling his own time in the studio, Monet asked him in a later letter, "Have you done your life-size figure?"[25] Struggling with the same processes that preoccupied his friend, Bazille was still making precisely drawn compositional studies for his pictures and superimposing grids on some of them to assist the transition from paper to canvas, steps that Monet himself seems to have disdained.[26] Over the ensuing months at Honfleur, Monet applied himself with unprecedented fervor to painting in several registers, completing at least two-dozen works that ranged from small oil sketches on panel to panoramic scenes of beaches and cliffs of considerable complexity. Among them are pictures of sites that would haunt his early career, such as the cliffs at Étretat, the beach at Sainte-Adresse, and the harbor and streets of Honfleur itself.[27] Further letters capture the palpable excitement of these events and give tantalizing hints of experiments with paint and rapturous responses to nature. For the first time, we can connect individual paintings with works in pastel made at the same moment. A suite of magnificent drawings in black chalk also had their origin in this stay, when Monet seems to have discovered a new, less conflicted rapport between his experiments on paper and those on canvas.

By accident or design, Monet spent a significant part of this period in the company of other artists who gathered annually at the Saint-Siméon farm near Honfleur. At this traditional Normandy farmhouse, situated a short distance to the west of Honfleur, in the Val-de-Grâce, members of the Tutain family had offered rustic accommodation and meals since at least the 1840s.[28] By day, a shifting population of painters would work in the local terrain, then gather on benches under the densely grown apple trees that surrounded the farm to enjoy home-brewed cider—a regional specialty—and relax together. Corot depicted part of the building and orchard in 1845, followed by Boudin and Jongkind in subsequent decades, then by such lesser names as Adolphe-Félix Cals, Emile Renouf, and Léon Barillat.[29] It is not known when Monet first stayed at the farm, but the Grand Journal tells us that he introduced the Beguin Billecocqs to its comforts in 1857, after showing them "the delicious chapel of Nôtre-Dame de Grâce." The party then enjoyed "an excellent fish dinner at an inn near the chapel . . . called the Toutain farm," where they also spent the night in rooms that were "simple but clean."[30] Returning in 1864, Monet again fell for its charms, writing to Bazille in July that the area was "simply gorgeous . . . each day I find something even more beautiful than the day before. It's enough to drive me crazy."[31] In the same letter, he explained, "When I look at nature, I feel as if I'll be able to paint it all" and insisted that "it is on the strength of observation and reflection that one finds a way."

A month later, on 26 August, Monet told Bazille, "we are quite a crowd here in Honfleur, several painters I did not know, and very bad ones at that . . . Jongkind and Boudin are here and we get on extremely well and stick together. Ribot is probably coming too: he's due to be painting a fishing boat with figures, in the open air. I'd be interested to see him do it. I'm very sorry that you're not here, since there's a good deal to learn from such company."[32] Monet's eagerness to absorb such lessons extended from the solemn realist Théodule Ribot (1823–1891) to his more familiar companions, Jongkind and Boudin, both prolific graphic artists who left their own records of the Toutain farm and its neighborhood. Among Boudin's drawings is a delicate study of apple trees such as those that surrounded the Toutain farm (fig. 71) and sketches of drinkers in the shade with their cider.[33] Given that Saint-Siméon was a short walk from the sea, we might also imagine that some of his countless pastels of beaches and lofty skies were executed during these seasonal residences.[34] Jongkind's witness to the events of this summer was even more explicit, covering at least four sheets that coincided with Monet's visit, such as the disarmingly simple *Tree at the Seine Estuary* (fig. 72), with its inscription in imperfect French, "Honfleur chez Mad Toutain St. Siméon le 24 septembre 1864."[35] More circumstantial evidence is found in a notebook reference to games of dominoes that Jongkind played with Monet, and in an elaborate watercolor of the church at Nôtre-Dame de Grâce, which Monet painted at this same time and from a similar viewpoint, by tradition in the company of his Dutch colleague.[36]

In letters he sent to Bazille, Monet's remarks about his own dramatically evolving work are numerous but fragmentary. He speaks enthusiastically of the large still life of flowers that was currently exhibited in Rouen—"undoubtedly the best thing I have done to date"—and of "a simple study . . . done entirely from nature" that had "a certain relationship with Corot."[37] Such references to "studies"—or *études*—occur

71

Eugène Boudin, *Apple Trees at Saint-Siméon*, c. 1850–54. Charcoal and pastel, 319 x 441 mm. Musée du Louvre, Paris

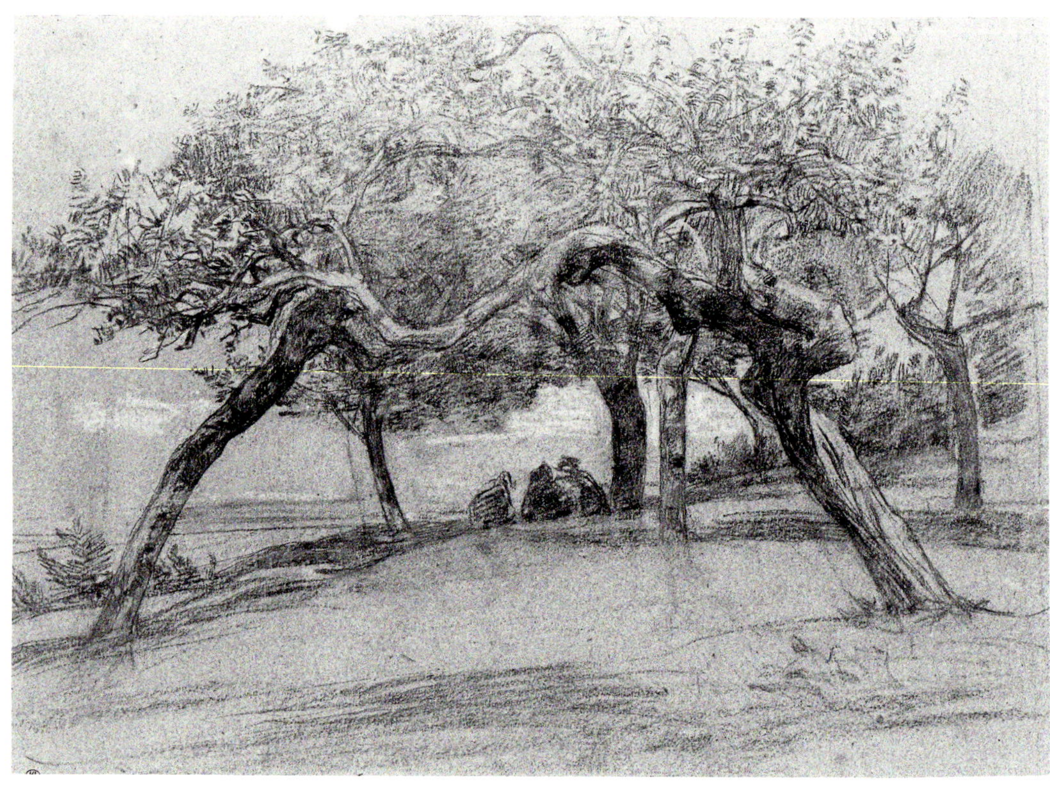

72

Johan Barthold Jongkind (Dutch, 1819–1891), *Tree at the Seine Estuary*, 1864. Watercolor and black crayon, 249 x 301 mm. Musée du Louvre, Paris

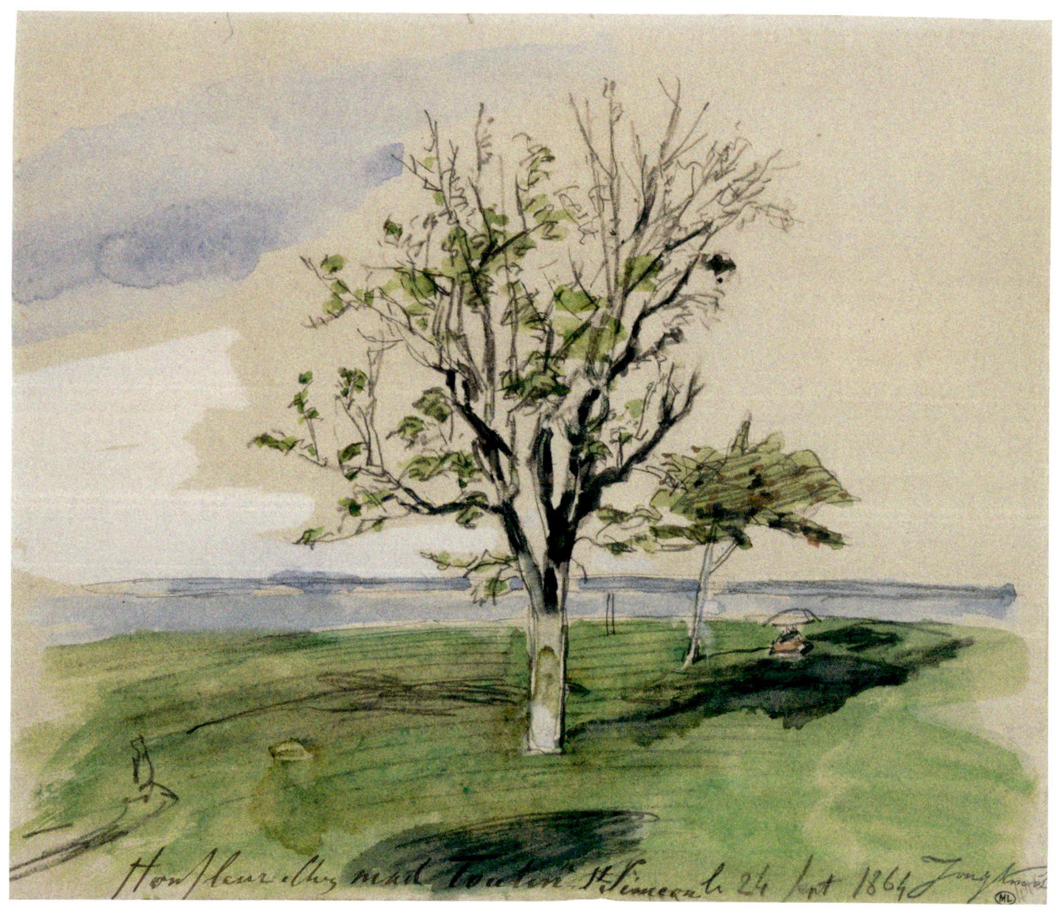

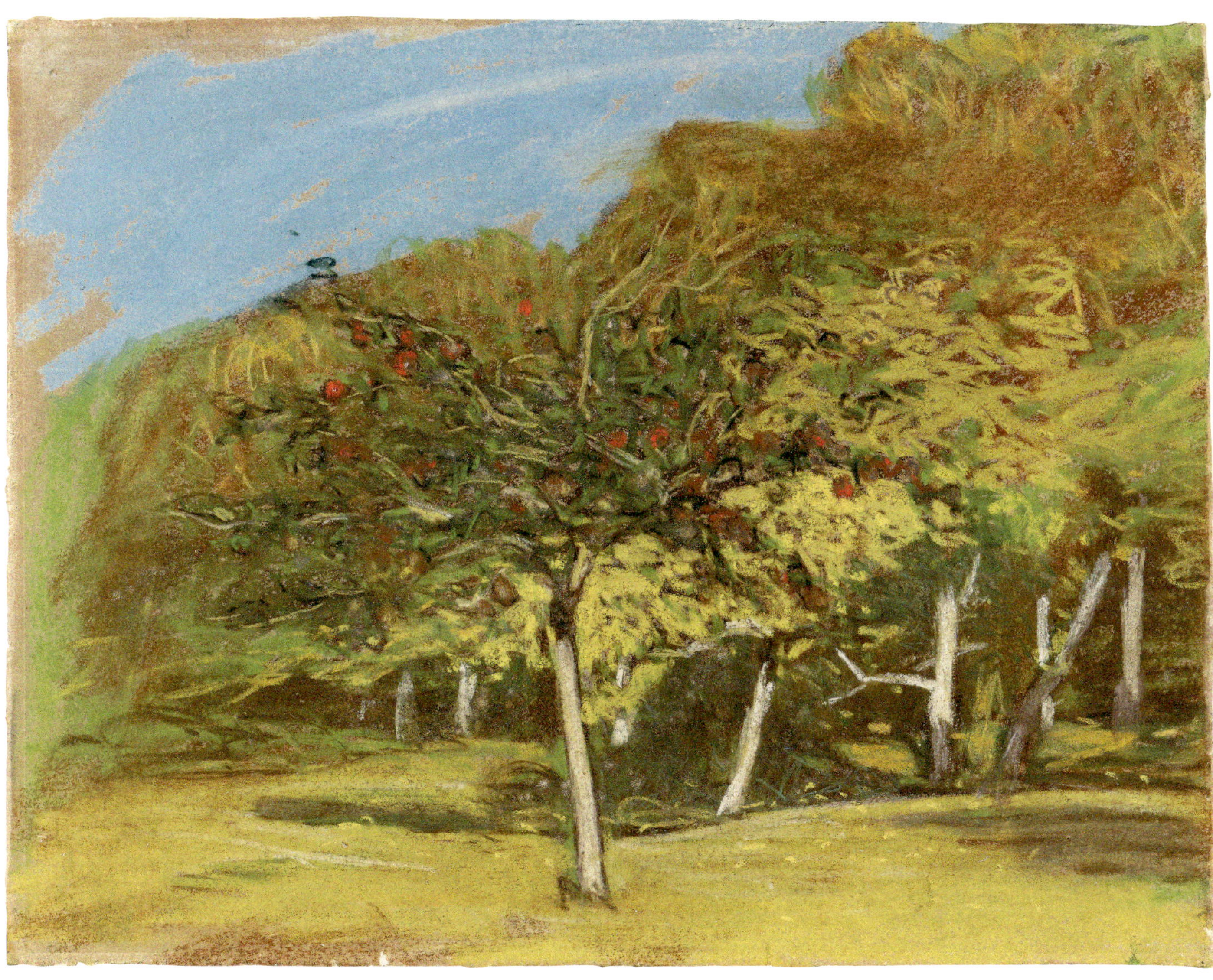

73
Fruit Trees, c. 1865–75. Pastel, 225 x 292 mm. Private collection, courtesy of Galerie Jan Krugier & Cie., Geneva [P75]

frequently, using an ambiguous term that occurs in Monet's correspondence throughout his life. In widespread currency in the nineteenth century, "study" could be applied to paintings, drawings, and other kinds of preliminary sketches or to improvised pictures on paper and canvas. In his July letter, however, Monet had a more specific sense in mind. "My studies are almost done," he announced to his friend, adding that he was still dissatisfied with some of them, but intended to "battle on, scrape off, and start again."[38] In this unmistakable reference to paint rather than pencil or crayon, Monet implied that he was making oil sketches, presumably "done entirely from nature." At least five modest-scale exercises of this type have been associated with the visit of 1864, all showing the rough, wooded track that approached the Toutain establishment, the *Route de la ferme Saint-Siméon*.[39] Though there are few obvious signs of them being "scraped" or battled with, these variants are consistent with a young artist's determination to master his craft and with Monet's self-imposed regimen of observation and reflection before nature.

With the impressionable young Monet involved in such activities among the company at the Toutain farm, we might expect to find further examples of technical advancement and cross-fertilization in both his painting and his draftsmanship. If he made drawings in the manner of Boudin, or used sketchbooks like those of Jongkind, they are now regrettably lost. More tangible traces can be identified, however, in a loosely related group of pastels and in the crayon studies of coastal scenes. Prominent among the former is the resonantly hued *Fruit Trees* (fig. 73), which has previously been linked to *Farmyard in Normandy*. With all the hallmarks of a Saint-Siméon motif, this warm, chalky image leads us directly to the pastel oeuvre of Boudin and his evocations of the region and its characteristic vegetation.[40] Monet's precocious sheet represents a cluster of trees heavy with apples, absorbing the warm light of late summer or early fall and is thus consistent with the last weeks of his stay in the Honfleur area, before he returned to Paris in late 1864. A similar subject occurs in a second pastel, *Normandy Farm under Trees*, which may represent a more detailed view of the same setting.[41] Firmly structured and boldly signed by the artist, this work was grouped by Wildenstein with pastels of the 1880s, when Monet certainly returned to Normandy and conceivably took a nostalgic look at the themes of his younger days. As we learn more about the sophistication of his graphic techniques in the earlier decade, however, it may be possible to reconsider such images as celebrations of the 1864 gathering at Honfleur.

Working beneath the eye of Eugène Boudin and using a still-unfamiliar medium, Monet made a number of trials with pastel during these months that were far from consistent with one another. Examined in detail in the next two chapters, these works could be painstakingly exact or brilliantly effusive, pursued as explorations of light and color on their own terms, or used to define new kinds of pictorial mode. The most immediately engaging group of such pastels, however, were those connected with his painting *Towing a Boat, Honfleur* of 1864 (see fig. 110), itself a virtual act of homage to Boudin. The fascinating suggestion considered in chapter 6, that the two artists were somehow complicit in this project, perhaps sharing notes or literally exchanging sheets of studies, is a further sign of the ebb and flow of advice and practical encouragement that characterized this crucial period. Monet's exploitation of his own *View of the Sea at Sunset* (see fig. 111) in the development of this painting is a rare event, in sharp contrast to the largely independent status of his pastel oeuvre as a whole. But it again reminds us of the transitional nature of these months, when new dialogues between his drawings and canvases, and between the example of one mentor and another, seem to emerge in bewildering succession.

Jongkind, Monet's "Real Master"

The second personality who had a critical bearing on Monet's art during the early 1860s, and particularly in the summer of 1864, was Johan Barthold Jongkind (1819–1891), whose influence was to rival that of Boudin himself. According to a later recollection, Monet first met Jongkind through his own draftsmanship. Working in this area in 1862 or 1863, perhaps when *Farmyard in Normandy* was begun, Monet saw a cow grazing in "the neighborhood of Le Havre, in a farm" and "conceived the idea of making a drawing of the noble beast."[42] His subsequent difficulties in restraining the animal required the assistance of an English tourist, who later offered to introduce Monet to Jongkind. It is probably fanciful to connect this anecdote with the black-chalk *Study of Cows* (see fig. 67), since an equally authoritative variant reports that a pastel, not a drawing, was underway at the time.[43] Whatever the precise circumstances, when the anonymous Englishman finally brought Monet together with Jongkind, the painter he had pronounced "dead to art" at the Salon of 1860 turned out to be "a simple, good-hearted man" who soon took the twenty-two-year-old under his wing.[44] "He asked to see my sketches, invited me to come and work with him, explained to me the why and the wherefore of his manner, and thereby completed the teachings that I had already received from Boudin. From that time on he was my real master, and it was to him that I owed the final education of my eye."[45]

Like Boudin, Jongkind (fig. 74) was an outsider at this date, a consequence of his uncompromisingly vivid art as well as his wild, flamboyant personality. Born in 1819, Jongkind spent most of his life in France and already

74
Nadar (Félix Tournachon) (French, 1820–1910), *Caricature of Johan Barthold Jongkind*, 1852. Charcoal on brown paper with white heightening, 227 x 150 mm. Musée du Louvre, Paris

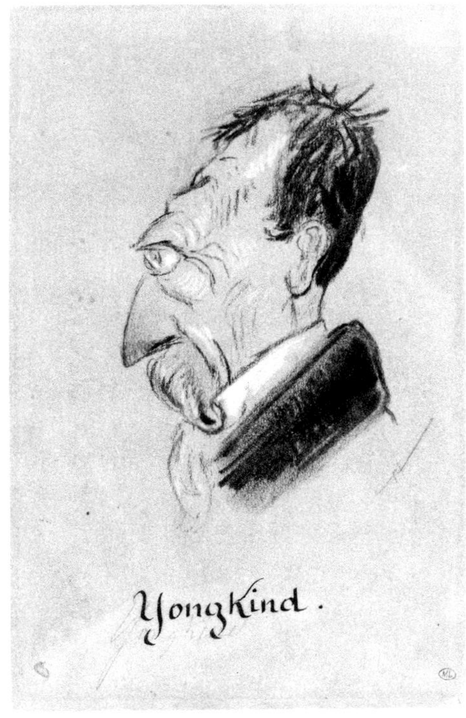

knew many of the artists Monet distantly admired, among them Courbet, Corot, and Millet. He was equally committed to painting city and countryside, often favoring areas in which Monet would later work, such as Yport, Le Havre, Honfleur, Sainte-Adresse, and Étretat, as well as Paris and Amsterdam. Regarded by some as the true father of Impressionism, Jongkind also shared Boudin's habit of making large numbers of energetic drawings in the open air, some of which stimulated the canvases he would then develop indoors. Jongkind settled in the French capital in 1861, where Monet continued to benefit from his willingness to explain the "why and wherefore" of art to the younger man. Happy to show both finished pictures and working studies to casual callers, Jongkind amazed Edmond de Goncourt in the next decade with countless "works on card, scrawls on paper, phantasmagorias of sky and water, colored fireworks in the ether."[46] In the early 1860s, Monet was inspired to experiment with a number of Jongkind-like motifs, such as the frontally approaching boat beneath an ominous sky, which appears in his *Seascape: Storm* (fig. 75). True to form, however, Monet was selective in his borrowings, learning from certain of his teacher's innovations, while almost willfully rejecting Jongkind's most characteristic drawing process.

A clear limit to Monet's virtuosity was watercolor, a medium he virtually ignored in his mature career, after making some youthful exercises that were reported by Théophile Beguin Billecocq and repeating the experiment in Algiers.[47] With a time-honored pedigree in landscape art, watercolor had been a common outdoor sketching tool for at least two centuries, as well as a more elaborate vehicle for large-scale paintings by his predecessors in France, England, and elsewhere. In this tradition, a lightly drawn image was often made in pencil or chalk to define the intended composition, followed by appropriate washes of color as the painting took shape. Jongkind, who is said to have instructed Boudin in the rudiments of the process, also combined watercolor with draftsmanship, though in a manner so unconventional that it has recently been labeled "heretical."[48] Many hundreds of Jongkind's works in the medium exist, some still bound in sketchbooks he used in the field, including thirty-two albums preserved in the collections of the Louvre and the Musée d'Orsay. Laboratory research has identified a remarkable feature in these works that appears to reverse conventional practice. In making studies such as *Dutch Fishing Boats* (fig. 76), Jongkind might begin the picture by spreading thinly diluted colors onto the blank paper, sometimes with considerable freedom, summarizing the broad features of the scene, its qualities of light, and dominant hues. Only at a secondary stage would he add emphatic lines to the already-existing watercolor, strengthening its brushed contours and introducing richer textures and more precise detail.[49] For reasons best known to himself, Jongkind thus turned the tables on centuries of custom, his superimposed graphic marks creating order in the painterly unruliness beneath.

Though he did not adopt this idiosyncratic procedure himself, Monet surely noted the contrary nature of Jongkind's watercolor technique and perhaps its implications for art in general. Later in his career he acquired one such

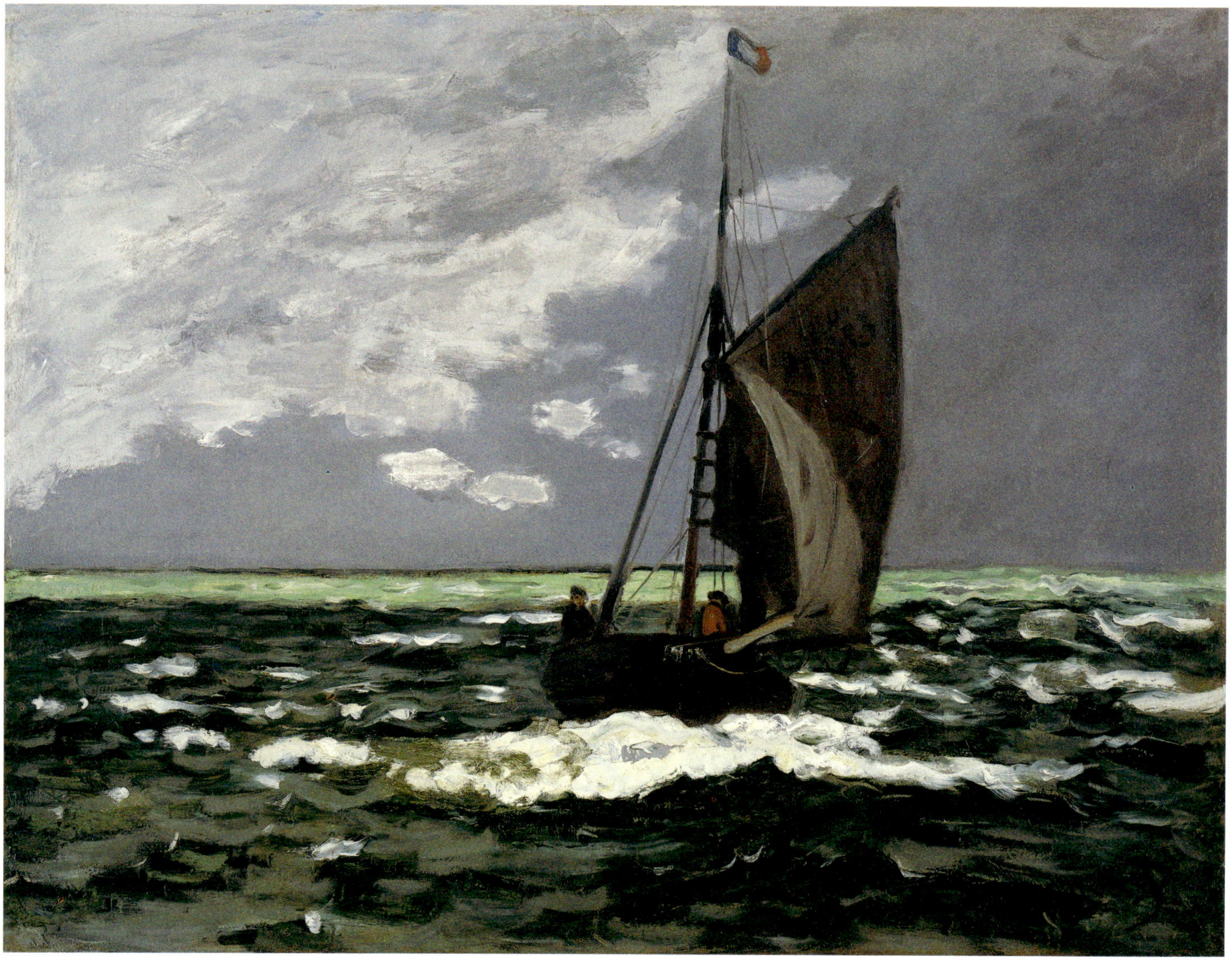

75

Seascape: Storm, c. 1866–67. Oil on canvas, 48.7 x 64.7 cm. Sterling and Francine Clark Art Institute, Williamstown, Massachusetts [W86]

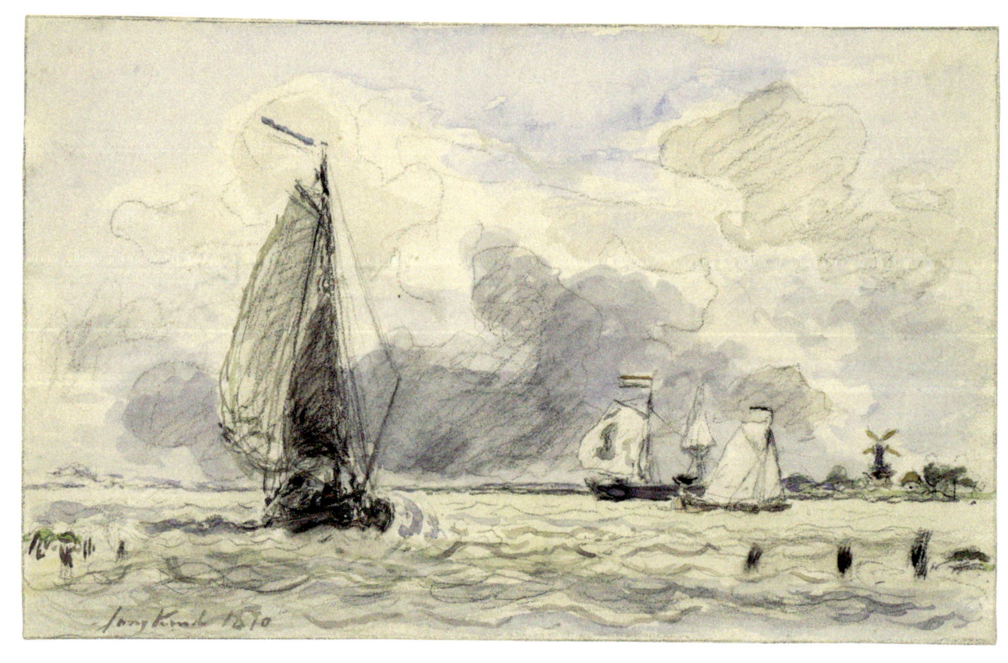

76

Johan Barthold Jongkind, *Dutch Fishing Boats*, 1870–72. Watercolor over black chalk; verso black chalk, 162 x 267 mm. The Metropolitan Museum of Art, New York. Mr. and Mrs. Isaac D. Fletcher Collection, Bequest of Isaac D. Fletcher, 1917

Jongkind sheet for his own collection, a harbor scene of 1880 entitled *Port-Vendre*, in which the interaction of line and color is vividly evident.[50] As a younger man, Monet had seen how color could be detached from line almost entirely in the pastel "enchantments" of Boudin, as Baudelaire called them. Jongkind's watercolors, by contrast, revealed how the relationship between these two elements might—quite literally—be inverted. The "absolute" value of line, as defined by Blanc, now became secondary, established only after the "relative" virtues of color had dominated the composition; the palette took precedence over the crayon, with the latter used almost as an afterthought. During the 1860s, Monet himself made a number of pastels and canvases in a similarly questioning spirit, apparently rethinking the orthodox roles of drawing or simply abandoning them. When painting his Jongkind-like *Seascape: Storm*, for example, there is no evidence that Monet used drawings or other kinds of preliminary study, and neither the naked eye nor radiography reveals any traces of draftsmanship beneath the paint itself.[51] Not only the marine motif brings to mind the work of his "real master," in other words, but also the way the picture was physically made. Having initially added his oil colors in broad, exploratory planes, Monet then applied some crisp, essentially linear brushstrokes on top of this layer of paint in order to tighten its visual structure. Clearly visible in areas such as the horizon, the rigging on the boat, and the foam on the waves, these last-minute demarcations are closely analogous to the pencil contours in Jongkind's watercolors and carry something of the same anarchic weight.

Monet's Black-Chalk Drawings

The most forceful example of Jongkind's influence on Monet's art, however, is found in the almost-unstudied group of black-chalk drawings that were made around mid-decade.[52] Numbering some dozen sheets, these drawings are exceptionally consistent in technique, scale, and subject matter, and are correspondingly unlike any other works in Monet's graphic oeuvre. In all of them we are conscious of the medium itself, a rich, dark, waxy crayon or fabricated chalk that is used both boldly and sensuously. Executed on off-white laid paper, most of the studies measure approximately 200 by 300 millimeters and may have originated in a single sketchbook.[53] The pervasive subject is the Normandy coast and the presence of the sea, which is variously flanked by cliffs, buildings, or—in one case—vegetation. Unified by their scale and their monochrome character, these images appear to have been conceived as a visually related set or series, the first of its kind in Monet's career. At least two have direct echoes in oil paintings he carried out in 1864 and a further pair was partly developed in pastel, but there is no evidence that they were intended as preparatory drafts for individual canvases or finished pastels. Rather, Monet seems to have self-consciously created them as a suite of black-and-white images, a focused celebration of the area in which he grew up and a display of draftsmanship with its own separate, if somewhat mysterious, identity.

Distinctive though they are, most of these drawings had an immediate source, a topographic link, or a close compositional precedent in the recent output of Jongkind. Between 1862 and 1864, Jongkind spent part of each year in the area between Le Havre and Honfleur, accumulating his eccentric pencil-over-watercolor scenes and working on associated paintings in improvised studios. One of his favorite structural devices was the plunging diagonal, which followed the line of a hill or cliff from the upper edge to the opposite lower corner of his compositions, as in the canvas *Coast at Sainte-Adresse* of 1862, and associated drawings and watercolors.[54] Hardly unique to Jongkind and also evident in the work of an artist such as Daubigny, this construction is nevertheless pronounced in the Dutchman's imagery at this time.[55] More than three quarters of Monet's black-chalk drawings also follow this same pattern, represented by the quintessential example now in San Francisco, *The Coast of Normandy*

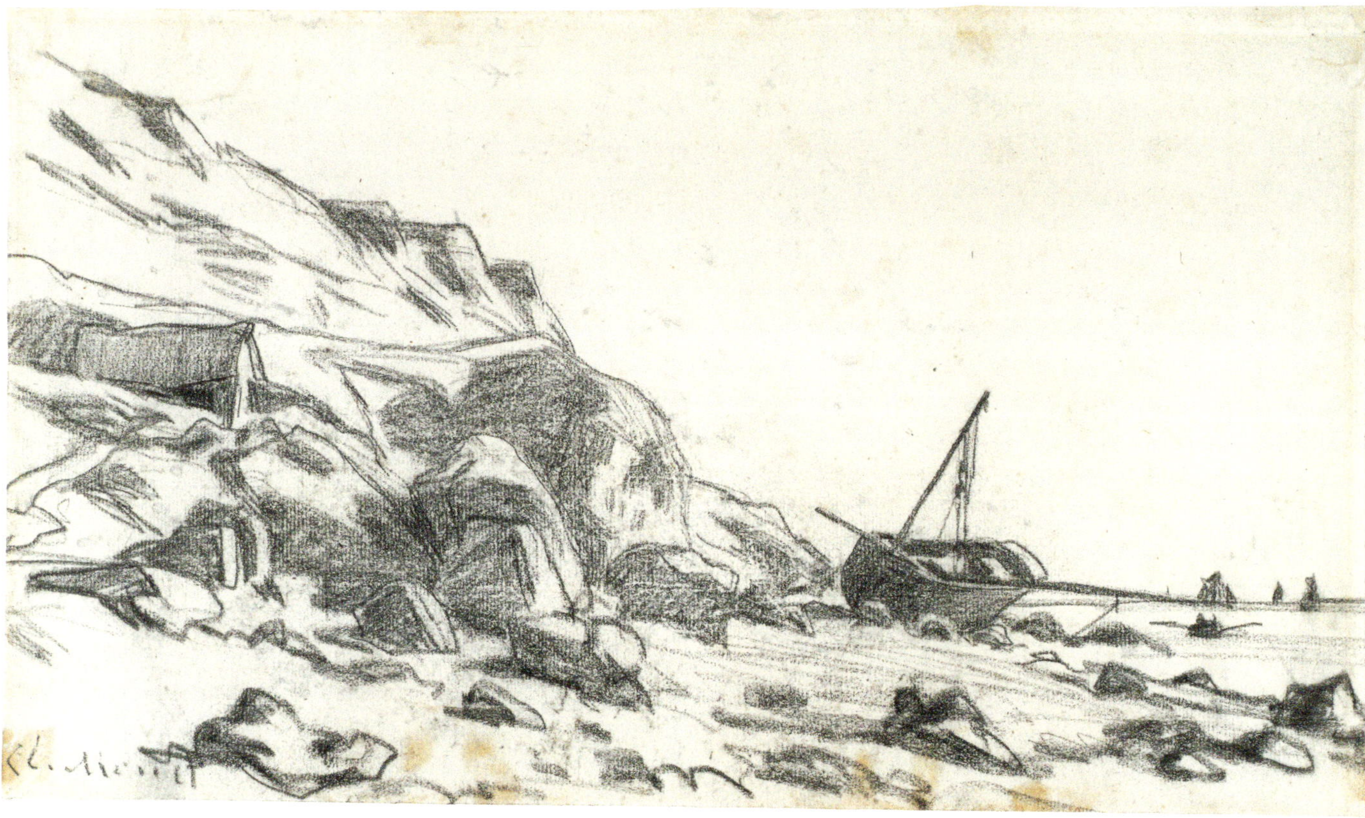

77
The Coast of Normandy Viewed from Sainte-Adresse, c. 1864. Black chalk on off-white laid paper, 175 x 308 mm. Fine Arts Museums of San Francisco. Memorial Gift from Dr. T. Edward and Tullah Hanley, Bradford, Pennsylvania [D419]

Viewed from Sainte-Adresse (fig. 77). Steep, rocky seashores of a similar kind, sometimes featuring a large boulder or a beached sailboat, were a recurring motif in Jongkind's art at this time, allowing him to break the monotonous line of the sea and hint at the drama of the engulfing elements. Monet brazenly appropriated these forms and their implicit theme, taking it one step further in a subgroup of studies linked to the San Francisco sheet. These seem to describe a sequential, pre-cinematic advance from frame to frame over at least six individual works. In the first, a fishing craft in full sail is seen from close quarters, where a storm has apparently left it stranded beneath a jagged cliff, here resembling several sites in the Honfleur area. Successive variants show the boat at a greater distance, as it is dismasted, abandoned, and then partly overturned, culminating in the sad hulk of *Cliffs and Sea, Sainte-Adresse* (fig. 78), in which two ships on the horizon offer the only note of hope.[56]

Such a parade of interconnected images was unprecedented in Monet's work but would soon take a different form in a brilliantly colored sequence of landscape pastels later in this decade.[57] Seen together, the larger group of black-chalk drawings suggests the work of a roving eye and a lively intelligence, accompanied by a remarkable technical command that Monet seemed able to activate as required. Using a medium that had not previously been featured in his graphic oeuvre, he showed exceptional confidence in his approach to the task and in his detailed execution of its complex imagery. Close examination of the individual sheets reveals that, in their early stages, some of the principal forms were lightly touched in, then firmly developed with dark contours, internal modeling, and a variety of tonal procedures, from casual hatching to dense accumulations of crayon. Where the handling of the San Francisco study seems relatively relaxed, almost sketchlike, the Chicago composition is a model of descriptive economy, balancing the rich textures of the bulky cliff against a broad expanse of empty sky. For an unknown artist in his early twenties, the series was a tour-de-force at many levels, yet Monet left behind no clues as to its origin or ultimate purpose.

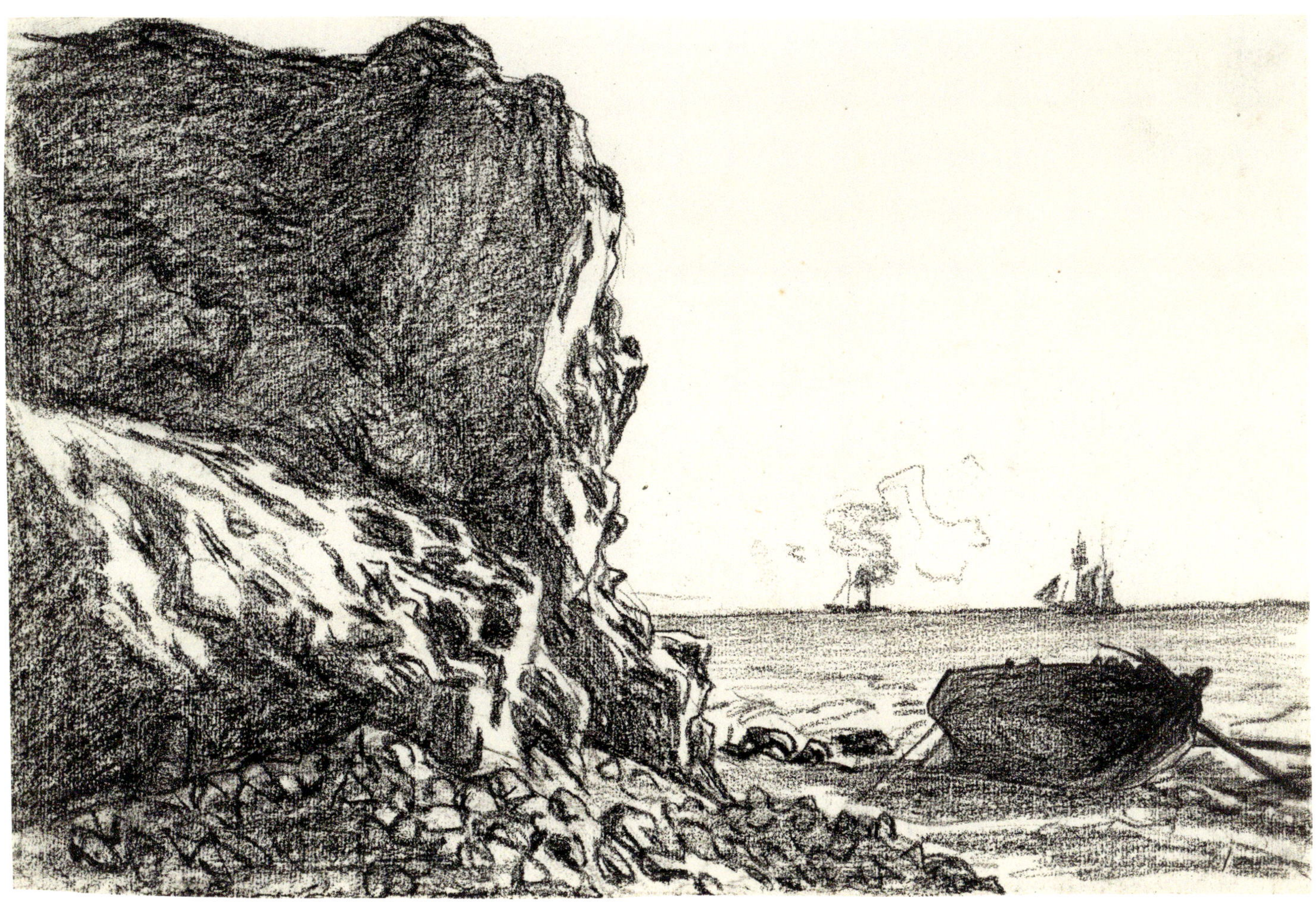

78
Cliffs and Sea, Sainte-Adresse, c. 1864. Black chalk on off-white laid paper, 206 x 314 mm. The Art Institute of Chicago. Clarence Buckingham Collection [D421]

A number of broad precedents for Monet's initiative can be found in the work of senior artists, such as Daubigny's pen-and-ink sketches based around his boat, *Le botin*, though these were widely disparate in their compositions.[58] More significant is the fact that Daubigny's drawings prompted a series of etchings that appeared in the early 1860s.[59] It is in this world of printmaking, then experiencing a major revival under the banner of the Société des Aquafortistes, that we discover a number of unexpected clues to Monet's project.[60] At its simplest, the production of a print typically involved the making of sequential states of a black-and-white image, as the artist gradually refined his subject from its linear beginnings to its tonally enriched conclusion. Both new and traditional processes were available to develop such designs, which could be executed as etchings, drypoints, engravings, lithographs, relief blocks, or other forms of print. Monet had already been exposed to several of these procedures at close quarters, during his friendship with Amand Gautier and in the transformation of his own caricature of Louis Laferrière (see fig. 48) into a *paniconographie*—a variation of relief printing—in 1860.

The significance of Amand Gautier in Monet's early technical formation has been largely overlooked, despite the closely overlapping careers of the two men at this period. Fifteen years older than Monet, Gautier counted among his acquaintances Courbet, Baudelaire, Boudin, and Jongkind, as well as Mme Marie-Jeanne Lecadre (Monet's aunt), and the Gaudibert family in Le Havre, with whom he spent some time in both 1858 and 1862.[61] Gautier's versatility can only have impressed his younger colleague, from the paintings he exhibited at the Salon and the printmaking activities of all kinds he

79

Johan Barthold Jongkind, *The Two Sailboats*, 1862. Etching, 178 x 166 mm. Sterling and Francine Clark Art Institute, Williamstown, Massachusetts

80

Johan Barthold Jongkind, *Houses beside the Canal*, 1862. Etching, 178 x 215 mm. Sterling and Francine Clark Art Institute, Williamstown, Massachusetts

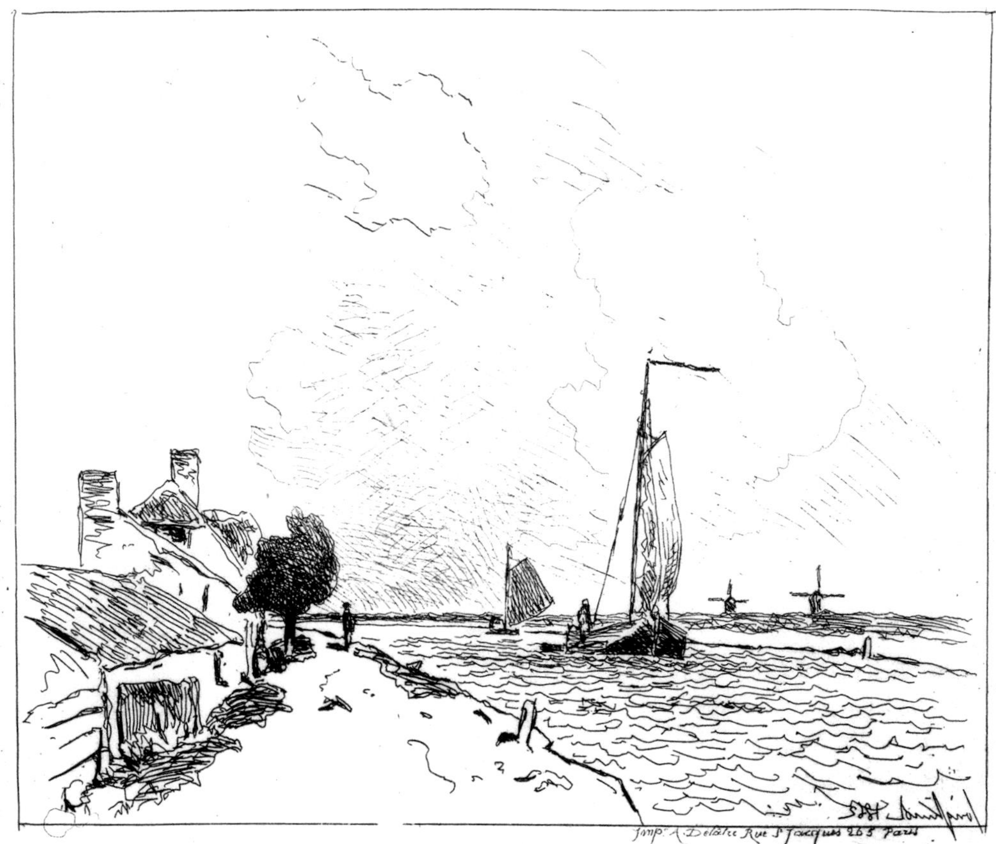

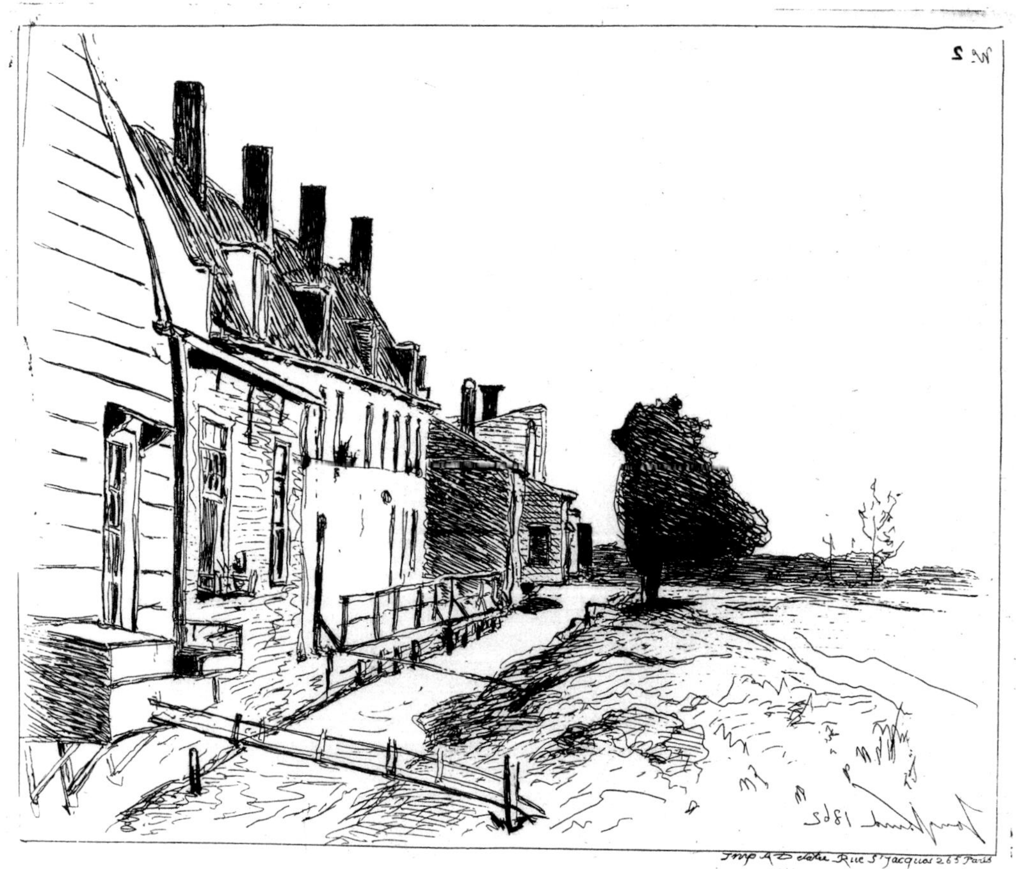

undertook, to the making of black-chalk drawings as illustrations for a novel by Champfleury.[62] When they met in Paris in 1859, Monet described how Gautier was "about to start work on a big lithograph," and would thus have witnessed the use of the black, wax-based crayons that were applied directly to lithographic stones at this date.[63] This was also the time when Gautier contemplated making an etching from the small canvas by Daubigny that Monet owned, though this scheme apparently came to nothing.[64]

Gautier's experiments were characteristic of a growing enthusiasm for printmaking in the circles in which Monet now moved, newly focused on the premises of Alfred Cadart (1828–1875) and the Société des Aquafortistes. Among Cadart's successes were discrete portfolios of prints by a single artist, such as the suite of eight etchings by Manet that appeared in 1862.[65] In this same year, Cadart published a similar set made by Jongkind, the *Cahier de six eaux-fortes, vues de Holland*, consisting of simple exercises in line drawing on a copper plate with tone sparingly indicated by roughly scratched hatching.[66] As Michel Melot points out, Jongkind's prints were themselves derived from a sequence of black-and-white drawings, executed in pen and ink close to the size of the finished etchings. Some of these drawings, which would all be reversed by the printing process, followed existing paintings by the artist, while others provided starting points for Jongkind's later canvases.[67] Nominally based on Holland, they show a variety of canal banks and seashores with occasional houses and isolated shipping vessels, backed by high, largely featureless skies and wisps of cloud. *The Two Sailboats* (fig. 79) typifies the unpretentious clarity of Jongkind's etchings and reintroduces us to the foreshortened sailing craft that

81
Houses by the Sea, c. 1864.
Black chalk on off-white laid paper, 246 x 334 mm.
The Museum of Modern Art, New York. Gift of Mr. and Mrs. Marion Joseph Lebworth [D422]

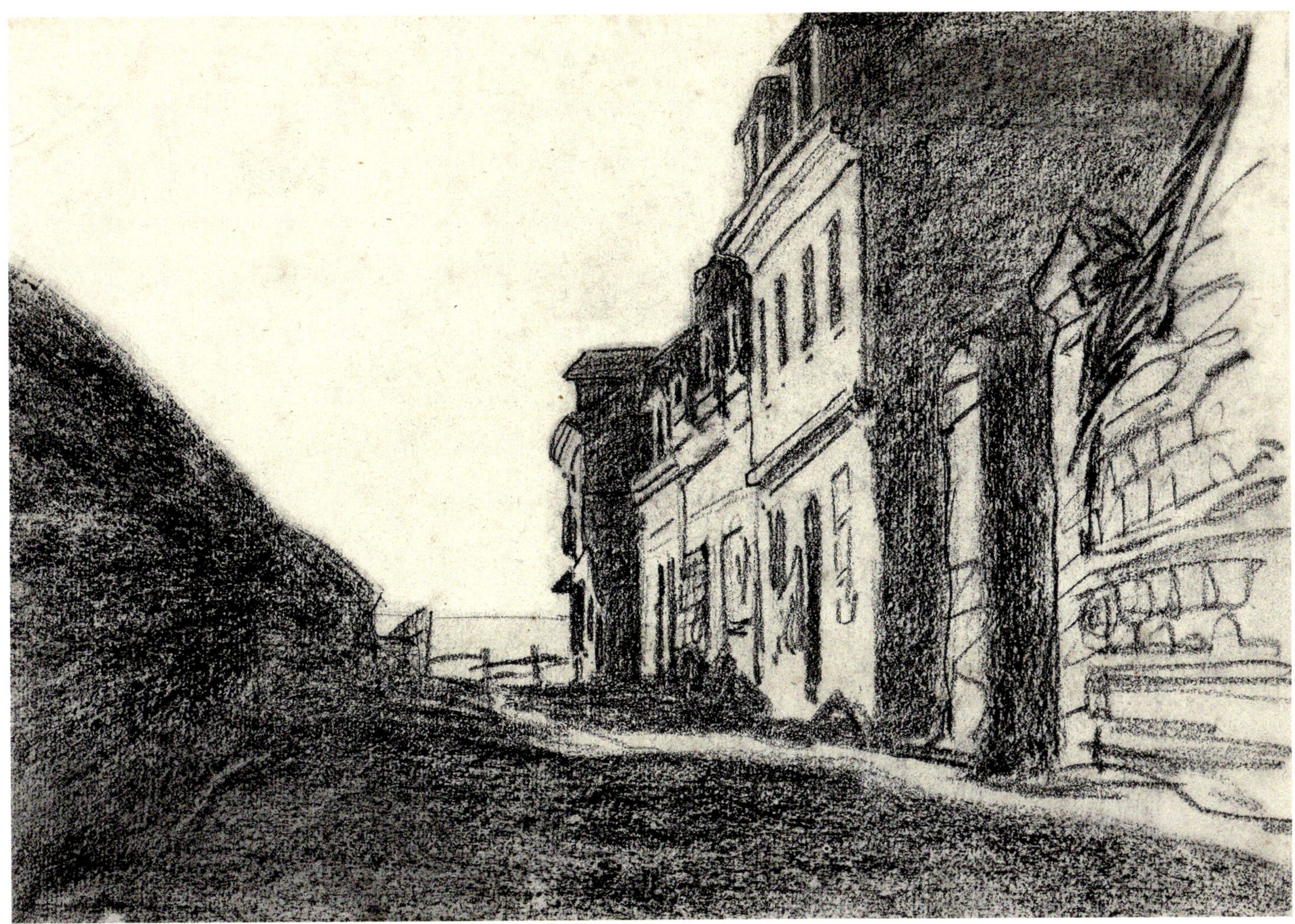

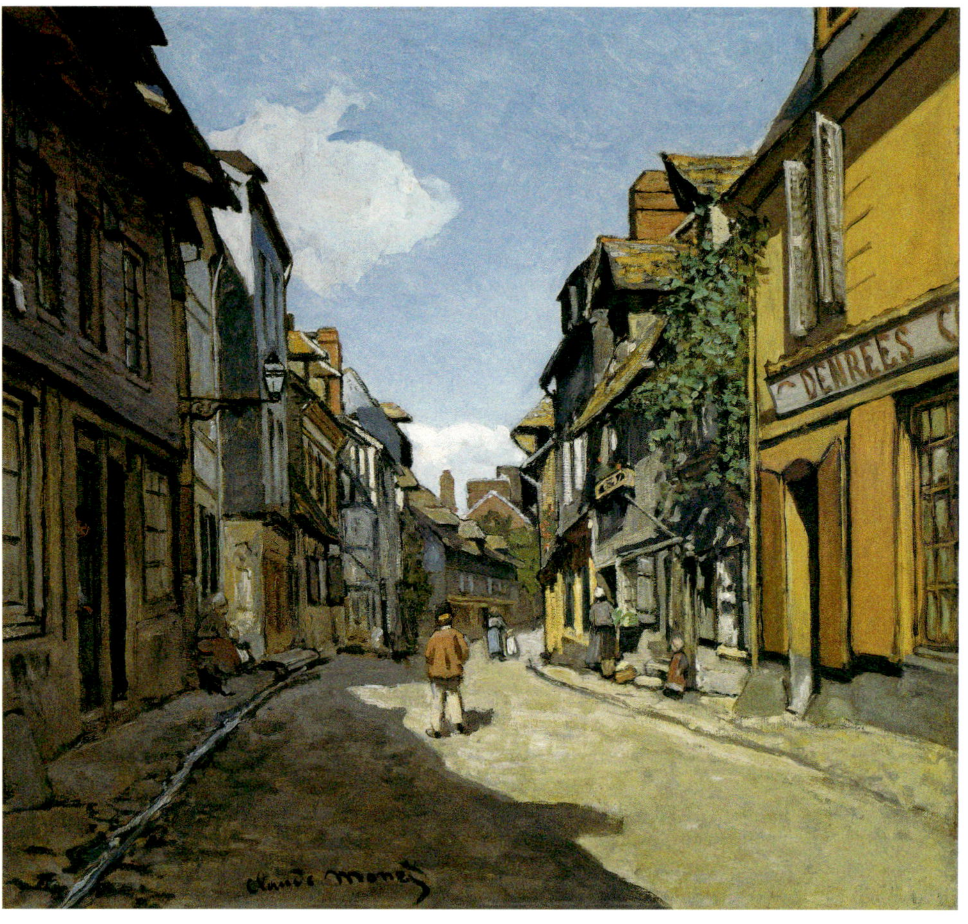

82
Rue de la Bavole, Honfleur, c. 1864.
Oil on canvas, 55.9 x 61 cm.
Museum of Fine Arts, Boston.
Bequest of John T. Spaulding
[W33]

Monet was to make his own in *Seascape: Storm*. The *cahier* attracted the attention of Baudelaire, whose review of April 1862 welcomed Jongkind's "singular abbreviations of his painting" and suggested that art-lovers habituated to reading "the soul of the artist" in such "rapid scribblings" would find these works as "calm as the banks of the great rivers and horizons of his noble homeland."[68] Jongkind himself actively promoted his prints, bringing them to the notice of the influential critic Philippe Burty, who also mentioned the series in the contemporary art press.[69] There is no record of when Monet became aware of them or whether his growing friendship with Jongkind gave him direct access to the preparatory drawings. What is beyond doubt, however, is that these works were firmly in Monet's mind when he undertook his own sequence of black-and-white drawings.

The most original design in Jongkind's suite of etchings was *Houses beside the Canal* (fig. 80), where a line of rooftops descends sharply to a low horizon to meet a strongly shaded tree. When Monet drew his own audacious *Houses by the Sea* (fig. 81), he clearly modeled it on Jongkind's composition, mirroring the thrust of the roofs and enlarging the dark mass of the tree into a triangular pool of shadow. His drawing is virtually the same size as the print and would, of course, have resembled Jongkind's own pen-and-ink design even more closely before it was reversed by the etching procedure. Monet may simply have improvised his motif, or perhaps used his ingenuity to seek out a comparable line of buildings in Honfleur as he reconstructed his mentor's coastal panorama. Uniting both views is the element of water, explicit in Jongkind's foreground canals and more subtly indicated in the strip of sea beyond the farthest dwelling in Monet's picture. Taking advantage of his richly tonal crayons, Monet heightened the play of light and shade in his version of the motif, carving into the dark recesses around the clifflike buildings and creating brilliant slabs of sunshine elsewhere.[70] These imaginative acts of appropriation were exceeded in the next step of his creative thinking; the creation of two oil paintings inspired by the same conceit. In the almost identical versions of *Rue de la Bavole, Honfleur*, one of which is in Boston (fig. 82), Monet introduced another line of houses to balance the right-hand row in his drawing but retained the dramatic patch of shadow at lower left.[71] The debt to Jongkind goes further, since in the previous year the Dutchman had painted his own canvas of a receding thoroughfare in the town, entitled *Street in Honfleur*, based on the same multifaceted traditional housing but using a less-extreme perspectival recession.[72]

In *Houses by the Sea* and his two associated paintings, it can be argued, Monet seized on one of Jongkind's pictorial motifs and took it to greater imaginative and expressive heights. The progression from Jongkind's etching to Monet's own crayon study and then to his canvas of Honfleur was a distinctly unorthodox one but not without its own logic. Printmaking is inseparable from reversal, which in turn prompts fresh structures and narratives, just as

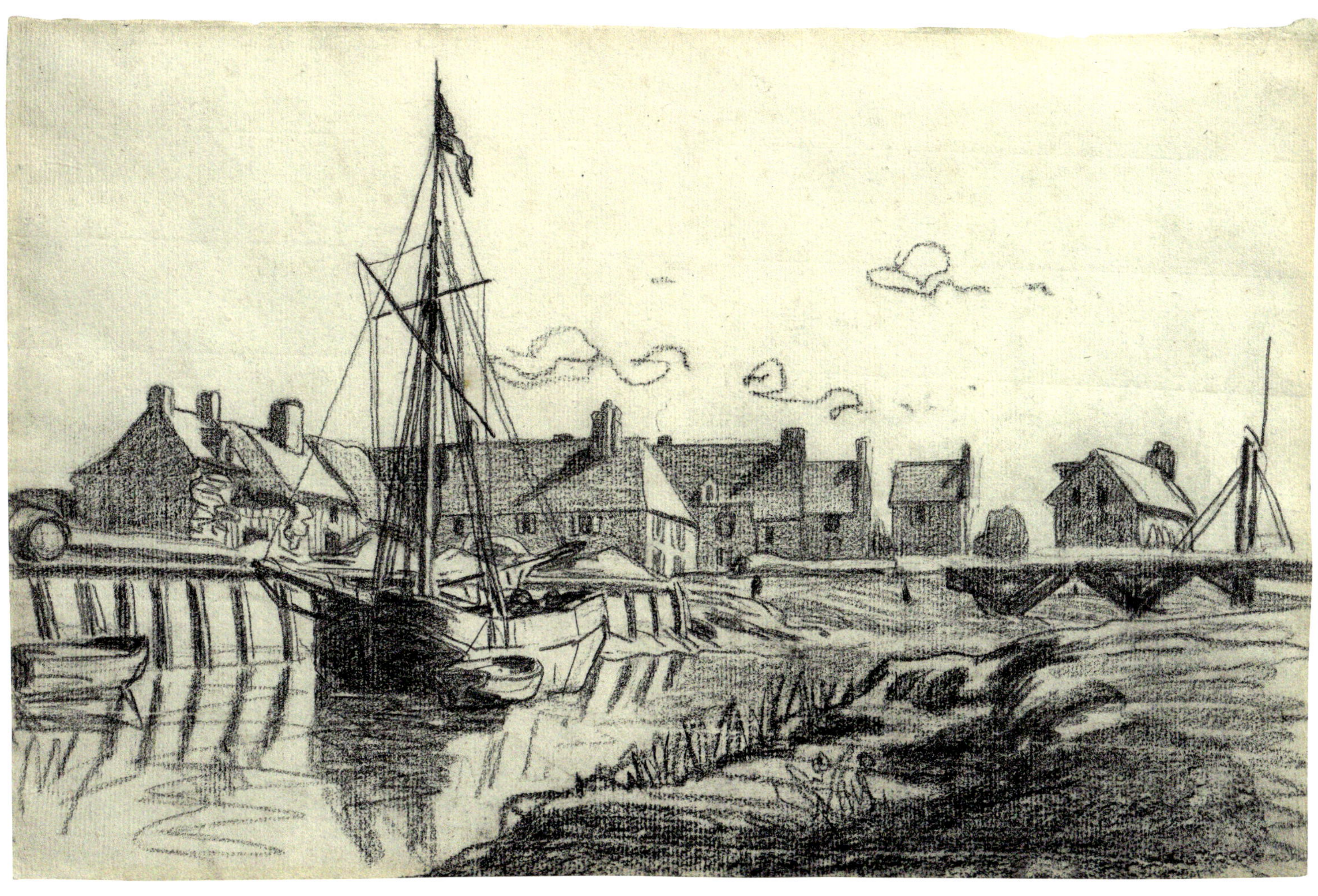

83
The Port at Touques, c. 1864. Black chalk on off-white laid paper, 210 x 330 mm. Sterling and Francine Clark Art Institute, Williamstown, Massachusetts [D415]

the manipulation of inks, grounds, and acid can lead to serendipitous qualities and patterns of tone. Clearly inspired by Jongkind's inventive approach, Monet may have toyed with the idea of a suite of presentation drawings, or even a *cahier* of etchings or lithographs of his own "noble homeland," the coast of Normandy. He was anxious for exposure and needed cash, and such an enterprise would have capitalized on the burgeoning trades in original printmaking and in travel illustration. Such a set of prints, however, would require visual variety as well as thematic unity, as Jongkind's own series demonstrated.

Other works in Monet's larger group of black-chalk drawings fit this description well. *The Port at Touques* (fig. 83) offers a variation on *Houses by the Sea*, presenting another row of substantial buildings near the water, here in a small settlement on the outskirts of Deauville and Trouville. With their steep roofs and blocky chimneys, these forms are again reminiscent of Jongkind's *Houses beside the Canal*, while the prominent ship in the foreground has many parallels in the older man's paintings and prints.[73] Conceivably representing the point of departure in Monet's graphic narrative, when the ill-fated barque set sail, this drawing shows the little harbor of Touques as the embodiment of tranquility. Lacking human participants of any kind, as does the rest of the sequence, the quietly monumental sheet is animated by a few curls of cloud — another signature Jongkind touch — that move across the sky.[74] Balanced horizontals and answering verticals establish the restful mood and are gently offset by the curving form of the riverbank at bottom right, a *repoussoir* — or distance-creating device — that helps generate the deep, untroubled spaces of *The Port at Touques*.

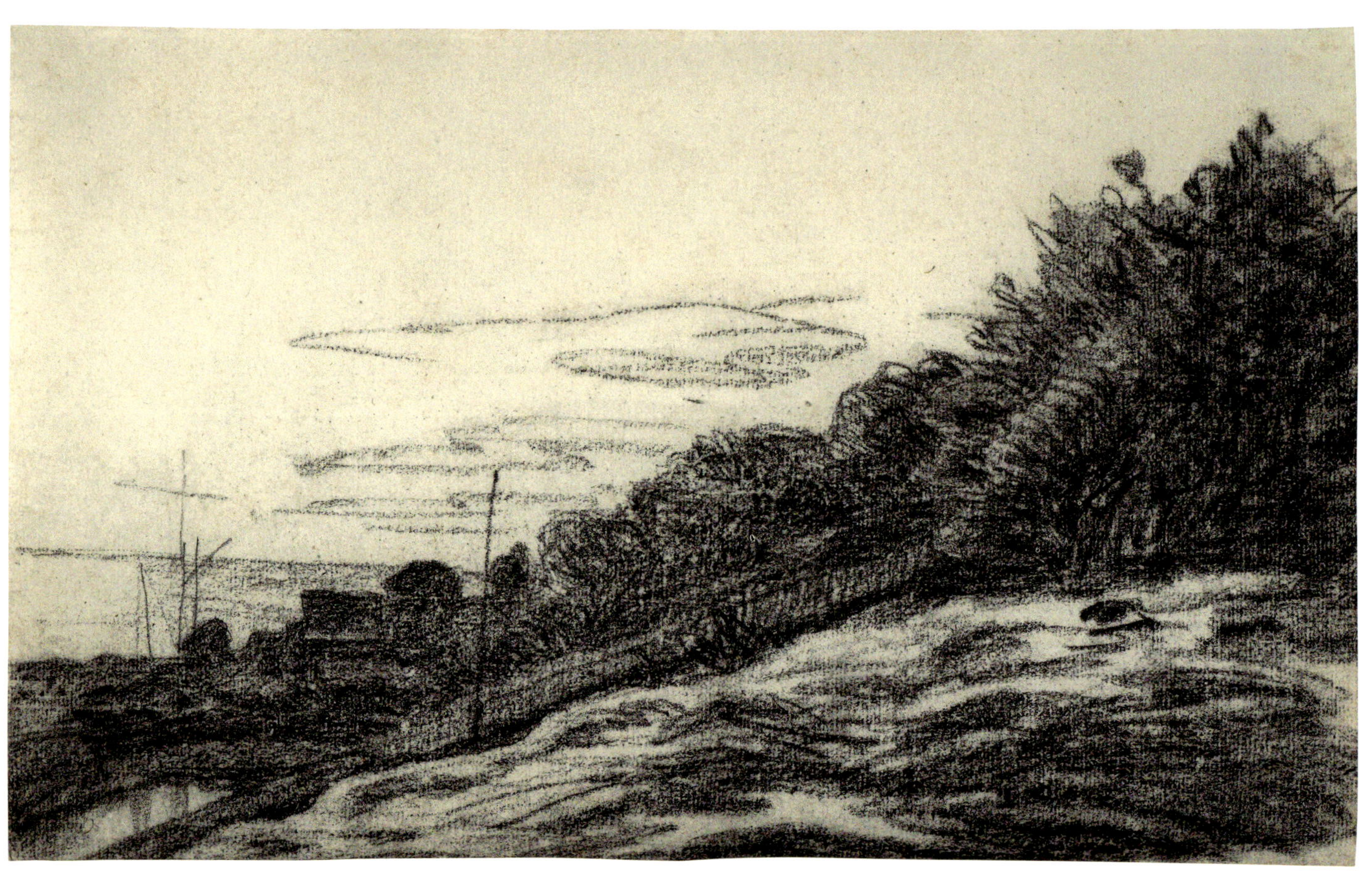

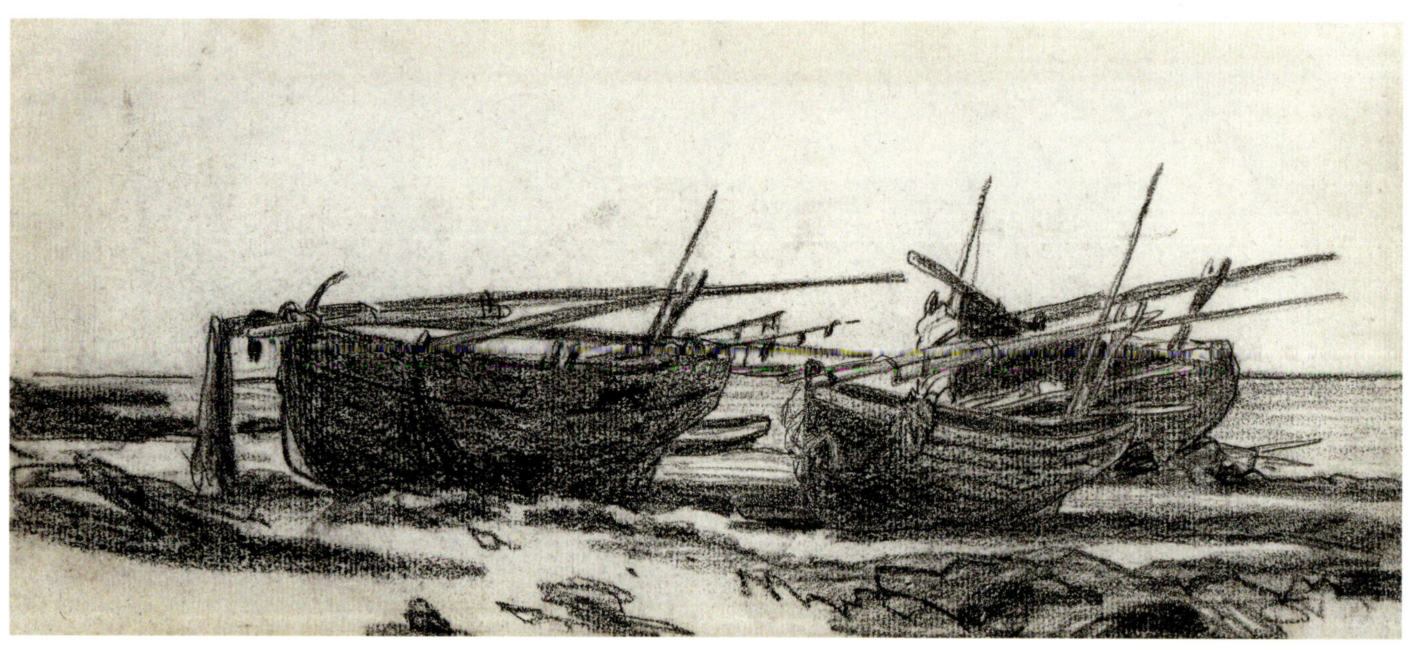

84
Coast of Lower Normandy, c. 1864. Black chalk on off-white laid paper, 180 x 300 mm. Private collection [D416]

85
Boats on the Beach in Normandy, c. 1864. Black chalk on off-white laid paper, 135 x 305 mm. Private collection, courtesy of Elrick-Manley Fine Art, Inc. [D433]

86
The Beach at Honfleur, 1864. Oil on canvas, 59.7 x 81.3 cm. Los Angeles County Museum of Art. Gift of Mrs. Reese Hale Taylor [W41]

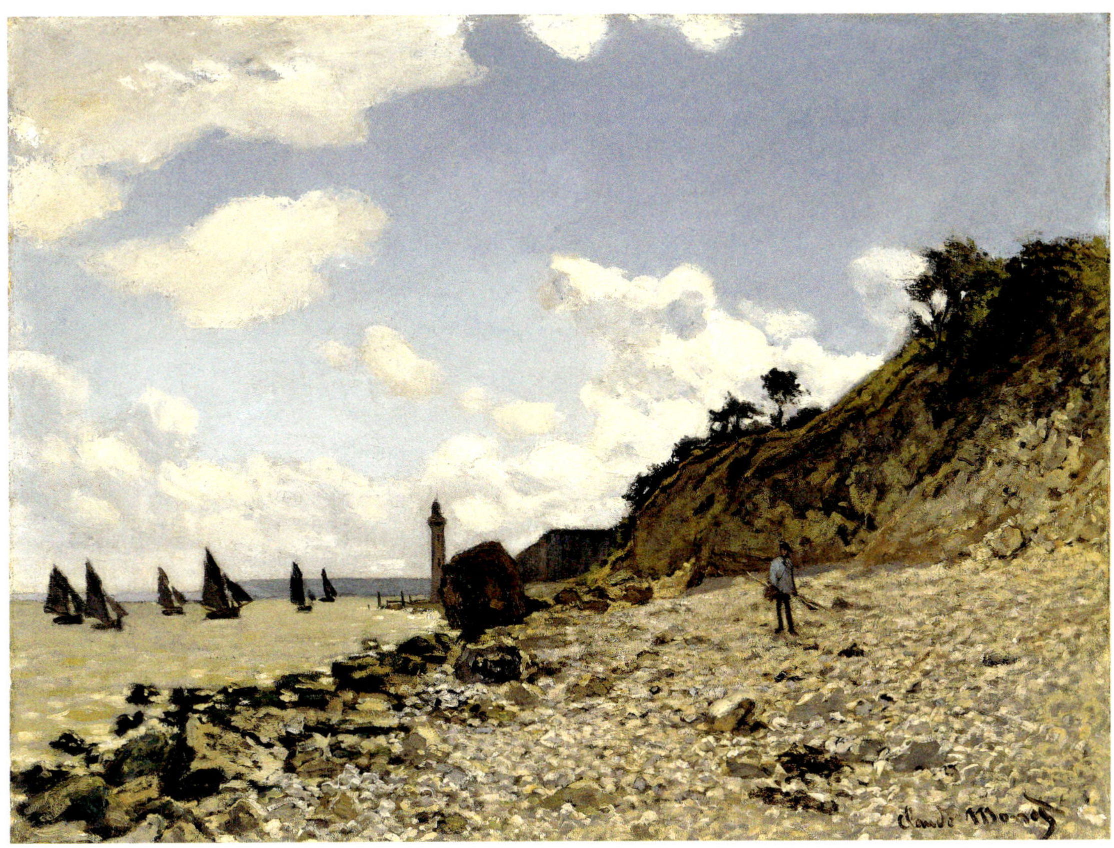

A similar matrix underlies *Coast of Lower Normandy* (fig. 84), another work built around a Jongkind-like corner-to-corner diagonal but with different textural qualities from the drawings already examined. With a skill beyond his years and his known formal education, Monet carries the spectator's eye from the animated foreground across a dense thicket that rises from the shore to a distant gleam on the ocean. Fine lines indicate masts and flagpoles, while a series of almost lazy flourishes introduce streaks of cloud into the plane of sky. All this was accomplished with rough, parallel strokes, crisp hatchings, and delicate touches of his waxy chalk, as the artist proceeded without second thoughts or corrections. Four or five other drawings from the set introduce variations on its central theme, carrying us to the cliff-overshadowed beaches of Yport and Étretat and introducing smaller fishing boats that have been pulled safely above the waterline in distinctly Boudin-like configurations.[75] Two of these, *Boats on a Beach* (see fig. 97) and *Boats on the Beach in Normandy* (fig. 85), conform to the technical character of the larger series and occupy sheets of identical width, though reduced in height to produce the double-square format much favored by Monet in these years. *Boats on the Beach in Normandy* is another sparkling exercise in draftsmanship, from its bold, matter-of-fact composition to the crisp detailing of spars and fittings. With its more topographically precise pair, these two works extend the central role of locally observed craft in Monet's drawn sequence and slightly enlarge its regional base.[76] Whatever Monet had planned for the black-chalk drawings, his efforts seem to have been in vain: almost half are confidently signed, but most remained with him until his death in 1926.[77] Perhaps discouraged by this adventure, Monet resisted any further involvement in graphic sequences or printmaking until the 1890s, transferring his interest in serial imagery to the making of pastels and oil paintings.

An exceptionally vivid canvas of 1864, *The Beach at Honfleur* (fig. 86), seems to have emerged from the same visual research that informed the monochrome drawings. Yet the relationship between this picture and Monet's current draftsmanship, like the larger issue of interaction between color and line in his output of the 1860s, continues to tantalize us. Most of the elements in his painting can be found in the black-chalk studies, yet no single sheet accounts for the entire composition. Was it derived from a now-lost sketch? Is there a similar linear design underneath its richly impasted surface? Could Monet have brushed it directly on the canvas, without preliminary drafting? When works of this period have been examined systematically, the results are often equivocal, partly because dense oil color often obscures their earlier stages and radiography fails to distinguish between early and later brushstrokes. In a relatively thinly painted work, such as the Kimbell Museum's *The Pointe de la Hève at Low Tide* of 1865, some fine lines can be seen with the naked eye beneath the more-developed areas but hardly constitute an appropriate drawing for such a major composition.[78] Compounding our difficulties is the lack of contemporary sketchbooks and the sparse documentation of the artist's thoughts, leaving us to wring meaning from a few surviving letters, a handful of extant studies on paper, and some brief references to drawings and related issues in Théophile Beguin Billecocq's Grand Journal.

"Bring Me Paper and Pencils": Luncheon on the Grass

In December of 1864, Théophile recounted how his father had just bought a painting of Honfleur from Monet to assist the artist financially, also acquiring some "crayon drawings representing Normandy farms."[79] The following spring, Monet wrote to Bazille from Chailly-en-Bière, where he was again painting the forest. Describing the weather as "superb," Monet urged his friend to join him and added a startling request: "Bring me paper and pencils," he wrote, "I absolutely need them."[80] Soon afterward, Monet must have heard that the Salon jury had chosen two of his paintings for the forthcoming exhibition, including *The Pointe de la Hève at Low Tide*. We now know for certain that Monet returned briefly to Paris for the occasion, celebrating his first Salon triumph over dinner and champagne with the Beguin Billecocq family.[81] One of the immediate consequences of his success was a commission to make a drawing from his other entry, *Mouth of the Seine at Honfleur* (see fig. 179), to be published in a weekly journal alongside the exhibition. Monet's response (see fig. 180), discussed in chapter 8, was carried out in pen and ink in a vivacious style that perhaps owed as much to Daubigny and his *Voyage en bateau* prints as it did to Jongkind.

Soon Monet was again writing from Chailly and demanding that Bazille hurry to his side "to pose for several figures," without which his "picture" would fail.[82] The work in question was to be one of the largest canvases Monet ever tackled, a *Luncheon on the Grass* that was intended to rival Edouard Manet's notorious 1863 painting with the same title and take the next Salon by storm. Gigantic in scale, the new picture also presented Monet with immense compositional and practical challenges that he had not previously encountered. His ten-foot-high bourgeois picnic scene required the painting of life-size male and female figures, who stood, sat, and reclined around a sumptuous spread of food and drink. Apart from a few modest portraits, Monet had no experience with such human narratives, nor of orchestrating poses, gestures, and fashionable behavior in a rustic setting. As a recent escapee from the studios of Suisse and Gleyre, the irony of this situation can hardly have escaped him. It was for precisely such projects that his teachers had urged the study of anatomy and deportment, as well as attention to the great figurative compositions of the past, which included celebrated *Concerts champêtre* and images of rural merrymaking. The young artist who had refused to make *académies* now found himself obliged to make drawings from the model, pleading with his friend to bring "paper and pencils" from the city and pose for certain of his imaginary characters. Camille Doncieux, Monet's new girlfriend, stood in for the female roles, aided by a certain "young Gabrielle," whose identity

87

Study for Luncheon on the Grass, 1865. Pencil, 255 x 340 mm. Sketchbook 1, fol. 24r. Musée Marmottan Monet, Paris [D106]

88

The Luncheon on the Grass, c. 1865. Black chalk on blue-gray laid paper, 305 x 468 mm. National Gallery of Art, Washington, D.C. Collection of Mr. and Mrs. Paul Mellon (1995.47.60) [not in Wildenstein]

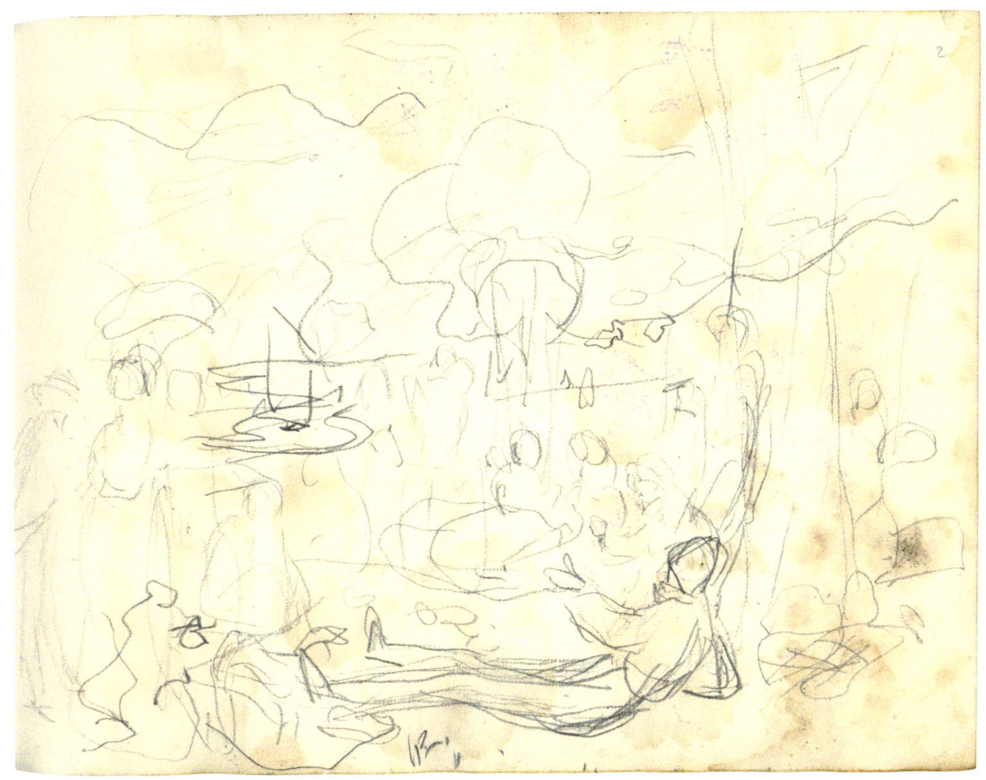

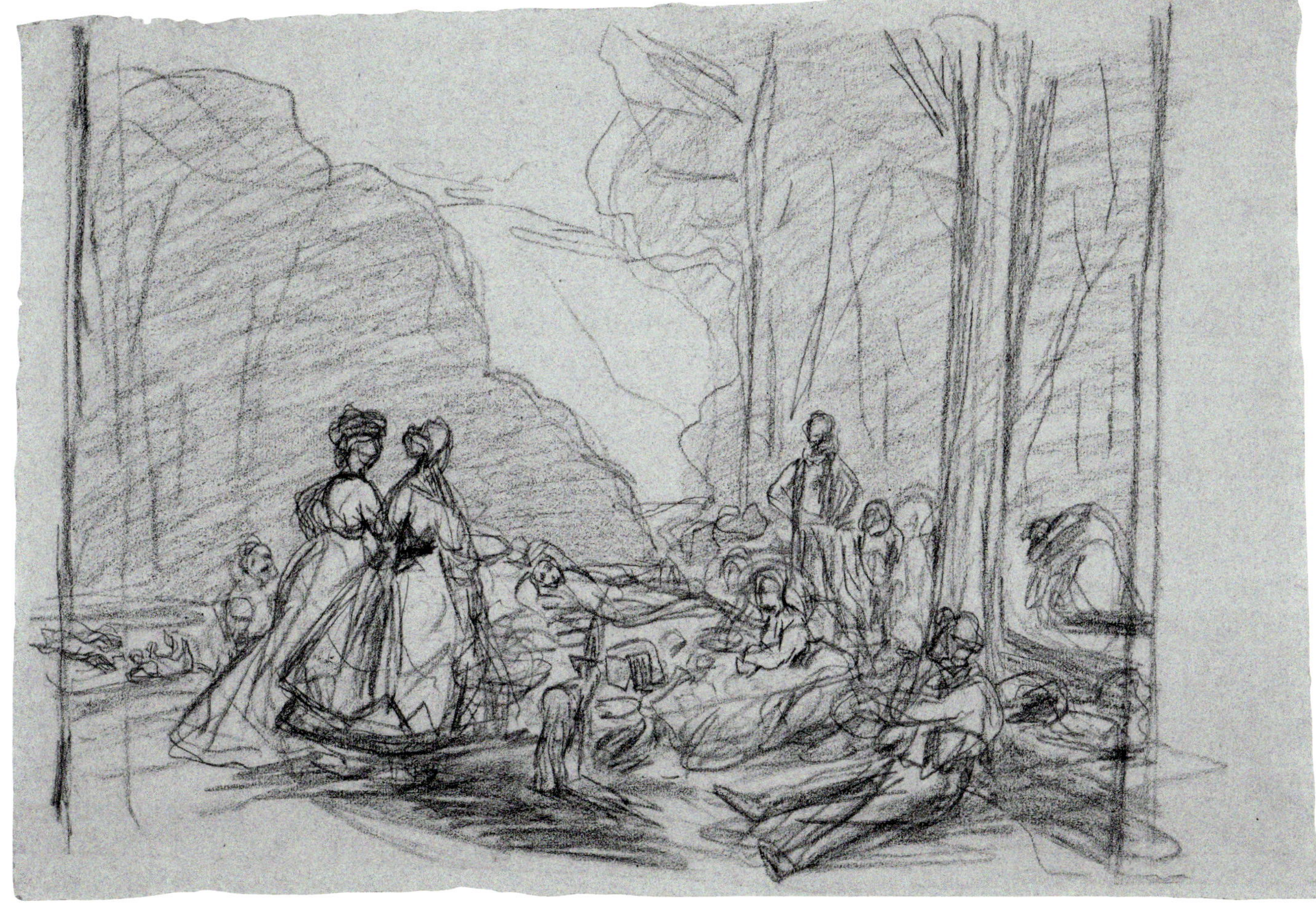

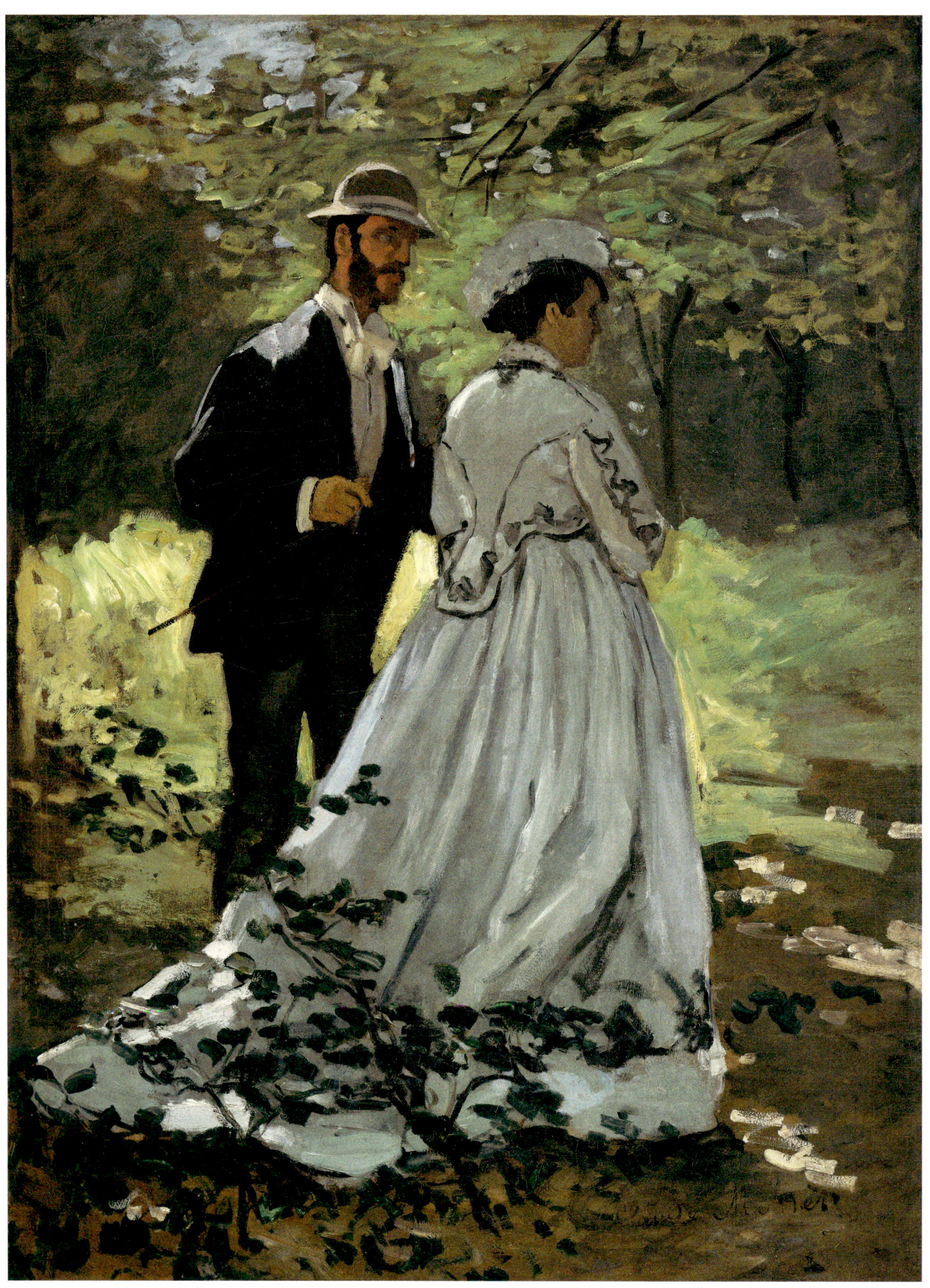

89

Bazille and Camille (Study for "Luncheon on the Grass"), c. 1865. Oil on canvas, 93.5 x 69.5 cm. National Gallery of Art, Washington, D.C. Ailsa Mellon Bruce Collection [W61]

remains a mystery.[83] For the first time, therefore, we are entitled to envisage a significant number of drawings made to aid Monet as he developed a major oil painting on canvas.

Only three such works from his hand appear to have survived, two of them found among Bazille's effects in Montpellier.[84] One was made in a sketchbook with pages a little larger than the black-crayon drawings, seeming to represent a primitive stage in the evolution of Monet's idea for *Luncheon on the Grass* (fig. 87). As crude as the Normandy coastal studies are sophisticated, this sheet shows cartoonlike figures scattered around a relatively open space, with the serpentine form of the famously tall Bazille prostrate in the foreground. Considerably looser in execution than the "scribble" described by Baudelaire in Jongkind's etchings, this drawing offers little more than a diagrammatic summary of the picture's contents, in what was surely some kind of private doodle or *aide mémoire*. The second study (fig. 88), now in the National Gallery in Washington, is more carefully constructed and closer in some respects to the finished painting. Here again, however, Monet showed an almost willful disregard for fine draftsmanship, despite executing the image with sophisticated materials. Using black chalk on bluish laid paper, he introduced meandering lines into the background that are reminiscent of some of Corot's landscape drawings and applied richer strokes to the figures themselves. But these roughly outlined and re-outlined forms are attempts at placement, not at individual articulation, and now recall the even-looser pencil visions of the young Cézanne—some dealing with similar outdoor groups—during this same decade.[85] Like the models depicted in Cézanne's sheets, they owe more to the imagination than to firsthand experience, a departure of an unusual kind for Monet. As with his earlier sketchbook page, this is self-evidently a working study for Monet's own purposes, an almost style-free exploration that reminds us of the sharp distinction between private and public in much of his graphic output.

The most prominent feature in the Washington drawing is the group at left, where two women stand side-by-side in elaborate dresses that reach to the ground. In the final version of the painting, these figures are joined by a black-suited gentleman, who also appears in an intermediate oil study with just one of his female companions (fig. 89). The third known sheet for this composition depicts the woman alone (fig. 90) and is the most decorous of all the preparatory drafts. Based on Camille, the drawing describes little more than her profile and tells us nothing about the person who would bear Monet's first son within two years and become the artist's wife in 1870. Effectively a portrait of a dress, it meticulously records each fold and tuck in what we have recently learnt was the fashion of the moment.[86] Knowing that he would not always have a model available, Monet took careful note of the black trim on bodice, sleeve, and hem, and observed the fall of fabric around Camille's body. This is drawing as documentation, the antithesis of his previous studies for the picture and one that distantly recalls the pencil sketches in his early sketchbooks. As things transpired, Camille's posture must have been reexamined at least twice more, initially for the oil study itself, where Monet swung her right shoulder a little further away from the viewer. In this area of the final, Salon-scale canvas, a section of which is preserved in the Musée d'Orsay, she is again transformed, the earlier drawing forgotten and a new red-trimmed robe bringing her even more up-to-date.[87]

Something of the appearance of his fifteen-by-twenty-foot painting can be deduced from the reduced-scale version in the Pushkin Museum of Fine Arts, Moscow (fig. 91). Despite the advice of many artist friends, including Gustave Courbet himself, Monet was unable to articulate this modern-life tableau to his own satisfaction. Failing to complete it in time for the 1866 Salon, he turned instead to the life-size *Camille, or the Woman with a Green Dress*, which is said to have been painted from life in four days and became an instant sensation with critics and public alike.[88] Especially telling in the Paris fragment of the *Luncheon on the Grass* is the costume of the second woman, where layer upon layer of yellows and ochers

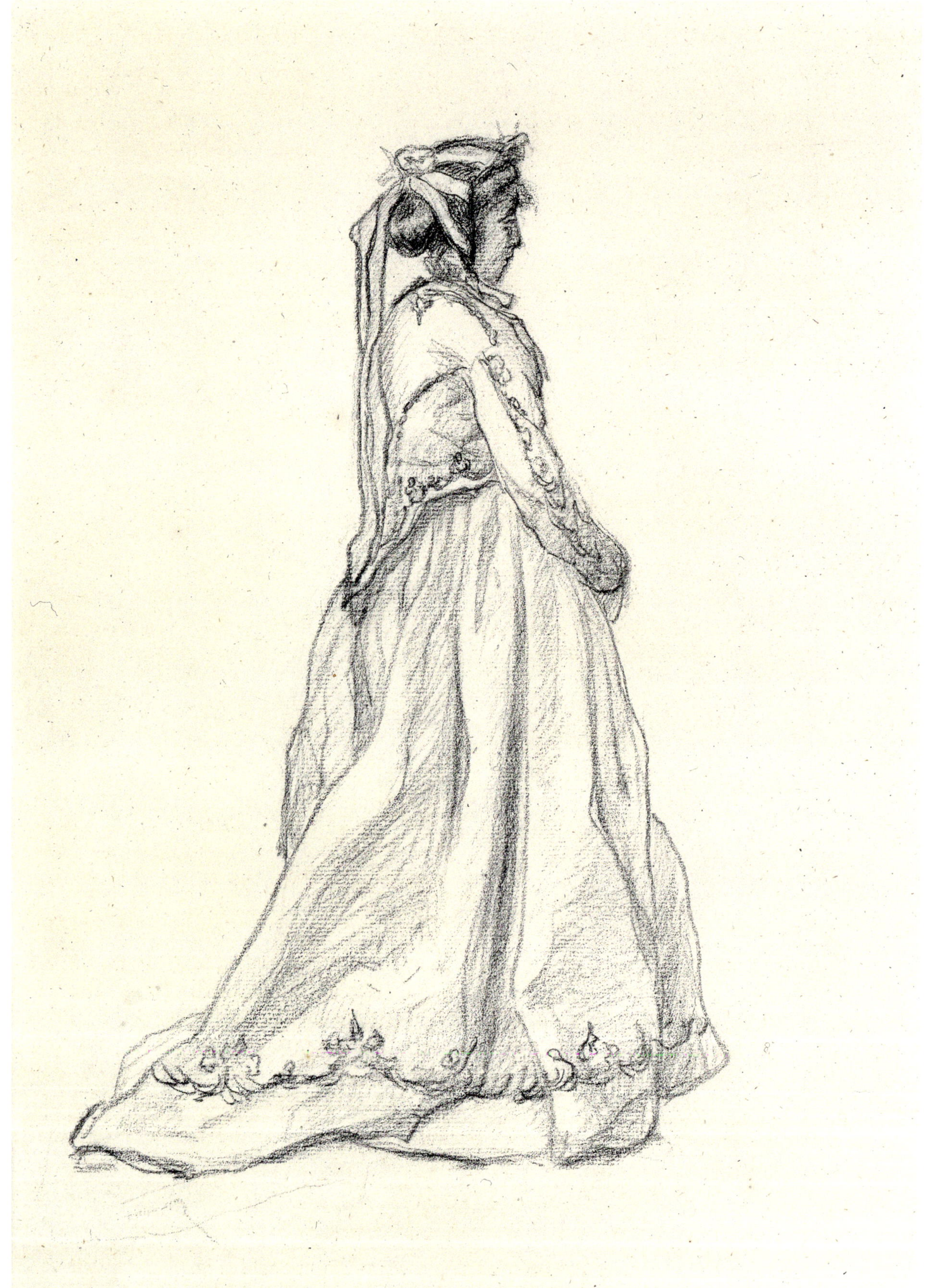

90

Figure of a Woman (Camille), c. 1865. Black chalk, 472 x 315 mm. Family of Richard S. Davis, courtesy of Stiebel, Ltd. [D424]

91

Luncheon on the Grass, 1866. Oil on canvas, 130 x 181 cm. Pushkin Museum of Fine Arts, Moscow [W62]

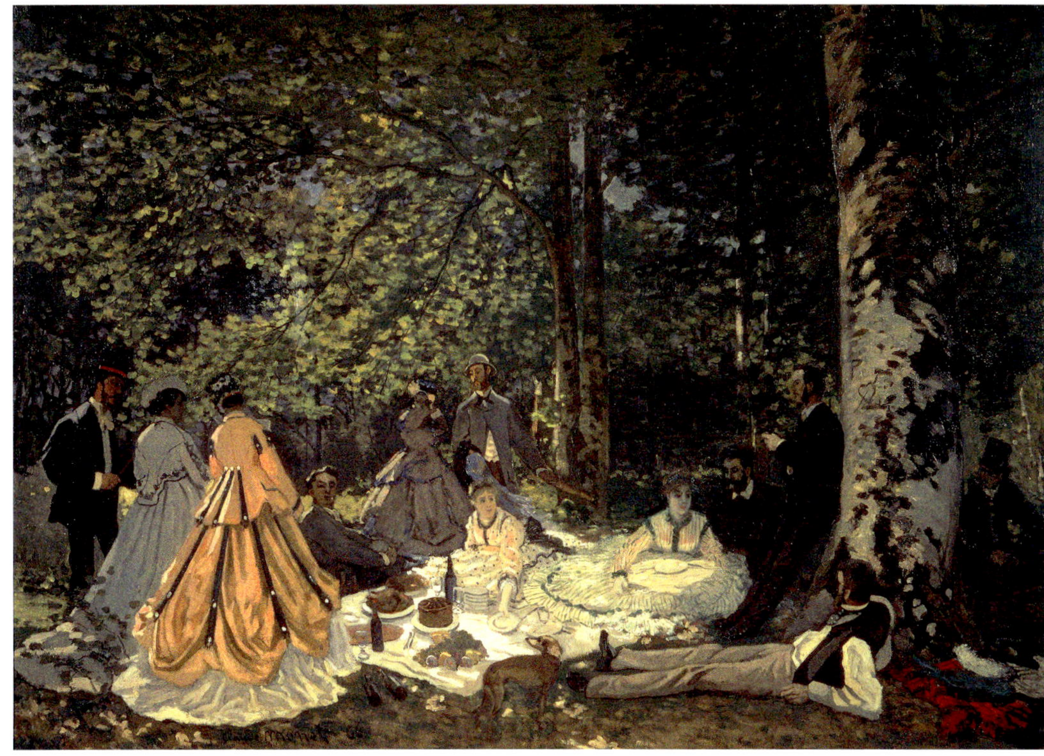

have been brushed onto the canvas, only to be wiped or scraped away by the frustrated artist. Within this stratified residue, countless darker strokes have left evidence of Monet's "drawing" as he defined the latest positions of folds and shadows, or moved the figure itself relative to its neighbors in an attempt to resolve his conundrum. Such linear brushwork undoubtedly lies beneath much of this vast composition, when Monet seems to have abandoned his studies on paper and improvised freely on the picture itself. Defeated by time and soaring ambition, as well as by deficiencies in his craft, Monet once again had reason to reflect on the fundamentals of his art.

Unquestionably a turning point in his early career, the great failed enterprise of the *Luncheon on the Grass* is too easily seen as an exception in the story of Monet's technical development. Striving to outperform Courbet and Manet in sheer painterly audacity, the young man from Le Havre fell back on the skills of the past, paradoxically making drawings from posed models and attempting to draft his extravagant composition on paper. But other evidence from these years now points to a more nuanced narrative. The link between certain of Monet's landscape canvases, such as *Rue de la Bavole, Honfleur* and *The Beach at Honfleur*, and his black-crayon drawings reminds us of the varied and still unresolved character of his working practice. Here it was line that preceded, defined, or accompanied his creations in color, a fact revealed only by the chance survival of the monochrome studies. Other such drawings, apparently now lost, are mentioned in the Beguin Billecocq Grand Journal, which also recalls Monet's characteristic arrival at the Normandy coast with equipment "for drawing and painting."[89] Added to this variegated picture of Monet as an anxious, versatile, and active draftsman is the knowledge that this very period, from the early 1860s to the years preceding the first Impressionist exhibition, was one of the most intense phases in his engagement with pastel.

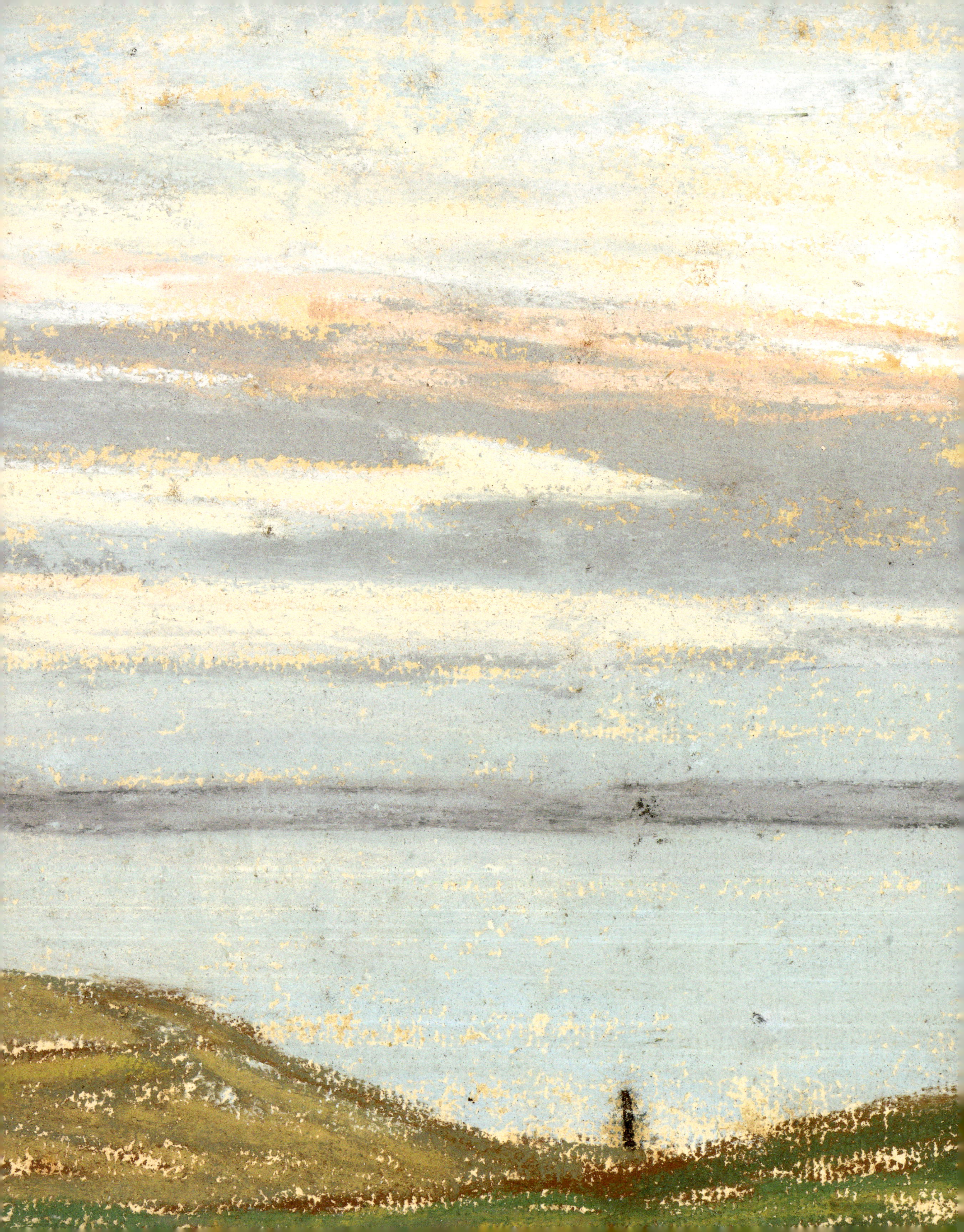

CHAPTER FIVE Monet's Pastels in Public

Claude Monet's public identification with the medium of pastel began surprisingly early, at the first exhibition of the group we now know as the Impressionists. Partly initiated by Monet, this event was held in Paris between April and May of 1874, at the studio of the photographer Nadar on the boulevard des Capucines (fig. 92).[1] The thirty artists involved had adopted an egalitarian approach to their organization and agreed to reject the jury system for the selection of works. Members were thus free to choose their own exhibits, as well as the subject matter, medium, and scale of the objects that best represented them.[2] The result was "strikingly eclectic," in Paul Tucker's words, embracing large canvases and ambitious sculptures by now-obscure individuals, such as Edouard Brandon (1831–1897) and Auguste-Louis-Marie Ottin (1811–1890), and brilliantly hued studies in oil by the figures who are most remembered today: Paul Cézanne, Edgar Degas, Berthe Morisot, Pierre-Auguste Renoir, Alfred Sisley, and Monet himself.[3] Often overlooked in this stylistic and technical mayhem, however, is the sheer quantity and variety of works on paper that were assembled. Félix Bracquemond, for example, opted for a sequence of more than thirty etchings; others presented lithographs, drypoints, drawings, and watercolors; and at least five contributors chose to show pastels.

In the catalogue of the 1874 exhibition, Monet himself listed five canvases, which shrewdly summarized his achievement of recent years: the large, boldly figurative *Luncheon* of 1868; two scenes of Le Havre, including the now-iconic *Impression, Sunrise*; his masterly view from Nadar's premises, *Boulevard des Capucines*; and the emphatically rural *Poppies at Argenteuil*.[4] Since their presentation in 1874, all five pictures have become internationally renowned, not only as emblems of his technical and conceptual precocity but as primary statements of Impressionist themes. Almost no attention, by contrast, has been paid to Monet's other works on display, also itemized in the catalogue and together exceeding in quantity his much-studied paintings. These additional pictures—seven in number—were imprecisely described as *croquis*, or sketches, but the medium in each case was specified as "pastel."[5] Monet left them untitled in the catalogue, following the practice of several other colleagues who referred to such entries simply as "watercolor," "etching," or "drawing."[6] Most of the smaller items of this kind attracted neither the admiration nor the withering scorn

92

Nadar's photograph of his studio at 35 boulevard des Capucines, Paris, c. 1855, the site of the first Impressionist exhibition

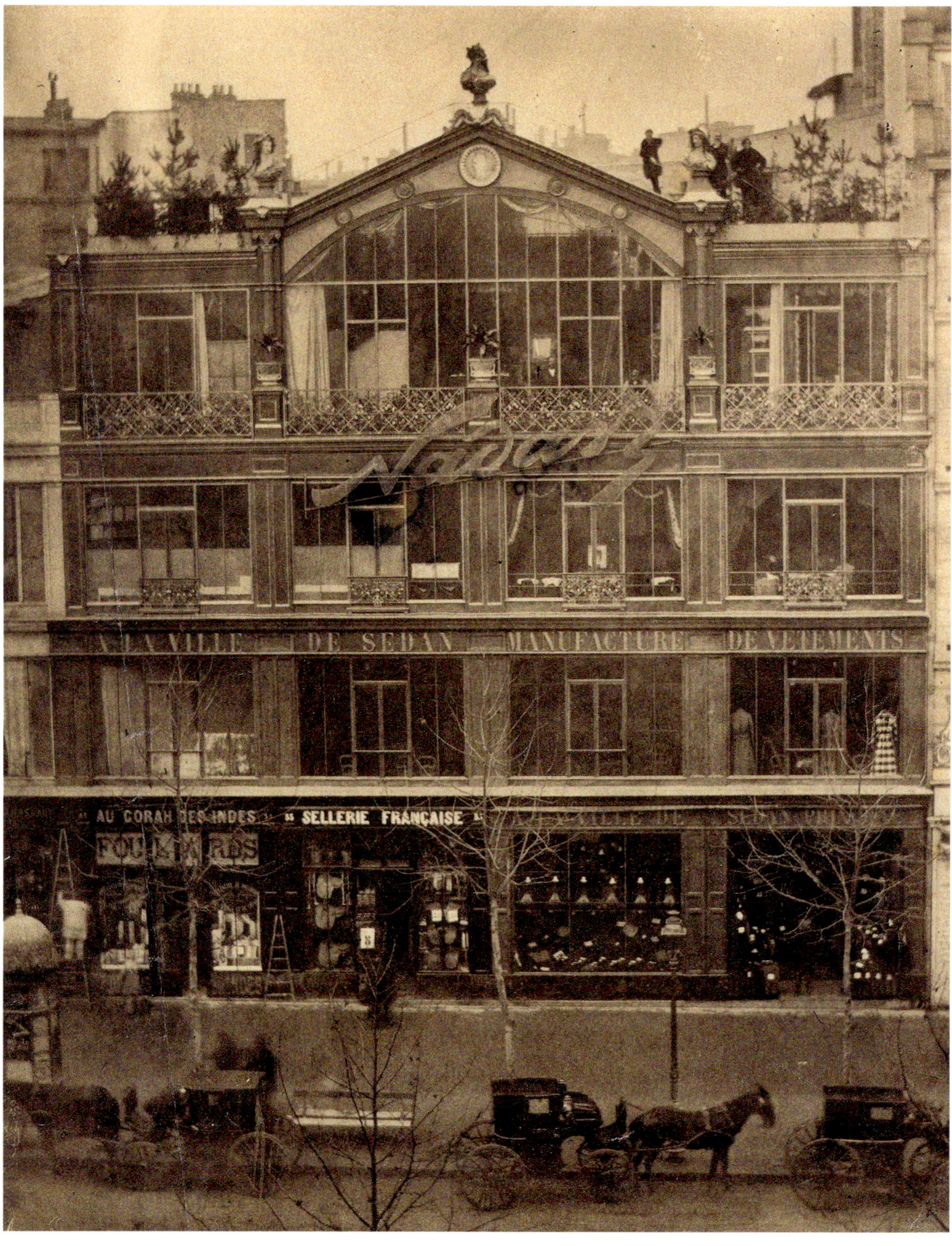

directed at the more conspicuous oil paintings in the exhibition, though Monet's pastels were briefly noted by one critic.[7] More remarkably, however, this neglect of Monet's full range of submissions has persisted into our own day. There has been no extended consideration of the pastels shown in 1874 or of their significance at this formative moment in his career, reflecting a larger disregard for the substantial body of similar works to which they belong.[8]

Monet's decision to include pastels in the first Impressionist exhibition raises a number of questions about his developing self-image as an artist and about the nature of such public displays at this date. At the age of thirty-three, he had yet to see more than two of his pictures accepted for any given exhibition in Paris, and all the works shown had been paintings. The many hundreds of studies on paper that Monet had certainly made were thus largely unknown outside his immediate circle, and there is no evidence that he—unlike Bracquemond and Manet, for example—had ever submitted examples of his graphic output to the Salon.[9] For all young and aspiring artists, opportunities for unveiling their recent work in any medium, to say nothing of controlling its presentation, were effectively curtailed by the dominance of the annual Salon. Provincial exhibitions, dealers' shows, and even impromptu installations in studios or other private premises offered some alternatives and might still have a critical effect on the advancement of a career, just as the choice of pictures for such occasions could initially circumscribe an artistic identity. When Monet chose to submit paintings to exhibitions in Rouen in 1864 and Le Havre in 1868, and cooperated with the Paris dealer Latouche in 1869, he was seizing on such marginal occasions and learning about their drawbacks. At the Rouen show, for example, Monet found that his one featured picture had been omitted from the catalogue and was hung in shadow "where it was completely impossible to see anything," as he reported to Bazille.[10]

Among its many historic and practical significances, the 1874 exhibition at Nadar's studio was crucial in allowing Monet and his peers to influence the presentation of their own art to the Parisian public. At the Salon, oil paintings had traditionally been given pride of place, hung frame-to-frame in several ranks, one above the other, with monumental canvases often reaching the ceiling. Works on paper were also shown in considerable numbers—at the 1874 Salon, for example, there were more than a thousand drawings, watercolors, pastels, and prints—but these were installed in separate rooms and thus at a distance from paintings or sculpture by the artist in question.[11] For the Impressionist generation, many of these practices seemed illogical and irksome. In 1870, Degas had addressed a long letter to the official Salon jury, in which he challenged their restrictive rules and proposed some changes. Benefiting from his experience of exhibiting at the Salon on several previous occasions, Degas argued that the paintings should be arranged more spaciously, with "no more than two rows of pictures" on any wall, and that each exhibitor should be given some say in the hanging of his or her own artifacts. He had also proposed a radical alternative to the scattering of an individual's submissions. Degas urged the Salon managers to "set up large and small screens" that would display drawings in the main galleries, so they became "mixed with the paintings, which they deserve."[12] Over time, the Salon would accommodate certain of these ideas, but in the spring of 1874, the fledgling Impressionist group clearly resolved to take the initiative.

No photographs or engravings of the boulevard des Capucines exhibition have survived, though fragmentary reports by participants, visitors, and critics enable us to reconstruct it in some respects. The previously unhappy experiences of Monet, Degas, and others seem to have been taken into account, as were the principles outlined in Degas's 1870 letter. Large windows along the length of Nadar's façade allowed good natural light for all, and a lottery ensured that there was no favoritism in the choice of position. According to Jules Castagnary, exhibits "were arranged by artist and hung in alphabetical order" and, as Martha Ward explains, "The display was spacious, with works hung in two horizontal rows and with larger works placed on the upper level."[13] Crucially, Ward adds that "Different media were exhibited but no mention made of their location, a fact that suggests that the entire show was probably rigorously governed by the progression of artists' names."[14] The nascent Impressionists, in other words, seem to have grouped together all the exhibits of each participating artist in turn, including paintings, studies on paper, and three-dimensional objects as chosen by the individuals themselves. As at the Salon, larger canvases were still hung above smaller items, though there was considerably more room around the works in general. This led to greater coherence in the arrangement, expressed in the alphabetical sequence that dominated the display. Most significant for our inquiry is the fact that the lower line of small pictures—presumably installed at eye level and embracing oil sketches as well as drawings, watercolors, pastels, and prints—were installed in close proximity to each artist's other submissions and thus contributed to a unified statement of his or her oeuvre. Walking from room to room, visitors would have encountered a series of miniature personal displays, following the sequence of the printed catalogue. At some point, therefore, they advanced from the offerings of the enamellist Alfred Meyer to the paintings of the now-forgotten Auguste de Molins, to arrive at the assembled canvases and pastels of Claude Monet.

In his 1874 installation, Monet chose to integrate pictures in two different media, presenting himself for the first time as a graphic artist, as well as a painter in oils. Given that the overwhelming majority of his pastels produced before this date were landscapes, there would have been an especially marked consonance between his studies on paper and his canvases, notably the three rural and coastal scenes. The Monet of Nadar's studio, in other words, appeared to the public as both a more coherent personality and a more technically versatile artist than has hitherto been acknowledged. He was not alone in taking advantage of this unusual freedom and the chance to parade his multiple skills. Probably on the row beneath his own unequivocally figurative paintings, Degas showed drawings, *essence* studies, and pastels; his friend Henri Rouart (1833–1912) added watercolors and etchings to a suite of Breton landscapes in oils; and Berthe Morisot included several watercolors and pastels with her painted scenes of family life. In total, around half the contributors to this exhibition installed such preparatory or supportive works with their paintings and sculpture, encouraging a more inclusive perception of their craft. Drawing was displayed by some as an activity in its own right, by others as a natural extension of their working procedures, and by many as a validation of their achievement through reference to traditional skills. It also had more pragmatic advantages; the modest prices of works on paper tended to encourage the timid collector and raise the likelihood of sales for their impecunious creators.

At this moment in Monet's career, many of these factors coincided with his drive to define and promote himself in the French capital, as he struggled to keep creditors at bay. As we now know from the Beguin Billecocq Grand Journal, Monet had been a prodigious draftsman in his youth and continued to produce drawings of many kinds throughout the 1850s and 1860s. The inclusion of pastels in his 1874 installation was a natural extension of this habit and a frank declaration of his continued graphic activity. Monet's display may also have carried more personal meanings. It is easily forgotten that a senior contributor to this same installation was the artist Monet regarded as his first master, Eugène Boudin, presumably encouraged to participate by the former pupil.[15] Significantly, Boudin himself also grouped together a balance of oil paintings and other works in Nadar's spaces, choosing three canvases of the Atlantic coast, four watercolors, and six pastels, among which were two of unspecified subjects and four entitled "sky studies."[16] More than a decade earlier, Baudelaire's rapture before the "prodigious enchantments of air and water" in Boudin's pastels had briefly highlighted the artist's originality. In the 1874 exhibition, further examples of these works were a reminder of Boudin's historical precedence and authority, and an unspoken endorsement of Monet's artistic lineage. Though most critics made no reference to Boudin on this occasion, his presence must have resonated for Monet on several thematic and perhaps sentimental levels. Monet's decision to introduce seven pastels of his own seems to acknowledge this, as did certain of his other choices. Hanging above, but in close proximity to his pastels, would have been his two canvases of Le Havre, the site of the first meeting between the two men. Both pictures depicted harbors and clusters of sail- and steamboats, motifs painted countless times by Boudin himself and perhaps offered here as another act of homage to Monet's mentor from Normandy.

A further element in Monet's selection of works, not just on this occasion but in later exhibitions, was a well-documented competitiveness with members of his own generation.

93

Edgar Degas, *Houses by the Sea*, c. 1869. Pastel, 314 x 465 mm. Musée du Louvre, Paris

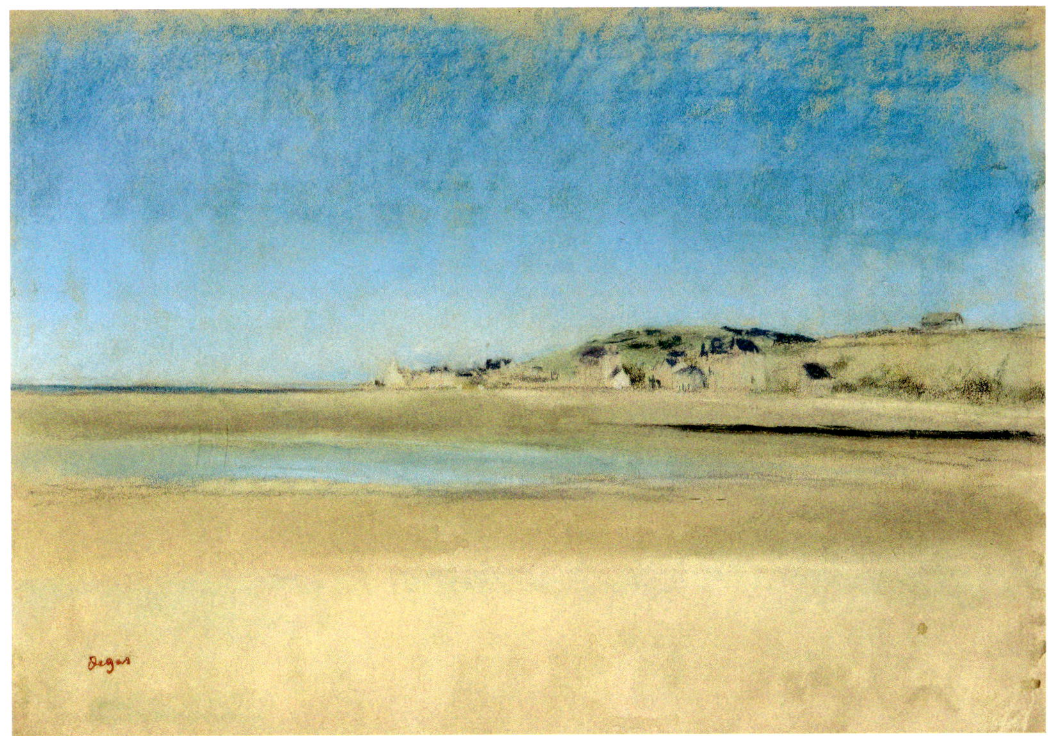

Apart from Boudin, the three other artists known to have shown pastels in 1874 were among Monet's closest professional collaborators in this enterprise: Renoir, Morisot, and Degas. Renoir had chosen to augment his group of paintings with an untitled and still unidentified "croquis, pastel"; Morisot offered three large, highly finished pastels that the critics found "charming," "full of light and vigor," and "delicious"; while the pastel *Laundress* presented by Degas was considered to be "among the outstanding works in the exhibition" by the pseudonymous critic, Marc de Montifaud.[17] As a fellow-organizer of the exhibition, Monet would almost certainly have been aware of his colleagues' growing engagement with this medium and their intention to display pastels on the boulevard des Capucines. Morisot had recently shown pastels at the 1872 and 1873 Salons, following Degas's similar success in 1870 with his pastel portrait of Morisot's sister, Yves Gobillard.[18] Monet may also have known about the suite of pastels of the Normandy coast made by Degas in the summer of 1869, including such expansive and frankly observed works as *Houses by the Sea* (fig. 93). Among the most unexpected and still unsung achievements of this period, Degas's inventive scenes of harbors, dunes, and beaches also seem to show an awareness of Boudin's work and a remarkably liberated approach to color and light.[19] Other colleagues, such as Pissarro and Sisley, had recently been investigating the potential of pastel, though most were relative beginners and chose not to show their efforts in 1874.

In such company, Monet had many reasons to demonstrate his mastery of pastel, and even to claim precedence over his peers. Contrasting with the controlled touch of Degas and the refinement of Morisot, Monet's vigorous pastel technique was already based on a decade of active experimentation, substantially longer than all but his most immediate rival, Degas. Even more remote from Monet's accomplishments were those of artists such as Renoir (fig. 94), Morisot, Cassatt, and Caillebotte, whose acquaintance with pastel had barely begun at this date. As a pastellist of the landscape, however, Monet was unquestionably the leader among his Impressionist contemporaries at the time of their first group exhibition, with at least sixty documented works already to his credit. The fact that Monet could present himself in 1874 as the preeminent maker of such

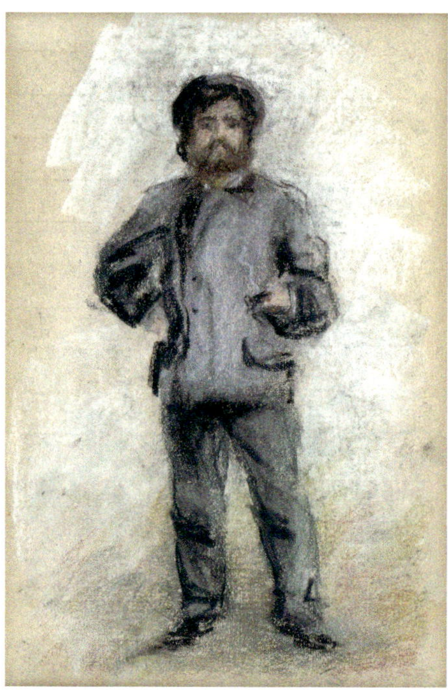

94
Pierre-Auguste Renoir (French, 1841–1919), *Portrait of Claude Monet*, 1875. Pastel, 440 x 330 mm. Musée Marmottan Monet, Paris

pastels is an astonishingly unexplored feature of his career. In the most immediate sense, it invites a detailed analysis of his pre-1874 pastel oeuvre and a consideration of his relationship with the medium in its broader historical context. Within this inquiry, the specific lack of information about the pastels shown by the artist in 1874 is inevitably taxing. Given that all but a fraction of his pastel output prior to this date consisted of rural and marine scenes, it seems highly likely that his exhibits conformed to this pattern. While several candidates have been proposed, among them *Broad Landscape* (see fig. 113) and *View of the Sea at Sunset* (see fig. 111), their claims seem to lack documentary support.[20] Such uncertainty, however, does not distract from the fundamental significance of Monet's decision to display this substantial cluster of works on paper. At the Impressionists' first collective exhibition, he chose to advertise his fluency in the making of both large and small-scale pictures, and his familiarity with several genres. And on the first occasion in his career when he could offer a self-selected body of work to a Parisian audience, Monet was visibly willing, perhaps eager, to be judged on the merits of his pastels.

Pastel in Monet's Public Career

How much do we know about Monet the pastellist before and after 1874? With the publication of the fifth volume of Daniel Wildenstein's catalogue raisonné in 1991, much new documentary and visual information concerning Monet's graphic activity became available, and the possibility of a critical survey of his pastel oeuvre emerged. One of many revelations from the Wildenstein archives was the extent of this little-known oeuvre: setting aside a number of dubious works and manifest forgeries—themselves a token of an established awareness of Monet's pastels—Wildenstein listed a total of one hundred and eight items.[21] Almost all of them are fully resolved compositions rather than casual sketches or unfinished drafts, and a substantial proportion are signed by the artist. Though few of the pastels are large—the exception is a trio of portraits on canvas, measuring 730 millimeters on their longest side—around a third approach half a meter in width.[22] Unsurprisingly, they are dominated by scenes of the sea and of cliffs, forests and farms, and by a variety of boating and pastoral subjects. Additionally, there is a score of discreet explorations of light over the river Thames, a few pastels of figures and animals, and a small number of purely domestic images.

Writing of this body of works in the final part of his publication, Daniel Wildenstein pointed out that "the study of the pastels has raised more questions than any other chapter in this volume, even in the entire catalogue raisonné."[23] Today, two principal issues still beset this subject. The first concerns the physical accessibility of Monet's pastels, which are exceptionally dispersed throughout the world's private collections and represented in just a handful of public institutions. As a consequence, few have been the subject of detailed technical or scholarly examination, while large numbers of pastels have disappeared from view for periods of half a century or more. Adding to this elusiveness is the second factor: the question of when Monet made these pictures and the phases of his main activity as a pastellist. Over ninety percent of the total output of pastels lacks any indication of a date in the artist's own hand and even some of the exceptions to this pattern have been challenged.[24] Wildenstein does not offer conjectural dates but arranges the works in a temporal sequence that takes into account the available documentary information. This evidence includes events in Monet's life that are related to the pastels' subjects or first owners; motifs linked in various ways to reliably situated oil paintings; and contextual references to early collectors, exhibitions, and publications. Such clusters as the family portraits of the early 1880s and the London pastels, which are firmly datable on both internal and external evidence, provide valuable points of reference, as do several works that are clearly associated with recorded visits to Monet's favorite locations. Toward the end of his life, Monet's voluminous

95
At Sea, c. 1860–70. Pastel, 210 x 420 mm. Private collection [P29]

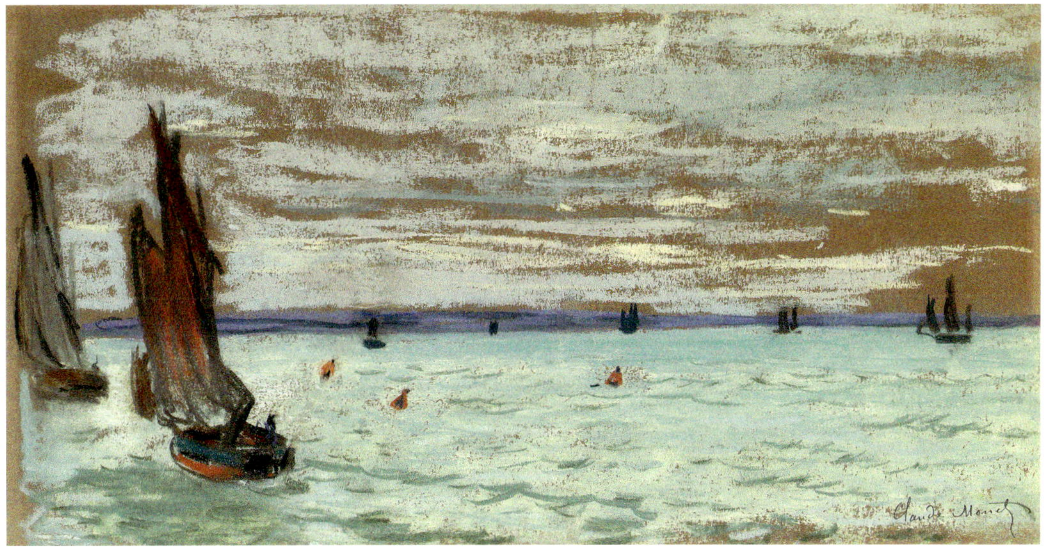

correspondence adds to this narrative, referring briefly to the dispersal of certain pastels and the making of the London scenes. This incomplete account, however, and the properly cautious approach adopted by the cataloguer, leaves us in no doubt that Monet's pastel oeuvre begins in his early Normandy years and ultimately reaches into the twentieth century.

If the current location and speculative dating of many of Monet's pastels remain problematic, the accumulated detail of their early histories can be revelatory. Almost from the beginning, it seems, a substantial number of pastels were given or sold by the artist to his close friends, some in circumstances that can be partially reconstructed. Before his untimely death in 1870, Frédéric Bazille, Monet's companion on early painting trips to Normandy, apparently acquired *Sainte-Adresse, the Villas*, a pastel depicting a site they had certainly visited together.[25] Another pastel related to Monet's paintings of this region is *Honfleur, Fishing Boat*, a work that belonged to the Realist novelist and art critic Edmond Duranty. Before he, too, died prematurely, Duranty was a leading theorist of Impressionism, writing admiringly of Monet at the time of the fourth group exhibition in 1879 and effectively crediting him, alongside Jongkind and Boudin, with the creation of the "school of bright sunshine."[26] The personal doctor and intimate of Pissarro, Van Gogh, and others, Paul Gachet (1828–1894) is recorded as the original owner of a woodland scene in pastel, *The Edge of the Forest*, while the composer Emmanuel Chabrier, an acquaintance of Degas and Manet during these years, collected no less than three of Monet's works in the medium.[27] One of these pastels carries a dedication from the artist to Chabrier himself, while the remaining two, which included *Study of Five Boys* (see fig. 108), are unusual in belonging to the very earliest works catalogued by Wildenstein.[28] Another intimate connection concerns a group of five pastels owned by Jean-Baptiste Faure, the renowned baritone at the Paris Opéra, who also accumulated a major collection of Impressionist canvases.[29] When Monet stayed at Faure's house in Étretat in 1885, he presented his host with at least some of the pastels in question, which Faure presumably hung with his two canvases of local scenes painted by the artist on the same trip.[30]

Beyond these private associations, it becomes clear that Monet was also willing to sell pastels and otherwise allow them into public circulation throughout much of his working life. In February 1876, perhaps prompted by his debut as a pastellist two years earlier, a scene of ships off the Normandy coast (fig. 95) was bought by Victor Chocquet, the courageous early patron of Cézanne, Renoir, and Monet himself.[31] The timing of his purchase and the nature of its subject, which is close to one of the marine views in Monet's 1874 installation, may even

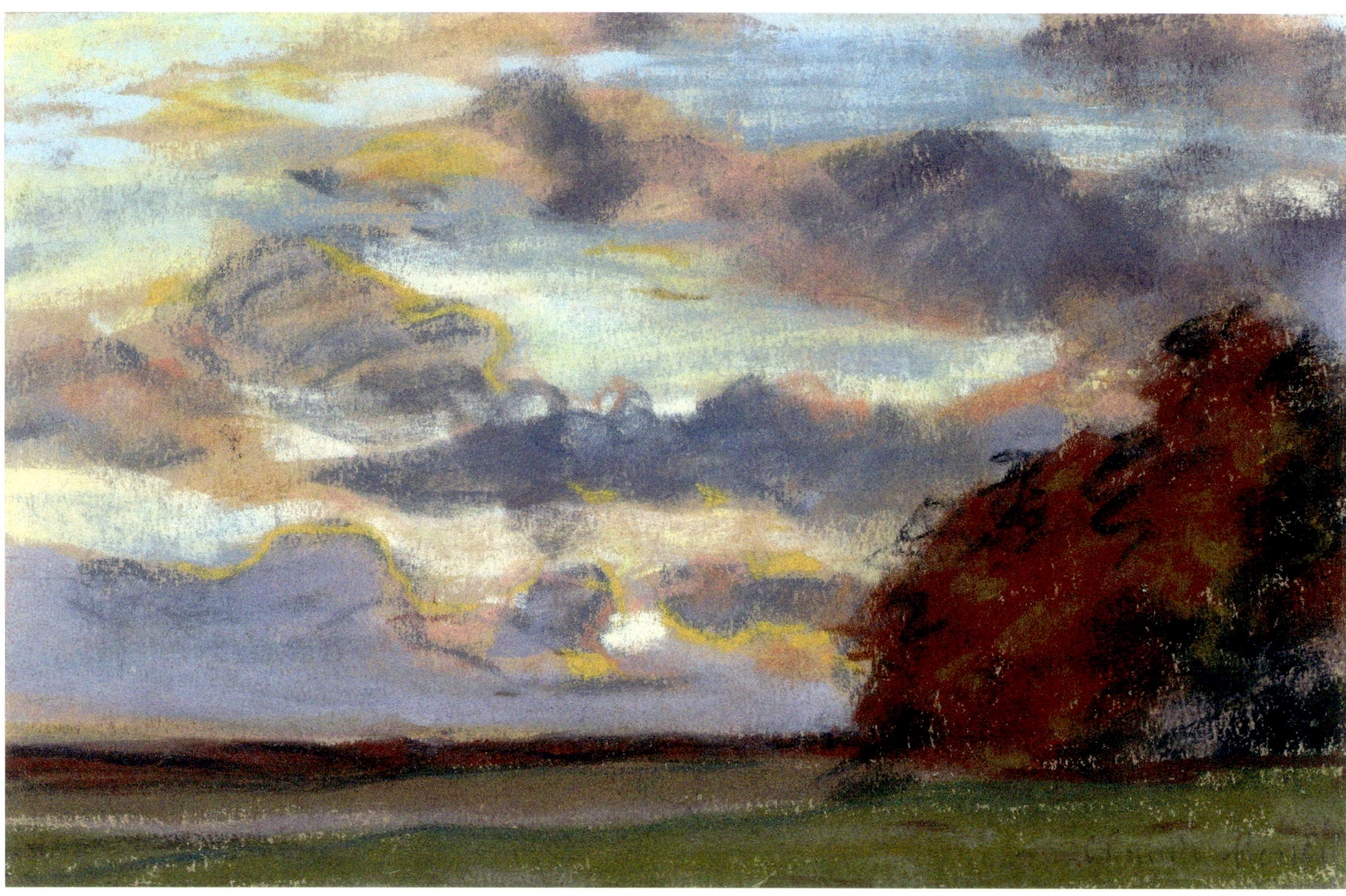

96
Sunset, c. 1865–70. Pastel, 210 x 315 mm. Private collection [P54]

indicate that Chocquet's pastel was among the seven works shown at that time. It is clear, however, that the two men did not meet until two years later; a letter from Monet written on 4 February 1876 reveals that Cézanne was about to introduce him to Chocquet, when the reclusive government employee added one of Monet's paintings—and perhaps the pastel—to his growing collection of Impressionist art.[32] Another pastel of a coastal subject joined Chocquet's holdings at an unrecorded date and—like the first—was sold at auction in 1899, when his widow died.[33] These studies thus joined a large and important group of at least fifty pastels that appeared on the market during Monet's lifetime, the majority following sales or gifts that have not been recorded in detail. Equally evident is that buyers of many kinds were anxious to acquire these pastels as they became available, including individuals from France, Germany, Britain, Russia, America, and Japan. Among these was the Russian collector Ivan Stchoukine, who amassed a celebrated gallery of paintings and pastels by Degas, Gauguin, Cézanne, Matisse, and Picasso. Before the turn of the century, Stchoukine purchased two pastels by Monet: a study of a Normandy headland, *Sainte-Adresse, Rocks at the Cap de la Hève*, and a dramatic view of the cliffs near Étretat (see fig. 139) though he apparently sold both within a few years.[34] One of the last documented lifetime sales was that of *The Thames in Fog* (see fig. 254), said to have been purchased directly from Monet in 1924 by a Mr. S. Yamashita and later given to the Bridgestone Museum of Art in Tokyo.[35]

In the decades immediately before his death in 1926, Monet would have witnessed a marked increase in the currency of his pastels, which were widely bought and sold, displayed by a number of art dealers in Paris, and formally exhibited in France, Germany, the United States, and elsewhere. By 1891, Durand-Ruel had bought two small sky studies at auction

97

Boats on a Beach. Lithograph after a drawing from c. 1864 by Claude Monet, 108 x 219 mm. From *Book of the Homeless*, ed. Edith Wharton (New York: Charles Scribner's Sons, 1916), pp. 100–101 [D432]

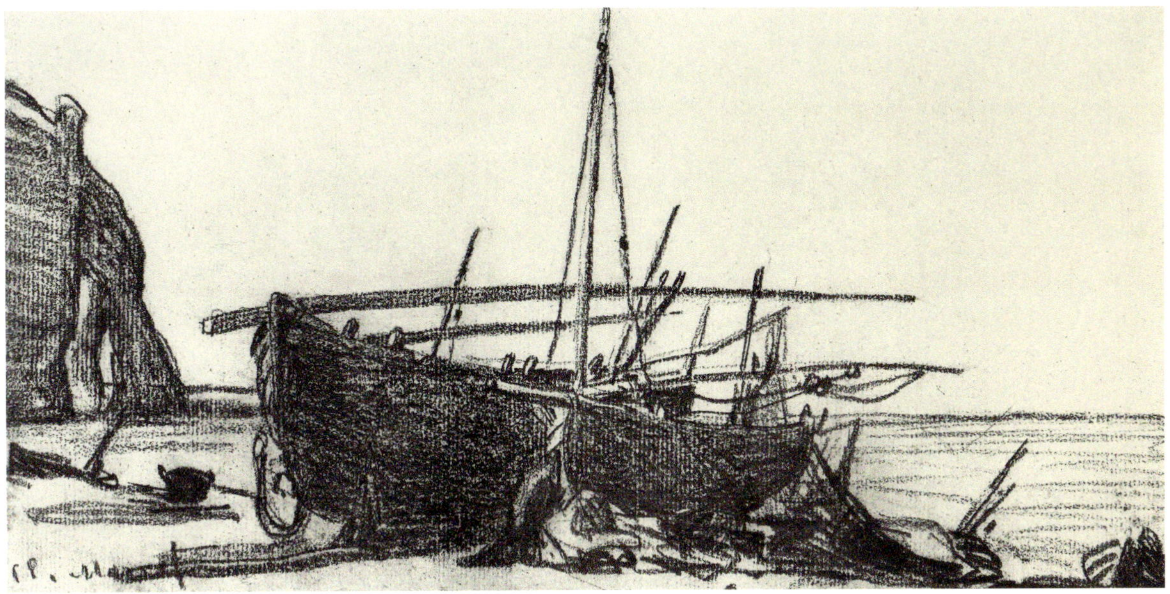

(see figs. 111 and 113), later selling them to the collector William T. Blake, who returned with them to Boston, Massachusetts; in 1906, a work from the beginning of the artist's career, *Yport and the Falaise d'Aval* (see fig. 59) was shown by Bernheim-Jeune, one of several dealers who competed to exhibit Monet's production in later life; in that same year, Bernheim-Jeune also acquired the pastel *Trees in Winter* and in 1909 added *The Clouds* to their stock, before Mme Sacha Guitry chose it for her collection.[36] Other works passed through the hands of Hector Brame, Georges Petit (fig. 96), and their colleagues, while Monet's reputation as a pastellist was spread abroad at Cassirer's gallery, Berlin, in 1909, and at the Kunstsalon Wolfberg, Zurich, in 1912.[37] According to Wildenstein's records, the same *Yport and the Falaise d'Aval* that earlier belonged to Bernheim-Jeune traveled widely in these years, appearing in Dusseldorf in 1911 and Leipzig in 1912, before returning once more to Paris. Especially noteworthy is the rapid dissemination of nine and perhaps more of Monet's London pastels, executed in 1901 but already present in personal collections and in the art trade from 1903 onward.[38]

An even greater exposure must have resulted from Monet's donation of pastels to charitable auctions, among them two events in aid of victims of World War I, in which the artist's own son Michel was currently bearing arms. One such offering was *Landscape with Houses* (see fig. 114), an austere scene given to a 1916 fundraising effort in New York and perhaps chosen by the artist for its solemnity.[39] The elegant volume edited by Edith Wharton for this occasion, *The Book of the Homeless*, also featured a monochrome drawing by Monet (fig. 97), along with studies by Sargent, Renoir, and Rodin, and texts by writers such as Henry James and William Butler Yeats.[40] Remarkably, Monet's pastel was reproduced in color, apparently the first time this occurred with one of his works on paper. Two other pastels had arrived in the United States some years earlier, as part of the collection of Theodate Pope Riddle, while one of the works formerly belonging to Victor Chocquet also crossed the Atlantic and was reputedly exhibited at the Metropolitan Museum of Art in 1924.[41] The earliest pastels to enter the collection of an American institution, however, were probably the two glowing sheets from the 1860s purchased by William T. Blake (see figs. 111 and 113), who presented them to the Museum of Fine Arts in Boston in 1922.

Among the prominent figures in the art world who owned Monet's pastels was the actor and pioneer filmmaker Sacha Guitry, who incorporated a brief sequence showing the artist at work on his *Water Lilies* in the remarkable

1915 film *Ceux de Chez Nous*. Several authors were similarly honored. Jean Dauberville, who collaborated with Guitry on his memoirs and later wrote on Impressionism, Bonnard, and other artists, was given a pastel in 1918.[42] The novelist Marçel Tendron, who wrote under the name of Marc Elder and published one of the earliest illustrated books on Monet in 1924, was presented in 1920 with two fiery sky studies (see figs. 103 and 104) for the collection of the Musée des Beaux-Arts at Nantes in Brittany, where they effectively became the first pastels by Monet to enter a public collection.[43] At an unknown date, the patron and intimate of the Nabis, Thadée Natanson, added an unusually vaporous pastel from the Thames series to his already considerable holdings of contemporary art, possibly during one of his visits to Monet at Giverny.[44] Changing hands yet again, *Yport and the Falaise d'Aval* (see fig. 59) was given in 1924 to Camille Mauclair, a senior chronicler of the Impressionist movement, some time after it appeared at public auction in Paris.[45] Of more local significance were works in the possession of Monet's friends and neighbors at Giverny, including the Comte Jacques de La Lombardière and Dr. Rivière, who received *Normandy Farm under Trees* and *The Seine at Giverny*, respectively.[46]

Monet's lifelong willingness to release his pastels into the larger world is crucial in defining their status: these were manifestly public images, not secretive experiments. Still in need of close study, however, is the place of Monet's pastels in the wider history of the medium and in his emerging identity as an artist, subjects on which he was entirely mute. Several aspects demand attention, among them the possibility that his attitude toward pastel changed radically across the decades. After 1874, Monet never again included pastels in exhibitions of his own work that he organized or selected, despite the fact that several—as we have seen—were shown in the early twentieth century in a variety of commercial and institutional settings, apparently with his blessing. Significant also was the occasional display of Monet pastels in dealers' shows alongside examples of his works on canvas, notably at Bernheim-Jeune in 1906 and 1922, and the first appearances of his pastels in museum exhibitions.[47] In the last quarter-century of his life, these small, radiant images made their contribution to his growing reputation in a number of ways. From their appearance as reproductions in books to the rapid spread of his pastels of London, Monet's graphic art had begun to take its place in history.

Line versus Color, Pastel versus Painting

In retrospect, Monet's decision to exclude pastels from his post-1874 exhibitions appears tied to his career-long effort to encourage specific perceptions of his art and persona. Gradually lowering his visibility as a draftsman as he emerged onto the public stage, Monet had increasingly concentrated the art world's attention on the ambitious nature of his oil painting. In his forties, Monet presented an outward stance as a leading painter of the modern age, following in the heroic tradition that had produced Delacroix, Courbet, and Manet, while placing an even-greater emphasis on impulsive, unrehearsed creativity. Texts written by his supporters in the 1880s stressed the immediacy and physicality of his art, accompanied by claims that Monet's canvases were made "in direct contact with the observed scene," by a painter who had "great facility with the brush: his touch is broad and swift," as Théodore Duret claimed.[48] Drawing was rarely mentioned and even the need for a studio was questioned: interviewed by Emile Taboureux in 1880, Monet is said to have protested, "I don't understand why anybody should want to shut themselves up in some room. Maybe for drawing, sure; but not for painting."[49] In 1889, another admirer conceded that Monet might begin a canvas with "a few charcoal lines," but insisted on the way "he attacks the painting all at once," completing it in "hardly an hour and sometimes much less."[50] Central to all these images was the brush rather than the pencil, which Monet actively engaged in his visual and tactile dialogues with the motif. Here, it seems, there was little room

98

Léon Riesener (French, 1808–1878), *Portrait of Mademoiselle Ehrler*, 1861. Pastel and charcoal, 1,300 x 974 mm. Musée du Petit Palais, Paris

for the preparatory sketch, the pondered design, or even the study in pastel.

From his first childish lessons in drawing and painting at Le Havre and his subsequent studies in Paris, Monet had encountered the complex historical resonance that surrounded all such statements and practices. Pastel, too, had its traditions and its symbolism, as well as a longstanding, contentious association with academic principles. Despite its deep roots in French art over preceding centuries, pastel had typically been marginalized as a hybrid technique, lacking the rigor of pure drawing on one hand and the rich complexity of oil painting on the other. Neither truly linear nor expressive of the full gamut of color, pastel rarely merited the most serious consideration. In his monumental *Grammaire des arts du dessin* of 1867, Charles Blanc briefly encapsulated this prejudice, arguing that pastel was best suited to representing "the brilliant tints of a young girl, the flesh of a child," and alerting his readers to the medium's physical frailty, a "tendency to fall into dust."[51] Blanc openly condescended toward the "feminine" qualities of pastels, contrasting them unfavorably with the "masculine" vigor of painting and suggesting their use to artists who wished merely "to capture fleeting colors."[52] A work such as *Portrait of Mademoiselle Ehrler* (fig. 98), made shortly before the publication of Blanc's book, neatly exemplified many of his assumptions. The artist, Léon Riesener (1808–1878), was a cousin of Delacroix and later a friend of the Morisot family who also used pastel for some atmospheric sketches of the Normandy coast.[53] Riesener's life-size portrait, however, seems to aspire to the condition of painting, while simultaneously exploiting the charms of its subject and the more ingratiating qualities of pastel itself. Hardly likely to raise the status of pastel in Blanc's eyes, this picture and many like it might well have been considered an affront to any artist or aesthete of principle.

In the early years of Impressionism, the public image of pastel was still defined and actively perpetuated by writers such as Blanc. Works in the medium tended to be smaller than oil paintings and only exceptionally—through the

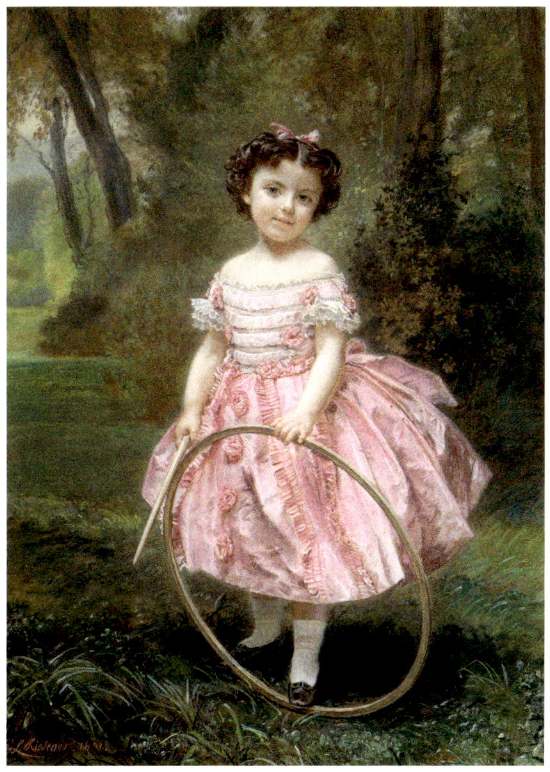

pasting together of several sheets of paper—achieved the grander pretensions of a major Salon canvas.[54] Inferior in scale and supposedly in durability, they were often assumed to be limited in creative ambition. Subjects typically chosen by pastellists included still lifes, flowers, landscapes, and domestic scenes, and the less rigorous kind of portrait—such as Riesener's—that concerned themselves with "the brilliant tints of a young girl." Artists of many callings, however, had continued to use the medium in their studios or in their outdoor exercises, especially when developing a composition for an oil painting or when working from motifs whose principal attraction lay in their colors. Delacroix's small, richly textured renderings of biblical themes, and his sketches of sunsets and North African scenes, are cases in point. But the association of pastel with women artists, whether amateur or professional, was also part of the established character of the medium, as Blanc's rhetoric clearly implied. From the eighteenth-century society portraits of Élisabeth Vigée-Lebrun to the more vivacious representations of family and friends by Berthe Morisot—a colleague much esteemed by Monet—pastel crucially lacked the "masculine" qualities of great art. Against this background, the reluctance of a highly ambitious male painter like Monet to be openly defined as a maker of pastels becomes a little more comprehensible.

Other factors contributed to Monet's ambivalence about pastel. At the hands of Ochard, Troyon, and Gleyre, the young artist had rapidly developed an aversion to the academic norms to which Blanc still clung. Dismissing their obsession with the purity of line and finding the strictures of figure-drawing arbitrary, he soon reverted to landscape and to an informal draftsmanship inspired by quite different traditions. For Monet and his fellow *pleinairistes*, the distinctions between line and color, the pencil and the brush, lost much of their significance, as a new set of priorities and techniques emerged. Critics at their first exhibitions often challenged them for this very reason, using the language of the past to note their supposed inability to draw and compose in the orthodox manner. Etienne Carjat railed against the group in 1874, announcing that "form" was "despised by them all, because it requires laborious and patient study," then damned their pictures as lacking "a well ordered subject, correct and animated drawing."[55] Paradoxically, Degas and those among his acolytes who shared his preoccupation with the figure were often spared such scorn. Noting that he was trained by a follower of Ingres, one writer argued that Degas "makes war on drawing with the weapons of draftsmanship," while Jules Castagnary simply exclaimed: "What precision there is to his drawing!"[56] Two years later, the critic Arthur Baignères summarized this polarity in perceptive and specifically historical terms, asking of the leading Impressionists: "Will they pass for masters one day? They might; then Degas will take the place that Ingres holds now, while that of Delacroix is saved for Claude Monet, the dazzling colorist of the group."[57]

This insight into the competing personalities of Monet and Degas also illuminates their respective attitudes to pastel. It is almost a commonplace to point out that an artist using pastel draws and colors in a single act: a line made in the medium is, by its nature, a mark of a certain hue, which will soon be joined by other strokes to form a mass of variegated color. As more of Degas's works in pastel were exhibited, his admirers came to celebrate this fusion of traditionally competing qualities in his art. In 1880, Joris-Karl Huysmans rhapsodized over a series of pastel portraits and dance images that revealed his exceptional achievement, now aligning Degas with Ingres's most famous rival. "No painter since Delacroix," he wrote, "has understood like Degas the marriage and adultery of colors; none today have a draftsmanship as precise and grand, a range of color as delicate."[58] Pastel, it seems, allowed the "Ingriste" Degas to lean toward Delacroix, reveling in color as much as in line. The reverse, it can be argued, applied to Monet, the youthful master of rural sketching who found that pastel integrated his draftsmanship with a passion for color in the natural world.

Pastel in Early Impressionism

For Monet and his circle, pastel had enormous potential: it could be used casually, spread in gossamer-thin veils or in dense, dynamic strokes of saturated hue and built up into multi-layered crusts that rivaled brushwork. It was also susceptible to manipulation on the paper surface, merging its powdery traces with previously applied colors and excelling in the representation of clouds, shadows, and reflections. Almost all the leading Impressionists adopted pastel to some extent, Caillebotte making landscapes on supports so large that they rivaled his canvases, and Degas and Cassatt choosing it as the principal vehicle of their maturity. Common to many of them was the sense that pastel could be remodeled to suit their energetic new art. As with Monet and Degas, there was also a marked tendency to narrow the divide between pastel and oil painting, by variously tackling the same themes and pictorial aspirations, and exploiting similar palettes and ranges of values in both media. They were also aware that their immediate

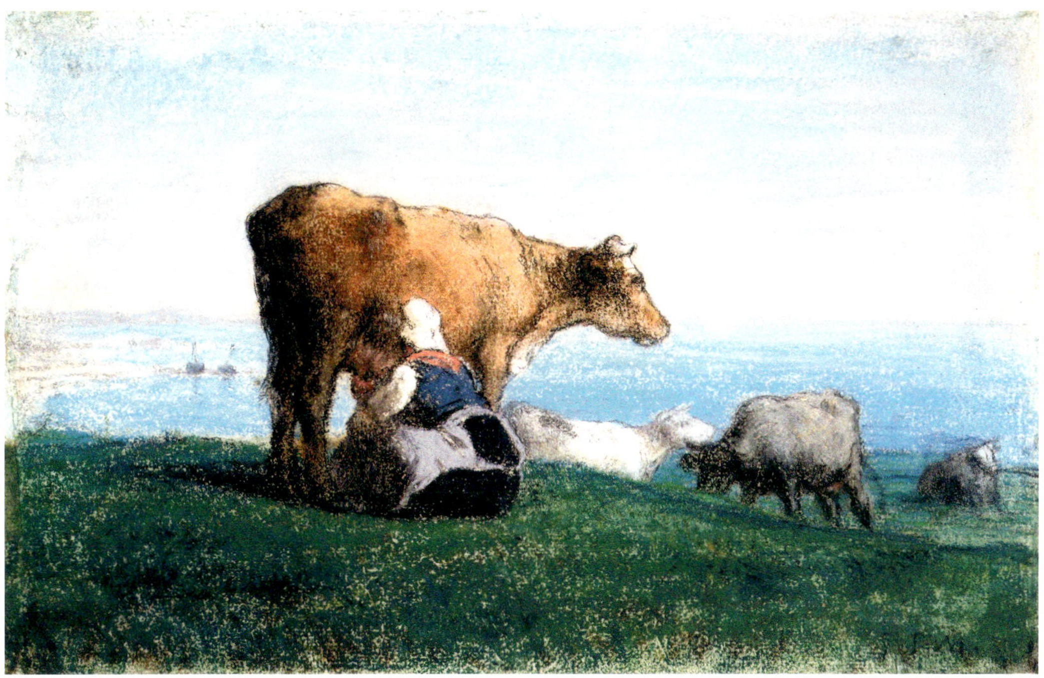

99
Jean-François Millet (French, 1814–1875), *The Milkmaid*, c. 1854–57. Pastel on blue-gray laid paper, 192 x 306 mm. Worcester Art Museum, Worcester, Massachusetts. Bequest of Mrs. Charlotte E. W. Buffington

predecessors had paved the way, seeking out their works at auction sales—such as that of Delacroix in 1864—and eventually acquiring examples for their own collections. In later life, Degas owned a landscape pastel by Delacroix and four studies in the medium by Boudin, while Monet hung a single Boudin pastel in his bedroom at Giverny and bought a spectacular early pastel-over-monotype by Degas.[59]

Less often cited in relation to Monet is the example of Jean-François Millet (1814–1875), some of whose densely worked pastel compositions could be compared directly, in both size and complexity of facture, with his current canvases. The extent to which pastels such as Millet's resonant *The Milkmaid* of c. 1854–57 (fig. 99) were known to the Impressionist group is difficult to establish and appears to have depended on firsthand contact with the artist or with his supporters.[60] Though only 306 millimeters across, this pastel has many of the structural attributes of a finished oil painting. A sophisticated pictorial space leads the viewer gently from foreground pasture to distant sea and pale sky, the delicacy of which is counterbalanced by the massive forms of the cows and the attendant figure. Combining two motifs that Monet himself would use a decade later (see figs. 67 and 119). Millet's sheet also set a precedent for the younger artist's luminous exercises in color and space, some of them in his own pastels of the Normandy coast. By tradition, Millet had met Monet's plein-air painting instructor, Eugène Boudin, when both men lived in Le Havre in the mid-1840s, and the latter is known to have acknowledged the importance of Millet's pastels for his own youthful formation.[61] It seems probable, therefore, that Monet was at least aware of the existence of such masterful pastels, just as it remains unlikely that he had sight of these works until after Millet's death in 1875, when the latter's studio contents and many pastels were sold.

Monet's close friendship with Boudin from the late 1850s onward exposed him to one of the most radical pastel-makers of the day, whose sky studies had briefly entered the consciousness of artistic Paris in 1859. Despite Baudelaire's advocacy, Boudin continued to struggle in finding patrons and seems to have sold few pastels during these years.[62] Largely self-taught, like Monet himself, Boudin was nevertheless prodigious in his use of the medium, making many hundreds of informal studies in his sketchbooks and on independent sheets, as well as elaborated, signed, and sometimes inscribed compositions

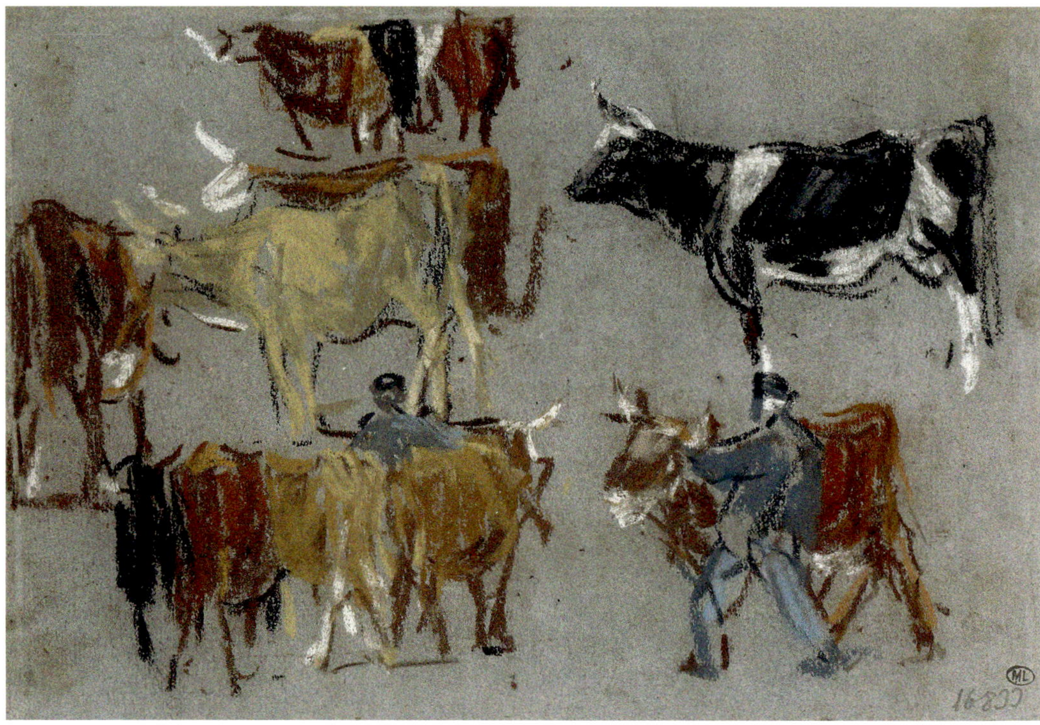

100
Eugène Boudin, *Peasants Herding Cows*, n.d. Charcoal and pastel, 151 x 220 mm. Musée du Louvre, Paris

that are clearly resolved works of art. Implicit in his oeuvre was the sense that Boudin's pastels had a life of their own, neither competing with his more successful canvases nor meekly supporting them, yet not entirely separate from his aspirations as a painter. Especially telling are the dense hues that characterize many of Boudin's pastels, evident in his much-admired "skies" but also in his fragmentary studies of Normandy and neighboring regions. Vivid scarlet and deep purple might describe a peasant's costume, for example; rich blacks, blues, umbers, and ochers will fix a herd of cows in the sun (fig. 100); and dazzling ultramarines and ceruleans can be mingled with the near-pink of a beach. These saturated colors speak to the world of brushes and paints as much as to the chalky paleness of traditional pastels, which were so easily dismissed by Blanc as lacking "the depth of oil painting."[63] As we shall see, the pastels made by Monet in the shadow of his teacher almost immediately adopted a similar rich palette and found a comparable relationship with his own youthful canvases.

Leaving its unmistakable mark on Monet, Boudin's example may also have stimulated the first pastels made by his companions. By a curious set of coincidences, one of the earliest such works by Berthe Morisot is entitled *Cows in Normandy*, made on an 1864 visit to Beuzeval, just south of Le Havre.[64] As it happens, her family had been introduced to the area by the pastellist Léon Riesener and spent their time on a stretch of coast much favored by Boudin. They were also near Honfleur, where — unbeknownst to the Morisots — the twenty-three-year-old Monet was occupied with paint and pastel during the very months of their vacation. Five years later, when he, too, had become an acquaintance of the Morisot family, Degas also traveled to the Beuzeval area to make his own suite of landscape pastels, again with Boudin partly in mind. Morisot herself waited almost a decade before absorbing the medium into her normal artistic practice, applying it to both landscape and figure subjects. Pissarro's beginnings were similarly delayed but somewhat less complex, leading to just a handful of documented trials in pastel from the mid-1860s onward and around a score achieved prior to 1874.[65] His case, however, is even more illuminating in the present context, for several reasons. The admiration of Pissarro for Monet at this period is a matter of record: in a forceful letter to Théodore Duret of 1873, Pissarro insisted that Monet's art was "very thoughtful, based on observation, and with an entirely new feeling, it is poetry through the harmony of true color, Monet is an admirer of true nature."[66] Pissarro's remarks carried considerable authority, since he had worked closely with Monet and observed him in action, literally sharing certain of his motifs. In his own pastels, Pissarro chose paper of similar dimensions to those of Monet and several times opted for rustic scenes that echoed works by his friend.

At the beginning of the new decade, pastel had acquired a modest momentum in the proto-Impressionist milieu and one that was informed by recent history. By this date, most of the major participants enjoyed some first-hand familiarity with the medium and even less prominent individuals, such as Alfred Sisley, Félix Bracquemond, and Armand Guillaumin (1841–1927), used pastel occasionally. These latter two figures can be seen to define some of the extremes to which pastel was taken. Bracquemond, a former Salon exhibitor, had clung to a rigorously precise technique for at least twenty years, achieving needle-sharp detail through close observation and disciplined craft. The semi-amateur Guillaumin, in total contrast, emerged as an artist from the liberating experience of the Académie Suisse, which Monet himself had briefly encountered in the early 1860s. Following Pissarro and Cézanne toward an open-air sketching practice, Guillaumin also developed a markedly relaxed pastel technique. Beside Bracquemond's works, many of Guillaumin's pastels seem almost haphazard, loosely arranged on the sheet and often left partly finished. Monet's own pastels seemed to propose a third way forward, one that was neither painstaking nor hasty, placing him in a different technical vanguard. Though never as ponderous as Bracquemond's, almost all of Monet's pastels are emphatically, self-consciously constructed within the rectangle of the sheet, as were his oil paintings within their respective canvases. Executed with considerable flair, they nevertheless distanced themselves from the output of Guillaumin and other colleagues by their completeness as visual statements. In virtually every instance, Monet's image has been developed and resolved to the point where he could sign it as an achieved work of art.

The notion that Monet saw each of his pastels as equivalent to a small oil painting, limited in scale but proportionately worthy of attention, helps to explain something of their distinctive character. It is also supported by a number of historical circumstances, prominent among them being the presence of Monet's signature on almost three quarters of his pastel output. By signing such works, as he would continue to do into the twentieth century, Monet unequivocally identified them as self-contained pictures that carried his endorsement into the wider world. His pastels in the 1874 exhibition shared this implication and were launched in public alongside much larger canvases, as items equally ready for the market. When Monet released these and other pastel compositions over the years, he necessarily embraced the fact that his densely hued scenes on paper would eventually coexist with his own painted oeuvre and with the works of his contemporaries. Selling or giving them to friends, he implicitly approved their presence on the walls of serious collectors like Chocquet and Chabrier, Faure and Stchoukine, Blake and Pope Riddle. Monet repeatedly chose such roles for his pastels, thrusting them into the limelight at charitable events and offering them in lieu of paintings on a number of occasions; toward the end of his life, for example, he pointedly gave three such pastels to a fellow artist, André Barbier (1883–1970), who had presented Monet with one of his own canvases.[67] Other pastels were dedicated to distinguished acquaintances and proffered on formal occasions, his signature assuring their authenticity and their definitive role in his art. It was only in Monet's personal exhibitions of paintings, where works in a rival medium and of near-miniature proportions might have distracted from the "broad and swift" touch of his brush, that their competition seems to have been unwelcome.

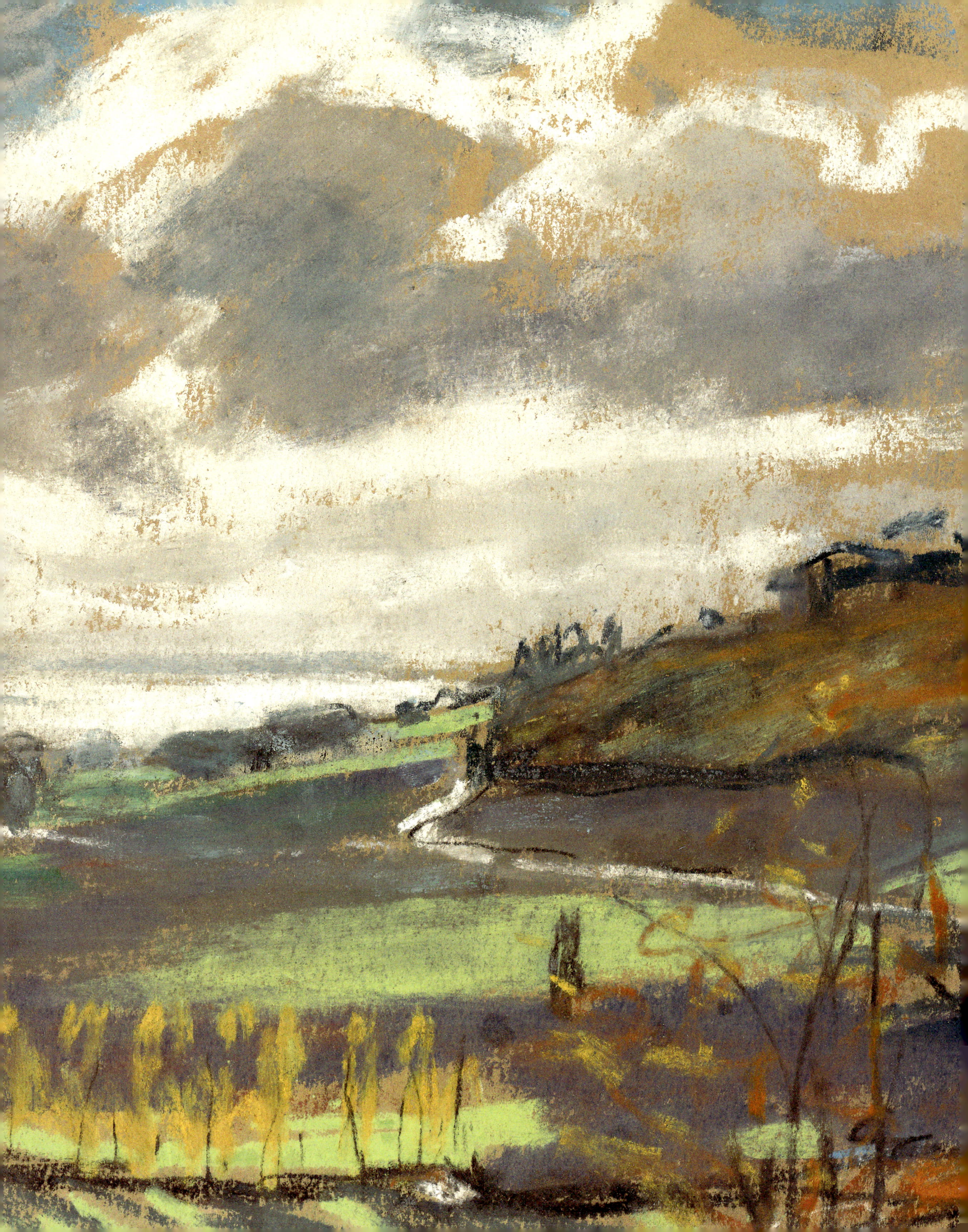

CHAPTER SIX Monet's Pastels in Private

The process by which Monet created his pastels within the larger narrative of his painting career, in contrast to their emergence into the contemporary art world, is virtually undocumented. Neither the artist's surviving letters, nor the reminiscences of his later years, refer to these works in more than a few words, while his first critics and biographers are almost as uninformative on the subject. Why Monet appears to have said so little is not clear, unless we see this reticence as another aspect of his image-building. By stressing one side of his professional achievement at the expense of others, it can be argued, Monet hoped to claim his place in the unfolding history of modern French painting, while emphasizing the originality of his practice. Whatever his motivation, the effect has been pervasive, almost removing his name from the roster of prominent pastellists of the nineteenth century and creating unusual obstacles for researchers. Any attempt to deal with Monet's pastels, therefore, must confront the simplest issues and begin from the most basic premises. What subjects do these largely unstudied pictures represent and what was their significance? When, where, and why did Monet spend time executing them? And what do his vigorous strokes and rubbings of color, accumulated chalky textures, and variously tinted papers tell us about the role of pastel in Monet's creative project as a whole?

The first of several surprising discoveries to emerge from such an inquiry concerns the relationship between Monet's pastels and his painted oeuvre. With the exception of the late London scenes, the bulk of his pastels turn out to be separate, independent works, not preliminary studies for a more complete or finished image in another medium. Unlike Morisot, for example, Monet rarely used pastel to draft out a composition that would culminate in a painting on canvas, or, like Degas, to explore a subsidiary feature—such as a figure or landscape element—for a larger design. In this definitive sense, the majority of Monet's pastels were conceived as extensions to his pictorial repertoire, parallel representations of the visible world with their own technical and imaginative history.

Two broad, subject-based categories can be identified in Monet's pastel oeuvre as a whole. The largest concerns his depiction of sites that are already well known from documented painting itineraries, such as those at Sainte-Adresse or Étretat. Typically, these pastels offer less-familiar viewpoints, differently nuanced conditions of light and weather, or more audaciously

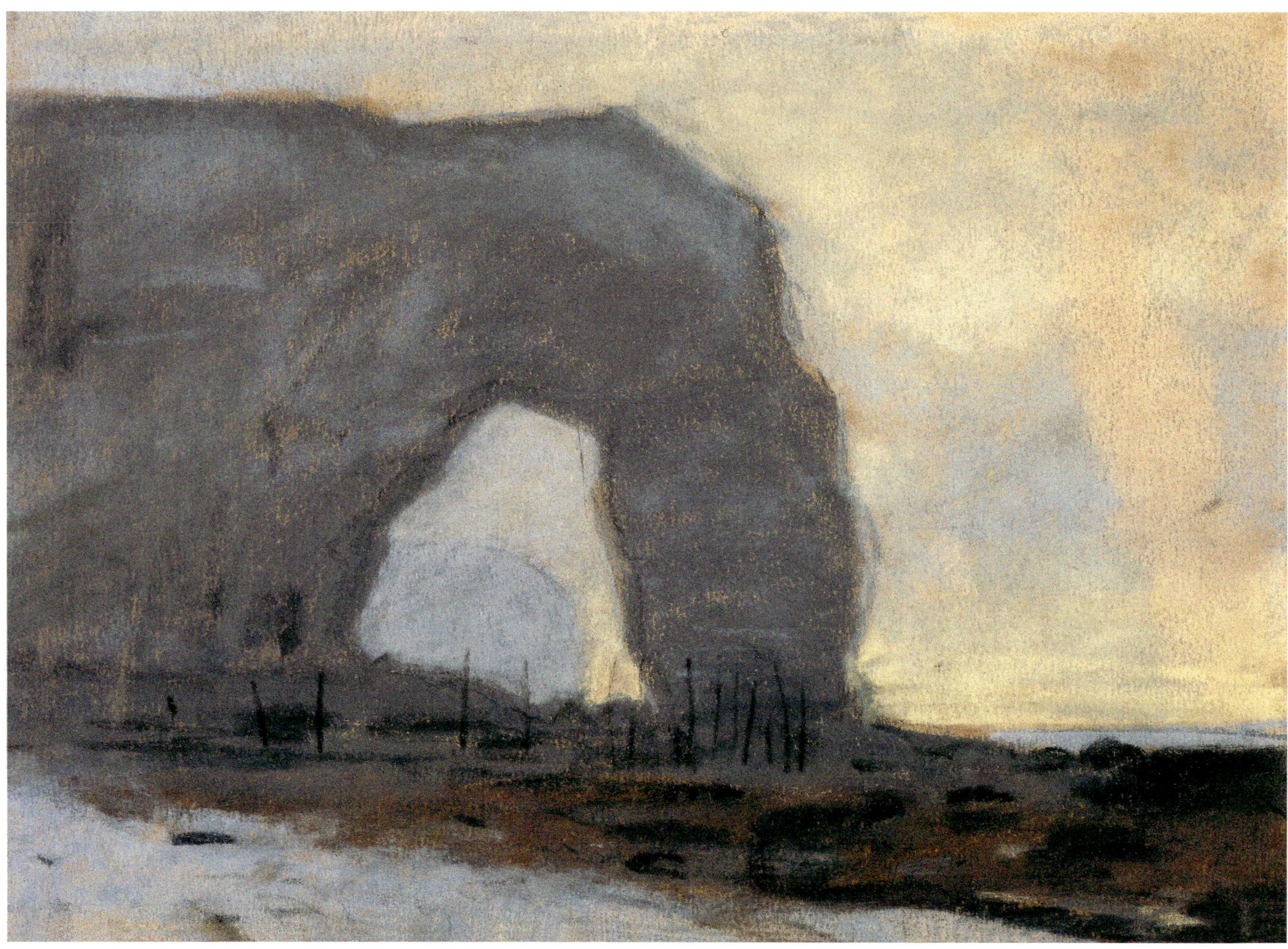

101
Étretat, the Manneporte at Low Tide, c. 1885. Pastel on beige paper, 230 x 330 mm. Private collection, London [P79]

pitched colors than his oil paintings made at the same locations. They thus have the effect of amplifying the artist's visual encounter with a given landscape, often in ways that exploit the distinctive properties of pastel itself. An illuminating case is the small but boldly conceived *Étretat, the Manneporte at Low Tide* (fig. 101), a work that has no direct counterpart among his painted canvases.[1] Here Monet adopted an unusually extreme view toward the southwest from the one of the beaches at Étretat, on an occasion when the sea was absent from the massive rock arch of the Manneporte. With the light behind the promontory, he produced a composition that is not only flatter and sparer than his other treatments of the same motif, but one that plays almost wittily with the alignment of near and distant cliffs. Unprecedented, too, are the limpid colors and their suggestion of evening light, expressed in a muted pastel palette and achieving a serenity that is rare in Monet's Étretat vocabulary.[2] Made on a visit to the area in 1885, when he completed around thirty paintings showing the arched cliff in different guises, this pastel is unmatched in its fresh simplicity by any of these canvases.

At the opposite extreme, a smaller class of pastels adds a number of entirely new motifs to Monet's oeuvre. Among them are views of Yport and Harfleur, small towns and their surroundings that would not reappear in his later oil paintings. Other works in this group are a cluster of rural landscapes that show fields, orchards, farmhouses, and country lanes, and a set of portraits, again with few if any connections to Monet's mature paintings. Though broadly conforming to the terrain we associate with the artist, these landscape images

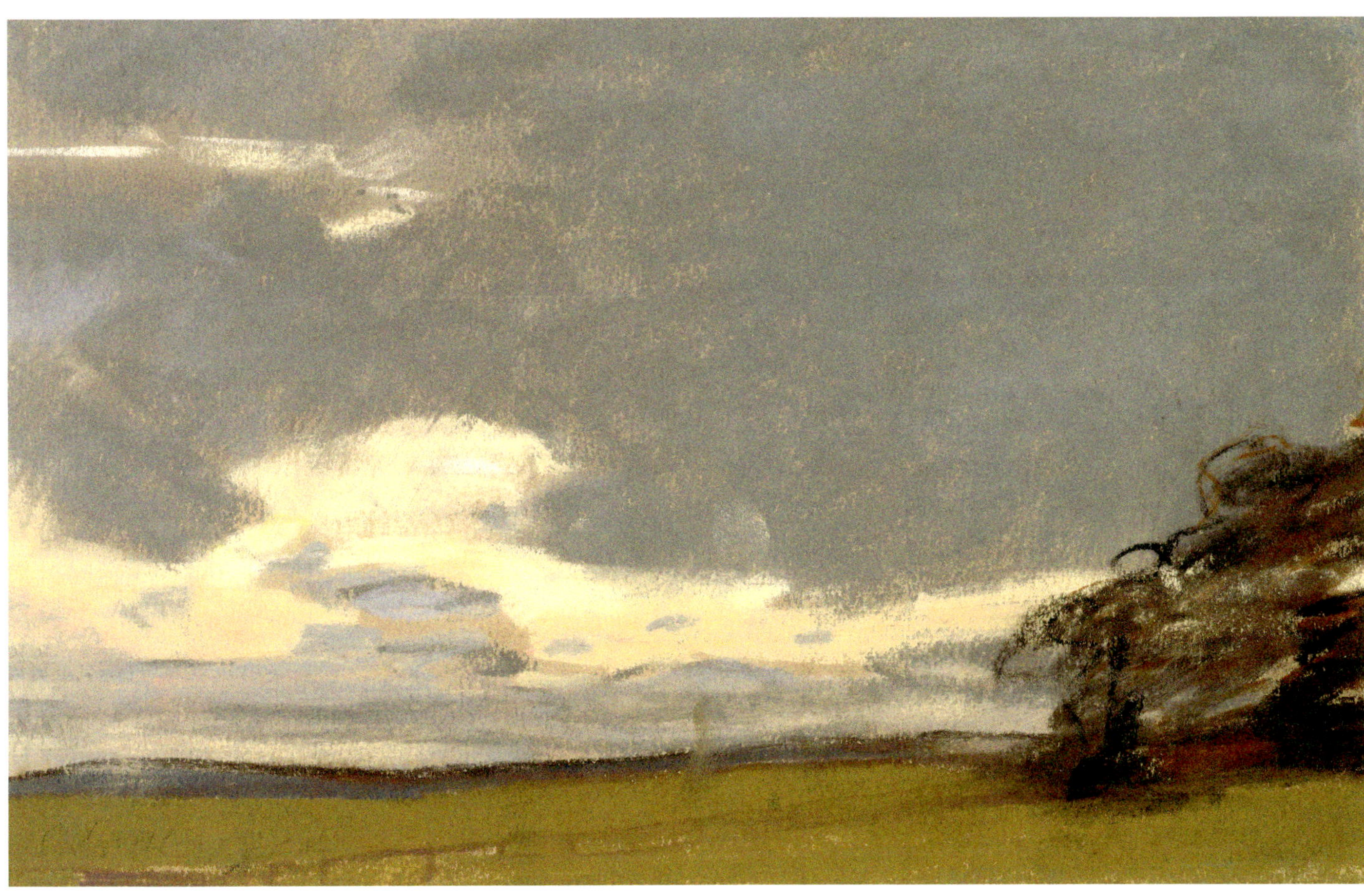

102
After the Rain, 1868. Pastel, 179 x 295 mm. Private collection [P48]

invite speculation about his motives for creating such singular scenes and about his use of pastel in general. One immediate possibility is that Monet chose pastel on these occasions to investigate a new subject, perhaps with a return visit and future canvases in mind. Such a strategy would be consistent with his occasional habit of attempting an oil painting at a previously unvisited location, then abandoning both painting and motif if the experience failed to satisfy him. More evident are those cases in which he used pastel to tackle a formerly neglected compositional challenge. In at least half a dozen pastels, for example, Monet made variants on the subject of a light screen of trees that crossed fields or meadows, dividing but not occluding the deeper space. *Three Cows in a Pasture* (see fig. 106) is a vividly colored representative of this type, as is the denser and more closely grained *The Meadow Lined with Trees* (see fig. 129), an elaborately finished pastel that was exhibited in his lifetime.[3] Yet for reasons that remain unknown, Monet began research into these motifs in the 1860s but chose not to pursue them in this form. While a scattering of canvases from these and later decades distantly recall the structure of such scenes, none is closely related to the earlier works on paper.[4]

Both the separateness of Monet's pastel vocabulary and his personal investment in the medium are encapsulated in works such as *After the Rain* (fig. 102). With no equivalent in his current paintings, this signed and dated composition is one of a cluster of ten or a dozen similar pastels that form a persuasive, unified sequence.[5] Despite the firmly indicated date on this work, there is some uncertainty about the precise place of this extended suite in his career.[6] It can be argued, however, that it represents Monet's first sustained exploration of serial imagery, undertaken at least a decade—and perhaps two—before he began the more celebrated canvases of grainstacks and poplars at Giverny.[7] In this case, it seems, pastel was

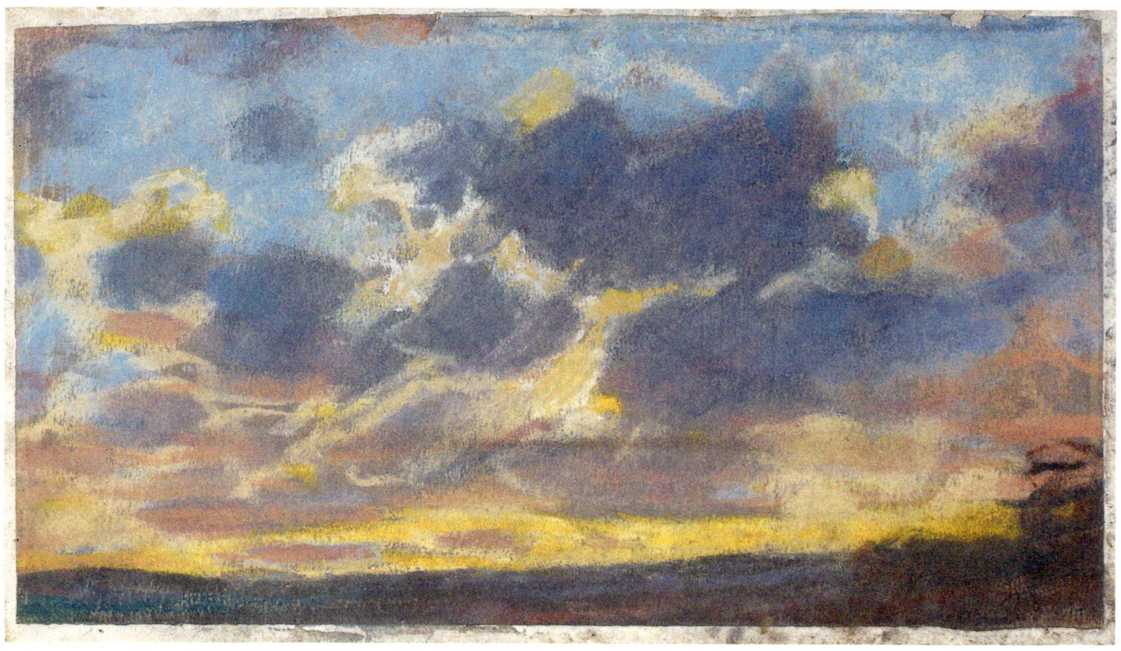

103
Nightfall, c. 1865–70. Pastel on gray paper, 212 x 379 mm. Musée des Beaux-Arts de Nantes. Gift of the Société des amis du Musée des Beaux-Arts de Nantes, 1968 [P55]

not only separate from paint, but significantly in advance of the artist's thinking on canvas. Each of the pastels in question records the play of light and weather above a largely featureless stretch of ground, their plainness often set against a hastily drawn bush or copse at the right-hand edge of the composition. Close in size and panoramic in format, they appear to have been conceived around the same time, perhaps within a few days or even hours of each other. In making *After the Rain*, Monet has seized a moment of heightened visual contrast, when the green of a freshly washed pasture still resonated with the pewter-gray of storm clouds passing overhead. Streaks of lemon and peach near the horizon suggest brightness to come, and perhaps herald the dazzling sunset hues of other works in the sequence, such as *Nightfall* (fig. 103) and *Twilight* (fig. 104), two pastels from the Musée des Beaux-Arts in Nantes. As we have seen, the immediacy of Monet's struggle with such natural events rapidly became part of his public identity, though more usually associated with what Duret called his "great facility with the brush." The suite of pictures to which *After the Rain* belongs is a reminder that Monet's technical deftness also extended to pastel, where his sensuous, responsive touch with the powdery sticks of color may have pioneered a more urgent fusion of seeing and art-making.

If the composition of *After the Rain* and the majority of Monet's landscape pastels are unique to the works in question, their physical origin seems to have been similar to his paintings of the same period. We know from the artist's letters that a visit to his old haunts or a survey of new terrain often began with long, meandering walks in search of a potential motif. Arriving for a working visit at Dieppe, Monet wrote on 7 February 1882 to his companion, Alice Hoschedé, "I've had a very tiring day, I've been all over the countryside, along all the paths below and above the cliffs. I've seen some lovely things and I was helped by superb sunshine."[8] Monet's sketchbooks show that he sometimes made small pencil drawings on these perambulations, and might hastily draft a composition that would define his next canvas (see fig. 140). It was only following the discovery of a suitable subject, and sometimes after the passage of several days, that he would return with canvas and easel to begin a painting. Other letters describe how Monet subsequently found that the atmosphere or wind direction had changed, the tides had advanced or retreated, and even that vegetation had grown to disrupt the view. At Dieppe, he told Alice that he "did some more exploring" before settling to work, but soon decided that

104

Twilight, c. 1865–70. Pastel on gray paper, 189 x 311 mm. Musée des Beaux-Arts de Nantes. Gift of the Société des amis du Musée des Beaux-Arts de Nantes, 1968 [P56]

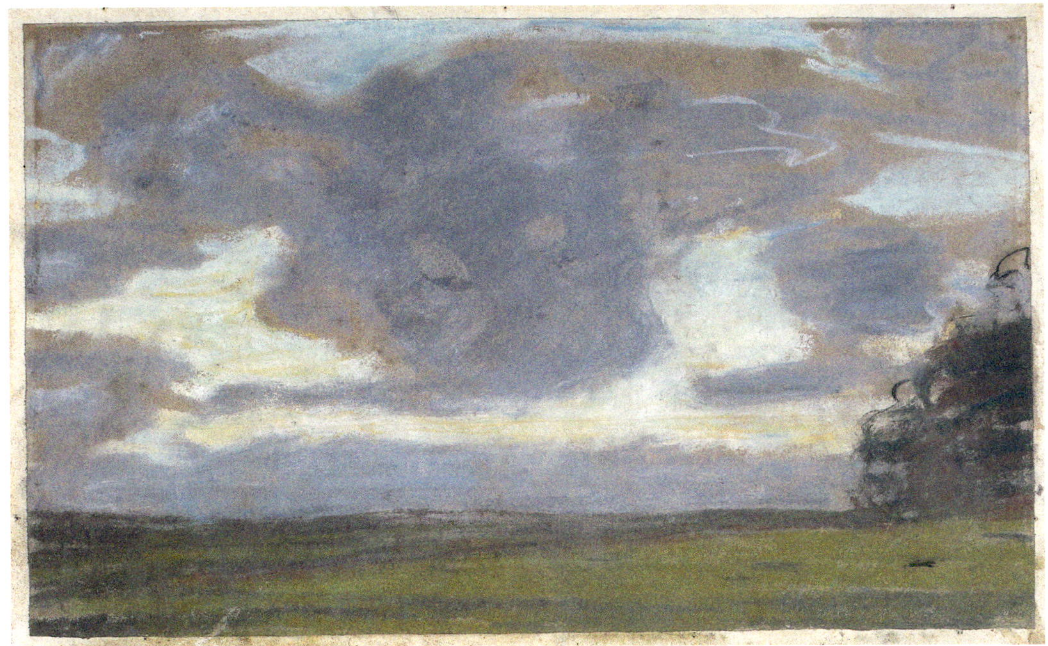

the area was unsuitable. Moving a little down the coast to Pourville, he "had an appalling day" and was soaked by the rain, but again found the countryside "very beautiful" before beginning a succession of radiant, light-filled canvases.[9]

Struggling with such uncertainties, Monet may sometimes have found that pastel simplified his predicament, allowing him to work rapidly and fix the scene when he first encountered it. Little apparatus was needed, beyond a simple box of pastels and a sketchbook page or small portfolio of paper. A sheet such as *After the Rain*, measuring less than 200 by 300 millimeters, might well have been finished on the spot, its principal structure and tones noted in a matter of minutes. The small, easily manipulated sticks of pastel were ideally suited to these circumstances, and their granular softness was unusually appropriate to the changeability of nature itself. Improvising textures and transitions of hue as the scene evolved in front of him, Monet could blur the edge of a moving cloud with his fingertips or add streaks of light as the sun suddenly illuminated a tree or path. As *After the Rain* approached completion, the sky may have begun to clear or the scene itself darken, defining the next frame in his cinematic sequence and encouraging him to follow the transformation of the landscape from composition to composition. *Nightfall* and *Twilight* have many characteristics in common with *After the Rain* and seem to represent successive images of this kind. Not only are they close to the paler work in size and facture, but both feature a similarly sweeping, low horizon line and a *repoussoir*-like knot of vegetation at right. Dominating all three pictures is the massive, stormy sky, becoming denser and more variegated in *Twilight* and extravagantly kaleidoscopic in *Nightfall*. The latter is especially notable for its richly worked surface, where Monet hurriedly superimposed further colors on previously applied layers, as in the central band of gold—which was formerly lemon—and in the blue added to the white at upper left. Yet another variant is *Sunset* (see fig. 96), in which streaks of multihued cloud are contrasted with a deep brown thicket at night. Works like these increase our sense of art being made under the pressure of time, with the artist literally keeping pace with external phenomena.

Pastel and Normandy

Monet's use of pastel as an exploratory medium, both in the geographical sense and as part of his tactile encounter with the landscape, is apparent in scores of similar works. In each case, we confront the issue of topography, often with startling results. The second revelation about Monet's body of pastels is the extraordinarily selective nature of the sites and locations chosen for these compositions. Though he remained dedicated to landscapes of many kinds throughout his long working life, Monet the pastellist narrowed his focus much further, touching on just a small fraction of the themes for which he is otherwise so well known. Hungry for new experiences as a painter, he traveled widely and often, tackling the Atlantic and the Mediterranean, the Seine and the Thames, the bulb fields of Holland and the mountains of Norway. Within France, he depicted small towns such as Honfleur and Trouville, Argenteuil and Vétheuil; the rugged cliffs at Varengeville and Belle-Île-en-Mer; the spectacular southern coast at Antibes and Menton; and such inland areas as Poissy, Vernon, and the Creuse Valley. As an artist of the city, he painted the railway stations and boulevards of Paris, the Houses of Parliament in London, the canals of Amsterdam and Venice, and the cathedral at Rouen, sometimes returning to these scenes for more than one campaign. Once settled at Giverny, Monet contrived entirely novel motifs that culminated in the water-lily pictures of his last years and continued to make occasional images of figures in the open air. Yet among his entire body of surviving pastels, we find that the great majority of these motifs are missing. Before 1900, there are no images in pastel of modern conurbations or foreign vistas; no glamorous resorts or architectural monuments; and no scenes related to the serial iconography that later brought him such fame. When Monet was at home, it seems, with his studio and professional equipment at hand, he dedicated himself to painting; conversely, when he visited far-flung places and exotic lands, Monet left his box of pastels behind. Even the late studies on paper of London's bridges follow this pattern, having been improvised when his paints, brushes, and canvases failed to arrive.

The extreme personal and regional focus of Monet's pastels is confirmed, and ultimately intensified, by a survey of the seventy-five or so landscapes made prior to the London scenes. Analysis of their subjects shows that all but one or two of these works is based on a single theme: the rural and coastal scenery of northwestern France. Even more precisely, the entire group of such pastels can be traced to a small corner of Normandy, within a fifty-mile radius of the Seine estuary. This was where Monet grew up and took his first faltering steps as an artist, in a territory to which he remained loyal throughout his life. The persistent echoes of this part of Normandy in his pastels are remarkable: among the forty or so works with a location defined in their titles, for example, every one is situated within this small area, usually at sites that reverberate with Monet's private history. There are depictions of Le Havre and Honfleur, where he went to school, made his first caricatures, and studied with Boudin and Jongkind; repeated images of Sainte-Adresse, which Monet visited on formative painting trips with Bazille and chose as the subject for some of his first large canvases; and around a dozen pastels of the dramatic bay at Étretat, recalling sojourns with his own young family and encounters with friends and supporters such as Théophile Beguin Billecocq, Jean-Baptiste Faure, and Guy de Maupassant.[10] Though the origin of many of the current titles is unclear, some can be traced to the artist himself and others are verifiable at first hand today.[11] Beyond question, however, is the intimate, pervasive connection of these works with the ground of Monet's childhood and adolescence.[12]

The settings for a number of Monet's less-specific images of boats, harbors, and marine views are harder to locate, but these works can also be attached to the larger body of Normandy scenes through their resemblance to dated paintings, and from expert analysis of such matters as rigging and sails.[13] The intriguing sheet, *Study of Sailboats and Harbor* (fig. 105), for example, is a mosaic of vignettes that initially appears to lack a context. Closer attention reveals a characteristic view of the jetty and robust lighthouse at Honfleur, which features in several canvases of this decade, among them

105

Study of Sailboats and Harbor, c. 1864–68. Pastel, 480 x 320 mm. Private collection [P25]

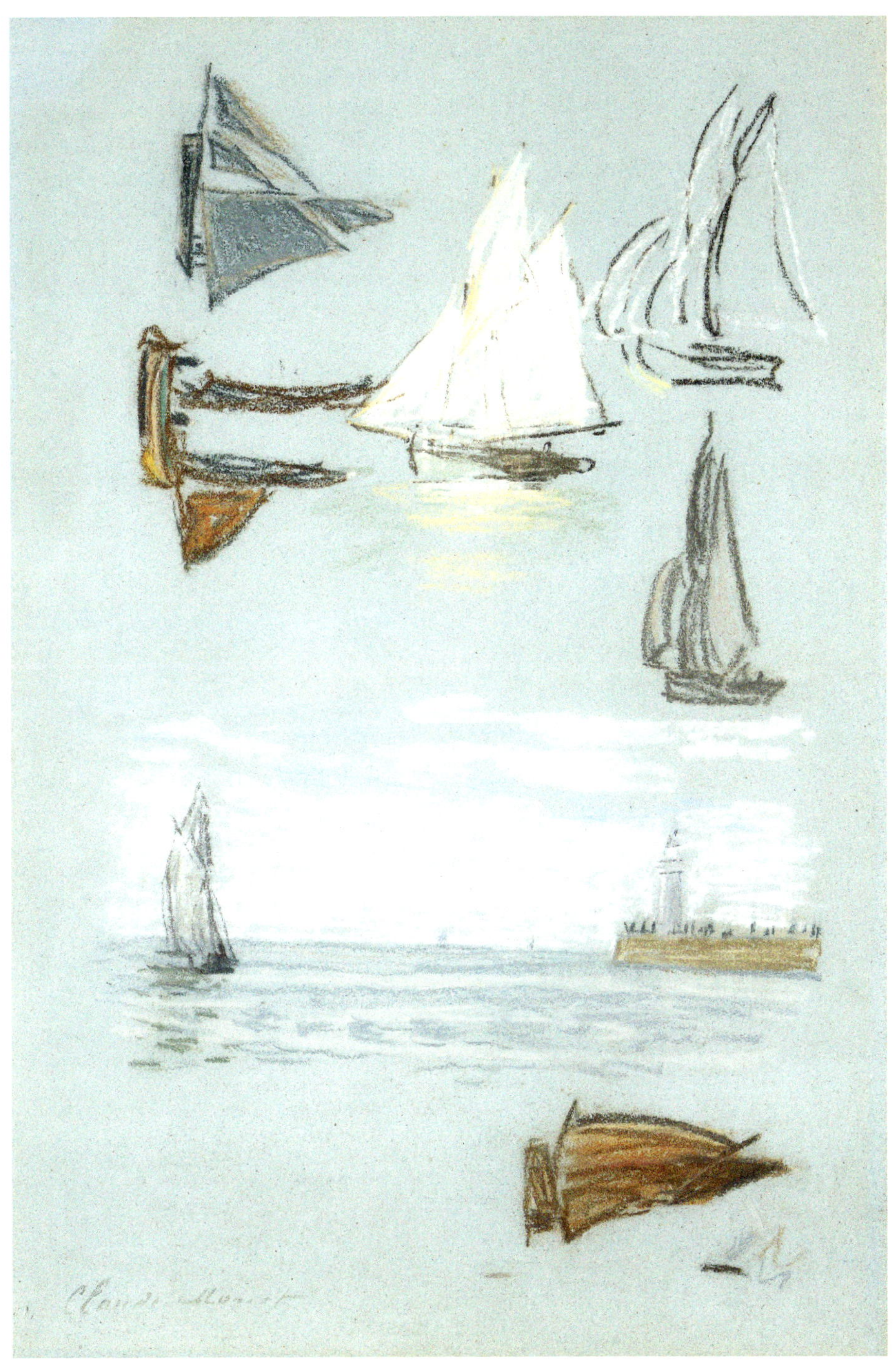

Towing a Boat, Honfleur (see fig. 110). Patient inspection has also identified the sailboats as belonging to traditional patterns from nearby Trouville and Villerville, testifying to both Monet's scrupulous observation and his local knowledge of such matters.[14] This sheet also permits a rare glimpse of his pastel practice in action, from the cursorily outlined single boat to more embellished variants, leading to the developed representation of Honfleur itself. Beyond this coastal area and its marine motifs, a group of inland subjects can also be traced to the Norman hinterland, its lush pastoral landscape and picturesque dwellings. *Normandy Farm under Trees* was signed by Monet and given to an acquaintance, and *Landscape near Le Havre* was initialed and perhaps titled by him, while studies of rich farmland, clustered

106

Three Cows in a Pasture, c. 1865–70. Pastel, 320 x 250 mm. Private collection [P47]

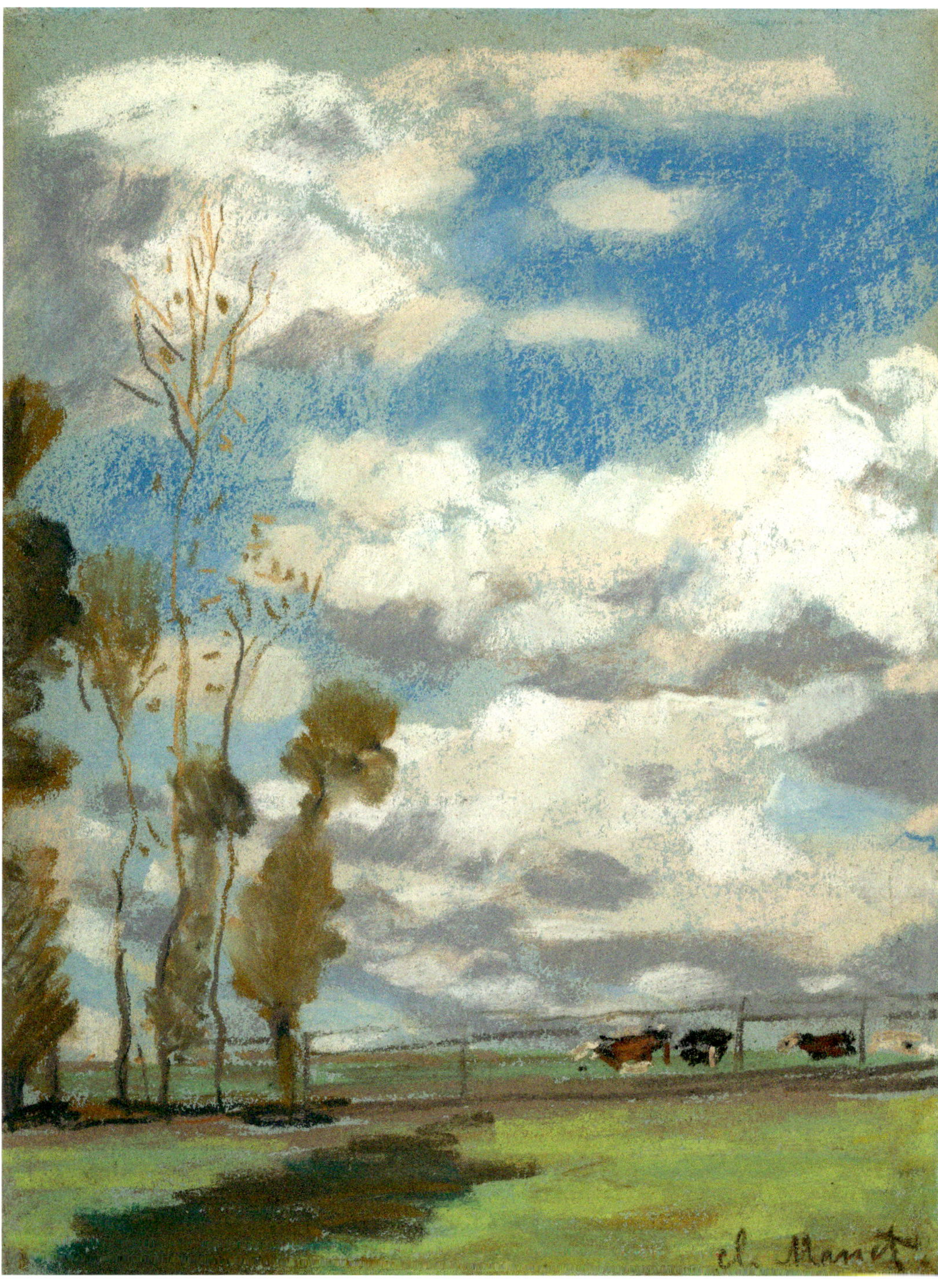

apple trees, and grazing cows evoke Normandy's celebrated rural produce.[15] *Three Cows in a Pasture* (fig. 106) is an almost quintessential image of the region, famous then as now for its cattle and orchards. Proud of his Norman roots throughout his life, Monet was said by Théodore Beguin Billecocq to appreciate "good meat and fine wines," and would continue to drink his Normandy cider in later years at Giverny.[16]

What can we deduce from the exclusively local character of Monet's pastel oeuvre prior to 1900? At the subjective level, he had many reasons to associate the medium with his youth, having first encountered it in the company of Boudin in the late 1850s and soon afterward undergone his own initiation as a pastellist. For the young Monet, pastel must have seemed inseparable from Boudin's Normandy motifs,

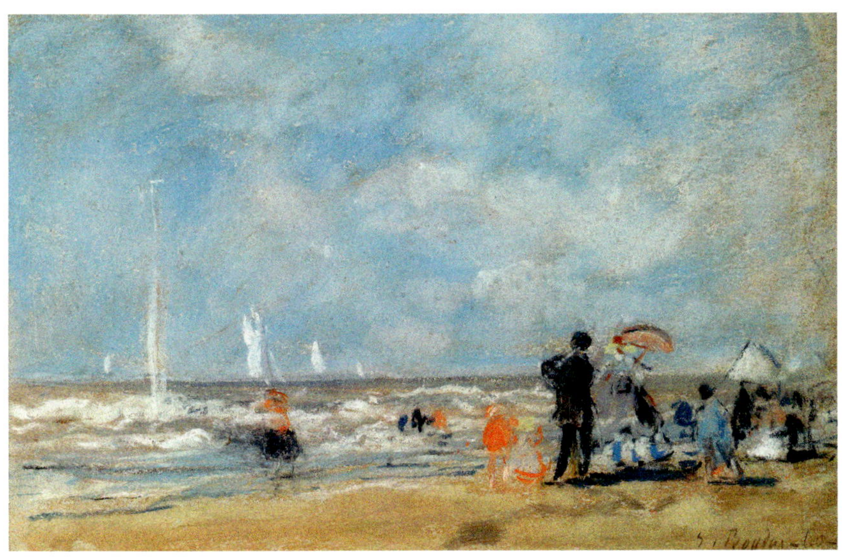

107
Eugène Boudin, *On the Beach*, 1863. Pastel, 190 x 300 mm. Musée Marmottan Monet, Paris

energizing the older man's beach panoramas and the "meteorological beauties" admired by Baudelaire, as well as his sparkling studies of regional costume, traditional markets, and local farm animals. More than a decade later, Monet's display at the 1874 Impressionist exhibition revealed that he was capable of both respect and nostalgia, sentiments that may well have extended to the substance of pastel itself. At some unknown date, Monet acquired two works by Boudin for his own collection, one of them a vivacious, richly textured pastel of seaside revelers, *On the Beach* (fig. 107). Recalling vacations with the Beguin Billecocq family and other friends on the sands of Normandy, such images were surely redolent of the colors and textures of Monet's early life. Historically, too, pastel was woven into the artistic fabric of the region, as Monet must have increasingly become aware. Several of his older heroes and admired fellow-practitioners had specifically worked in the medium while sojourning in Normandy: Millet in the 1840s and 1850s; Delacroix, who stayed in Dieppe in 1852 and 1854; while marginal figures like Paul Huet, Léon Riesener, and Camille Flers, and the regulars at the Saint-Siméon farm, seem to have instinctively reached for their pastels as they approached the Atlantic Ocean.

As the years passed, long after the deaths of his parents and the dispersal of his youthful acquaintances, Monet continued to pay extended visits to this area. Making not just oil paintings but also pastels of its cliffs, seascapes, dense green fields, and tangled copses, he naturally returned to some of the territory associated with his beginnings. From the 1880s onward, the center of Monet's activities on the Norman coast moved further north, beyond Étretat to Fécamp, Le Petites Dalles, Varengeville, and Dieppe, and thus to areas with fewer personal ties. Pastel, too, became less prominent, disappearing entirely from his responses to Normandy after his fiftieth year, when his intimate connection with the region came to an end.

The pastels of Normandy were concentrated in two phases of sustained activity, both of them in decades that preceded Monet's final determination to settle at Giverny, a village that was itself situated on the region's border. The earlier period was centered on the 1860s, the later more specifically tied to his travels between 1881 and 1886. As a student in Paris and an aspiring Salon exhibitor, Monet made frequent trips to the Normandy coast around Le Havre, where his father and his supportive aunt, Mme Lecadre, still lived. These included expeditions to Honfleur in 1864 and 1866; Trouville in 1865; Sainte-Adresse in 1864, 1865, and 1867; and Le Havre and Étretat in 1868. During these years he completed dozens of accomplished pastels, some of which were presumably among those shown at the 1874 Impressionist exhibition. Over the next decade, the 1870s, Monet remained close to successive bases in and around Paris, spending time in other cities, such as London and Amsterdam, but otherwise painting most consistently at Argenteuil and Vétheuil. As we have already noted, none of these sites provided subjects for new pastels, though a recently discovered, unpublished work, *Bank of the Seine* (see fig. 127), can now be identified as a depiction of the Parisian suburb of Bougival.[17] After 1880, Monet journeyed persistently over several years, experiencing the brilliant light and color of the Mediterranean at Antibes, Menton, and Bordighera but turning to the relative sobriety of Normandy on numerous occasions. Pastel again came into its own on these later outings, though it was used less frequently. The creation of the pastel *Cliff at Pourville*, for example, almost certainly coincided with paintings of similar scenes that Monet undertook during one of his coastal sojourns in 1882, such as the occasion when he was "soaked to the skin" during an exploratory walk.[18] Four stays in Étretat followed, resulting in an invigorated response to its stony architecture in such spectacular pastels as *Étretat, the Manneporte at Low Tide* (see fig. 101) and *Étretat, the Needle Rock and Porte d'Aval* (see fig. 138). Extensive trips to Dieppe and Varengeville produced no identifiable images in pastel, though two handsome studies of Norman orchards were speculatively grouped in this later period by Wildenstein.[19]

Beginnings with Pastel

Any study of the developing character of Monet's pastels over the course of these decades hinges on several criteria: the perceived progression of his technique itself; the evolution of a distinctive relationship between the medium and Monet's growing intimacy with the landscape; and, underpinning all these considerations, the documented or estimated dates when these single or sequential pastels were made. Necessarily interlinked, these issues are best considered through a chronological study of individual works, chosen to exemplify Monet's personal approach to pastel and its atypical relationship with his painted oeuvre. The earliest items in the Wildenstein catalogue raisonné are two sheets of assorted figure studies, including *Study of Five Boys* (fig. 108). Arbitrarily composed but vigorously handled, both sheets provide an instructive link between Monet's 1856 and 1857 sketchbooks on the one hand, where remarkably similar individuals appear on certain pages, and the figures in certain oil paintings from the early 1860s, on the other.[20] In *Farmyard in Normandy* (fig. 109) and *Rue de Bavole, Honfleur* (see fig. 82), for example, childish bystanders introduce a human element into their respective canvases, their awkward, staring poses marking the flow of quotidian life and the artist's intrusive presence. Allowing us to date the two pastels no later than 1864, these links also place them in the very small group of extant working studies made for known paintings.[21] When Monet began *Study of Five Boys*, the forms of the children were outlined in dark crayon or pastel, then their costumes and faces tinted with his box of chalky colors. As we have seen, the presence of such preliminary drawing is often instructive, here suggesting caution in Monet's handling of pastel and an orthodoxy of approach that may still reflect the teaching of Ochard or Gleyre. These conventions had already begun to disappear from Monet's craft by the early 1860s, soon to be replaced by a new confidence in working with color alone. Though susceptible to oversimplification, not least in the self-image projected by Monet, such a leap from preliminary delineation toward a more audacious fusion of design and hue is one of the most revealing trajectories of his formative years.

The earliest of the small number of Monet's pastels that carry dates are all landscapes, beginning with the intricate and ambitious *Yport, les Grottes*.[22] Inscribed on the verso "Yport, 1861. Claude Monet," this work is almost twice the size of *Study of Five Boys* and was evidently made in quite different conditions. We know little of Monet's activities in this period prior to his departure for Algiers in June, though the Beguin Billecocq Grand Journal has greatly enhanced our information about his movements in the previous year and the ease with which he and his Parisian visitors traveled in Normandy. During the summer of 1860, Théophile and his family vacationed at Honfleur, where Monet joined them for a series of "artistic excursions," on foot, by boat, and in a horse-drawn carriage, to such resorts as Trouville and Villerville, and across the estuary to Le Havre. Such outings involved communal drawing sessions, typically led by "young Oscar," and on one occasion they were all introduced to Eugène Boudin.[23] It also seems likely that Monet returned to visit his family in Le Havre before leaving for North Africa the following spring, and perhaps wandered a little way north to work at nearby Yport with his pastels.

Situated some eight miles from Étretat, Yport was then a small village dominated by

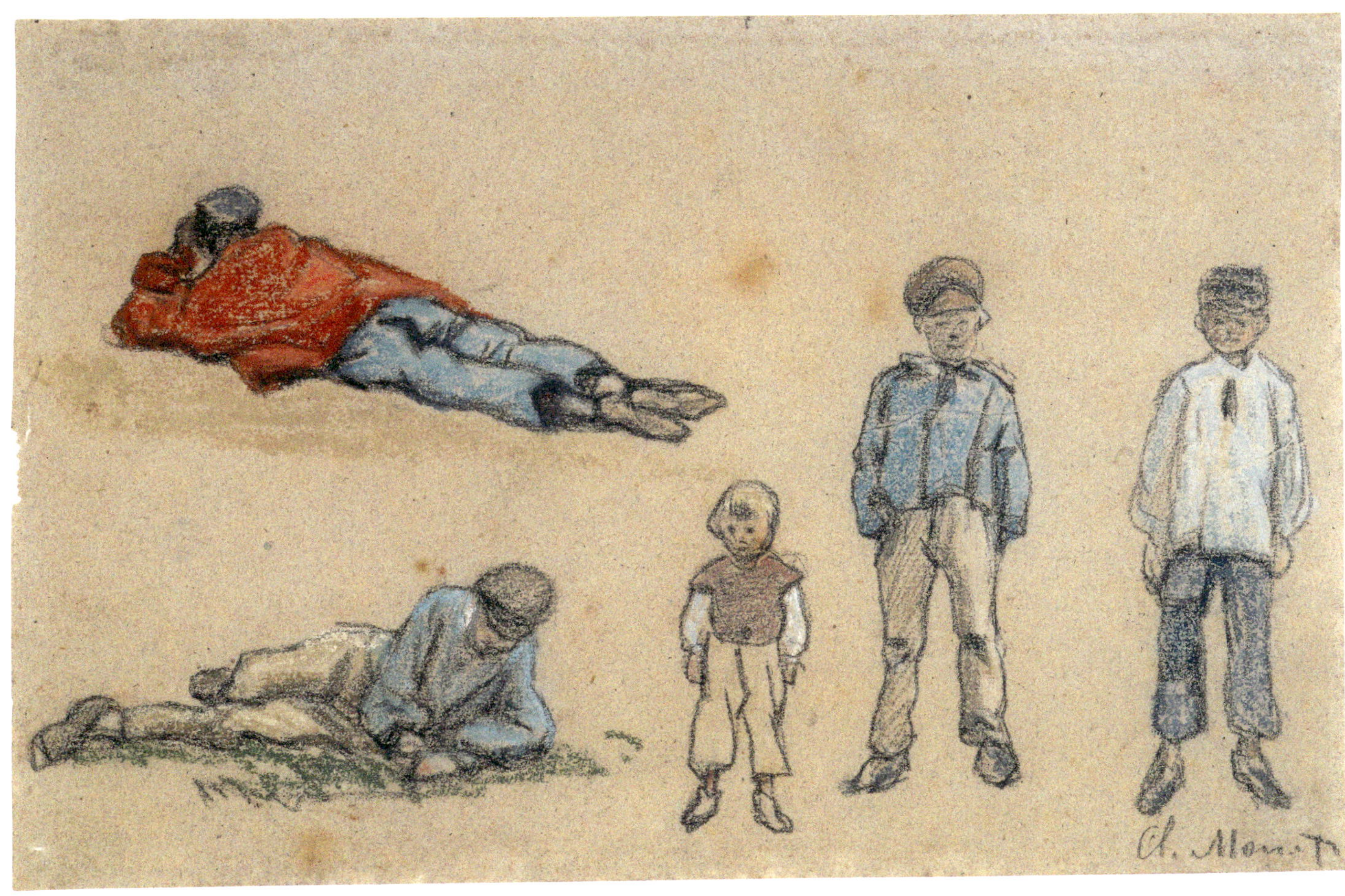

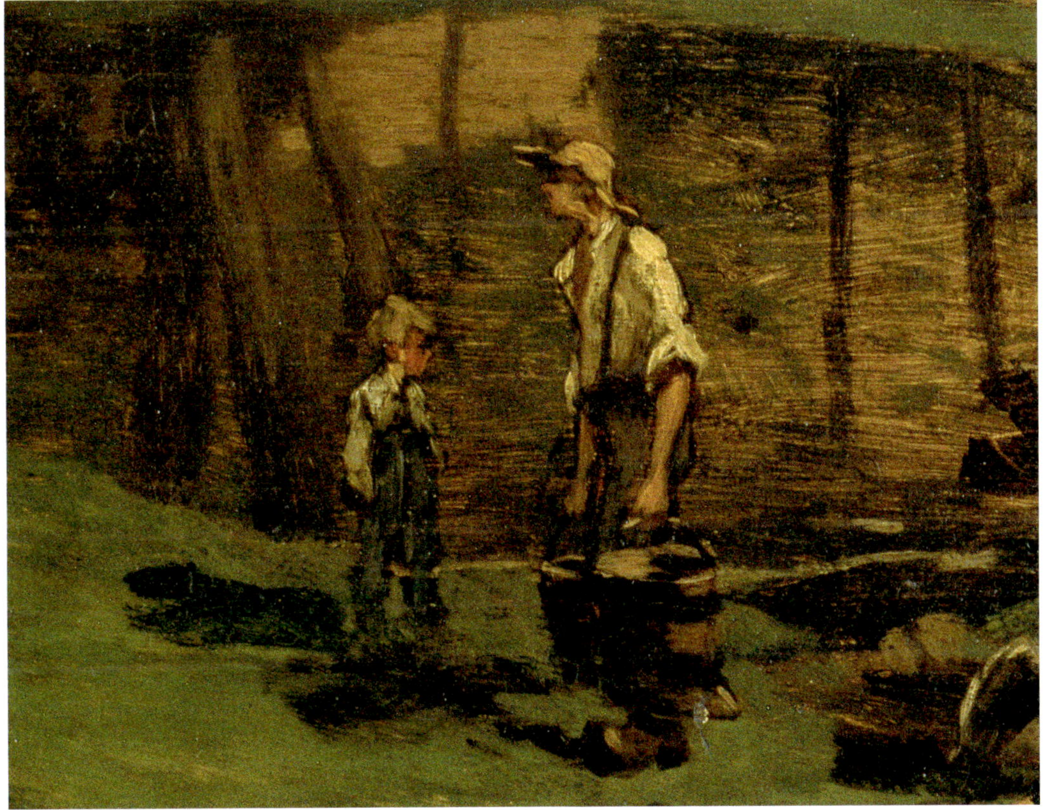

108
Study of Five Boys, c. 1864. Black chalk and pastel on buff paper, 140 x 250 mm. Museum Boijmans Van Beuningen, Rotterdam. Koenigs Collection [P2]

109
Detail of *Farmyard in Normandy* (fig. 66)

110

Towing a Boat, Honfleur, 1864. Oil on canvas, 55.2 x 82.1 cm. Memorial Art Gallery of the University of Rochester. Gift of Marie C. and Joseph C. Wilson [W37]

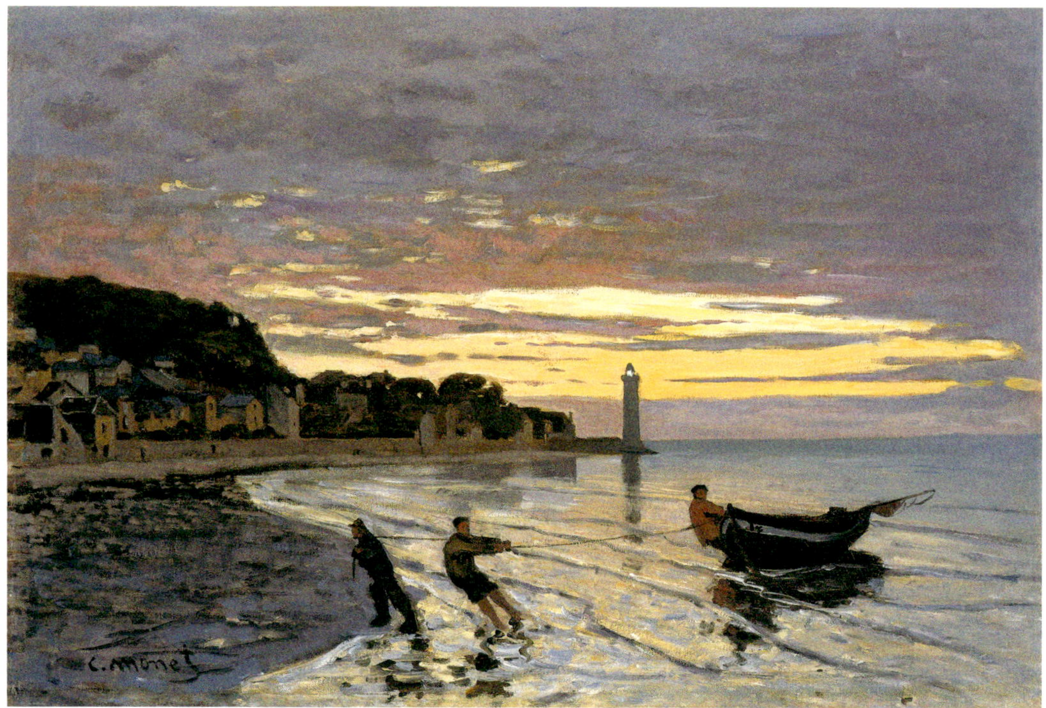

the rocky escarpment that looms over Monet's composition, into which caves or grottoes had been cut long ago. Following the pattern of *Study of Five Boys*, Monet initially established this scene in monochrome, then heightened it with pastel in an essentially traditional sequence of operations. A companion study, *Yport and the Falaise d'Aval* (see fig. 59) was presumably made at the same time, offering a more distant view of the rugged cliff, a broader prospect of the village, and a glimpse of the sea. Examination of this richly worked pastel reveals something of its technical history, during which layers of color were gradually built up across the sheet. Beneath the bright green in the foreground, for example, a substratum of purplish gray can be detected, echoing a pale gray layer that is still visible under the blue of the sky. This more somber early state, followed by Monet's increased boldness in the application of local color, might be expected of a relative novice, as might the addition of dark lines to clarify certain foreground forms at the end of the process. His exploitation of the paper's texture and the inspired completion of the work with touches of bright pink and grass green illustrate the young Monet's responsive engagement with the medium and his determination to capture the distinctive qualities of this spartan subject.[24] A group of pastels made at Sainte-Adresse may well date to the years after his return from Algeria, when the Grand Journal again takes up the story.[25] According to the diarist, the Beguin Billecocqs holidayed in the same area that year and met up with "Oscar, who was actively applying himself to his canvases."[26]

After these tentative beginnings, Monet's pastels show a gradual increase in inventiveness, in the mastery of color, and in the flexibility with which he applied his discoveries to work in other media. As we have seen, all these elements were combined in the memorable months spent at the Saint-Siméon farm, between the early summer and late fall of 1864. Manifestly enjoying the company of Boudin and Jongkind, the twenty-four-year-old Monet was surrounded by the making of drawings, watercolors, pastels, and oil paintings, by these and other residents at the inn. Though few such works from his own hand have been specifically traced to these months, we are told that members of the Beguin Billecocq family bought several "delicious" Normandy landscapes from Monet when he returned to Paris, as well two "pencil drawings,

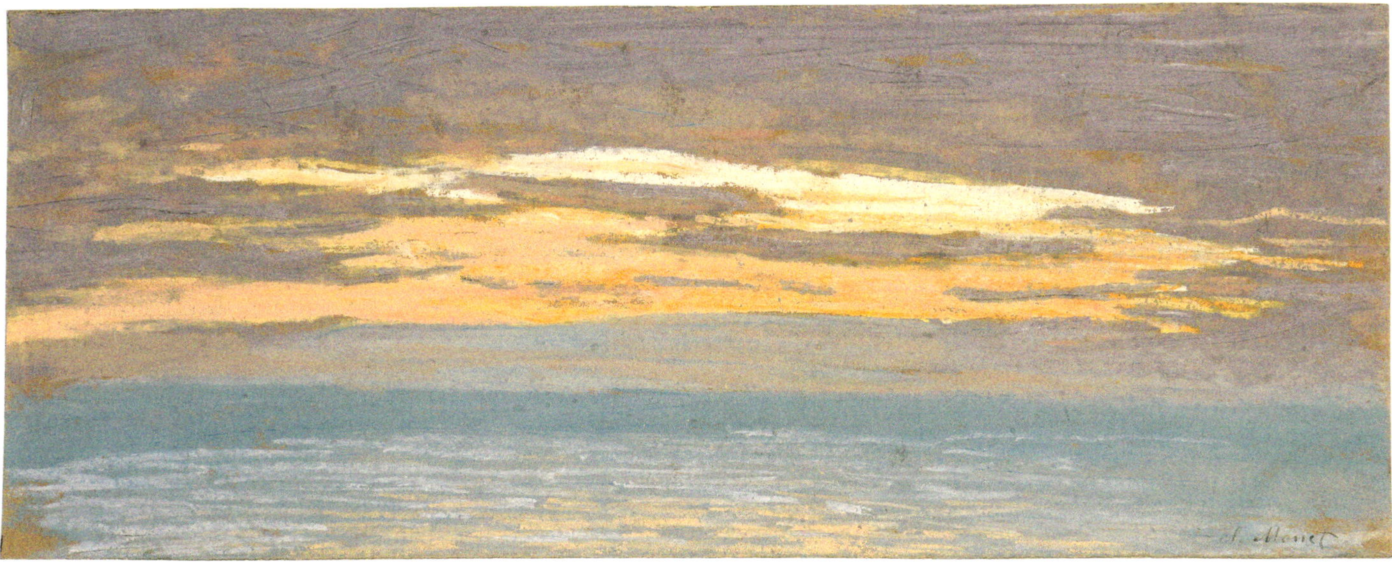

111
View of the Sea at Sunset, c. 1862–64. Pastel, 153 x 400 mm. Museum of Fine Arts, Boston. Bequest of William P. Blake in memory of his sister, Anne Dehon Blake [P34]

representing Normandy farms."[27] Given his previous, somewhat tentative experience with pastel at Yport and perhaps Sainte-Adresse and elsewhere, it is hardly surprising to find him making dramatic progress in the medium as the months passed.[28] It is also understandable that Monet should occasionally fall back on the notion of pastel as a subsidiary medium, still one of its habitual functions in the artistic community. In Monet's case, the earliest and most securely documented examples of this kind are a small set of studies that relate loosely to *Towing a Boat, Honfleur* (fig. 110), a precocious canvas made at this time.[29] The painting directs us toward the west of the Seine estuary, with Honfleur's small harbor and unmistakable lighthouse on the horizon, while high on the left are the trees bordering the Val-de-Grâce, where the Saint-Siméon farm was situated. While nothing is known about its inception, Richard Brettell has argued that this canvas "best exemplifies Monet's status as a direct open-air painter," noting that it was executed at speed to capture "a moment at sunset," and thus "its very imagery is of short duration."[30]

This approach to *Towing a Boat, Honfleur* can be further inflected in several ways. In 1864, Monet was still a virtual novice at outdoor painting and could be reduced to frustration by its complex demands. Given the thrilling yet elusive subject of this canvas, he may well have found that its execution taxed his powers considerably. Citing the picture's surface, Brettell notes that "Monet could not have made this work in one sitting," and we might speculate that the still-inexperienced artist also resorted to other means to achieve his goal. The existence of *View of the Sea at Sunset* (fig. 111), a substantial pastel study at the Museum of Fine Arts, Boston, that corresponds closely to the central area of sky in the painting, seems to point to an intermediate stage in this procedure. Pastel, already somewhat familiar to Monet, could be manipulated at will and applied with extreme rapidity in front of the most fugitive natural events. The richly mingled golds, mauves, and warm grays in the Boston work, therefore, may well represent Monet's first response to the unfolding sunset, to be consulted over the hours and perhaps days in which the Rochester composition progressed. Compared to the static scenes at Yport, this pastel was remarkably ambitious in its own right, approaching the spontaneity of the sky studies made by Boudin at this very period. Signs of improvisation in *View of the Sea at Sunset* endorse its status as an on-the-spot study, where certain colors have been dragged through earlier pastel marks, other areas brushed or wiped, and water perhaps applied at some stage.[31] The immediate link with Boudin, the "king of skies," who certainly exploited his own pastel studies when

112
Sunset over the Sea, c. 1862–64. Pastel and gouache on buff-colored paper, 172 x 332 mm. Ashmolean Museum of Art and Archaeology, University of Oxford [P30]

113
Broad Landscape, c. 1864–66. Pastel, 174 x 359 mm. Museum of Fine Arts, Boston. Bequest of William P. Blake in memory of his sister, Anne Dehon Blake [P32]

114
Landscape with Houses, c. 1864–66. Pastel on beige paper, 219 x 425 mm. The Metropolitan Museum of Art, New York. Bequest of Susan Dwight Bliss, 1966 [P38]

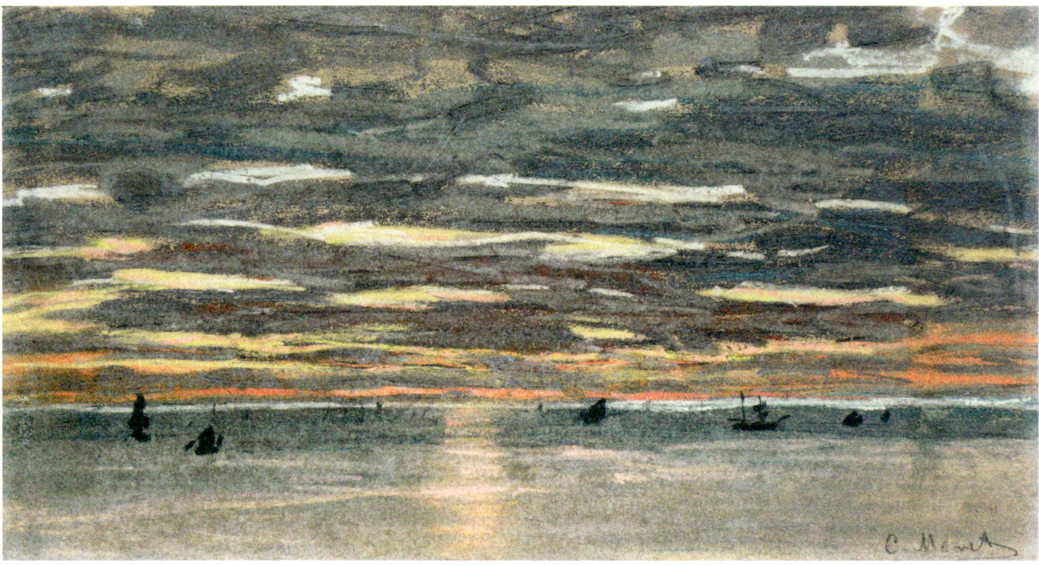

embarking on major paintings, increases the likelihood that Monet experimented in this way. Even more suggestive is the discovery that certain features of the Boston pastel come close to a painted cloudscape by Boudin, raising the possibility that the two artists worked side-by-side or even shared each others' preparatory studies at this date.[32]

Monet's choice of a long, narrow sheet of paper for *View of the Sea at Sunset* associates it with at least fifteen similarly proportioned pastel images from his early years.[33] Each approximately twice as broad as it is high, these works recall a format much favored by Daubigny, both in his drawings and paintings on canvas, where a sweeping gaze across a wide vista is often implied. In this group of Monet's pastels, similarly broad prospects of earth and sea are laid out before us, beneath skies that range from the ominous to the serene. The Ashmolean Museum's *Sunset over the Sea* (fig. 112) is a denser version of the Boston pastel, unrelated to any known painting but—like *View of the Sea at Sunset*—also signed by the artist.[34] As if surveying the gamut of atmospheric effects, Monet produced other variants in this informal sequence that show night descending, and a handful of studies that may represent the dawn. In *Broad Landscape* (fig. 113), powdery pinks and pale eggshell blues hint at the innocence of an early morning sky, set against a simple landscape whose bareness is relieved only by an enigmatic central pole. Such minimal terrain is in quiet contrast to the Saint-Siméon imagery and remains rare in Monet's oil paintings of his early and middle years.

As in the somewhat later series around *After the Rain*, though less directly concerned with seriality, this group suggests the use of pastel as an investigative process, here dealing with insubstantial qualities of light that are largely detached from notable structures or topographic forms. In *Broad Landscape*, Monet has conjured the atmosphere from fine, misty color brushed across a pale laid paper, exploiting the subtle qualities of its surface to evoke the brightness of the day. His understated composition mirrors the rising curve of the cloudscape in the symmetrical profile of the cliff, distantly recalling the elemental conception of nature in the work of Monet's Romantic predecessors. Remote from most of his own paintings of this period, these pastels explore a panoramic structure and a minimal narrative that Monet had neither the occasion nor perhaps the courage to take up in his larger canvases at this date. If they have a progeny, it may be the oils of his last decades, with their eruptions of disembodied luminance and materiality on a massive, wall-size scale.

An exception to this general pattern is the unusual *Landscape with Houses* (fig. 114), which is among the most severe of Monet's pastel

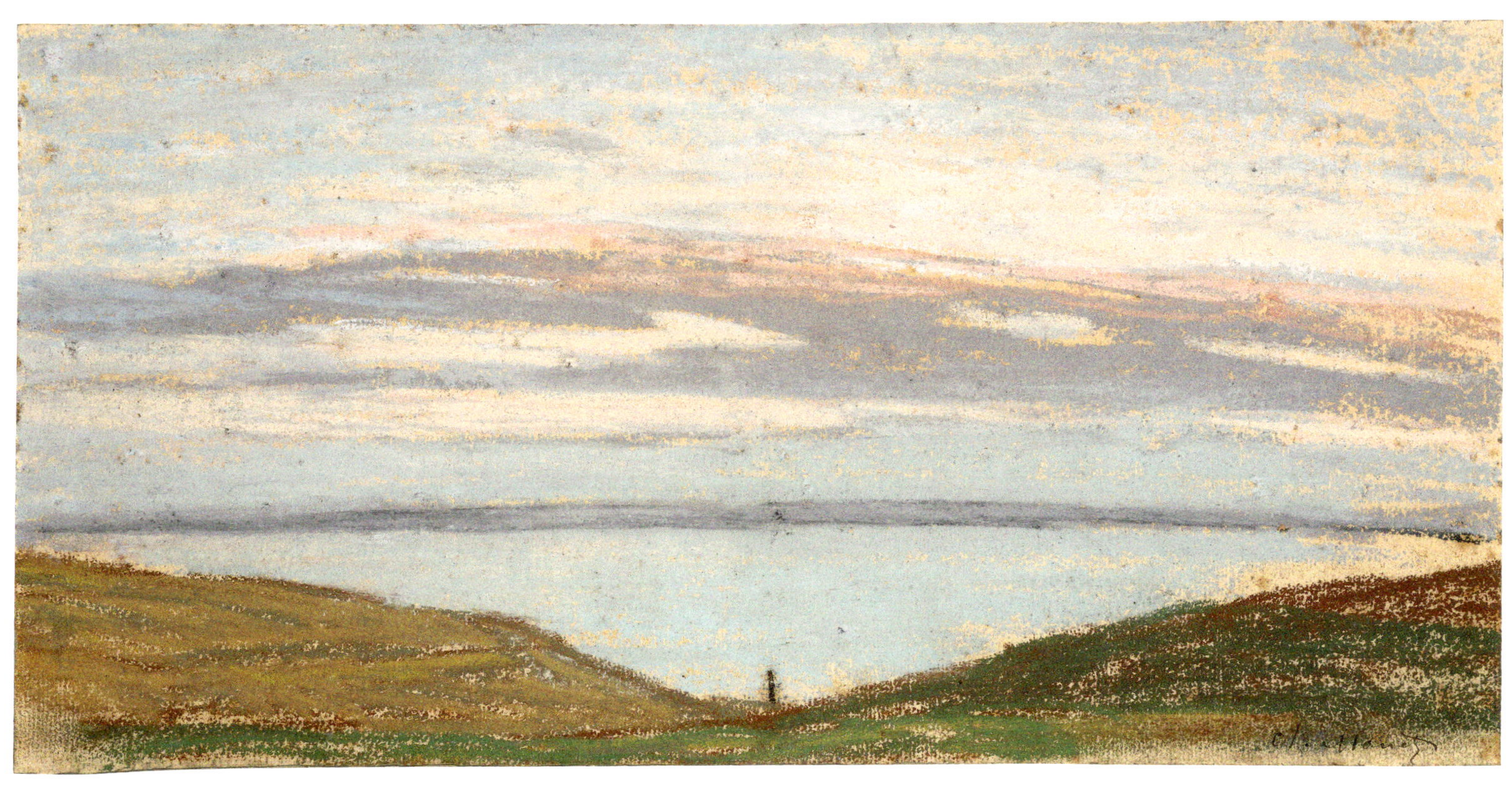

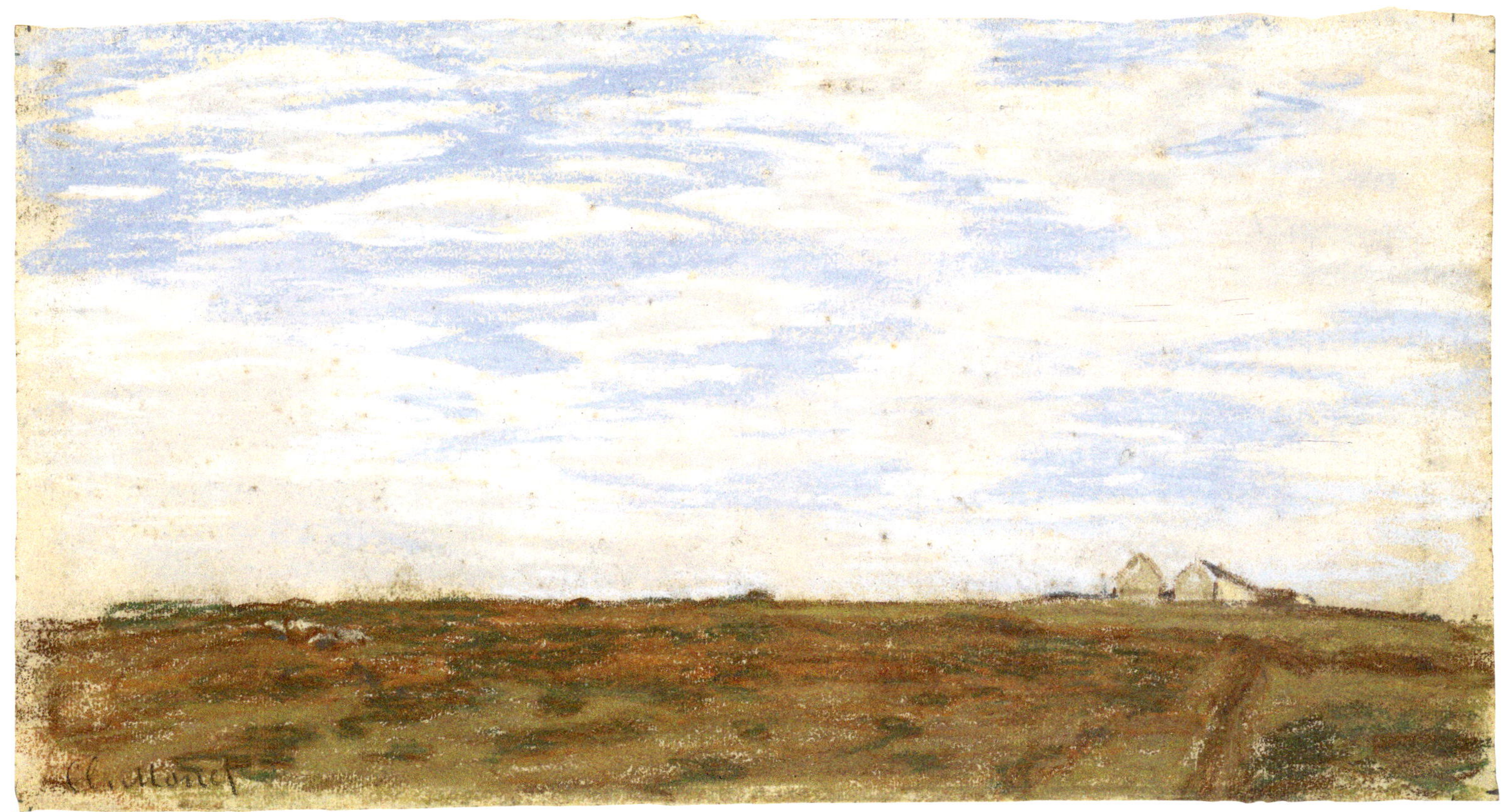

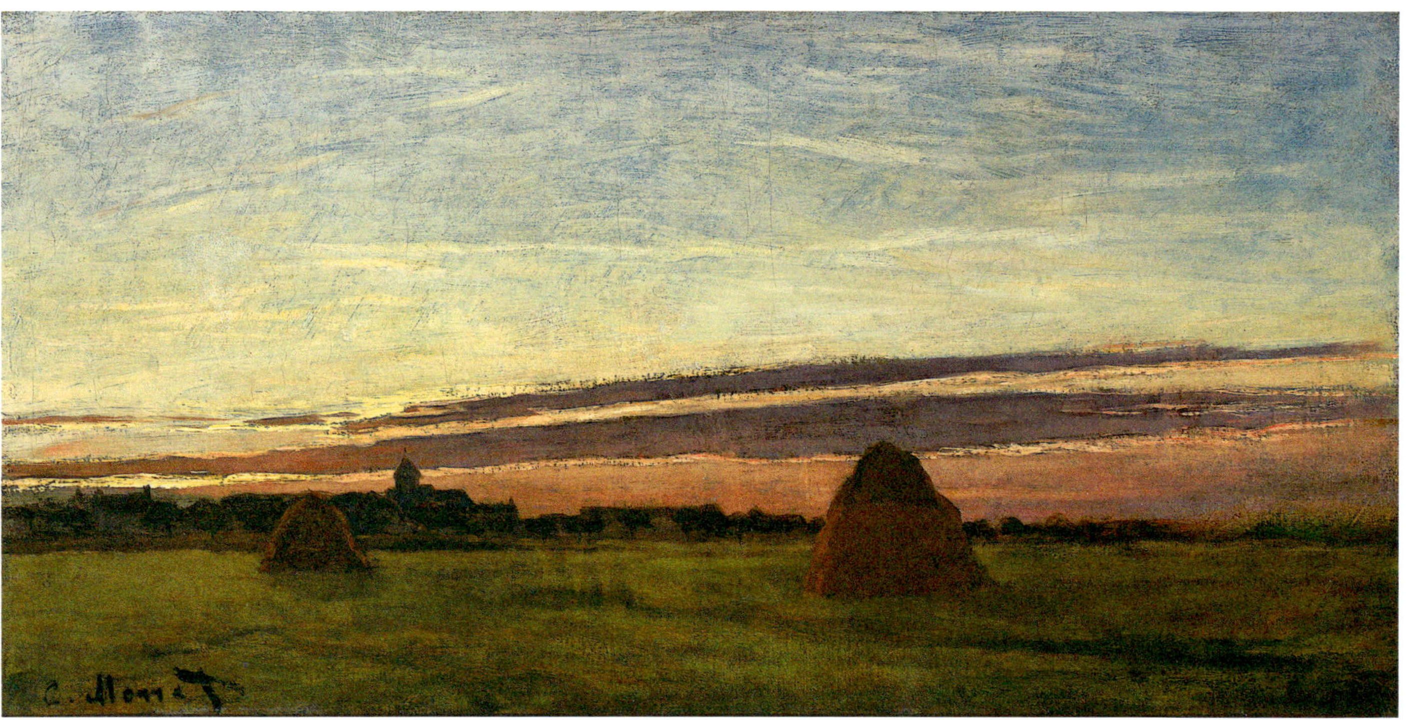

115
Grainstacks near Chailly at Sunrise, 1865. Oil on canvas, 30.2 x 60.3 cm. San Diego Museum of Art (Museum Purchase) [W55a]

subjects and one that relates tantalizingly to a contemporary canvas. No prominent clouds or rich colors invade this lightly textured sky, while the bare landscape gives few clues to its location. The coarse, dark texture of the earth may suggest recent rain or agricultural activity, and we might guess that an ill-defined building at far right indicates a farm. Monet's reasons for selecting this empty scene are not immediately apparent, unless he wished to test his resources against extreme compositional and chromatic simplicity.[35] As with several works from this loose sequence, however, a firm signature was added to *Landscape with Houses*, indicating that Monet saw it as a complete and viable creation. In 1916, he gave the pastel to a charitable cause organized by the writer Edith Wharton, who illustrated it in color alongside other donated images and texts, in *The Book of the Homeless*.[36] The same landscape may also have inspired Monet to conceive his enigmatic small canvas *Grainstacks near Chailly at Sunrise* (fig. 115), an undated picture that has been related to his third stay at Fontainebleau in 1865.[37] Combining the low horizon and double-square format of pastels such as *Broad Landscape* with the streaked clouds of *View of the Sea at Sunset* and *Sunset over the Sea*, this work represents a rare case in which a Monet painting may have grown directly out of a colored work on paper. Not precisely identical in design, the canvas and the Metropolitan Museum pastel nevertheless show a similar distribution of land and sky, as well as signs of distant habitation, and both include a variant of a conical, grainstack-like form. Made at a time when the role of pastel in his working practice was still undefined, this pairing is rich in significance, not least in its inference that Monet sometimes carried pastels with him on painting expeditions.

Several pastels with markedly more complex surfaces and imagery appear to have been prompted by Monet's visits to Honfleur and the Saint-Siméon farm in the mid-1860s. Unlike the sky studies and empty plateaus, these works show steep hills and deep valleys, expansive views of distant habitation, and dramatic meteorological events. Many represent the place where the river Seine, after its long passage from Paris, flows into the ocean between Honfleur and Le Havre. In *The Seine Estuary* (fig. 116), the delicately pointed spire at left is that of the church at Harfleur, a small town on the outskirts of Le Havre.[38] An engraving by Daubigny (fig. 117),

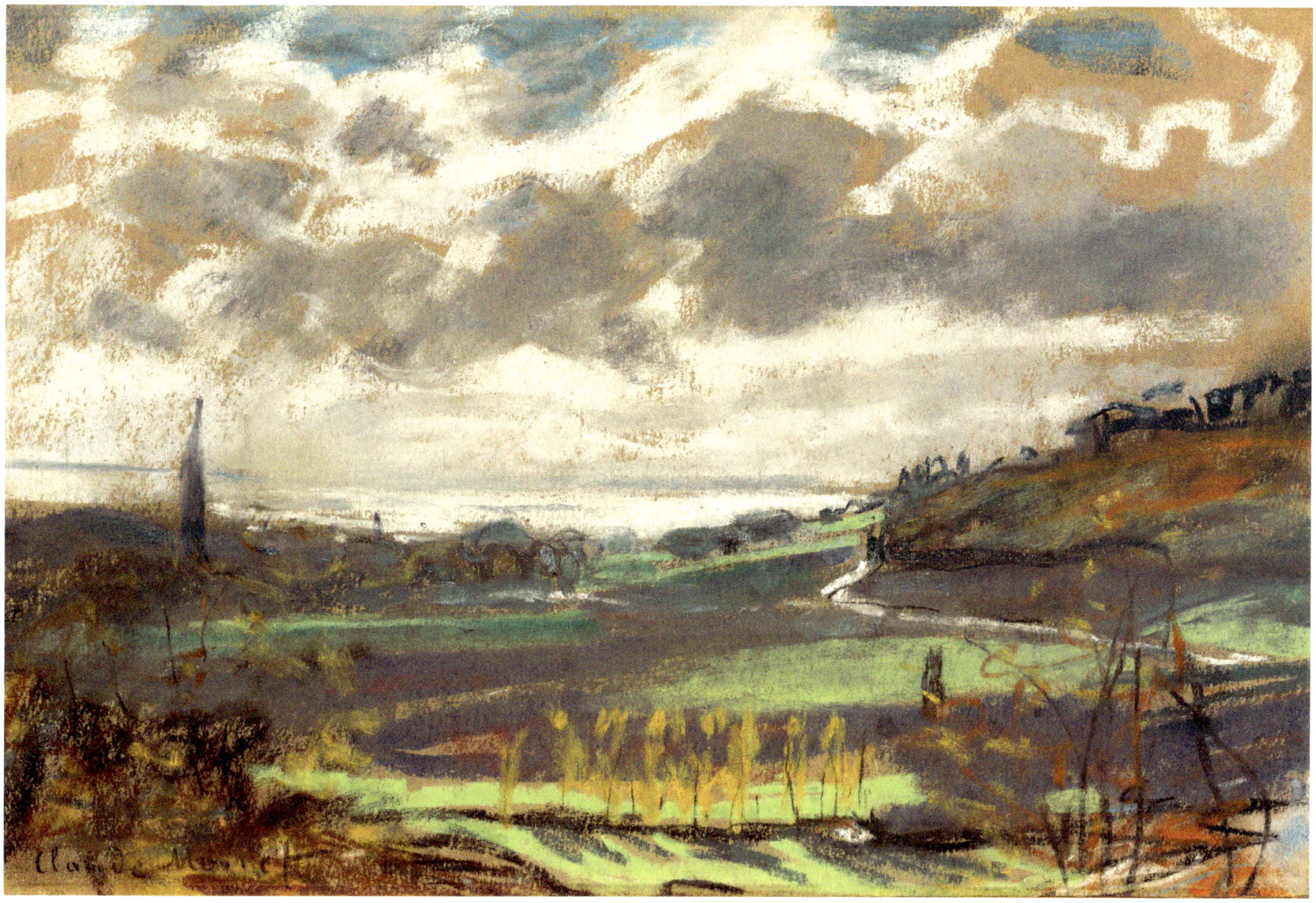

116
The Seine Estuary, c. 1864–70. Pastel on paper laid down on canvas, 251 x 375 mm. Private collection [P63]

117
After Charles François Daubigny, *View of Harfleur*, c. 1855. Wood engraving, 70 x 89 mm. From Eugène Chapus, *Guides Itinéraires de Paris au Havre* (Paris: Librairie de L. Hachette et Cie., 1855), p. 183

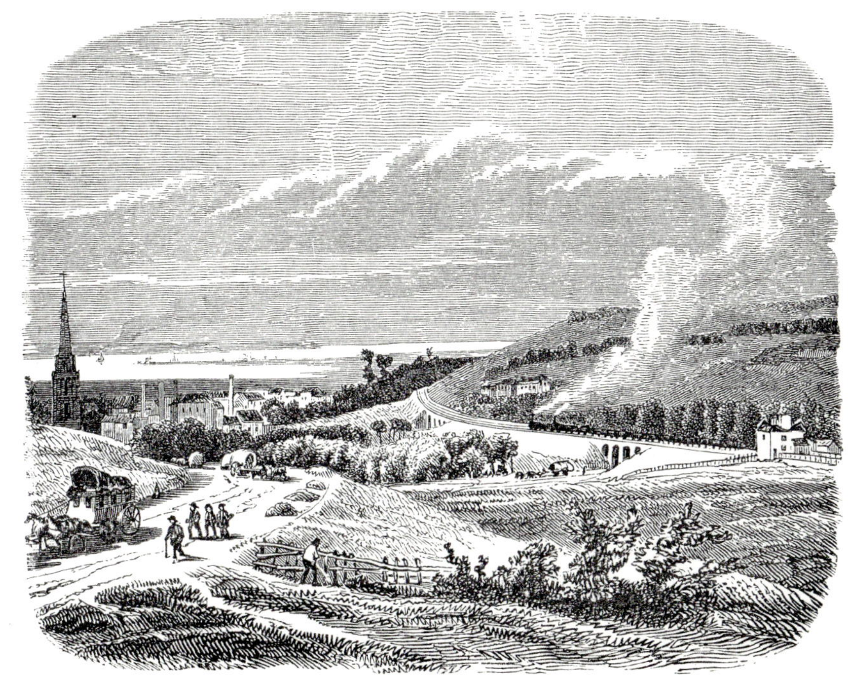

Vue d'Harfleur.

reproduced in the 1855 *Guides Itinéraires de Paris au Havre*, shows almost the same view from a greater distance and emphasizes a railway track at right that is hardly featured in Monet's composition.[39] Looking south over the water toward the site of the Toutain farm, Monet chose to focus on the scintillating movement of sunshine across this landscape, rather than the finer points of the area's geography. Color was applied with extraordinary gusto, in broad, flourishing strokes that simultaneously defined the volatility of Monet's subject and the impromptu character of his enterprise. Dark lines in the foreground are almost slashed onto the paper, while a hasty ribbon of white pastel in the sky captures the scudding clouds. Just as vivid is the palette, spanning brilliant silvers, deep purple-grays, and saturated lilacs, with telling touches of warm red-brown and vivid lime green, and strokes of gold where the sun catches a line of saplings. Presumably made on one of his visits to Normandy later in this decade, when Monet's pastel technique was well advanced, this was by any standard a tour-de-force of observation and rapid execution. Tonally and gesturally more extreme than even Boudin's most uninhibited studies, it may owe more to Jongkind's dynamic interweaving of intense color with an energetic graphism. Whatever its origin, we are left in little doubt about Monet's enthusiastic embrace of pastel as he approached his late thirties.

Pastel in the Late 1860s

A pastel of a very different kind is the vivacious *Fruit Trees* (see fig. 73), an undated work that Wildenstein places at a later period. Another eloquent testimony to Monet's love of Normandy, this study of an apple-laden orchard seems to belong with his visit to Saint-Siméon in 1864, or perhaps to the time Monet again spent in the area with his now-pregnant companion, Camille Doncieux, from late 1866 until early 1867.[40] A gap of four years separates the first Saint-Siméon pastels from the next group of such works that were dated by Monet himself, which center on the year 1868. In the intervening period, at least thirty undated pastels can be traced to local sites he is known to have visited, on the basis of their broad affinity with well-documented paintings. During this crucial phase in Monet's developing use of pastel, we sense an increased confidence and versatility, the result of both private experimentation and continuing contacts with older colleagues. As so often in his career, such productivity does not necessarily correspond with a settled personal existence. The second half of the 1860s was a period of exceptional turbulence in Monet's life, so extreme that a letter to Bazille hinted at an impulsive attempt to commit suicide.[41] Money was a persistent problem: his successes at the 1865 and 1866 Salons were vital in attracting the attention of critics, fellow artists, and dealers but failed to secure sufficient sales to finance a regular studio or pay for his travels and domestic expenses. Support from his family was intermittent, often obliging him to implore friends like Bazille and Gautier for assistance or letters of support. Along with several recorded gifts, we now know that the Beguin Billecocq circle made frequent purchases from him at this time, of both works on canvas and paper.[42]

When Théophile first met Monet's new companion, in December of 1865, he was instantly charmed by the "ravishing" Camille. Previously a shadowy figure in Monet's life, Camille emerges vividly from the pages of the Grand Journal, where we are told that she soon joined with Monet in the Beguin Billecocq "theatrical evenings" in Paris and was judged to be "an excellent comedienne." Clearly impressed, Théophile was untroubled by their irregular relationship; "this young woman had an excellent manner," he wrote, "wearing elegant but simple outfits and engaging in conversation."[43] At the next Salon, Camille achieved further distinction as the subject of Monet's well-received *Camille, or the Woman with a Green Dress*, a work fulsomely admired by Théophile when he visited the exhibition. At the end of the year, Camille seems to have returned with Monet to Normandy, staying at Saint-Siméon once more as work continued on his paintings. His correspondence over this

118
Cat Sleeping on a Bed, c. 1865–70. Pastel, 110 x 210 mm. Private collection, courtesy of Jill Newhouse and Neffe de-Gandt Fine Art, London [P60]

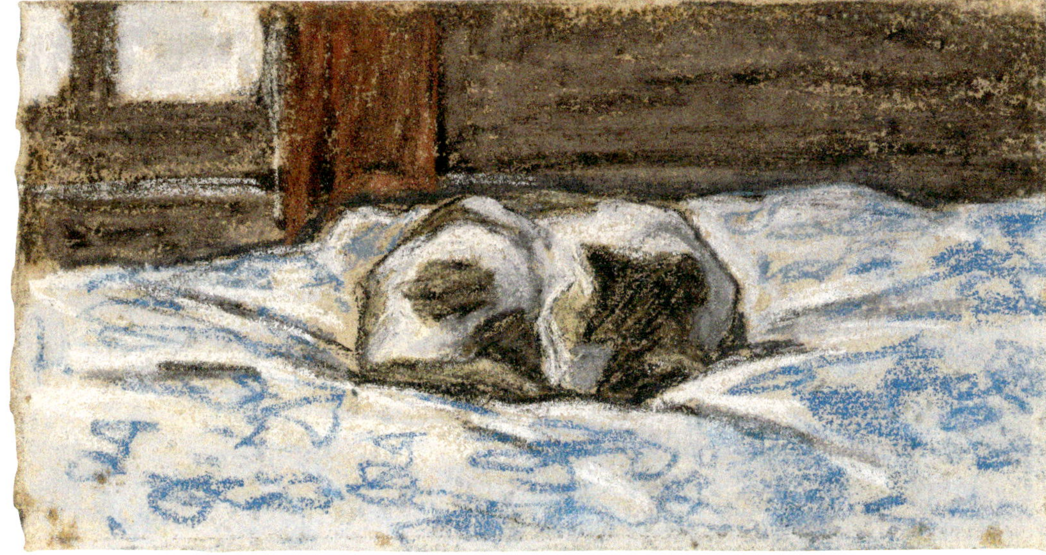

period describes the extreme financial hardship of the couple, when food, rent, and even the materials of his craft were almost beyond their means. Adding to their woes, Monet's liaison with Camille was disapproved of by his father, who refused to receive her at his home in Sainte-Adresse. Camille was the model for several important canvases during these years and posed for his only known drawing of a single figure, for *Luncheon on the Grass* (see fig. 90). The birth of their son Jean in August of 1867 increased the couple's needs and the pressure on Monet to create and sell works of art. His characteristically violent mood swings and self-dramatizations continued; in June, for example, he wrote to Bazille from Sainte-Adresse, "I am as happy and well as could be," only to tell him six weeks later, "I'm going through the most terrible torments."[44]

One result of this predicament that directly affected his paintings and pastels was that Monet, sometimes accompanied by Camille, moved frequently from cheap rented houses to borrowed lodgings and work spaces, and shuttled to and fro between Paris and Normandy. During one such sojourn, he executed a pastel portrait of Camille as she reclined on a sofa, and took the apparently unique step of producing a counterproof of the image.[45] It was perhaps at a similar moment of domestic calm that Monet made the charming *Cat Sleeping on a Bed* (fig. 118), another exceptional pastel that unites pattern and rhythmic form in ways that prefigure the work of Bonnard and the Nabis. The focus and direction of Monet's painting could be similarly improvised, ranging over elaborate suburban portraits and chaste still lifes, storm-swept harbors and rustic woodland, scenes of the metropolis and paintings of the beach at Trouville. Monet's fragmentary correspondence reveals that these works were already impelled by the clash of imperatives that would vitalize his output for decades. At Étretat in late 1868, he declared, "I'm surrounded here by all that I love. I go into the country which is so lovely that I perhaps find it even more agreeable in winter than in summer."[46] Telling Bazille that he no longer missed the distractions of Paris, Monet asked: "Don't you think that, face to face with nature and alone, one can do better?"[47] Earlier letters had been concerned with the very Parisian marketplace he was now rejecting, enjoying gossip about Manet and Courbet, and including appeals for aid to influential figures, such as the critic Arsène Houssaye.[48] These twin drives, to paint nature head-on and to survive from day to day, almost overwhelmed him.

In such chaotic times, two phases of relative tranquility in Monet's art—if not in his practical affairs—resulted in vigorous, masterful groups of pastels. The first dates from 1867, when Monet left Camille in Paris and lodged

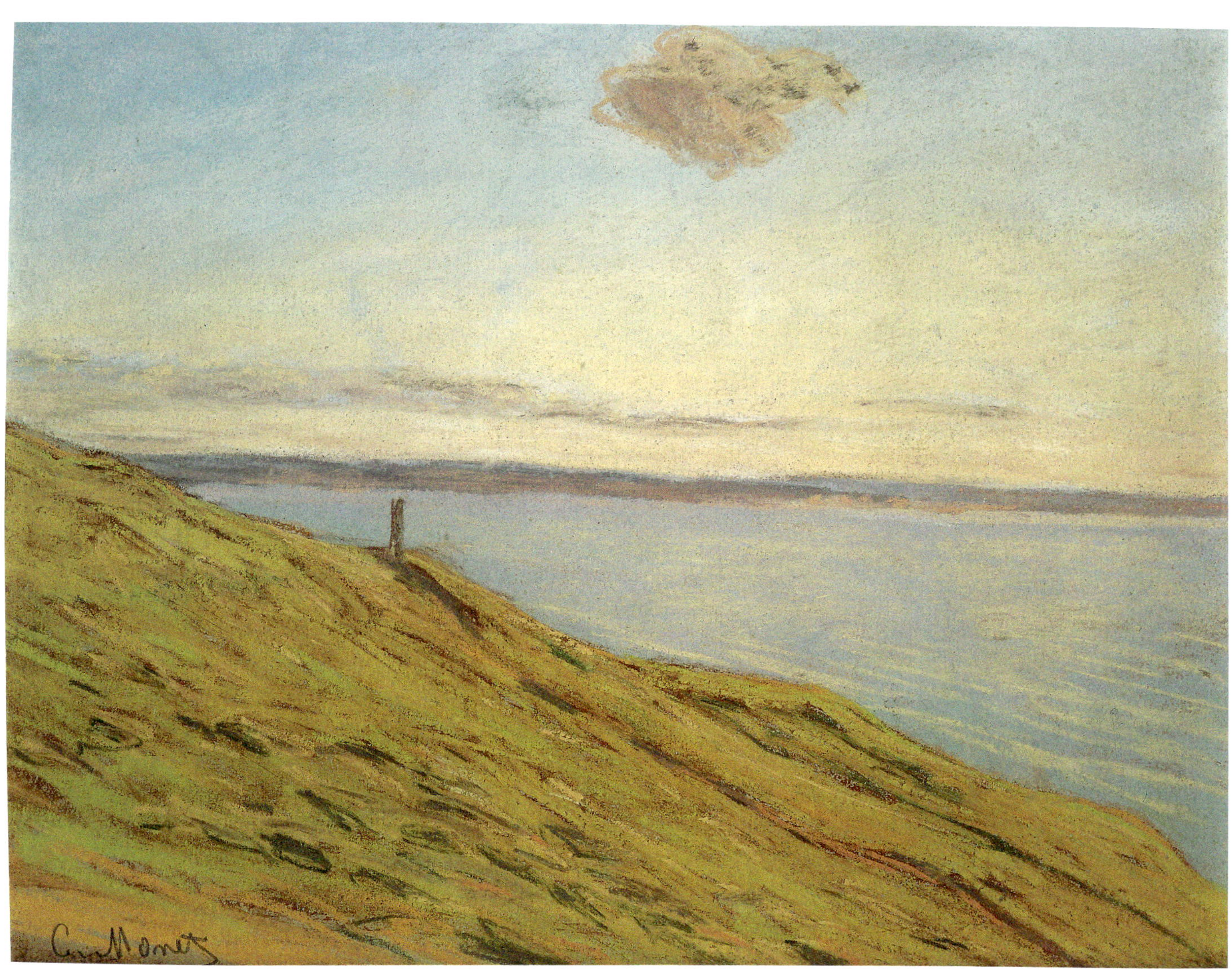

119
Sainte-Adresse, View across the Estuary, c. 1865–70. Pastel, 216 x 279 mm. Private collection [P12]

with members of his family in Sainte-Adresse. Fired with ambition, he began work immediately after his arrival: "I've twenty or so canvases well under way," he informed Bazille; "Stunning seascapes, figures and gardens, something of everything in fact. Among my seascapes, I'm painting the regattas at Le Havre with lots of people on the beach and the shipping lane covered with small sails. For the Salon I'm doing an enormous steamboat."[49] More than a century later, several of these pictures are counted among his early masterpieces: the subdued *Sainte-Adresse*, now in the National Gallery of Art in Washington, carried the subject of one of Monet's first Salon entries to new heights of grandeur and again acknowledged his debts to Daubigny and Jongkind, while the meter-wide *Regatta at Sainte-Adresse*, in the Metropolitan Museum of Art, encapsulated the translucency of the sea and the airy spaces beloved of Normandy vacationers.[50] In these and other coastal canvases, Monet developed a structural model that would serve him throughout his middle years. Characterized by high skies and pronounced horizons, they are typically offset by a powerful wedge of coastline that emphasizes the underlying geometry of the image. This asymmetrical matrix also provided the foundation for the pastel *Sainte-Adresse, View across the Estuary* (fig. 119) and at least six similar works on paper from this sojourn.[51] Daringly stripped of incident, from substantial buildings and landmarks to such devices as "a shipping lane covered with small sails," the sumptuously textured triangles

120

Taking a Walk on the Cliffs at Sainte-Adresse, 1867. Oil on canvas, 73 x 100 cm. Matsuoka Museum of Art, Tokyo [W93a]

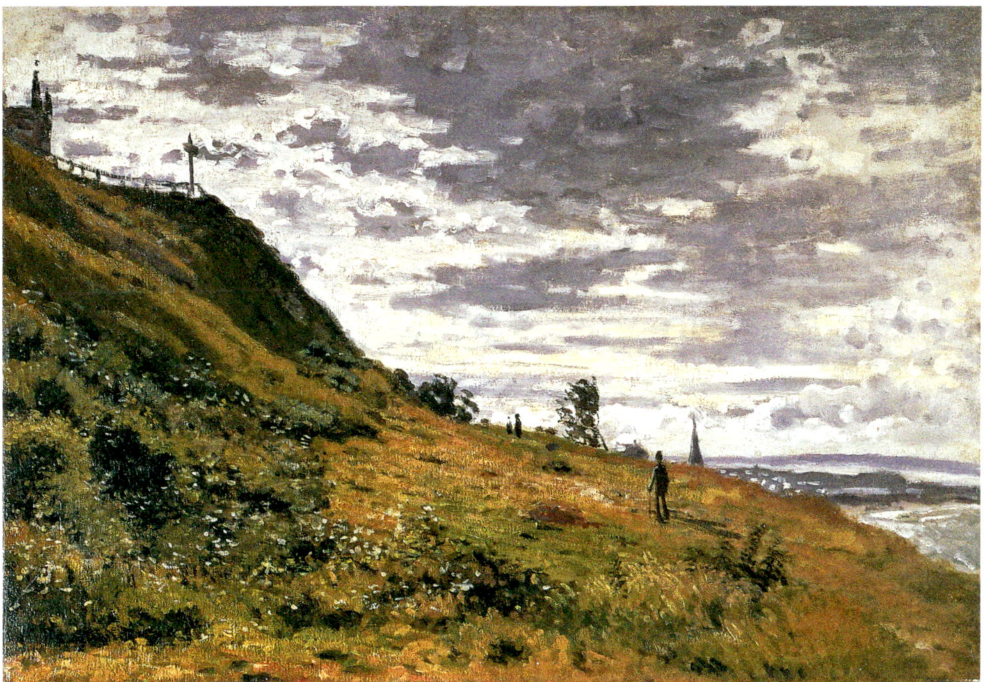

of sea and headland in this work, suspended beneath a parallel strip of sky, belong with Monet's most expansive inventions to date.

The clarity of this pastel was perhaps inspired by his earlier exercises in the medium, such as *Broad Landscape* and *Landscape with Houses*, though *Sainte-Adresse, View across the Estuary* exceeds them all in its rich facture, which might almost be described as painterly. In the foreground, for example, energetic ribbons of green, yellow, ocher, and red-brown are braided together like rapidly applied brushmarks, apparently unsupported by a linear draft beneath. Color has been stroked into color, its cumulative warmth intensified by planes of bright blue above and beyond the headland. The exuberance of this work seems to capture the euphoria felt by Monet when he arrived at Sainte-Adresse in June, as well as his excitement at the "stunning seascapes" also underway. An oil painting from the same period, *Taking a Walk on the Cliffs at Sainte-Adresse* (fig. 120), is unusual in excluding the ocean almost entirely, but otherwise provides a bridge between the two contrasting media. Both canvas and pastel are based on the view from the Cap de la Hève, the westernmost point of the landmass above Le Havre, where Monet looked over the town toward the Seine estuary and the Côte-de-Grâce in the distance. An even more extensive pastel, *Sainte-Adresse, View of Le Havre*, reaches nearly 500 millimeters in width and combines elements of both works, now showing the same vista from a higher vantage point.[52] These two sheets, along with contemporaneous paintings, illustrate the potential for creative interplay between Monet's different techniques and materials at this stage in his career. Allowing him to work rapidly or reflectively, to test a new angle of view or an untried combination of hues, or to note a theme for future investigation, these studies on paper and canvas seem like steps in the same forward progression.

The possibility of a reciprocal, mutually dependent relationship between pastel, drawing, and painting, with the former sometimes setting the pace, has already been noted in the context of *After the Rain* and its serial companions, some dated 1868. It is again strikingly apparent in Monet's depictions of Étretat from the late 1860s. Traveling a mere fifteen miles north of Le Havre and the Cap de la Hève, Monet had been visiting the spectacularly eroded bay of Étretat at least since his teenage years. From the pages of the Beguin Billecocq Grand Journal, we have already learned of an excursion to the town in 1857, when

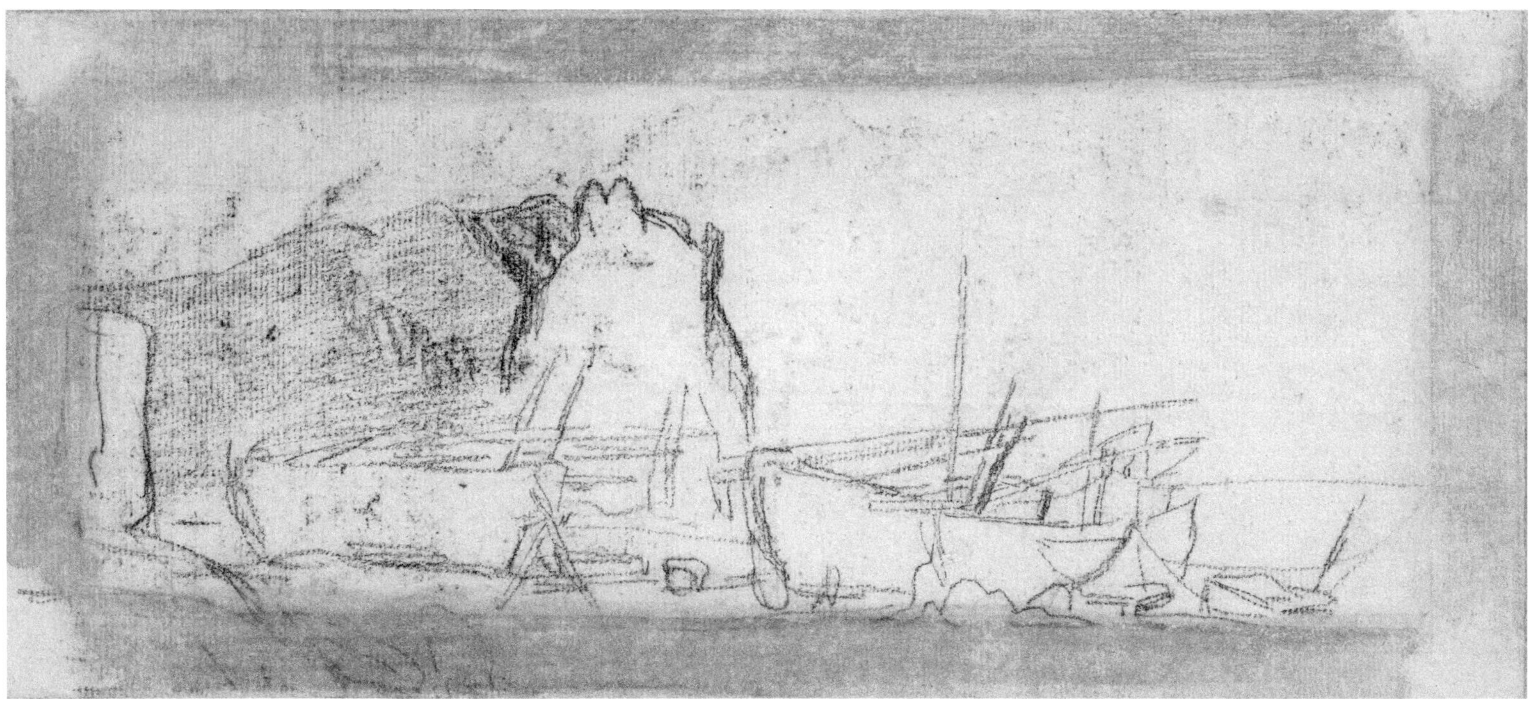

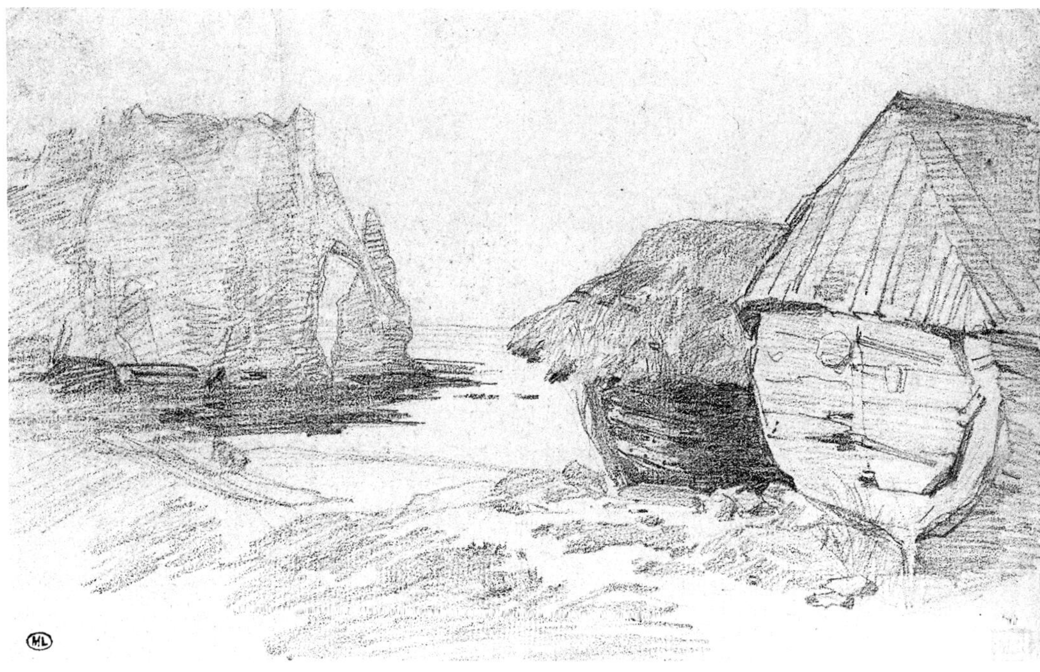

121
Boats on the Beach in Normandy, c. 1864. Black chalk, 135 x 305 mm. Private collection, courtesy of Elrick-Manley Fine Art, Inc. [verso of D433]

122
Eugène Boudin, *Boats Beached beside the Sea and Roofed to Provide Shelter*, n.d. Black crayon. 141 x 227 mm. Musée du Louvre, Paris

the sixteen-year-old artist "realized exquisite little sketches of the cliffs," to the delight of his companions.[53] Two unsigned and undated canvases of this same subject are also attributed to these intermediate years by Wildenstein, who implicitly dates them around 1864.[54] As both cases show, Étretat was already an established tourist destination and a lure for painters of all kinds, a phenomenon that Robert Herbert has thoughtfully set against Monet's own obsession with the bay.[55] Over the years, Monet would return repeatedly to this spectacular site, recording it in his sketchbooks, in scores of canvases, and in some of the most audacious pastels of his career.

A modest new insight has been added to this story during research for *The Unknown*

123

The Luncheon, 1868. Oil on canvas, 232 x 151 cm. Staedel Museum, Frankfurt [W132]

Monet, with the discovery of an unpublished drawing of the Porte d'Aval and its flanking cliff (fig. 121). Executed on the verso of *Boats on the Beach at Normandy* (see fig. 85), this study was concealed for many years by the mat and backing board of the catalogued work. The technique and graphic manner of both studies identifies them with the monochrome drawings made by Monet around 1864, such as *Cliffs and Sea, Sainte-Adresse* (see fig. 78) and *Coast of Lower Normandy* (see fig. 84), while adding a new location to that graphic repertoire. The revealed sketch shows Monet tackling one of the most frequently depicted prospects at Étretat, which also features in a canvas of unknown location that is grouped by Wildenstein with works of 1864.[56] Only slightly larger than the drawing, this small painting is known from a black-and-white photograph, but clearly depicts an unobstructed view of the cliff and its instantly recognizable arch. In the unfinished drawing, the scene is wider and cluttered by a group of beached boats and their variously angled spars, stressing its day-to-day actuality rather than its grandeur. Perhaps dissatisfied with this informality, Monet turned the sheet over and began his second composition of the fishing craft alone, situating them against the plainer background of the sea.[57] A sketchbook study in pencil by Boudin (fig. 122) shows a similar glimpse of the cliff at Étretat, here with the fishing boats replaced by *caloges*, hulks that had been abandoned and thatched to use as storage, though we can only guess at the likelihood of Monet's awareness of this prototype.[58] Like Monet's other monochrome studies of this period, his drawing may have been created as the basis for an etching, as a work for sale, or as a preliminary step toward painting a novel subject, or conceivably for all of these reasons.

In December of 1868, Monet, Camille, and their young son moved to a house at Étretat and remained there through a snowy winter. Their plain, dimly lit surroundings are known to us through a quartet of canvases showing family mealtimes, one of which, *The Luncheon* (fig. 123), Monet was planning to submit to the Salon. Despite the adversities of the season, he

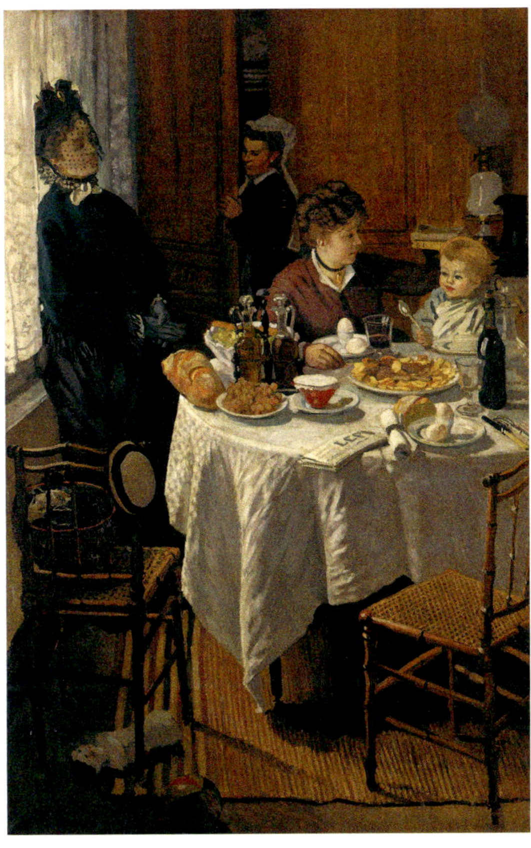

preferred to work: "I spend my time out-of-doors on the shingle when the weather is stormy or when the boats go out fishing," he reported to Bazille.[59] The elaborate *Caloges and Boat at Étretat* (fig. 124) presumably grew out of such experiences, though its refined details must have been completed in more sheltered conditions. At right is one of the unmistakable short, sturdy wooden craft that carried the Étretat fishermen out into the bay, here draped with nets and ropes from a recent expedition. Beyond it, at left, are several *caloges*, closely echoing Boudin's drawing, while situating Monet's pastel unequivocally in the famous bay. Distinguished from Monet's two previously discussed drawings of boats by the addition of color, *Caloges and Boat at Étretat* is exceptional in its densely recorded textures and maritime minutiae, as well as the complexity of its design and the precision of its finish.

In a way that is highly unusual in Monet's surviving oeuvre, these three variants on related Étretat motifs invite us to follow his technical procedure, from tentative beginnings with line

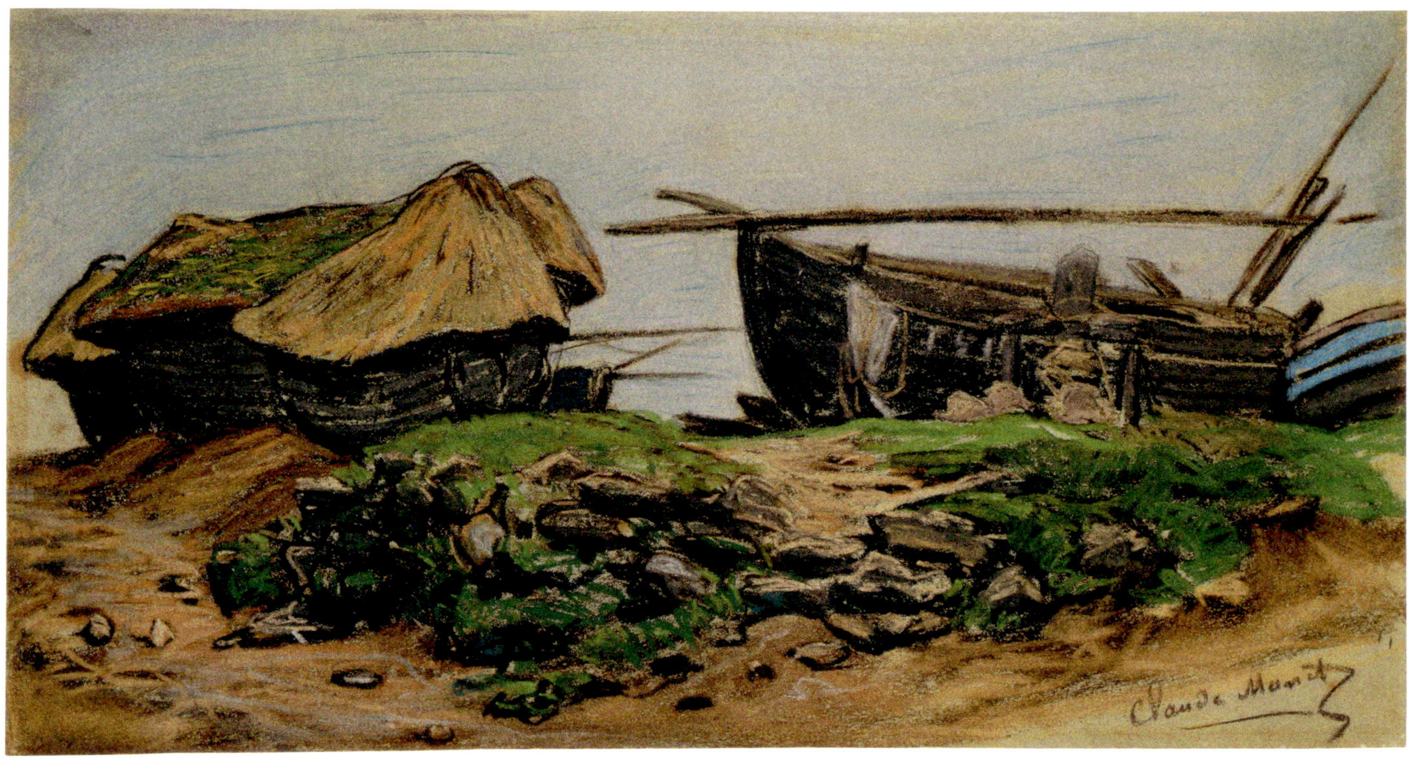

124
Caloges and Boat at Étretat, c. 1865–70. Pastel, 207 x 405 mm. Israel Museum Collection, Jerusalem. Gift of Abraham M. Adler, New York, to America-Israel Cultural Foundation, 1971 [P23]

to a polished formal construction that—once again—invokes the language of painting. *Caloges and Boat at Étretat* exploits the gamut of pictorial possibilities, from Monet's subtle differentiation of sea and sand, and his delight in the textures of thatch and foliage, to his exploitation of a palette that spans the delicate blue sky and the richly weathered timbers of the boats. Within this sophisticated image, the linear underpinnings of the composition reveal its origins in Monet's draftsmanship and perhaps a concern to display the full range of his skills as he achieved a marketable end product. It would be almost two decades, however, before he carried the subject to its logical conclusion, in a series of exceptionally sensuous paintings of beached boats, such as *Three Fishing Boats* (see fig. 234).

Monet had completed a wide variety of other pastels by the time he left Étretat in January 1869, including a second arrangement of *caloges* and fishing boats; a more conventional view of the local church; and three further studies of the cliffs.[60] Most of them were initialed or signed with a flourish, and we can imagine Monet, on his return to Paris, offering these picturesque scenes to collectors or galleries to boost his meager income. Rarely cynical in such situations, however, Monet had accepted new pictorial and physical challenges in these works, most conspicuously when he exposed himself to the tempest in making two energetic pastel studies of storms lashing the beach and rocks. One of these is very close to the Musée d'Orsay's painting, *Rough Sea at Étretat*, perhaps following it in time and certainly exceeding it in chromatic daring.[61] Setting the tone for later works in both media is *Étretat, the Arch, and the Aval Cliff* (fig. 125), where a blazing sunset expires behind the rocky massif that had inspired so many of Monet's precursors. Composed of broad, almost wild flourishes of just a few colors on coarse laid paper, this arresting scene was probably carried out in a matter of minutes. As in the studies for *Towing a Boat, Honfleur* of 1864, we instinctively respond to Monet's urgent mingling of salmon pink, pale greens, and a catalogue of different blues, with the sun slipping out of sight as he worked.

The audacity of this conception may owe something to the recent landscapes of Gustave Courbet, with whom Monet was often in contact during these years. The sky and sea

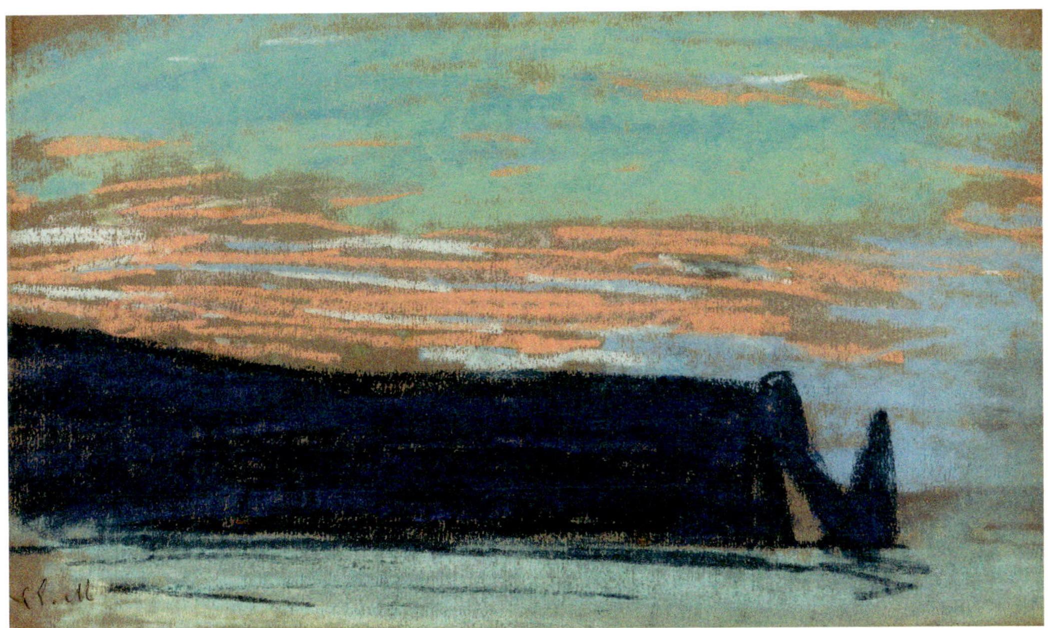

125

Étretat, The Arch, and the Aval Cliff, c. 1885. Pastel, 210 x 370 mm. Musée Marmottan Monet, Paris [P19]

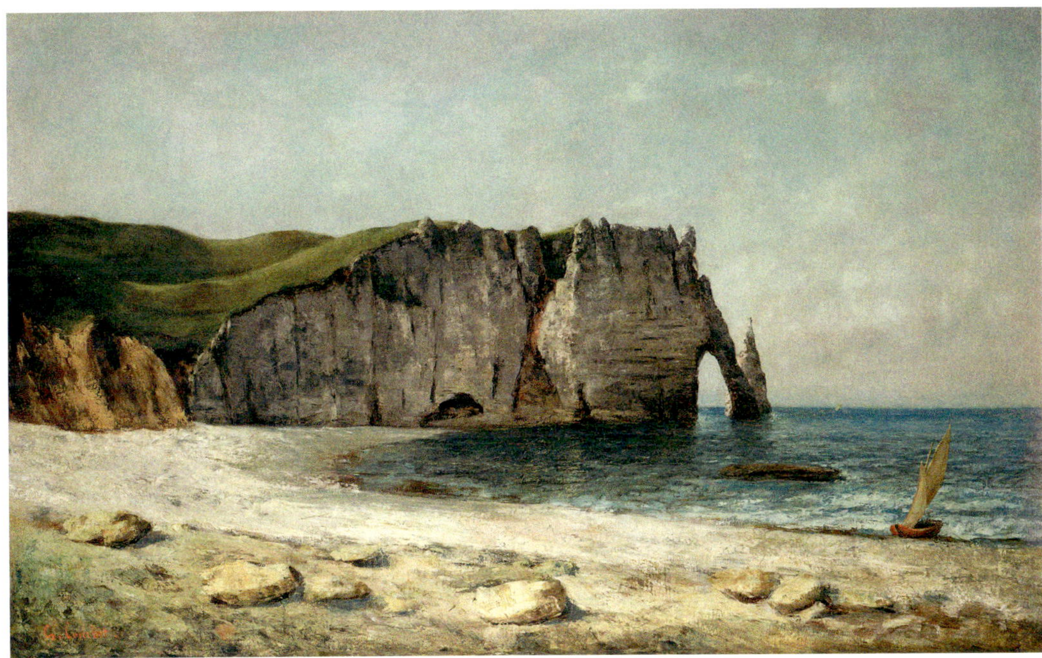

126

Gustave Courbet (French, 1819–1877), *Cliff at Étretat*, 1869. Oil on canvas, 76.2 x 123.1 cm. The Barber Institute of Fine Arts, University of Birmingham, Birmingham, England

paintings made by Courbet at Trouville in 1865, for example, had proposed new color harmonies and a breadth of execution that almost certainly encouraged Monet's experiments on canvas and perhaps his works on paper. In 1866, Monet and Camille had dined with Courbet in Deauville, during an expedition that may have resulted in the latter's first pictures of Étretat scenes, which depict the less characteristic northeastern sweep of the bay.[62] Three years later, Courbet returned to Étretat in the summer, some months after Monet and Camille had left. Paradoxically, therefore, Courbet was to follow Monet on this occasion, completing his definitive panoramas of the cliffs and beach between August and September, including several that have features in common with Monet's recently identified drawing (fig. 126).[63] In contrast to his young follower, and to his own stormy reputation, Courbet opted for sobriety, describing Étretat to his parents as "a charming little seaside town."[64] His paintings favored clear daylight and calm

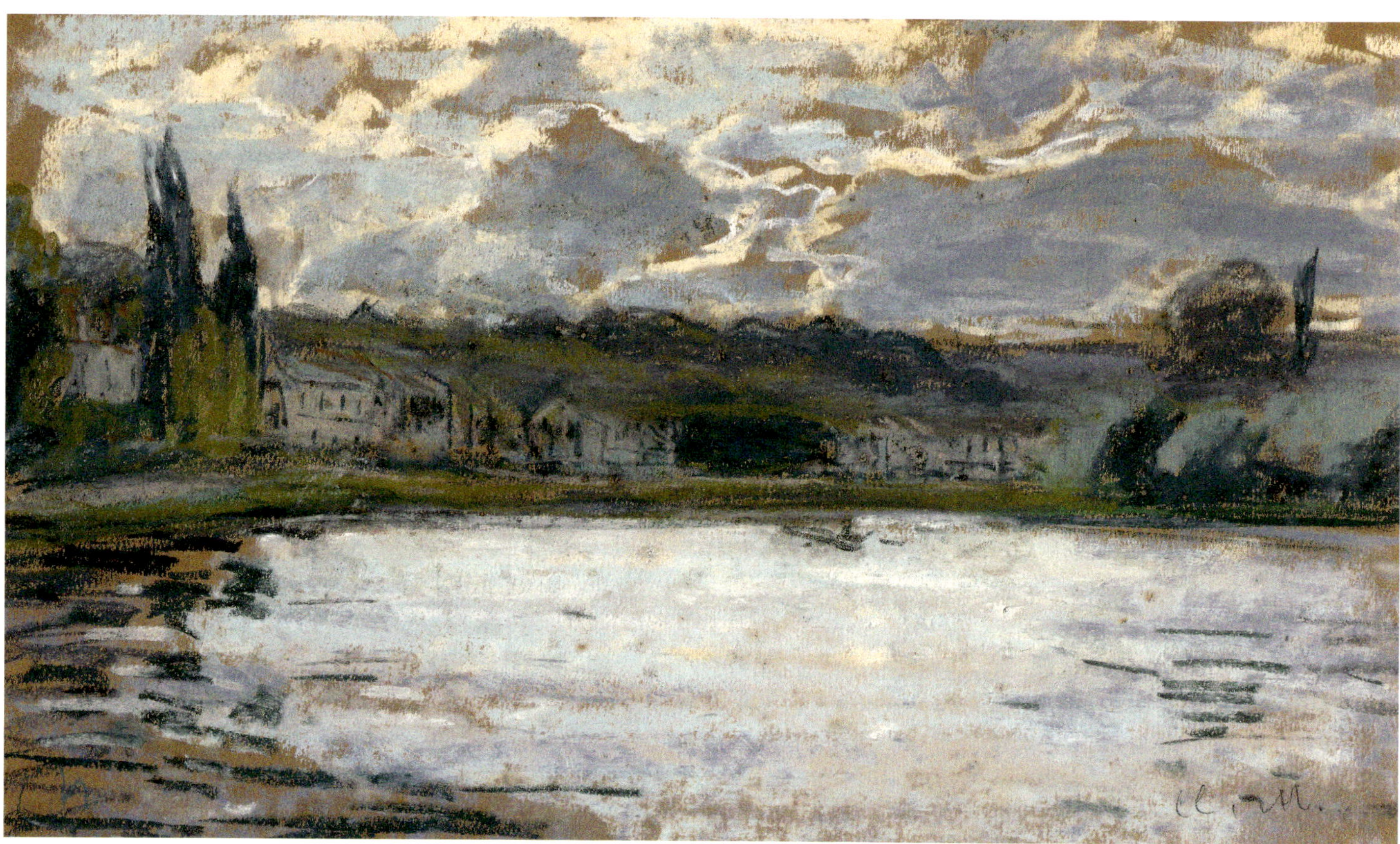

127
Bank of the Seine, c. 1869. Pastel on tan paper, 245 x 425 mm. Private collection [not in Wildenstein]

seas, and a muted range of browns, moss greens, and blue-grays; for all their monumentality, they already seem sedate beside the experiments of the twenty-year-old.

If Monet had hoped to alleviate his dire situation by selling pastels in Paris, it seems that he was disappointed: none of the works from Étretat have a recorded owner from this period and several remained with the artist until the end of his career, though it remains possible that some were included in the 1874 exhibition.[65] Similar setbacks on a number of personal and professional fronts continued to haunt Monet's existence from 1869 to 1874, distantly acted out against the national humiliation of the Franco-Prussian War and its violent political aftermath. In 1870 and 1871, the successive deaths of his Aunt Marie-Jeanne, his friend and occasional patron Frédéric Bazille, and his own father, tore three important figures from Monet's immediate circle. It also loosened his ties with Normandy and brought to an end many prospects for future aid. Refusals at the Salon brought more disappointment, when *The Luncheon,* begun at Étretat, for example, was rejected in 1870, only to be defiantly displayed by Monet at the 1874 group show. Paul Tucker has argued that Monet's income from the sale of paintings at this time was far higher than his pleas for help would suggest, a proposal supported by the Beguin Billecocq memoirs.[66] From 1872 onward, the young dealer Paul Durand-Ruel became an increasingly important factor in Monet's financial survival, eventually buying dozens of pictures and proselytizing on behalf of the nascent Impressionists generally. Monet also found a renewed solidarity with colleagues from earlier times, enjoying months of productive painting with Renoir at La Grenouillière, with Boudin at Trouville, and with Pissarro at Louveciennes. This phase was crucial in forming their group identity, as the loose confederation experimented boldly with outdoor painting and with radical ways of engaging with light, matter, and the transience of sensation.

Until now, there has been no documentary evidence that Monet made either pastels or independent drawings in the decade following

128
The Seine at Bougival, Evening, 1869. Oil on canvas, 60 x 73.3 cm. Smith College Museum of Art, Northampton, Massachusetts. Purchased [W151]

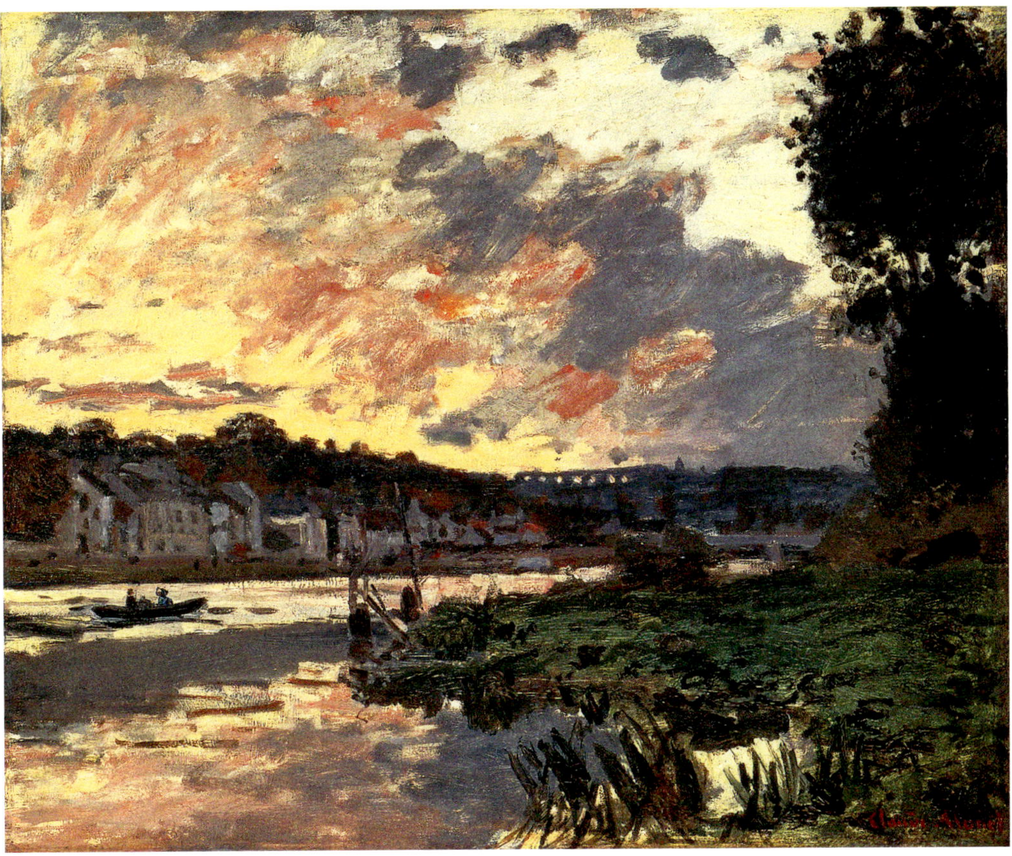

his departure from Étretat. Though many studies on paper remain undated and may well have originated during this period, the standard catalogues of Monet's work reveal not a single example that can be unequivocally associated with his career between 1869 and the beginning of the 1880s; the exceptions are the summary drawings found in his sketchbooks, which will be discussed in chapter 7. But given the intense graphic activity of Monet's earlier years, so vividly endorsed by the Beguin Billecocq archives and augmented by our examination of the first pastels, this decade-long hiatus seems baffling. As in his youth, we might reasonably postulate quantities of lost or destroyed works on paper, even as we introduce new candidates for consideration and evaluate freshly discovered information.

A recently discovered, uncatalogued sheet that evokes Monet's new life before his move to Argenteuil in 1871 is *Bank of the Seine* (fig. 127).[67] Through its resemblance to documented oil paintings, this muted but sensuous work can be situated with confidence in Monet's immediate post-Étretat period. The line of houses seen across the water, interspersed with poplars and other vegetation, is also found in a painting belonging to the Smith College Museum of Art, Monet's *The Seine at Bougival, Evening* (fig. 128), which shows part of the same motif from a more oblique angle. Bougival was then a village on the western outskirts of Paris, where Monet and Camille resided for a year in nearby Saint-Michel after leaving Normandy. True to form, the artist investigated his unfamiliar surroundings in several trial canvases, though this pastel seems to be the only extant response to the site in another medium.[68] When making *Bank of the Seine*, Monet used his preferred pale tan paper, countering the warmth of its surface with cooler blue and green pastels, and mixing white into the larger areas to suggest a cloudy sky and silver reflections. The low westerly light indicates the end of day, a progression that effectively continues into the sunset of the Smith College canvas. Such sequential affinities between pastels and oil paintings remind us of Monet's months at Honfleur and Étretat, while the vigorously gestural skies in both Bougival images share the dynamism of a work such as *The Seine Estuary* (see fig. 116). Much less characteristic of Monet's studies on paper is the continuity between a coastal and an inland theme, and the transposition of aspects of a Norman project to the edge of the metropolis.

After taking refuge in London from the war, Monet rented a house near the Seine at Argenteuil, where he was soon visited by Théophile Beguin Billecocq. In his narrative for June 1872, we read how the diplomat was again greeted by Monet's "delicious wife," Camille, and also by "his two friends, the painters Sisley and Pissarro."[69] After listing some of the subjects of Monet's new paintings, the memoir continues, "His drawings have become less precise than in his youth, but he always handles line with intelligence and feeling. He now represents what he sees with lines and curves, seeking to re-create the landscapes in their broad outlines through these contours."[70] In November, Théophile bought from Monet "for 200 francs some pencil drawings representing Normandy and a little canvas representing the banks of irises along the Seine."[71] Five years later, after enjoying dinner with Monet and Camille in Paris, Théophile noted his purchase of "some small pencil drawings depicting Normandy landscapes," which he describes as "scenes of woodland, work in the fields, farms."[72] One of many occasions when the older man offered assistance by buying such works for cash, it is unclear how accurately Théophile recorded the pictures he saw or acquired. The French word *dessin* can be extended to a variety of studies on paper, including pastels, watercolors, and works in other media. Few surviving drawings by Monet correspond to the objects Théophile mentioned, though several pastels come closer to his descriptions.[73]

Lacking much of his former motivation for travel, Monet made only three brief visits to Normandy in this new decade. When he and Camille were married in 1870, they stayed in Trouville long enough for Monet to paint her on the sands and beside the sea. The result of two subsequent working sessions in the Le Havre area in 1873 and 1874 was a mere dozen canvases, his entire painterly response to the immediate region prior to 1881. It was from this small cluster of works that Monet selected a pair of harbor scenes to be shown in the first Impressionist exhibition, alongside the still unidentified "seven pastels" listed in the catalogue. If he used pastel on these short provincial expeditions, we would perhaps expect the results to have been considered for the 1874 installation, but there is no specific evidence for the inclusion or exclusion of such works. Two sheets have been loosely connected with the period as a whole, both with contested dates: one, a rural subject entitled *Landscape, near Le Havre*, carries the artist's initials and the date "78"; the other, *The Sea at Le Havre*, is inscribed "Claude Monet 72."[74] A further ten pastels of unidentified countryside motifs may also be the products of this phase, conceivably corresponding to Théophile Beguin Billcocq's description of "scenes of woodland, work in the fields, farms" from Normandy, though equally plausible as studies of terrain near Bougival or Louveciennes, or even Vétheuil and Poissy.[75]

The Musée Marmottan Monet's *The Meadow Lined with Trees* (fig. 129) is among the latter group, summarizing the frieze-like compositions and lack of central features or incidents that characterizes many of them. Distinguished from the majority of Monet's current canvases by their exclusively terrestrial subjects — neither the sea nor the Seine make an appearance — these pastels are predominantly textural and atmospheric. Monet was clearly proud of *The Meadows Lined with Trees*, apparently exhibiting it at least twice, though failing to find a buyer.[76] Somewhat self-effacing as an image, it nevertheless shows the considerable refinement of his pastel technique in a rural context, here directed at nuance rather than high drama. Using tan paper, Monet exploited a wide range of touch, rubbing, and interweaving of colors to establish, then inflect, the variegated planes of sky, trees, and field. Significantly, the principal branches and trunks appear to have been drawn in black

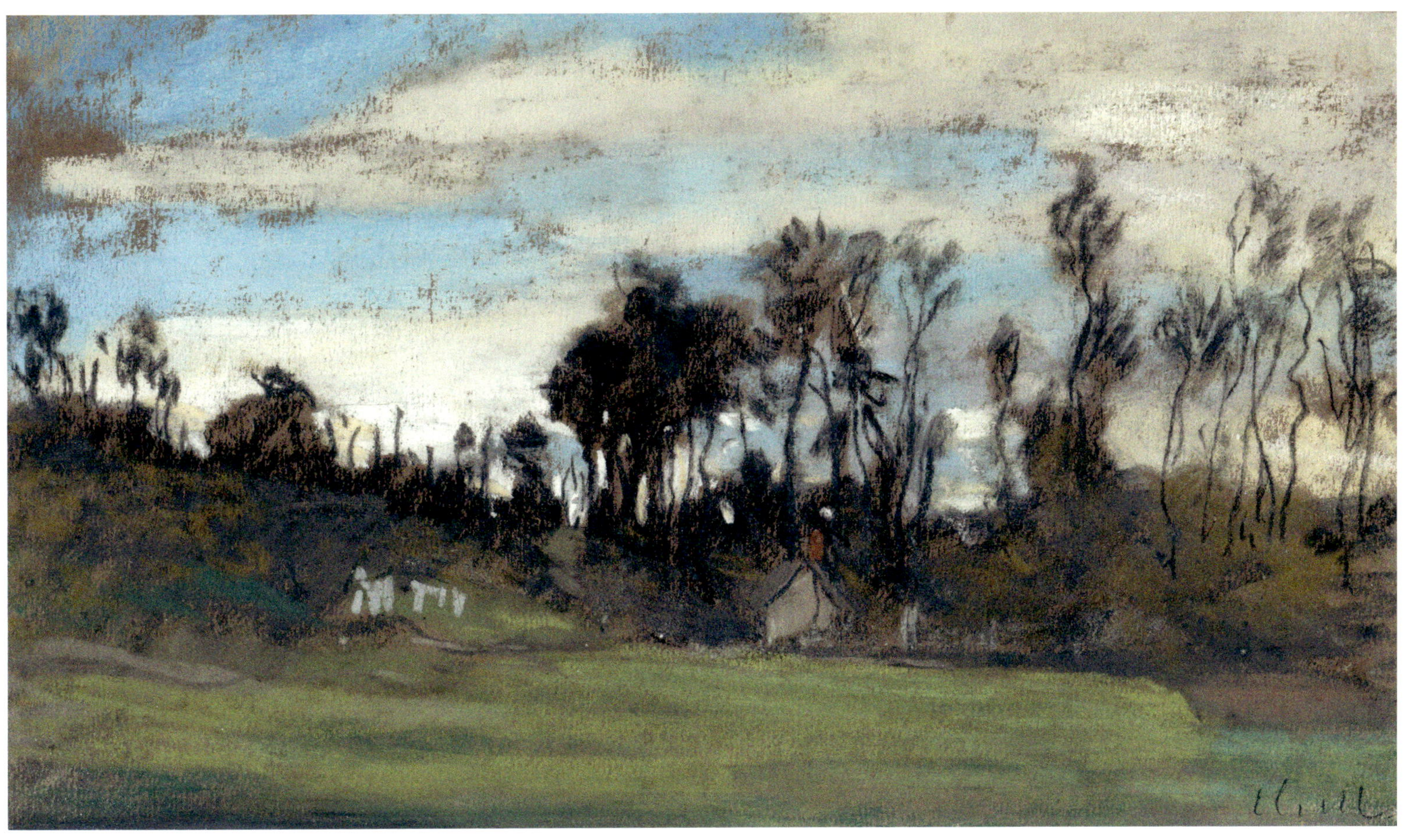

129
The Meadow Lined with Trees, c. 1870–80. Pastel and gouache, 220 x 370 mm. Musée Marmottan Monet, Paris [P67]

chalk or even charcoal, insisting on their linear identity and sounding a note of formality in this otherwise rich composition. Common to the Marmottan sheet and several of the other catalogued works is a flattened, tapestry-like space in which the viewer's imagined progress from shallow foreground into pictorial distance is slowed by a lattice of saplings, fences, and foliage. A similar device appears repeatedly in Monet's oil paintings of the 1870s, which may well have developed out of, or in parallel with, such explorations on paper, as in comparable pairings from the Normandy coast.[77] In each instance, the effect is to direct our eyes across the picture surface, rather than to the artist's mastery of perspective and visual illusion. Color and mark, palpability and sensation take on a heightened significance, partially replacing the lure of narrative or the seduction of fine detail. We do not marvel at Monet's sleight of hand, in other words, but at the intensity and subtlety of his grasp of the experienced subject.

Line and Color in Monet's Emerging Career

In the 1870s, the beginnings of a consensus about Monet's gifts as a painter emerged from the barrage of critical writing that greeted successive Impressionist exhibitions. Apart from a few often-quoted dissensions, his work was frequently singled out for praise: when the Étretat *Luncheon* was shown in 1874, for example, it was admired for its vivid realism, "a photograph with color, movement and light," claimed Edouard Drumont.[78] On the same occasion, Castagnary remarked more cautiously on the lack of "finish" in several of Monet's canvases, a note repeated by Chesneau and echoed in responses to his paintings over the years.[79] The critic Victor Fournel, writing as "Bernardille," repeated the claim in 1877, but Bertall was more explicit in asserting that Monet's colors were placed "a little randomly on the canvas, without much attention to planes and perspective."[80] In time, the argument that Monet's relation-

130

Road in a Hollow, Pourville, 1882. Oil on canvas, 60.3 x 81.6 cm. Museum of Fine Arts, Boston. Bequest of Mrs. Susan Mason Loring, 1924 [W762]

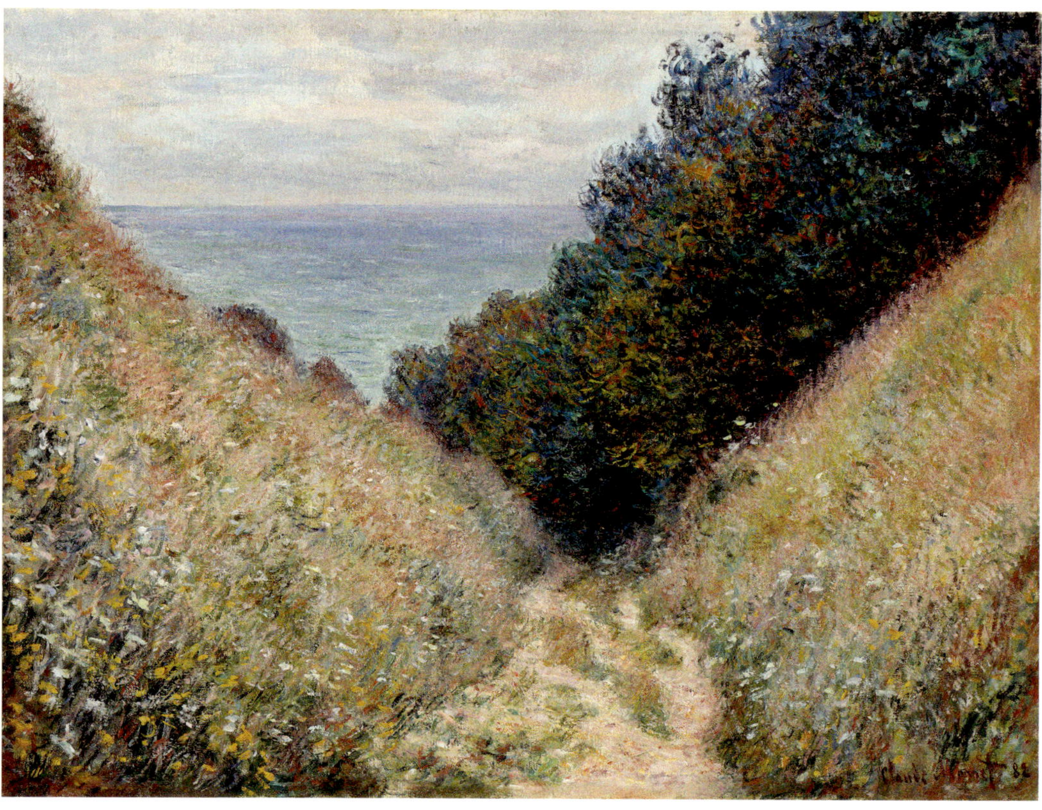

ship with drawing was a defining quality of his art—for better and for worse—would gather momentum, perhaps fueled by the painter's own suppression of his draftsmanly activities. By 1880, when Monet opted to exhibit separately from his companions, Théodore Duret could celebrate the fact that the artist no longer required "masses of preliminary sketches, no more pencil or watercolor drawings to be used in the studio, but, rather, one integral oil painting begun and completed out of doors in nature, in the presence of the subject, which is interpreted and rendered at first hand."[81]

Reversing these arguments three years later, however, Joris-Karl Huysmans saw only "a carelessness, an all-too-obvious lack of training" in Monet's pictures, while Gustave Geffroy chose to occupy the middle ground. In a display that probably included *Road in a Hollow, Pourville* (fig. 130), Geffroy acknowledged "the drawing is summary" and imagined that Monet "sketches only a few lines on the bare canvas."[82] Geffroy was nevertheless ecstatic about the sheer painterliness of these new works, where "the sun plays across the humid air and brings everything fully to light; and the gradations of light, the transparency or opacity of the atmosphere, and the density of air around the objects are always expressed with infinite delicacy."[83] Later becoming Monet's friend and biographer, Geffroy did not meet him until a chance encounter on Belle-Île in 1886, but he was among the first to identify the originality of the artist's visual project. "One will recognize the quality of M. Claude Monet's drawings in *Sunken Path in Pourville*, for example—a painting composed of three straight lines, two leafy, grassy slopes whose bases intersect with the sea in the background."[84]

Geffroy's prose captured brilliantly the idea that line and color, drawing and painting, had become inseparable in Monet's new art, fused together in the single act of creation. Monet's surviving graphic oeuvre from his middle years, though far from complete, provides an intriguing endorsement of this conception. After 1880, there are no separate signed and dated drawings beyond those made specifically for the processes of reproduction, a phenomenon discussed in chapter 8. These remarkable works

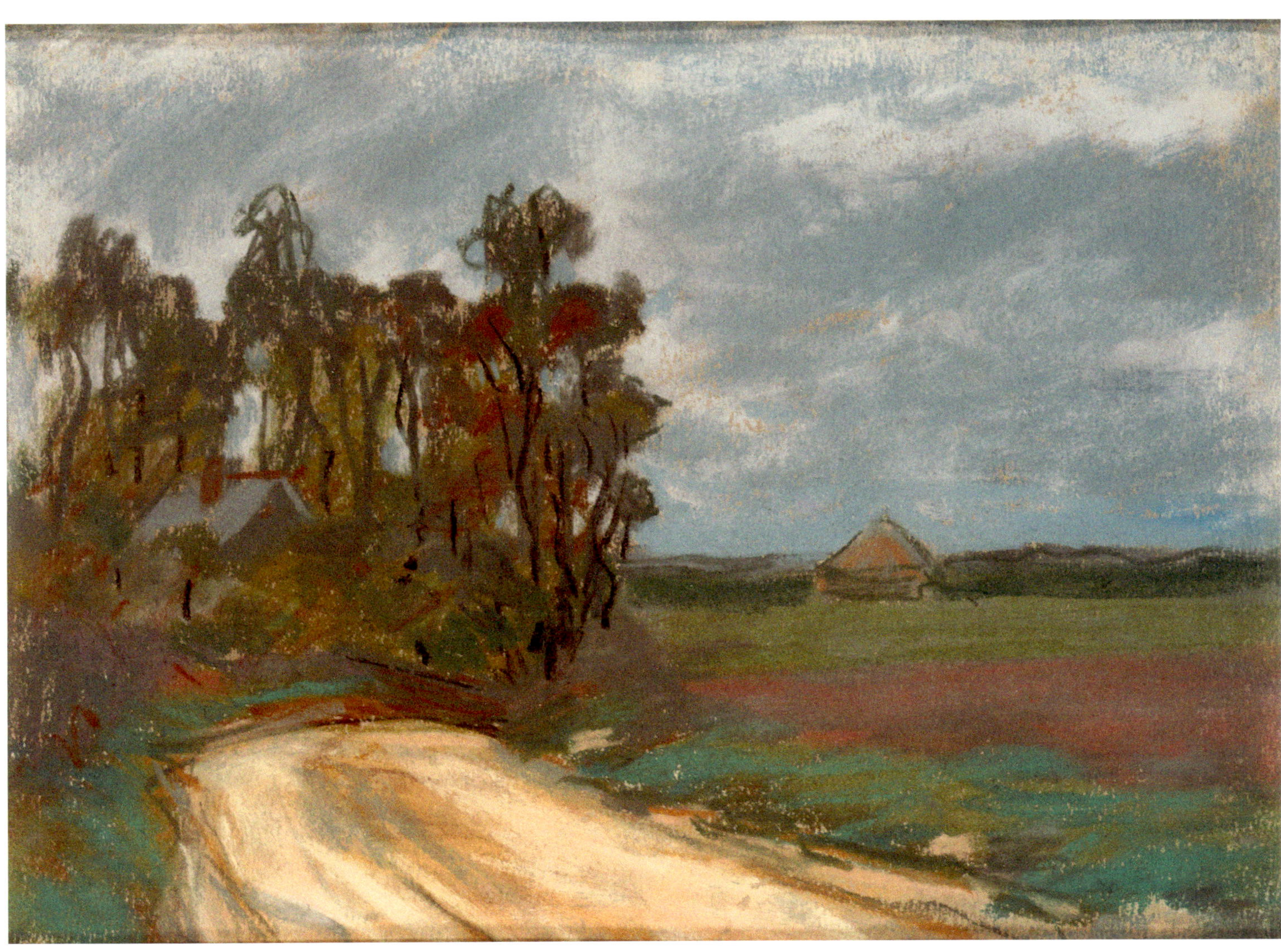

131
The Road and the House, c. 1885. Pastel, 210 x 292 mm. Private collection [P42]

might almost be used as a retrospective gloss on Geffroy's text; inevitably drawn after the completion of the canvases to which they relate, not in preparation for them, they remind us of the high level of skill in Monet's works on paper and his ability to command line in many different circumstances. A further subtext in this many-layered narrative is found in Monet's sketchbooks, which were demonstrably used throughout this decade. Dominating all these categories, however, is the small, mixed body of pastels produced by Monet in the 1880s, which includes some of his finest achievements in the medium, as well as some oddities. Wildenstein lists fourteen works in pastel from this period, none of them directly dated but the majority traceable to documented events or individuals.[85] The list begins with a group of highly uncharacteristic exercises in portraiture, largely based on the children of Alice Hoschedé, who would become Monet's second wife. They are followed by several pastels of rustic Norman motifs, provisionally inserted into this decade, along with a solitary view near Giverny.[86] Unquestionably the stars in this category, however, are the last items: Monet's five final pastels of Étretat.

Before turning to the Étretat works, two instances of Monet's less characteristic use of pastel should be considered. The first concerns a dramatic rural composition known simply as *The Road and the House* (fig. 131), which Wildenstein places with a much earlier sequence of pastels. Arguably the most energetically drafted of all the pastels considered in our survey, this near-expressionist configuration rushes us headlong into a previously unidentified

132

The Rocks at Falaise, c. 1885. Pencil, 115 x 195 mm. Sketchbook 5, fol. 15r. Musée Marmottan Monet, Paris [D298]

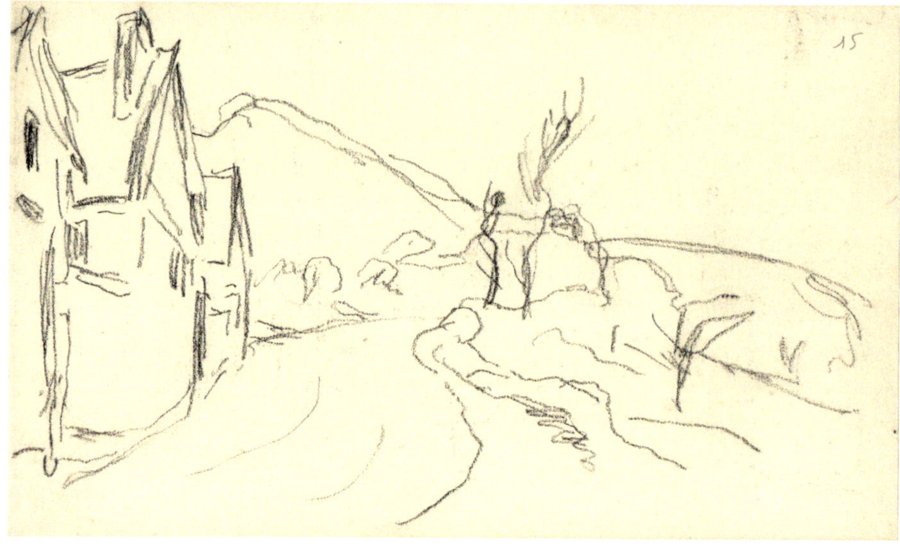

corner of rural France. Unlike most of Monet's studies from the 1870s, this lively scene exhibits a correspondingly dramatic facture and an insistent graphism. Broad swathes of color are applied with painterly confidence, while heavy, gestural lines have been used to circumscribe the highway, the horizon, and the wild copse around the larger house. Prominent in the foreground is the curved sweep of an ocher-hued road, while easily overlooked in the distance is a squat, pyramidal grainstack. Both these features take us to the early years of Monet's residence in Giverny, where in 1885 he made a sequence of sketchbook drawings and associated canvases of the nearby village of Falaise (fig. 132). In these paintings, such as *Road to Giverny in Winter*, an angled track occupies the lower part of the composition, and in several there are clusters of trees with dark, serpentine trunks and glimpses of wayside houses.[87] Among the drafts in the sketchbook in question, there is also a solitary study of a grainstack, smaller and rounder than the example in the pastel but implicitly part of the genesis of its motif. Establishing an unusual rapport between these three media, Monet used his lines, his sticks of color, and his paintbrushes with a similar fervor, making the only work in pastel of his new home and perhaps the first, modest contribution to his series of grainstacks.

The second departure from his practice resulted in the pastel portraits, which also help to illuminate Monet's changed circumstances. Camille had died tragically in 1879, from complications that followed the birth of the couple's second child, Michel. Yet again, Théophile Beguin Billecocq fills out the story, recounting her gradual descent into illness, his attempts to secure better medical advice, and gifts of money.[88] In 1881, Monet and his sons moved to Poissy, west of Paris, a site he had first visited as a young friend of the Beguin Billecocqs in 1858.[89] Soon after this relocation, Madame Hoschedé and her children joined the three Monets, effectively forming a single household. The fusion of the two families has been much analyzed, but we are left to speculate about the reasons for the artist's unexpected recourse to portraiture at this time. From the ages of the depicted children, it seems that the pastels were made early in the decade, against the immediate background of loss and upheaval.[90] Apparently improvised and executed in haste (three of them are inexplicably on canvas), they are distinctly conventional in manner and may have been partly based on photographs.[91] It seems likely that these group likenesses were undertaken as the enlarged family took stock of itself and perhaps sought comfort in one another. A reluctant portraitist, on this occasion Monet embraced all the children pictorially, if hurriedly, adding Michel to one of the works as he had earlier welcomed the new Hoschedé baby, by painting him around the same time as his own young child.[92] Apart from such personal resonances,

133
Self-Portrait in His Atelier, 1884. Oil on canvas (unfinished). Musée Marmottan Monet, Paris [W891a]

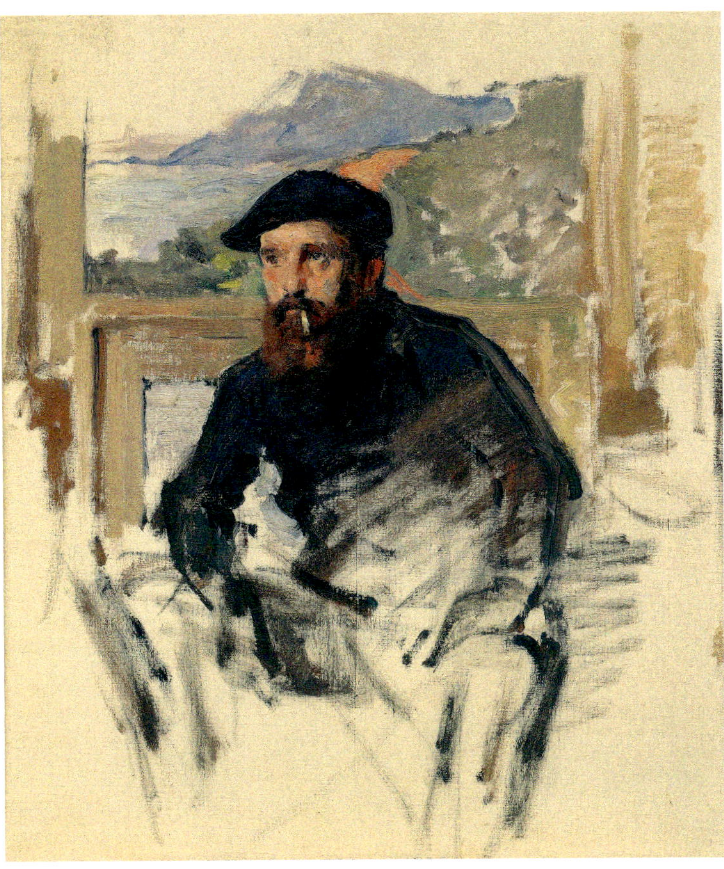

these pictures tell us that his new family was exposed to Monet's working practices and sometimes participated in them. More vivid still is a group of studies in a later sketchbook, when the artist manifestly joined in a drawing session with Germaine and Jean-Pierre Hoschedé and Michel Monet (see fig. 157).[93]

Later Pastels of Étretat

Now settled with the Hoschedés, first at Poissy and after 1883 at Giverny, Monet found new energy for his travels (fig. 133). At times taking members of the family with him, he accelerated his itineraries as the decade advanced, returning to Normandy several times and reaching Provence, the Italian border, and Holland before 1886. Some of the sites of his youth again enticed him, notably in four working visits to Étretat; the first, in 1883, when he completed at least twenty canvases; the second, brief and largely unproductive, in 1884; and finally, a ten-week sojourn from September to December 1885, with a shorter return in early 1886, that together resulted in an astonishing fifty or so completed paintings. Away from his new home, Monet corresponded with Alice and his friends energetically, reporting his frustration with the changeable weather and his exhilaration when work went well. Absent yet again from the letters are references to the drawings made in his sketchbooks, and to the pastels he is known to have committed to paper on this visit. A simple process of deduction allows us to identify at least some of these works, providing a rare point of certainty in their otherwise elusive history. Monet's letters show that he initially occupied a house at Étretat that belonged to Jean-Baptiste Faure, who invited the artist and his extended family to enjoy a vacation there before much of the painting was begun.[94] When Alice and the children returned to Giverny, Monet moved to a hotel on the beach, but at an unrecorded date he repaid Faure's generosity by giving him some pastels of local scenes. Three such works have been identified in Faure's collection, presumably left behind by the grateful artist or presented to

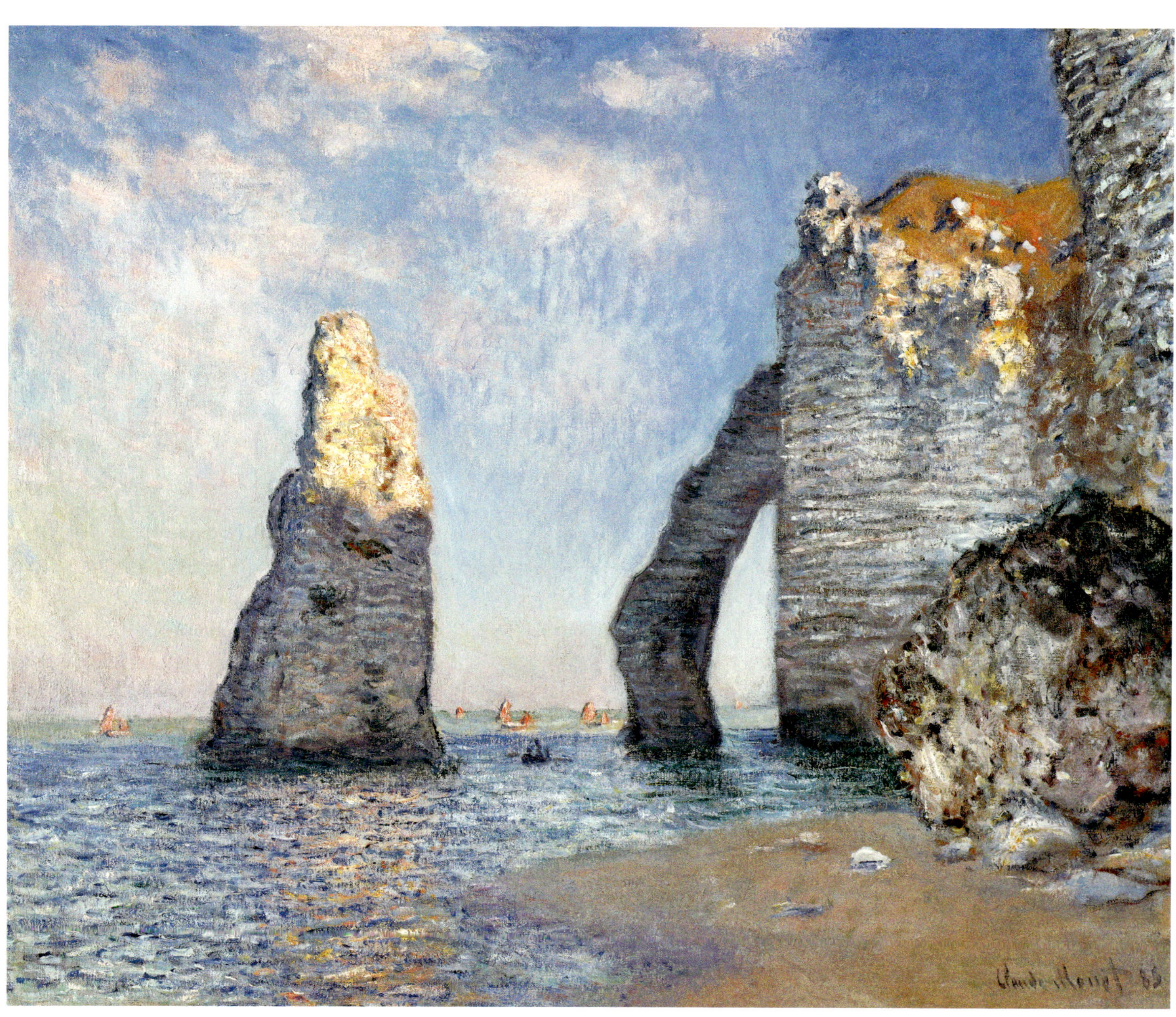

134

The Cliffs at Étretat, 1885. Oil on canvas, 64.9 x 81.1 cm. Sterling and Francine Clark Art Institute, Williamstown, Massachusetts [W1034]

135
Étretat, View from the Falaise d'Aval, c. 1884–86. Pencil, 110 x 195 mm. Sketchbook 4, fol. 27r. Musée Marmottan Monet, Paris [D264]

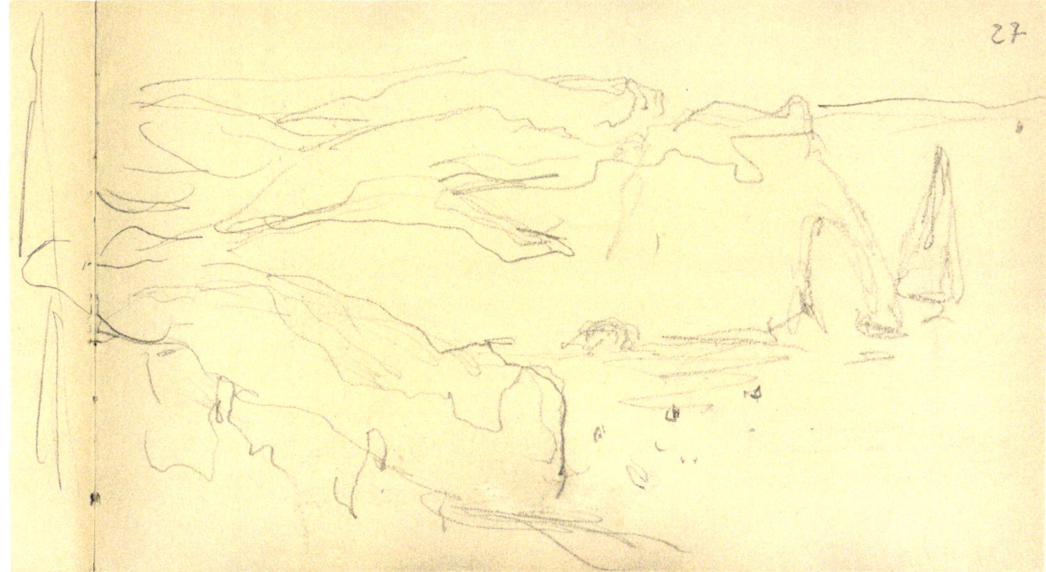

the host subsequently.[95] His satisfaction with these offerings seems to be reflected in Faure's decision to acquire two further works from this visit, both of them substantial canvases of Étretat subjects.[96]

One of the pastels owned by Faure was *Étretat, the Needle and Porte d'Aval, Sunset*, currently of unknown location, a classic view of the headland to the southwest of the bay and its curiously weather-sculpted arch.[97] Drawn and painted hundreds of times by Delacroix, Boudin, Jongkind, Courbet, and their contemporaries of different persuasions, the same vista had already provided the subject for Monet's early chalk study (see fig. 85) and a similarly titled pastel of the late 1860s (see fig. 125), as well as eight canvases from the visit of 1883. Later in life, he was to acquire a watercolor by Delacroix of part of this view for his own collection, a further gesture of homage to a predecessor on the Normandy coast.[98] In a letter written in February of 1860, Monet had already acknowledged his audacity in following such works by Courbet as *Cliff at Étretat* (see fig. 126), while insisting that he would "try to do it differently."[99] A motif with such a resonant history was both a perennial challenge to the younger man and a benchmark against which to judge his own developing art. By 1885, Monet was clearly determined to push further, taking up where he had left off two years earlier and exploring new extremes of color and structural invention. More than a dozen oil paintings of this view resulted in variants that embraced brilliant pink, lemon, and even greenish skies, cascades of golden light and opalescent reflections in the ocean, and scenes of both dawn and dusk. In the pastel of this subject given to Faure, the cliff is seen from virtually the same angle as the study of the 1860s, but now Monet's field is subtly more panoramic. On a sheet that is twice as wide as it is high, he gave himself enough space to accommodate the rocky mass and a broad expanse of sea, as well as a towering, almost theatrical sunset.[100]

During his first weeks at Étretat in 1885, there was clearly enough sunshine for Monet to work vigorously in the open air, directly reengaging with a site he had known since childhood. Now, it was not only touristic views and glamorous vistas that attracted him but a range of entirely novel combinations of cliff and beach that emerged from his restless wanderings on foot and from short trips by boat. One of the latter produced the spectacular *The Cliffs at Étretat* (fig. 134), a view from the almost inaccessible western flank of the headland, close to the rock arch, or Porte d'Aval.[101] Deserted except for the tiny fishing boats near the horizon, this extraordinary corner of the Normandy coastline distills the natural grandeur of Étretat and something of its charismatic place in French

136

Eugène Boudin, *Cliff Hollowed by the Sea, Étretat*, 1883–85. Black chalk, 308 x 461 mm. Musée du Louvre, Paris

137

The Manneporte near Étretat, 1886. Oil on canvas, 81.3 x 65.4 cm. The Metropolitan Museum of Art, New York. Bequest of Lillie P. Bliss, 1931 [W1052]

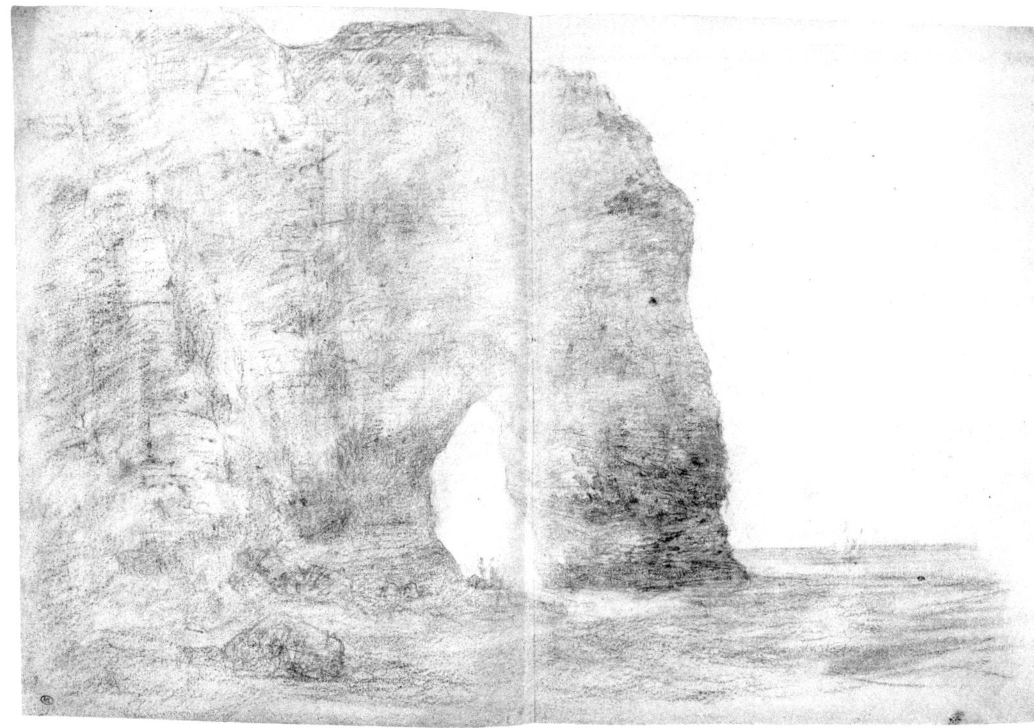

history and culture. Long since identified as a key site for geologists, the multilayered limestone of the region was laid bare at Étretat and provided vital insights into the primeval past of the entire Paris basin.[102] At the same time, it was frequently likened to the soaring architecture of France's Gothic cathedrals, thus fusing into a single structure one of the major ideological conflicts of the age: that between religion and science. Monet's response to such wider issues has been generally neglected, though it may offer a key to his longstanding fascination with the timeless aspects of Étretat, and perhaps inflect the criticisms of Robert Herbert and others of his disregard for the life of the town. Apart from the Porte d'Aval and needle, and the Manneporte, Monet also tackled its beaches and storms; both wings of the bay, including the rival arch—the Porte d'Amont—at the northeastern extremity; the contiguous cliffs and pathways, precipices and rural surroundings; and, above all, the elemental character of Étretat itself. Few geographical locations have been so thoroughly surveyed and so expressively represented in a single artist's drawings, pastels, and oil paintings

More completely than any of his previous expeditions, the 1885 campaign at Étretat reveals an interrelationship between the multiple strands of Monet's mature creative practice. Several major canvases unquestionably had their origin in his sketchbooks, used as the artist scouted the area on foot and investigated original sight lines and new combinations of form. His letters allow us to reconstruct strolls around the headland and along its steep tracks: on 28 October 1885, when rain prevented him from painting, Monet informed Alice that he had returned from a walk, having searched "all the corners" of Étretat, and a week later that he had "taken a walk and looked again at my motifs."[103] It was presumably on such perambulations that he made a pocket-size view of the arch from a distance (fig. 135) and the even more dynamic sketch from the edge of the cliff itself (see fig. 154), as unexpected motifs came into view and possibilities for new canvases presented themselves. The sheer vivacity of these studies suggest a little of Monet's excitement, as well as the potency of line in defining form in a few seconds of frantic draftsmanship.

Pastel was also part of this project, sometimes complementary to his paintings of Étretat and occasionally carrying their experimental

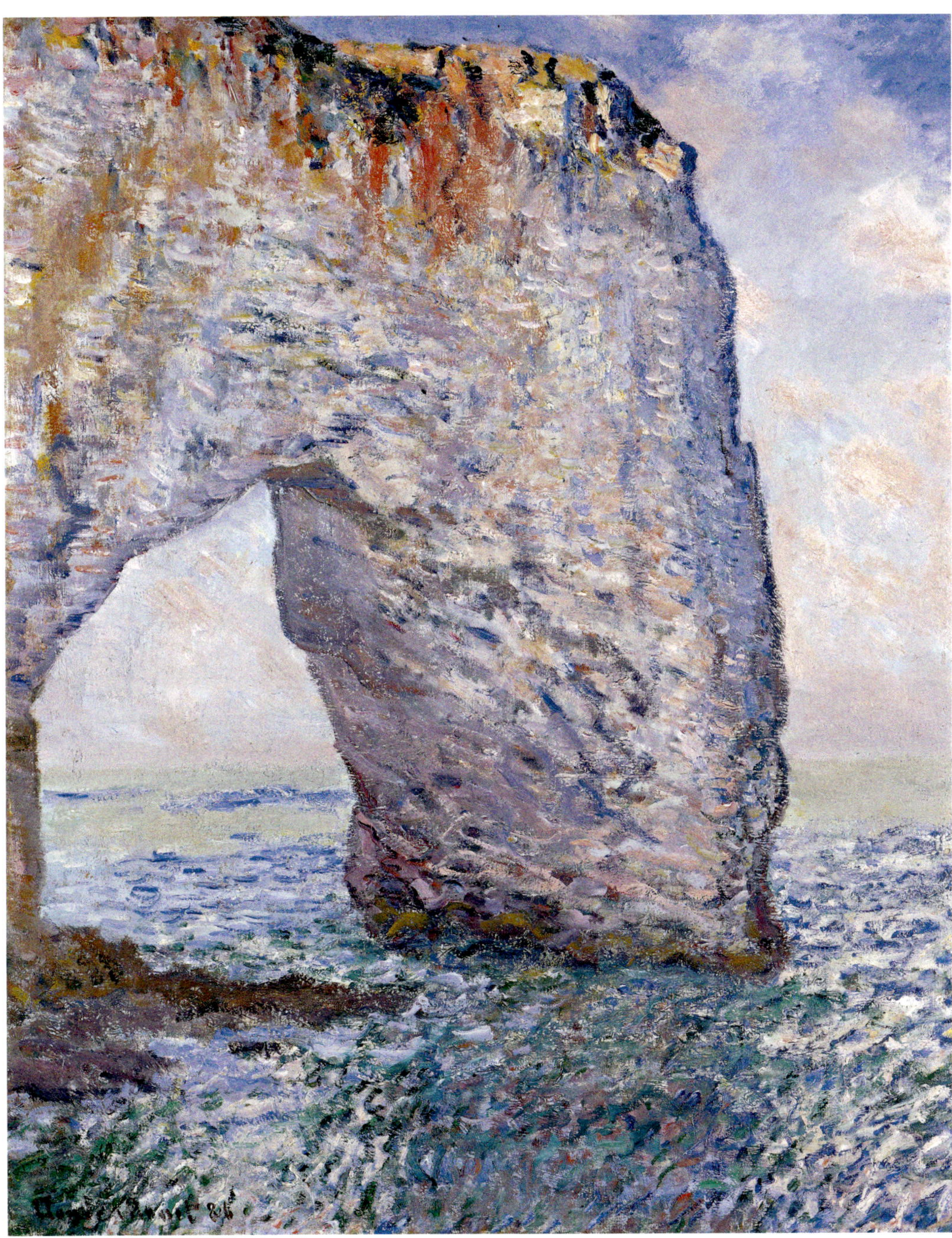

strategies to new extremes. One evening, he was clearly struck by the sight of the westernmost rock arch, finding it largely cast into shadow.[104] *Étretat, the Manneporte at Low Tide* (see fig. 101), also given to Faure, was probably made on the spot, a substantial distance from Monet's lodgings at the Hotel Blanquet and probably reached by boat. Altogether more original in design than *Étretat, the Needle and Porte d'Aval, Sunset*, this delicate image was new to his repertoire, while perhaps recalling a sketch from one of Boudin's notebooks of earlier years: *Cliff Hollowed by the Sea, Étretat* (fig. 136). During his 1883 and 1885 residences at Étretat, Monet made several other dramatic images of the Manneporte at close quarters, all of them on canvas and emphasizing the ponderous bulk of the stone and its crumbling, multihued surface (fig. 137). The opposite qualities of the subject, however, are celebrated in this solitary pastel, as the artist gently fused its silhouette with the empty beach and the evening sky. Appropriate

138
Étretat, the Needle Rock and Porte d'Aval, c. 1885. Pastel on tan paper, 400 x 235 mm. Private collection [P78]

to such an understated approach, Monet's chalky colors evoked the ancient limestone and the pale, particulate mist above the beach, in one of the quiet masterpieces of his middle years.

Whereas *Étretat, the Manneporte at Low Tide* is tranquil, perhaps reflecting the calm beginnings of the 1885 visit, the extraordinary *Étretat, the Needle Rock and Porte d'Aval* (fig. 138) strikes a note of unexpected sobriety, even gloom. After Alice's departure with the children in early October, Monet repeatedly bemoaned the wind, rain, and occasional snow that drove him indoors and prevented work: "I am desperate about the weather," he wrote to Durand-Ruel on the 28th, after telling Alice, "I have been unable to return to any of my motifs of the Manneporte."[105] Beset by the problems of keeping warm and by local visitors, one of whom was the novelist Guy de Maupassant, Monet longed to be alone, to paint, and to explore what he confessed was his "love for the sea."[106] Solitude is an implicit theme in many of his canvases, where the beaches and promontories are empty and idle boats represent absent fishermen (see fig. 235).[107] It pervades his pastels too, most poignantly in *Étretat, the Needle Rock and Porte d'Aval*, which was also formerly owned by Faure. A unique vertical depiction on paper of the rock arch and its needle, this is also a rare case in which a dark mood in a work by Monet changes a familiar subject almost beyond recognition. Pervaded by the shadowy blues, creams, and browns of an overcast dawn or approaching night, the scene has an elegiac air of the kind favored by Monet's friend and occasional correspondent James Abbott McNeill Whistler (1834–1904).[108] The looming foreground cliff and brittle outlines in the distant arch also hint at gothic dread, suggesting an early exploration of a bleak psychological register that Monet would return to in canvases of Belle-Île in 1886 and in Fresselines three years later. Not the least claim of this exceptional image, therefore, is the possibility that Monet chose pastel to embark on an often-underestimated journey into his psyche.

In *Étretat, the Needle Rock and Porte d'Aval*, the arch and needle are seen from high above the sea, more extreme and unexpected than even the Clark's *The Cliffs at Étretat*. The pastel, however, has no equivalent in Monet's painted oeuvre, except for a scattered group of solemn, idiosyncratic canvases that include two in a similar format, each with remote views of the Manneporte.[109] Part of this project appears to have been the self-conscious extension of Étretat's iconography as laid down by his forbears, in which Monet again attempted to "do it differently." One further image in pastel, *Étretat, the Cap d'Antifer* (fig. 139), took the challenge another step by moving slightly beyond the bay itself. Here Monet has walked southwest along the cliff tops, then gazed along the coast with his back toward Étretat. The moment is captured in a solitary sketchbook drawing (fig. 140), rendered in characteristically serpentine pencil lines and divided across the center, where the composition first took shape in the artist's mind. Though less picturesque than most of his other motifs, this subject enabled Monet to emphasize the bulk of the Normandy massif and its precipitous conjunction with the sea.

In *Étretat, the Cap d'Antifer*, a meandering path and a customs officer's hut are the only signs of passing humanity in a winter landscape now dominated by wind and cold. In late November, Monet contemplated the short trip by boat to Antifer, the site in question, but stormy seas prevented his departure.[110] Slightly better conditions are indicated by the pastel, but its earth tones and steely blues remain unrelieved by the sunshine that eluded him throughout these weeks. An oil painting of the same scene was presumably carried out around this time, its sharper areas of focus in the distant cliff, and nearby path and hut, suggesting that it was made after the work on paper.[111] Grand and uncompromising, the canvas was among several works from the 1885 campaign that soon attracted discerning collectors. It was sold within months and exhibited in New York at the end of April 1886, while the pastel was also recorded in the collection of a Mme Materne by 1894 and subsequently acquired by Ivan Stchoukine.[112] Despite the anguish of his lonely vigil at Étretat in 1885, Monet himself also seemed pleased with the final

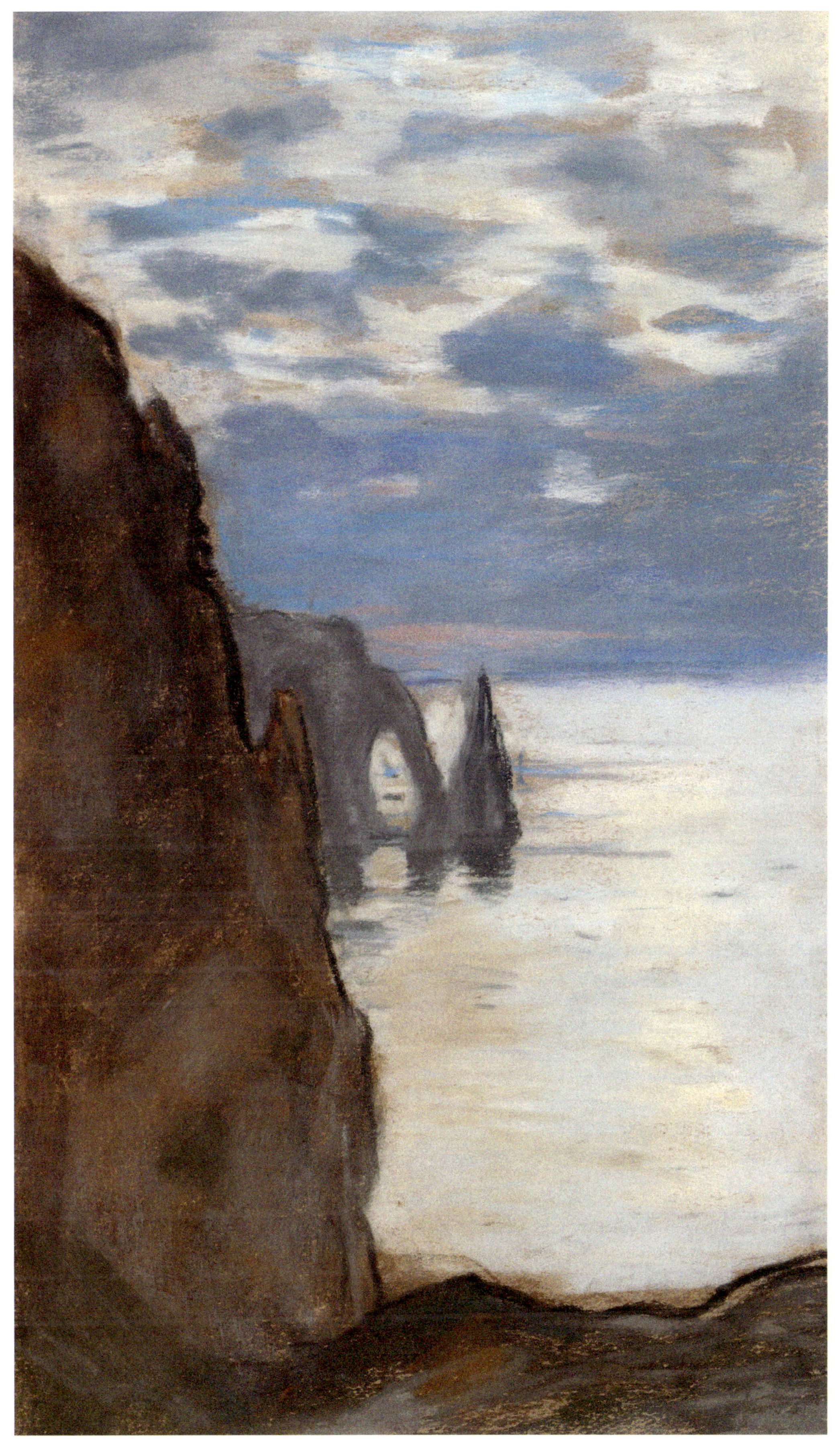

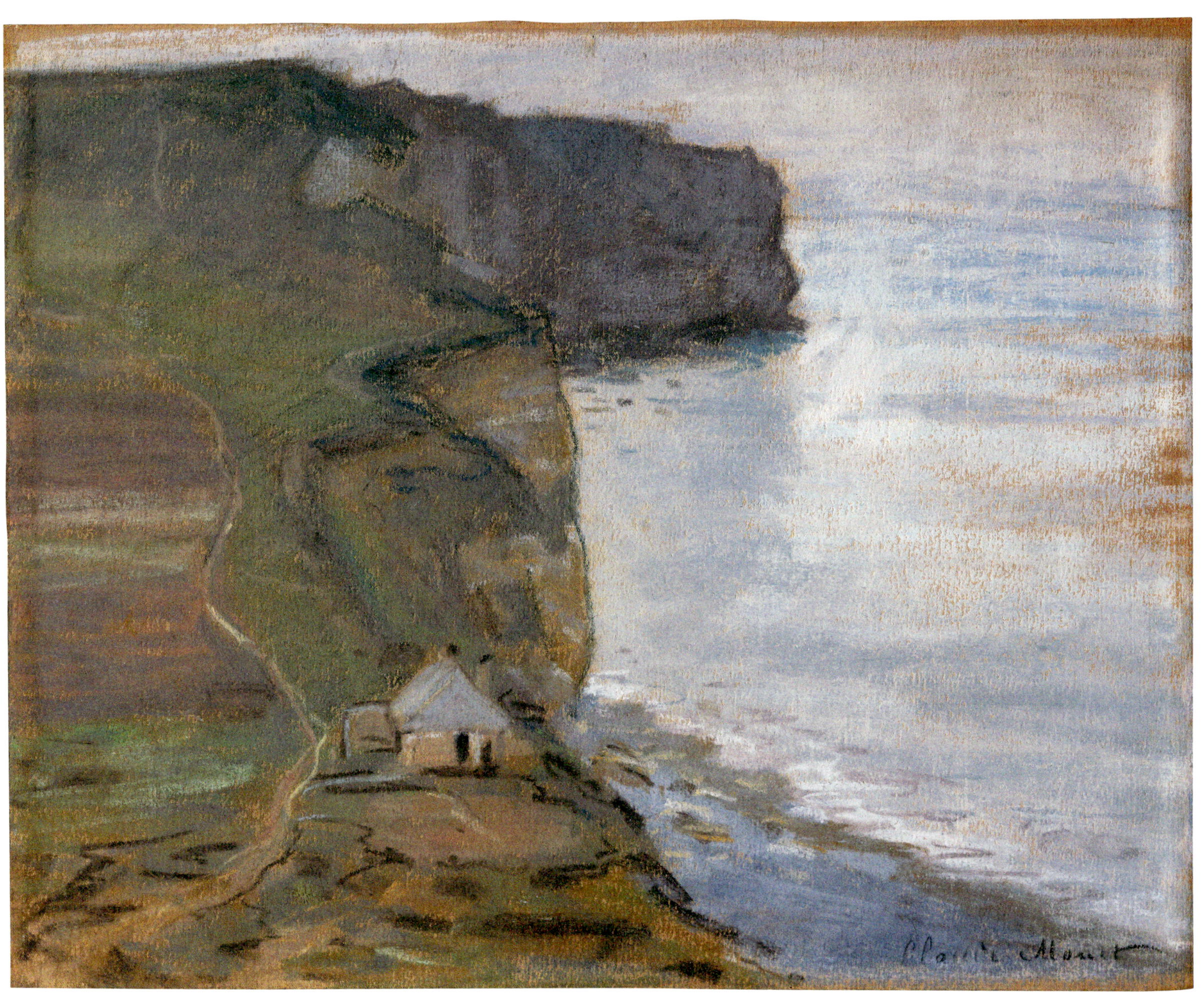

139

Étretat, the Cap d'Antifer, c. 1885.
Pastel, 270 x 346 mm. Private collection [P80]

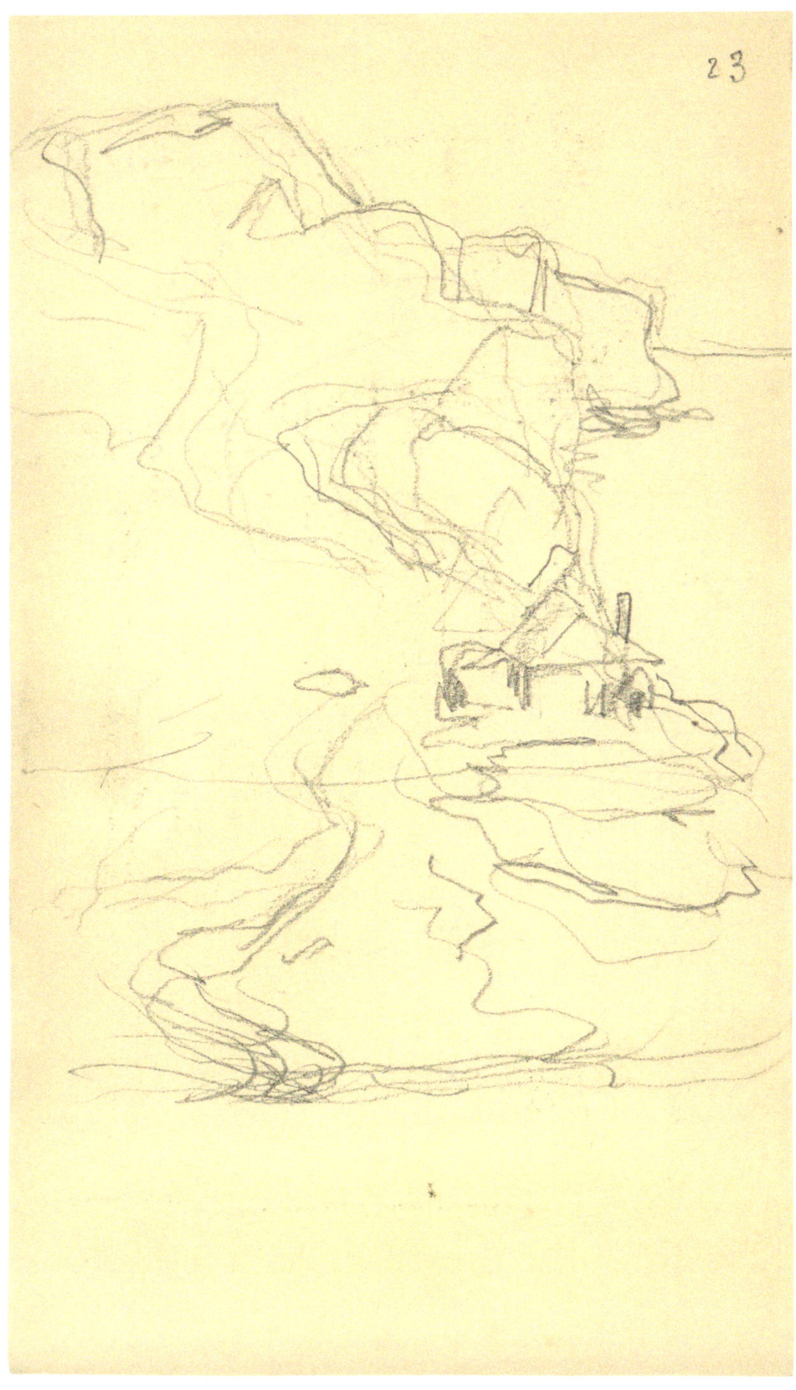

140

Étretat, the Cap d'Antifer, c. 1885. Pencil, 195 x 110 mm. Sketchbook 4, fol. 23v. Musée Marmottan Monet, Paris [D257]

outcome, choosing four paintings of this site to be reproduced in color by William Thornley in 1894 (see Appendix, p. 273).

At Étretat in the 1880s, Monet found a new flexibility in the roles of drawing and painting, and in the dense, mutual dependency of the rituals that contributed to his art. Certain canvases are dominated by muscular contours, created with a color-loaded brush and dedicated to the rhythms of the landscape and the containment of its extravagant textures. Others seem to shimmer, their myriad broken touches dissolving into one another, just as the grains of deep-hued pastel in *Étretat, the Cap d'Antifer* merge sky, sea, and cliff top. The evolution of this image, from pencil sketch to pastel to oil paint, or in some other sequence that remains unknown, takes us to the heart of Monet's project at mid-career. Linear and painterly together, all these works show an artist in dynamic control of his technical practice, achieved through decades of experimentation and struggle. After the Étretat campaigns, it would be more than ten years before he again took up his pastels, a period in which drawing itself seems to have faded as an independent activity. A delightful coda to the story, however, is provided in a letter written from Étretat on 12 November 1885, when Monet offered some advice to the teenage Blanche Hoschedé, who was beginning to consider herself a painter. Monet told Alice, "I am happy to know that Blanche is working: if she is willing to go to some trouble, she will do well"; explaining that Blanche needed practice in "putting things in their place," the former rebel from Gleyre's studio then urged her—without a hint of irony—to work at drawing.[113]

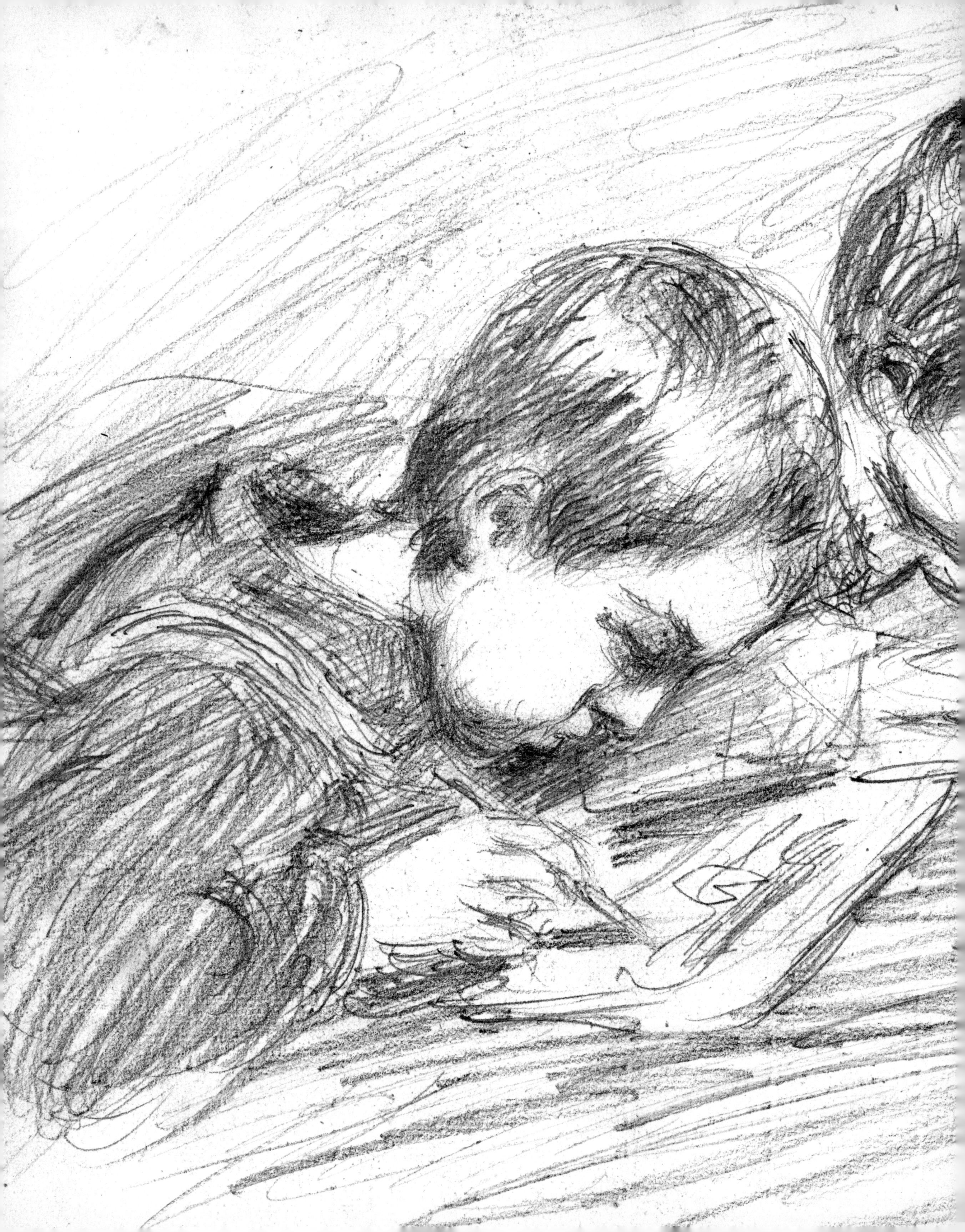

CHAPTER SEVEN Rough Drafts: The Sketchbook Drawings

Essential to Claude Monet's public image was the denial of the role of drawing in his working method. Snapshots of the older artist frequently show him with a cigarette in hand but never a pencil, and sketchbooks, among a painter's basic tools, are nowhere to be seen in photographs of his successive Giverny studios. Journalists, critics, and biographers avoided the subject altogether. As noted earlier, in setting Monet apart from his predecessors Corot and Courbet, Théodore Duret wrote at the time of his first one-man exhibition in 1880, "Claude Monet, who follows them, has succeeded in accomplishing what they began. In his case there are no longer masses of preliminary sketches, no more pencil or watercolor drawings to be used in the studio, but, rather, one integral oil painting begun and completed out of doors in nature, in the presence of the subject, which is interpreted and rendered at first hand."[1] Duret's statement has all the makings of an effective sound bite: it is clear, concise, and unequivocal.

It is also inaccurate. Monet never relinquished the habit, formed in his teenage years, of carrying sketchbooks with him on his frequent expeditions into the landscape as he searched for new subjects to paint. For this artist, the page of a notebook offered a private space in which to jot down visual ideas, a place to think on paper. To Monet, such drawings were of strictly utilitarian significance, utterly lacking in commercial or even aesthetic value. None of the folios was sold or exhibited during his lifetime. With few exceptions, the majority of Monet's mature sketchbook drawings relate to the first rather than the last stages of his creative process. Liberated from conventions of perspective, proportion, and modeling, these studies represent unself-conscious rehearsals rather than polished performances, "rough drafts" rather than presentation pieces of the kind found in his *carnets* of 1856–57. Monet's later sketchbooks preserve his least refined yet among his most intimate artistic utterances.

Monet made use of sketchbooks from the beginning of his professional career in the 1860s through his final decade of activity in the 1920s. Our primary evidence for this aspect of his working method consists of eight *carnets* that the artist left to his son, Michel, who in turn bequeathed them to the Musée Marmottan Monet in 1966.[2] Of the relatively few scholars who have devoted significant attention to Monet's sketchbooks, only two have considered them in relation to his complete painted oeuvre.

In the appendix to his 1986 monograph *Monet: Nature into Art*, John House offered a concise preliminary study of the dates and subjects found in the Marmottan sketchbooks.[3] Their complete contents — some 300 individual drawings — remained unpublished until the appearance of the fifth volume of Daniel Wildenstein's catalogue raisonné in 1991.[4] Besides reproducing nearly every sheet in the form of small photographic halftones, Wildenstein and his team carried out an ambitious effort to match individual sketches with specific sites and oil paintings.

Combined with the 104 studies in Monet's three youthful *carnets* of the 1850s (discussed in chapter 1), the Marmottan holdings bring the known tally to just over 400 individual drawings in eleven sketchbooks. While the *carnets* comprise a substantial body of work that encompasses the artist's entire career, we should be wary of forming definitive conclusions based on what must be an incomplete sample. Evidence of removed pages, as well as chronological and geographical gaps in Monet's known sketchbook drawings at various stages of his career, may be attributed to the unintentional loss or deliberate destruction of an unknown quantity of individual sheets and entire *carnets*.[5] Recognizing that the same proviso applies to the sketchbooks of his contemporaries, it is still illuminating to compare some statistics relating to their activity in this specific realm of graphic production.

Of the elder draftsmen that Monet admired, both Boudin and Jongkind left an exponentially greater number of sketchbook drawings than their protégé. Upon the death of Boudin in 1898, over 6,000 individual sheets of paper with studies in oil, watercolor, pastel, chalk, and pencil were found in his studio. The majority of these were given to the state, and eventually passed from the Musée du Luxembourg to the Cabinet des dessins of the Louvre, where they were mounted in twenty-two albums. Boudin did not avail himself of commercially manufactured sketchbooks, but rather amassed and glued together individual sheets of colored papers into sketchpads that he systematically disassembled as he worked his way through them.[6] Jongkind, in contrast, regularly employed bound *carnets* of the kind used by Monet; thirty-two of at least forty-one documented *carnets*, containing more than 1,100 drawings, are in the Louvre's collection.[7]

The next generation of French painters left relatively few sketchbooks that have survived intact. Just two *carnets* have been published in the literature on Renoir[8] and Bazille,[9] one each by Manet[10] and Sisley,[11] and none by Caillebotte.[12] Pissarro left a large corpus of drawings that originated within sketchbooks, none of which is known to have survived intact. Although a catalogue raisonné of his drawings has yet to be compiled, Richard Brettell and Christopher Lloyd published the holdings of the Ashmolean Museum, Oxford, the major repository of his drawings, and in the process identified leaves from at least twenty-seven different sketchbooks; two others have been deduced from drawings in other collections.[13] Pissarro employed sketchbooks of various sizes, favoring large books during his travels in South America and using smaller pocket-sized *carnets* in Louveciennes and London. Like Monet, he used his sketchbooks primarily to work out compositional formulas rather than to create highly finished studies.

Relative to his fellow Impressionists, Degas was unquestionably the most classically accomplished and prodigious draftsman. His graphic legacy comprises thirty-eight virtually intact notebooks consisting of over 2,500 pages housed mainly at the Bibliothèque Nationale, Paris.[14] In his authoritative study of this corpus, Theodore Reff characterized Degas's private tomes as "notebooks" rather than "sketchbooks," as they contain not only drawings but also a significant component of manuscript notations including travel agendas, diaries, original poetry, and technical notes.

Next to Monet and Degas, Cézanne was the only other major figure among the leading French painters of the late nineteenth century to have left a number of sketchbooks that remain more or less intact. Seven out of as many as nineteen of Cézanne's documented *carnets* survive in at least a partial state.[15] Cézanne's

TABLE 4 Monet's Sketchbooks at the Musée Marmottan Monet

SKETCHBOOK NO.	WILDENSTEIN NOS.	MARMOTTAN INV. NO.	APPROX. DATES OF USE	DIMENSIONS OF ALBUM
1	D105–39	5128	1865–1919	263 x 352 mm*
2	D140–59	5130	1874–81	250 x 320 mm*
3	D160–222	5134	1873–1900	120 x 186 mm
4	D223–74	5131	1881–85	120 x 200 mm*
5	D275–333	5132	1884–88	126 x 202 mm
6	D334–80	5129	1886–1925	242 x 322 mm*
7	D381–403	5133	1895	120 x 203 mm
8	D404	5135	1908	147 x 96 mm

* *modern binding*

sketchbooks are filled with fragmentary visual ideas, compositional studies, and the occasional shopping list. In Reff's eloquent words, "though his notes in them were restricted to practical matters, his sketchbooks were indeed his journals; if we read them perceptively, they reveal as fully in a visual as they could in a verbal form the whole span of his emotions from the most exalted to the most sober."[16]

Order and Chronology

Wildenstein's catalogue raisonné presents Monet's eight Marmottan sketchbooks in a rough chronological sequence based on the earliest drawings he identified in each book (see table 4). At an unknown date and by an unknown hand, the individual leaves of each sketchbook (including blank pages) were numbered consecutively in pencil on both sides of the sheet. Wildenstein accepted this pagination, which established the front and back of each *carnet*, and assigned sequential catalogue numbers to the drawings within. If a drawing continued across two pages, he assigned it a single number. In a few instances Wildenstein skipped a page with markings on it if he believed that they did not constitute an original drawing by Monet (for instance, sheets containing only inscriptions, random test strokes, or what are presumed to be children's sketches).

Notwithstanding the relative imprecision of his ordering of the *carnets* (sketchbook 3 was probably first, used slightly earlier than sketchbook 2), Wildenstein's numbering system is retained here for the sake of consistency with the catalogue raisonné. Ultimately, the numbering of Monet's sketchbooks and the drawings contained therein bears little relation to their actual chronology of use, which remains elusive. Given the overlapping dates of several of the sketchbooks and the artist's tendency to utilize the same *carnet* over the course of many years, the complex issue of their sequencing might best be dealt with on a page-by-page rather than a book-by-book basis. Even then, the fact that many pages cannot be related to specific paintings or geographical locations makes it impossible to establish a complete chronology.

It is of some significance that the first edition of Wildenstein's catalogue raisonné, which appeared in five parts between 1974 and 1991, relegated the drawings and pastels to the fifth and final volume. This privileging of Monet's painted oeuvre, while altogether appropriate, meant that the sketchbooks were not fully published until all of the oils had appeared in print. There is an undeniable logic to this approach, one added benefit of which was that it enabled the author to cite related paintings by Wildenstein number in the notes for individual drawings. Conversely, where the painting entries mention related sketchbook drawings, they are referenced by the Musée Marmottan's accession number for each *carnet* and by folio number within the book.[17]

The only basic element of cataloguing information lacking in Wildenstein's sketchbook entries is a precise date or date range for each drawing. Rather than assign specific years to individual pages, he adopted a slightly less user-friendly approach by merely indicating in his descriptive notes when a drawing relates to one or more oil paintings. Wildenstein connected roughly half of the sketchbook drawings in some way to Monet's painted oeuvre. It is left to the reader, based on the dating of the oils, to extract this crucial bit of information from the relevant painting entries and apply it to the drawings.

In enumerating the various kinds of relationships that exist between Monet's sketchbook drawings and his paintings, Wildenstein employed a number of relatively noncommittal terms. His most frequent and ambiguous phrase used in sketchbook entries that reference related canvases is the simple Latin abbreviation "Cf.," for "compare" or "see also." For example, in his entry on folio 37 recto of sketchbook 3 (D216), a drawing of cliffs near Pourville-Varengeville, the note reads "Cf. DW no. 788. Only the framing at the left is different," a reference to a canvas dated 1882 in the Rijksmuseum Twenthe, Enschede.[18] Although such comparisons can be extremely useful, this expression evades the issue of whether a given drawing might be considered a direct study for a specific painting. Another somewhat ambiguous term employed frequently in the sketchbook entries is *annonce* (literally "announce"), as in: the disposition of forms in a particular drawing *announces*—that is, signals or indicates—a similar formal structure in a series of related canvases. In some instances, Wildenstein confidently denoted that a specific sketchbook drawing is a "study" (*étude* or *esquisse*) or "preparatory sketch" (*croquis preparatoire*) for one or several related paintings.

In carefully reviewing the copious and intricate links that Wildenstein established between the pages of Monet's *carnets* and his enormous output of paintings, which numbers almost 2,000 works, one finds that the author occasionally failed to take into account the primacy of the sketchbook drawings and exploit the internal physical evidence that they might offer in his dating of the oils. For instance, sketchbook 6 contains four drawings on consecutive pages of the village of Bennecourt (fols. 29–32 verso, D371–72, 375, 377). Wildenstein identified the first two drawings as studies for W1126, a canvas signed and dated 1887 that Monet immediately sold to John Singer Sargent. He identified the latter two drawings as studies for W989 and W990, two undated canvases that he assigned to 1885. Based on the evidence of the four sketches, which appear to have been carried out on the same occasion, the two undated paintings of Bennecourt's church might be reassigned to 1887.[19]

Physical Characteristics

The Marmottan sketchbooks are relatively homogenous in their physical composition, belonging to a grade of commercially manufactured artists' materials that were widely available in Monet's day. They are simple in construction and modest in scale, ranging from approximately 90 by 140 millimeters to 250 by 340 millimeters, and consist of anywhere from 29 to 49 extant folios.[20] Of the five pocket-sized *carnets*, numbers 3, 5, and 7 are fitted with small fabric loops to hold a pencil, and numbers 3 and 5 have elastic straps attached to the binding edge to keep them fastened when not in use. After the Musée Marmottan acquired the sketchbooks in 1966, the museum's circular collection stamp was imprinted in red ink either on the recto or verso of each sheet (see fig. 143). Several of the books entered the museum's collection in a tenuous state of preservation without their original cloth covers.[21] In 1997, sketchbooks 1, 2, 4, and 6 underwent conservation including rebinding.[22]

Two of the books retain evidence of the

141
Label for E. Troisgros, from sketchbook 6, Musée Marmottan Monet, Paris

142
Emilio Aickelin's seal on the inside cover of sketchbook 8, Musée Marmottan Monet, Paris

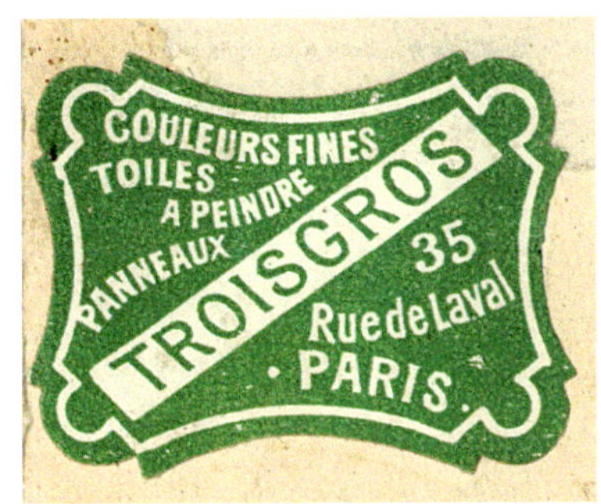

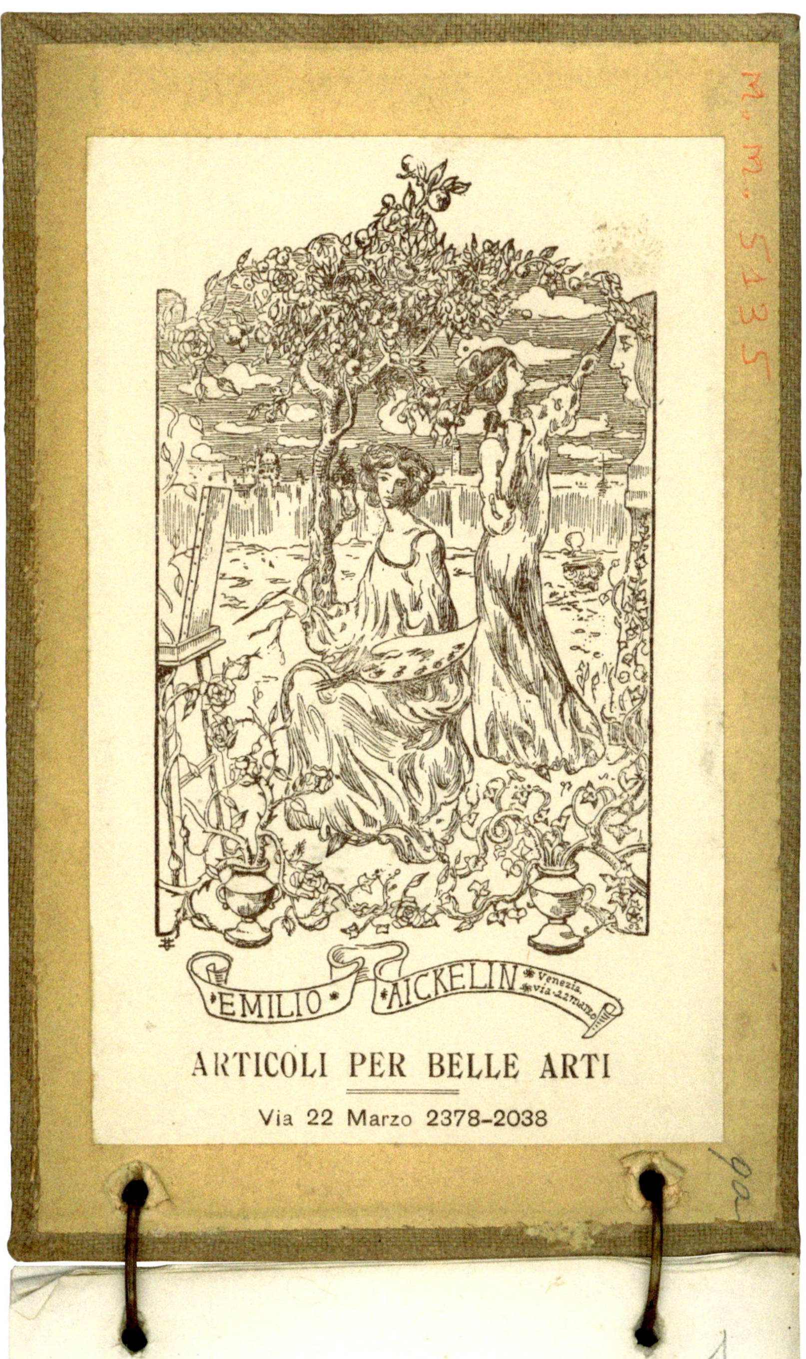

merchants from whom Monet purchased them. Sketchbook 6, which he used from the mid-1880s through the mid-1920s, bears a small green label on the guard sheet of E. Troisgros (fig. 141), an artists' supply shop at 35 rue de Laval (now the rue Victor-Massé) in Paris from which Monet bought pigments, canvases, and frames as early as 1881.[23] In the immediate aftermath of his 1885 mishap on the beach at Étretat, when his painting equipment was swept out to sea, he telegraphed Troisgros to have a new traveling easel fabricated and sent up to him along with other unspecified art supplies to replace what was lost.[24]

Monet's Venetian sketchbook (number 8) is the only one of the eight Marmottan *carnets* without a sewn binding. Instead, it takes the form of a cloth-covered flip pad held together by two metal rings. A printed supplier's label mounted on the inside cover shows that Monet purchased this petite album during his roughly two-month stay in Venice in 1908. The source was Emilio Aickelin, a retailer of *articoli per belle arti* and publisher of postcards on the Via 22 Marzo (fig. 142), a major commercial street just a short walk from the Grand Hotel Britannia where Monet and his wife Alice relocated around 19 October 1908 after staying several weeks in the Palazzo Barbaro. John Singer Sargent was another of Aickelin's customers; his supplier's stamp also appears on a watercolor by the American artist dating from the same period in the collection of the Metropolitan Museum of Art.[25]

In general, the Marmottan *carnets* consist of medium-thickness, neutral cream-colored paper, both of the laid (books 1 and 2) and wove (books 3–8) varieties. A portion of sketchbook 3, which is otherwise composed of cream-colored paper, consists of three sheets each of tan and blue-gray toned paper.[26] Unlike his youthful sketchbook of 1857, in which he favored specific paper colors for certain subjects, there is nothing to suggest that Monet's use of the toned sheets in this book was in any way influenced by his subject matter. Indeed, he seems to have been oblivious to the presence of tinted sketchbook pages, as is evidenced by the continuation of a single drawing of cliffs begun on

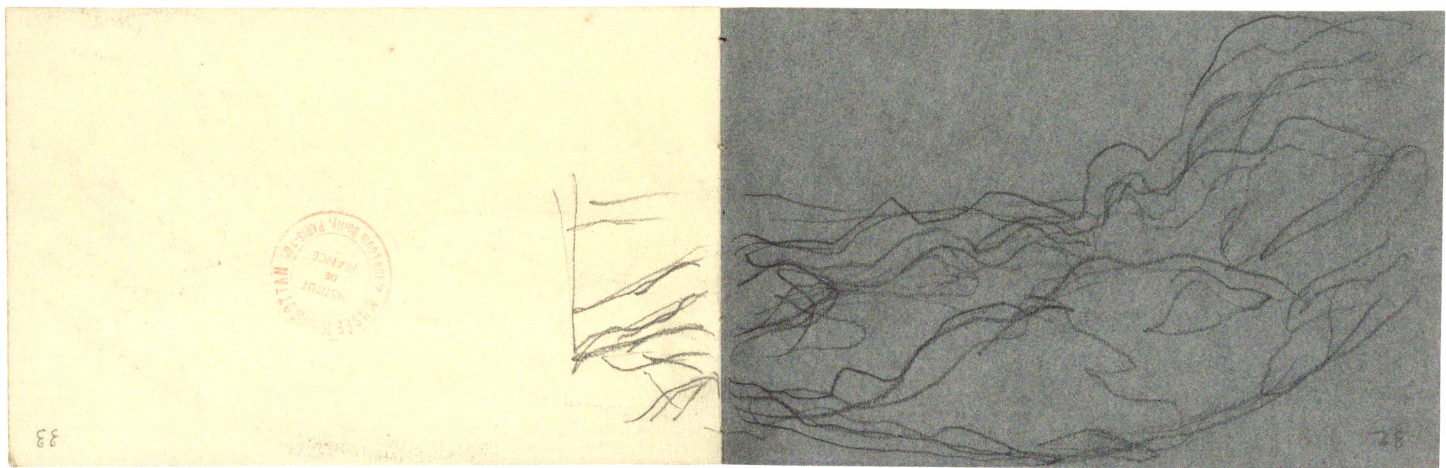

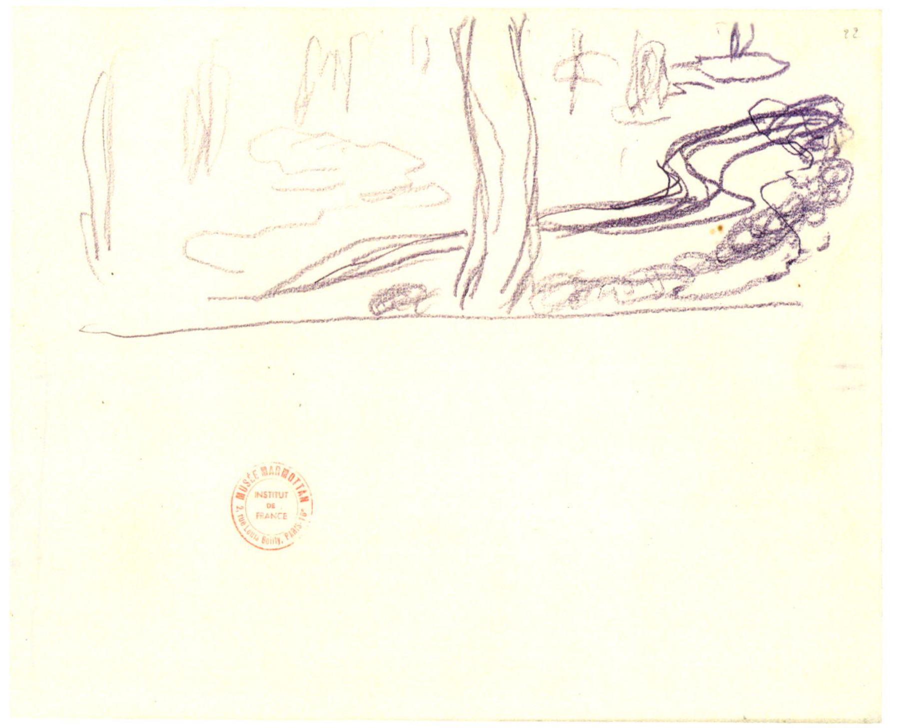

143

On the Cliff near Pourville, c. 1896–97. Pencil on cream and blue-gray paper, 110 x 360 mm (full spread). Sketchbook 3, fols. 32v and 33r. Musée Marmottan Monet, Paris [D208]

144

Willow and Water Lilies, c. 1914–19. Violet crayon, 255 x 340 mm. Sketchbook 1, fol. 22v. Musée Marmottan Monet, Paris [D124]

blue-gray paper onto a facing cream-colored sheet (fig. 143).

Monet executed the majority of his sketchbook drawings with either soft or hard pencils. Exceptions include black-chalk drawings in sketchbooks 1, 4, and 5 and a number of studies of the 1910s (iris, water lilies, weeping willows) in violet[27] and black crayons (fig. 144).[28] The smooth wove papers in the sketchbooks were not particularly conducive to the pastel medium, and Monet generally refrained from using pastels within their pages. The recto of folio 21 in sketchbook 1 bears the counterproof in pastel of what appears to be the drawing of a girl's head (not in Wildenstein). Another exception occurs in sketchbook 5: the verso of folio 30, identified by Wildenstein as *Tree on the Coast? (Arbre au bord de la mer?)* (D318), was carried out in black crayon and pastel. John House recognized that this badly rubbed sheet was related to the 1888 oil *Antibes* in the Courtauld Institute of Art, London (W1192), proposing that it was a copy after the painting rather than a study for it.[29]

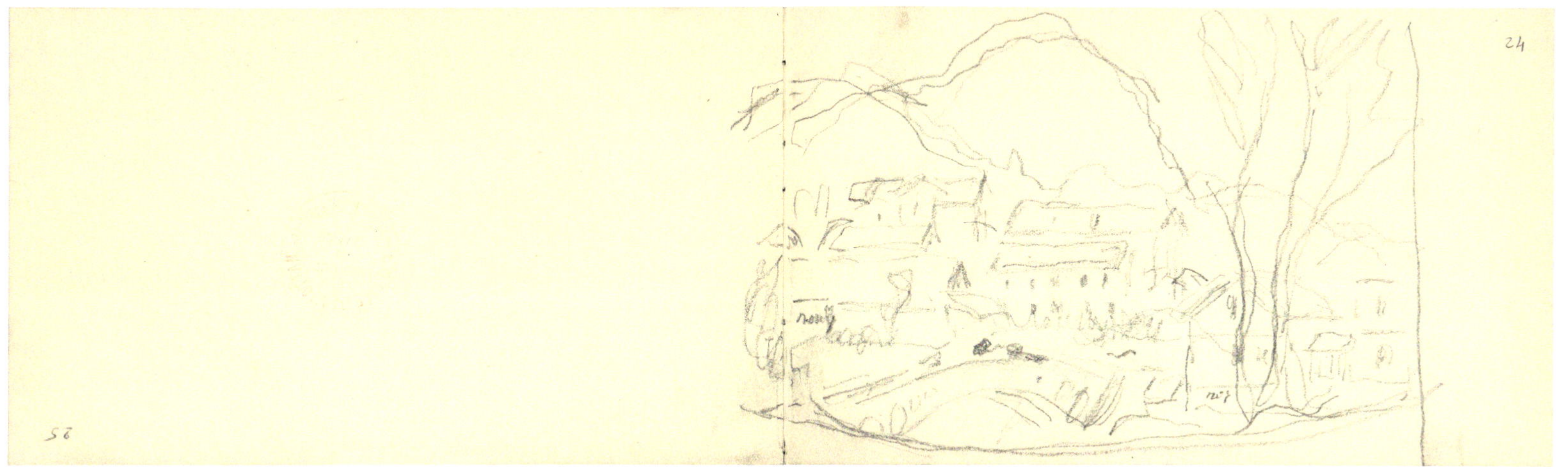

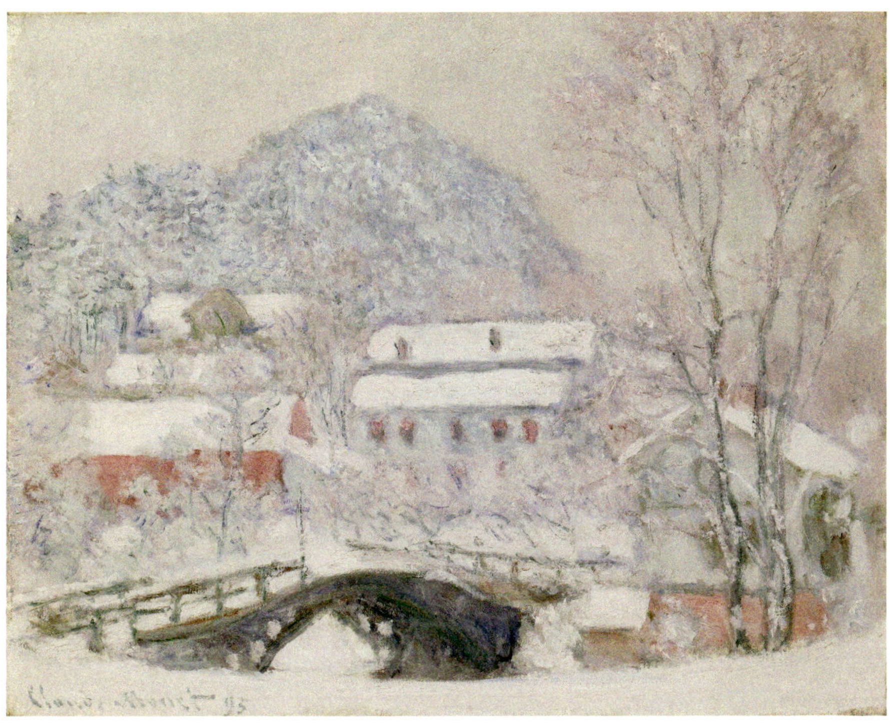

145
The Village of Sandvika and the Lökke Bridge, 1895. Pencil, 115 x 400 mm (full spread). Sketchbook 7, fols. 24v and 25r. Musée Marmottan Monet, Paris [D399]

146
Sandvika, Norway, 1895. Oil on canvas, 73.4 x 92.5 cm. The Art Institute of Chicago. Gift of Bruce Borland [W1397]

Manuscript Annotations

Relatively few manuscript annotations are to be found within the pages of Monet's sketchbooks. The inside front cover of sketchbook 3 contains a record, in the artist's hand, of various expenses from an undetermined trip, including 44 and 48 francs for two railway tickets and 63 francs 50 centimes for a stay at the Hotel St. Nicolas. The last page and inside back cover of the same book contains a list of fifteen plant and flower names in Latin, probably related to one of his ambitious gardening projects at Giverny. Monet's Norway sketchbook (number 7) gives his host's name and mailing address at Sandvika on the first page ("Fru Björnson / Björnegaard / (Smestad) Sanviken" [Sandvika]), and the location "Dalebo" [Dalbo] on the otherwise blank folio 3.[30] On one of the final pages of sketchbook 4, the artist made out a list of twenty-one paintings that is only partially legible but may represent a preliminary selection of works he planned to submit to the seventh group exhibition of independent artists that opened in March 1882.[31]

The kinds of color notes that one occasionally finds on black-and-white sketchbook drawings by other artists (for instance, Pissarro) are almost entirely absent from Monet's *carnets*. Sketchbook 1 contains a single drawing, in mauve crayon, of an iris flower labeled "mauve pale" (D108). The Norway *carnet* contains an elaborate drawing of the village of Sandvika and the Lökke Bridge in which the word "rouge" appears in two places (just to the right of the binding roughly 40 millimeters from the lower edge, and near the base of the trees at the bottom right) to indicate the colors of particular buildings that will appear in a painting (figs. 145 and 146).

Most interesting are the annotations that appear on three sketchbook drawings recording the hour of their creation. In sketchbook 4, a view of houses in Varengeville is inscribed "9h-" (D249); and in sketchbook 6, two drawings of Bennecourt are annotated "Midi à 1hre"

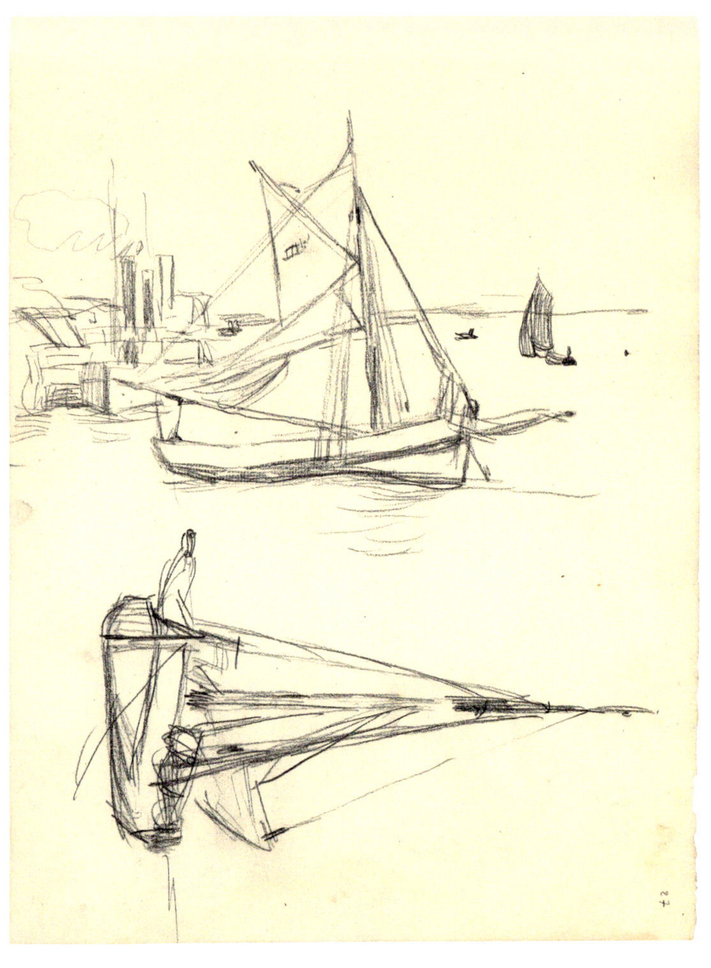

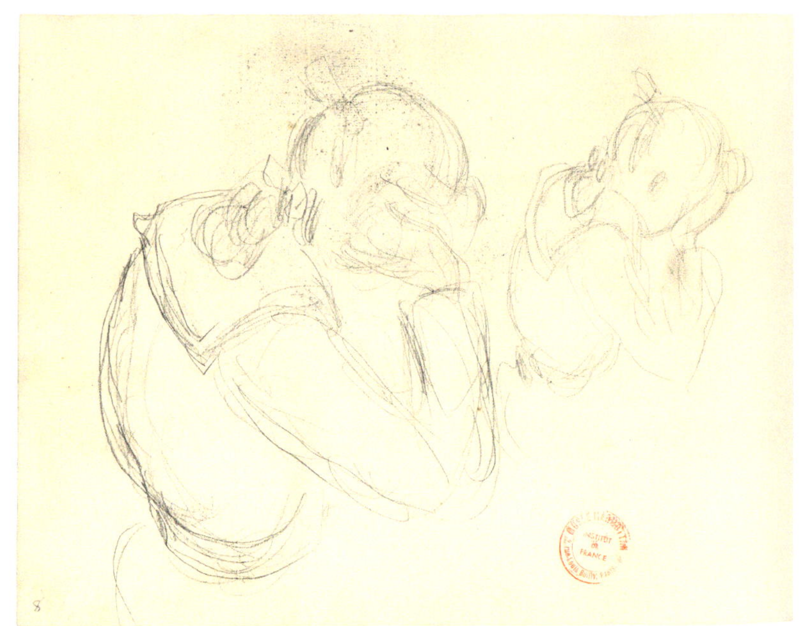

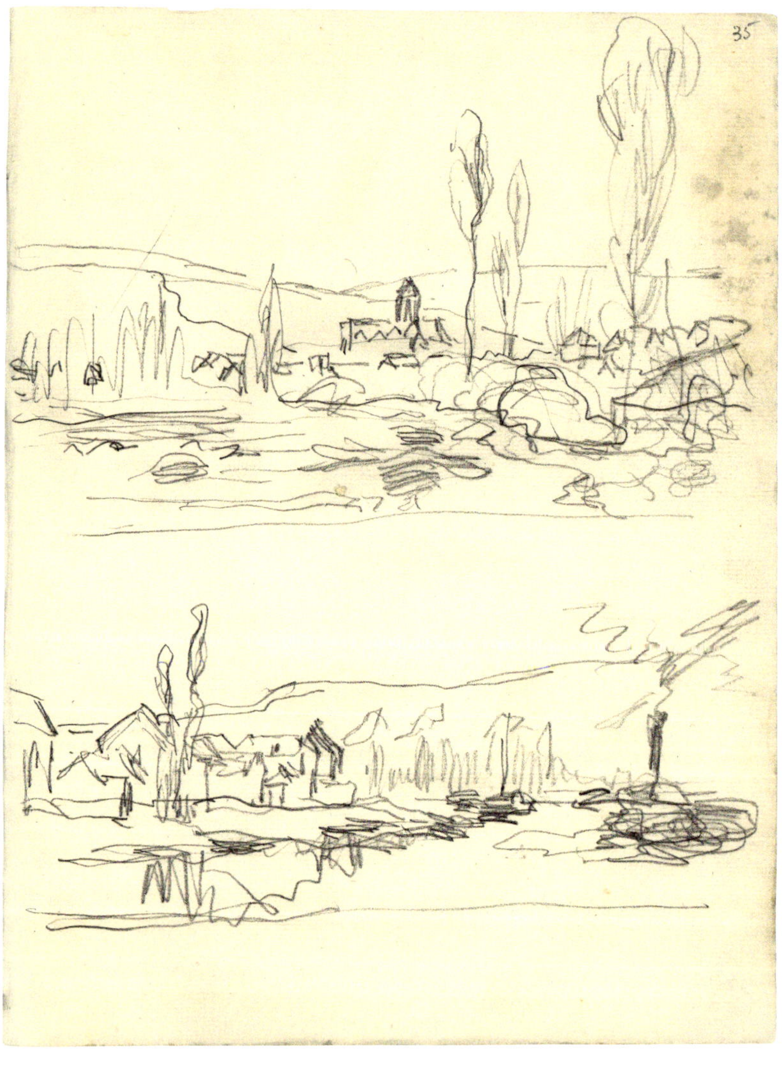

147
Studies of Boats, c. 1866–69. Pencil, 340 x 255 mm. Sketchbook 1, fol. 27v. Musée Marmottan Monet, Paris [D130]

148
Germaine Hoschedé Reading, c. 1885. Pencil, 255 x 340 mm. Sketchbook 1, fol. 8r. Musée Marmottan Monet, Paris [D111]

149
Vétheuil Seen from Île Saint-Martin and *Tugboat on the Seine in front of Lavacourt*, c. 1878–80. Pencil, 310 x 240 mm. Sketchbook 2, fol. 35v. Musée Marmottan Monet, Paris [D159]

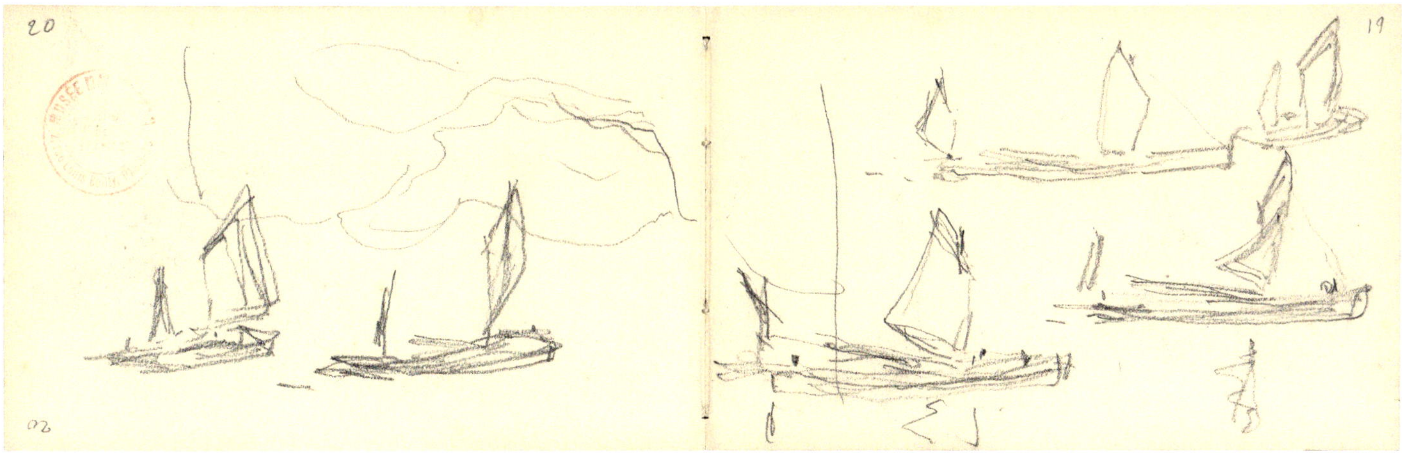

150

Boats on the Thames, c. 1899–1900. Pencil, 110 x 360 mm (full spread). Sketchbook 3, fols. 19v and 20r. Musée Marmottan Monet, Paris [D184–85]

and "Midi à 1hre / extraordinaire de / gris / lumineux" ["1 o'clock in the afternoon, extraordinary luminous gray"] (see figs. 168 and 169). These notes are the only explicit indication in the *carnets* of an increasingly essential tenet of Monet's landscape painting: namely, that the time of day, and hence the light conditions, were critical to his selection of a particular vantage point for setting up his canvas.

Mise en page

Some general observations may be offered concerning the *mise en page* of Monet's sketchbook drawings, which is to say, his approach to placing forms within the boundaries of a single blank sheet or a two-page spread. For a painter whose reputation is based in part on his systematic approach to serial imagery, his sketchbooks offer a startling glimpse into another side of his artistic personality. If there is anything deliberate about these books, it is the very casualness with which he filled them in, throwing them open almost at random, continuing studies across the binding, and paying little attention to composing each page. It is hardly an exaggeration to state that organized chaos reigns within the covers of Monet's sketchbooks.

Monet's non-sequential use of the *carnets* has already been observed, but what might be added concerning their consistency of orientation? A quick glance at the layout of their contents in Wildenstein's catalogue raisonné may be visually misleading because each drawing is reproduced individually from its correct viewing angle. In making basic decisions regarding the order and "primary" orientation of each book, Wildenstein followed the lead of whoever was responsible for inscribing folio numbers on each page, placing them in most cases on what was decided to be the upper-right corner. A close examination of Wildenstein's scrupulous entries finds an indication, through the abbreviation "(p.i.)" (for "*position inverse*" or inverted position), of the actual viewing angle of each drawing. For many of the drawings, Monet held his sketchbooks vertically like a flip pad rather than horizontally like a book. Compiling this information for the large sketchbook 1, for example, we find that only ten of thirty-three studies are in the "proper" orientation; in this case, the predominant viewing angle (i.e., of more than two-thirds of the drawings) is the opposite of what was accepted by Wildenstein. As if to thwart the efforts of future cataloguers, Monet did not recognize a primary orientation in his sketchbooks; to him they had no front or back, no up or down (fig. 147).[32]

On occasion, Monet reused the same folio or two-page spread to make multiple studies either during a single session (fig. 148) or at disparate places and times (fig. 149). Like his youthful sketchbooks of 1856–57, the mature *carnets* include a number of pages filled out with composite studies of sailing vessels (fig. 150, for instance), but these are altogether lacking in the fine detail of his student work. In a few instances, Monet allowed two studies to overlap

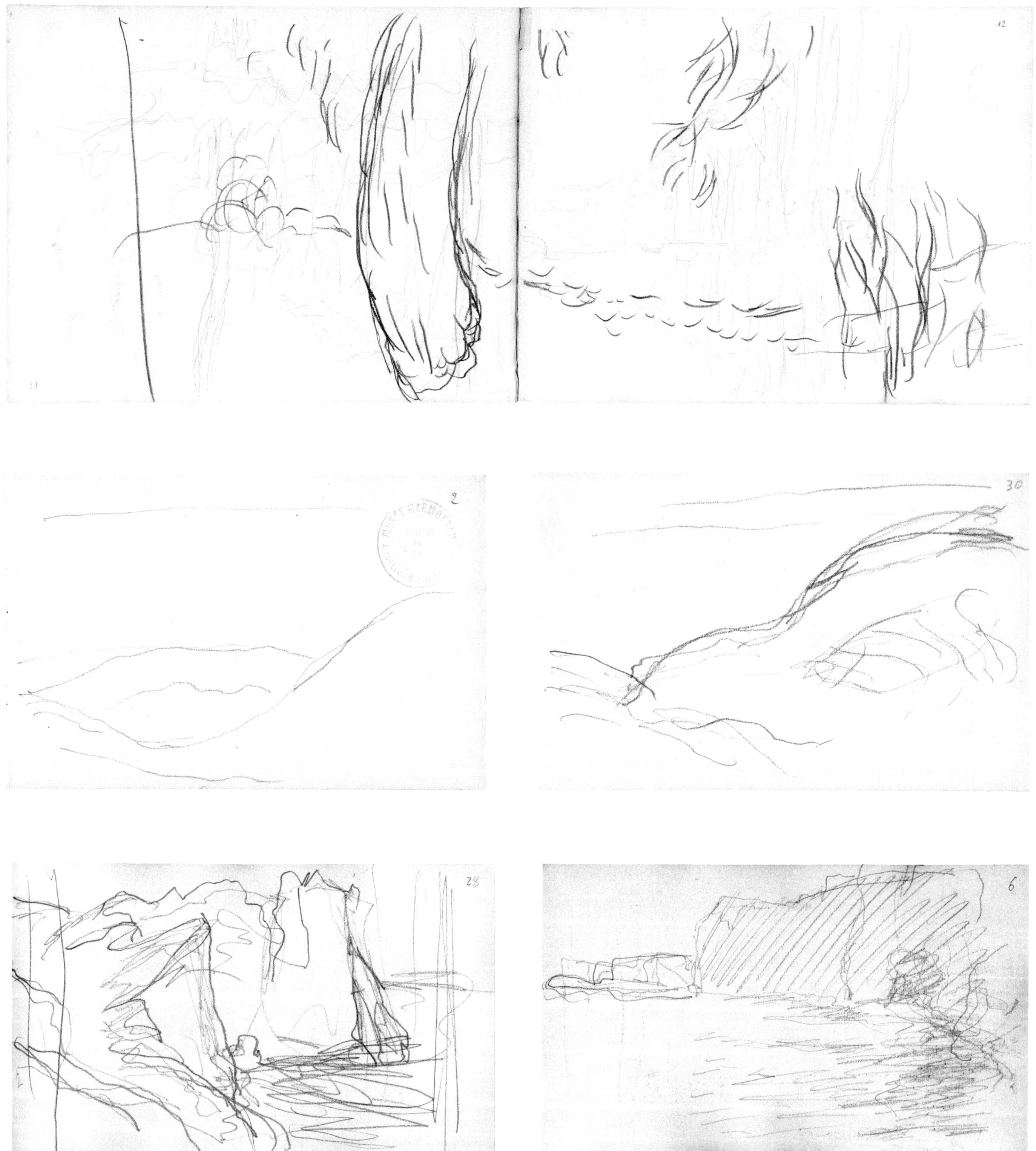

151

Weeping Willow at the Giverny Pond, c. 1914–19. Waxed crayon, 235 x 630 mm (full spread). Sketchbook 6, fols. 11v and 12r. Musée Marmottan Monet, Paris [D351]

152

Rolling Landscape, after 1887. Pencil, 110 x 180 mm. Sketchbook 3, fol. 2r. Musée Marmottan Monet, Paris [D161]

153

Cliff Downstream from Dieppe, c. 1896. Pencil, 110 x 180 mm. Sketchbook 3, fol. 30r. Musée Marmottan Monet, Paris [D203]

154

The Porte d'Aval Seen from the Cliff Path, c. 1885. Pencil, 110 x 195 mm. Sketchbook 4, fol. 28v. Musée Marmottan Monet, Paris [D267]

155

The Cliffs of Varengeville, 1882. Pencil, 110 x 195 mm. Sketchbook 4, fol. 6r. Musée Marmottan Monet, Paris [D231]

(for example, adjoining studies, in opposite senses, of a cliff at Varengeville [D177, fol. 13 verso] and grainstacks at Giverny [D178, fol. 14 recto] in sketchbook 3).

Particularly in his old age, Monet recycled entire sketchbook pages by making vigorous new drawings over more lightly rendered earlier studies, a simultaneous act of creation and eradication. For instance, he sketched a two-page spread of boats on the Thames over a spare earlier drawing, in the opposite sense, of the simple contours of an unidentified landscape (see fig. 150). While it is possible that his failing eyesight played a role in this unorthodox methodology[33]—the majority of such redrawn leaves are water-lily studies from the mid-1910s (fig. 151, D348–52, 369, 379)—several were carried out before the onset of his cataracts.

The Graphic Language of Monet's Sketchbook Drawings

If one were to characterize the style of Monet's sketchbook drawings, accolades like "beautiful" or "refined" do not immediately come to mind. The sketches in the *carnets* are functional remnants of his working process, fragments rather than finished works of art, patently intended for private consumption. In his early years, Monet proved with the greatest confidence his skills as a draftsman. His large caricatures (see chapter 2) as well as the extraordinary series of black-chalk drawings of the mid-1860s (discussed in chapter 4), which are concurrent with the earliest studies in the Marmottan *carnets*, reveal an accomplished hand, fluent not only in multiple languages of line but in tone, texture, and chiaroscuro.

In his sketchbooks we find Monet working in an altogether less-polished graphic mode, one characterized by spontaneous animated lines of varying intensities. At one extreme are the most lightly executed studies, almost minimalist in their spare and fine outlines (fig. 152). On other folios, Monet lingered a bit, allowing his hand to double back and retrace his first marks (fig. 153). On certain of these sheets, the intensity of retracing builds to an extreme, suggesting the artist's exhilaration in finding and fixing a particular viewpoint in both his mind's eye and the page of his sketchbook (fig. 154). At the opposite end of the spectrum from the most sparsely drawn folios are a number of studies in which the reassertion and multiplication of superimposed lines reach a ferocious, even riotous crescendo.

The primary function of line in Monet's sketchbooks was to demarcate the principal contours of motifs or elements in the landscape. Rarely did he fill in these outlines with any attempt at tonal mark-making. In those few instances, he attended to defining darker values using quick zigzag strokes, or rapidly scrawled loose parallel hatching (fig. 155). Only in his independent portrait studies of his children and stepchildren did he seek to model forms, evoking naturalistic textures and light effects with his unsystematic shading (see fig. 157).

Among the most heavily worked of his sketchbook drawings is a view of the Auteuil platform of the Gare Saint-Lazare contained in the same *carnet* as the child portraits (fig. 156).[34] Five other studies of the station's interior and exterior are found in sketchbook 2, but the drawing in sketchbook 1, clearly executed on a different occasion and using a harder pencil, is at once the most vigorous, chaotic, and "finished" of the group.[35] It may be characterized as a graphic rehearsal for the painted version in the Musée d'Orsay that was likely exhibited in the third Impressionist exhibition of 1877 (W438). Conservative critics were shocked by the gritty urban subject matter.

Relative to Monet's other sketchbook drawings, this folio offers an abundance of "content": the interior of a modern train shed (the Gare Saint-Lazare), a fragmented cityscape (buildings in the rue de Rome), an iron trellis over the tracks (the Pont de l'Europe), a steam locomotive (the Auteuil train), gas lamps, barriers to direct pedestrian traffic, and a scattering of a half-dozen figures, several of whom wear station workers' caps. At the same time, none of this content is rendered in sufficient detail to serve as a visual reference for later use. From the hand

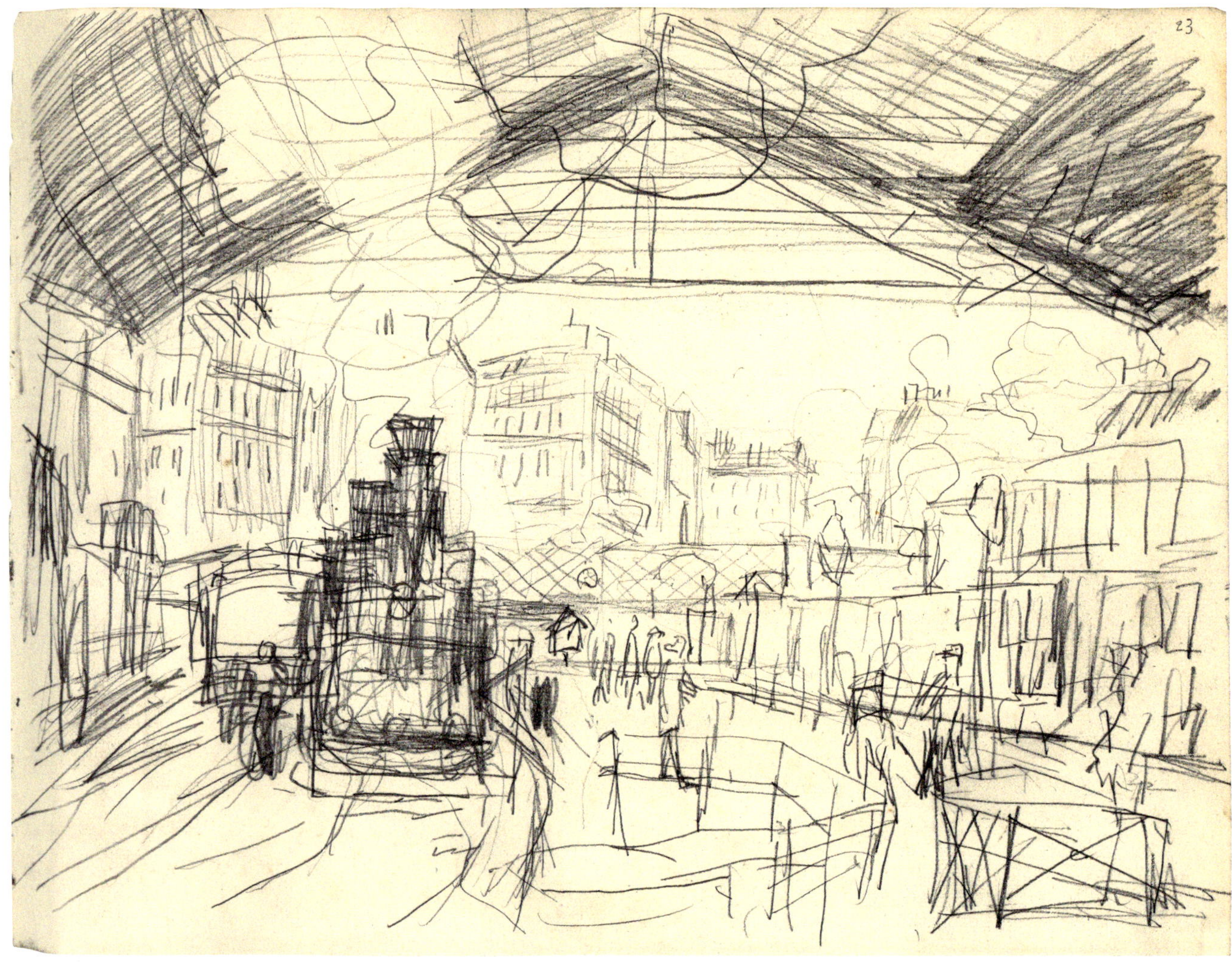

156
The Gare Saint-Lazare (Suburban Lines), 1877. Pencil, 255 x 340 mm. Sketchbook 1, fol. 23v. Musée Marmottan Monet, Paris [D125]

157
Jean-Pierre Hoschedé and Michel Monet Drawing and *Germaine Hoschedé Writing*, c. 1885. Pencil, 255 x 680 mm. Sketchbook 1, fols. 9v and 10r. Musée Marmottan Monet, Paris [D114–15]

158
Michel Monet Reading, c. 1885. Pencil, 255 x 340 mm. Sketchbook 1, fol. 7v. Musée Marmottan Monet, Paris [D110]

of a painter so admired for the softness of his brushwork, this sheet offers a startlingly frenzied, even brutal exploit as a draftsman.

Categories of Drawing

In the broadest possible terms, the contents of the Marmottan *carnets* may be divided into three loose categories according to their original functions: drawings made for their own sake that are independent of the artist's painted oeuvre; exploratory drawings made as preliminary attempts to fix vantage points or as *aides memoires* in surveying sites to paint; and preparatory studies for specific paintings or groups of paintings. It should come as no surprise that the vast majority of Monet's sketchbook drawings belong to the second category: hastily executed rough sketches often made during the course of long hikes through the landscape.

Of the few sketchbook drawings that are entirely independent of Monet's painted oeuvre, perhaps the most touching are the sensitive portrait studies of several of the young people in the artist's household at Giverny contained in the large sketchbook 1 (D110–15). From the apparent ages of the sitters (Michel Monet [1878–1966] and Jean-Pierre [1877–1961], Germaine [1873–1968], and possibly Jacques Hoschedé [1869–1941]), the six consecutive pages probably date from the middle of the 1880s. The subjects are all seated at a table, quietly reading, writing, and drawing (fig. 157). One page representing young Michel engrossed in a book, his head propped against his right hand, bears in the lower-left corner the unmistakable graffito of a child (fig. 158).[36]

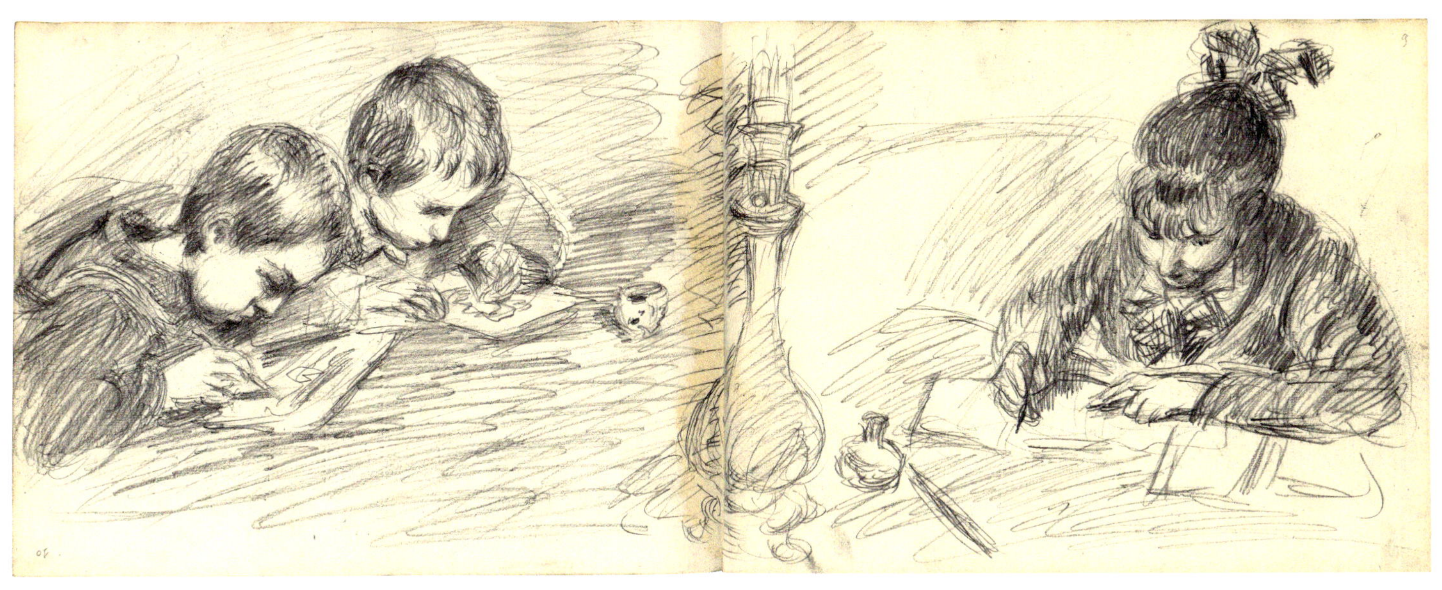

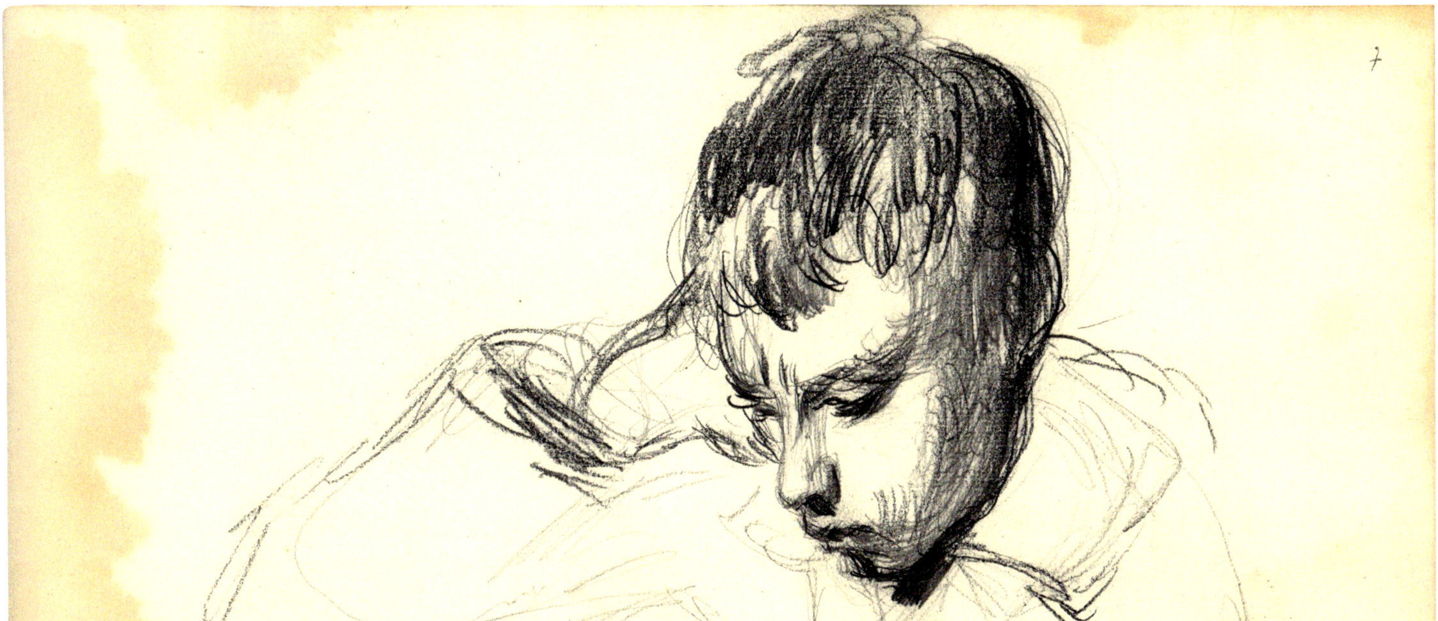

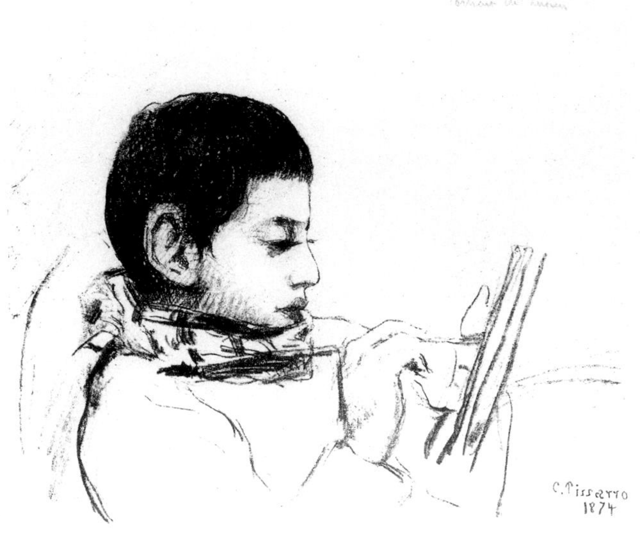

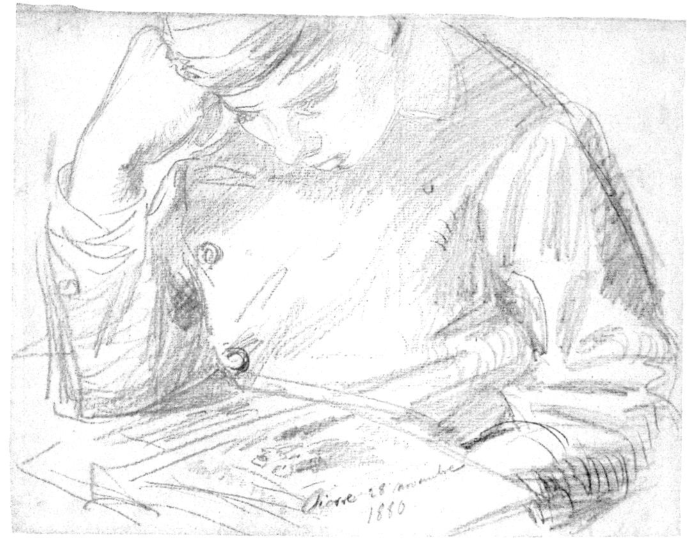

159
Camille Pissarro (French, 1830–1903), *Portrait of the Artist's Son, Lucien*, 1874. Lithograph, 237 x 300 mm. Museum of Fine Arts, Boston. Stephen Bullard Memorial Fund

160
Alfred Sisley (English, active in France, 1839–1899), *The Artist's Son, Pierre*, 1880. Black chalk, 230 x 310 mm. Walsall Museum and Art Gallery, Walsall, England. Garman-Ryan Collection

Although the Monet and Hoschedé children were the subjects of a number of portraits from the late 1870s onward, the sketchbook drawings bear no direct relationship to any of these canvases. They reflect something more informal: a rare occasion in which Monet took an almost certainly forced break from his all-consuming occupation to spend time with his family, guiding his brood in recreational activities that undoubtedly included drawing. Yet these are not boisterous scenes of children at play—they are scenes of children at work, in which everyone is immersed in his or her individual project and no one makes eye contact. The present but unseen father sets the example by burying his nose in his own sketchbook.

Similar glimpses of the domestic life of the other Impressionists' children may be found in graphic works by Morisot, Pissarro (fig. 159), Cézanne, and Sisley, whose unfortunately cropped black chalk study of his thirteen year-old son, Pierre (1867–1929), is dated 28 November 1880 (fig. 160). When Sisley died of cancer in 1899, Monet came to the aid of his bereft family, organizing a sale for the benefit of his son and daughter.[37] As a young man, Pierre Sisley became an unsuccessful suitor of Monet's attractive stepdaughter, Germaine Hoschedé; he later became an equally unsuccessful decorator and draftsman, and died impoverished, like his father.

Between the categories of independent studies and exploratory drawings lies a gray area, the product of another way of using sketchbooks commonly exercised by Monet's elders (e.g., Jongkind and Boudin) but infrequently practiced by him as a mature artist. For this older generation, the *carnet* could serve as a personal archive of isolated motifs, a store of images drawn on speculation with the idea that they might find their way into future canvases. Although this synthetic approach to composing pictures would seem to stand directly at odds with Monet's artistic agenda, his sketchbooks contain a number of drawings potentially of this type, which therefore invite special scrutiny.

The most frequent appearance of such possible stock imagery occurs in the many isolated representations of sailing vessels that are scattered throughout sketchbooks 1 through 5 (fig. 161). These studies were carried out in a variety of locales, including Argenteuil, Honfleur, Trouville, Villerville, Zaandam, and London. In simple, practical terms, the prominent inclusion of watercraft in Monet's seascapes and riverscapes poses an obvious problem from the point of view of his plein-air, direct-to-canvas painting technique. Unless a boat is moored, it cannot be captured instantaneously with an artist's brush on canvas. Monet grew up on the water and during his teenage years perfected his ability to draw every type of sailing vessel. That he continued to make drawings of boats in his mature sketchbooks may simply reflect

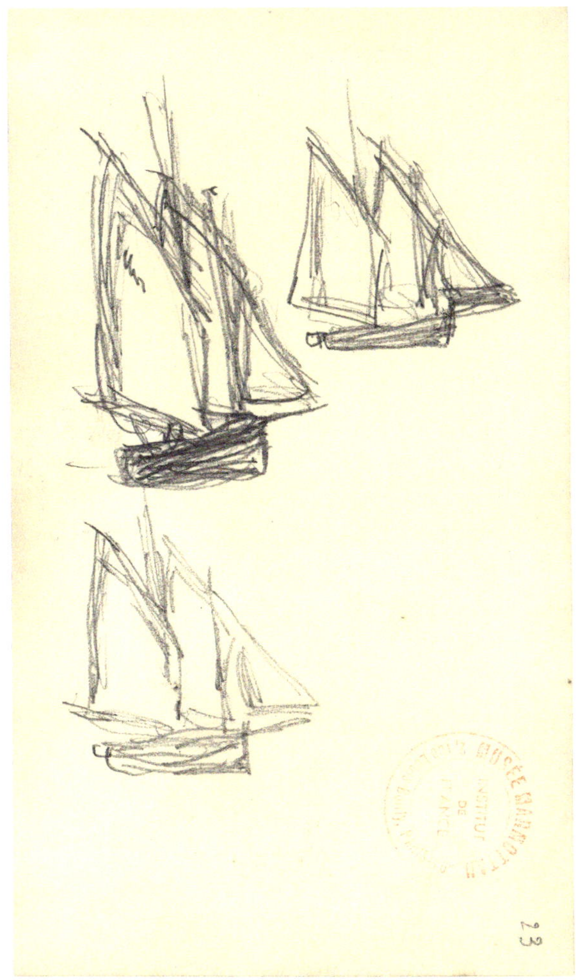

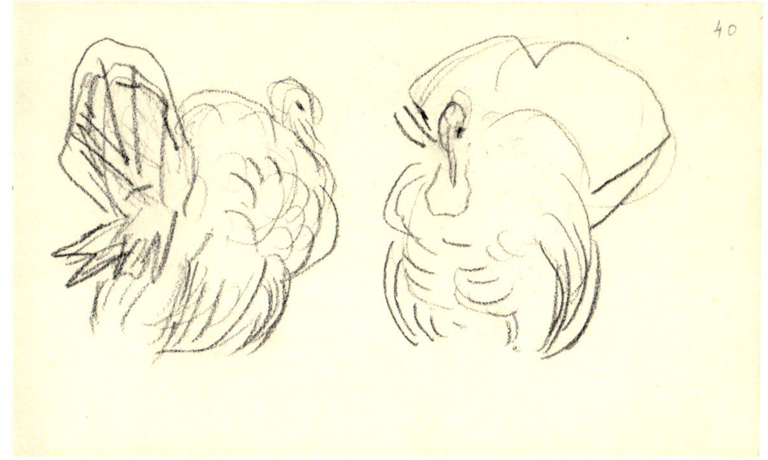

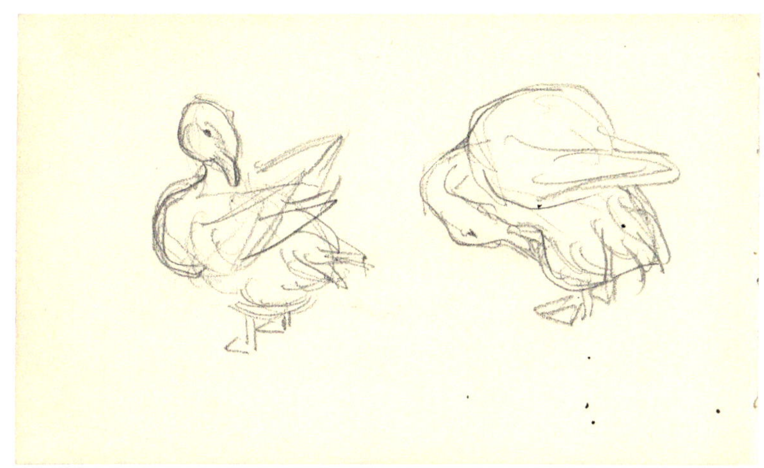

161
Plattes of Villerville, c. 1883. Pencil, 195 x 110 mm. Sketchbook 4, fol. 23r. Musée Marmottan Monet, Paris [D256]

162
Study of Turkeys, 1884–88. Black chalk, 115 x 195 mm. Sketchbook 5, fol. 40v. Musée Marmottan Monet, Paris [D324]

163
Study of Ducks, 1884–88. Black chalk, 115 x 195 mm. Sketchbook 5, fol. 42v. Musée Marmottan Monet, Paris [D328]

an impulsive activity, a kind of intellectual and manual exercise that he enjoyed. As has been already noted, most of the later boat studies are lacking in the kind of detail that would be necessary for them to function effectively as visual sources. Still, Wildenstein has identified several instances in which a boat drawn in isolation on a sketchbook page appears in a particular canvas,[38] suggesting that Monet may have considered such studies an archive of stock motifs.

Another potential collection of stock images may be found in the small-format sketchbook 5: nine consecutive studies of turkeys (fig. 162) and ducks (fig. 163), perhaps drawn in the artist's own poultry yard.[39] On some sheets the same bird appears to be depicted from more than one angle or engaged in several different actions. These highly conventional and charming folios pose vicious problems in dating. The other drawings in this *carnet*, which Monet used mainly in Bordighera, Rouen, and around Giverny, derive from the mid-1880s, but none of the poultry studies relate to his canvases of this period.

Exploratory Drawings

"It's easy to get used to not going for walks, but you must get back to it all the same and make a habit of what really is the best thing about living in the country," Monet wrote to Alice from Bordighera in January 1884.[40] "Mine is a dog's life and I never stop walking; I walk here, there and everywhere. As a break between studies, I go on explorations down every path I find, always on the lookout for something new." Each of Monet's landscape paintings represents the fruit of his attempt to fix the sensations of color and light of a particular place and time in the medium of oil on canvas. The vast majority of

TABLE 5 Itineraries of Monet's Sketchbooks

PLACE	YEAR	SKETCHBOOK NO.: FOLS.
Holland (Zaandam)	1871	1: 29v–34v
Varengeville	1882	4: 3v, 5v, 6r, 10r–14r, 16r, 18v–21r
Étretat	c. 1883–85	4: 2v, 22v, 23v–28v
Italy (Bordighera, Sasso)	1884	5: 1r–2r, 3r, 4r, 5r, 6r, 7r–8r, 9r, 10r–12r
Rouen	c. 1884–85	5: 2v, 8v, 9v
Port-Villez	188	4: 39v–42r
Falaise	1885	5: 4v, 5v, 14v–19r
Creuse Valley (Fresselines)	1889	6: 20v–21v, 25v, 32r, 33r
Rouen	1892–93	3: 1r, 2v–9v, 10r–11r
Norway	1895	7: 5v–29v (entire book)
Pourville and Varengeville	c. 1896–97	3: 13v, 27v, 28v, 29v–33r, 34r, 35r, 37r
London	1899	3: 18v–21r

the landscape studies in his sketchbooks represent an earlier stage in the process, one of exploration, discovery, and endless hikes through the countryside. This procedure is outlined in another letter to Alice, sent shortly after his arrival in Dieppe in February 1882:

I've had a very tiring day, I've been all over the countryside, along all the paths below and above the cliffs. I've seen some lovely things and I was helped by superb sunshine. . . . Tomorrow I'll do some more exploring and the day after I'll set to work and depending on how I do, I'll see whether I should stay here.[41]

Although he failed to mention it in his letter, Monet did not go empty-handed on his wide-ranging rambles. The simplest and most vigorous of sketches that fill his pocket-sized *carnets* record moments in which he paused to make visual notes in a kind of graphic shorthand as he sought appropriate viewpoints to paint.

Like a film director scouting locations, Monet traversed every conceivable type of terrain during the course of his long career, from the dramatic cliffs of Étretat to the Côte d'Azur and the mountains of Norway and Italy. Extending the cinematic analogy, we might imagine several discreet groups of drawings distributed throughout the sketchbooks to read like a filmmaker's storyboards, in which the first-person narrative follows an artist trudging through the landscape looking for something to paint. The complete list of sites recorded in this manner is extensive. A partial account of Monet's itineraries as mapped in significant clusters of sketchbook drawings is given in table 5.

A sequence of four folios in sketchbook 6 provides a succinct case study, enabling us to visualize Monet's stroll from the countryside into the village of Bennecourt, a small commune southeast of Giverny, on an unspecified day during the late 1880s (fig. 164). In the first view a screen of spindly tree trunks obscures the distant village, which is identifiable by the steeple of its sixteenth-century church rising in the center of the composition (fig. 165). Two vertical framing lines anticipate the square-format canvas that Monet will select to paint roughly this viewpoint (W1126). For the next study (fig. 166),[42] he rotated his sketchbook ninety degrees to draw the same scene on a vertical sheet, adding horizontal lines across the top and bottom edge to help envision a square composition. A third sketch (fig. 167), also occupying a discrete section of a vertical page, depicts the

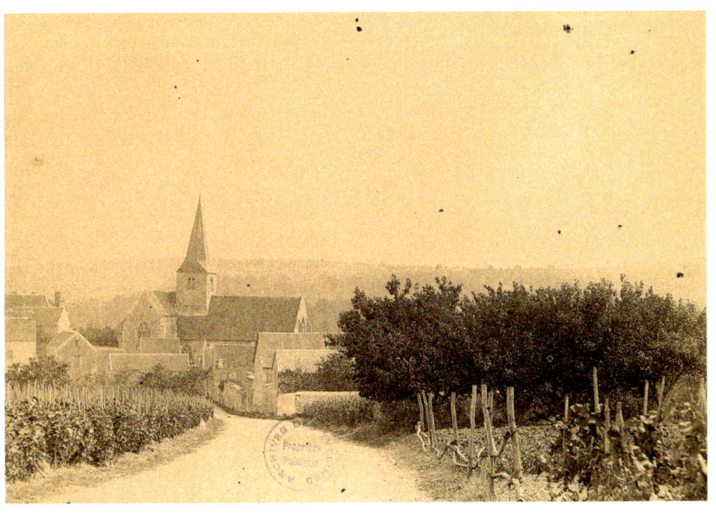

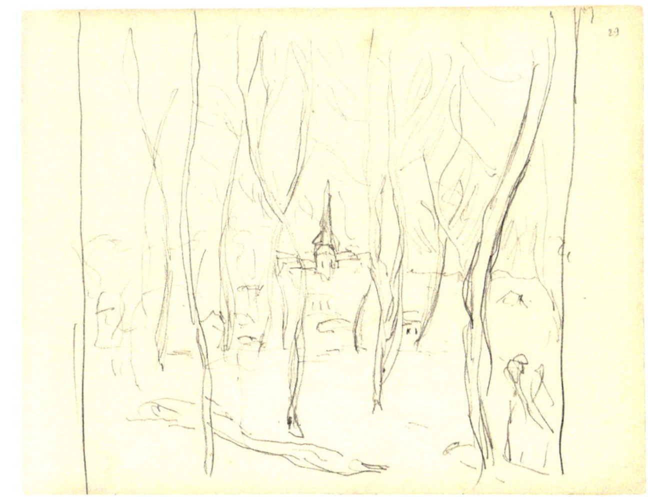

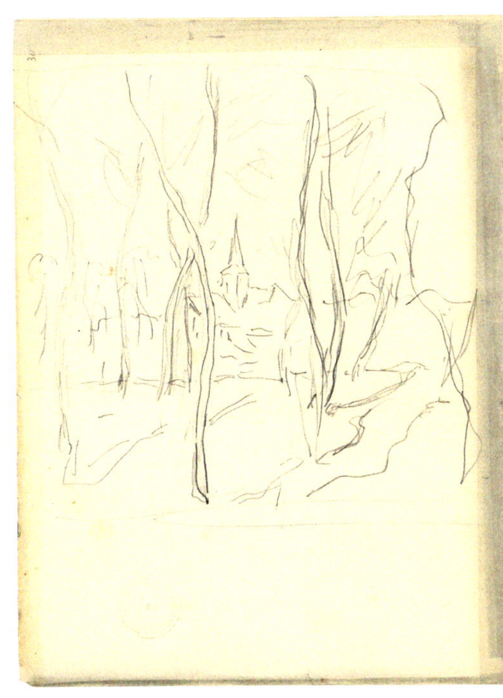

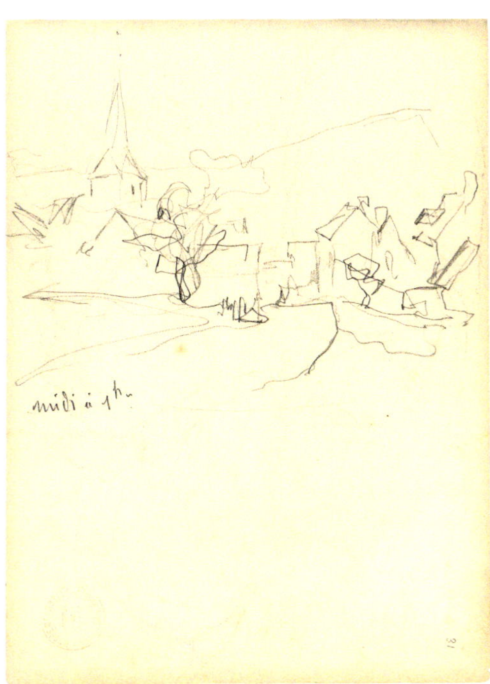

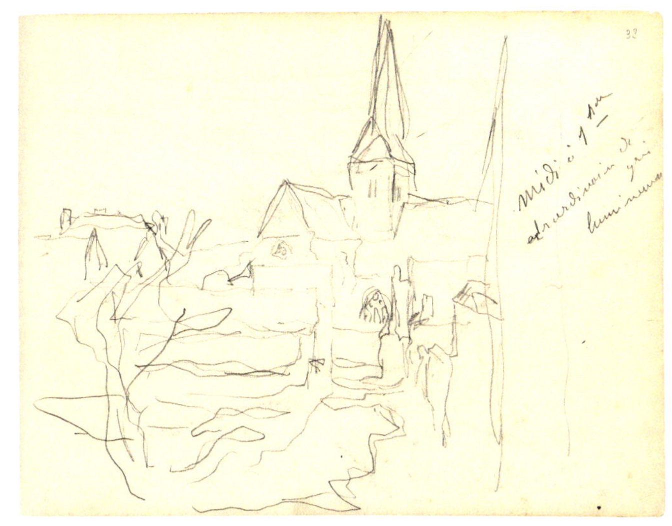

164
Entry to the village of Bennecourt, c. 1889

165
Bennecourt Seen through the Trees, c. 1887. Pencil, 235 x 315 mm. Sketchbook 6, fol. 29v. Musée Marmottan Monet, Paris [D371]

166
Bennecourt Seen through the Trees, c. 1887. Pencil, 315 x 235 mm. Sketchbook 6, fol. 30v. Musée Marmottan Monet, Paris [D372]

167
Bennecourt, c. 1887. Pencil, 315 x 235 mm. Sketchbook 6, fol. 31v. Musée Marmottan Monet, Paris [D375]

168
The Church at Bennecourt, c. 1887. Pencil, 235 x 315 mm. Sketchbook 6, fol. 32v. Musée Marmottan Monet, Paris [D377]

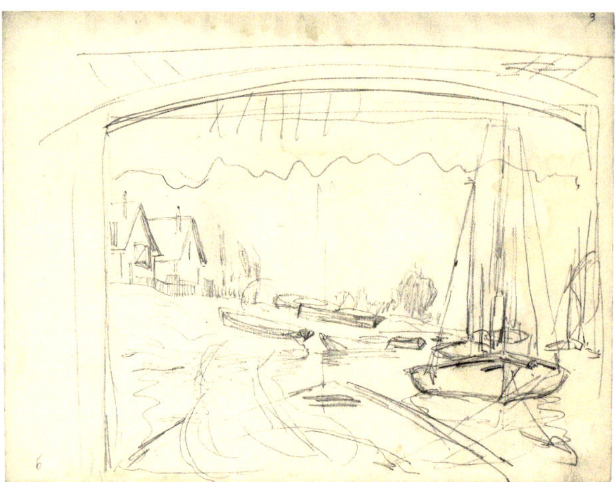

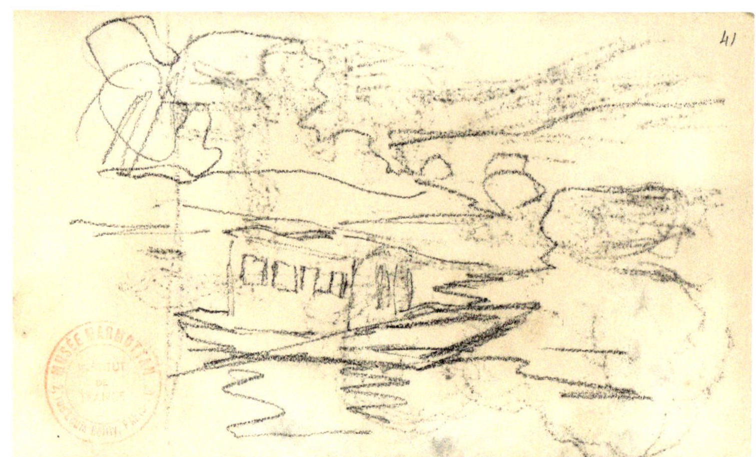

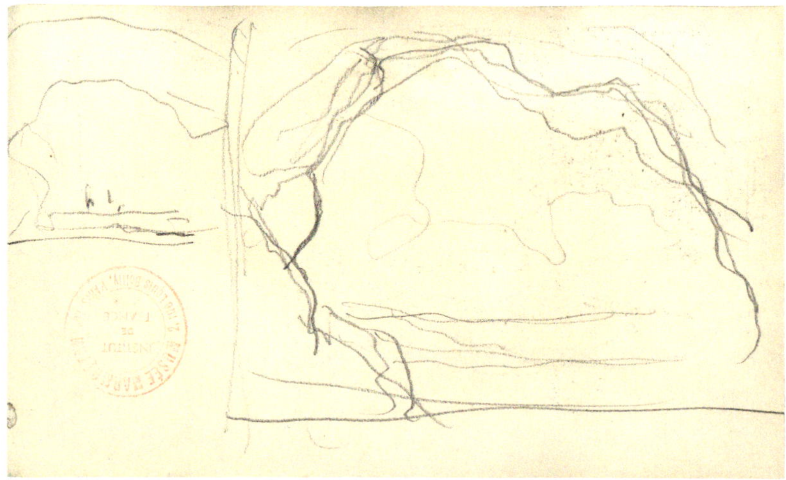

169
In the Studio Boat in Front of Petit Gennevilliers, c. 1875. Pencil, 240 x 310 mm. Sketchbook 2, fol. 9r. Musée Marmottan Monet, Paris [D148]

170
The Studio Boat at the Isle of Nettles, c. 1883–85. Black chalk, 110 x 195 mm. Sketchbook 4, fol. 41r. Musée Marmottan Monet, Paris [D270]

171
Étretat, Close View of the Manneporte, c. 1883–85. Pencil, 110 x 195 mm. Sketchbook 4, fol. 27v. Musée Marmottan Monet, Paris [D265]

vague silhouette of the village, the steeple of Saint Ouen rendered in simple outline. A notation below the drawing records the time of day: one o'clock in the afternoon. A similar inscription on the next drawing, marking the same hour, indicates that Monet continued his approach to the church straight away, pausing just down the road to carry out another square-format view (fig. 168) that would establish the perspective of two oil paintings (W989–90). His sketch records just enough architectural detail to establish the angle of view for his oils.

On some of his expeditions, Monet availed himself of modes of transportation besides walking. He carried out a sequence of drawings on the first ten folios of sketchbook 2 while comfortably ensconced in the little *bateau-atelier* ("studio boat") that he employed in Argenteuil during the mid-1870s.[43] Two of the drawings include, as a rough framing device, an indication of the boat's doorway and cloth canopy, which protected him from the elements (fig. 169). Sketchbook 4 includes several black-chalk studies of a nettle-covered island in the Seine around Giverny, where he built a boat-house and moored his *bateau-atelier* after moving to the area in 1883 (fig. 170).[44] In Norway, Monet traveled around the frozen countryside on foot, as well as by railway and sleigh, recording his impressions throughout the pages of sketchbook 7.

Although the *mise en page* of Monet's sketch-book drawings is casual in the extreme, many of the exploratory studies are themselves primarily concerned with the business of selecting and framing. His final touch was often the addition of rough horizontal and/or vertical framing lines, sometimes more than one set, corresponding to the proportions of the canvas that he had in mind. Except in his late water-lily decorations, Monet generally favored relatively square over panoramic-shaped canvases. Thus, the long, thin format of the smaller sketchbooks lent themselves to wide-angle views that he would then crop with framing lines (fig. 171). The prevalence of these simple compositional devices throughout the *carnets* might be cited to refute the frequent claims of hostile critics that "the hatred of composition is the characteristic sign of Impressionism."[45]

Lines of Thought: Studies for Paintings

Having settled on a specific motif or viewpoint, Monet would have us believe that the next and final stage of his working process was to return with his portable easel, open his paint box, and attack his canvas. A relatively small number of sketchbook drawings, perhaps fewer than ten percent, show the artist continuing to work through compositional problems with pencil and paper. These sheets represent an intermediary stage loosely connected with and following the prospecting sketches but preceding the application of paint on canvas. John House suggested that the drawings of young girls in a rowing boat (1887) and poplars (1891) belong to this uncommon category;[46] to these we might offer some additions, including the studies for the Grainstacks (1889–91) and Rouen Cathedral façade series (1893) and the *Grand Décorations* (1920–26), all to be discussed further in chapter 10.

One occasion on which the function of Monet's sketchbook drawings transcended mere prospecting is recorded in sketchbook 3: four studies (figs. 172–75) for the painting in the National Gallery, London, *Le Havre Museum* (fig. 176), signed and dated 1873 by the artist.[47] The ostensible subject of this canvas is the city's original museum of fine arts and public library, built in 1845 on the Grand Quai and destroyed during the Second World War, but Monet allowed the architecture to be significantly obscured by a layer of sails. He was able to situate himself on a dock running parallel to the quay in order to render the museum and its neighboring buildings from the water, giving the viewer the impression, perhaps, of floating in the harbor. A similar prospect appears in numerous photographs and postcards of the site dating from the late nineteenth and early twentieth centuries.[48]

There is no way of working out the sequence of the four studies within the pages of the sketchbook. They appear on the versos of folios 34 (a cream sheet) and 35 (a blue-gray sheet), and both the recto and verso of folio 36 (a tan sheet). A total of 42 folios are extant in this *carnet*. Although the four drawings are situated near the "end" of the sketchbook, we should be reminded that the later numbering of the pages from the book's other extremity in no way reflects its sequence of use by Monet. In fact, these four drawings are the earliest sketches in book 3, which was apparently cast aside by the artist and not taken up again until the late 1880s.

What sets these sheets apart from the majority of the prospecting studies is the fact that all four drawings were made from virtually the same perspective. It was unusual for Monet to stand still and draw the same vista several times, yet having identified a potential viewpoint and set down his first impression in the *carnet*, he proceeded to carry out three more drawings of the identical site. These are not successive studies in the sense of becoming progressively more finished from one to the next. Instead, they seemingly offer a time-lapse view, in which the architectural background remains much the same while the deployment of boats in the foreground changes. The various configurations of sailing vessels represent either the artist's direct observations over the course of time, or compositional experiments as he considered several alternate design solutions to organizing these elements in his painting. One of the drawings includes a vertical framing line cropping the page to approximate the proportions of his canvas (see fig. 174), but ultimately Monet shifted the point of view for his painting so that the museum structure appears off-center in the finished work.

Drawings in sketchbooks played a significant role in the development of several of Monet's late series paintings. Ten studies of grainstacks are to be found in sketchbooks 3 and 5,[49] and twelve of Rouen and the cathedral façade in sketchbook 3.[50] Many of the these sketches are of the exploratory variety, drawings that record Monet's search for just the right view, the perfect angle, the proper framing. Before narrowing in on the western façade of Rouen Cathedral as seen from directly across the street (D167–68), Monet executed several distant views of the city in which the cathedral is reduced to a few

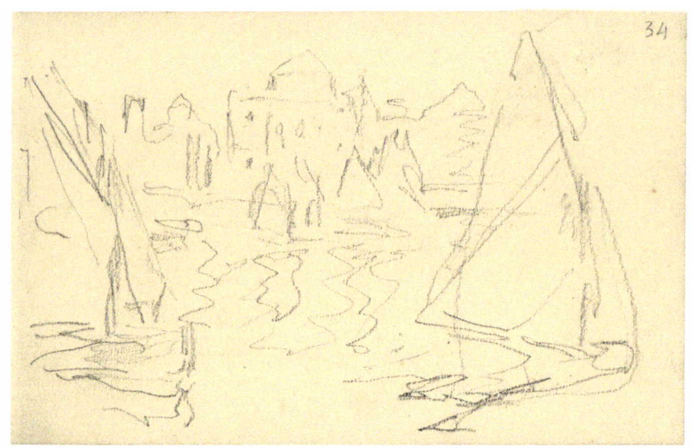

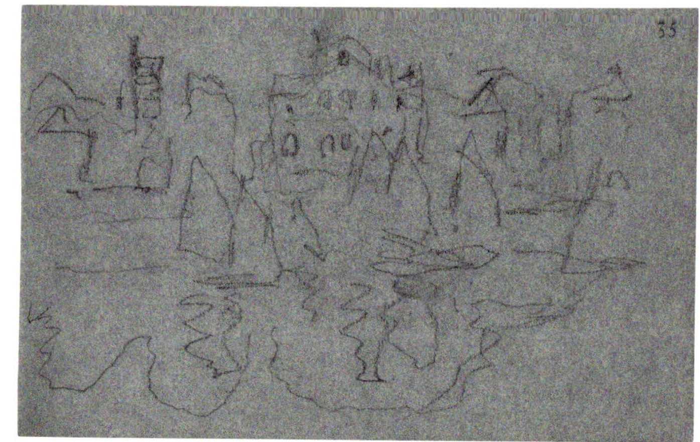

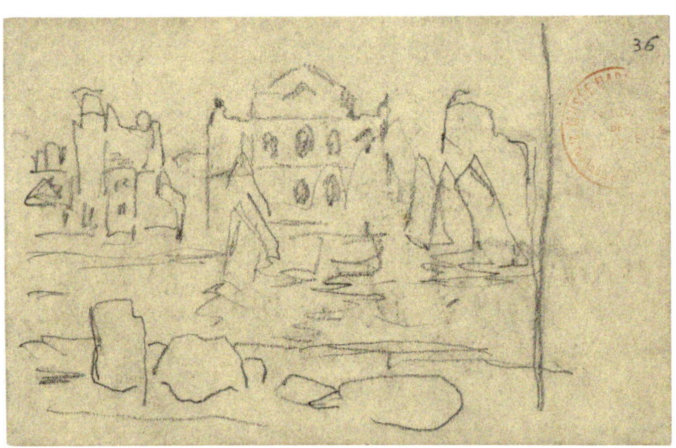

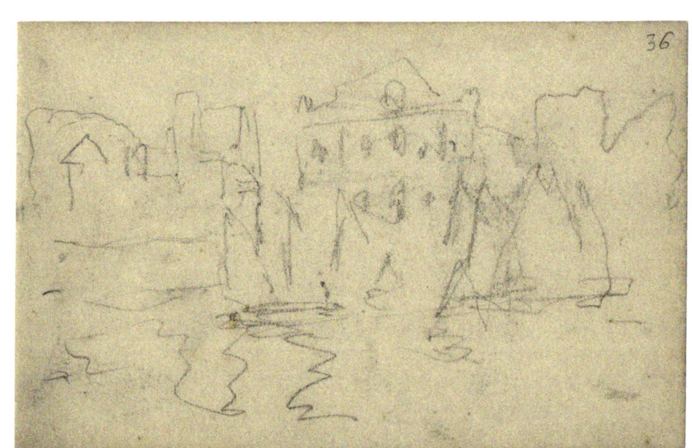

172
The Old Outer Harbor of Le Havre, c. 1873. Pencil, 110 x 180 mm. Sketchbook 3, fol. 34v. Musée Marmottan Monet, Paris [D211]

173
The Old Outer Harbor of Le Havre, c. 1873. Pencil on blue-gray paper, 110 x 180 mm. Sketchbook 3, fol. 35v. Musée Marmottan Monet, Paris [D213]

174, 175
The Old Outer Harbor of Le Havre, c. 1873. Pencil on tan paper, 110 x 180 mm. Sketchbook 3, fol. 36r and v. Musée Marmottan Monet, Paris [D214]

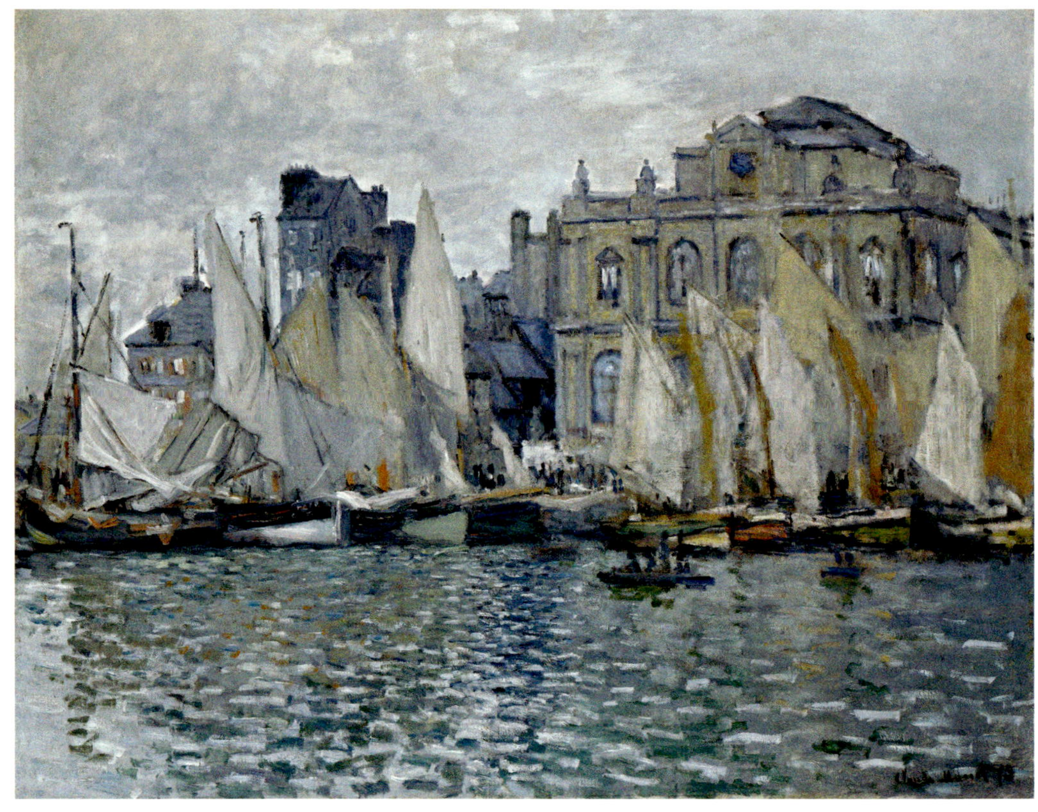

177
The Seine at Rouen, c. 1892–93. Pencil, 110 x 180 mm. Sketchbook 3, fol. 4v. Musée Marmottan Monet, Paris [D165]

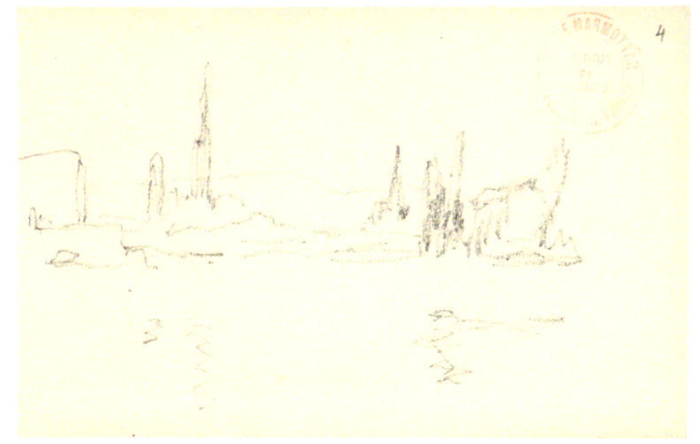

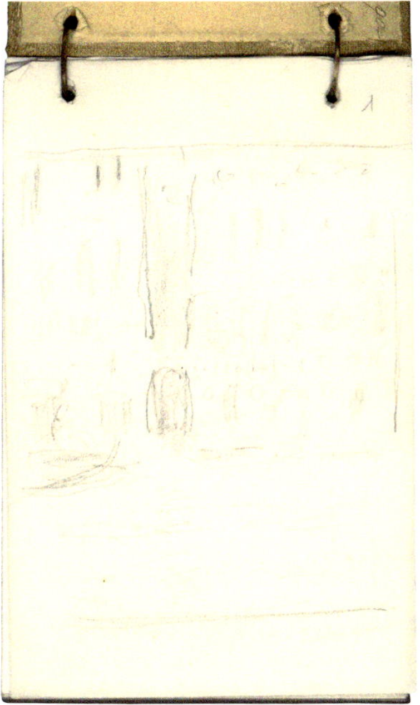

178
Venice, Palazzo Dario, 1908. Pencil, 145 x 95 mm. Sketchbook 8, fol. 1r. Musée Marmottan Monet, Paris [D404]

OPPOSITE: 176
Le Havre Museum, 1873. Oil on canvas, 75 x 100 cm. The National Gallery, London. Bequeathed by Helena and Kenneth Levy, 1990 [W261]

parallel vertical lines. One of these exploratory drawings (fig. 177) records a very similar perspective to a painting of 1872 (see fig. 188).[51]

Twenty studies of water lilies are divided between sketchbooks 1 and 6,[52] comprising the last of Monet's sketchbook drawings and, second only to his London pastels, forming the largest concentration of works on paper devoted to a single subject within his graphic oeuvre. Limited to two of the three large-format *carnets*, and executed in pencil and violet and black crayons, many over previous sketches, the water-lily studies are the most abstract drawings within the pages of Monet's sketchbooks (see the discussion in chapter 10). The majority of these studies spread across facing pages, filling the entire surface in a 3:7 format more closely approximating the wide ratio of the panels used for his *Grand Décorations*; a few are cropped or contained by framing lines. The purpose of these drawings—their precise role in the evolution of the great project—is as indistinct as the surfaces they represent, a play of reflections and real objects, natural motifs and perhaps imagined forms, intermingling on paper, on canvas, and in the draftsman-painter's weakening eyes.

Lost Sketchbooks?

Unlike his sketchbooks of the 1850s, in which the very act of drawing marked the beginning and end of the creative process, the majority of the drawings in the Marmottan sketchbooks offer incomplete artistic statements. In these *carnets*, Monet quietly turned his back on his earlier schooling in draftsmanship and allowed himself the freedom of expression to draw first and think afterward. Although they represent his smallest extant works, the tiny pages of his sketchbooks preserve some of his most vital and expressive creations. Even more than his letters, they offer us the voyeuristic pleasure of reading the artist's mind.

If we accept that the *carnets* played an essential role in Monet's working method, then one question naturally arises: what of the major painting campaigns for which few or no drawings have been identified?[53] Although the Marmottan sketchbooks span the limits of Monet's entire professional career, there are a number of significant lacunae. Conspicuous by their absence are studies from Belle-Île on the rocky Atlantic coast of Brittany, where Monet painted around forty canvases over a three-month period in the autumn of 1886. He spent four months in Antibes on the Côte d'Azur in the winter and early spring of 1888, producing another forty paintings. Only a single sketchbook drawing is datable to this trip (sketchbook 6, fol. 24v, D365). Shortly after his arrival, he reported in a letter to Alice that he had hiked twenty-five kilometers from Monte Carlo to Nice.[54] It is difficult to imagine him not carrying a sketchbook on this picturesque excursion, but if he did bring one along, it has vanished without a trace. Finally, it has been noted that only a single drawing in an otherwise empty *carnet* is attributable to Monet's roughly two-month stay in Venice in 1908 (fig. 178). It seems more appropriate to ponder not if, but how many, of Monet's sketchbooks have been lost.

In many ways, it is surprising that upon his death, Monet left as many as eight sketchbooks lying about, allowing them to fall into the hands of his son, Michel, and then pass from him into the Marmottan, a museum governed by the Institut de France. Once inside this prestigious institution, they became the prey of art historians, eventually entering the painter's official corpus in the catalogue raisonné of his work. In the end, it was probably Monet's casual attitude toward the sketchbooks, fueled by his presumed belief in their worthlessness, that resulted in them slipping out of his control, and into his published oeuvre.

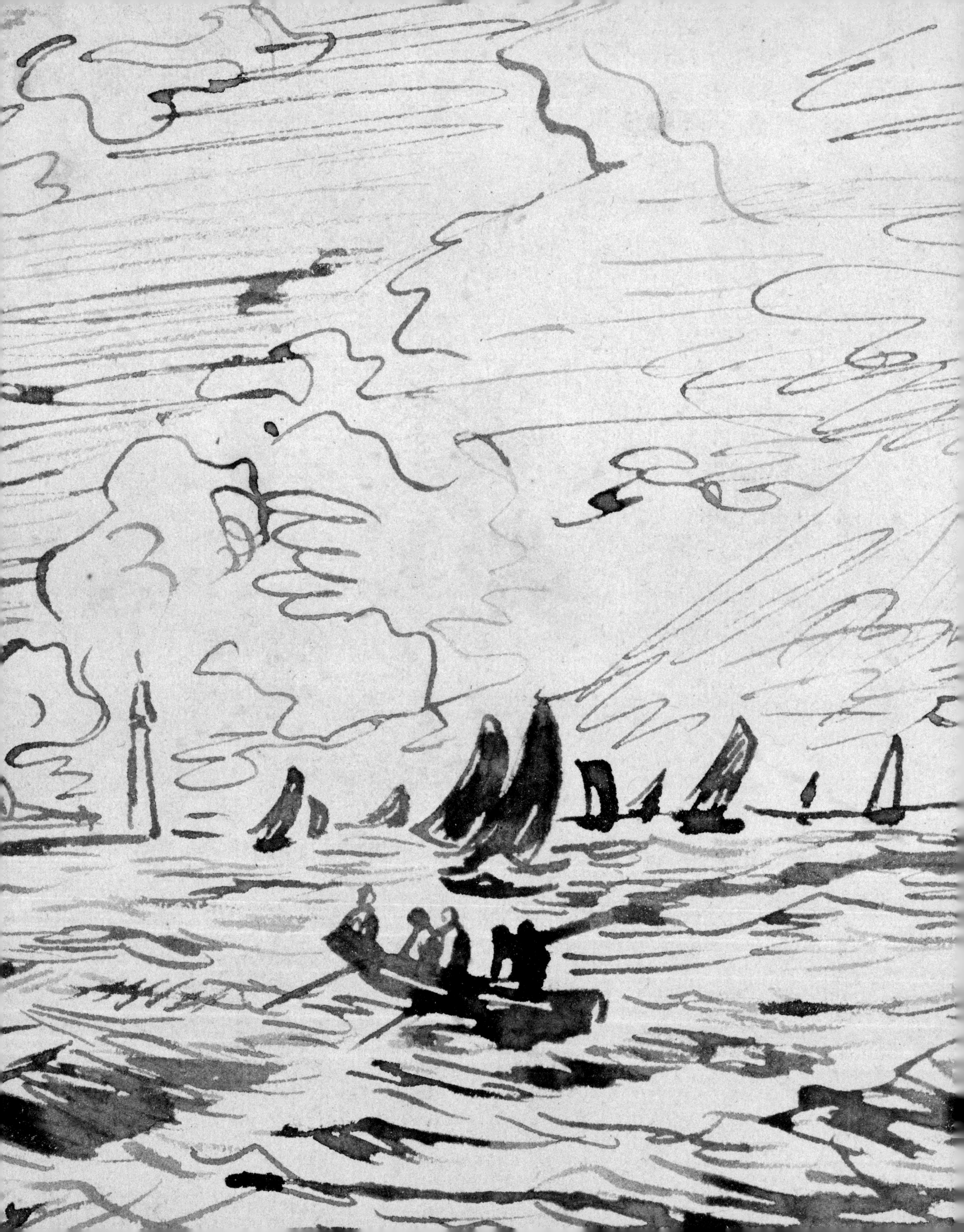

CHAPTER EIGHT Drawing for the Mass Media

The rise of Monet's reputation from his debut at the Salon of 1865 through his participation in the Impressionist exhibitions and a series of one-man shows in Parisian galleries was both chronicled and promoted by the popular press. His career coincided with a new era of cheap publishing—the birth of the "mass media" as it would come to be known—and an international upsurge in the field of illustrated art journalism. The interrelationships between artists, dealers, critics, and publishers during the late nineteenth century were complex and frequently defy modern standards of journalistic objectivity. It is clear that Monet, in league with his dealers, played a crucial role in the construction of his public persona, both in the manipulation of his life story (as described in chapter 1) and in the articulation of his aesthetic. At the heart of this public-relations campaign was an effort to portray Monet as *the* master of plein-air painting, an artist who toted his canvases into the landscape and painted at the speed of light. Yet while his defenders consistently suppressed the notion that he might have recourse to preparatory drawings, Monet played an active role in promoting his work in the media by producing reproductive or more appropriately "interpretive" drawings after his own paintings. These drawings appeared in the form of relief etchings in such widely read journals as *La vie moderne*, the *Gazette des beaux-arts*, *L'Art dans les deux mondes*, and *The Studio*.

Monet is on the record as stating that his reproductive drawings were of no importance, and after they had served their purpose he was more than willing to abandon them with their publishers. As in his larger graphic oeuvre, scholars have been all too quick to follow Monet's cue and dismiss this specialized body of work as mere public relations potboilers. Yet to do so is to miss a unique opportunity to climb inside the artist's head and see his paintings through his own eyes. The products of intense looking and thinking, Monet's drawings for the mass media represented a stimulating, if unnatural task, their apparent spontaneity masking the challenge they posed. Monet was a master at painting from nature, but drawing from painting required a different mindset.[1]

Within the printmaking industry, the job of translating paintings into black-and-white drawings suitable for engraving was for centuries a specialized task. It involved converting color values into shades of gray by transmuting continuous tones and textures into systematic crosshatching. Paintings with strong linear structures, works made up of straight lines and hard edges, were easier to translate than more painterly canvases, but in truth, anything could be captured by engraving's so-called "net of rationality," converted into a highly evolved language of dots and lozenges.

That the reproductive drawings were commercially motivated is not a reason to disregard them, for the same impulse lay behind the paintings they reprise. The drawings were made to be seen, to both connect and communicate with the public. Today, public-relations professionals speak of "impressions" in calculating the effectiveness of how their messages reach their audiences. An impression represents a literal glance, the moment in which a reader or viewer's eye fixes on a word, a phrase, or an image and makes a connection. There is no way to estimate how many impressions Monet's reproductive drawings made, but it is safe to assume that many more people experienced them in print form than viewed the original paintings that were their models.

The publication of Monet's drawings in art journals raises a number of larger issues around the production and reception of these printed images: what did publishers and editors of illustrated periodicals see as the added value of engaging artists like Monet to make reproductive drawings after their own paintings, rather than farming the work out to professional copyists? How were the printed images identified and referenced within the texts they accompanied? And how would casual readers have comprehended these images: as literal reproductions, original works of art in their own right, or (erroneously) as preparatory studies for the paintings represented?

Despite the growing fascination with serial imagery evidenced in his paintings and his devotion to collecting Japanese woodblock prints, during the course of his long career Monet showed neither interest nor firsthand experience in direct printmaking. Among the academic strictures eroded by the vanguard artists of his generation was the traditional hierarchy of media that elevated painting over printmaking and kept the two separated in the annual Salons. In the Impressionist exhibitions, no such barriers existed; works on paper—pastels, watercolors, black-and-white drawings, and prints—were integrated into the installations alongside oil paintings. Within the Impressionist group, a relatively small faction developed a special interest in etching. Degas was at the center of this bloc, which came to include Mary Cassatt, Marcellin Desboutin, Ludovic-Napoléon Lepic, Camille Pissarro, Jean-François Raffaëlli, Alphonse Legros, and Félix Bracquemond. Between the fourth and fifth Impressionist exhibitions in 1879–80, Degas and his friends pooled their resources in planning a cooperative artists' review, *Le Jour et la nuit*, that was meant to include illustrations in the form of original etchings; although the journal never appeared, a number of prints were created in anticipation of its publication.[2] Monet remained outside this coterie, and in fact the timing of the preparations for *Le Jour et la nuit* coincided with his retreat from the larger Impressionist group. Not a single etching can be attributed to his hand. His abstention from etching was extraordinary among this circle of artists. Even colleagues like Frédéric Bazille, Gustave Caillebotte, Paul Cézanne, and Vincent van Gogh, who had little interest in printmaking at least tried their hands at etching.

By the 1890s, the attention of French painter-printmakers had largely shifted from intaglio processes to lithography. While he stayed just as aloof from the color revolution that swept fin-de-siècle lithography as he had from the earlier etching revival, Monet authorized and signed an edition of prints by William Thornley (1857–1935) that translates his nuanced brushstrokes into the binary language of lithography. Like his own drawings for gillotage, the lithographs that comprise the Thornley portfolio effectively isolate line from color and thereby contradict Monet's principal rhetorical position with regard to the graphic arts.

By the early twentieth century, significant advances in photographic and photomechanical technologies rendered all of these autographic approaches obsolete and set off a tidal wave of printed reproductions originating in the lens of a camera. During the 1920s, Monet's studio at Giverny was invaded by photographers intent on presenting his last great project to the masses even before it was placed on public view. He grudgingly accepted the intrusions, while trying his best to maintain control over how his work would appear in print. But the floodgates were open, and Monet was on his way to becoming one of the most frequently reproduced painters of the modern age.

Monet and Gillotage

All of Monet's commissioned drawings appeared in the form of relief etchings, a process best known for its commercial applications in the popular press and commonly the domain of reproductive rather than original printmaking. The technique was called gillotage and it was relatively new, having been patented by its inventor, the Parisian printer Firmin Gillot (1820–1872) in 1850.[3] Gillotage in its first incarnation may be crudely summarized as follows: an artist's original drawing in greasy ink is transferred from a sheet of paper to a zinc plate, after which the lines of the drawing are coated with resin to make them resistant to acid. The plate is then etched, leaving the design standing in relief and, after mounting on a woodblock, suitable for letterpress printing. Setting aside the medium's many variations and intricacies, it is important to note that from an artist's point of view, making a gillotage print is virtually as straightforward as the act of drawing. In this sense, it was the ideal technique for a painter like Monet with no interest in mastering the etching needle or learning to draw on the temperamental surface of a lithographic stone. Like transfer lithography, gillotage provided a purely mechanical method for disseminating drawings in a large edition that was not subjected to interpretation on the part of a reproductive etcher, wood engraver, or lithographer.

The proliferation of gillotage in mid-nineteenth-century art journals and illustrated books is explained by its flexibility and viability as a means of combining text with image, and not by its inherent efficiency or aesthetic qualities. As a relief process, it offered the benefit of printing by the same method as letterpress, and thus could be easily integrated into a page layout. This significant advantage made up for its two major drawbacks: the preparation of the zinc plate was extremely labor-intensive, and with careless handling the result could be less faithful in its finest details to the artist's original drawing than transfer lithography.

Monet's first gillotage print was his *portrait-charge* of the actor Laferrière published in the third issue of the weekly newspaper *Diogène* on 24 March 1860 (see fig. 48). Clearly inscribed in the lower-left corner of the image is the word "PANICONOGRAPHIE," leaving no doubt that the print is a gillotage rather than an original lithograph. While the nature of this technique prior to the 1870s was such that Monet's original drawing would have been destroyed in the course of transferring it to the zinc plate,[4] the transfer process caused a double-reversal, so that the printed image at least preserves the orientation of his design.[5] As a result, Monet was spared the challenge of mirror-writing the titles of the plays that appear on a series of placards behind Laferrière.

Despite the promise shown by this early commission, the nineteen-year-old Monet had greater ambitions than to spend his life as a newspaper illustrator. It would be five years of intense work, interrupted by a stint in the military, before the artist would make his debut as a painter at the annual Salon de Paris. The acceptance of two seascapes in the Salon of 1865 would also provide his next opportunity to produce a drawing specifically for publication.

L'Autographe au Salon, 1865

In the spring of 1865, Monet crossed a major professional hurdle when he learned that the jury had accepted two canvases he submitted to the annual Salon des Beaux-Arts. *Mouth of the Seine at Honfleur* (fig. 179), at the Norton Simon Foundation in Pasadena, and *The Pointe*

179
Mouth of the Seine at Honfleur, 1865. Oil on canvas, 89.5 x 150.5 cm. The Norton Simon Foundation, Pasadena, California [W51]

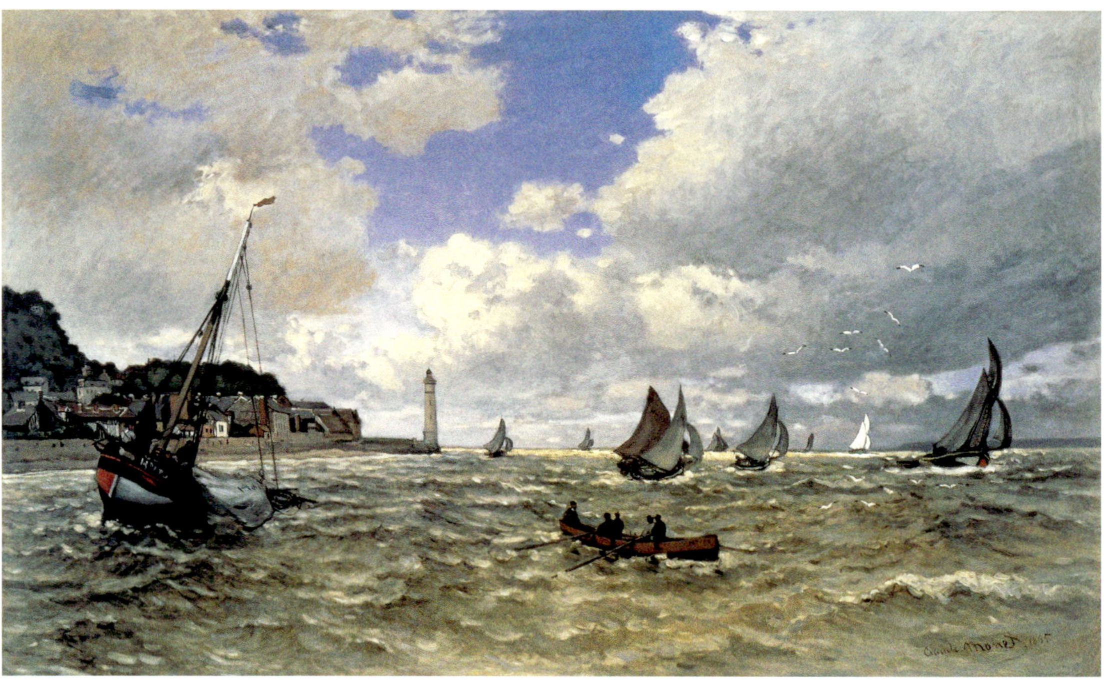

de La Hève at Low Tide, now owned by the Kimbell Art Museum in Fort Worth, attracted considerable attention upon the opening of the Salon on 1 May. "Here we must mention a new name," Paul Mantz remarked in the *Gazette des beaux-arts*:

> *We were not aware before of M. Claude Monet, creator of* Pointe de La Hève *and* Mouth of the Seine at Honfleur. . . . *As we passed along, his* Mouth of the Seine *brought us to an abrupt halt, and we shall never forget it. As a result, we shall follow the future efforts of this sincere seascapist with great interest from now on.*[6]

Monet's arrival was confirmed by an invitation to submit a drawing of his *Mouth of the Seine at Honfleur* for reproduction in *L'Autographe au Salon de 1865 et dans les ateliers,* the first time one of his paintings would appear in print. In its second year of publication under the auspices of the newspaper *Le Figaro, L'Autographe au Salon* was a large-format picture journal offering highlights of the current Salon reproduced in gillotage with brief captions penned by "Pigalle." A new issue appeared each Saturday from 29 April through 15 July 1865, offering anywhere from twenty-three to forty-two reproductions arranged in a rich visual patchwork over eight to twelve pages. The layouts in *L'Autographe au Salon* adhere successfully to the principle of controlled anarchy, with the composition of each sheet not locked in a grid but free flowing, much like a spontaneously compiled scrapbook of images, captions, and facsimiles of artist's statements in their own handwriting. The price per issue was 60 centimes on white paper, 75 centimes for the deluxe edition on chamois (admission to the Salon itself cost one franc, except on Sunday). During the course of a dozen issues, *L'Autographe au Salon de 1865* presented 430 drawings by 352 artists; in the same year, 2,243 paintings were listed in the catalogue of the Salon.

In order to streamline this ambitious publishing venture and ensure that the volume would be complete before the closing of the exhibition, the editors employed a staff of seven professional draftsmen who created the facsimiles on lithographic transfer paper of the original works submitted. These copies would then be handed over to specialists in gillotage for transfer and etching in relief on zinc plates. Thus, the Salon exhibitors were kept clear of the mechanics of reproduction and were free to make their submissions in whatever technique and on

180
Mouth of the Seine at Honfleur, 1865. Pen and ink, 245 x 360 mm. Private collection, courtesy of Brame & Lorenceau, Paris [D423]

181
A. Belloguet, after Claude Monet, *Mouth of the Seine at Honfleur,* 1865. Gillotage, 165 x 280 mm. From *L'Autographe au Salon de 1865* 9 (24 June 1865), p. 76

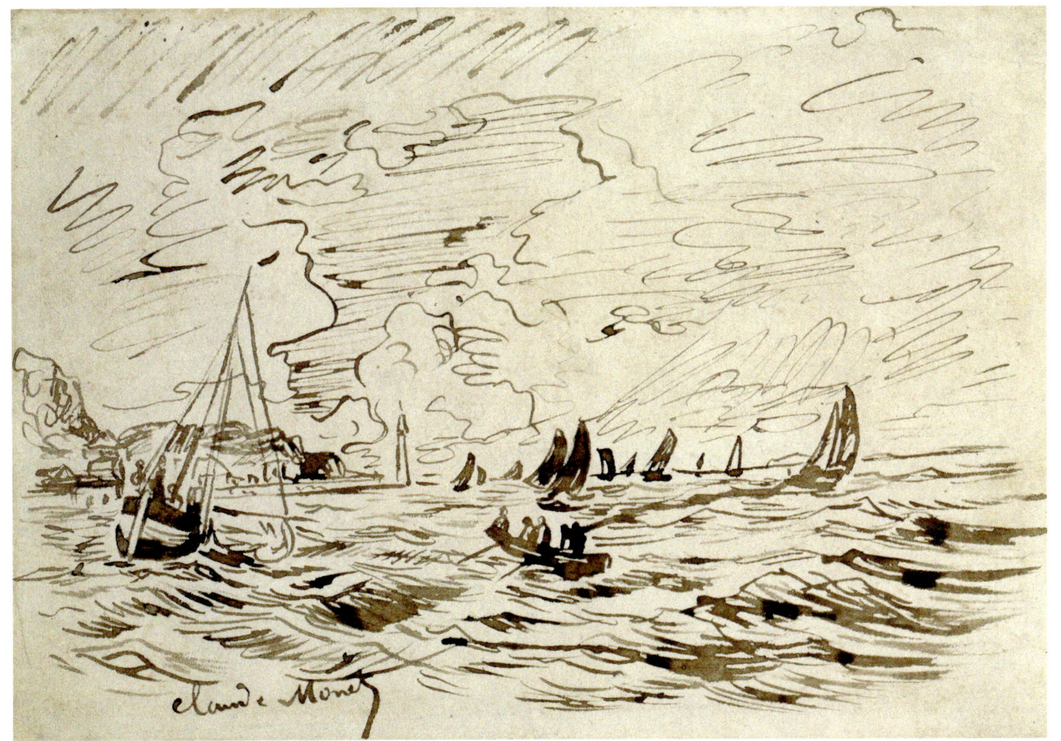

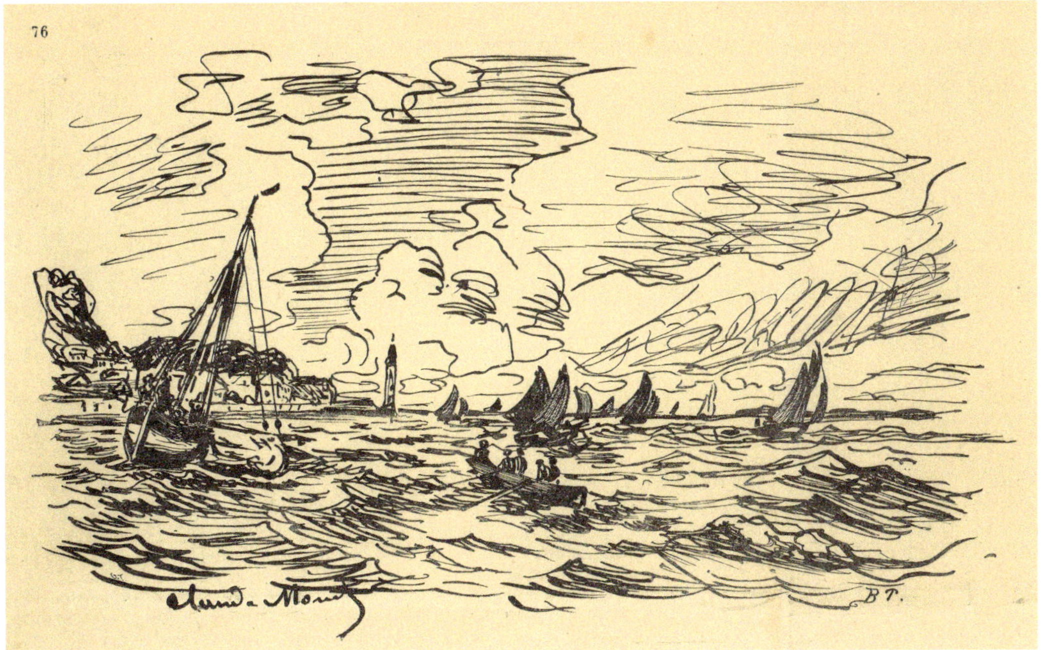

whatever type of paper they chose; through this method, their original drawings were preserved, and only the facsimiles were lost in the transfer.

Monet's drawing of *Mouth of the Seine at Honfleur* appeared in the ninth issue of *L'Autographe au Salon* on 24 June 1865. His original pen-and-ink drawing (fig. 180) was copied by A. Belloguet, a professional illustrator employed by the paper; Belloguet's facsimile, in turn, was transferred to a relief plate by Firmin Gillot. The print (fig. 181) is featured prominently, taking up a third of the page and accompanied by a relatively generous caption by the standards of this publication. Pigalle's enthusiastic commentary extols Monet as "the author of the most original, supple, and the most solid

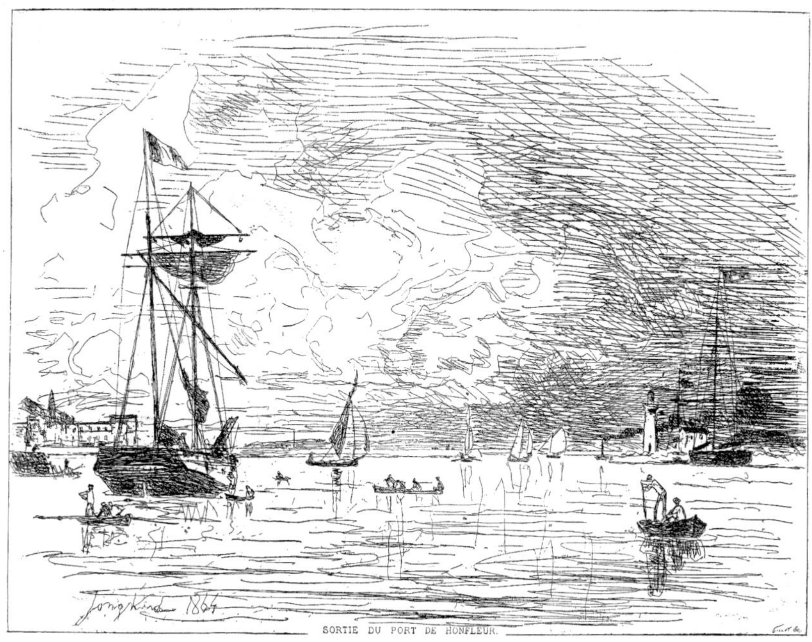

182
After Johan Barthold Jongkind, *Exit from the Port at Honfleur*, 1865. Gillotage, 231 x 305 mm. From *L'Autographe au Salon de 1865* 5 (27 May 1865), p. 37

and harmoniously painted seascape that has been exhibited in a long time—A tonality a bit heavy, like that of Courbet; but what richness and what originality of observation! M. Monet, unknown yesterday, has made his reputation at his first attempt with this one painting."[7]

In approaching this assignment, Monet was faced for the first time with translating one of his finished paintings into a black-and-white drawing suitable for reproduction. In taking on this task, he could have chosen from a vast range of approaches, all of which were demonstrated in the pages of *L'Autographe au Salon*. Some of the published drawings were highly finished, even pedantic transcriptions with disciplined crosshatching in the manner of engraving to convey tone and texture; at the opposite extreme were spare neoclassical-style drawings preserving only the outlines of the compositions they reproduced.

From this array of possibilities, Monet settled on a manner of drawing that was most consistent with his colleagues Daubigny and Jongkind, particularly the energetic style of the latter's etchings. Two of Jongkind's works had appeared in the fifth issue of *L'Autographe au Salon*: his etching *Exit from the Port of Honfleur* (fig. 182) and *Dutch Canal near Rotterdam, Moonlight,* a drawing after his oil paintings exhibited in the Salon.[8] The spontaneity and coarseness of Jongkind's graphic manner was admired by the younger generation of painters, and his etchings were praised by Charles Baudelaire in 1862 as "curious observations for a painter, sketches which any art-lover accustomed to reading the mind of a painter in his most rapid *scribbles* (*gribouillages*) will know how to interpret. Scribbles is the term used a little facetiously by the good Diderot to characterize Rembrandt's etchings."[9]

Monet's adoption of Jongkind's "scribble"-style for his debut in *L'Autographe au Salon* represented an audacious public statement on the part of the young painter and a radical departure from the highly finished manner that he had perfected in his independent black-crayon drawings of the mid-1860s that more closely approximates the rough drafts in his mature sketchbooks. There is nothing remotely academic or systematic in the bold strokes of his pen. Two thirds of the sheet is taken up by the cloud-laden sky, which becomes the site of the most abstract and rapidly executed passage in any of Monet's published drawings. The gillotage print, two generations removed from Monet's drawing, preserves the overall impression of the original without slavishly replicating his pen's every stroke, and as a by-product of the relief printing technique, produces lines of uniform blackness. The result is an even darker and more aggressive image that closely approximates the syntax of Jongkind's deeply etched lines.[10]

La vie moderne

While Monet kept well outside the clique of etching enthusiasts centered on Degas, he did get caught up in another trend that attracted many of the Impressionist painters during the late 1870s: namely, promoting one's paintings by drawing copies for reproduction in newspapers. There were several factors that fueled the popularity of artist-drawn facsimiles in the popular press. A graphic translation made by a painter was seen as retaining a particular sense of authority, not photographic in nature but derived from the assumption that only the inventor of a work of art understands it from the inside out. This unique insight privileged an artist's own interpretation over a drawing by a professional copyist. In addition, from the perspective of an arts editor, a previously unpublished drawing made by a painter exclusively for one's journal had a special cachet.

Monet's first known invitation to publish a drawing after *L'Autographe au Salon* arrived via Gustave Caillebotte in April 1879. It was only after fierce prodding by Caillebotte that Monet had agreed to show his work in the fourth Impressionist exhibition. At the end of the opening day, Caillebotte wrote to report on the turnout to his absent colleague. He enclosed a number of newspaper clippings, and added, "I have been charged by Duranty to ask you for a drawing for a journal. He asked for one of your *Drapeaux* or *Pommiers*, or something else of Vétheuil if you prefer. Send it as soon as possible to the exhibition office."[11] Monet seems not to have responded to this request; Duranty's review appeared in *La Chronique des arts et de la curiosité*, a supplement to the *Gazette des beaux-arts*, on 19 April without an illustration.

In that same month, the collector Georges Charpentier founded a new weekly paper called *La vie moderne* that promoted art and literature as a kind of public extension of the private salons that his wife famously hosted. Joining the editorial staff was Auguste Renoir's brother Edmond, a professional journalist who was charged with organizing a series of contemporary art exhibitions in a gallery located on the premises. In the newspaper's inaugural issue, he articulated the hoped-for synergy between the periodical and its exhibition space on the boulevard des Italiens: "Having at their disposal perfectly suitable quarters in a most Parisian atmosphere, the founders of *La vie moderne* have very naturally been brought to organize an artistic exhibition which will serve as a kind of corollary to their publication."[12] He went on to describe the modest gallery as having the potential to be "nothing less than the studio of the artist transported momentarily to the boulevard."[13] After a series of installations devoted to such figures as Giuseppe de Nittis (1846–1884) and Antoine Vollon (1833–1900), Renoir was given the opportunity to stage his first one-man show at the Galerie de La Vie Moderne in June 1879, accompanied by an article in the review written by his brother.[14] Manet showed his latest paintings there in April 1880, and Monet's first opportunity followed in June.

The pictorial program of *La vie moderne* was as ambitious—and innovative—as its exhibition schedule. *La vie moderne* became the most proactive journal in promoting photography-based gillotage ("photo-gillotage"), a state-of-the-art photomechanical process developed by Firmin Gillot's son, Charles (1853–1903), as a revolutionary medium for the reproduction of artists' drawings. In its first issue, editor-in-chief Émile Bergerat (1845–1923), the son-in-law of Théophile Gautier (1811–1872), had outlined his vision for a lively journal in which illustrations by prominent artists would intermingle with texts by leading writers. In the first few months of publication, *La vie moderne* kept this promise, with drawings by artists exhibiting in the fourth Impressionist exhibition (most notably Degas and Cassatt) as well as the official Salon des Beaux-Arts (Jules Bastien-Lepage [1848–1884] and Léon Bonnat [1833–1922]). Renoir became one of the journal's most prolific contributors, his illustrations running the gamut from portraits of writers and artists (fig. 183) to vignettes of daily life, reproductive drawings after his own paintings and works by other artists, and even ornamental designs.

Bergerat claimed that its illustration program made *La vie moderne* nothing less than the standard-bearer for innovation in the French illustrated press. At the end of its first semester of publication (4 October 1879), he wrote, "It is correct to say that the means of expression placed in the service of our admirable contributors was perfectly designed to seduce them, as it placed in their hands a system of reproduction that preserves of their drawings the individuality of touch, the mystery of tone, and all the texture of the surface. Moreover . . . artists had grown tired of being betrayed by lithographic or wood-engraved translations to which they

183

Pierre-Auguste Renoir, *Portrait of Léon Riesener (Study for the illustration in "La vie moderne")*, 1879. Black crayon with scratchwork on scratchboard, 325 x 244 mm. Smith College Museum of Art, Northampton, Massachusetts. Bequest of Selma Erving, Class of 1927

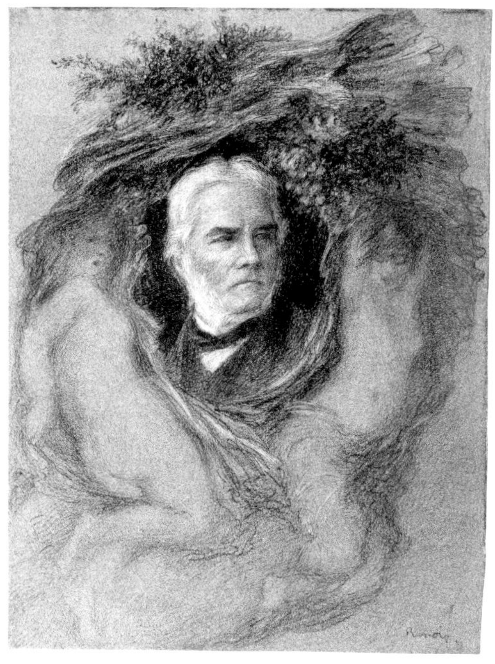

had been submitted unceasingly for so many years."[15] In one of his most forceful defenses of this modern printing technology, Bergeret further emphasized the superiority of photo-gillotage over the time-honored medium of wood engraving, or xylography, which it had largely displaced: "On occasion, some readers have reproached us for failing to include wood engravings (*bois*) in *La vie moderne* perhaps without realizing that one of the clauses of our program has been precisely to lead the renewal of public taste, fatigued by thirty years of xylography. Given the gradual perfection of the means of reproduction known under the name *gillotage*, and the many advantages offered by this system, we count among its followers loyal and even stubborn practitioners."[16] A writer for the *Nieuwe Rotterdamsche Courant* praised *La vie moderne* for employing the best French draftsmen and painters and applying the "celebrated gillotage process" for reproductions of the greatest fidelity.[17]

Although *La vie moderne* incorporated the same kind of printing matrices as *L'Autographe au Salon* in the 1860s—typographic blocks, or zinc plates etched in relief mounted on woodblocks—the process by which the drawings were transformed into prints represented a significant departure, which in turn signaled a major technical advance in gillotage that had taken place since the earlier publication. By the late 1870s, photography had become the preferred method for transferring drawings to zinc plates.[18] Put simply, an artist's drawing could now be photographed and the negative placed on a zinc plate coated with a light-sensitive ground. The coated areas exposed through the negative hardened when exposed, and the rest of the acid-resistant ground was subsequently washed away. The plate was then etched as usual. While this innovation allowed for the preservation of the original drawing, it continued to influence the choice of drawing medium, the style of draftsmanship, and even the scale of the original illustration. Photo-gillotage also required the artist to draw on specially grained papers.

These distinctive papers were meant to address a persistent problem faced by Monet, Renoir, and their contemporaries in creating drawings for reproduction by photo-relief: the inherent difficulty of replicating halftones.[19] A solid black line on a white sheet of paper posed no problem, but a pale line or an area of shading in gray might fail to register in the photographic negative and disappear in the final print or become exaggerated to the same value as the darker lines, upsetting the tonal balance of the image. Further, relief printing cannot produce areas of gray; it can yield either pure black from those areas of the plate standing in relief or pure white from areas that have been etched down. A number of workarounds were available by the 1880s, most involving scratchboard or specially textured papers designed to break up the tonal areas of the drawing into fine networks of lines or dots suitable for letterpress printing. Professional printers specializing in photo-gillotage had to supply illustrators with appropriate materials and instruction so that the result would best preserve their intentions.

La vie moderne's graphic commissions provided an additional revenue stream for the journal. Subscribers received a discount on deluxe printed editions of selected illustrations as single sheets, and in the summer and fall of 1879 its gallery presented an installation entitled *Les dessins de la vie moderne*. The editors explained,

184
Edouard Manet, *Portrait of Monet (Head of a Man)*, 1874. Pen and ink wash, 170 x 140 mm. Musée Marmottan Monet, Paris

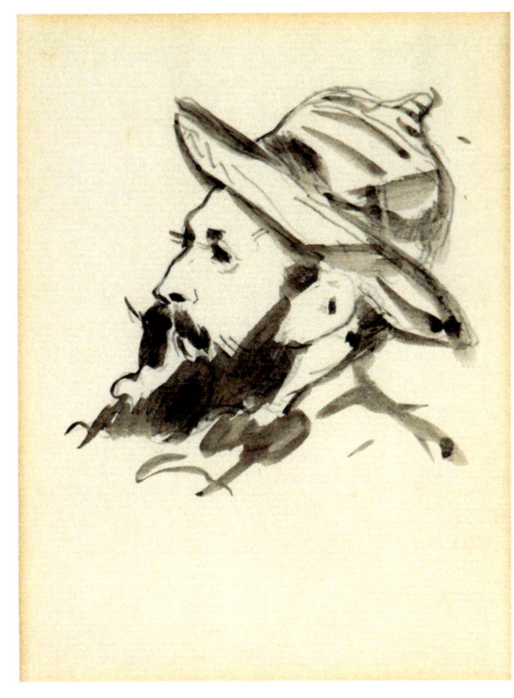

"Until now perhaps nobody has attempted to organize an exhibition of this nature, composed exclusively of materials that served to supply an art publication during its first three months of existence," proclaiming the show a "complete microcosm of contemporary art."[20] A writer in *L'Année artistique* praised this effort for showcasing drawings "executed for the journal itself by the most illustrious living artists, drawings reproduced directly by means of the Gillot process, without being subjected to translation by engraving (often an act of treason)."[21]

Exhibition at Galerie de la Vie Moderne, 1880

For Claude Monet, the year 1880 brought both disappointment and opportunity. Faced with mounting financial difficulties, he resolved early in the new year to break away from the Impressionists, who were planning their fifth group exhibition for the month of April, and try his hand at submitting once again to the official Salon. In the pages of *Le Gaulois*, a mock funeral notice appeared on 24 January on behalf of Monet's "ex-friends, ex-students, and ex-supporters," chiding the artist for his decision to join Renoir in this act of desertion and announcing that his funeral would take place in the "church" of the Palais de l'Industrie at ten o'clock in the morning on the first of May, the opening day of the Salon.[22] This satirical notice was not entirely off the mark; of the two canvases Monet submitted, one was summarily rejected, while the other was skied so that visitors to the exhibition could barely make it out. Even worse, the reviews of his submission, a large landscape of Lavacort, were decidedly lukewarm.

In the midst of this debacle, Monet was already looking ahead to his first one-man exhibition scheduled for June 1880 in the gallery of *La vie moderne*.[23] This exhibition of eighteen canvases provided a welcome opportunity for the artist to redeem himself after the disappointment of the Salon, and prompted two significant texts: the exhibition catalogue essay by Théodore Duret and an interview with Monet by Émile Taboureux, which was transcribed in the pages of the journal.[24] Duret's essay contains the first extended statement of Monet's plein-air method of landscape painting, an approach defiant in its renunciation of preliminary drawings: "The fleeting impressions once garnered by the landscape artist sketching out of doors and then lost and forgotten in the process of transforming the sketch into a picture in the studio can now be seized by the artist working in nature," Duret proclaimed. "He can rapidly capture the most ephemeral, the most delicate effect at the very moment it appears before him."[25] This theme was picked up in the interview with Taboureux (see chapter 5, p. 112), which was illustrated by a gillotage print after Manet's pen-and-ink portrait of his colleague that also graced the frontispiece of the exhibition catalogue (fig. 184).

Although the texts by Duret and Taboureux effectively cast Monet in the role of anti-draftsman, the editor of *La vie moderne* saw no incongruity in asking him to make a reproductive drawing in order to promote the exhibition, and ever hungry for publicity, Monet accepted the invitation. The subject was first broached in April, when Taboureux interviewed the artist in Vétheuil and asked whether he would consider providing a drawing to illustrate the article;

NOTRE EXPOSITION

CLAUDE MONET

Nous avons publié dans notre dernier numéro un portrait littéraire du peintre Claude Monet par M. Émile Taboureux. Nous n'avons donc plus besoin de présenter à nos lecteurs l'artiste dont les œuvres nouvelles sont exposées en ce moment dans notre galerie du boulevard des Italiens et du passage des Princes.

Claude Monet nous a apporté dix-huit tableaux, tous exécutés d'après nature, avec cette science du plein air dont il est l'un des maîtres. Cette exposition a remporté un très grand succès dans le public amateur et parisien, et la plupart des toiles ont été achetées dès le premier jour.

Parmi les toiles les plus remarquées, citons : *la Marine*, dont nous donnons la reproduction; *le Dégel au soleil couchant*, tableau très important et d'un effet on ne peut plus décoratif; diverses vues de Vétheuil à des heures variées; *les Bateaux d'Argenteuil*, dont l'éclat et les reflets rappellent les colorations vénitiennes; *la Gare Saint-Lazare*, et plusieurs études d'arbres et de fruits.

M. Théodore Duret a, du reste, consacré à cette exposition une monographie précédée d'un portrait de Claude Monet par Édouard Manet. On la trouve au bureau de la *Vie Moderne*.

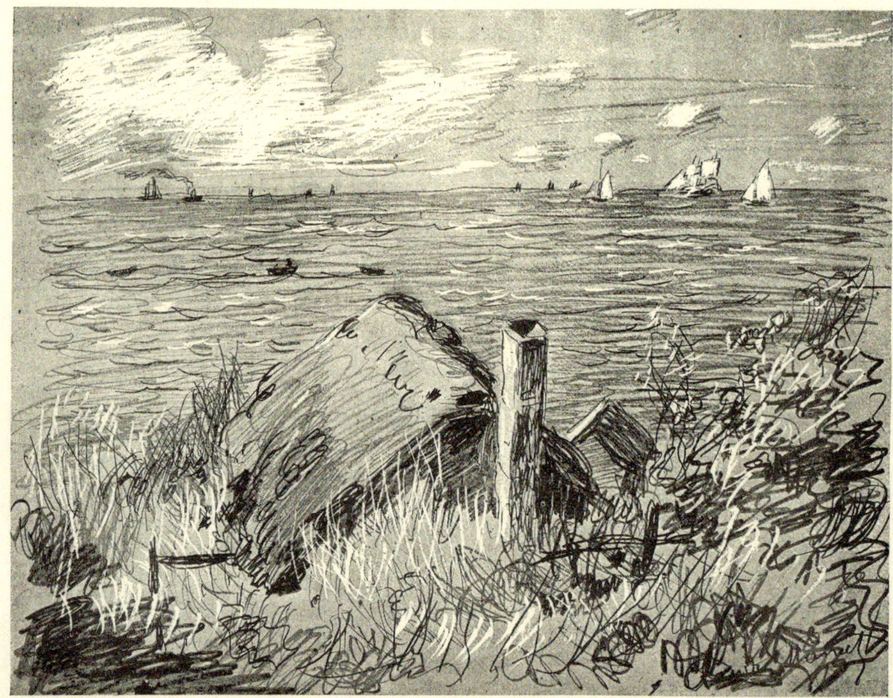

EXPOSITION DE LA « VIE MODERNE » : *PAYSAGE*. — Dessin de CLAUDE MONET.

CHRONIQUE FINANCIÈRE

Le train s'est remis en marche. Et quelle vitesse! C'est un train éclair. Jamais nos rentes n'avaient été à pareille fête. Elles ont escaladé les plus hauts sommets. A quels cours ne peuvent-elles pas prétendre désormais? Tous les précédents justifient leurs prétentions, même les plus exagérées.

La conversion a reçu encore un coup de bas parlementaire. Ce n'est pas seulement M. Magnin, c'est la Chambre à peu près unanime qui a enterré la question posée par un conversionniste. De longtemps l'horizon de la cote ne sera assombri par ce nuage.

Les fonds étrangers ne se sont pas fait répéter l'invitation. Les voilà au pinacle et fort disposés à ne pas s'attarder en si beau chemin. Seuls les timides et les sages ont tort. Le succès n'est plus que pour les téméraires. Je ne voudrais pas voir malheur leur arriver, mais vraiment n'en prennent-ils pas trop à leur aise? Les crédits douteux passent aujourd'hui presque au premier plan. Gare au revers de la médaille!

Les sociétés de crédit ont l'élan plus tempéré. Il y a pourtant de bien vifs entraînements aussi de ce côté. Voyez la Banque de Paris, une institution hors ligne, j'en conviens. Mais ce n'est pas d'hier qu'elle est en brillante situation, au vu et su de tout le monde. Quelle enjambée pourtant cette semaine!

Le Crédit Foncier n'est pas resté en arrière. Chaque bourse lui a fourni son contingent de progression. La solide institution! Et comme le public, qui ne peut se hisser au prix des actions, a raison de se disputer ses obligations communales et foncières! Ce sont des placements de premier ordre, avec des chances de lots mirifiques, ce qui ne gâte jamais rien. Avant peu, il faudra payer plus cher ces excellents titres. Les derniers stocks seront épuisés.

La Société Financière a secoué enfin son engourdissement. Son allure a été bien meilleure depuis huit jours. Ce ne peut être là qu'un premier pas. Cette valeur a encore bien du chemin à faire avant d'avoir atteint les prix qui lui sont légitimement dus.

La Société Générale mérite même faveur. Elle aussi vaut beaucoup mieux que les cours sur lesquels elle s'attarde. Gardez-vous d'en douter, elle aura son jour, et prochain. Le public ne persiste jamais longtemps dans ses erreurs d'évaluation.

La Banque d'Escompte a été très ferme. Ce serait une faute d'oublier que cette Société va détacher le 1er juillet un coupon de 25 francs. Il y a là une marge de reprise indiquée d'avance.

J. CONSEIL.

Paris. — Typ. G. CHAMEROT, 19, rue des Saints-Pères. — 9709.

Le Directeur-Gérant : Emile BERGERAT.

185
After Claude Monet, *The Cabin at Sainte-Adresse*, 1880. Gillotage, 145 x 191 mm. From *La vie moderne* 2 (19 June 1880), p. 400 [D436]

Monet wrote to his editor, Bergerat, to explain that he did not have the proper type of paper to execute a drawing for reproduction.[26] We may be sure based on the complaints of his fellow painters that this "commission" was unpaid, its value to be derived solely from its marketing potential rather than any direct remuneration from the journal. As Renoir later explained to Vollard, "We were to be paid by future benefits—that is to say that we did not get a penny."[27] Pissarro refused a request to produce a drawing for *La vie moderne*, remarking to his son Lucien that "from the financial point of view it's not worth it, in fact I believe they only reward their illustrators with the publicity!!!"[28]

The gillotage based on Monet's painting *Cabin at Sainte-Adresse* of 1867 (Musée d'Art et d'Histoire, Geneva) did not accompany the Taboureux interview but appeared a week later with a short unsigned article entitled "Notre Exposition Claude Monet" (fig. 185).[29] Although the exhibition featured more current examples of his work, Monet chose to reproduce a canvas painted thirteen years earlier. It was a picture that had been first shown in a maritime exhibition held at Le Havre in 1868 and again in the third Impressionist exhibition of 1877. Since 1873 it had been in the collection of Duret.

As he had done for *L'Autographe au Salon*, Monet produced a drawing that looks anything like a plodding reproduction of a painting; Bergerat described it as a "sketch . . . of a free and charming improvisation."[30] Monet translated the rapid brushstrokes and layering of colors on his canvas into a monochromatic image constructed from three major elements: a gray ground, rapidly scrawled black lines, and scraped highlights, the three-toned effect harkening back to the landscape vignettes from his 1857 sketchbook. In this instance, his drawing support—the special paper he needed from Bergerat—was a prepared piece of scratchboard. Known variously as "scraperboard," "scraping paper," or "Gillot paper," this support is typically made up of a heavy sheet of cardboard that has been coated with bright white chalk and, in the case of the *Cabin at Sainte-Adresse*, overprinted with a layer of middle-tone in gray ink. Monet is known to have used scratchboard on one previous occasion, for his small watercolor of Dieppe dating from around 1856 (see fig. 10). For the *Cabin at Sainte-Adresse*, he used pen and black ink to create the dark lines in the image, while producing the highlights with a sharp engraving tool to scratch or scrape through the black areas and the layer of toned ground. The additive and subtractive lines freely intermingle. In some areas, Monet scraped highlights through the dark lines, while in others he drew over the highlights. The result is an animated surface that preserves the tonal structure of the original painting. The foliage in the foreground, especially along the right edge, is transformed into a riot of black-and-white scribbles.

Working with scratchboard can be challenging for a novice, as it combines aspects of drawing and engraving. Even an experienced practitioner like Renoir found it unwieldy. Reminiscing over his experience as an illustrator for *La vie moderne*, Renoir complained to Ambroise Vollard: "The most terrible of all is that they forced upon us, for our drawings, a paper . . . that requires the use of a scraper to render the whites: I have never been able to get used to it."[31] We do not know whether Monet was satisfied with his own handling of the technique. He wrote to Charpentier on 15 June and asked him to forward one or two copies of the forthcoming issue containing the reproduction of his drawing, but no further communications between them have surfaced.[32]

Exhibition at Durand-Ruel Gallery, 1883

Monet's next one-man exhibition, a larger show of at least fifty-six paintings at Paul Durand-Ruel's new gallery on the boulevard de la Madeleine, resulted in even greater publicity and provided several new opportunities for the artist to promote his work through reproductive drawings in the art journals. The March 1883 exhibition eventually attracted attention from a range of influential critics, including Alfred de Lostalot (writing for *Gazette des beaux-arts*),

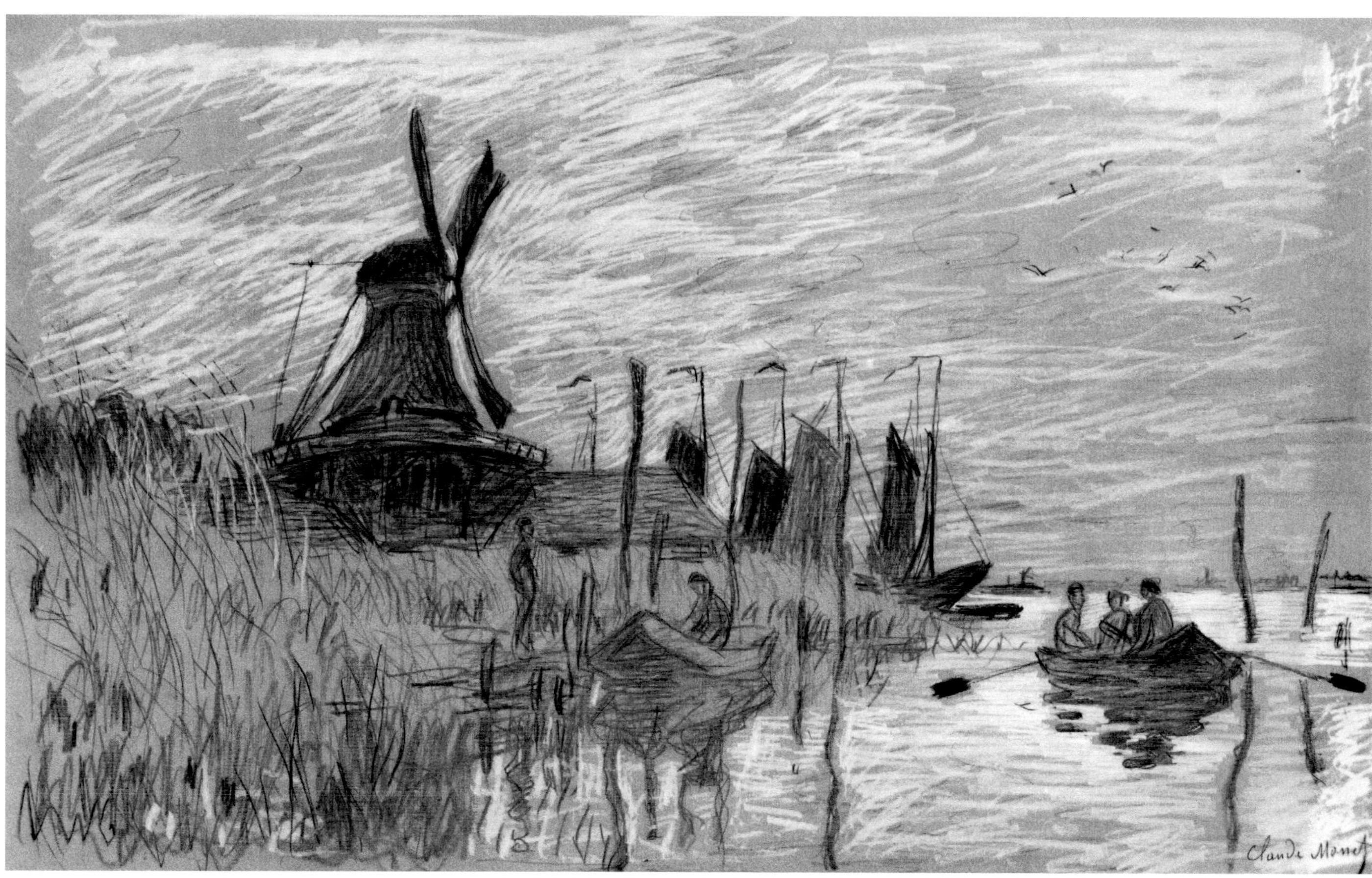

186
Windmill at Zaandem, 1883. Black crayon and scratchwork on Gillot paper, 145 x 290 mm. Location unknown [D438]

Ernest Chesnau (for *Annuaire illustré des beaux-arts*), Armand Silvestre (*La vie moderne*), Philippe Burty (*La République française*), Emile Bergerat (*Le Voltaire*), and the young Gustave Geffroy (*La Justice*). In the words of Steven Levine, "The year saw Monet's consecration in print, if not yet in sales."[33]

In the early days of the exhibition, the public-relations situation looked bleak. The show had opened on 28 February, and after the first week, Monet grew anxious at the apparent lack of interest in the press. Several agitated letters addressed to Paul Durand-Ruel give insight into the artist's views on the vital role of newspaper articles in driving gallery attendance. In a state of dejection, he wrote on 6 March:

I find that if one addresses the public and is greeted with silence and indifference, then that is a failure. As for me, I pay almost no attention to the opinions of the journals but it is important to recognize that in our epoch, you can't do anything without the press, and I must say that if the colleagues you have mentioned find the silence of the newspapers of little importance for me, I guarantee you that they will certainly know to secure their cooperation when it is their turn for an exhibition, and they will be right to do so, because without question the press excites public curiosity and, in my case, there isn't a person who has spoken with me about this silence and not deplored it.[34]

The next day Monet was still brooding over the lack of press coverage, and sent another letter to Durand-Ruel, this one more accusatory in tone:

This new and unfamiliar indifference has affected me deeply. When we were attacked and even vilified in the newspapers we could always comfort ourselves with the thought that it was all a measure of our worth since no one would have bothered about us if that weren't the case. So how should this silence be interpreted? You mustn't imagine that I want to see my name in the newspapers. I really am above all that and I couldn't care in the least about what the press and so-called art critics

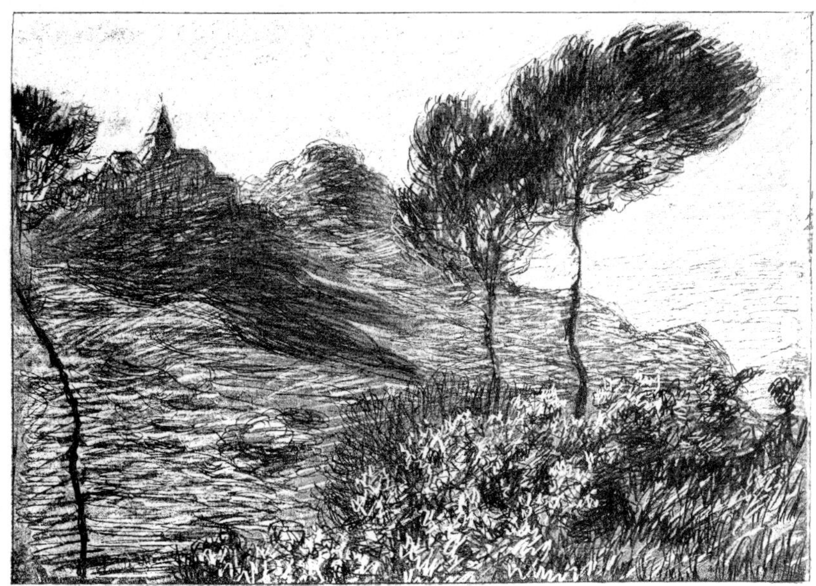

187
After Claude Monet, *The Church at Varengeville, Sunset*, 1883. Gillotage, 135 x 192 mm. From *Gazette des beaux-arts* 27, no. 4 (1 April 1883), p. 347

think, since they rival each other in their stupidity. Indeed, it doesn't affect the artistic side of things at all. I know my worth, and am harder on myself than anyone else could be. But things have to be looked at from the commercial angle. And we'd be blind not to see the truth staring us in the face, not to recognize that the exhibition was ill-prepared and poorly advertised. It is necessary at all costs to secure in advance the cooperation of the press, since even intelligent art-lovers are more or less responsive to the noise made by the newspapers.[35]

In Monet's view, there was no such thing as "bad press," and despite his stated aversion to drawing, he would relent to join in the noise-making in the only way that he could. In all, he consented to produce four scratchboard drawings related to the 1883 exhibition for reproduction in gillotage: *Windmill at Zaandem* (after his painting of 1871 in the collection of Jean-Baptiste Faure, published in the 17 March issue of *La vie moderne*; fig. 186), *View of Rouen* (after his painting of 1872, published in the 1 April issue of the *Gazette des beaux-arts*; see fig. 190), *The Church at Varengeville, Sunset* (after the painting of 1882 in Durand-Ruel's stock, also in the April issue of the *Gazette des beaux-arts*; fig. 187), and *The Two Anglers* (after the painting of 1882 apparently still with the artist, in the April issue of *L'Art moderne*, see fig. 194).

The earliest of these paintings, *View of Rouen* (fig. 188) was a work that Monet had sold to the artist Michel Lévy in January 1873.[36] As the Durand-Ruel exhibition was being pulled together in the middle of February 1883, Monet contacted Lévy, whom he had first met in Holland, to request the loan of the painting.[37] It was then hanging in the home of Lévy's brother on the boulevard de Clichy, and it is conceivable that Monet had not set eyes on it in a number of years. While Monet remained at Étretat, Durand-Ruel arranged for the picture to be transported to the gallery for the opening on 28 February.

The painting is remarkable in ways that transcend its modest scale. Its palette is subtle, emphasizing chalky and atmospheric violets punctuated by a tricolor flag that juts into the scene from the right edge of the canvas. With its low horizon and vast expanse of sky, the composition is organized by a series of strong vertical forms, from rows of tall, thin poplar trees to attenuated boat masts, distant smokestacks, and the spire of Rouen's great Gothic cathedral, all reflected in the calm surface of the water. The city's Nôtre-Dame cathedral here makes its first known appearance in a painting by Monet, a subject to which he would return with great passion some two decades later. Joachim Pissarro has suggested that the inclusion of this work in the spring 1883 exhibition at Durand-Ruel's may have inspired Pissarro to travel to Rouen in the fall of that year and embark on his own series of landscapes and urban views, several of which offer a vista very similar to Monet's 1872 painting.[38] Curiously, when the painting was sold at auction from Lévy's collection in 1892, Monet harbored an unsympathetic opinion of the work, writing with some incredulity to his wife, "Did you know that a mediocre and ancient *View of Rouen* was just sold at Drouot for 9500 francs?"[39] After it resurfaced three years later in a New York auction, the painting again appeared in print, this time in the form of a wood engraving in *Scribner's Magazine* (see fig. 191).[40]

The *Gazette des beaux-arts* editor's decision to solicit drawings of the *View of Rouen* as

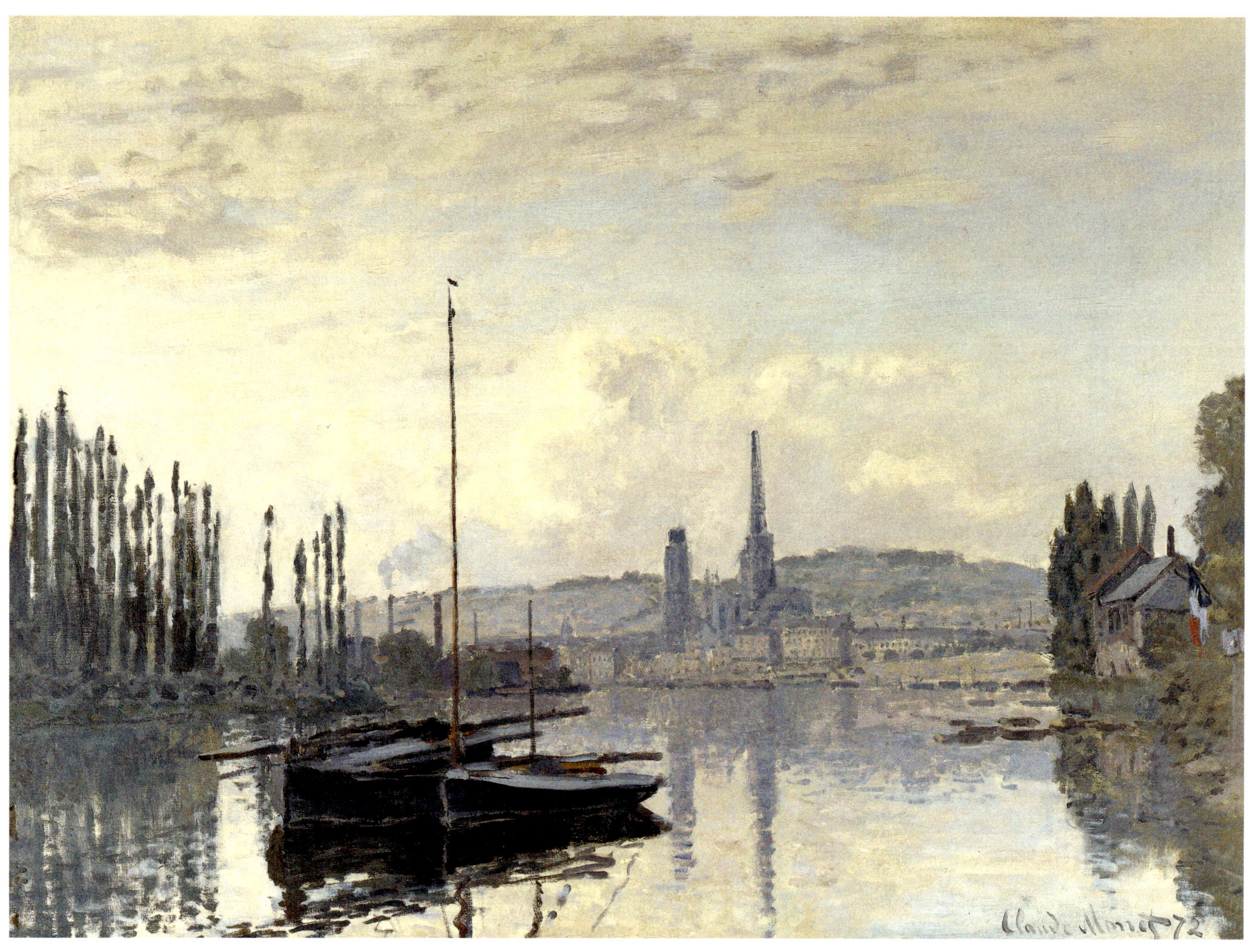

188
View of Rouen, 1872. Oil on canvas, 54 x 73 cm. Private collection, courtesy of Pyms Gallery, London [W217]

well as the more recent *Church at Varengeville, Sunset* must have been prompted by the critic De Lostalot, since these two paintings were among only four specifically named in his article. De Lostalot cited both works in his discussion of Monet's distinctive use of the color violet in rendering effects of sunlight. In an aside that can only be read as a form of official sanctification, the conservative critic compared the *View of Rouen* favorably with the work of the Dutch Baroque painter Aelbert Cuyp (1620–1691).[41]

At 313 by 475 millimeters, the Clark drawing (fig. 189) is roughly two-thirds the size of the painting it reproduces (54 by 73 cm). The relative grandeur of the sheet was dictated by the process of photo-gillotage, which typically calls for a reduction on the order of two to four times the size of the original drawing.[42] As printed in the *Gazette des beaux-arts*, the final image measures 135 by 205 millimeters (fig. 190). The drawing (and print) modify the proportions of the composition slightly, stretching the scene horizontally to make it more rectangular than square. Lightly rendered vertical lines in the area of the poplars and just to the left of the tall mast indicate his first efforts to set down the principal motifs. Perhaps for the sake of legibility, the artist chose to alter the relationship between the distant cityscape and the empty sailboats

189
View of Rouen, 1883. Black crayon and scratchwork on Gillot paper, 313 x 475 mm. Sterling and Francine Clark Art Institute, Williamstown, Massachusetts [D434]

190
After Claude Monet, *View of Rouen*, 1883. Gillotage, 135 x 205 mm. From *Gazette des beaux-arts* 27, no. 4 (1 April 1883), p. 345

191
Walter Monteith Aikman (American, 1857–1939), after Claude Monet, *View of Rouen*, 1896. Wood engraving, 116 x 158 mm. From *Scribner's Magazine* 19, no. 1 (Jan. 1896), p. 2

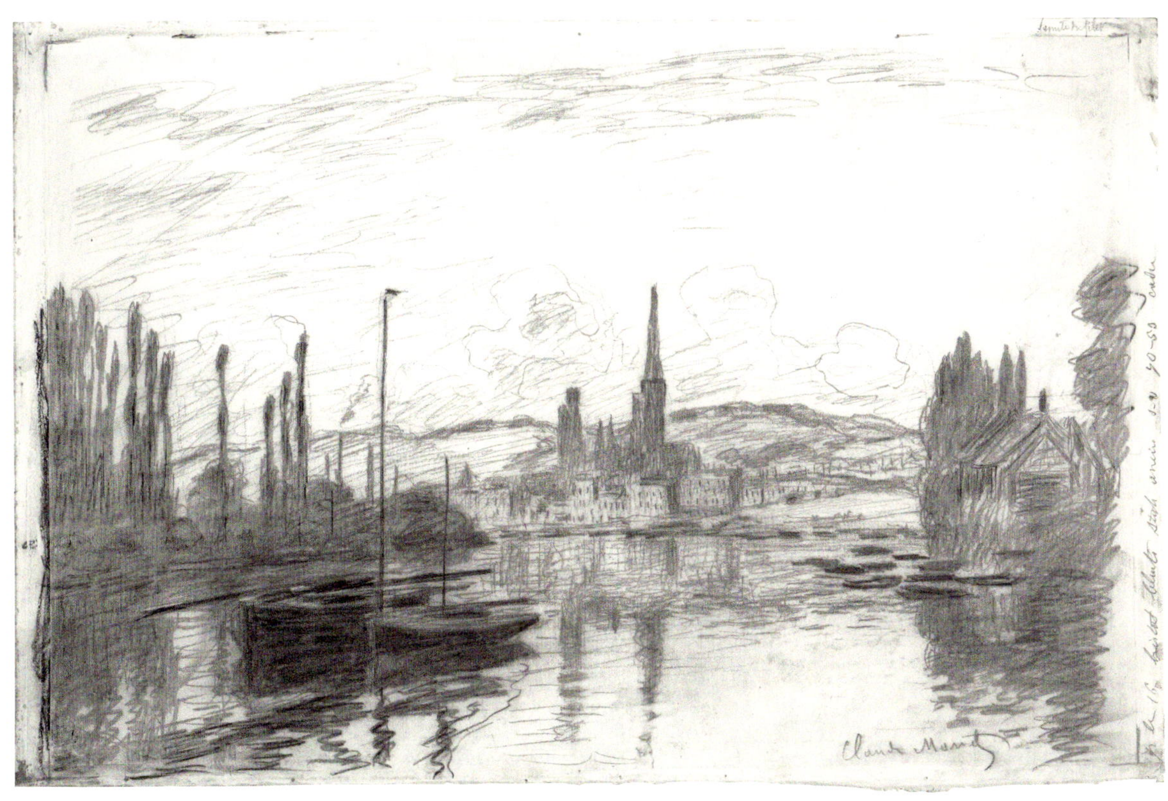

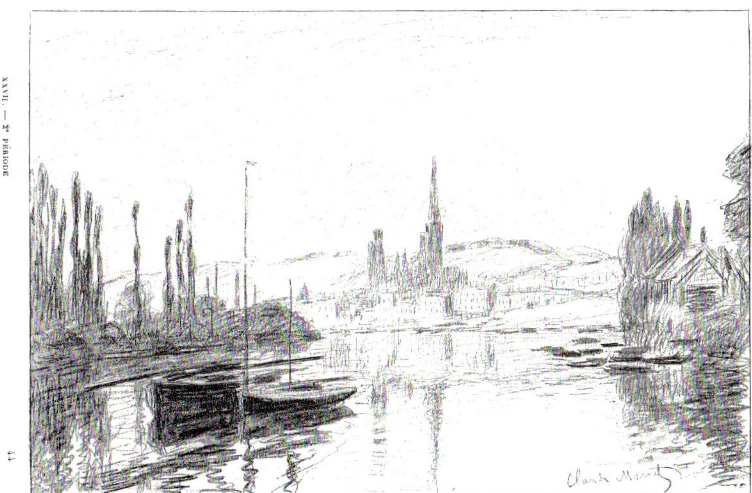

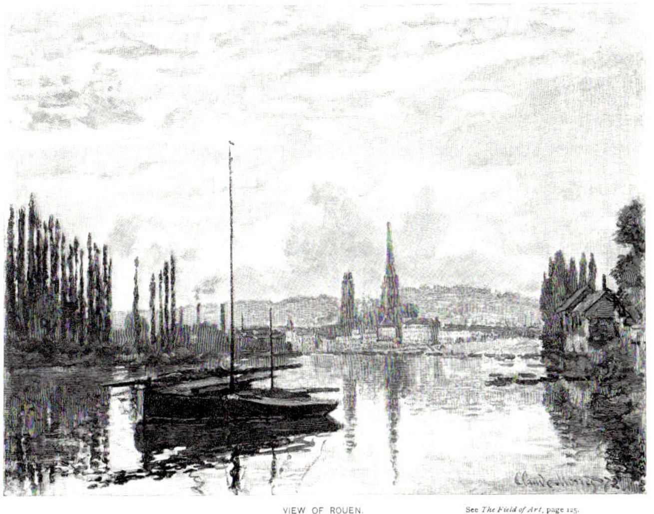

moored in the foreground. Compared with the telescoping of these elements in the painting, the space of the drawing is compressed in a way that increasingly characterized Monet's landscapes of the 1880s and 1890s, so that the cathedral and surrounding buildings appear closer to the viewer. Besides enlarging the background, Monet reduced the height of the tallest flagstaff so that it no longer towers above the cathedral's great northern spire.

The manner in which Monet translated brushstrokes into *gribouillages*, especially in the areas of reflections on the water, is consistent with the style of his previous reproductive drawings. Once again, the Impressionist who disavowed drawing adopted what might be called

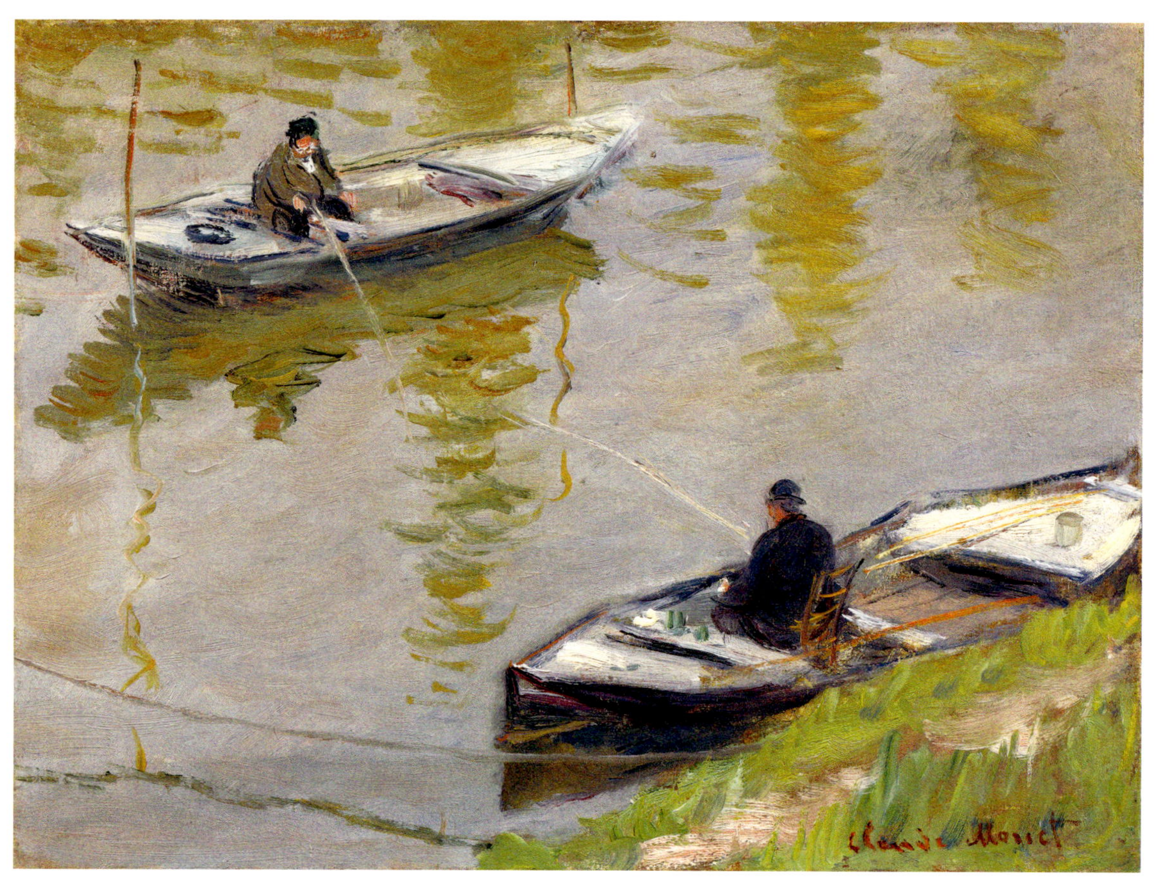
Claude Monet

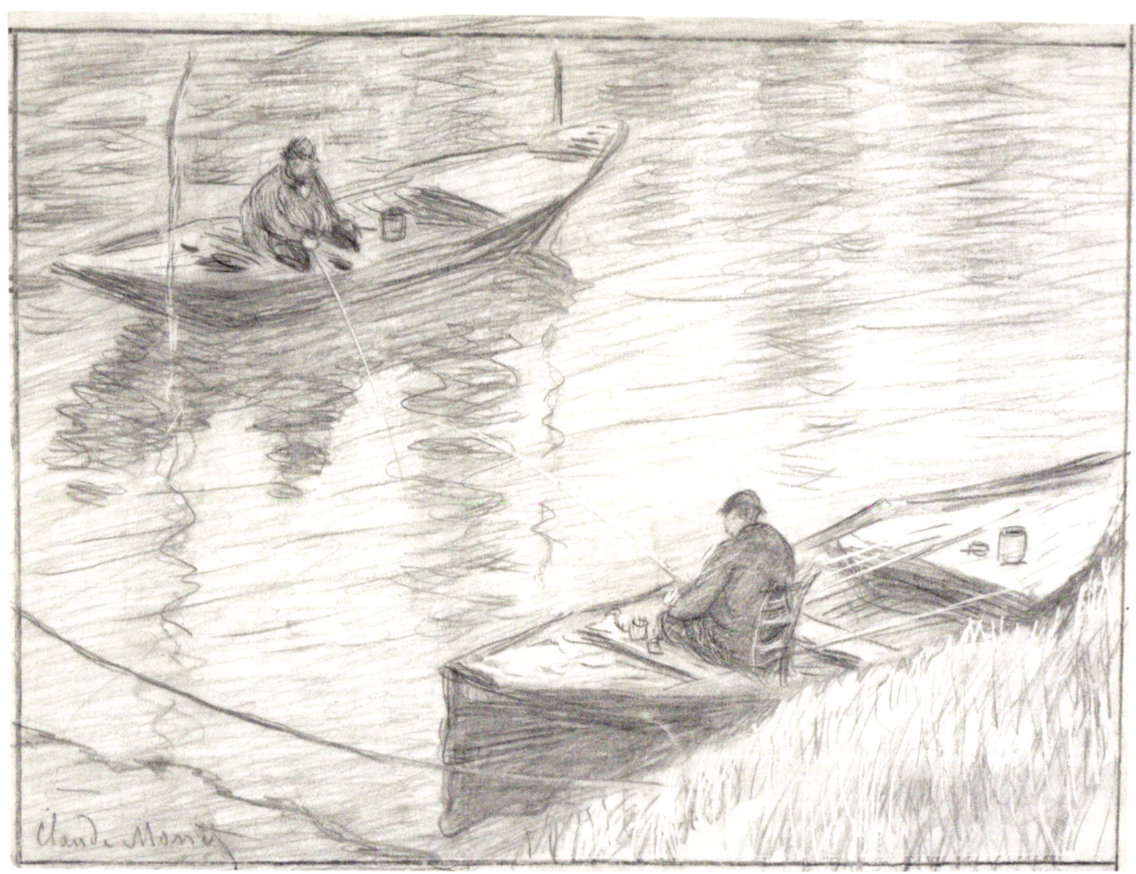
Claude Monet

192
The Two Anglers, 1882. Oil on canvas, 38 x 52.5 cm. Private collection [W749]

193
The Two Anglers, 1883. Black crayon and scratchwork on Gillot paper, 256 x 344 mm. The Fogg Art Museum, Harvard University Art Museums, Cambridge, Massachusetts. Bequest of Meta and Paul J. Sachs, 1965 [D435]

194
After Claude Monet, *The Two Anglers*, 1883. Gillotage, 167 x 234 mm. The Fogg Art Museum, Harvard University Art Museums, Cambridge, Massachusetts. Drawing Department Fund for Special Acquisitions

a gestural approach to mark-making that does everything to call attention to itself, that is, to the action of the artist's hand.[43] To heighten the sense of aerial perspective, Monet applied varying degrees of pressure with his black crayon on the ridged paper, from the most forceful marks on the boats and poplars in the foreground to moderate pressure in drawing the cityscape and even lighter force in delineating the sky. In this sheet he made only spare use of the medium's ability to create highlights by scratching through the drawing to reveal the white gesso ground.

To some extent the unrestrained effects of the drawing are toned down in the print. This byproduct of the transfer process is explained in an artist's manual of the mid-1890s, which advised:

For drawing in general or the use of effects in drawing it should be noted that with all these [prepared Gillot] papers the drawing may be somewhat overdone, and this is necessary in order to obtain the corresponding vigorous action in the reproduction. The printing ink is, as a rule, never such a deep black as the drawing ink, nor is the paper which is used for printing ever so white as the lines of the toned paper. The contrasts would, therefore, in printing become too little, and flat unsatisfactory pictures would be obtained. With these drawings, therefore, the two opposites, "black and white," may be used to the extreme, even if the drawing is not satisfactory to the artistic eye.[44]

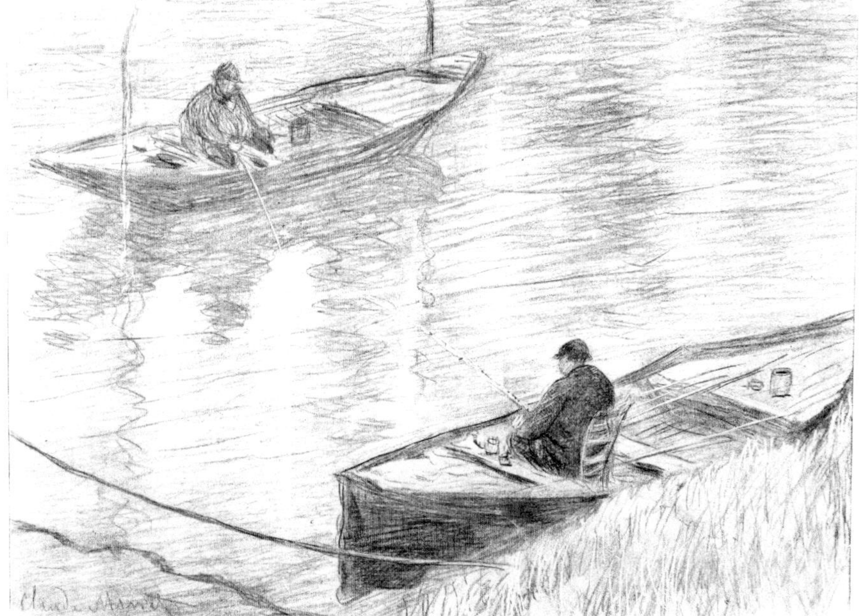

Monet's drawing of *The Two Anglers* in the Fogg Art Museum appeared in the form of a gillotage print on a full page in the April 1883 issue of *L'Art moderne*, where it accompanied a brief review of the exhibition penned by an anonymous "Amateur."[45] Like the *View of Rouen*, this drawing is approximately two-thirds the size of the original painting (figs. 192 and 193); the gillotage print (fig. 194), in turn, is roughly two-thirds the size of the drawing. The subject and viewpoint of this work are perhaps more typical of Caillebotte than Monet, with its close portrayal of two Poissy fishermen and the placement of the horizon above the upper limit of the canvas (and the sheet) at the expense of an open view of the surrounding landscape. Of the fifty-six canvases shown in the 1883 exhibition, only three others painted since 1880 included figures of any comparable significance.[46] Not merely *staffage*, the fishermen and their activities play a major role in this composition. At the same time, Monet used this rather mundane subject to explore one of his favorite themes: the reflections of light and other forms on the broken surface of the water.

It is tempting to interpret his decision to submit a reproductive drawing of this atypical work for publication as a proclamation that his talents transcended pure landscape painting and embrace modern life subjects. What makes his choice of this painting especially puzzling is the fact that the work was not actually shown in the 1883 exhibition. Instead, a closely related canvas, *Anglers on the Seine at Poissy* (Österreichische Galerie, Vienna), from the collection of Jean-Baptiste Faure, was listed in the catalogue.[47] The latter painting, slightly larger in scale and populated with additional fishermen and boats, was mentioned in passing by reviewers H. Marriott (in *Le Journal des arts*), Gustave Geffroy (in *La Justice*), and Paul Labarrière (in *Journal des artistes*). Why Monet copied the smaller, alternate version for the article in *L'Art moderne* rather than the picture included in the exhibition is not known. One possibility is that since the request for a drawing must have reached the artist while the show was still on view, he chose the most expeditious means of fulfilling the request by copying a painting still in his possession — the smaller version — rather than venturing into Paris to make a drawing after one of the works hanging in Durand-Ruel's gallery.[48]

Like the Clark drawing of Rouen, the Fogg sheet is executed in a vigorously calligraphic manner with black crayon on white scratchboard. It makes greater use of toolwork to gouge white lines into dark areas of the drawing, and covers the entire prepared surface of the sheet with marks of varying degrees of intensity. Scratched lines define the tall grasses of the riverbank, details of the boats and the fishing poles. Although a few inconsequential details are changed from the original painting, particularly in the anglers' accessories onboard their respective vessels, the translation from color to black-and-white successfully preserves the relative values of the model. Monet's gestural brushwork, most evident in the reflections, is echoed in his calligraphic black-crayon marks.

L'Art dans les deux mondes and the Exhibition at Durand-Ruel, 1891

For twelve short days in May 1891, Monet was given a one-man exhibition in Paul Durand-Ruel's gallery on the rue Le Peletier in which he placed on view fifteen recent paintings of grainstacks and seven additional canvases dating from 1886 to 1891.[49] Since his previous solo exhibition at Durand-Ruel in 1883, he had temporarily severed relations with the dealer and shown his work in a number of other venues, including the Boussod and Valadon Gallery that was run by Theo van Gogh, the Goupil Gallery in London, and Durand-Ruel's major competitor, the Galerie Georges Petit. The 1891 exhibition marked his reconciliation with Durand-Ruel and was accompanied by a significant public-relations effort by the dealer. The exhibition catalogue contained a short essay by Gustave Geffroy and prompted a number of substantial reviews. As he had done in 1883, Monet produced four drawings for reproduction in the press.

Durand-Ruel promoted the exhibition in his own journal, *L'Art dans les deux mondes*. He had founded the weekly newspaper in November 1890 with a publicly stated double-aim: "first of all to publish a series of retrospective studies on the old masters and to follow, not only in Europe but also in America, Modern Art in all of its transformations."[50] According to its masthead, the newspaper was printed in an edition of 10,000 and distributed both in Paris and New York. The editors were Yveling RamBaud (pseudonym for Frédéric Gilbert) and Camille de Roddaz, and the list of principal contributors included such luminaries as Émile Zola, Octave Mirbeau, Claude Roger Marx, Maurice Maeterlinck, and Edmond de Goncourt. Illustrations took the form of photo-gillotage prints, some from original drawings but most from photographic negatives. From his letters to his son Lucien we know that Camille Pissarro was an avid reader of *L'Art dans les deux mondes,* even while taking every opportunity to disparage its publisher; seeing through the journal's grand mission statement, he wrote, "(Durand's) review is just so much self-advertisement and nothing more."[51]

L'Art dans les deux mondes featured two articles on Monet in the spring of 1891, around the time of his exhibition at Durand-Ruel's. The first was a study by Octave Mirbeau (1848–1917; fig. 195) published in the 7 March issue and accompanied by three gillotage prints after drawings by Monet; a fourth drawing intended for the same issue remained unpublished.[52] The Mirbeau article was in the planning stages at the same time as the exhibition, and its publication preceded the show by two months. The second article by Gustave Geffroy appeared during the run of the exhibition in the 9 May issue and consisted of a reprint of his catalogue essay without any illustrations.[53]

The genesis of the collaboration between Mirbeau and Monet on the March article may be followed through a fascinating series of letters that survive between the writer, the painter,

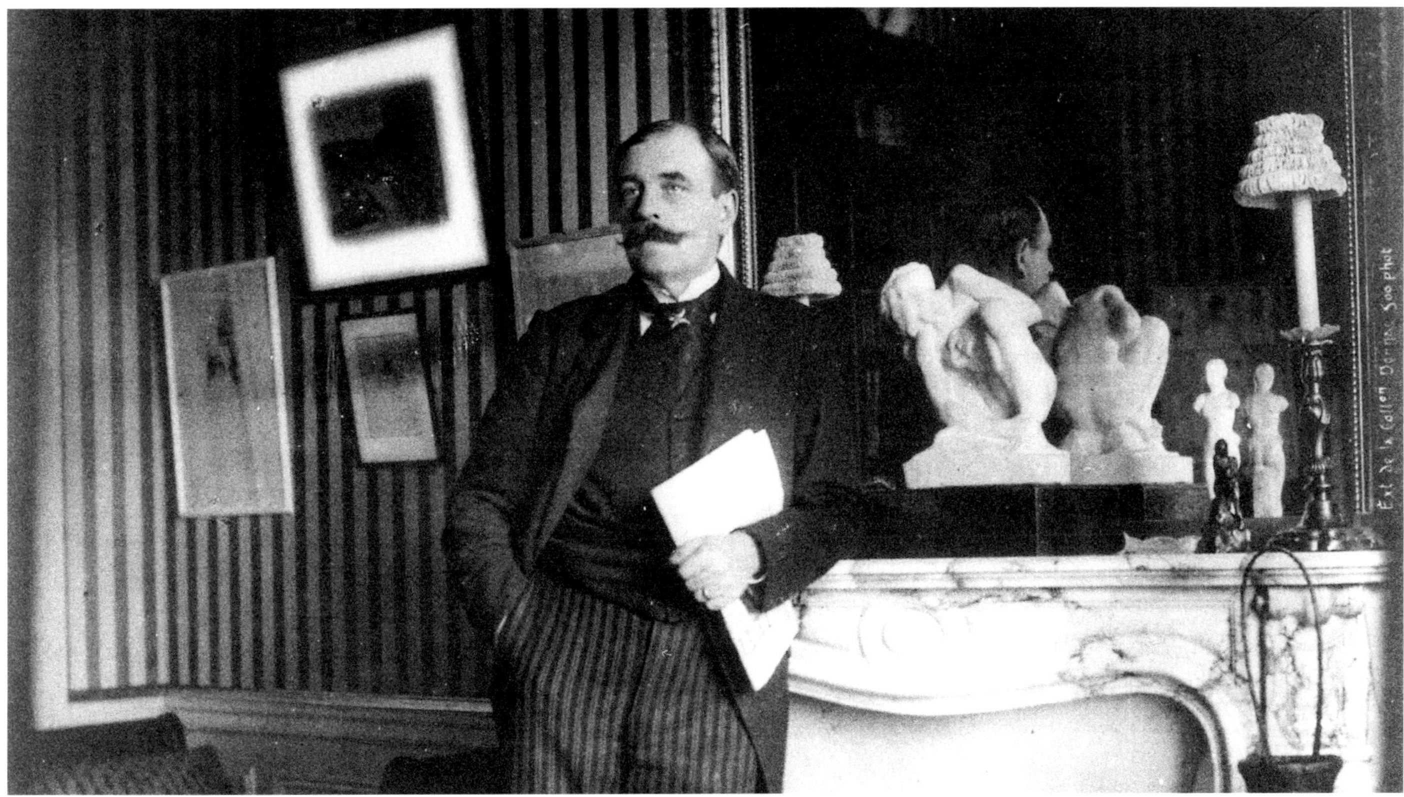

195
Octave Mirbeau in his study, c. 1890

and the dealer responsible for bringing them together. It was Durand-Ruel who had first introduced Mirbeau to Monet in November 1884, when the journalist was interviewing artists for a series of newspaper articles. In gratitude for the piece that appeared in the 21 November issue of *La France*, Monet presented the writer with a version of *The Customs House* (Fogg Art Museum, Cambridge).[54] The two men bonded, and entered into a lengthy correspondence.[55] Mirbeau subsequently reviewed Monet's 1889 exhibition at Boussod and Valadon, and then enlarged his essay for the catalogue of Monet's enormous joint exhibition with Rodin at the Galerie Georges Petit later in the same year.

The first reference to an article for *L'Art dans les deux mondes* is found in the postscript of a letter sent from Monet at his home in Giverny to Paul Durand-Ruel on 3 December 1890: "I have heard that you are arranging for something to be published in the newspaper *L'Art dans les deux mondes*; if so, I would be happy to receive copies of the issues that have already appeared, if that is possible."[56] The dealer replied immediately with copies of the first two issues as well as a plea for drawings based on the artist's recent work suitable for reproduction. Monet's response was lukewarm:

I am going to busy myself making the drawings that you have requested for Monsieur RamBaud, but you know that it is not my strength; in short, I will do my best. As for the study to be made of me, Mirbeau recently told me that it had been requested from him, and that he thought if he did not have too many other things to do, he would write it. I sent him a note and you will be apprised of his response.[57]

Although Mirbeau's name had appeared on the masthead of the first issue, he had abruptly resigned when he came to recognize the journal as a predominantly commercial enterprise designed to sell paintings. In response to Monet's direct appeal, which is lost, Mirbeau responded between 7 and 10 December:

I had tendered my resignation as collaborator on the newspaper in question. But to collaborate with you, and for you, has nothing to do with commerce,

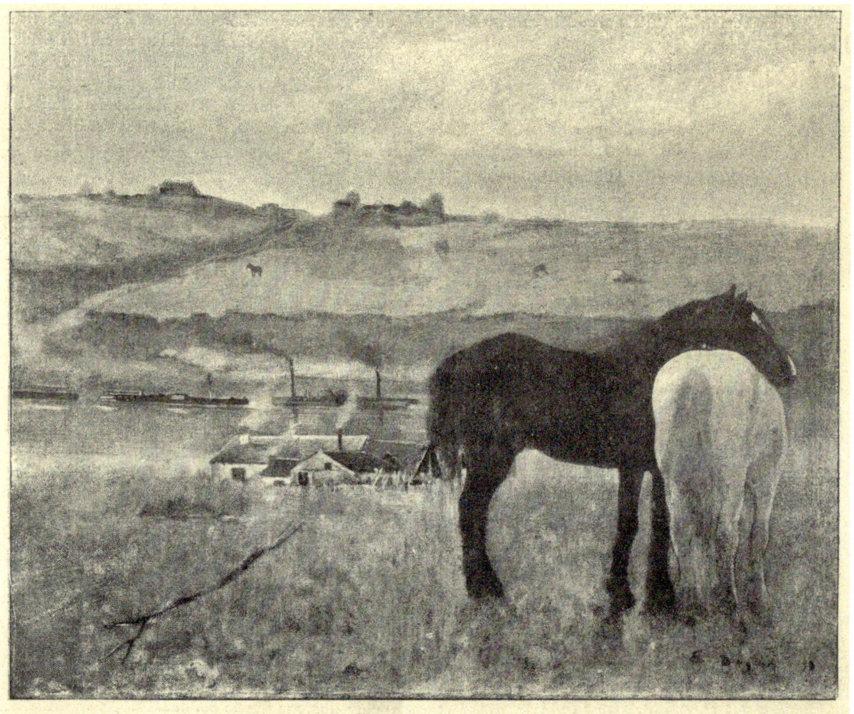

196
After Edgar Degas, *Horses in a Meadow*, 1890. Gillotage, 145 x 180 mm. From *L'Art dans les deux mondes* 1 (20 Dec. 1890), p. 45

and I accept to write the article with joy. I will write to Durand senior to whom I owe a response, because it has been at least eight days since he had written to ask me to reconsider my decision. I return there with you. So let's get going![58]

Mirbeau's use of the expression "collaborate" *(collaborer)* is significant, as it suggests that he saw this invitation as more than a straightforward journalistic assignment, but as an opportunity to enter into a creative partnership with the artist, to paint a series of his own word pictures and to produce a text that unlike his previous efforts would also be illustrated by Monet. The writer immediately paid a visit to Giverny to acquaint himself with the artist's latest paintings as well as the environment in which he lived and worked. Monet reported on the meeting briefly to Durand-Ruel in a letter of 14 December:

Mirbeau, who came to see me two days ago, told me that you wrote to him, in any case you will be able to count on his participation, and he is going to write the study of me. So write to tell him when you want to have it. I will busy myself with the drawings but I will ask you to wait a little bit because of everything that I'm in the middle of doing outdoors. The weather is so beautiful that I want to take advantage of it as much as possible.[59]

In subsequent letters to Durand-Ruel, Monet continued to make excuses for his failure to produce the requested drawings. "When you write, tell me if you have received a response from Mirbeau and for when you would like to have the drawings," Monet wrote on 21 December, "It may seem like nothing, but it frightens me a great deal, because I am so maladroit with white and black, and I am so absorbed by what I am doing that I am not able to do anything else."[60] Having emphasized his uneasiness with the assignment by transposing the expression "black and white," he proceeded with a new avoidance tactic:

I just received the current issue of L'Art dans les deux mondes*, and I found the reproduction of the Degas to be very well done. Wouldn't it be possible to reproduce a painting of mine in the same manner? The image of* L'Eglise de Vernon *belonging to Monsieur Vever, for example, came out very well.*[61]

Three works by Degas were reproduced in the 20 December issue of the journal, one of which was the painting *Horses in the Meadow* (1871; National Gallery of Art, Washington, D.C.) then in Durand-Ruel's own collection (fig. 196).[62] Rather than commission a drawing from Degas, the editors employed a photographic negative of the painting for direct transfer to the line block. While Monet was impressed with the results (and desperate for a way out of making the drawings), Degas and Pissarro were not as enthusiastic. In a letter to Lucien, Pissarro reported, "Durand cares less for art than ever, he is having some reproductions of my paintings made by the Michalet process. Degas is furious, he says that Durand probably hopes to get the Legion of Honor."[63] Compared with the original painting, the photomechanical reproduction of *Horses in the Meadow* is relatively harsh in its translation of the subtly colored landscape into black and white. Also, retouching of the relief plate led to the inadvertent removal of some details, including a small structure that vanished from the distant horizon.

Four days into the new year, Monet's procrastination continued, and he wrote to Durand-Ruel to ask again if a photograph could spare him the dreaded obligation:

Concerning the drawings, I mentioned in one of my letters to try to make a good reproduction of one of my paintings by the process employed for the Degas, but you have not responded. See if there is a way and otherwise I will try to get on with the sketches.[64]

While the journal used photographic negatives to reproduce paintings by Degas, Pissarro, and Sisley, among others, Durand-Ruel persisted in his requests for drawings from Monet, and as of 21 January, his request was still unfilled. On that date, Monet reported that he was still hard at work painting grainstacks in the snow:

Please apologize for me to Monsieur RamBaud about my drawings; he will receive them soon, but at the moment I am in the thick of work. I have so many things going that I can't be distracted for a minute, as I want above all to profit from the splendid effects of winter.[65]

By early February, Monet had at last found time to set aside his brushes and tackle the onerous task of drawing. RamBaud had shared the results with Gustave Geffroy, who reported on them with great enthusiasm to Mirbeau. In a letter sent to Monet around 10 February, Mirbeau made a good-natured quip concerning the painter's stance as an anti-draftsman:

Geffroy has told me that you have sent some drawings of great beauty, and that he doesn't know anything more admirable than the Woman with a Parasol [*see fig. 206*]. *For a man who* doesn't know how to draw, *that must have surprised you. As for me, I was sure of that, because given what you are, my dear Monet, it is impossible for you not to inject into the smallest of things the grandeur of your genius. Have faith that in the article, while predicting the Monet that you will be, I will not forget what you are.*[66]

With the text and images in place, it would be another month before the article appeared in print. "It looks like you haven't passed through the pages of *L'Art dans les deux mondes* for several weeks," Mirbeau noted. "They have many things to push, and Rambaud told me they want to dedicate more space to you than the others."[67]

The article was published in the 7 March issue. Even before setting eyes on it, Mirbeau was disgruntled. He complained to Monet:

I think that my article must have appeared today. I am furious. They did not want to send me the proofs. I had many things to correct in it, and I anticipate typographical errors of which the house is far too prodigious in making. It's the same as always, my dear Monet: don't be angry with me for this stupid article. The intention is good; the execution, bad.[68]

Regardless of the author's exasperation with the editorial staff, his study would make an important addition to the growing body of criticism on the artist. Among its contributions was an extraordinary description of Monet's garden at Giverny, the first extended literary treatment of this important site. Mirbeau relished the opportunity to paint a picture of Monet's garden in words, and his portrayal of Giverny in three different seasons is more vivid than any form of photography or reproduction available at the time. His hyperbolic vision of the garden in summer reveals his expertise in botany:

On either side of the sandy path, nasturtiums of every hue and saffron eschscholtzias collapse into dazzling heaps. The surprising fairy-tale magic of the poppies swells on the wide flower beds, covering the withered irises; it is an extraordinary mingling of colors, a riot of pale tints, a resplendent and musical profusion of white, pink, yellow, and mauve, an incredible rolling of blond flesh tones, against which shades of orange explode, fanfares of blazing copper ring, reds bleed and flare, violets disport themselves, black-purples are licked with

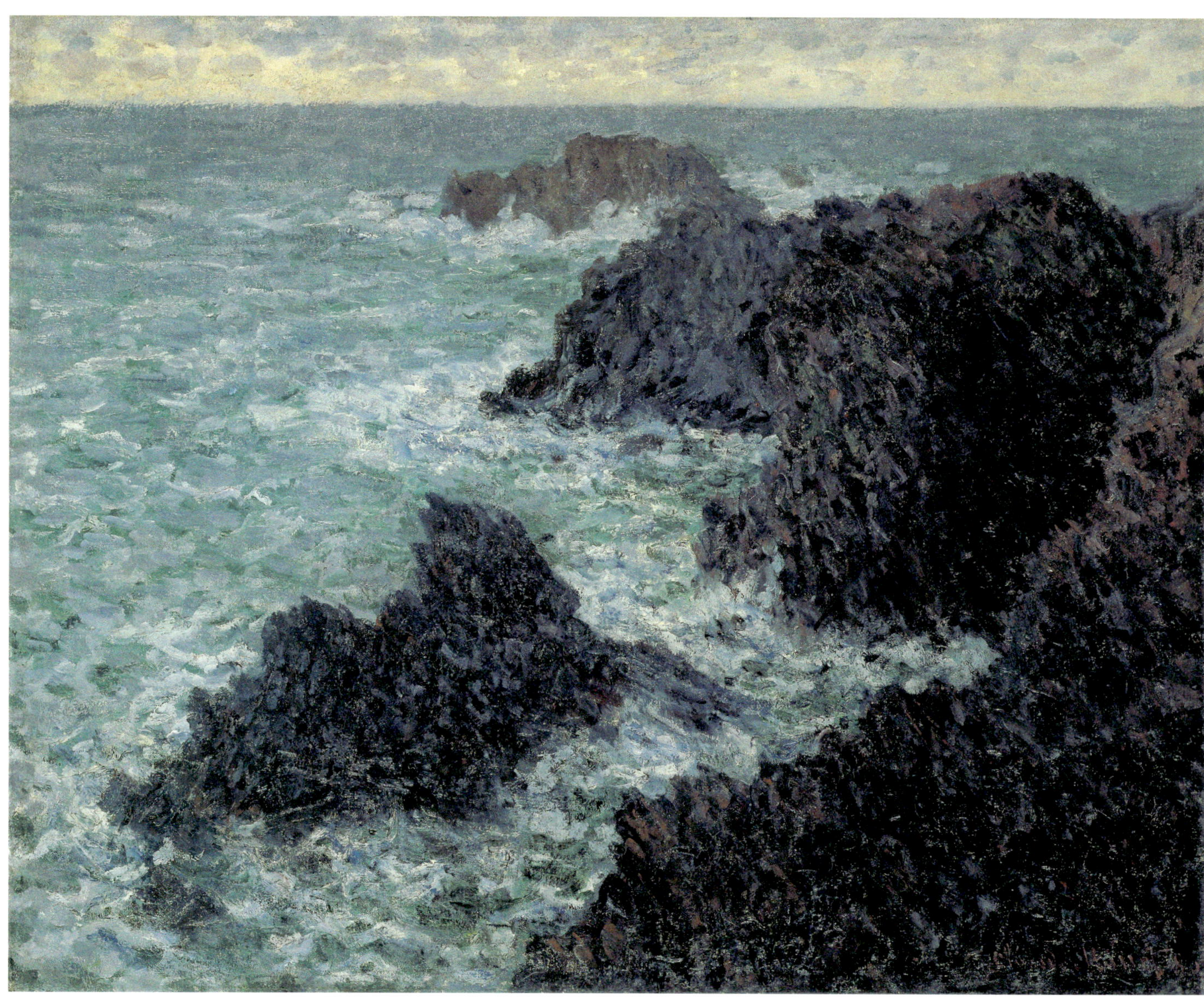

197
The Côte Sauvage, the Cliffs of Belle-Île, 1886. Oil on canvas, 65 x 81.5 cm. Musée d'Orsay, Paris. Bequest of Gustave Caillebotte, 1894 [W1100]

flame. And here and there, rising from this marvelous wave, from this marvelous flow of flowers, the hollyhocks dress their masts with exquisitely rumpled fabrics, as light and vaporous as gauze, their creases satin-brilliant; they bear little dancers' skirts that balloon and billow. The suns of the Texas roses reach out their long bracts heavy with buds, and the great California sunflowers leap, shoot their green eyes upward, their tousled flower heads crested with gold, like fabulous angry birds. In the air, the fresh breath of the mignonette mingles with the nasturtiums' peppery scent.[69]

Mirbeau's prose attempts nothing less than a vivid recreation of the garden in the reader's mind, and so takes the place of a visual (painted or photographic) representation of Giverny.

In the article, Mirbeau contrasted the tranquility of Monet's garden with the "tragic rocks and the howling gulfs" of Belle-Île-en-Mer.[70] Monet's drawing of *The Côte Sauvage*, after his painting of 1886 (figs. 197 and 198), appeared on the journal's front page (fig. 199) above the caption "Dessin inédit de M. Claude Monet" ("unpublished drawing by M. Claude Monet"). His work at Belle-Île had figured prominently in recent exhibitions held at Georges Petit's gallery, and the source for this illustration was a canvas acquired from the artist by Gustave Caillebotte that was among those previously shown;

198
The Côte Sauvage, 1891. Black crayon, 234 x 315 mm. National Museum of Western Art, Tokyo [D443]

199
After Claude Monet, *The Côte Sauvage*, 1891. Gillotage, 249 x 309 mm. From *L'Art dans les deux mondes* 1 (7 March 1891), p. 181

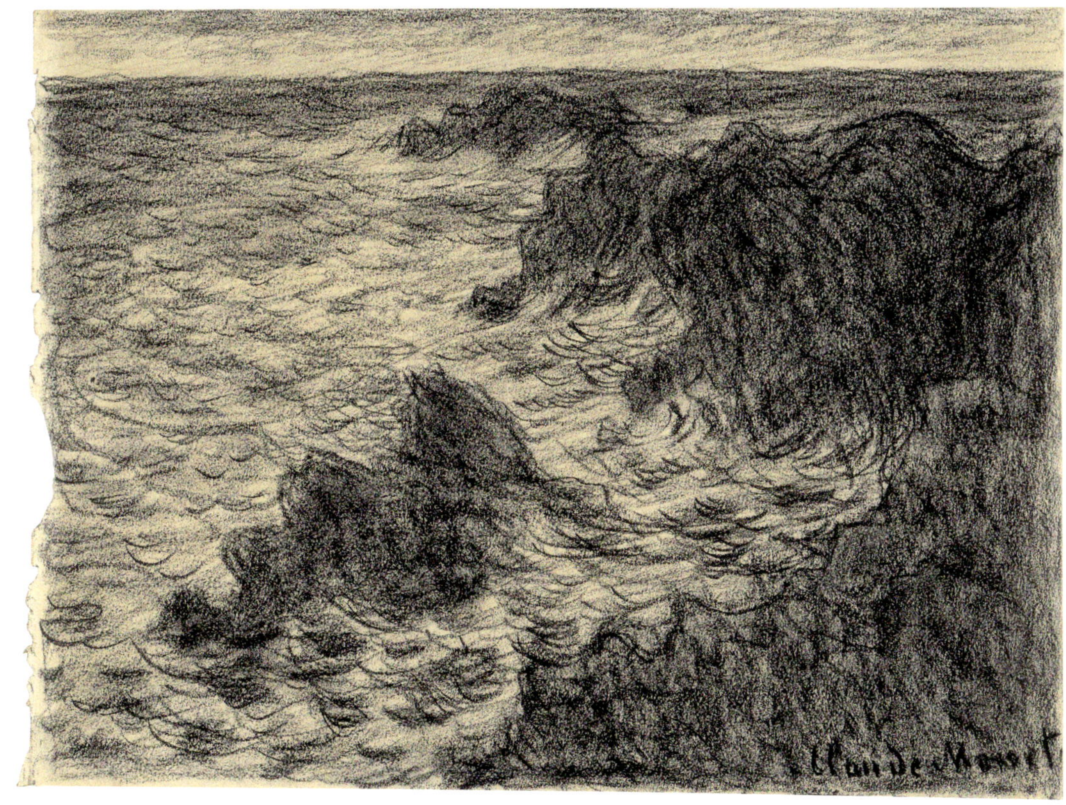

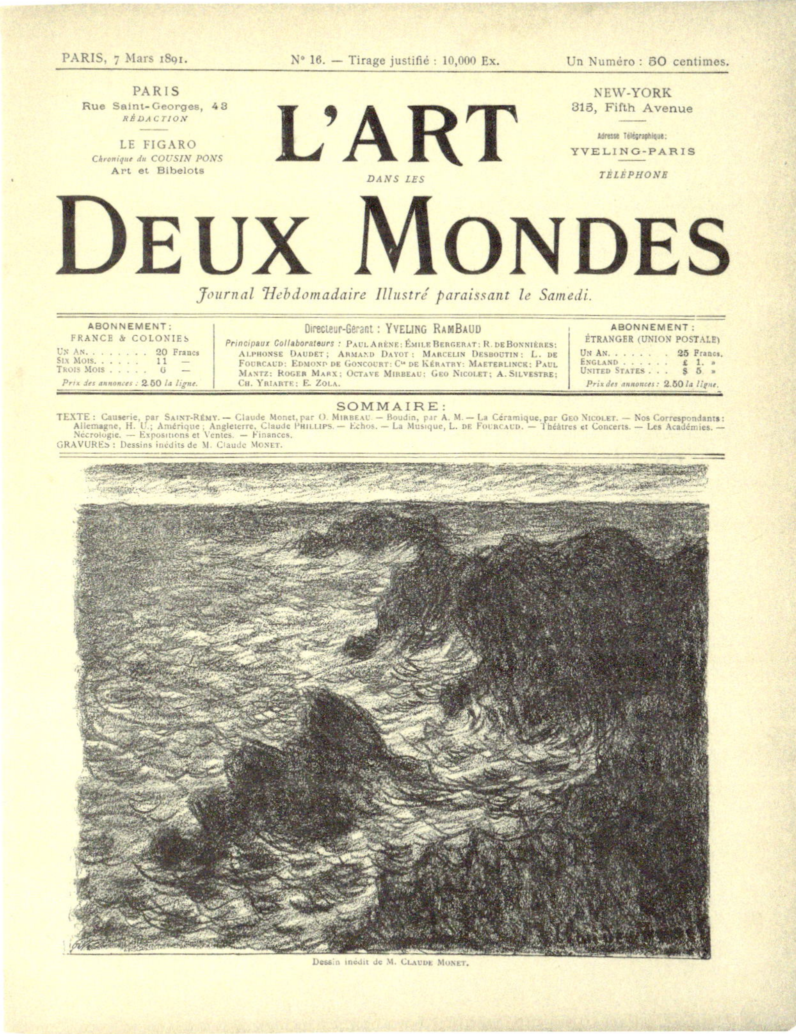

PARIS, 7 Mars 1891. N° 16. — Tirage justifié : 10,000 Ex. Un Numéro : 50 centimes.

PARIS
Rue Saint-Georges, 43
RÉDACTION

LE FIGARO
Chronique du COUSIN PONS
Art et Bibelots

L'ART
DANS LES
DEUX MONDES

Journal Hebdomadaire Illustré paraissant le Samedi.

NEW-YORK
315, Fifth Avenue

Adresse Télégraphique:
YVELING-PARIS

TÉLÉPHONE

ABONNEMENT :
FRANCE & COLONIES
Un An. . . . . 20 Francs
Six Mois. . . . . . 11 —
Trois Mois . . . . . 6 —
Prix des annonces : 2.50 *la ligne.*

Directeur-Gérant : YVELING RAMBAUD
Principaux Collaborateurs : Paul Arène; Émile Bergerat; R. de Bonnières; Alphonse Daudet; Armand Dayot; Marcelin Desboutin; L. de Fourcaud; Edmond de Goncourt; Cte de Kératry; Maeterlinck; Paul Mantz; Roger Marx; Octave Mirbeau; Geo Nicolet; A. Silvestre; Ch. Yriarte; E. Zola.

ABONNEMENT :
ÉTRANGER (UNION POSTALE)
Un An. . . . . . . 25 Francs.
England . . . . . . £ 1. »
United States . . . $ 5. »
Prix des annonces : 2.50 *la ligne.*

SOMMAIRE :
TEXTE : Causerie, par Saint-Rémy. — Claude Monet, par O. Mirbeau. — Boudin, par A. M. — La Céramique, par Geo Nicolet. — Nos Correspondants : Allemagne, H. U.; Amérique; Angleterre, Claude Phillips. — Echos. — La Musique, L. de Fourcaud. — Théâtres et Concerts. — Les Académies. — Nécrologie. — Expositions et Ventes. — Finances.
GRAVURES : Dessins inédits de M. Claude Monet.

Dessin inédit de M. Claude Monet.

200
After Claude Monet, *The Côte Sauvage*, 1893. Gillotage, 154 x 204 mm. From *The Studio* 1 (1893), p. 242

201
William Thornley (French, 1857–1935), after Claude Monet, *The Côte Sauvage*, c. 1894. Transfer lithograph printed in black on blue-toned chine appliqué, 210 x 277 mm. Collection of Dr. Morton and Tobia Mower

202
William Thornley, after Claude Monet, *The Côte Sauvage*, c. 1894. Transfer lithograph printed in black on olive-toned chine appliqué, 210 x 277 mm. Bibliothèque de l'Institut National de l'Histoire de l'Art, Paris. Collections Jacques Doucet

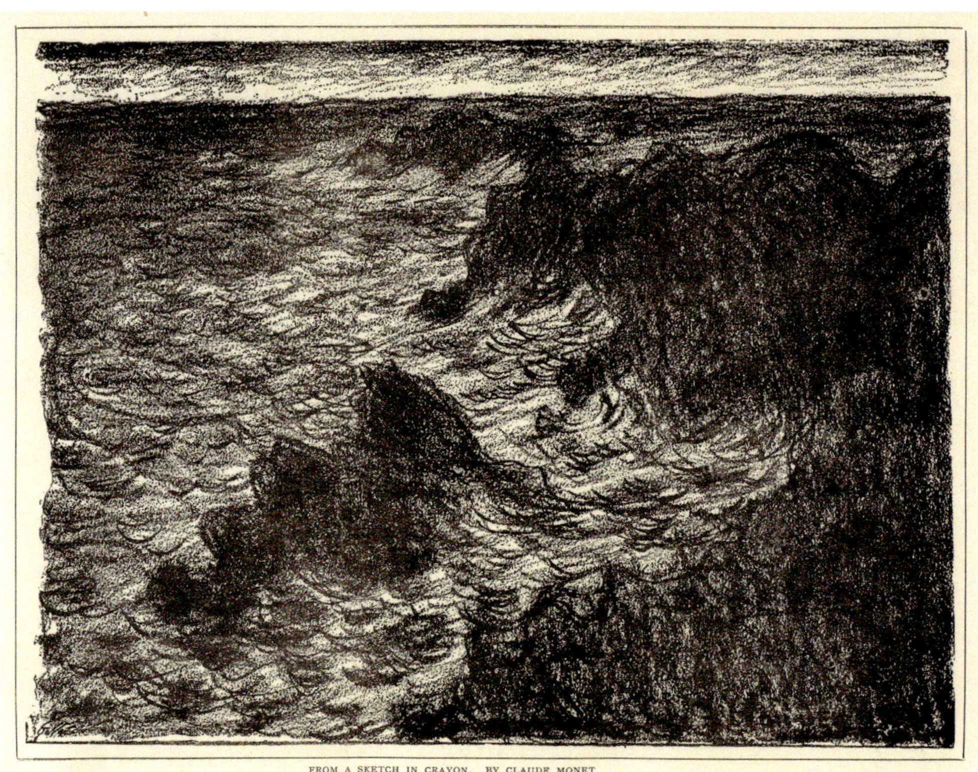

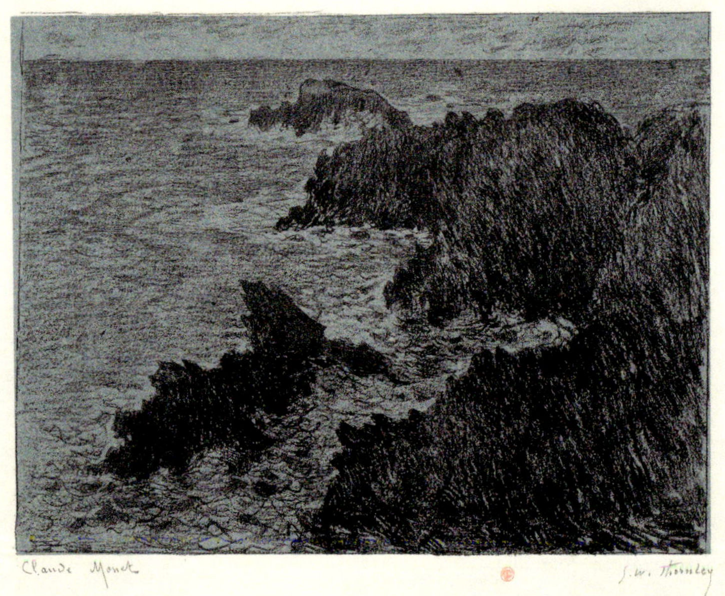

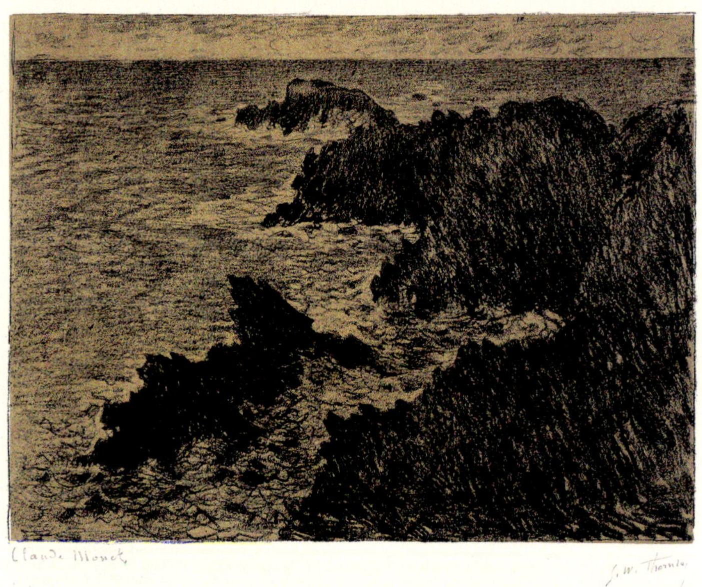

it would not feature in the 1891 exhibition at Durand-Ruel, but it would be reproduced in a later journal (fig. 200) and then in William Thornley's portfolio of lithographs after Monet in two color variants (figs. 201 and 202).[71]

Unlike his previous submissions to *La vie moderne* and the *Gazette des beaux-arts*, *The Côte Sauvage* was not executed on lined scratchboard but on a grained paper that broke up the black-crayon marks into halftones for transfer to the relief etching plate. With its high horizon, the composition provided Monet with another opportunity to fill the sheet with a variety of expressive lines. Although the seascape is more turbulent than either the *Cabin at Sainte-Adresse* or the *View of Rouen*, there is a greater delicacy

203
Grainstacks, 1891. Black crayon, 233 x 292 mm. National Museum of Western Art, Tokyo [D444]

204
After Claude Monet, *Grainstacks*, 1891. Gillotage, 80 x 200 mm. From *L'Art dans les deux mondes* 1 (7 March 1891), p. 183

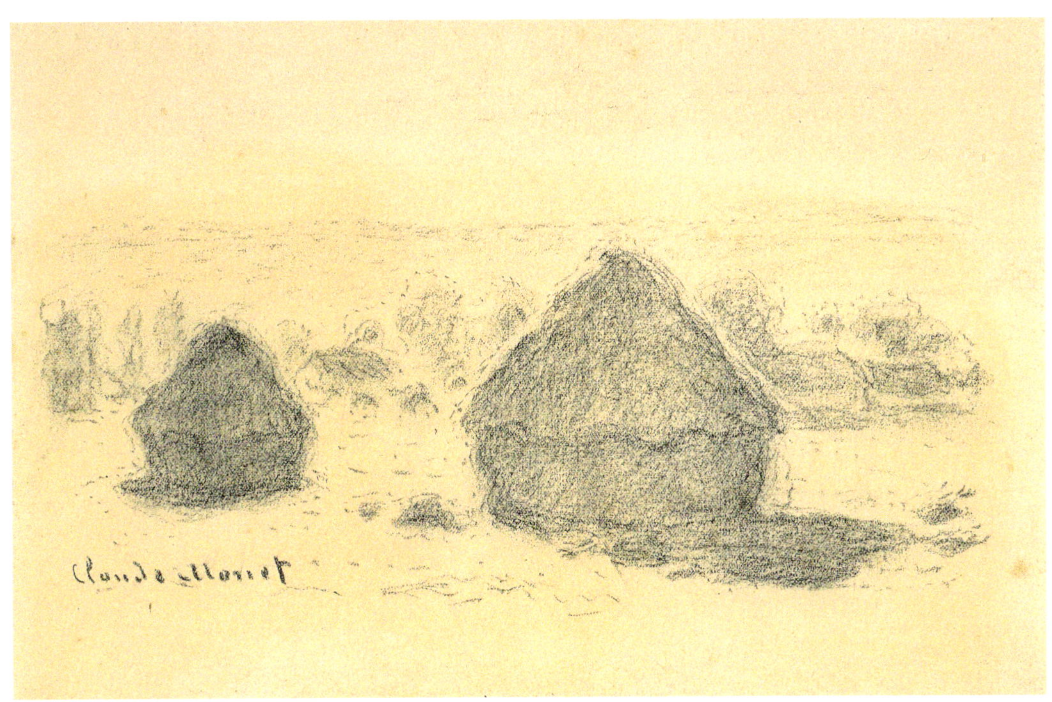

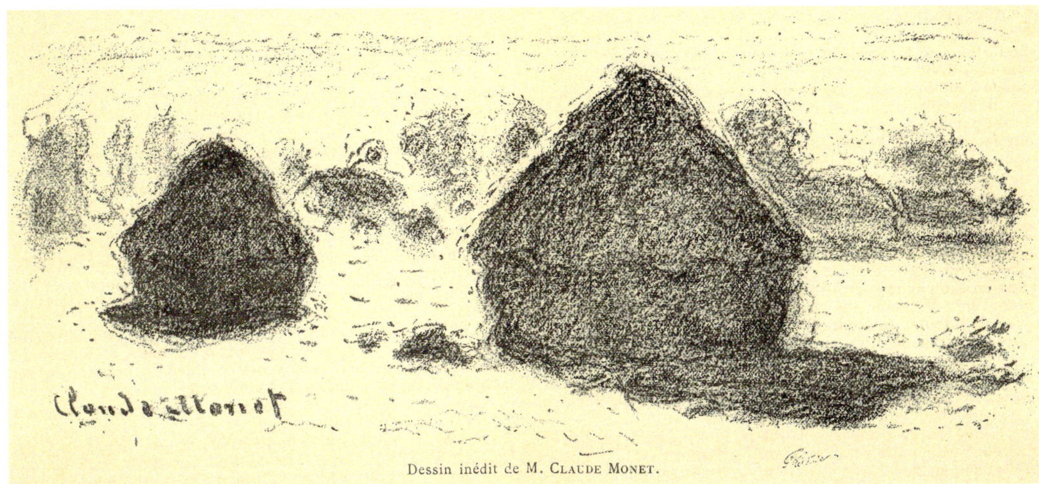

in Monet's translation of the painting's layered patches of brushwork into a series of overlapping cursive marks that define the waves. With the sea drained of its brilliant blue-green color, the drawing accentuates the raw, elemental power of the sea cliffs' irregular profiles. Within these silhouettes, Monet suggested the rough surfaces and textures of the rocks by rubbing the chalk; a few lines drawn over the smudged areas add definition to the forms. The soft chiaroscuro effects of the original drawing, one of Monet's most striking forays in this genre, are preserved remarkably well in the published gillotage print.

The second "Dessin inédit de M. Claude Monet" to appear with Mirbeau's article (figs. 203 [crayon] and 204 [gillotage]) was based on *Grainstacks in Bright Sunlight* (Hill-Stead Museum, Farmington, Connecticut), a canvas dated 1890.[72] While the Grainstacks series would comprise the bulk of Durand-Ruel's forthcoming exhibition, Mirbeau only touched on these works in passing:

Claude Monet's landscapes illuminate, so to speak, the planet's states of consciousness and the extrasensory shapes of our thoughts. And he has no need to vary his themes and change his settings in order

205
Woman with a Parasol, 1886. Oil on canvas, 131 x 88 cm. Musée d'Orsay, Paris [W1077]

to inspire in us a panoply of impressions. A single theme—as in his stunning series of haystacks in winter—is enough to allow him to express the manifold and so various emotions that the drama of the earth undergoes from dawn to nighttime.[73]

The Grainstacks series was an immediate success with collectors; two thirds of the works featured in the 1891 exhibition had already been sold prior to its opening. Curiously, Durand-Ruel's competitors Boussod and Valadon acquired the Hill-Stead painting just prior to its publication in Mirbeau's article; consequently it was not among the fifteen Grainstack canvases shown in May.

Compared with the Belle-Île drawing, Monet's graphic translation of his painting of grainstacks is more tonalist than calligraphic in its syntax. Sharp line plays less of a role in this sheet than soft, shaded forms made by gently rubbing the side of the crayon against the fine-grained paper. Dotted lines, merely flicks of the crayon, surround the principal motifs to enhance the effect of dissolving light and atmosphere. The composition of the drawing was somewhat compromised in its published form; although lightly indicated framing lines delimit the original drawing, the upper and lower registers were cropped out in the gillotage print, compressing the image into an oblong rectangle.

Of the three paintings rendered by Monet for *L'Art dans les deux mondes*, the *Woman with a Parasol* (fig. 205) was the subject of Mirbeau's most extended and imaginative description. In a sense, taking the large-scale canvas of 1886 as a starting point, both men were charged with the same task: translating an Impressionist painting into an entirely different language, a language of black and white, lines of text and lines of black crayon (figs. 206 and 207). Here, across the printed page, Monet's masterful graphic translation literally faces off against Mirbeau's poetic exegesis (fig. 208):

On a sunlit hillside—we see only the summit, the rose-pink earth, the dry grasses—against the sky, against the sweet-toned sky, among the white and rose clouds that race across the azure of the firmament, a woman makes her way, slender, light, imponderable; a gust of wind is in the fluttering chiffon of her veil, the bottom of her dress is raised in back, tossed by the flight of her stride; she seems to skim across the grass. In her modernity, she has the distant grace of a dream, the unexpected charm of an airy apparition. Observe her closely. It is almost as if she will be gone shortly. The parasol she carries, with her arm in a delightful attitude, bathes her face in golden shadow, and blossoms over her like a great flower. No arabesques, nothing but simple, straight, fleeting lines of extraordinary elegance, of truly masterly and surprising purity and sensitivity and breadth of drawing. These are exquisite landscapes, this woman's supple body, and this dress made of an unidentifiable fabric of fused reflections, gentle shadows, and vivid light.[74]

It is in this remarkable juxtaposition of image and text that the act of "collaboration" imagined by Mirbeau came the closest to realization. After the publication of the article, it would be two months before Parisians could see the *Woman with a Parasol* in person, when Monet allowed it to be shown for the first time in Durand-Ruel's May exhibition.

Monet made a fourth drawing for *L'Art dans les deux mondes* that was never published in the form of a gillotage print, probably because the work it reproduced was neither included in the 1891 exhibition nor mentioned anywhere in Mirbeau's text. Alternately titled *The Customs-Officer's Cabin near Pourville*, it was based on his painting *The Fisherman's House, Overcast Weather* (location unknown) of 1882 that was with Durand-Ruel in the early 1890s.[75] The subject, a tiny customs shed perched on the channel coast at Petit Ailly, was one that Monet painted repeatedly; he had presented another version to Mirbeau in 1884.[76] His graphic reprise of the painting further emphasizes tone and texture over line, evoking the soft grasses on the cliff in a manner closer to his drawing of *Grainstacks* and his black-chalk drawings of the 1860s than the nervous energy of his *Woman with a Parasol*, or his work for *La vie moderne* and the *Gazette des beaux-arts*. For all of the angst he expressed to Durand-Ruel, Monet conquered the specialized

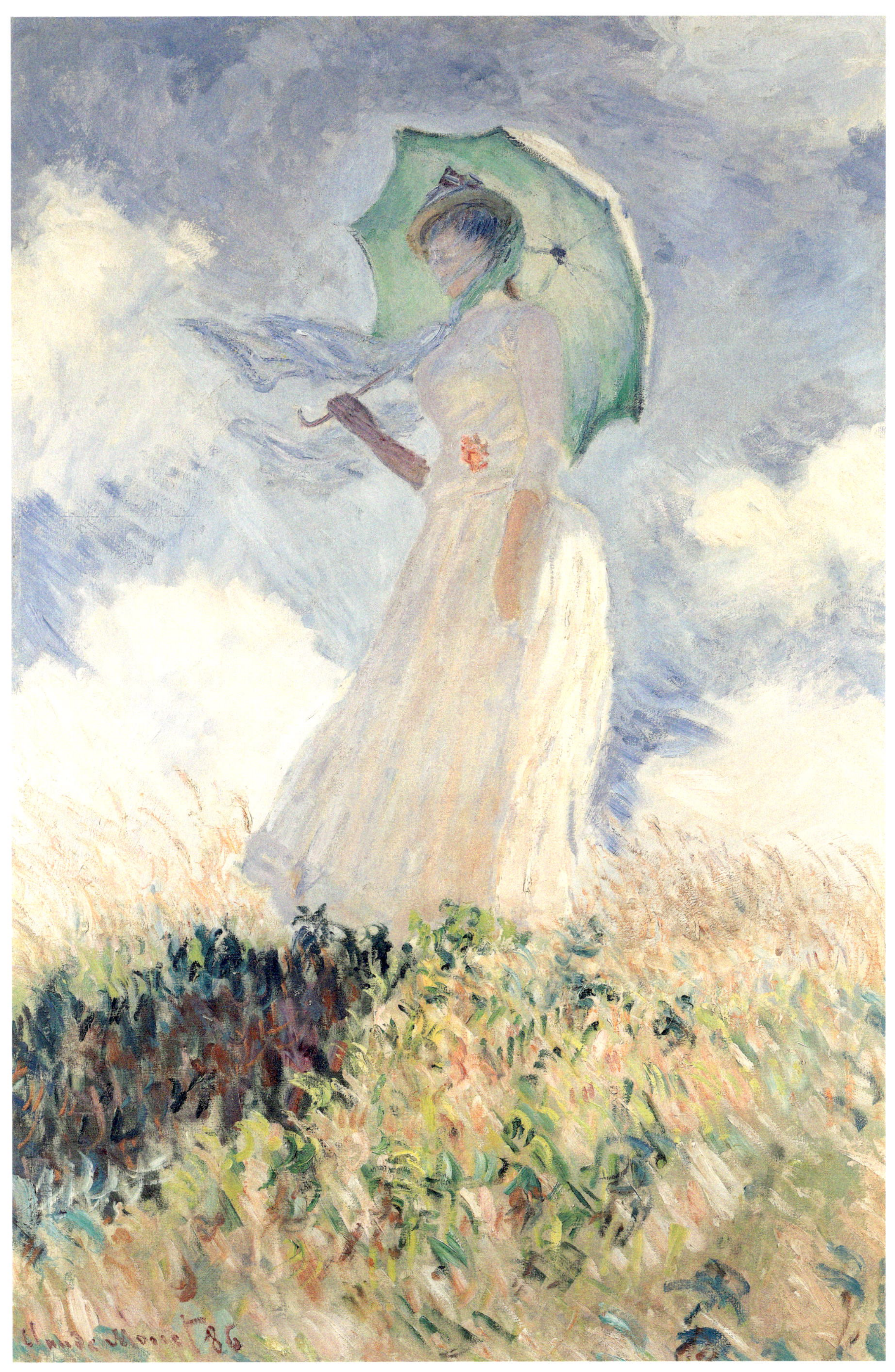

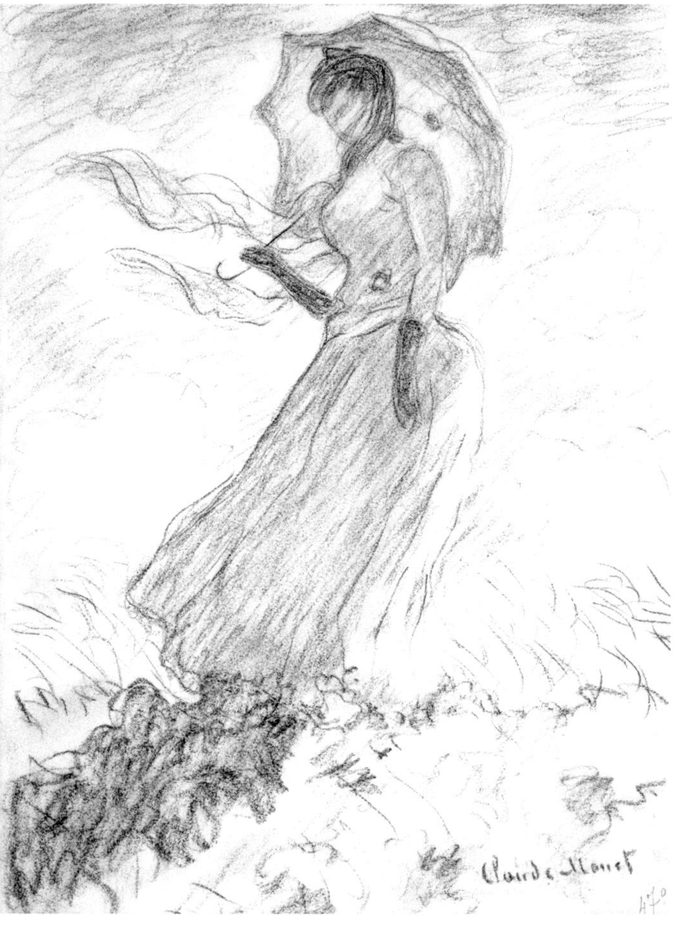

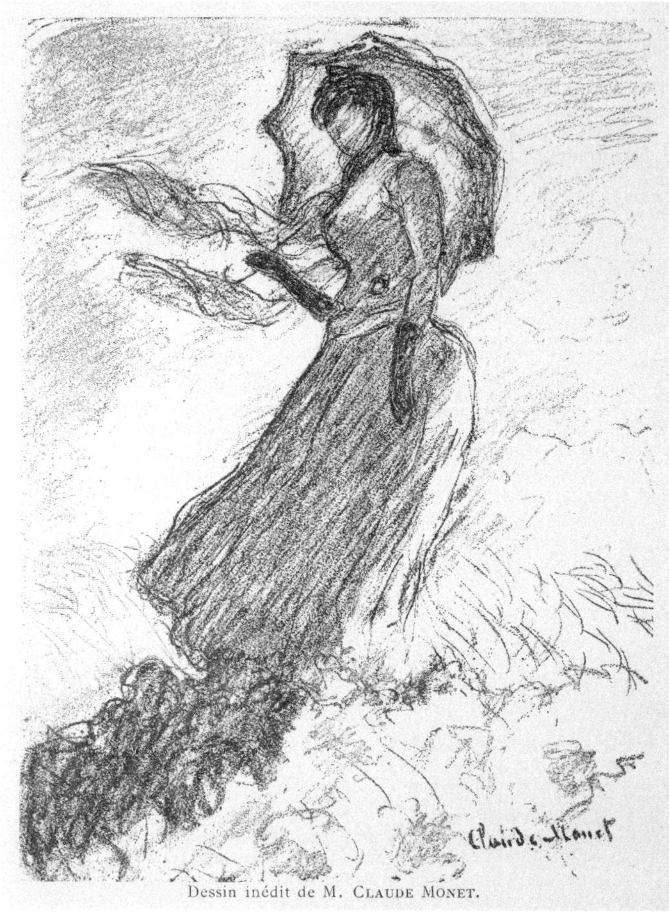

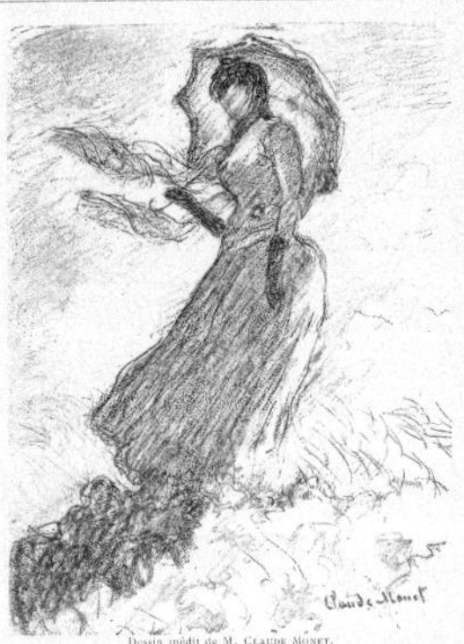

206

Woman with a Parasol, 1891. Black chalk on Gillot paper, 320 x 230 mm. Private collection, Tokyo [D446]

207

After Claude Monet, *Woman with a Parasol*, 1891. Gillotage, 143 x 108 mm. From *L'Art dans les deux mondes* 1 (7 March 1891), p. 184

208

Pages 184–85 of *L'Art dans les deux mondes* 1 (7 March 1891), showing the gillotage after Claude Monet juxtaposed with text by Octave Mirbeau

genre of reproductive illustration, showing himself to be the master of several different modes of drawing within this narrow field.

After the publication of Mirbeau's article, a surprising role reversal took place when Gustave Geffroy asked Monet to intervene on his behalf to procure drawings from James Abbott McNeill Whistler for an article that he was preparing for *L'Art dans les deux mondes*. Monet wrote to Whistler on 2 April:

You must have received a letter from one of Mirbeau's and my best friends who wants to write a study on you in the new journal (L'Art dans les deux mondes) *and who would like to see some drawings by you in order to appear at the same time as the article in said journal. Our friend Geffroy who I believe visited you this winter in London is a man of great talent who admires you, naturally, and who will write a very beautiful article. You can thus be without fear of compromising yourself in sending the drawings that he wants. The journal is in its infancy but it appears to me destined to have a future. I am sending you several issues so you can judge for yourself.*[77]

It seems that Whistler was even less responsive than Monet had been to Durand-Ruel's persistent requests. When Geffroy's article appeared on 27 June, it was illustrated with a photographic image of Whistler's *Portrait of Théodore Duret* (fig. 209) rather than an interpretive drawing by the painter.[78] After reading the study, Monet wrote to its author both to congratulate him and to express his displeasure at the quality of the accompanying illustration:

I want to tell you the pleasure your article on Whistler gave me; the beginning, above all, was delicious. This arrival, this evocation of the Nocturnes *of Whistler, is an exquisite godsend. So accept all of my compliments. But there is one thing that is disastrous, and that is the* Portrait of Duret *and it is most unfortunate that your article already appeared because you would have certainly had a tasty drawing. He has just (Whistler) written me at length on this subject, praying for you to wait so he could send you something very good,*

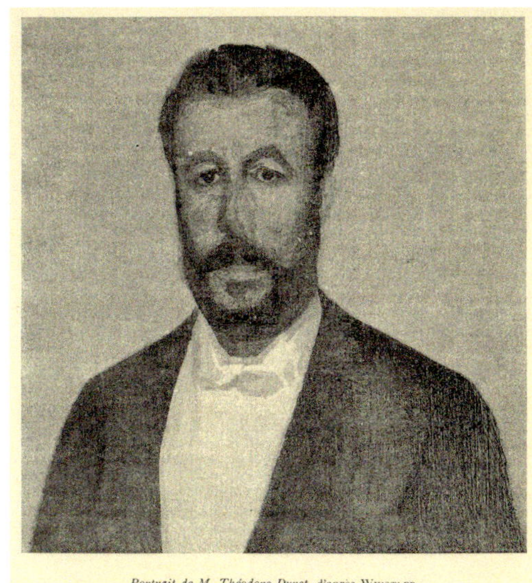
Portrait de M. Théodore Duret, d'après WHISTLER.

209
After James Abbott McNeill Whistler (American, 1834–1903), *Portrait of Théodore Duret*, 1891. Gillotage, 122 x 118 mm. From *L'Art dans les deux mondes* 1 (27 June 1891), p. 63

asking for me to send his apology to you. Eventually I will show you the letter if you don't ever come to Giverny. In short, I am sure, as I know him, he will be sorry and perhaps angry at this terrible reproduction.[79]

In the end, it would appear that despite all of his reluctance, Monet appreciated that qualitative difference between handmade drawings by artists after their own works and images derived from photographs.

Contrary to Monet's promise to Whistler, *L'Art dans les deux mondes* did not have a future. Two months after this exchange, the journal abruptly ceased publication. The final issue, published on 11 July 1891, contained a fuzzy photographic reproduction of Monet's *The Seine at Lavacourt (Vétheuil)* (Fogg Art Museum, Cambridge) from Durand-Ruel's stock (fig. 210).[80] While this form of reproduction captured, to some extent, the artist's brushstrokes, and pointed the way to the future, it produced a less than satisfactory image. On 14 July 1891, Pissarro sent the final issue to Lucien, wryly observing:

You will see from the article "Causserie" *that the review's purpose was to put the Impressionists over, and since this objective has been attained, there is no reason for it to continue. Hum! Hum! Does this mean that it is without funds? You never know what's up with that devil of a Durand. I learned lately, in Paris, that Durand had to take back a*

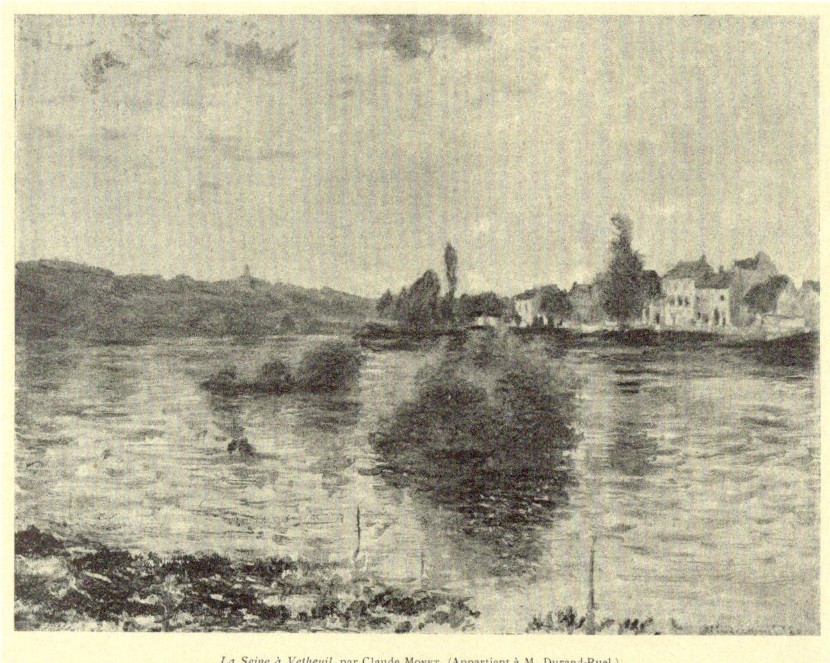

210
After Claude Monet, *The Seine at Vétheuil*, 1891. Gillotage, 143 x 194 mm. From *L'Art dans les deux mondes* 1 (11 July 1891), p. 89

number of paintings sold for a considerable sum to a collector who went bankrupt. Is this the case? Mysterious![81]

In the immediate aftermath of the journal's demise, Charles Durand-Ruel wrote a letter to Monet asking him to request the return of his four drawings from Yveling RamBaud. Monet responded:

It is difficult for me to do what you have asked, considering that I do not have any relationship, so to speak, with the director of L'Art dans les deux mondes. *It was your father who asked me for the drawings, and it was to him that I sent them. The dealer, upon seeing them, only said to me that he would take the four drawings, because, he said, they may be able to appear later on another occasion, and that's all. Therefore, in these circumstances I am not able to send him a personal request, and besides these drawings are of no importance, so it would be better if he gives them to you.*[82]

After Monet effectively disowned the drawings, Durand-Ruel succeeded in retrieving them from RamBaud.

The four drawings that Monet had created with such reluctance for *L'Art dans les deux mondes* became the most frequently reproduced and exhibited of his works on paper during his lifetime. Their relatively high visibility is explained by the Durand-Ruels' generosity in sharing (i.e., marketing) their holdings. The drawings were not filed away in dusty portfolios but were at various times framed and displayed in the family's adjoining apartments on the rue de Rome as part of a collection that was more public than private: visitors were admitted on Tuesday afternoons from two to four.[83] With the passing of time, as the tradition of making copies for reproduction in black and white slowed and then ceased altogether, the status of Monet's drawings as *reprises* of paintings was forgotten. Contributing to the confusion, undoubtedly, was the improvisational quality of line that effectively disguised the drawings' reiterative nature. For instance, in an article published shortly after the artist's death entitled "La Technique de Claude Monet," Jean-Gabriel Goulinat observed:

We never saw (Monet) paint from a drawing as was done by all of his predecessors. Consequently, his drawings are rare, and to tell the truth, if they are evocative of anything, it is the desire to see the canvas that comes out of them. That is the case most especially of the sketch that exists of the Young Woman with a Parasol.[84]

In 1893, Durand-Ruel gave permission for the editors of the new English periodical *The Studio: An Illustrated Magazine of Fine and Applied Art* to republish the line block of Monet's *The Côte Sauvage*, along with some smaller gillotage prints from a study on Boudin's drawings that had also appeared in *L'Art dans les deux mondes*.[85] Occupying a full page, *The Côte Sauvage* was captioned "From a Sketch in Crayon. By Claude Monet" (see fig. 200). The accompanying article made no reference to the fact that the drawing reproduces a painting, but rather implied that it is a typical plein-air sketch by the artist:

In the last number of THE STUDIO *a number of characteristic sketches by English artists were given as illustrations to Mr. Hartley's* Sketching from Nature *and Mr. George Thompson's* Sketch-book in the Street. *Here we are reproducing from* L'Art dans les Deux Mondes *(by the kind permission of Messrs. Durand-Ruel & Co., of Paris) a very typical instance of Claude Monet's black and white work, and a group of sketches by Eugène Boudin.*[86]

The author went on to defend the artist's style against unnamed English critics who accused him of leading painting in the direction of anarchy, concluding, "Monet has not yet conquered either English hearts or English art entirely; yet, on the other hand, to those who love him he represents the last word of modernity in landscape."[87]

Monet's original drawings, rather than the gillotage prints derived from them, were photographed and reproduced in several publications before 1926. *The Côte Sauvage* and *Grainstacks* appeared in Théodore Duret's *Histoire des peintres impressionistes* (1906)[88]; *Woman with a Parasol* was reproduced in Georges Grappe's monograph *Claude Monet* (1909)[89]; and *The Côte Sauvage* accompanied an article by Adolphe Tabarant in *Bulletin de la vie artistique* (1921).[90] All four drawings appeared in *A Giverny, chez Claude Monet* (1924) by Marc Elder (pen name of Marçel Tendron), bound into the text as deluxe facsimiles on faux-Japan paper.[91] While Elder made no specific reference to the drawings in his text, their captions include dates that correspond with the original paintings (for instance, the drawing of the *Customs-Officer's Cabin near Pourville* is dated 1882, and *The Côte Sauvage*, 1886), leading readers to assume that they were studies for, rather than after, the respective canvases.

Durand-Ruel lent the drawings to a Monet exhibition at the Galerie Bernheim-Jeune, Paris, in 1906, the only occasion on which they were shown together.[92] He sent all but the *Woman with a Parasol* to Brussels in 1908 for the great *Salon jubilaire* marking both the twentieth anniversary of the arts festivals organized by the Libre Esthétique and the twenty-fifth anniversary of the founding of the group Les Vingt.[93] *The Côte Sauvage* and *Grainstacks* were shown together again in Belgium at the Salon du Dessin in Liège, 1909.[94] Several of the drawings made a second appearance at the Galerie Bernheim-Jeune in exhibitions of works on paper mounted during the early 1920s.[95]

In 1926, the Japanese collector Lord Hosokawa Moritatsu persuaded Joseph Durand-Ruel to part with two of the drawings, *The Côte Sauvage* and *Grainstacks*. Eventually they entered the collection of the National Museum of Western Art, Tokyo. During a visit to Durand-Ruel's in September 1927, René Gimpel saw the two remaining works and recorded his impressions in his diary. After noting that the artist had a reputation for destroying most of his drawings, he observed:

Some of them have had a miraculous escape, as he had sent them to be reproduced in journals, and for this reason they were all signed. They showed me two: a study for one of the two women with the parasol which Monet's son has just given to the Louvre, the other depicting the top of a cliff. The wind and the movement of the woman with the parasol are caught in it; it is marvelously rendered, although his drawing has the insubstantiality of his painting, save that the outlines are forcefully set off. It is also very graceful.[96]

Woman with a Parasol and *Customs-Officer's Cabin near Pourville* remained with Joseph Durand-Ruel's daughter Marie-Louise until her death in 1991, after which they were sold at auction and disappeared into private collections.[97]

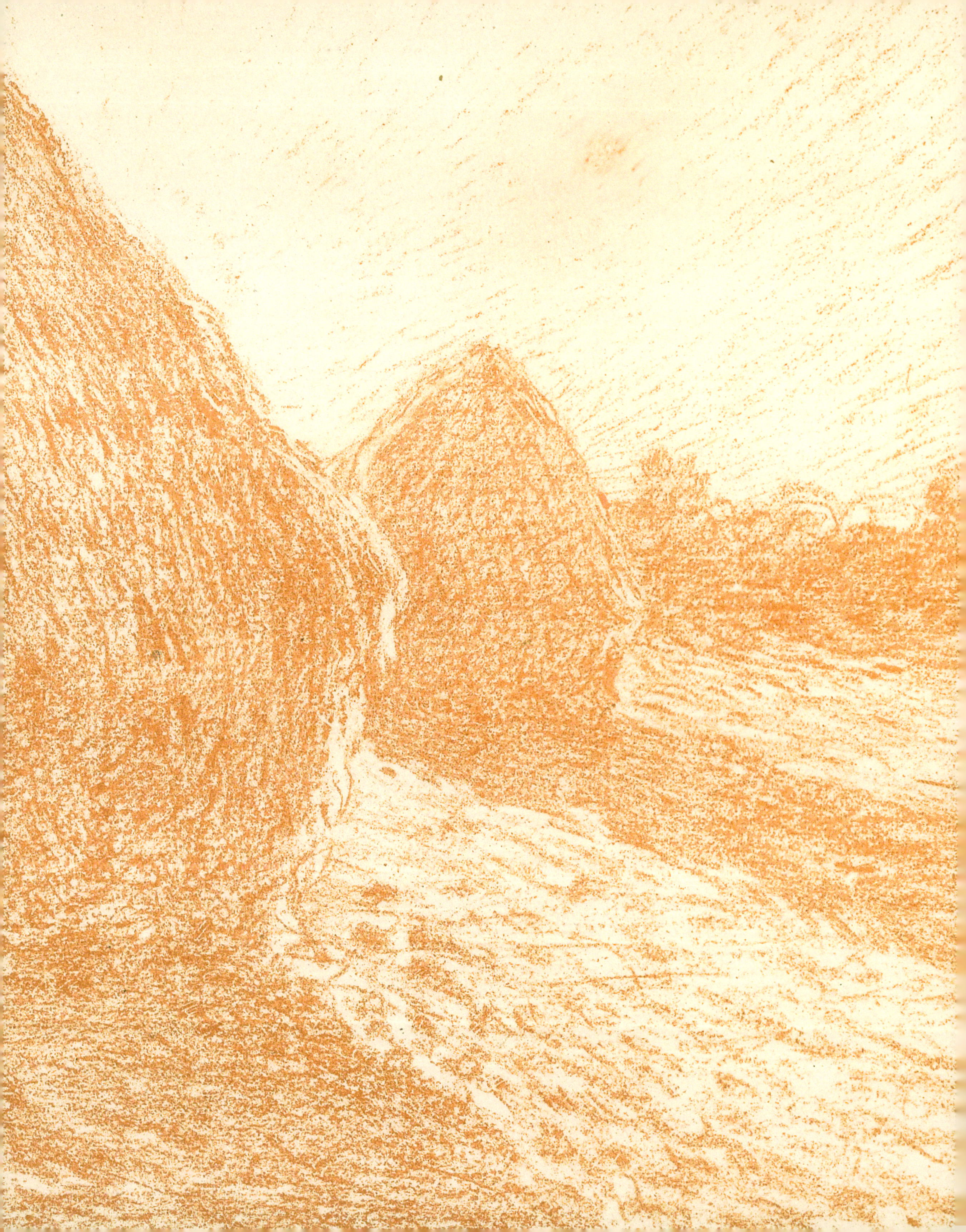

CHAPTER NINE Monet in Print

A clear gauge of Monet's growing reputation was the increasing attention his work received in the international art press from the 1870s onward. In addition to the publication of his own drawings as described in the previous chapter, his paintings began to appear in books and periodicals in the form of professionally rendered reproductive prints. One of the first of these publications was Paul Durand-Ruel's three-volume *Galerie Durand-Ruel, Recueil d'estampes gravées à l'eau-forte* (Paris, 1873), with an introduction by Armand Silvestre, which contained four black-and-white etchings after Monet's recent paintings by Léon Gaucherel (1816–1886), Henri-Émile Lefort (b. 1852), and François Flameng (1856–1923; fig. 211).[1] Georges Lecomte's *L'Art impressioniste d'après la collection privée de M. Durand-Ruel* (Paris, 1892) included eight etchings by Auguste Lauzet (1865–1898) after paintings by Monet dating from the 1880s.[2] Several of Lauzet's plates were printed in toned inks, including the *Rocks of Belle-Île,* which appeared in brown (fig. 212), and *Grainstacks at the End of Summer (Meules à Giverny)*, which was sepia-toned (fig. 213). After 1900, Monet's paintings were etched by two of the last members of the dying breed of printmakers to specialize in this genre, Gustave Greux (1838–1919) and Charles Waltner (1846–1925), both working for the *Gazette des beaux-arts* in 1904 (fig. 214).[3]

As opposed to the cold precision of engraving, etching was appreciated for its painterly qualities, with some critics going so far as to claim for it the ability to evoke a full palette of colors in black and white. Yet if one were to summarize the interpretive strategies in processing Monet's paintings taken by etchers like Flameng, Lauzet, and Waltner, they would be mainly concerned with communicating form over facture. While they eschewed the rigid graphic syntaxes of their colleagues in the fields of metal- and wood-engraving, these reproductive etchers also put down dense patterns of dots and dashes and spun intricate, though irregular, webs of tight crosshatching to evoke tone and texture. Seen up close, the great variety of marks they created with their etching needles and other tools is fully apparent; from a distance, the fine work tends to coalesce into more mechanical overall images.

Thanks in part to the enthusiasm of the young American artist Theodore Robinson (1852–1896), several of Monet's paintings appeared in the form of reproductive wood engravings in the American popular press during the early 1890s.

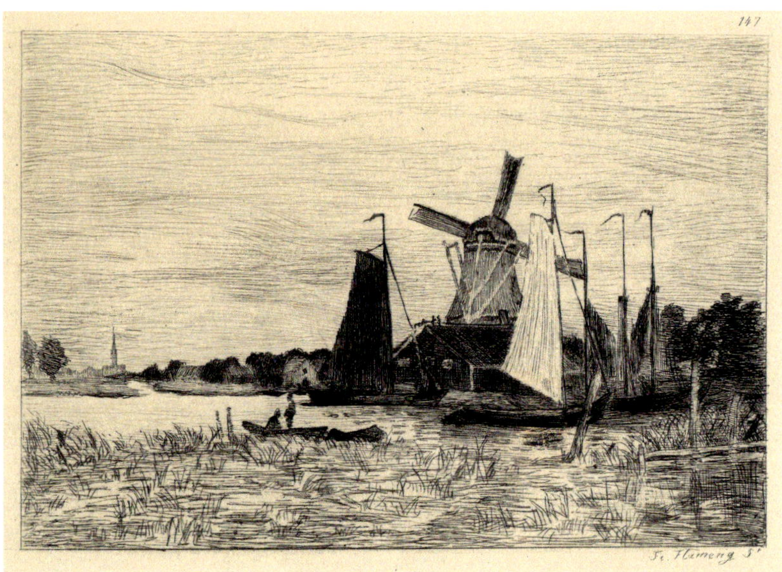

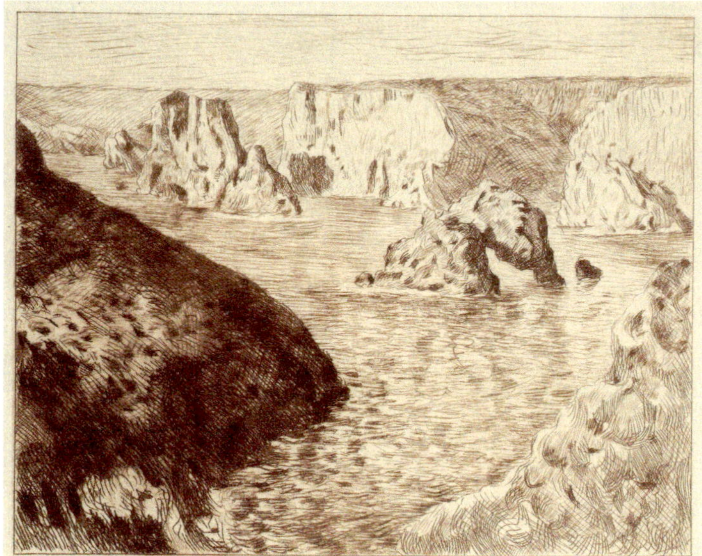

211
François Flameng (French, 1856–1923), after Claude Monet, *Windmills in Holland*, 1873. Etching, 90 x 134 mm. From *Galerie Durand-Ruel* 3 (1873), no. 147

212
Auguste Lauzet (French, 1865–1898), after Claude Monet, *Rocks of Belle-Île*, 1892. Etching printed in brown, 106 x 135 mm. From Georges Lecomte, *L'art Impressioniste* (Paris: Chamerot et Renouard, 1892), p. 103

213
Auguste Lauzet, after Claude Monet, *Grainstacks at the End of Summer*, 1892. Etching printed in sepia, 83 x 129 mm. From Georges Lecomte, *L'art Impressioniste* (Paris: Chamerot et Renouard, 1892), p. 249

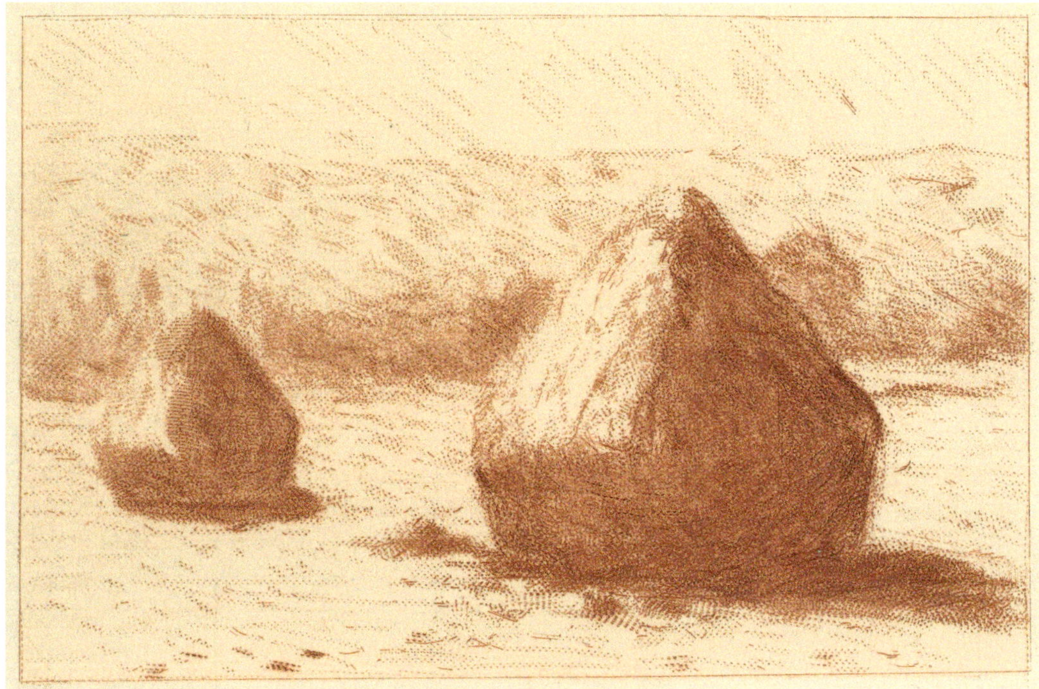

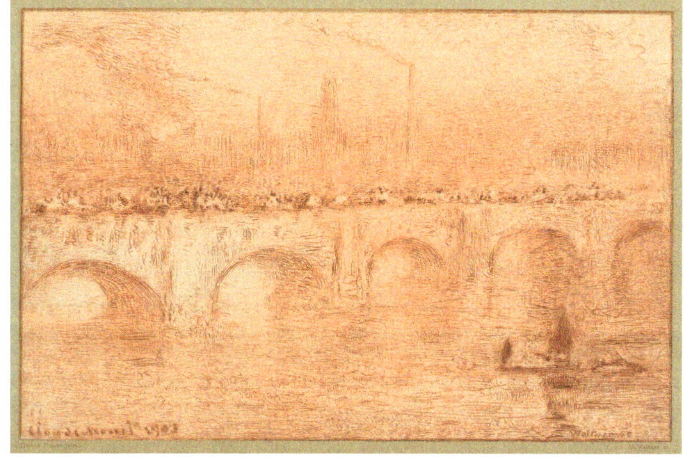

214
Charles Waltner (French, 1846–1925), after Claude Monet, *Waterloo Bridge*, 1904. Etching printed in sepia, 140 x 218 mm. From *Gazette des beaux-arts* 32 (1 July 1904), pp. 86–87

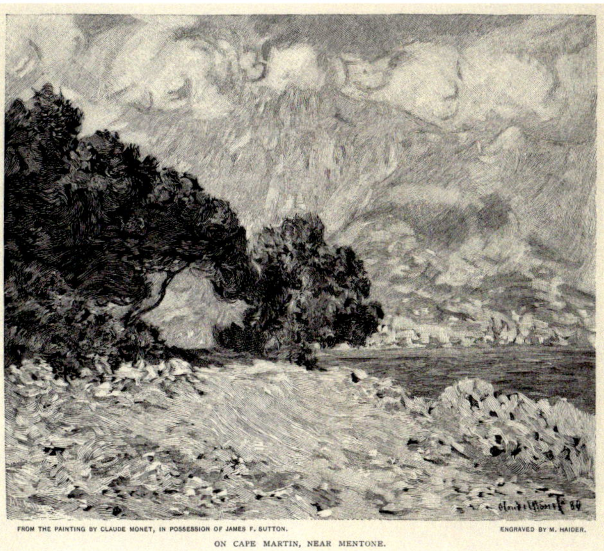

215
M. Haider, after Claude Monet, *On Cape Martin, Near Mentone*, 1892. Wood engraving, 106 x 128 mm. From *The Century* 44 (Sept. 1892), p. 700

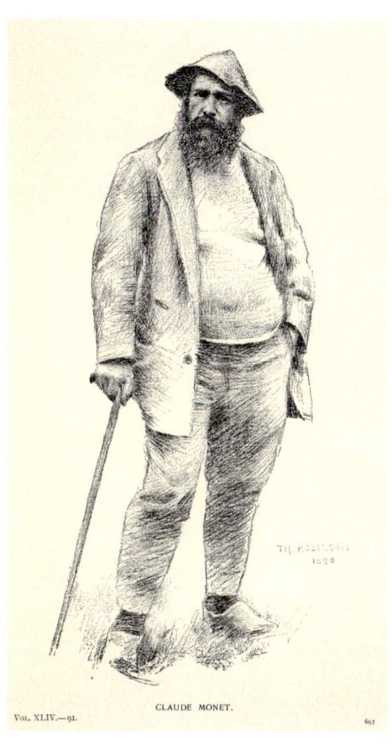

216
After Theodore Robinson (American, 1852–1896), *Portrait of Claude Monet*, 1892. Gillotage, 241 x 166 mm. From *The Century* 44 (Sept. 1892), p. 697

Robinson had trained at the Chicago Academy of Design and the National Academy of Design prior to enrolling at the École des Beaux-Arts in the 1870s. He became a committed Francophile, spending significant periods of time in Paris and traveling around the French countryside in the company of other American painters. During a stay in Giverny in the 1880s he made the acquaintance of Monet and became a frequent visitor and correspondent until his untimely death in 1896.

In 1890 Robinson began writing an article on Monet that would eventually be published in the September 1892 issue of *The Century*, one of the earliest extended pieces of writing devoted to the French painter to appear in the American press.[4] In 1886 Durand-Ruel had staged a successful exhibition of Impressionist paintings at the American Art Association in New York, and during the early 1890s solo exhibitions of Monet's work took place at New York's Union League Club and the Saint Botolph Club in Boston. A week before the Boston opening, Robinson wrote to Monet in March 1892 to report on the growing interest in his paintings and "a great desire to learn" about his art among the American public.[5] Without going into detail concerning the text, he took pains to describe the illustration program for his forthcoming article, which would include two wood engravings and one photomechanical reproduction after canvases belonging to American collectors James F. Sutton and William H. Fuller.[6] Given his intimate knowledge of Monet's likes and dislikes, and wanting to remain on favorable terms, Robinson sensed that the quality of the reproductions would be Monet's primary concern.

When the article at last appeared, Robinson wrote in his diary, "It is a disappointment *quant aux illustrations*, and they have not used one of Monet's sketches—much to my disgust."[7] The meaning of this note is not clear, as there are no other references in Robinson's papers to his requesting drawings from Monet for reproduction in his article. Upon presenting the publication to Monet, Robinson noted that he "thanked me for my article (*Century*) and was civil about the illustrations—liked best perhaps the 'near Mentone,'" a wood engraving by M. Haider after a canvas in Sutton's collection now in the Museum of Fine Arts, Boston (fig. 215).[8] He added that Monet found his portrait drawing (fig. 216), based on a photograph Robinson had taken during a visit to Giverny around 1888–90 (see fig. 2), "not bad."[9]

Robinson contributed to a second short item on Monet for the January 1896 issue of *Scribner's Magazine*.[10] The previous March, Robinson had previewed an auction at the American Art Association that featured, among other works, Monet's *View of Rouen* of 1872 (see fig. 188) from Sutton's collection. At the sale in late April, the painting brought $2,500 and entered the collection of Mr. and Mrs. Henry O. Havemeyer. *Scribner's* art editor August Jaccacci subsequently commissioned Walter Monteith Aikman (1857–1939) to produce a wood engraving after the painting (see fig. 191) and invited Robinson to write a description of it for his January column, "The Field of Art."[11] Robinson's uncredited contribution gushes:

In the "View of Rouen," with what directness and justness of vision has a chef-d'oeuvre been created! Everything moves and vibrates in the delicious summer air, the little boats rock gently at anchor, the tall poplars nod, and clouds sail across the luminous sky. One likes his work of this period for its youth and gayety; never has landscape painting, unhampered by non-essentials, spoken so directly to the heart of the charm of nature and the joy of living.

In February, less than two months before suffering a fatal asthma attack, Robinson sent his last known letter to Monet. With it he enclosed the January issue of *Scribner's*. "M. Jaccaci who is in charge of art affairs at *Scribner's Magazine* went to much trouble for the engraving," Robinson wrote, "and it seems to me it isn't too bad although it is almost impossible to convey the charm of such a painting with wood engraving."[12] Compared with Monet's vigorous reinterpretation of the canvas for the *Gazette des beaux-arts*, Aikman's print for *Scribner's* is both technically polished and lifeless. Monet's reactions to the article and the print are unrecorded.

The Thornley-Monet Portfolio

In 1894, J. Mancini, a recently established picture dealer who had set up shop in the heart of the Paris gallery district, entered into an agreement to publish a limited-edition portfolio of lithographs after paintings by Claude Monet. Each impression bore Monet's signature in pencil, as well as the autograph of a less famous, though equally entrepreneurial artist, the painter-lithographer William Thornley (1857–1935). The album *20 Lithographies d'après Claude Monet* (20 Lithographs after Claude Monet) represents one of the most inadequately documented and misunderstood collaborative projects of Monet's career.[13] The very obscurity of this collection of prints is extraordinary, for by the time of its appearance, Monet had crossed a threshold of public visibility that would only continue to increase into his old age and beyond. By the 1890s he was at last earning a reliable and respectable income from sales of his paintings and with each new gallery exhibition solidifying his reputation in the eyes of international critics and amateurs as one of the foremost living artists. Although it did not relate directly to any of his one-man exhibitions of this busy era, the portfolio was itself a mini-retrospective in print form, offering a concise survey of Monet's paintings of the previous fifteen years and featuring a number of works that would not be otherwise made public during his lifetime.

The publication of the Thornley-Monet portfolio coincided with an unprecedented surge in the practice, promotion, and appreciation of lithography, both in the industrial-commercial sphere, as well as in the fine art market. Put simply, the 1890s in Paris was *the* decade of the original color lithograph, and virtually every leading artist participated in some fashion in this contemporary printmaking movement. Certain artists, like Degas, Pissarro, and Toulouse-Lautrec, took up lithography with great enthusiasm, while others, like Cézanne, Rodin, and Sisley, approached the medium only tentatively, through the vigorous intervention of dealers and professional lithographic printers.

In terms of his personal experience with lithography, Monet remained a holdout, one of a tiny faction of vanguard painters who shunned hands-on lithographic production altogether. He declined an invitation to produce a lithograph for André Marty's print series *L'Estampe originale* (1893–95).[14] In December 1898, when he was invited by the Société libre des gens des lettres to contribute to a group album of lithographs with a preface by Octave Mirbeau entitled *Hommage des artistes à Picquart*, he replied, "I regret terribly that I am not able to respond according to your wishes, for despite my great admiration for Colonel Picquart, I have never made a lithograph and so I am incapable of producing anything that would be the least bit appropriate for the Album you are planning."[15] Few painters of Monet's generation could have made this blunt admission, as the medium of lithography had become so tightly woven into the fabric of French artistic life of the 1890s.

Another more persistent request came from Gustave Geffroy as he was in the process of completing the eighth and final volume of *La vie artistique* (1892–1903), an anthology of his art criticism. The frontispieces of each of the previous installments consisted of etchings, drypoints, and lithographs by the artists most admired by Geffroy, including Renoir, Rodin, Pissarro, and Fantin-Latour. At last, in April

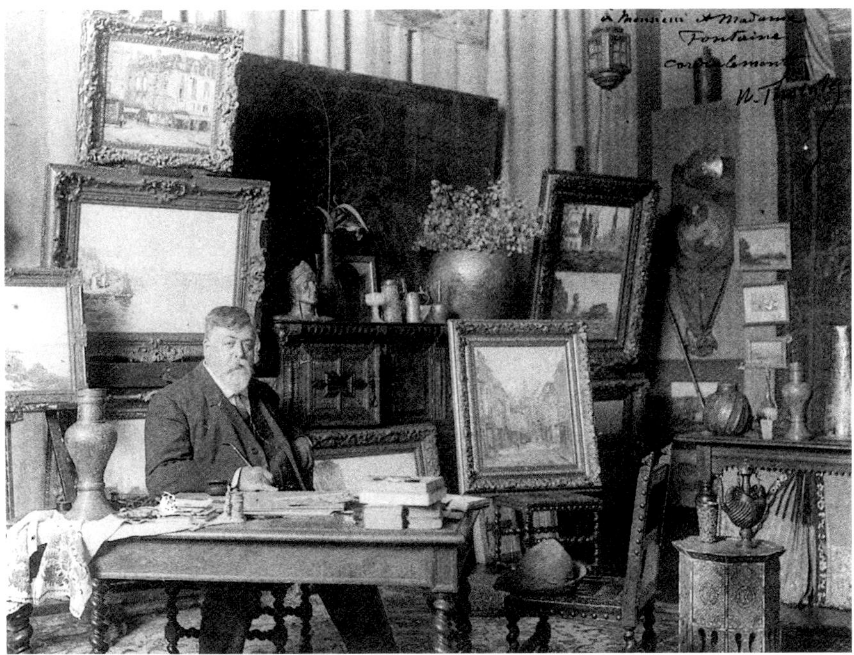

217
William Thornley in his studio at Osny, c. 1900

1903 the author asked Monet to contribute a lithograph, and to facilitate the task, he dispatched several small stones and lithographic crayons.[16] In response, Monet made the usual excuses, months passed, and as the publication deadline approached in August, Geffroy continued his assault. Monet spoke of his uneasiness with the medium and threatened to throw the stones and crayons "to the devil."[17] Geffroy wrote, "You're wrong to be afraid of this. You could draw (like your drawings!) some undulating coastlines, or the portal of Rouen Cathedral, or something else."[18] The appeal was unsuccessful; on 1 September 1903 Monet returned the materials to Geffroy's publisher, and at the last minute a lithograph by Adolphe Willette was substituted for the frontispiece.[19]

As an album devoted exclusively to the work of Claude Monet, the Thornley portfolio was obviously more selective in scope than the "gallery" publications of Durand-Ruel. It also differed from those earlier productions in that it was conceived with the artist's blessing and participation. In a sense, the portfolio represented another turning point in the public image of Monet the draftsman. Having personally entrusted the task of reproducing his paintings to a professional painter-lithographer, he would never again consent to make drawings after his own canvases. A number of mysteries surround the Thornley-Monet portfolio, including the circumstances of its production and the nature of the collaboration between lithographer and painter. Before turning attention to the prints themselves, it is necessary to introduce several shadowy individuals, each of whom had a hand in the portfolio's creation.

The Lithographer William Thornley

Painter-lithographer William Thornley (fig. 217) played a unique role in the annals of Post-Impressionism. Born George William Thornley Thistlewood in Val-de-Marne to an English father and French mother, he first learned drawing and watercolor painting from his father Julian Thornley Thistlewood (born c. 1808), an amateur who seems not to have exhibited his work.[20] He later studied painting and lithography under Achille Sirouy (1834–1904), Eugène Ciceri (1813–1890), and Edmond Yon (1836–1897).[21] Thornley showed his first watercolor in the Salon of 1878, his first lithograph (after Diego Velázquez) in the Salon of 1879, and his first oil painting in the Salon of 1880. Early in his career he achieved his greatest commercial and critical successes as a reproductive lithographer, starting with a series of twenty-five color lithographs after François Boucher printed by Joseph Lemercier in 1881. He exhibited lithographs after Camille Corot and Constant Dutilleux in the Salon of 1880, and after Pierre Puvis de Chavannes throughout the 1880s.

Thornley's reproductive lithographs came to the attention of Theo van Gogh, director of the Boussod and Valadon Gallery. It was Theo who bestowed on him a momentous print commission: a portfolio of fifteen lithographs after paintings and pastels by Edgar Degas (fig. 218).[22] Several of the prints were exhibited at Boussod and Valadon in April and September 1888, while the series was still incomplete. On both occasions Thornley's lithographs were reviewed by the avant-garde critic Félix Fénéon, who admired them as evocative "equivalences" rather than dry facsimiles:

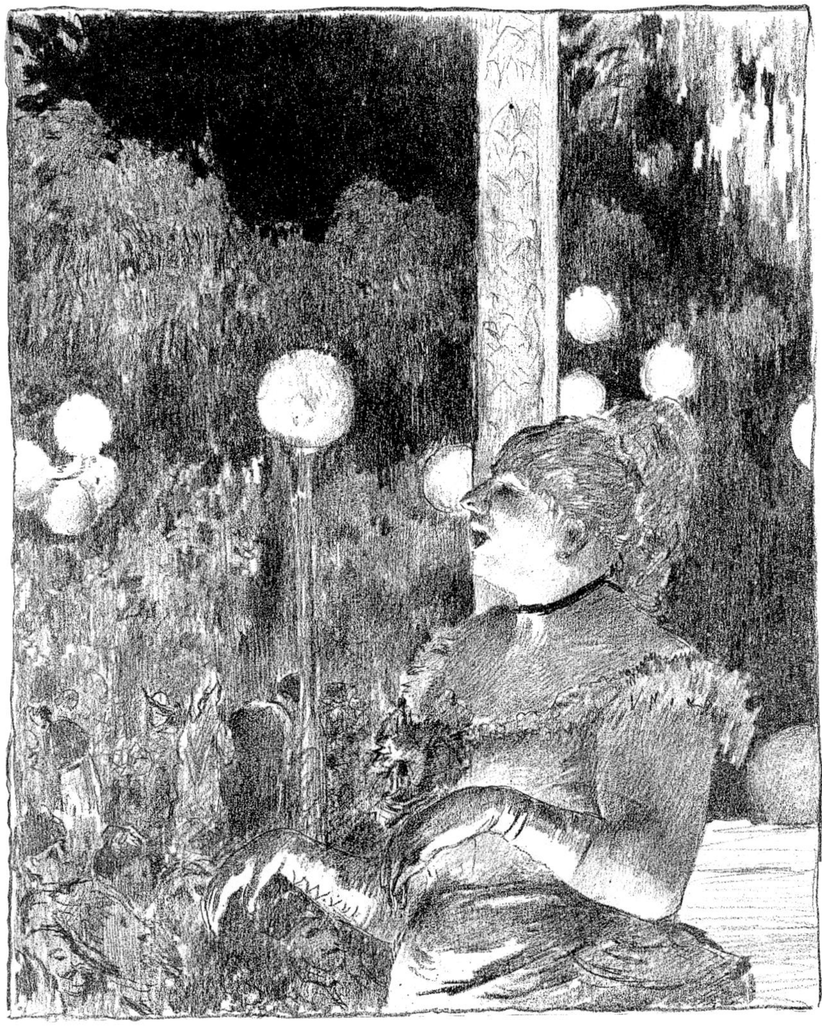

218
William Thornley, after Edgar Degas, *The Song of the Dog: Thérèse Valdon*, 1889. Transfer lithograph on chine appliqué mounted on blue paper, 240 x 200 mm. Musée Goupil, Bordeaux. Gift of the Societé des amis des musées de Bordeaux, 1996

Here [Thornley] demonstrates a sagacity that is truly disconcerting: it is Mr. Degas's very spirit, at its most intimate, that he has imprinted on these plates. In order to achieve this secondary reality, he has freely treated his text, and has found remarkable equivalences when it would have been a disservice to translate the idiom of painting too literally.[23]

Thornley's achievement was undoubtedly facilitated by Degas's direct involvement in the project. An experimental lithographer in his own right, he paid close attention to Thornley's progress and did not hesitate to stop the presses when he saw something that displeased him. A congenial letter from Degas to the newlywed printmaker on 28 April 1888 documents one such occasion and sheds light on their working relationship:

Before persecuting you about the stones, I shall congratulate you on your marriage, here you are a happy boy. Moreover you were proceeding at such a pace that one could not help suspecting something as important. A few days after your flight they brought me two proofs from [the printer] Bécquet (women trying on hats). I told them to stop the printing and warned them that I would go to the printing office. It was impossible for me to go there, or to return to Rouart [who owned the pastel being reproduced] with your drawing on transfer paper. I wanted to make a few alterations on the drawing; and I hardly regret not having made them as you were not there. I shall return to Paris about 15 September and we shall finish with all that. You were in too much of a rush, my dear Mr. Thornley. Art requires more leisure than that. But I now see the reason for your impatience.[24]

The task was not to be completed until February 1889, when Boussod and Valadon began offering the portfolio in a regular edition of one hundred impressions with a printed signature of Thornley (at a price of 100 francs), and twenty-five impressions signed in pencil by both Thornley and Degas.

Thornley's collaboration with Pissarro on a similar portfolio in the late 1890s is better documented than his relationship with either Degas or Monet, and helps establish his working method in carrying out projects of this kind (fig. 219). The first mention of this undertaking is found in a letter from Pissarro to his son Lucien dated 14 April 1898, in which he reported that he had been approached by the "dessinateur lithographe" who had reproduced works by Degas and Monet to ask permission to make a similar album of twenty-five prints based on his painted views of Paris and Rouen. Thornley proposed an edition of one-hundred impressions with a deluxe portfolio cover.[25] It is evident from Pissarro's correspondence that the project's sole mastermind was the lithographer. Indeed, it was Thornley who took the initiative of approaching Pissarro even before he had secured the backing of a publisher or the services of a printer. Pissarro informed Lucien that Thornley wanted to complete the prints before

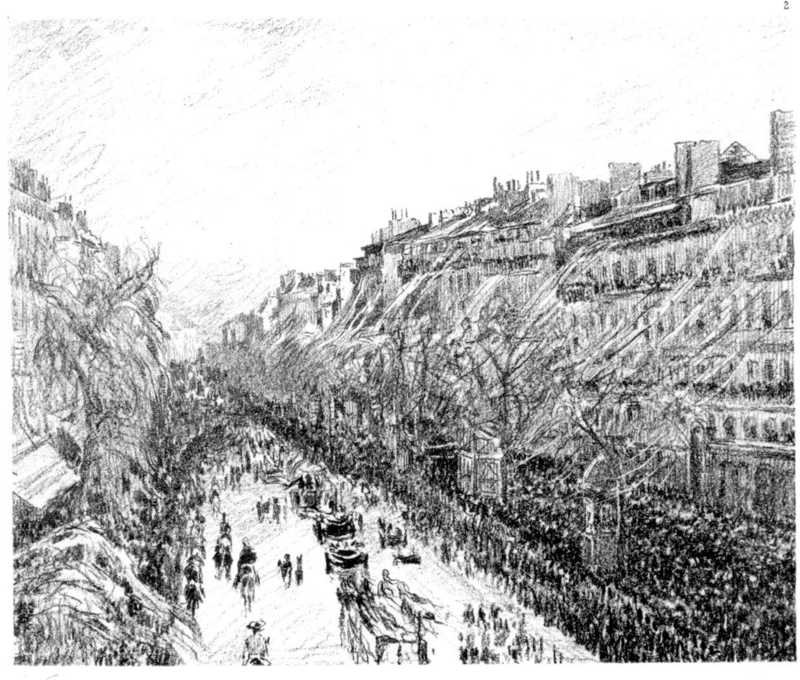

219
William Thornley, after Camille Pissarro, *Shrove Tuesday on the Boulevards*, 1900. Transfer lithograph with scraping printed in brownish-black on off-white chine appliqué, 197 x 248 mm. Collection of Dr. Morton and Tobia Mower

speaking to potential distributors.[26] At first, Pissarro questioned the suitability of lithography for the print album and proposed that Octave Mirbeau be engaged to write an introductory text; eventually Gustave Geffroy would accept the commission.[27]

The project was not mentioned again in Pissarro's correspondence until late October 1899, when he wrote to Lucien:

There will soon appear a series of portfolios [sic] *with lithographs by an artist of great talent after my principal paintings; it is Mr. Thornley who is going to execute this work, the one who reproduced a series after Degas and one after Monet. If the occasion arises to place it in London, we will have to give it some thought at the appropriate time. You can well imagine that I am a tad interested. Does [Elbert Jan] Van Wisselingh [1848–1912] handle these types of publications?*[28]

Lucien responded that upon the appearance of the lithographs he would contact Van Wisselingh, the Dutch art dealer and printseller who operated a gallery in Hanover Square, but asked his father to clarify who was actually publishing the album.[29] Pissarro reported Thornley's intention to self-publish the prints, since for the time being he was without a publisher.[30] In the end, he entered into an agreement with a print dealer on the rue Laffitte named Charles Hessèle to sell the lithographs and arrange for their distribution in London, yet the title page gave no indication of a printer or publisher.[31] The project was delayed until June 1900 because of Geffroy's tardiness in writing the preface, "Hommage à Camille Pissarro."[32]

With the impending release of the Pissarro album, Thornley lost no time in attempting to line up a new job. He next set his sights on Pierre-Auguste Renoir, who was at first receptive to the proposition. Renoir wrote to Durand-Ruel from Grasse on 3 April 1900 to inform him of the offer:

Mr. Thornley must come to see you in order to have some paintings of mine to reproduce in lithography as he has done for Degas, Monet, etc. He asked me if I wanted it done, and I told him yes, for what else could I do? But I would like you to kindly tell him to await my return before proceeding on the work. I want to discuss it with you beforehand.[33]

Renoir returned to Paris in May, but any subsequent communications on the matter with Durand-Ruel and Thornley are undocumented. He must have thought better of the arrangement, as nothing came of the proposed Renoir-Thornley portfolio. A few years later Ambroise Vollard convinced Renoir to produce a portfolio of a dozen original transfer lithographs that remained unpublished until the artist's death in 1919.[34]

Pissarro's correspondence reveals that Thornley experienced a financial crisis around 1901. It was then that Pissarro wrote a letter of introduction on his behalf to the Bernheim brothers, encouraging them to consider buying his colleague's paintings. Pissarro also extended him a number of loans totaling 6,400 francs that Thornley was unable to repay. Janine Bailly-Herzberg has suggested that Pissarro's initial generosity grew out of a sense of responsibility for the presumed failure of the Thornley-

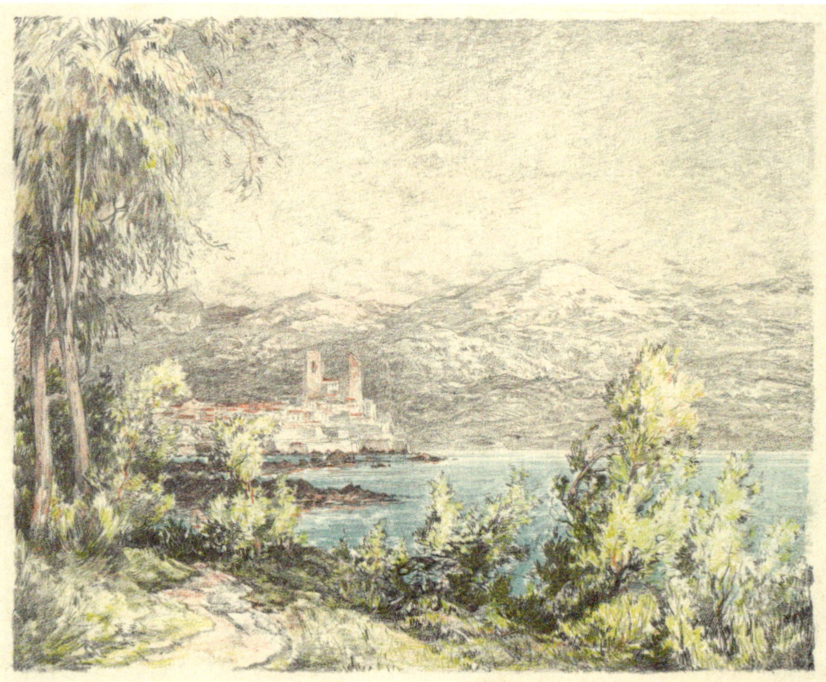

220

William Thornley, *Antibes*, c. 1890s. Transfer lithograph with scraping printed in gray, blue, green, and orange, 275 x 348 mm. Private collection

Pissarro portfolio to recoup its costs.[35] In fact, the financial agreement between the two men over the portfolio, and its ultimate success or failure in the marketplace, are both undocumented. In the end, Pissarro was forced to bring a lawsuit against his former collaborator, which was finally decided in 1903 by an order requiring Thornley to settle the debt in regular payments to Pissarro and his heirs over the course of the next seven years.[36]

At this time Thornley had been living for over a decade in Osny, a small village near Pontoise where Pissarro had resided in the early 1880s. Osny would serve as Thornley's home base until his death in 1935. While he stopped exhibiting at the Salon after 1889, he showed his works in a number of other venues, including the salons of the Société Nationale des Beaux-Arts (where he was *hors concours*), the Société des Beaux-Arts in Antibes (of which he was the founder and president), and Georges Petit's gallery. He also opened his Osny studio to the public on Thursdays, Sundays, and holidays from 2 to 6 P.M. during the summer months.[37] In a short review of his June 1899 exhibition of paintings and watercolors at Georges Petit's gallery, Gustave Geffroy noted that the artist who had made his debut as a reproductive lithographer after Boucher, Puvis de Chavannes, Degas, and Monet had now become a painter, and that "many of his landscapes were conceived in the manner of Monet. The influence is above all visible when Monsieur Thornley tackles views of the cliffs and waves of Varengeville [where he owned property], Dieppe, or the rocks of Antibes melting in the light"[38] (fig. 220; see also fig. 230). Like Monet, he was an incessant traveler, always on the lookout for fresh marine and landscape motifs. His paintings, watercolors, and lithographs document his extensive journeys around France, Italy, Belgium, Holland, and Norway. Until the end of his life, he continued to paint in what had become a *retardataire* style rooted in modes of representation that were no longer at the cutting edge even when he took them up in the 1890s.

The Printer Henry Belfond

The lithographic printer Henry Belfond was named by André Mellerio as one of the top professionals in his field in his famous essay of 1898, "La lithographie originale en couleurs," although he described him as a specialist in black and white.[39] Belfond started out as a trial proofer in the large firm of Lemercier. By 1890 he set up his own printing establishment in the rue Gaillon off the avenue de l'Opéra, and there he catered to such artists as Jean-Louis Forain, Alexandre Lunois, Charles Dulac, and Adolphe Willette. James Abbott McNeill Whistler worked closely with him on a proposed album of color lithographs entitled *Songs on Stone* between 1891 and 1893 (fig. 221). At first the American expatriate was enamored with the French printer, but in November 1893 Whistler severed ties with Belfond upon discovering that he had sold a dedicated proof the artist had presented to him. Whistler wrote to his former printer Thomas R. Way to complain, "In Paris as I make out there is only one man who prints with intelligence and feeling—and I have just discovered that he is not to be trusted!"[40] That Belfond's business had closed within the year is attested by another letter from Whistler to Way

221
James Abbott McNeill Whistler, *Draped Figure, Standing*, 1891. Lithograph printed in red-orange, pale ocher, orange-brown, and peach, 280 x 170 mm. Sterling and Francine Clark Art Institute, Williamstown, Massachusetts

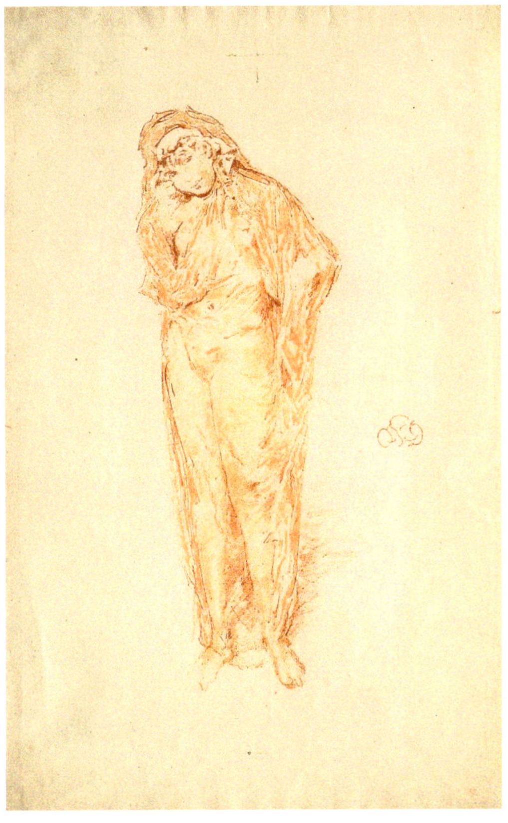

dated 2 November 1894 in which he reported, "I will attend to what you asked about the odd proofs printed in Paris—but it is not easy, as the firm in question has broken up, and gone to the dogs!!!"[41] After closing his own shop, Belfond offered his services to several other Parisian firms, including those of F. Dupont, Eugène Marx, and Engelmann.[42]

The Publisher J. Mancini

By far the most elusive personality connected with the Thornley-Monet portfolio was its publisher, J. Mancini. Even his forename remains a mystery. Fortunately, the expatriate American print collector and art agent George A. Lucas (1824–1909) frequented his shop and annotated his address book; thanks to him we know that Mancini was the nephew of Adolphe Beugniet (active 1848–93), a well-established frame and picture dealer who operated a gallery at 10 rue Laffitte.[43] Beugniet sold modern paintings by Delacroix and members of the Barbizon School and was seen as a potential alternative to Durand-Ruel by Degas and Pissarro; "that devil Beugniet," Pissarro wrote, "only has one eye, but the good one is terribly clairvoyant."[44]

Mancini's gallery was initially located one block away from Beugniet's at 47 rue Taitbout, a street running parallel to the rue Laffitte that like its neighbor was home to a number of art galleries. In fact, 47 rue Taitbout had been for many years the address of Hector Brame, senior, the founder of a long dynasty of dealers.[45] Brame opened his gallery at this location in 1864, but by 1891 he had moved down to number 36; his son relocated the business to the rue Laffitte in 1892.[46]

Mancini appears to have inaugurated his gallery in 1894. In the previous year Beugniet retired and handed over his own business to his son, Georges-Albert-Félix. Assuming that Mancini was also in Beugniet's employment, we might expect to find him strike out on his own shortly after his cousin took over the family business, keeping in mind that it would have taken Mancini additional time to establish a new gallery. The Paris *Annuaire-Almanach du Commerce Didot-Bottin* first listed "Mancini (J.) tableaux" at 47 rue Taitbout in 1894. George Lucas recorded his first visit to the gallery in the company of the print collector Samuel Avery on 22 May of that year.[47] He continued to frequent Mancini's until April 1899.

Mancini remained active as a paintings dealer throughout the first two decades of the twentieth century. He bought and sold works by the modern French school, including Delacroix, Boudin, Degas, Pissarro, Lautrec, Gauguin, Vuillard, and Matisse. In 1905 he moved from the rue Taitbout to 45 rue de l'Opéra, and in 1909 he was listed at 63 boulevard Haussmann.[48] At this point he revised his entry in the Parisian business directory to read "*expert en tableux*." Interestingly, of Mancini's documented clients, several were Argentine, including Dr. Eduardo Mollard, whose important collection later entered the Musée d'Orsay. In the early 1920s Mancini's activity in the sales rooms appears to have come to a halt. There is a possibility that he retired at that time and spent his final years in Buenos Aires.[49]

222

Portfolio cover of *20 Lithographs after Claude Monet*, c. 1894. Bibliothèque de l'Institut National de l'Histoire de l'Art, Paris. Collections Jacques Doucet

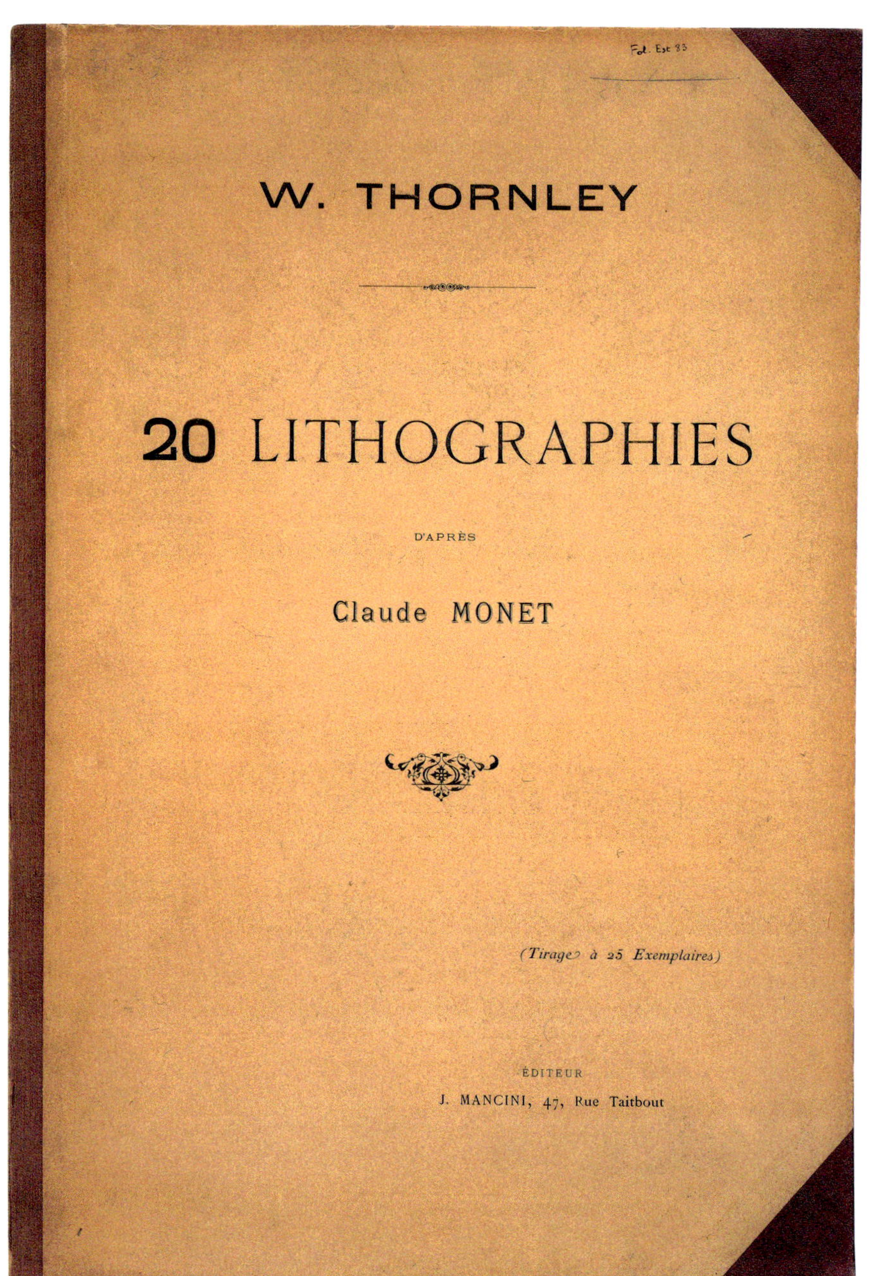

Dating the Portfolio

Previous attempts to assign a date of publication to the Thornley-Monet portfolio (fig. 222) have been contradictory, suggesting a range of possibilities from 1890 to 1906.[50] The earliest published reference to the album occurs in the final volume of Henri Béraldi's compendium of prints by nineteenth-century artists that appeared in late 1892. However, given the date of Mancini's inauguration, the portfolio could not have been published before 1894. This discrepancy is explained by Béraldi's own *modus operandi*: his lists of prints by living artists were often informed by the artists themselves and sometimes included forthcoming productions.[51] For instance, when Béraldi contacted Pissarro in 1889 while preparing the catalogue of his prints for the eleventh volume of his guidebook that would not appear until 1891, the artist responded with an annotated list that included, by his own admission, a number of prints that were not yet finished.[52]

It is likely that Thornley, perhaps late in

1891 or early in 1892, provided Béraldi with a similar list that incorporated not only his past efforts but his current work-in-progress, the planned Thornley-Monet album. This scenario would explain why Béraldi identified Goupil as its publisher, when in fact the new and inexperienced firm of Mancini eventually took on the responsibility. The lithographer's specification of the largest international publisher of reproductive prints may have been a case of wishful thinking that did not work out the way he planned. Even if Béraldi's catalogue cannot be used to determine the portfolio's date of publication, the fact that he listed it in his 1892 volume is still of some use, as this reference establishes that the project was already in production by that year.

Contributing to the dating problem is a lack of publicity at the time the portfolio appeared and the fact that nowhere in his surviving correspondence does Monet make any reference to it. Thornley's name occurs only in the various lists compiled by Monet of contributors to the fund he set up to purchase Manet's *Olympia* for the Louvre, a major preoccupation of his around 1889–90.[53] Consequently, we can only speculate as to the precise circumstances surrounding the genesis of Thornley's print project. It is possible that Monet was first introduced to Thornley's work when selections from the Degas portfolio were shown at Boussod and Valadon in 1888. It was just at that time that Monet had fallen out with Durand-Ruel and signed a contract with Theo van Gogh to show ten of his Antibes canvases at Boussod and Valadon. Perhaps it was Van Gogh himself who first suggested a Thornley-Monet collaborative portfolio to follow the Thornley-Degas album; alternately, Thornley could have taken the initiative, as he would later do in the case of his Pissarro and (unrealized) Renoir portfolios.

There are several factors that help pinpoint the date of publication of the Thornley-Monet portfolio to the middle of 1894. The first is George Lucas's previously cited diary entry of May 1894, which provides the earliest evidence that the publisher Mancini had opened his gallery on the rue Taitbout. Whistler's letter to Thomas Way from November 1894 establishes that the album's printer, Henry Belfond, was already out of business by that date, so it seems most likely that the portfolio appeared during the second or third quarters of that year. It is conceivable that Thornley began work on the lithographic transfer drawings after the twenty paintings by 1892, the date of the latest painting to appear in the album, and that he did not finish the task for twelve to eighteen months. It would have taken at least another month for Belfond to transfer Thornley's drawings to stones and print the edition of twenty-five impressions of each subject, totaling five hundred proofs. Unlike Thornley's earlier Degas and later Pissarro portfolios, a larger unsigned edition of one hundred impressions was not produced.

A One-Man Show in Print

As the study of his work for reproduction in gillotage makes clear, Monet devoted a great deal of energy to the presentation of his paintings in a series of gallery exhibitions that took place during the last two decades of the nineteenth century. After the dissolution of the Impressionist group, the individual members were left to fend for themselves in securing venues for the promotion and sales of their latest work. Increasingly, Parisian dealers mounted single-artist exhibitions on a modest scale (generally under two dozen paintings), often for a period of a month or less. Monet's first one-man show of eighteen paintings took place at Charpentier's Galerie de la Vie Moderne in June 1880 and was followed by solo exhibitions at Durand-Ruel (1883, 56 works; 1891, 22 works; 1892, 15 works; 1895, 49 works), Boussod and Valadon (1888, 10 works), the Goupil Gallery, London (1889, 20 works), Durand-Ruel, New York (1895, 40 works), the American Art Galleries, New York (1896, 14 works), and Galerie Georges Petit (1898, 61 works). Exhibitions of Monet's paintings were also held in New York at the Union League Club (1891, 32 works) and the Lotos Club (1899, 22 works), and in Boston at the St. Botolph Club (1895, 27 works; 1899, 28 works).

TABLE 6 Prints in the Thornley-Monet Portfolio

PRINT NO.	DATE / TITLE / WILDENSTEIN NO. FOR CORRESPONDING PAINTING		
1	1877	*Arrival of the Normandy Train, Gare Saint-Lazare*	W440
2	1879	*Vétheuil in the Fog*	W518
3	1882	*The Customs House, Afternoon Effect*	W737
4	1885	*Beach and Falaise d'Amont, Étretat*	W1012
5		*Fishing Boats at Étretat*	W1013
6		*Three Fishing Boats*	W1029
7		*Cliff and the Porte d'Aval, Étretat*	W1019
8	1886	*Woman with a Parasol*	W1077
9		*Portrait of Poly*	W1122
10		*Rocky Coast and the Lion Rock, Belle-Île*	W1090
11		*The Côte Sauvage*	W1100
12		*Port-Domois at Belle-Île*	W1109
13		*Storm at Belle-Île*	W1117
14	1888	*View from the Cap d'Antibes*	W1174
15		*Young Girl (Germaine Hoschedé) in the Garden at Giverny*	W1207
16		*The Bridge at Vervy*	W1234
17	1889	*The Creuse, Dark Weather*	W1224
18		*Gorge of the Petite Creuse*	PROBABLY W1230
19	1890	*Grainstacks, Last Sunrays*	W1272
20	1892	*Blanche Hoschedé Painting*	W1330

The largest single gathering of Monet's canvases prior to 1900 took place at Galerie Georges Petit, a gargantuan exhibition timed to coincide with the Exposition Universelle of 1889 that included 145 paintings by Monet and 36 sculptures by Auguste Rodin.

The appendix in this volume (see pp. 273–78) provides a catalogue of the twenty lithographs that make up the Thornley-Monet portfolio of 1894, a product that may be seen as extending the concept of the one-artist gallery exhibition into the "virtual" realm of the printed image. John House has stressed Monet's evolving view of the dealer exhibition, showing how his conception of this key mechanism was transformed from a strictly commercial enterprise to a consideration of "the exhibition as an art work in its own right."[54] While engaged in the act of applying paint to the surface of an individual canvas, Monet was increasingly aware of how the object before him would eventually hang in an ensemble of related works on the wall of a public gallery. His approach to selection and installation seems to have evolved as part and parcel of his adoption of serial imagery. In a sense, the print portfolio was the literal manifestation of two interrelated ideas that came to define Monet's artistic program of the 1890s: the aesthetic of serialism and the construction of the public exhibition as a synthetic form of art.

To date, only one full set of the twenty lithographs has been discovered (from the collection of Jacques Doucet [1853–1929] in the Bibliothèque de l'Institut National de l'Histoire d'Art, Paris). A partial set of nine prints presently in the collection of Dr. Morton and Tobia Mower may be traced to Michel Monet and in all probability to Monet himself. As the album was unbound and not accompanied by a descriptive text or table of contents, we cannot be sure

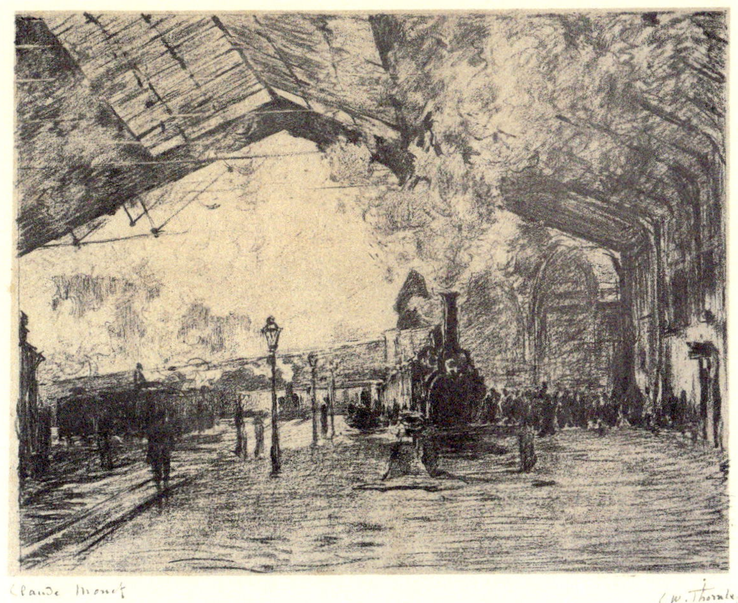

223

William Thornley, after Claude Monet, *Arrival of the Normandy Train, Gare Saint-Lazare*, c. 1894. Transfer lithograph printed in warm gray on off-white chine appliqué, 212 x 260 mm. Bibliothèque de l'Institut National de l'Histoire de l'Art, Paris. Collections Jacques Doucet

224

William Thornley, after Claude Monet, *Vétheuil in the Fog*, c. 1894. Transfer lithograph printed in turquoise on off-white chine appliqué, 212 x 249 mm. Bibliothèque de l'Institut National de l'Histoire de l'Art, Paris. Collections Jacques Doucet

if there was an intended sequence. Although Monet himself paid little attention to chronology in planning the installations of his exhibitions, the prints are listed in table 6 according to the dates of the corresponding paintings that they reproduce.

From the vantage point of the mid-1890s, when the portfolio first appeared, the selection provides an idiosyncratic snapshot of Monet's oeuvre that may in all probability be attributed to the painter rather than the lithographer. Instead of emphasizing his most recent work—the Grainstacks, Poplars, and Rouen Cathedral series—the selection is weighted more heavily to canvases of the mid- to late-1880s, documenting Monet's return to Étretat (four prints), his Belle-Île campaign (five prints), his work in the valley of the Creuse River (three prints), and his renewal of interest in figure painting at Giverny (three prints). These subjects seemed to have a personal meaning to the artist as he looked back on his life and career from the perspective of his mid-fifties.

The earliest painting represented in the portfolio, the *Arrival of the Normandy Train, Gare Saint-Lazare* (fig. 223; see also fig. A1), was a picture that had been shown on at least three prior occasions. Ernest Hoschedé had purchased it directly from the artist shortly after it was painted in March 1877 and lent it the following month to the third Impressionist group exhibition. He sold it a year later to Georges de Bellio. The painting was not seen for another decade, when Monet made a direct appeal to de Bellio to borrow it for his contribution to the sixth annual International Exhibition at the Galerie Georges Petit, the nucleus of which was a selection of his Belle-Île paintings. He wrote to de Bellio on 29 April 1887, "I would like to show a note very different from my marines and I thought of exhibiting one of your *Gares*: they have never been seen at Petit's."[55] The painting would appear again in the Monet-Rodin exhibition at Georges Petit's in 1889, and in 1894 would enter the collection of Ernest Donop de Monchy.

The ethereal *Vétheuil in the Fog* (fig. 224; see also fig. A2), the other work of the 1870s represented in the portfolio, had a similar history of public exhibition. Like the *Arrival of the Normandy Train, Gare Saint-Lazare*, it was featured in the sixth International Exhibition of 1887 and the Monet-Rodin dual retrospective in the summer of 1889. In addition, it was among sixteen canvases shown at Boussod and Valadon in February–March 1889, and appeared subsequently in the exhibition *Impressions by Claude Monet*, organized by Theo van Gogh for the London branch of the Galerie Goupil in April

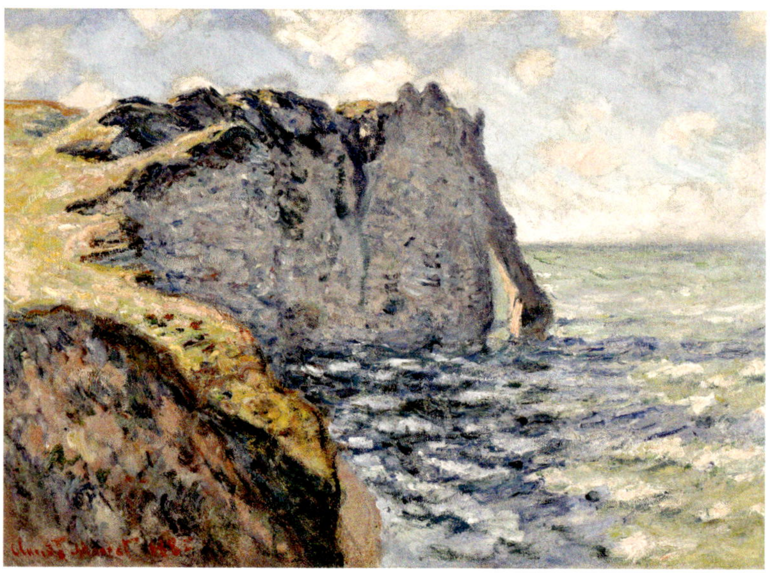

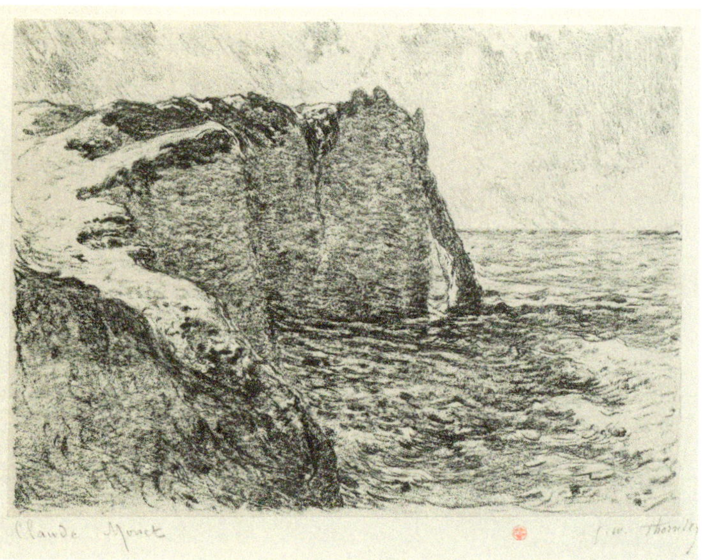

225
Claude Monet, *The Cliff and the Porte d'Aval, Étretat*, 1885. Oil on canvas, 65 x 92 cm. Bequest of Marie Dabek, Paris, to the State of Israel, in memory of Jack and Mimi Dabek. On permanent loan to The Israel Museum, Jerusalem, from the Administrator General of the State of Israel [W1019]

226
William Thornley, after Claude Monet, *The Cliff and the Porte d'Aval, Étretat*, c. 1894. Transfer lithograph printed in greenish-gray on off-white chine appliqué, 187 x 260 mm. Collection of Dr. Morton and Tobia Mower

1889. *Vétheuil in the Fog* seems to have acquired an emblematic meaning for the artist. It was a painting he installed proudly on an easel in his first Giverny studio and never sold. Georges Clemenceau recorded an anecdote relating to this vaporous work that might explain its frequency of public display in the short span of seven years (it was shown five times between 1887 and 1894) culminating in its reproduction in the Thornley portfolio, its final appearance during the artist's lifetime.[56] Some time earlier Jean-Baptiste Faure had turned down an offer to buy the work for fifty francs, criticizing its lack of finish and complaining that the too-white canvas did not have enough paint on it; Monet, bruised and defiant, subsequently bestowed on it a special status, that of an ideological talisman.

The four Étretat paintings represented in the portfolio had much less public exposure prior to their translation into lithographs. The works originated in Monet's intensive late autumn/early winter 1885 painting campaigns on the Channel coast. Three of the four canvases upon which the prints were based (*Fishing Boats at Étretat* [see fig. A5], *Three Fishing Boats* [see fig. A6], and *The Cliff and the Porte d'Aval, Étretat* [figs. 225 and 226]) were still with the artist as of the date of publication; the early provenance of the fourth, *Beach and the Falaise d'Amont, Étretat* (see fig. A4), is unrecorded. Seen as a group, the four prints neatly encapsulate Monet's experience of this dramatic site, with views of both the Porte d'Amont and the Porte d'Aval; only the Manneporte is excluded. Fishing vessels are the primary subjects of the three beach scenes, which arranged in a particular sequence give an almost cinematic effect of zooming in from a distant overview of the beach looking toward the Porte d'Amont with small boats dotting the shore to a view of the immediate coastline with boats protruding into the foreground and finally a close-up "portrait" of three fishing boats.

At the heart of the Thornley portfolio is a remarkable sequence of Monet's most otherworldly landscapes, the rugged cliffs at Belle-Île (fig. 227; see also figs. A10–13) and the desolate valley of the Creuse River in the Massif Central (see figs. A16–18). These highly expressive, though somber works had met with near-universal acclaim when large groups of them were shown in the Monet-Rodin exhibition of 1889. For anyone who associated Impressionist landscape painting with blissful images of sunlit gardens, this nexus of seven prints in which the primary subjects are rock formations may come as a surprise. The monumental solid forms were particularly well suited to Thornley's incisive process of lithographic distillation. Almost as an antidote to the stark views of Belle-Île and the Creuse Valley appear four luminous figural compositions, including the most recently painted canvas in the suite (see figs. A8, A9,

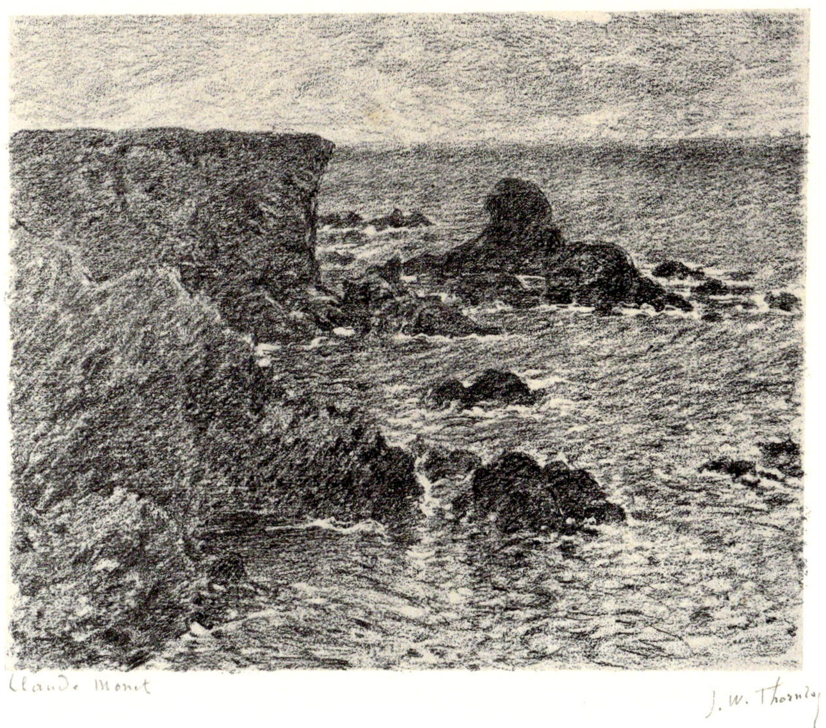

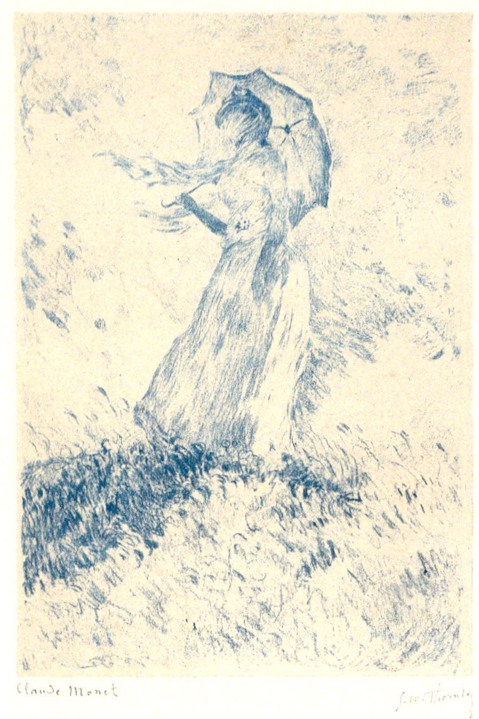

227
William Thornley, after Claude Monet, *Rocky Coast and the Lion Rock, Belle-Île*, c. 1894. Transfer lithograph printed in warm gray on beige chine appliqué, 195 x 240 mm. Bibliothèque de l'Institut National de l'Histoire de l'Art, Paris. Collections Jacques Doucet

228
William Thornley, after Claude Monet, *Woman with a Parasol*, c. 1894. Transfer lithograph printed in dull blue on off-white chine appliqué, 274 x 196 mm. Bibliothèque de l'Institut National de l'Histoire de l'Art, Paris. Collections Jacques Doucet

A15, and A20). Although Monet had started out as a virtuoso portraitist in the specialized field of caricature, his mature public image was as a pure landscapist. And just as his considerable drawing skills effectively went underground, so too did his talent for representing the human figure after such early canvases as the *Luncheon on the Grass* (1865), *Camille, Woman in a Green Dress* (1866), and *The Luncheon* (1868–69). From 1886 to the early 1890s, he revisited figure painting in a loose series of canvases attempting to integrate large-scale figures and plein-air settings. The models were drawn from the Hoschedé girls, including Suzanne (fig. 228; see also fig. A8), Germaine (see fig. A15), and Blanche (see fig. A20), who became the artist's stepdaughters upon his marriage to their mother, Alice, in 1892.

In a letter to his brother Theo written in the spring of 1888, Vincent van Gogh looked to the future and asked, "Who will be in figure painting what Monet is in landscape?"[57] Had he been privy to this exchange, Monet might have been equally flattered and resentful of the implication that his talent was limited to a single genre. Of the body of experimental figure paintings he embarked on in the late 1880s, Monet wrote to Geffroy, "I so want to prove that I can do something different," and the next year he showed four of the paintings in a discrete section of the Petit gallery retrospective under the title *Essais de figures en plein air*.[58] Within the more concisely edited presentation of his work in the Thornley album, the inclusion of three of these *essais*, in addition to the half-length *Portrait of Poly* (see fig. A9), must be taken as an emphatic declaration by Monet that his range extended beyond landscape to embrace figure paintings.

Given the portfolio's date of publication, one might expect it to showcase Monet's most recent and distinctive contribution to Neo-Impressionism: his adoption of serial imagery in his paintings of grainstacks, poplars, and the façade of Rouen Cathedral. In fact, the only series represented is that of the Grainstacks, and the specific painting chosen to appear did not belong to either of the predominant compositional types, in which single grainstacks or pairs of larger and smaller stacks appear in the middle ground, centrally framed within the picture plane (as in Monet's gillotage for *L'Art dans les deux mondes*

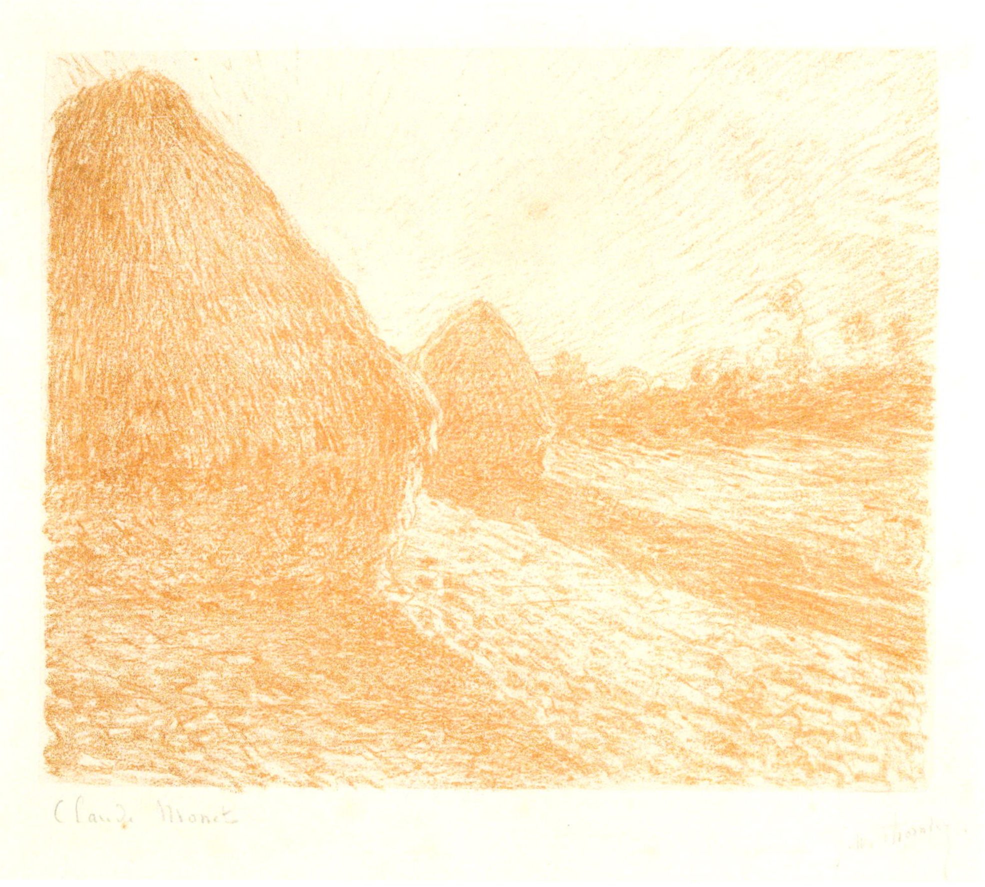

229
William Thornley, after Claude Monet, *Grainstacks, Last Sunrays*, c. 1894. Transfer lithograph with scraping printed in orange on off-white chine appliqué, 217 x 262 mm. Collection of Dr. Morton and Tobia Mower

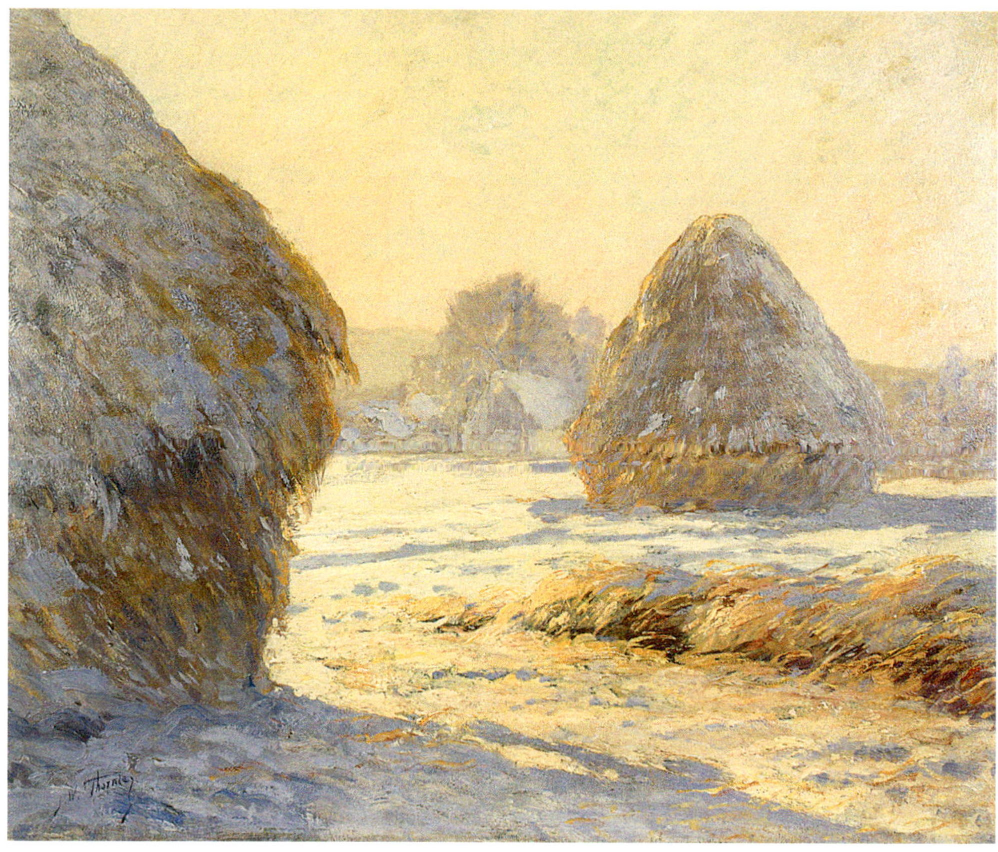

230
William Thornley, *Grainstacks in Winter at Osny*. Oil on canvas. Private collection, Jean-Claude Barrié (Reproduced from *William Thornley Retrospective*, exh. cat. [Osny, 1994])

231
Claude Monet in his studio at Giverny, 1890s

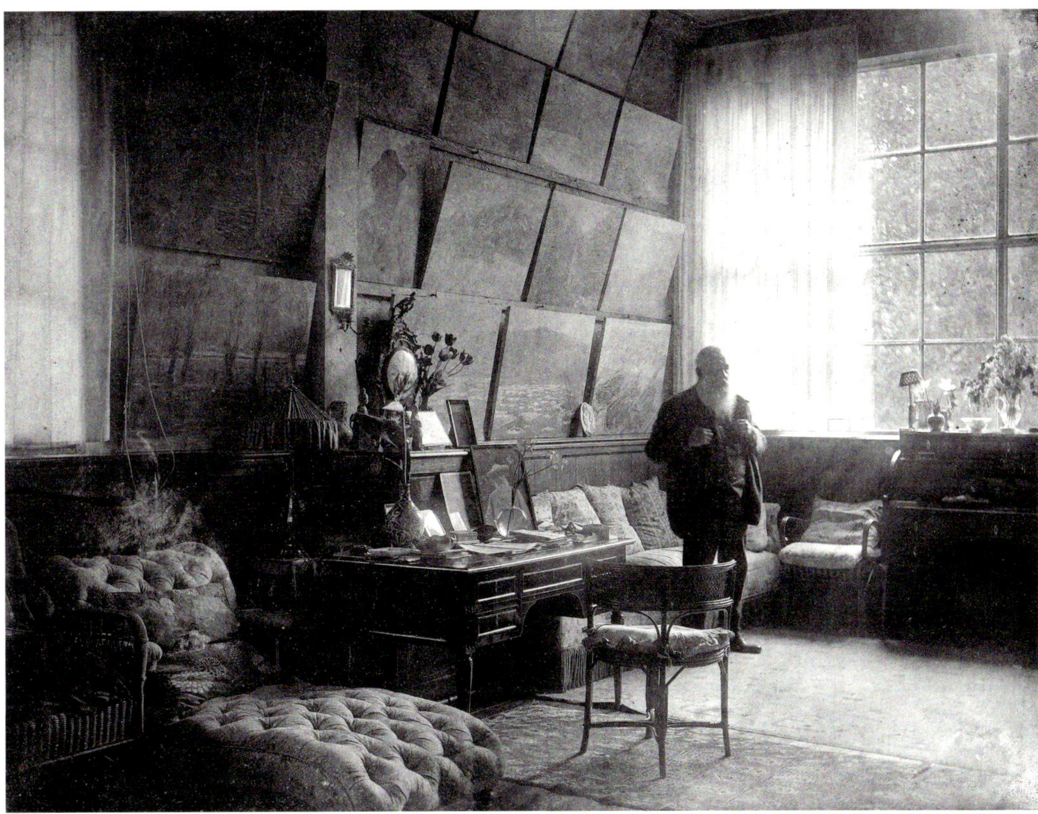

(see fig. 204). Instead, the decision was made to include *Grainstacks, Last Sunrays* (fig. 229; see also fig. A19), one of a smaller subset of the main series in which Monet moved in closer to his subject and placed himself at an oblique angle, allowing a grainstack to be cropped by the edge of the canvas. Thornley seems to have been particularly inspired by this choice, as it served as the template for one of his own paintings of *Grainstacks in Winter at Osny* (fig. 230).[59]

Beyond the subject matter, another way of looking at the selection of works for the Thornley-Monet portfolio is to consider the ownership of the original canvases during the period in which the project was underway, roughly between 1891 and 1894. Perhaps the most striking discovery is that just one of the twenty pictures originated in the inventory or private collection of Paul Durand-Ruel.[60] After showing his work exclusively with Durand-Ruel in the past, Monet had become more of a free agent by the early 1890s, selling his canvases directly to collectors and through Durand-Ruel's competitors Boussod and Valadon and Georges Petit. For instance, Monet sold *Grainstacks, Last Sunrays* directly to Paul Gallimard at the end of January 1891,[61] and *The Creuse, Dark Weather* (for the print, see fig. A17) to "Hamman," acting as an agent for Isidore Montaignac and M. Knoedler & Company later in the same year.[62] A likely explanation for the omission of Durand-Ruel's paintings from the selection was Thornley's anticipation of publishing and/or distributing the portfolio through the Galerie Goupil and its branch Boussod and Valadon. Monet had sold one of the paintings, *View from the Cap d'Antibes* (for the print, see fig. A14), to Boussod and Valadon in December 1888.[63] Goupil exhibited it in London in 1889.

Even more telling than the virtual exclusion of Durand-Ruel from the album is the predominance of works held by the artist at the time of its publication. At least eight paintings fell into this category (and possibly several others, because their date of sale from Monet is unrecorded), and of these, Monet held onto six until the end of his life. Several of the paintings are documented in photographs taken of Monet's studios at Giverny (fig. 231). Personal favorites of the artist included *Woman with a Parasol*,

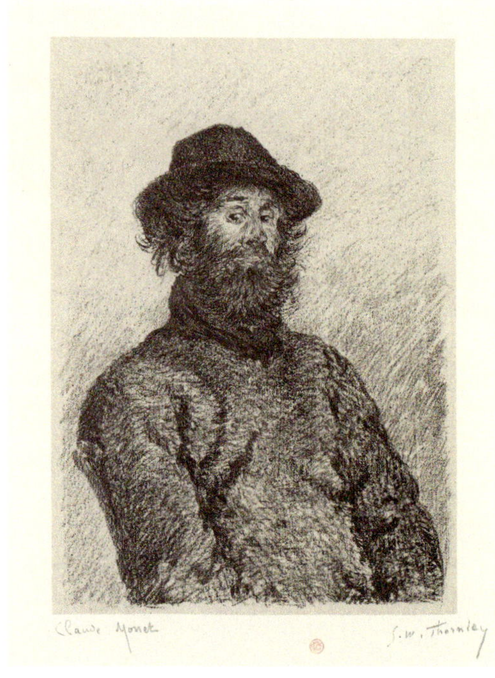

232
William Thornley, after Claude Monet, *Portrait of Poly*, c. 1894. Transfer lithograph with scraping printed in dark gray on off-white chine appliqué, 223 x 164 mm. Collection of Dr. Morton and Tobia Mower

for which Suzanne Hoschedé had posed; *Blanche Hoschedé Painting*; and the *Portrait of Poly* (fig. 232). If there remains any doubt that Monet was responsible for the selection of works in the portfolio, the presence of the latter painting would seem to set the matter to rest. Monet had a special fondness for the sitter, a fisherman from Kervilahouen who acted as his porter during his Belle-Île expedition, and he was especially proud of the painted likeness he created in November 1886.[64] He exhibited the portrait at Georges Petit's gallery in 1887 and again in his large retrospective of 1889, and hung the canvas directly above his desk in his studio at Giverny. When he was painting in the Creuse Valley in the spring of 1889, Monet wrote Alice to ask her to send a photograph of *Portrait of Poly* to present to the poet Maurice Rollinat (1846–1903).[65]

Color and Line in the Thornley-Monet Portfolio

With the exception of a few hand-colored caricatures of his paintings that had appeared in the popular press, the publication of *20 Lithographs after Claude Monet* represented the first time any part of Monet's painted oeuvre was reproduced in printed images that were not strictly monochromatic.[66] The artist's own graphic translations of his paintings were all carried out in black ink or crayon on white paper for reproduction in single-tone gillotage. Under William Thornley's direction, Henry Belfond printed the suite of lithographs in a variety of colored inks on several different tints of *chine appliqué*, thin sheets of China paper affixed to heavier wove supports commonly employed in the printing of fine lithographs and etchings. In addition, two of the twenty lithographs were designed for printing from multiple stones inked in several different colors. The color choices generally reflect the chromatic effects of the corresponding paintings, although certain prints exhibit divergent, seemingly arbitrary color schemes.

It is worth remarking that in lithography, as in all other printmaking methods, color and line are truly autonomous, relegated to discrete stages in the process and often to two different hands. The act of creating the printing matrix, as in the conveyance of Thornley's drawings from sheets of lithographic transfer paper to the surface of a limestone, is entirely independent of printing an impression. Consequently, the color of the lithographic crayon used to make the drawing is altogether irrelevant to the color of ink applied to the stone in the printing process.

In approaching each subject, Thornley and Belfond selected a hue of ink that would act as a keynote for distilling Monet's palette into a lithographic impression. In several cases, this chromatic keynote was clearly derived from the dominant color scheme of the original oil. For example, the lithograph after the predominately blue-green *Véthueil in the Fog* (see fig. 224) was printed in shades of both green and grayish blue, while *Grainstacks, Last Sunrays* (see fig. 229) was printed in orange to evoke the brilliant sunset effect of the original painting. For the most part, the printing inks employed in the Thornley-Monet portfolio were not especially intense, but rather grayed down and subdued, particularly among the suite of images of Belle-Île and the Creuse Valley, where the sensation given is appropriately melancholic. Greater emphasis was placed on the formal structures

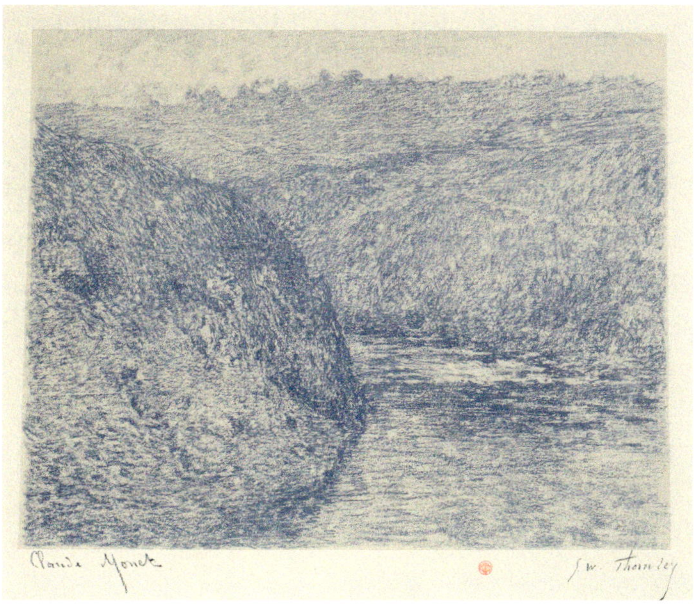

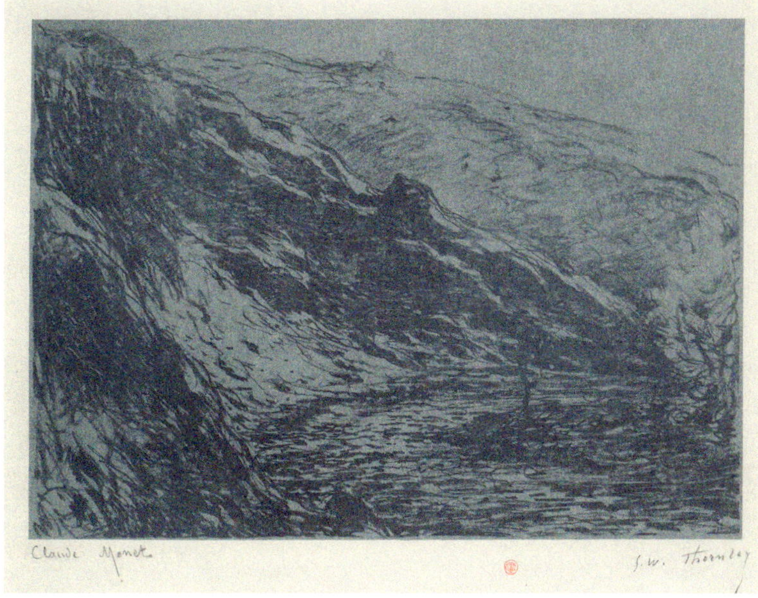

233
William Thornley, after Claude Monet, *The Creuse, Dark Weather*, c. 1894. Transfer lithograph printed in dark blue on off-white chine appliqué, 204 x 254 mm. Collection of Dr. Morton and Tobia Mower

234
William Thornley, after Claude Monet, *Gorge of the Petite Creuse*, c. 1894. Transfer lithograph printed in purplish-gray on olive-toned chine appliqué, 208 x 292 mm. Collection of Dr. Morton and Tobia Mower

of the images rather than dynamic color effects. Belfond's sensitivity and restraint recall the work he had carried out with Whistler a few years earlier on the abandoned *Songs on Stone* project.

If only by technical necessity, the restricted chromatic range of the lithographs echoes Monet's increasingly non-descriptive and restricted, or "atmospheric," approach to color in his paintings of the 1890s. The young Neo-Impressionist painter Paul Signac (1863–1935) verbalized this phenomenon in his diary of 1894 in an imaginary exchange with Monet: "But no, M. Monet, you are not a naturalist," he argued. "Trees in nature are not blue, people are not violet . . . and your great merit is precisely that you painted them like this, as you feel them, and not just as they are."[67] Signac's observations on Monet's paintings would not have been contradicted by the even more extreme distillation of color in Thornley's lithographs.

While Belfond printed the majority of the lithographs on neutral shades of chine appliqué, in a few cases he employed more striking tinted papers to work in conjunction with the key tone of printers' ink. Through the mixing and matching of a few permutations of printers' ink and tints of chine appliqué, color variants were introduced into the editions of several of the lithographs. Such inconsistencies in a published edition, rather than merely within a set of artist's proofs, were most unusual, but we must recall that by affixing his signature, Monet effectively gave all the variant printings his seal of approval. Impressions of *View from the Cap d'Antibes* (see fig. A14) have been located in both bluish-gray on rose-toned chine appliqué, and green on off-white chine; similarly *The Creuse, Dark Weather* was printed both in greenish-gray on rose-toned chine, and dark blue on off-white chine (fig. 233). Both *The Côte Sauvage* and *Gorge of the Petite Creuse* (fig. 234) exist in impressions on both dark blue and olive-toned chine appliqué (see figs. 201 and 202). Viewed alongside each other, the color variants might be seen as evoking the serialist aesthetic of Monet's oils.

Two of the prints combined separately inked lithographic stones to more literally approximate the color schemes of the corresponding paintings: *Three Fishing Boats* (figs. 235 and 236; see also fig. A6) and *Blanche Hoschedé Painting* (fig. 237; see also fig. A20), a pair of canvases of roughly identical dimensions that were photographed hanging side-by-side in Monet's second Giverny studio in 1900 (fig. 238).[68] The lithograph of *Three Fishing Boats* is the more elaborate of the two, with the composition broken into four components: on the Doucet impression, a blue-gray keystone for the principal forms and individual accent elements on

235
Three Fishing Boats, 1886.
Oil on canvas, 73 x 92.5 cm.
Szépmüvészeti Múzeum, Budapest
[W1029]

236
William Thornley, after Claude Monet, *Three Fishing Boats*, c. 1894. Transfer lithograph printed in blue-gray, green, acidic yellow, and light pinkish beige on off-white chine appliqué, 210 x 265 mm. Bibliothèque de l'Institut National de l'Histoire de l'Art, Paris. Collections Jacques Doucet

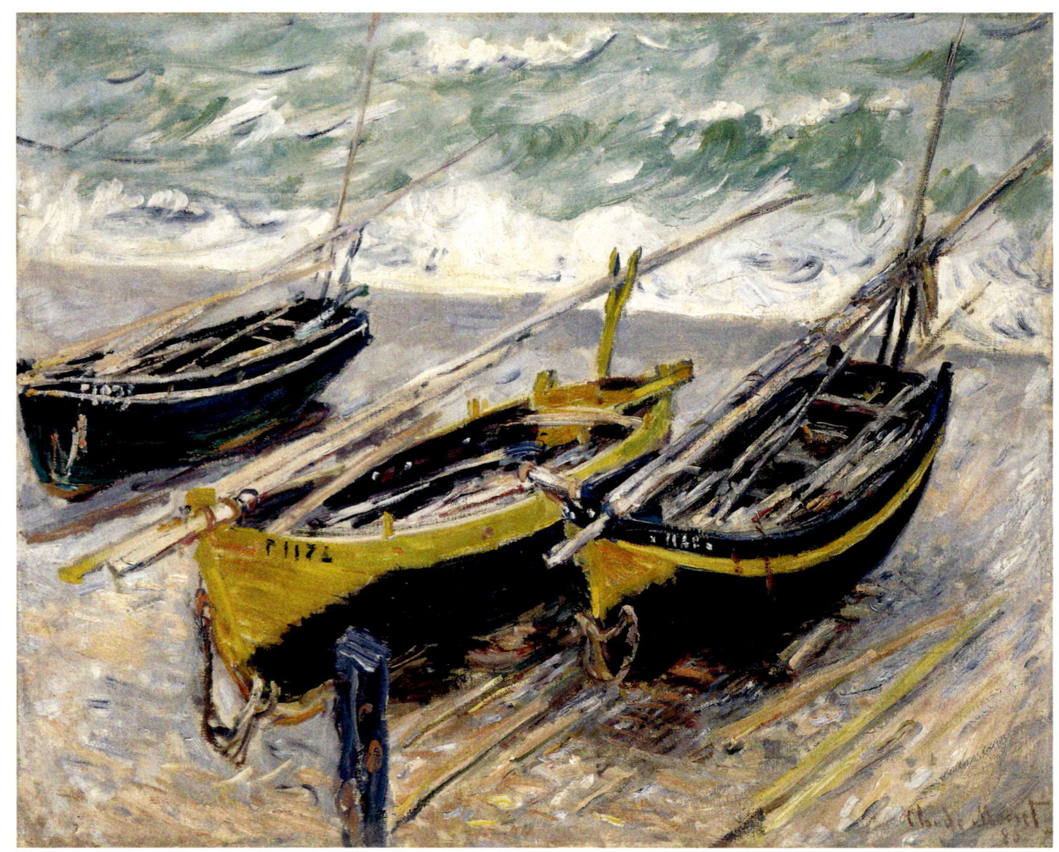

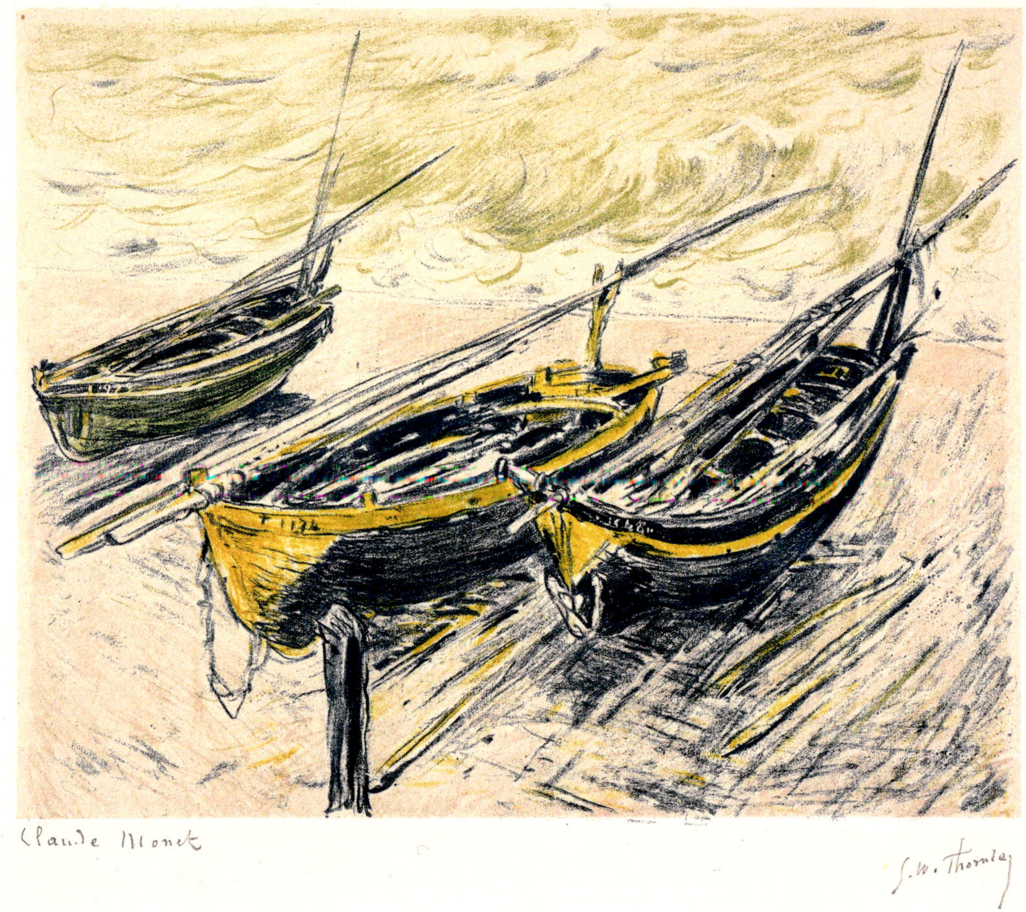

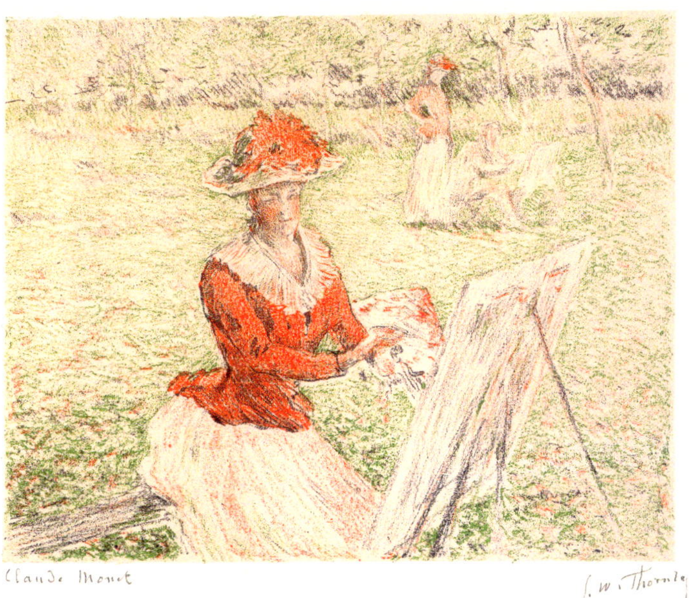

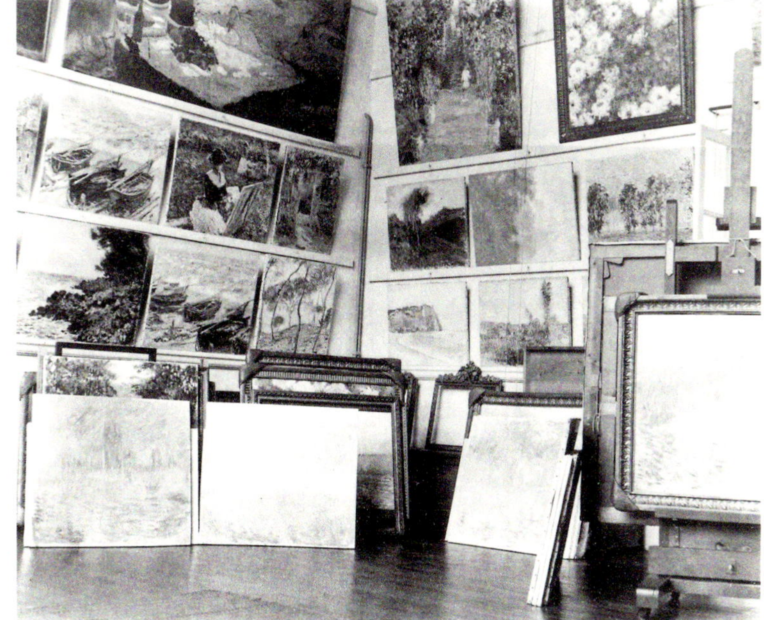

237
William Thornley, after Claude Monet, *Blanche Hoschedé Painting*, c. 1894. Transfer lithograph printed in gray-black, green, and red on off-white chine appliqué, 160 x 200 mm. Bibliothèque de l'Institut National de l'Histoire de l'Art, Paris. Collections Jacques Doucet

238
Interior of Monet's second studio at Giverny, c. 1900

separate stones in green, acidic yellow, and light pinkish beige. *Blanche Hoschedé Painting* was printed from three stones: black-gray (keystone), green, and red. By the time the Thornley portfolio was put into circulation, this labor-intensive method of color lithography was well on its way to becoming an essential feature in the explosion of artists' lithographs that has been characterized as the "color revolution" in fin-de-siècle printmaking. Belfond was considered a pioneer among the lithographic printers who mastered this technology and made it available to artists in the early 1890s.

Finally, the reappearance in the Thornley portfolio of two of the same works recently translated by Monet into gillotage drawings for *L'Art dans les deux mondes* gives us the opportunity to compare the painter's distinctive graphism with the handling of a professional reproductive draftsman. As might be expected, Thornley's manner of drawing is stylistically more conservative than Monet's. For instance, whereas the painter's own graphic translation of the *Woman with a Parasol* gives an impression of vigor and spontaneity, with the kind of rough lines identified with rapid preparatory sketches, Thornley's interpretation is more polished and more literal, providing a heightened level of detail and a greater sense of solidity in the masses (see figs. 205 and 228). To a lesser extent the same stylistic divergence characterizes the two graphic reprises of *The Côte Sauvage*, with Monet's placement of lines less structured and Thornley's more deliberate (see figs. 197 through 202).

Success or Failure?

In the final analysis, should the Thornley-Monet portfolio be considered a success or a failure? There are, of course, many different ways to measure its performance, from applying purely aesthetic criteria (qualities of draftsmanship, color, printing, the degree to which the prints were faithful to the original paintings) to cold, hard sales figures. An essential question is how the portfolio was received upon its initial appearance. Unfortunately, this publication of lithographs seems to have been met with silence in the art press. Attempts to locate contemporary reviews of the portfolio have thus far proven futile. We do not even know whether Mancini organized an exhibition of the prints in his rue Taitbout gallery on the occasion of their publication.

When it came to promoting exhibitions of his own paintings, Monet would not have tolerated this kind of critical apathy, but his letters

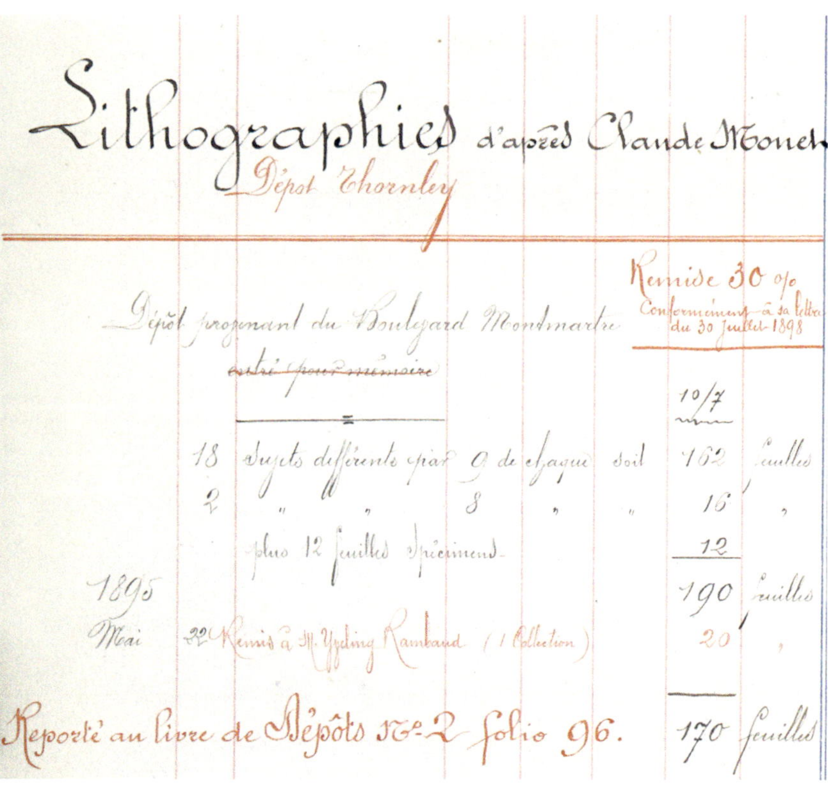

Lithographies d'après Claude Monet
Dépôt Thornley

Remise 30 o/o
Conformément à sa lettre du 30 Juillet 1898

Dépôt provenant du Boulevard Montmartre
~~entré pour mémoire~~

		10/7	
	18 Sujets différents par 9 de chaque soit	162	feuilles
	2 " " " 8 " "	16	"
	plus 12 feuilles spécimens	12	
1895		190	feuilles
Mai	22 Remis à M. Yveling Rambaud (1 Collection)	20	"
	Reporté au livre de Dépôts No. 2 folio 96.	170	feuilles

239
Goupil ledger recording sales of William Thornley's lithographs after Monet, c. 1895. Courtesy Musée Goupil, Bordeaux

make no reference to the print project's genesis, production, or reception. Were it not for a brief passage in Yveling RamBaud's final book *Silhouettes d'artistes* (1899) we would have no record of Monet's reaction to the lithographs. During a visit to Thornley's studio in Osny, the former editor of Durand-Ruel's *L'Art dans les deux mondes* testified that the painter-lithographer proudly showed him correspondence from both Degas and Monet, two artists "difficult to please and incapable of holding back their opinions under the pretext of politeness."[69] The letters reportedly offered praise and gratitude for his efforts on their behalf.

We have a slightly clearer picture of the portfolio's commercial fortunes. According to the title page, the size of the edition was set at twenty-five, indicating a total print run of 500 individual impressions. It should be acknowledged, however, that there were often disparities between announced and realized editions, with the size of the actual print run sometimes failing to reach the number indicated on the colophon. It is not known whether Belfond printed the complete edition of twenty-five sets of the Thornley-Monet portfolio before going out of business. Also undocumented is the retail price of either the complete set or individual impressions of the prints.

What we do know is that the lithographs were distributed through at least three sources: the publisher of record J. Mancini, the Boussod and Valadon Gallery on the boulevard Montmartre, and the Galerie Goupil in the Place de l'Opéra. While the portfolio was not advertised in Goupil's print catalogues, the publication did enter its ledger books (fig. 239). The records indicate that by May 1895, 190 impressions joined Goupil's inventory from the "Boulevard Montmartre," that is, from Boussod and Valadon, although the consigner is identified as "M. Thornley à Osny près Pontoise." This shipment was made up of eight complete sets, one partial set (missing two subjects), and twelve sample sheets.[70] The remainder of the edition is unaccounted for. The ledger indicates that on 22 May 1895, one "collection" was given to the journalist RamBaud, perhaps in the hope of generating publicity. The remainder of the prints languished unsold in Goupil's stock until 30 July 1898, when an agreement was finally reached with Thornley for the gallery to receive a 30 percent commission on sales.[71] The subsequent ledgers record little interest in the prints, which could be purchased individually: Goupil sold only 102 impressions, or the equivalent of just over five sets, through 1917.[72]

If the Thornley-Monet lithographs were largely ignored by critics and performed relatively poorly, it may have been because of their status as reproductive rather than original prints. Indeed, the portfolio ran counter to the growing fashion for artist-designed and executed lithographs as promoted by such figures as André Marty and Ambroise Vollard. In discussing artist's lithographs, French critics of the 1890s took pains to draw a distinction between "original" prints conceived and drawn by a single artist and "reproductive" or "facsimile" lithographs that were typically designed by painters but drawn on stone or zinc plates by specially trained artisans. In light of the medium's technical requirements, which were far more elaborate and expensive than those of etching, very few painters possessed the ability to initiate a lithographic project without the cooperation of a skilled professional. Some degree of collaboration was a given, although the nature of the collaboration between individual painters and professional lithographers like Thornley and Auguste Clot might vary significantly on a case-by-case basis.

Speaking out vehemently against the kind of lithographic collaboration exemplified by the Thornley-Monet portfolio, André Mellerio, for one, claimed "the modern print was no longer a facsimile reproduction of just any original work in color, but a personal conception, something realized for its own sake."[73] He went out of his way to denounce the phenomenon of the lithograph of interpretation, particularly the productions of its foremost practitioner Clot, who created reproductive lithographs after a number of leading artists, including Rodin, Sisley, and Redon. While acknowledging their technical virtuosity, Mellerio panned Clot's efforts, advising collectors that "readymade displays of brilliance, with which a facile printer can easily but treacherously seduce one, must be rejected out of hand. The artist has to acquire his craft himself, actually put his hand to stone."[74] In fact, Clot's publisher Ambroise Vollard actively suppressed the role of the reproductive lithographer, whose name appears nowhere on the prints he generated. By omitting this information, Vollard led potential buyers of certain prints to believe that they were the sole creations of the painters whose signatures graced the lower margins. In Vollard's publications, Auguste Clot was an invisible man.

The Thornley-Monet prints fall squarely in the category of the lithographic facsimile. While the title page clearly disclosed the roles of painter and lithographer, the signatures of both Monet and Thornley on the individual impressions asserted their joint contribution to the finished product without indicating exactly who did what. In the absence of attention from the modern community of Monet scholars, a century after the album first appeared the nature of the painter's role in this project has remained uncertain. A review of recent auction catalogues finds the notion that Monet had a hand in both designing and drawing the lithographs has persisted, at least in the art market. While they do not, in fact, belong to Monet's proper graphic oeuvre, the prints do indeed reflect his intellectual property as a unique and personally selected anthology drawn from his original paintings, a visual autobiography translated from paint into print by a sensitive disciple.

In all fairness to both Thornley and Monet, the apparent failure of their collaboration to achieve commercial success should be seen in the broader context of the fin-de-siècle print market. For despite the enthusiasm of later generations of art historians and collectors, virtually none of the great lithographic productions of the 1890s that were so passionately promoted by critics like Mellerio and Roger-Marx and publishers like Marty and Vollard turned an immediate profit.[75] Many explanations have been put forward for the failure of these projects, including oversaturation of the fine-print market and confusion among the general public concerning the differences between original and reproductive prints.

After Thornley: Color Photography of Monet's Paintings

Monet lived late enough into the twentieth century to witness significant technological advances in the field of polychromatic photography that made it possible to give the illusion of reproducing a full range of colors. Having long since relinquished any hands-on role in making graphic reproductions of his paintings, he continued to assert control over how his work appeared in print. When the artist was in his eighties, Arsène Alexandre, Gustave Geffroy, and the novelist Marc Elder (Marçel Tendron) published important monographs on his life and oeuvre that would incorporate plates from photographic negatives printed in color. The artist's surviving correspondence with Alexandre and Geffroy as well as others involved in their book projects reveals his ongoing active interest in matters related to reproduction, in particular to the accuracy of photomechanical color illustrations.

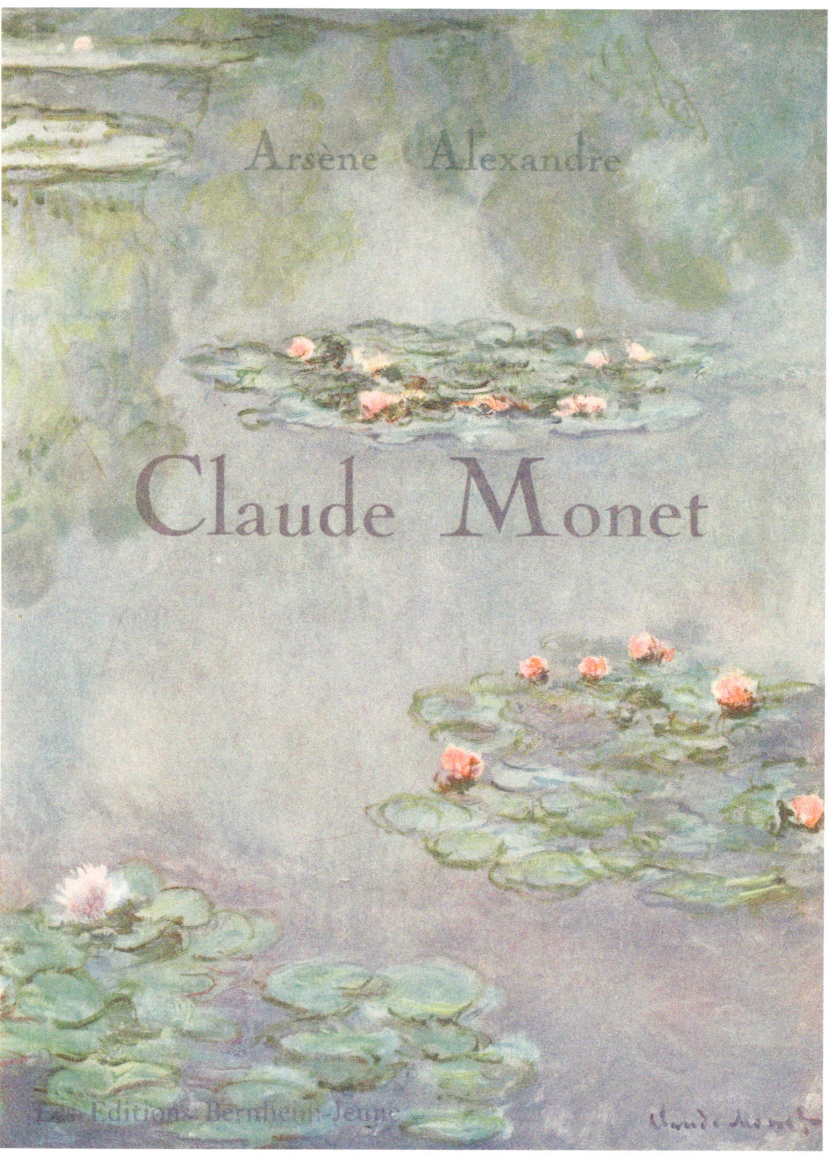

240
Frontispiece for Arsène Alexandre, *Claude Monet* (Paris: Editions Bernheim-Jeune, 1921). Halftone printed in magenta, cyan, and yellow, 355 x 265 mm

In 1920 Monet wrote to Alexandre that he was "a little scared" of color photography as preparations were underway to shoot several of his paintings for his forthcoming monograph *Claude Monet* (1921) (fig. 240).[76] The book's publisher, the Bernheim brothers, sent a crew of photographers to Monet's large studio at Giverny for several days in February 1921, disrupting his labor on the water-lily murals. The team was overseen by André Marty, the former promoter of color lithography who was now proficient in the field of color photography. After this unwelcome interruption, Monet expressed his concerns regarding the quality of the reproductions, demanding final approval over the photographs that would be printed, especially those in color. He explicitly forbade the publication of specific images, warning, for example, that a certain photograph of the Grainstacks painting from the Gallimard collection was "ghastly" and that its "reproduction in color . . . is absolutely impossible."[77] His wishes were respected, and the plate, representing the same canvas in the Thornley portfolio, appeared in the book in black and white.[78]

Geffroy, whom the Bernheims had originally engaged to write the volume ultimately penned by Alexandre, published his own monograph, *Claude Monet, sa vie, son temps, son oeuvre,* in 1922. Geffroy's book is illustrated with fifty-four collotypes (a form of photomechanical reproduction) of which three were printed in color by the Parisian firm of Léon Marotte.[79] Shortly after receiving a copy, Monet wrote to express his profound thanks for the author's sensitive scholarship and "everything that is beautiful in the book."[80] He was unhappy, however, with a color plate representing the *Group of Rocks at Port-Goulphar* (fig. 241) from the author's own collection. Marotte had reneged on his promise to submit color proofs to Monet, who was now so incensed by the mediocre quality of this one image that he went on the record to oppose its publication and requested that the full edition of 1100 copies of the book be suppressed. Geffroy seems to have successfully deflected Monet's objection, and his book circulated to wide acclaim.

Judging by his surviving letters, Monet was less heavy-handed in his dealings with Marc Elder, whose book *A Giverny, chez Claude Monet* appeared in November 1924 under the publishing arm of the Galerie Bernheim-Jeune. By this time he was fully preoccupied with the completion of his last great project, the *Grand Décorations,* and was plagued by worsening vision problems resulting from cataracts. Accompanying Elder's text are forty-one plates, thirty-four of which appear in the form of black-and-white collotypes. In addition to these, three color plates present Monet's paintings in trichromatic halftone, the same process used in Alexandre's volume.[81] In this technique, filters were placed

241
After Claude Monet, *Group of Rocks at Port-Goulphar*, 1922. Collotype printed in magenta, cyan, and yellow, 134 x 133 mm. From Gustave Geoffroy, *Claude Monet, sa vie, son temps, son oeuvre* (Paris: G. Crès et cie, 1922), pp. 192–93

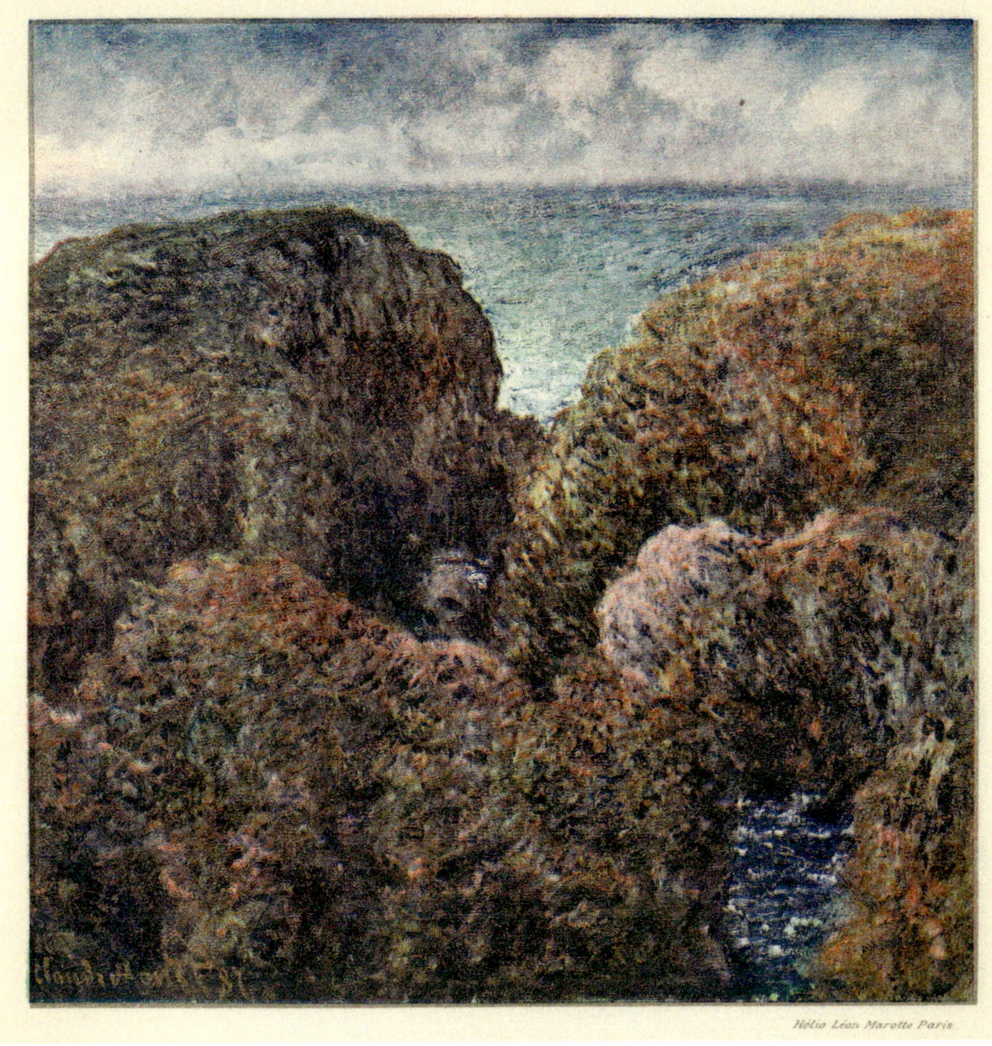

on the camera lens to separate the image into the primary colors magenta, cyan, and yellow; the three resulting negatives were used to produce halftone relief blocks that were recombined to give the impression of a full range of colors. Viewed under magnification, the plates give the appearance of pointillist paintings in which separate dots of pure color are placed in close proximity to each other so as to coalesce in the eye of the viewer.

Although the results were far from perfect, the way of the future was clear. Photomechanical techniques like relief color halftone relieved painters like Monet of making graphic translations of their own canvases and put reproductive printmakers like Auguste Lauzet and William Thornley out of business. The state of the art had been transformed, yet Monet never forgot his experience in this specialized genre. When Alexandre was preparing his monograph, he sought to reproduce one of Monet's first submissions to the Salon of 1865 and wrote to the artist for assistance. Monet replied that he had lost track of the two canvases that had been acquired out of the Salon by Alfred Cadart but could provide two small and not very clear photographs of the works. He mentioned that one of the canvases had been reproduced in *L'Autographe au Salon* in the form of a print he had designed (see figs. 180 and 181). In the typically self-effacing manner that he adopted when referring to his own drawings, he added, "This reproduction was a scribble ("*gribouillage*") of mine in pen. Try to find it, as it is interesting, and if it isn't impossible for you to have an example, that would please me."[82]

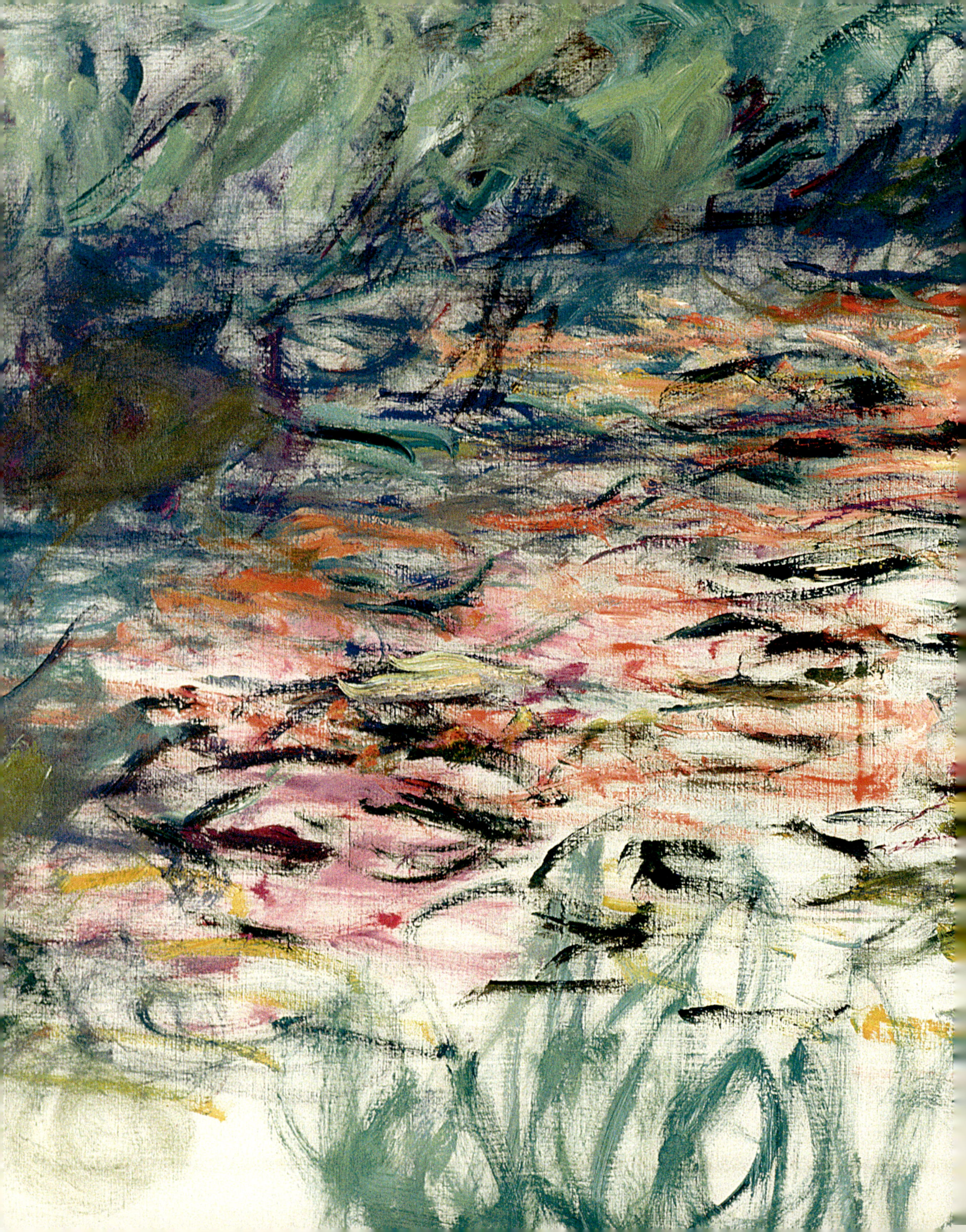

CHAPTER TEN Lines of Color: Drawing in the Late Years

From our vantage point in the twenty-first century, the paintings of Monet's final decades seem inseparable from what Georges Clemenceau once called their "flights of color whose wings carry us beyond imagination's heights."[1] Color dominates our apprehension of the series pictures of the 1890s, the rainbow-hued Giverny garden canvases, and the kaleidoscopic *Grand Décorations* of Monet's last years, in which subject matter seems to lose its central role. In one of the most substantial books on his art to appear in recent years, *Color and Time: Claude Monet*, Virginia Spate argues that Monet "increasingly fused earth, sky, solid matter, water in one shimmer of color."[2] The association of Monet's later work with the liberated colors of abstraction has also been examined with a thoroughness that was previously lacking. Two ambitious exhibitions have been devoted to this theme, while the writings of Michael Leja and others have done much to document the impact of Monet's final paintings on the Abstract Expressionist generation in America.[3] For the leading critic of that period, Clement Greenberg, the late works challenged conventional approaches to the picture surface and to illusionism, but were above all "chromatic and symphonic."[4]

Widely neglected in studies of his oeuvre in general, Monet's draftsmanship has been absent from almost all such considerations of his late career. Our intoxication with the artist's color, it might be argued, has blinded us to the structural, rhythmic, and descriptive qualities of his later paintings and to the drawings that sometimes accompanied them. There is some justification for this neglect. Several of the patterns established in Monet's youth and middle life for the production of works on paper manifestly faded or even disappeared by the turn of the century. The surviving sketchbooks, for example, point to their vigorous but intermittent usage in the 1850s and between the 1870s and 1890s, a practice that lessened quantitatively thereafter. Pastel, too, follows a trajectory that soars in the years prior to the Impressionist exhibitions, then again briefly when the artist was in his forties, only to decline toward the century's end. As our examination of Monet's early years has demonstrated, allowance must always be made for missing clusters of works on paper and lost individual sheets, but the execution of specific drawings for known oil paintings also seems to become less frequent—though not entirely negligible—in the 1890s and beyond.

The widespread assumption that drawing played no role in Monet's later life is, however, seriously flawed in at least two respects. The first is strictly historical and concerns several periods of activity in which studies on paper can be documented and their role in his art precisely described. These include substantial groups of small line drawings made in several sketchbooks that were demonstrably involved in the formulation—even the initial conception—of his Grainstacks, Rouen Cathedral, and certain other serial paintings. An additional case has already been examined in chapter 8, where the artist's participation in various printmaking schemes in the 1890s and his creation of a number of related black-crayon drawings was surveyed. The most familiar exception to the rule is the suite of pastels begun in London in 1901, a dramatic late blossoming of a medium that we now know to have been a significant feature of his late public career.[5] Finally, and most unexpectedly of all, Monet again turned to drawing in the very last years of his life, when he took up paper and sketchbooks as he labored over the great water-lily friezes of the 1920s. Contrary to the orthodox view of Monet's achievement and perhaps to certain canons of modernism, his broader engagement with line in the second half of his career was both persistent and critical to his practice.

The second neglected factor in existing assessments of Monet's later oeuvre is a more elusive one but no less fundamental. Earlier chapters have revealed that at most stages in his development as an artist the element of line was part of Monet's imaginative thinking and his practical activity. Rarely consistent as a draftsman for any length of time, Monet would take up his graphic materials when occasion demanded and rapidly adapt them to the subject and the technical challenges at hand. Specific ventures—such as the making of a series of drawings of the Normandy coast, or a late return to the bay at Étretat—would stimulate an idiosyncratic response with his pencil, chalks, or crayons, which might never be used in the same way again. Common to most of these phases was an implicit sense of drawing in dialogue with painting, whether as a direct exchange or through some oblique relationship with another medium, such as printmaking. The drawn line, in other words, had a rapport and perhaps an equivalence with the stroke of the brush, though one that was not well defined or ever entirely comfortable for this most self-conscious of artists.

In Monet's final decades, we find a continuation of this sporadic conversation, more than once occurring at a key moment of transition or at the birth of a new visual theme. Keeping his graphic skills in the background, and even denying them on occasion, Monet evolved new ways of painting with entwined line and color that radicalized certain of his later canvases. He was not, of course, alone in this research, at a time when several of his former Impressionist colleagues—notably Degas and Cézanne—were finding their own distinct paths through the same contested territory.[6] But Monet's experiments were unique, in the technical and conceptual sense, though they have yet to be acknowledged as such or subjected to careful consideration. In works such as *Charing Cross Bridge* (see fig. 255) and *Water Lilies* (see fig. 265), we may encounter an unexpected visual language in ribbons of color and brushed arabesques, glowing contours and densely hued hatchings that aspire toward a large-scale, color-saturated draftsmanship.

Drawing for the Grainstacks and Rouen Cathedrals

The beginnings of Monet's serial painting coincided with some remarkable and still-underestimated groups of sketchbook drawings. At their most minimal, these are represented by a sequence of pencil studies made in the Creuse Valley in 1889, when Monet briefly noted a half-dozen potential motifs in a large drawing book.[7] The purpose of these sketches seems to have been conventional, allowing him to seize the broad outlines of the landscape at several points on his early perambulations. Monet immediately referred to three of them as he made canvases in the proto-series that resulted

242
Grainstacks at Giverny, c. 1888–91. Pencil, 110 x 180 mm. Sketchbook 1, fol. 21v. Musée Marmottan Monet, Paris [D188]

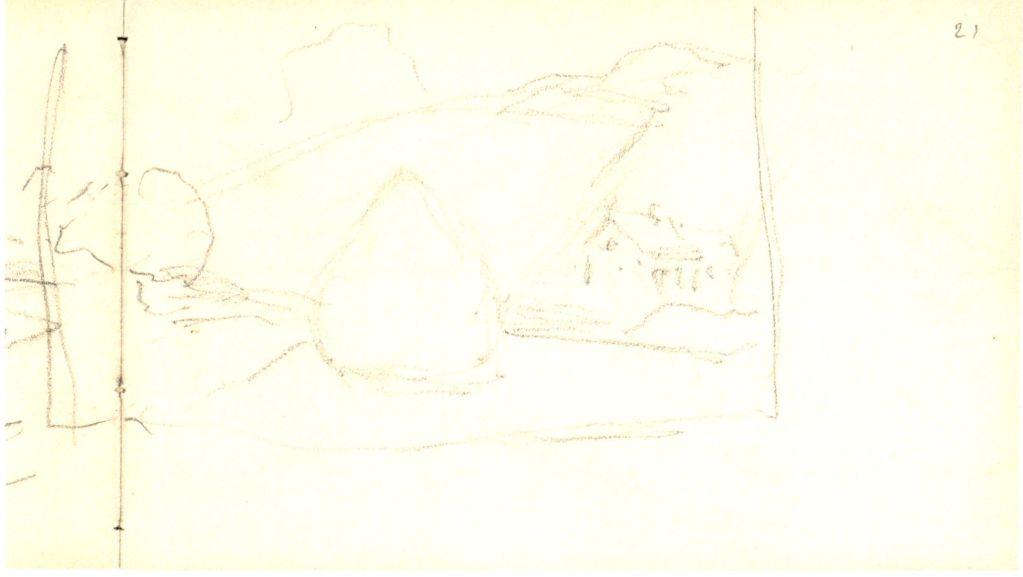

from this visit.[8] A much more complex process is signaled by a cluster of drawings that relate to the artist's first true series, the Grainstacks. On one or more occasions in the years before and possibly after 1890, Monet took a smaller sketchbook with him into the fields near his house at Giverny. This sketchbook, which he had already owned for almost twenty years, measures only 110 by 180 millimeters and could be comfortably carried in his pocket or held in the hand while drawing.[9] Its pages were mainly unused, though it contained a few sketches reaching back to Le Havre in 1873 and a scattering from more recent times. As he wandered in the locality, he accumulated a total of ten simple studies in pencil that were linked by their theme. In the background of most of them are the low-lying hills that border the valley around Giverny, and glimpses of its houses and farms, while their foregrounds all feature the curiously bulbous, conical forms of grainstacks (see figs. 242–44).[10] Some of these images are related as pairs or trios, where the artist has apparently shifted his viewing angle or rotated around a chosen feature. In at least three cases, the design has spread to part of the opposite page, and in a single example Monet added vertical and horizontal lines, as if to define a potential composition (fig. 242). Almost miniature in scale and rudimentary in technique, they seem like impromptu drafts, casual in their execution and carelessly treated thereafter, as some became rubbed or partly erased on subsequent expeditions.

Like almost all of Monet's sketchbook drawings, these works carry no dates or inscriptions and are generally located in his career through their links with better-documented paintings. Several authors have mentioned certain of the studies in question, though without clarifying their roles in the emergence of Monet's now-renowned canvases.[11] The majority of this sequence of almost thirty paintings was made between 1889 and 1891, while some preliminary attempts at less-distinctive scenes appear from 1885 onward and a final reprise of the theme occurs in 1893.[12] The early and later painted variants are more diffuse, showing smaller grainstacks and a greater emphasis on the surrounding countryside. In the classic phase of this motif, Monet brought the grainstacks closer to the picture plane and typically reduced them in number, to just one or two forms that define the picture both compositionally and chromatically. Roughly comparable images for several of these arrangements can be found in Monet's sketchbook drawings; a faint outline on folio 23 corresponds to an 1886 canvas, for example, and there is a bold study of two stacks on folio 22 (fig. 243) that anticipates such works as *Grainstacks (Sunset, Snow Effect)*, while an isolated sketch of a single stack in front of a screen of trees on folio

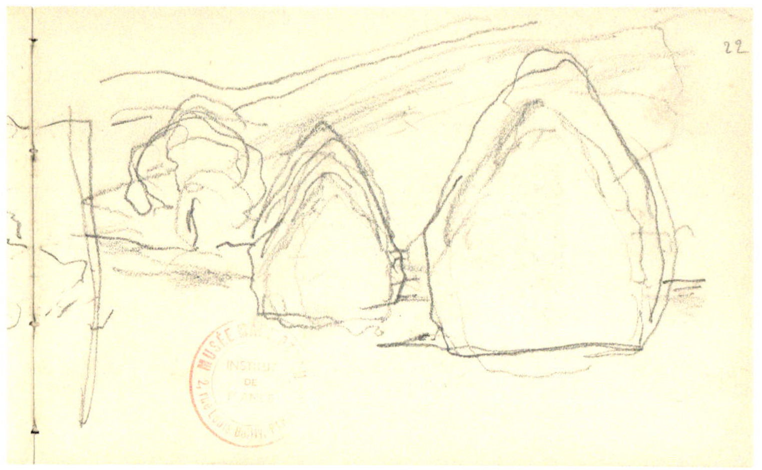

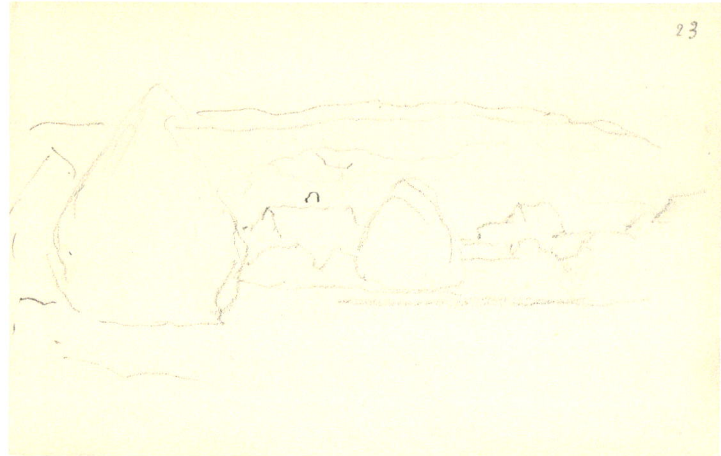

243
Grainstacks at Giverny, c. 1888–91. Pencil, 110 x 180 mm. Sketchbook 3, fol. 22r. Musée Marmottan Monet, Paris [D189]

244
Grainstacks at Giverny, c. 1888–91. Pencil, 110 x 180 mm. Sketchbook 3, fol. 23v. Musée Marmottan Monet, Paris [D192]

39 verso somewhat resembles his last painted treatment of the motif.[13]

What function did these modest, monochromatic sheets serve in the conception and realization of Monet's Grainstack paintings? The spread of drawings in this sketchbook, seeming to correspond to canvases made over a seven-year period, is initially baffling. Did the artist draft the first of such pencil compositions around 1886, subsequently adding new drawings to the same section of his sketchbook over the years as the canvases in his studio progressed? If this possibility seems unlikely, the alternative is almost as untenable: that at some point during his walks of the late 1880s, Monet surveyed an entire vocabulary of grainstack scenes on these tiny rectangles of paper, which he then realized in color, one by one, without returning to the sketchbook to make further drawings.

This conundrum can be partly resolved through further analysis of the drawings and their relationships to the Grainstack paintings. Several drawn studies have a generic relationship to part of the painted series; others, such as that on folio 23 verso (fig. 244), seem to anticipate specific compositions in oil; and some are unlike any of Monet's known canvases.[14] Conversely, designs for one of the most distinctive subgroups of paintings in this series that features a single grainstack (W1280–90) are notably absent from the sketchbooks. Neither the severe, repeated horizontals of hill and field, nor the pyramid-like silhouettes of the solitary grainstacks in these works have direct precedents in his drawings. Typically, Monet's sequence of pencil sketches are curvilinear and free flowing, their stacks invariably irregular in form and their placement less systematic than in his canvases. A drawing of a roughly comparable motif (see fig. 242) illustrates this difference and shows the tendency for such drafts to include a number of distracting subsidiary features, such as prominent trees and bushes, substantial woodland, or a large cloud in the sky. Even when they are close thematically, in other words, Monet's paintings and drawings of grainstack motifs do not match up precisely.

Some of these discrepancies can almost certainly be accounted for by the circumstances in which the Grainstack paintings were made. Monet himself made it clear that these works emerged from direct contact with the subject and from the experience of observing and painting outdoors in all types of weather.[15] In such conditions, of course, a pocket-size drawing became irrelevant and the forms of each picture would have been arrived at through intense negotiations of color and value, texture and space, as so eloquently described by Paul Tucker.[16] As he painted, the placement of the stacks within each canvas became both deliberate and artful, just as the streamlining of the landscape and the stripping away of lesser elements was aimed at resolving the image as a whole. Even the shifting shapes and proportions of the stacks themselves, while possibly reflecting varying local patterns, times of year, and even specific crops, were also subject to

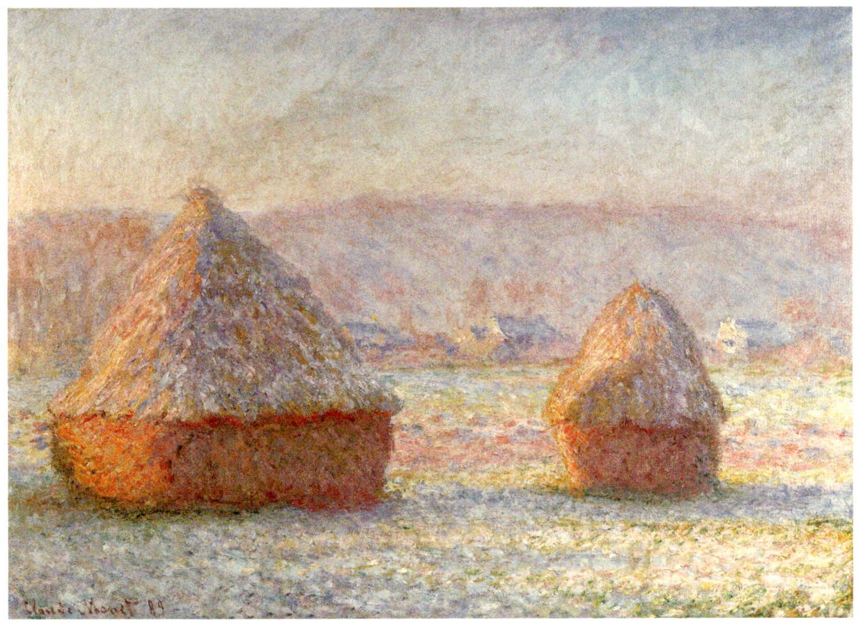

245
Grainstacks, White Frost Effect, 1889. Oil on canvas, 65 x 92 cm. Alfred Atmore Pope Collection, Hill-Stead Museum, Farmington, Connecticut [W1215]

the geometric imperatives of Monet's compositional program.

An examination of the sketchbook drawings for the Grainstacks pictures leads to a single, overarching conclusion: that most of Monet's drawn studies for this motif were provisional in character and executed at an early stage in the project.[17] Perhaps made over successive days or weeks as the artist pondered his new series, these sketches are consistent with a preliminary, questioning phase in his ambitious enterprise. Tentativeness is evident in their facture, which required the redrawing of contours and the almost playful rearrangement of forms, as if grainstacks were chess pieces to be moved on a fixed board. Spillage of lines onto adjoining pages also suggests improvisation, as does the linear framing of a scene in anticipation of a painted composition. These are inventive and mobile creations, the characteristic result of Monet's walks in the landscape and of the stalking of his visual prey, using the simplest of linear marks to keep track of his thoughts. Leafing through his sketchbook, we can follow the emergence of the central motif, as the rounded forms of grainstacks against their planar backcloth asserted themselves in his imagination. As in most of Monet's series—the Rouen Cathedral façade, the stands of parallel poplars, the Japanese bridges—the Grainstacks were based on a profoundly economical concept. Groping toward this core image through drawing, the most primitive and direct of all art-making processes, Monet could then proceed to his canvases and his colors.[18]

Before leaving this episode, we should return briefly to the independent drawing of grainstacks discussed in chapter 8. In this sheet, Monet reversed the procedure he had used when working from nature in his sketchbook, now transcribing his already-completed oil painting *Grainstacks, White Frost Effect* (fig. 245) back into monochrome. Choosing the same black, waxy crayons that had animated his studies of Normandy in the mid-1860s, Monet summarized the vibrantly colored forms of this scene on conventional paper, and again on Gillot paper, as a prelude to its reproduction in black and white. The subsequently printed image (see fig. 204) was yet another example of Monet's willingness—albeit after persuasion—to cross the boundaries between media, sometimes in both directions, to creative effect. This case also highlights the paradoxical nature of many such collaborations during his career. The crayon study attempts the impossible, translating a densely hued canvas into the stark, monochromatic language of line, mark, and tone. By contrast, in his sketchbook drafts for the Grainstacks, as in the drawings for other serial imagery, Monet adopted one of the most traditional functions of his craft, using a pencil line to circumscribe a number of yet-to-be-painted scenes. Drawing, in this sense, was a time-honored shorthand made potent by its association with color, allowing him to use lines to define the armature on which his richly colored oil paints would be modeled.

Monet used the same easily portable sketchbook when he set out on his second great series, the paintings of the Rouen Cathedral. On this occasion, the logic of his use of drawing was entirely straightforward and even more literally connected to the process of exploration. Arriving in Rouen early in 1892, Monet looked for suitable sites for a new group of paintings. By 12 February, he was becoming disillusioned: "Towns really do not suit me," he wrote to Alice, but also remarked that he had just installed himself in a

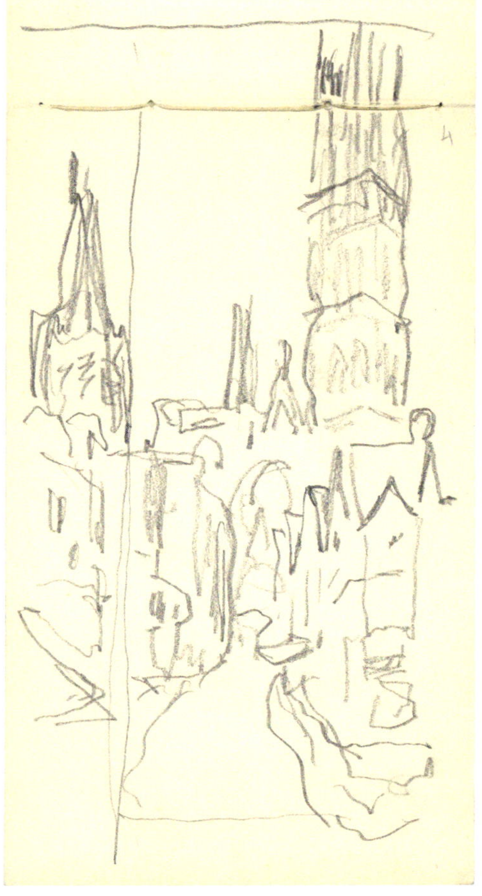

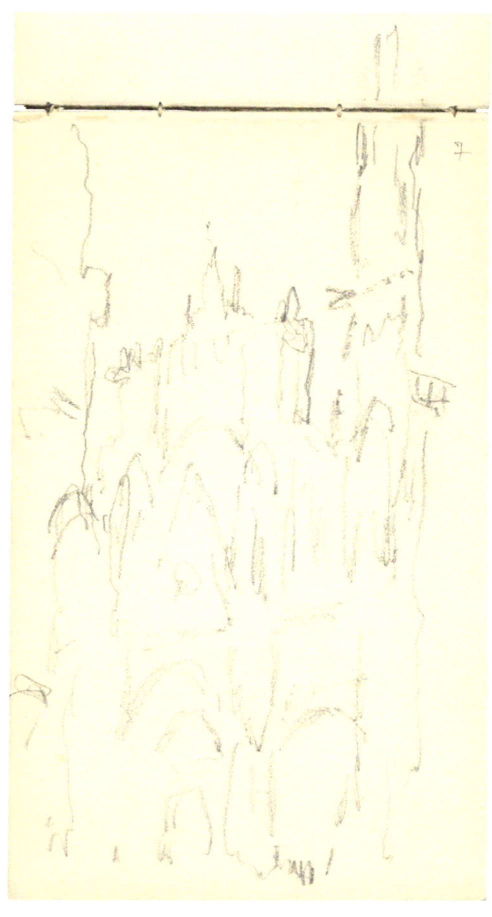

246
The Portail de la Calende and the Central Tower, c. 1892. Pencil, 180 x 110 mm. Sketchbook 3, fol. 4r. Musée Marmottan Monet, Paris [D164]

247
The Façade of Rouen Cathedral, c. 1892. Pencil, 180 x 110 mm. Sketchbook 3, fol. 7r. Musée Marmottan Monet, Paris [D168]

room opposite the cathedral.[19] None of the artist's correspondence describes how he arrived at this particular view of the building, and few commentators have reconstructed the process through his sketchbooks, which seem to invite such an interpretation. Some caution is appropriate, since we cannot assume that Monet moved from page to page in a consistent manner, but the cumulative evidence is suggestive. On the very first leaf of sketchbook 3, for example, the artist made a drawing of Rouen from a distance, with its spires and towers rising from a mist-engulfed city. A small, hastily brushed oil painting of this view was carried out, but Monet chose not to develop it in further canvases.[20] Three of the next four pages bring us into Rouen itself, where he sketched a winding medieval street and the clustered houses, rooftops, and pinnacles rising above it (fig. 246). A second rapidly executed painting that featured the cathedral in the background took the experiment further, but again failed to result in a satisfactory motif.[21] Perhaps disheartened, Monet then returned in his sketchbook to a more remote view of Rouen, looking at the city across the Seine, almost as if it were a rural landscape.

It is at this point that the sketchbook drawings change. The following three pages are different in handling, composition, and focus from all those that preceded them and appear to record a moment of imaginative transition. Each is a summary sketch, in which Monet confronted the west façade of Rouen Cathedral at close quarters, with the building itself cropped by all four edges of his sheet (fig. 247). Thrust against the massive Gothic structure, he used a tremulous line to distill its essential character, its weather-beaten buttresses, arched window recesses, and crumbling pinnacles. Astonishingly, these three drawings seem to have captured the qualities Monet needed, a combination of density and overall simplicity that announced a new motif. More remarkable still is that this trio of pencil images surveyed most of the elements that were explored in his subsequent series of almost thirty

248

Rouen Cathedral, Façade, 1894. Oil on canvas, 106.3 x 73.7 cm. Sterling and Francine Clark Art Institute, Williamstown, Massachusetts. Acquired in memory of Anne Strang Baxter [W1358]

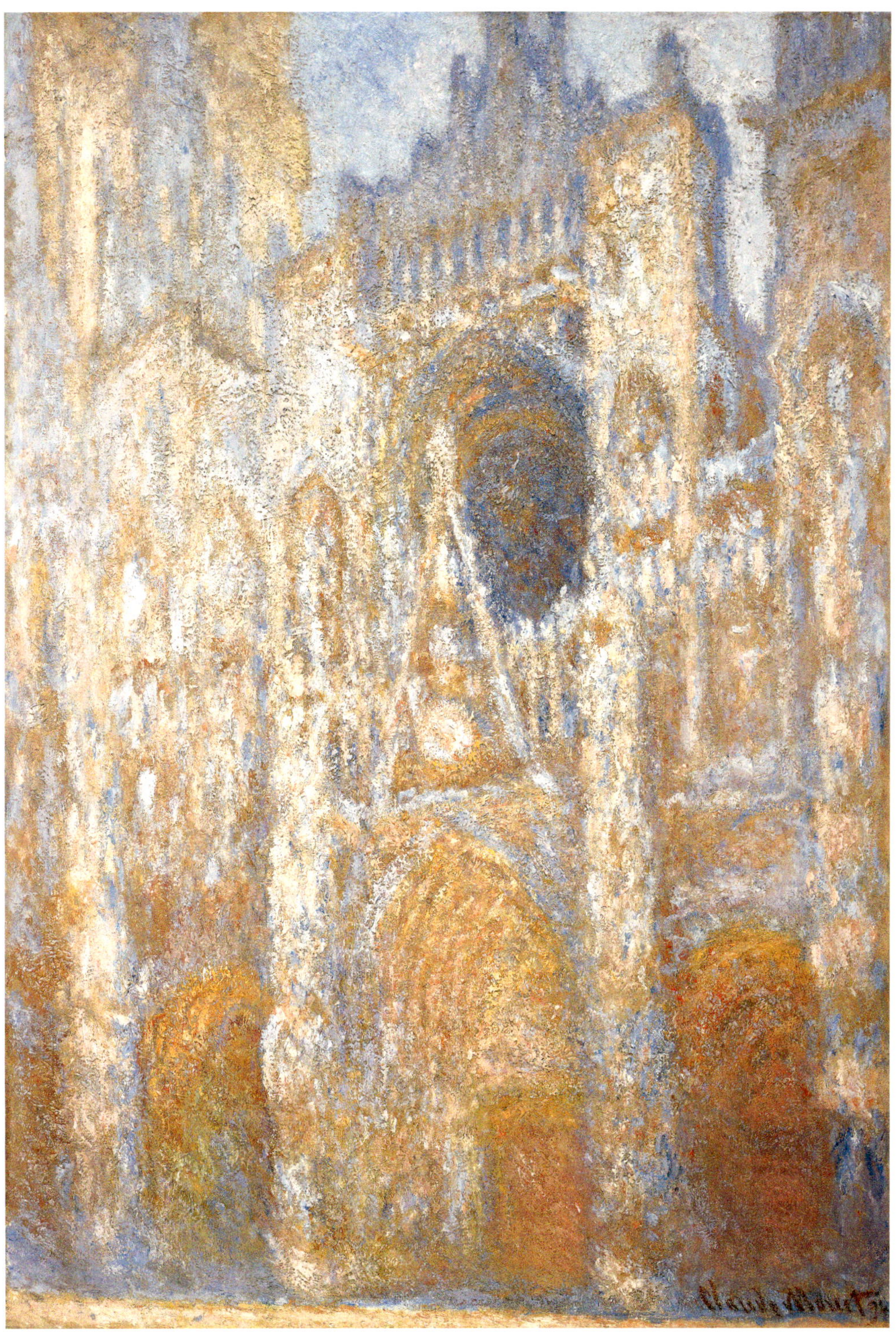

canvases. Unlike the story of the Grainstacks, no other drawings appear to have been necessary, and the artist would spend many months in both 1892 and 1893 unraveling the consequences of his initial discovery in successive paintings. In the canvas belonging to the Sterling and Francine Clark Art Institute (fig. 248), for example, aspects of all three initial designs can be found; Monet has effectively reframed the sketch on folio 7 (fig. 247) by slightly reducing the margins at the top, left, and right. The painting's emphasis on the central window is closer to the two preceding drawings, and there is a slight shift in his viewing angle that corresponds to known changes of his working location. In the last analysis, the sequential drama of the sketchbooks need not be insisted upon. But as with the Grainstacks, there can be little doubt that these small, gray pencil drafts were made before their meter-high painted counterparts and—in some barely comprehensible way—seem to have encapsulated for Monet their light-splitting radiance.

After the critical and financial success of the exhibited Grainstacks and Rouen Cathedral paintings in 1891 and 1894, Monet had good reason to feel that the new momentum of his art had been vindicated. Other series followed or overlapped with the complex stages of completion of canvases already in progress, until the programmatic resolution of grouped motifs accounted for almost all his production. Several of the campaigns of the 1890s seem to have originated in his sketchbooks, though none as circuitously as the Grainstacks or as dramatically as the Rouen Cathedrals. A few pencil studies of trees arranged in lines or screens, for example, apparently marked the beginning of the Poplars, and a more extended cycle of drawings executed in a new sketchbook devoted to his travels in Norway at mid-decade may have been made with a similar intention.[22] Significantly, however, only four or five of the latter cluster of nineteen sketches are related to canvases that survive from this trip. Hampered by freezing temperatures and "endless snow," Monet was to leave this country frustrated by his inability to achieve a sustained working routine.[23] Most of his drawings were false starts, almost touristic glimpses of trees and of settlements he passed through, and it was only a group of eight studies of Mount Kolsas that coalesced into a satisfying motif and led to a limited sequence of canvases.[24]

It cannot be overlooked, however, that the occasional demands placed on Monet's sketchbooks were to continue until the very end of the century and even beyond. In 1896 and 1897, he made winter expeditions to the stretch of coast north of Le Havre, painting at Varengeville, Pourville, Dieppe, and related sites. In one sense, this was a nostalgic return to the region of his upbringing and to the coast that had inspired many of the definitive paintings of his early adulthood; in another, it is significant that Monet chose to distance himself from localities such as Honfleur and Le Havre, where family ties no longer called him. As in previous sojourns, the bulk of his new work was dedicated to the theme of sea and cliffs, with almost every sub-series leaving its traces in his pocket sketchbook, the same one that had been carried to Rouen and into the fields of Giverny. By now a virtual compendium of his serial art, this sketchbook and its peripatetic use seem to have become essential stages in his working pattern. A dozen wandering lines on a single page were sufficient to fix a view at Le Petit-Ailly or nearby Dieppe (fig. 249), yet Monet was apparently unable to proceed toward painting without them. There are fewer suggestions that he compiled these drafts while strolling through nature, but the need to pin down his motif at a crucial moment in its conceptualization was still unshakeable.

The Pastels of London

On a different occasion and at another point in his "series" sketchbook, following a curiously random sequence of drawings of Rouen, Varengeville, and sites near Giverny, Monet made a single study of the Houses of Parliament in London (fig. 250).[25] Few drawings in this book are less substantial, yet this slight outline has several claims to our attention. First, it shows that Monet continued his long-established habit of carrying such sketchbooks on painting trips at the turn of the century, if only to use them occasionally or perhaps not at all. A similar case occurred as late as 1908, when a visit to Venice was marked by a solitary study in an otherwise empty drawing book, purchased while he was in the city.[26] Second, this small image of London provides an initial link between Monet's late draftsmanship and one of the most extreme painterly phases of his art, when his depicted subject matter was seen by a contemporary to dissolve in an "enchanted, misty vision."[27] The square Victoria Tower in Westminster and the pointed silhouette of Big Ben, both identifiable in his drawing, were to appear in the distant

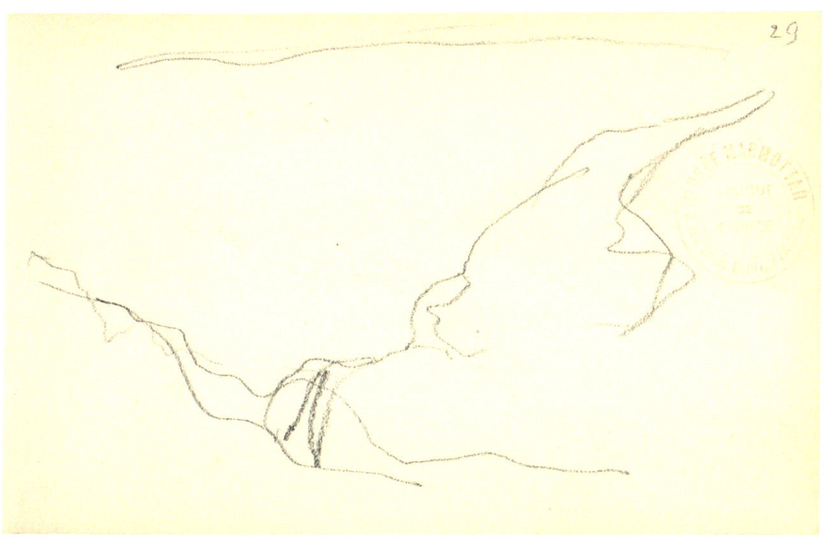

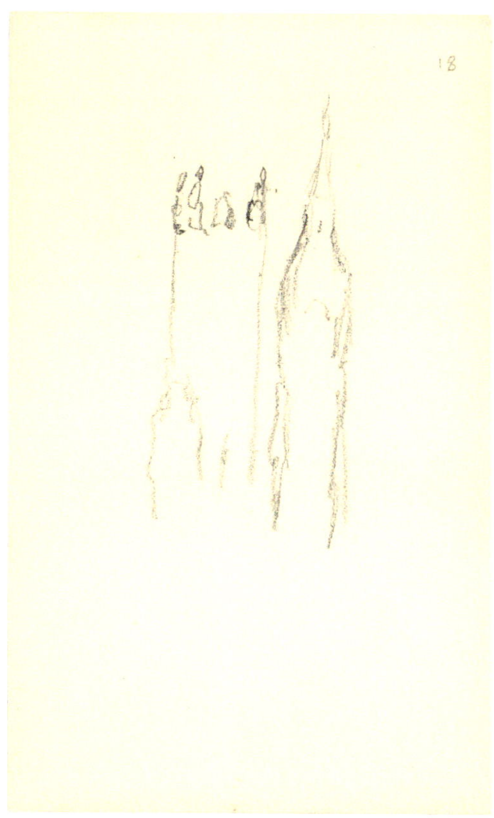

249

Cliff to the West of Dieppe, c. 1896. Pencil, 110 x 180 mm. Sketchbook 3, fol. 29v. Musée Marmottan Monet, Paris [D202]

250

London, The Towers of Parliament, c. 1899–90. Pencil, 180 x 110 mm. Sketchbook 3, fol. 18v. Musée Marmottan Monet, Paris [D183]

haze of several of his London pictures (see fig. 255), though never with this degree of detail. Even in the English rain and fog, it seems, drawing had its place, as his slowly unfolding cycle of canvases of the River Thames further attests.

Monet's extensive correspondence shows that he stayed in London three times between 1899 and 1901. There he labored on almost a hundred canvases, taking works in progress back to France after each trip and returning with them to England the next year for further refinement, finally completing the series at Giverny. He stayed at the exclusive Savoy Hotel in the center of the city, where he could look down from the north bank of the Thames across the busy river to the wider industrial landscape. Facing east, Monet saw the deep stone arches of the old Waterloo Bridge, topped by its crowds of pedestrians and rush-hour traffic; as he turned west, he confronted the grid of the modern steel structure that carries trains into Charing Cross railway station to this day. Two major sequences of paintings were based on these views and a third was begun when he acquired permission to paint opposite the Houses of Parliament at Westminster, beyond Charing Cross. Monet explained that it was above all the atmospheric effects that fascinated him, reporting to Alice how "torrential rain" could be followed by "appallingly clear" conditions, without a "wisp of fog," the sun "so dazzling I found it impossible to see," and an occasion when "the Thames was all gold."[28]

Arriving in London for his third visit, on Friday, 25 January 1901, Monet discovered that his boxes of canvases and equipment had yet to appear and found himself unable to work. The next day, his letter to Alice complained of restlessness but mentioned that he had "tried in vain to make some sketches in pastel" which "had not helped" his mood.[29] After some "superb weather" on Sunday, 27 January, it rained heavily and Monet told Alice that he "continued to try" with his pastels. Acknowledging that he had lost touch with the medium, he added "this amuses me a lot, even though I'm no longer accustomed to it, it occupies me and may be useful."[30] On Monday, his luggage

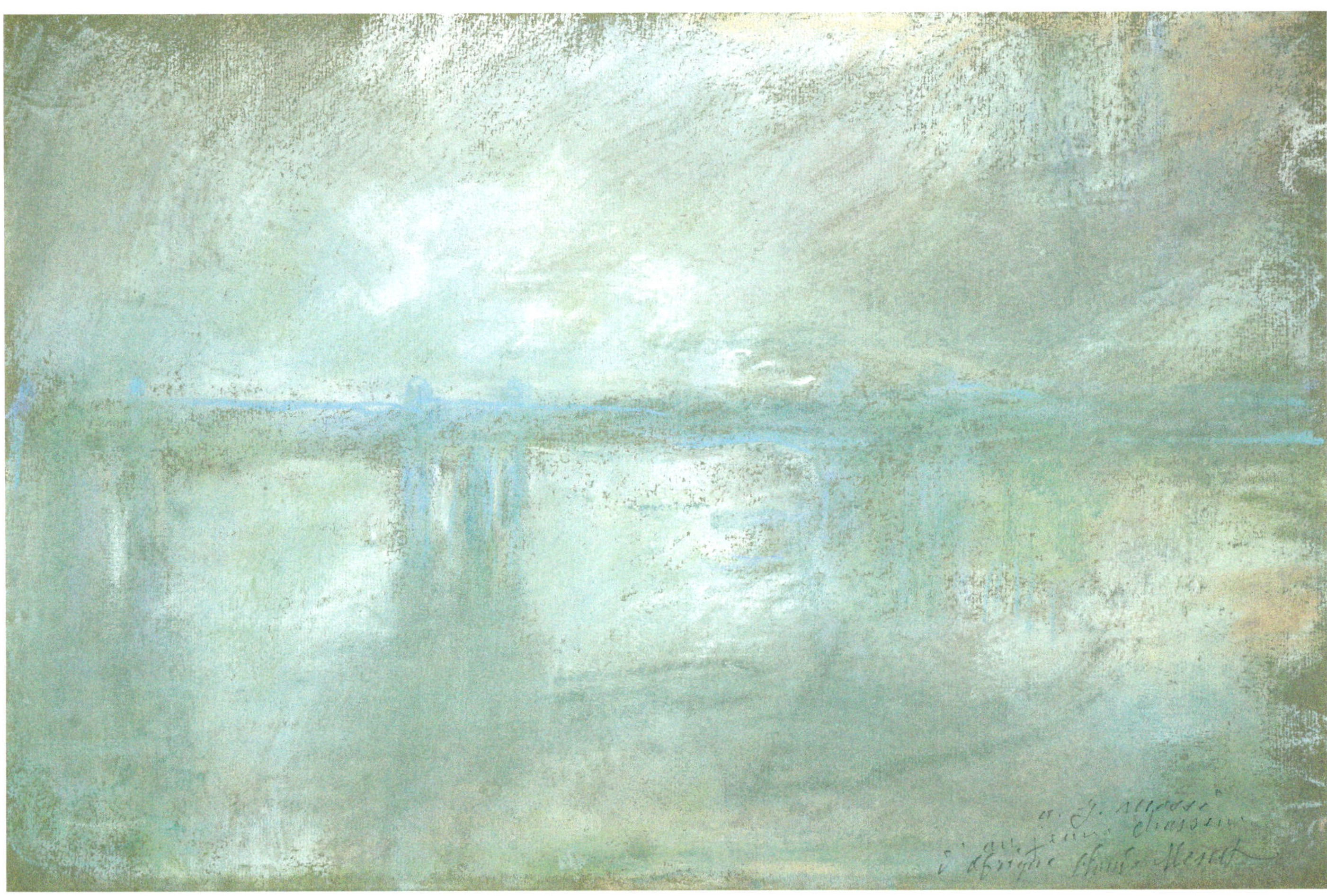

251
Charing Cross Bridge, c. 1901. Pastel, 310 x 485 mm. Triton Foundation, The Netherlands [P84]

was still missing and he again worked at "many pastels," now describing them as being "like exercises" as he prepared for the task ahead.[31] A week after his arrival, Monet could finally turn to his painting and almost immediately conceded that things had gone well; "It's thanks to my promptly made pastels that I saw what I had to do," he explained.[32] No further mention of the pastels is made in his letters, as painting filled his waking hours.

A total of twenty-six works in pastel on paper have been preserved from this period of unexpected effort in 1901, all of them based on the river and two adjacent bridges. Since Monet had already painted these same subjects many times in 1899 and 1900, and anticipated returning to his canvases any day, he made little attempt to explore new motifs in the pastels. Conceived in quite different circumstances from his sketchbook drawings and made for quite different reasons, the pastels represented the continuation of a well-defined project and made no claims to thematic originality. *Charing Cross Bridge* (fig. 251), for example, recapitulates the composition of one of the earliest oil paintings in the series, a work sold to Boussod and Valadon in Paris in November 1899 that is now in the Shelburne Museum, Vermont.[33] Both pastel and canvas show the extreme formal simplicity that characterizes the entire London oeuvre, balancing strong horizontal and vertical elements against the more fragile qualities of shifting light.[34] In this case, the Shelburne painting and the related pastel share the middle range of the palette, though other variants in both media explore the gamut from icy blues and deep purples to shocking collisions of peach, mineral green, and charcoal black. *Charing Cross Bridge* is both majestic and delicate, almost seamlessly merging a wide spectrum of hues and even introducing fine lines of pure color—such as the blues on the bridge—as part of the principal design.

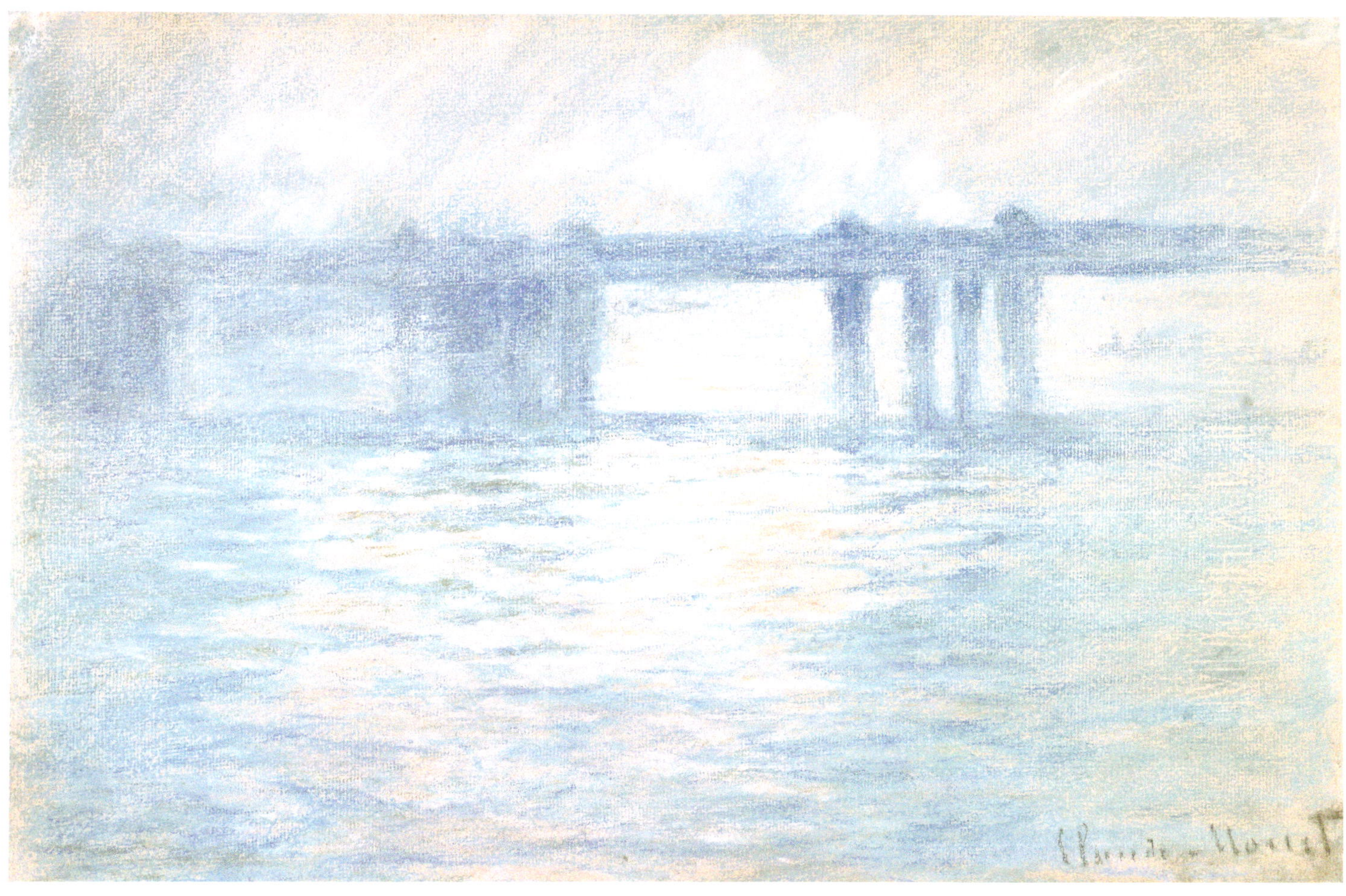

252
Charing Cross Bridge, London, c. 1901. Pastel, 300 x 470 mm. Private collection, New York [P83]

Following a general tendency among these works, the pastel shows a closer view of the bridge than the oil version, as if the artist has zoomed in on his subject as he planned the smaller study. Using sheets of paper that were approximately a quarter the size of his meter-wide canvases, Monet modified his ambitions accordingly. Some pastels resemble sections or details of the larger motif that have been simplified as designs and reduced in overall complexity to allow his chalky medium greater expressive latitude.

Monet attempted just five pastels of his view of Charing Cross, each intricately varied from the others in its tonal values and in the placement of its principal forms. In *Charing Cross Bridge, London* (fig. 252) he lifted the edifice nearer to the upper edge of the rectangle and depicted its structure with greater precision than in the previous work. Now we are more conscious of the water, a subtly inflected expanse of pearl-pinks and grays that vies with the bridge for prominence. Such nuanced evocations of visual experience, endlessly varied by slight shifts in the weather and the drifting pollution from London's factories, were at the heart of Monet's fascination with his London subjects, as the titles of certain of these works declare. Pastels sold in his lifetime and probably identified by him include *Charing Cross, Sun Effect in the Mist* and *Charing Cross, Fog*, while related oil paintings specify "veiled sunshine," "pink effect," and "effect of sun in the fog."[35] Friends who visited him described how Monet would watch the occluded vista patiently, then announce, "The sun is out again" as his companions saw "nothing but that gray-muffled space, a few hazy shapes, the bridges that seemed to hang in nothingness, the smoke that rose only to quickly dissolve, and a few surging waves of the Thames, visible at the river's edge."[36]

Some of the physical features of these pastels offer insights into their making and their

253
Waterloo Bridge, Boats on the Thames, 1902. Pastel on blue-gray paper, 310 x 480 mm. Private collection [P105]

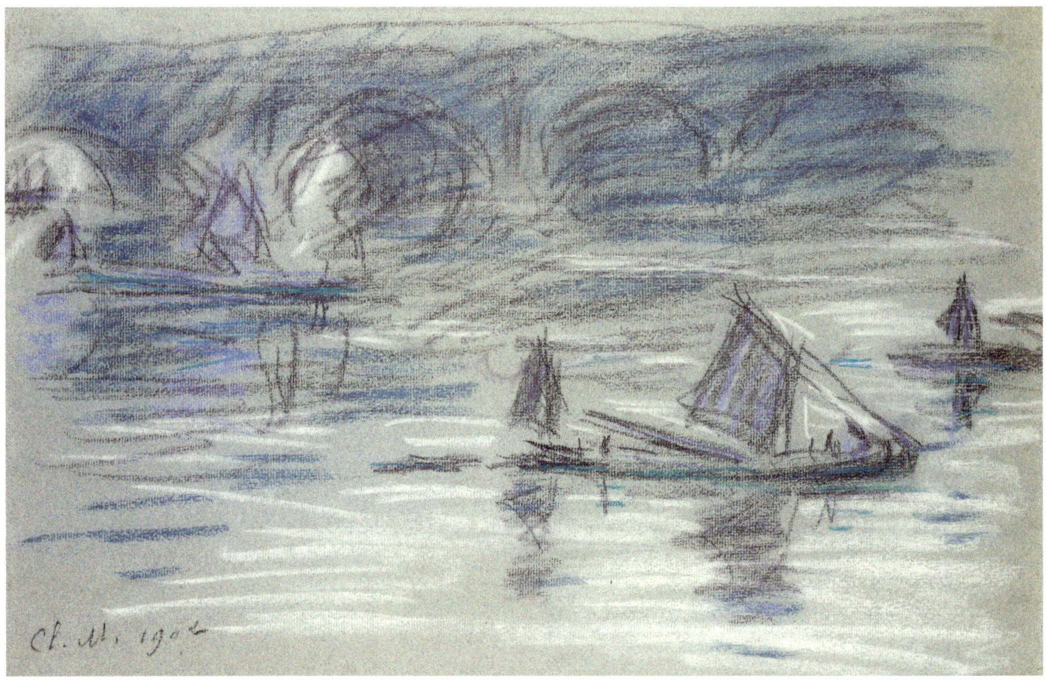

subsequent history. The laid paper on which *Charing Cross Bridge, London* and at least one other pastel was made bears a "Michallet" watermark, suggesting that Monet brought this French-made material with him or found a supplier in London.[37] Many of the series were carried out on a pale, tan-colored paper, its warmth offsetting the dominantly cool hues of his pastel images. *Waterloo Bridge, Boats on the Thames* (fig. 253) and some other works, however, are on bluish or gray sheets.[38] Both of the Charing Cross scenes already discussed were signed by the artist, as were the great majority of his Thames pastels. Given Monet's professed reluctance to make these works, he was notably eager to give or sell them to acquaintances, and released several to the commercial market. Another Charing Cross scene was dedicated to a comrade from his military service in Algeria, a certain A. Massé—"jeune chasseur d'Afrique," as the inscription puts it—and others were passed to Sacha Guitry and the painter André Barbier.[39] Other examples went through the art trade before the painter's death in 1926, and the unusual *The Thames in Fog* (fig. 254), in which Waterloo Bridge and a fleet of barges almost disappear behind a burst of colored light, was sold by Monet himself to a Japanese visitor at Giverny in 1916.[40]

Soon after his crates of canvases had finally arrived, Monet explained that the making of the pastels already showed him the way ahead: "I saw what I had to do." The suggestion that his works on paper anticipated some of his forthcoming challenges on canvas provides a rare glimpse of Monet's thinking on such matters. Applied retrospectively, it might rationalize certain of the pastels made at Honfleur or Étretat, which perhaps enabled him to see what he "had to do" in terms of the color harmonies and radical compositions of the 1860s and 1880s. In London in 1901, this remark pointed to a direct, sympathetic relationship between his pastels and his unfinished works on canvas that is dense with unexplored significance. Such a rapport is evident in the mesmerizing surface of *Charing Cross Bridge* (fig. 255), a painting from the Indianapolis Museum of Art that is both unsigned and undated. Clearly left in an incomplete state, it is impossible to deduce from which of the three painting campaigns this work emerged or to guess at Monet's reasons for preserving it in such a broadly sketched condition. Whatever its history, the canvas gives us tantalizing access to Monet in mid-action by the River Thames, as he worked toward the definition of another sun-infused

254
The Thames in Fog, 1901.
Pastel, 312 x 480 mm.
Bridgestone Museum of Art, Ishibashi Foundation, Tokyo [P106]

255
Charing Cross Bridge, c. 1900.
Oil on canvas, 66 x 92.7 cm.
Indianapolis Museum of Art. Gift of Several Friends of the Museum [W1530]

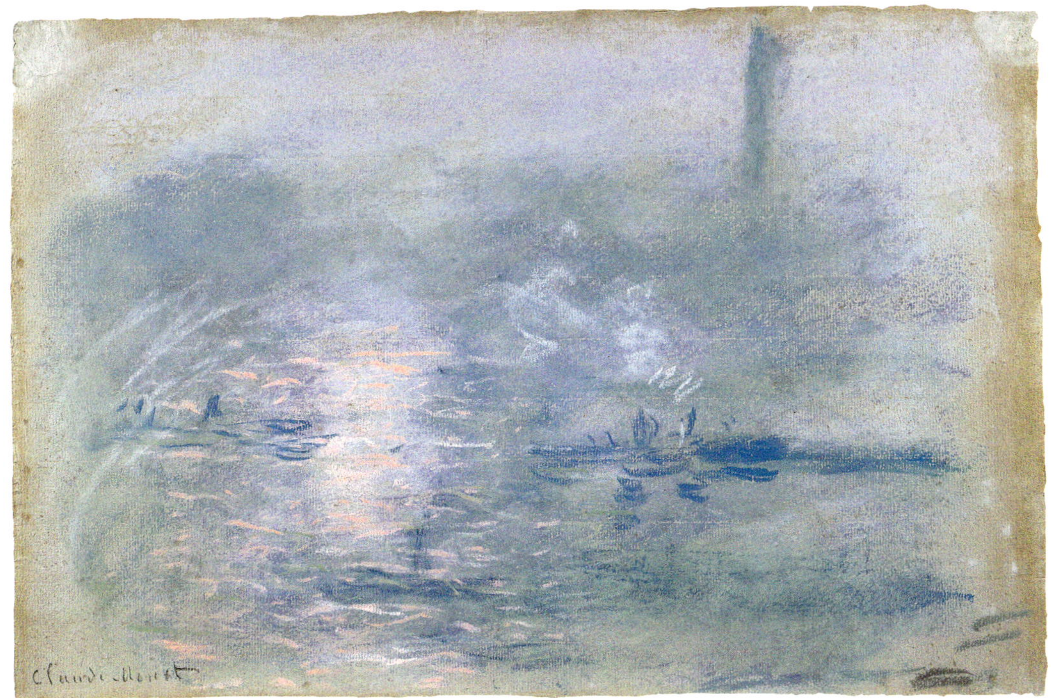

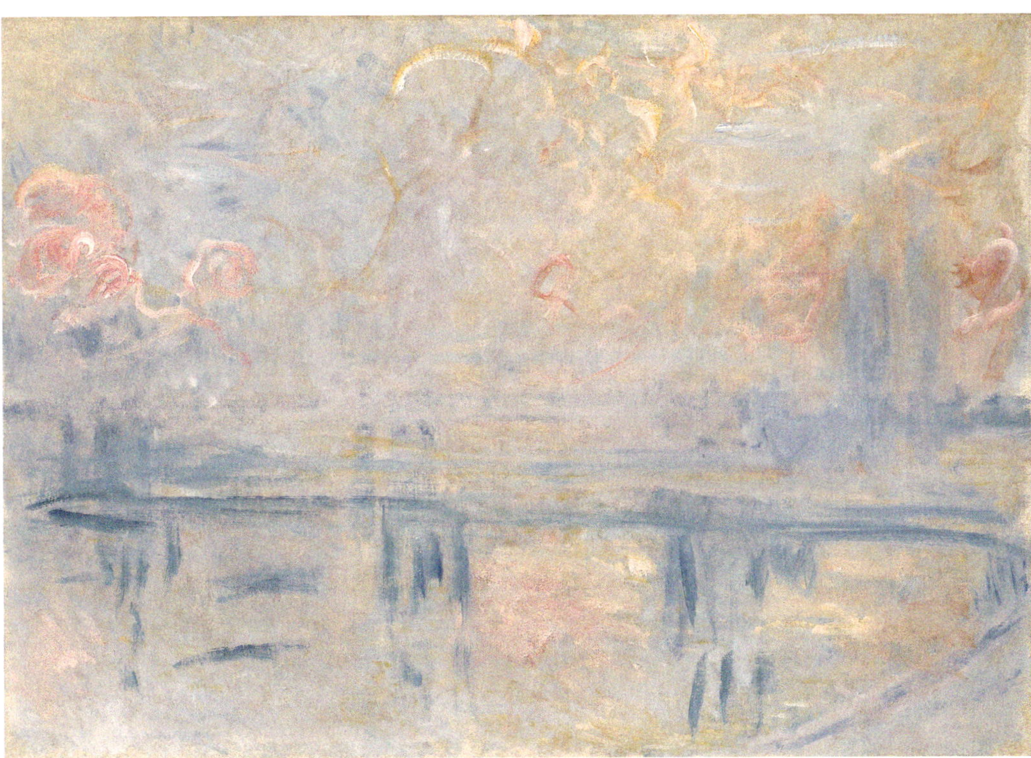

painting of a now-familiar motif. Every aspect of this image seems to be under negotiation, even the position of the bridge itself, which began in the upper half of composition and is now well below the horizon. Progressively heavier strokes of gray-blue paint record its gradual descent, earlier marks having been painted over with lighter hues. The palette, too, is manifestly in transition, with yellow cloud or smoke swirling above, blue mist at center, pink steam rising from the trains, and the Thames "all gold" toward the lower-right margin.

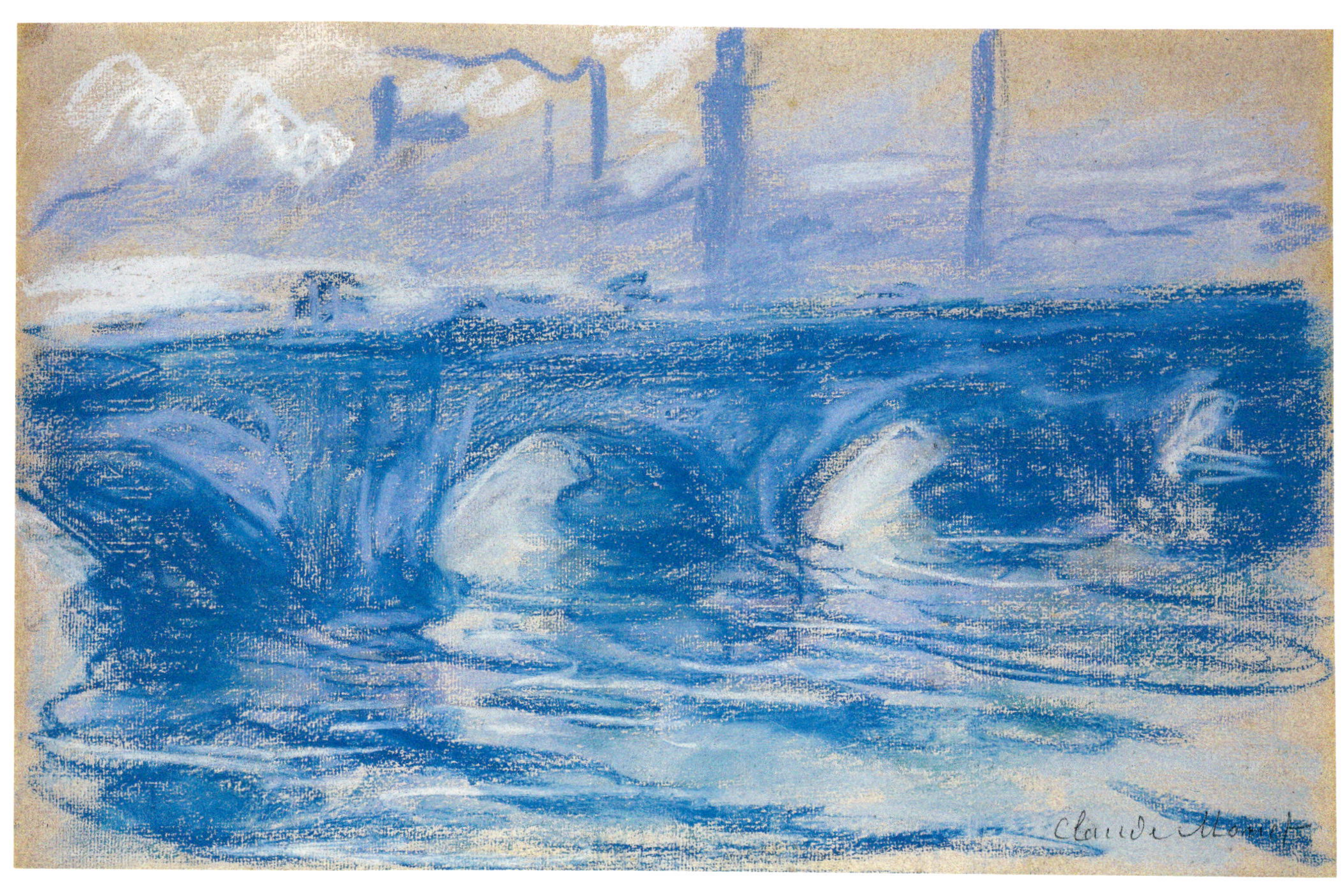
Claude Monet

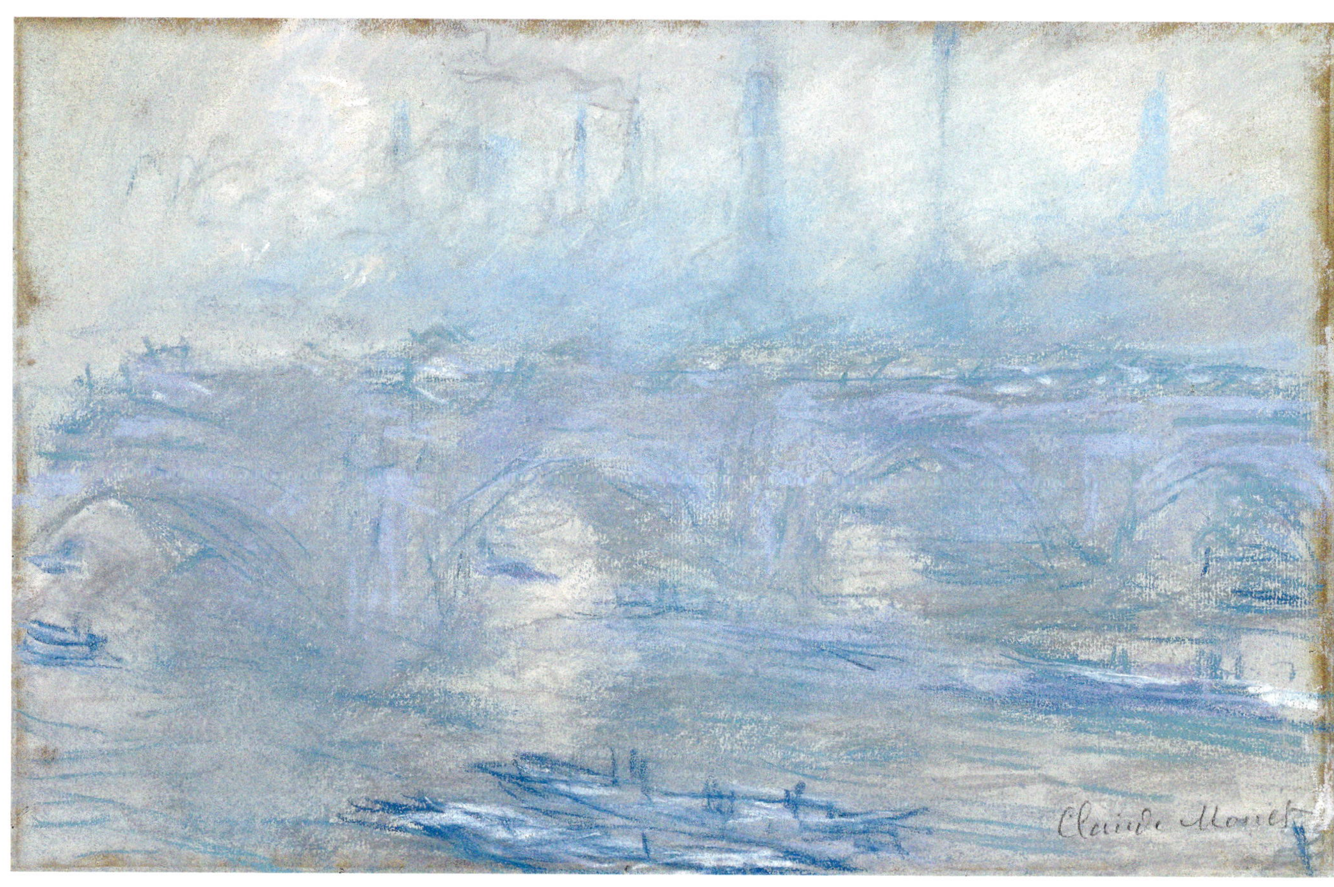
Claude Monet

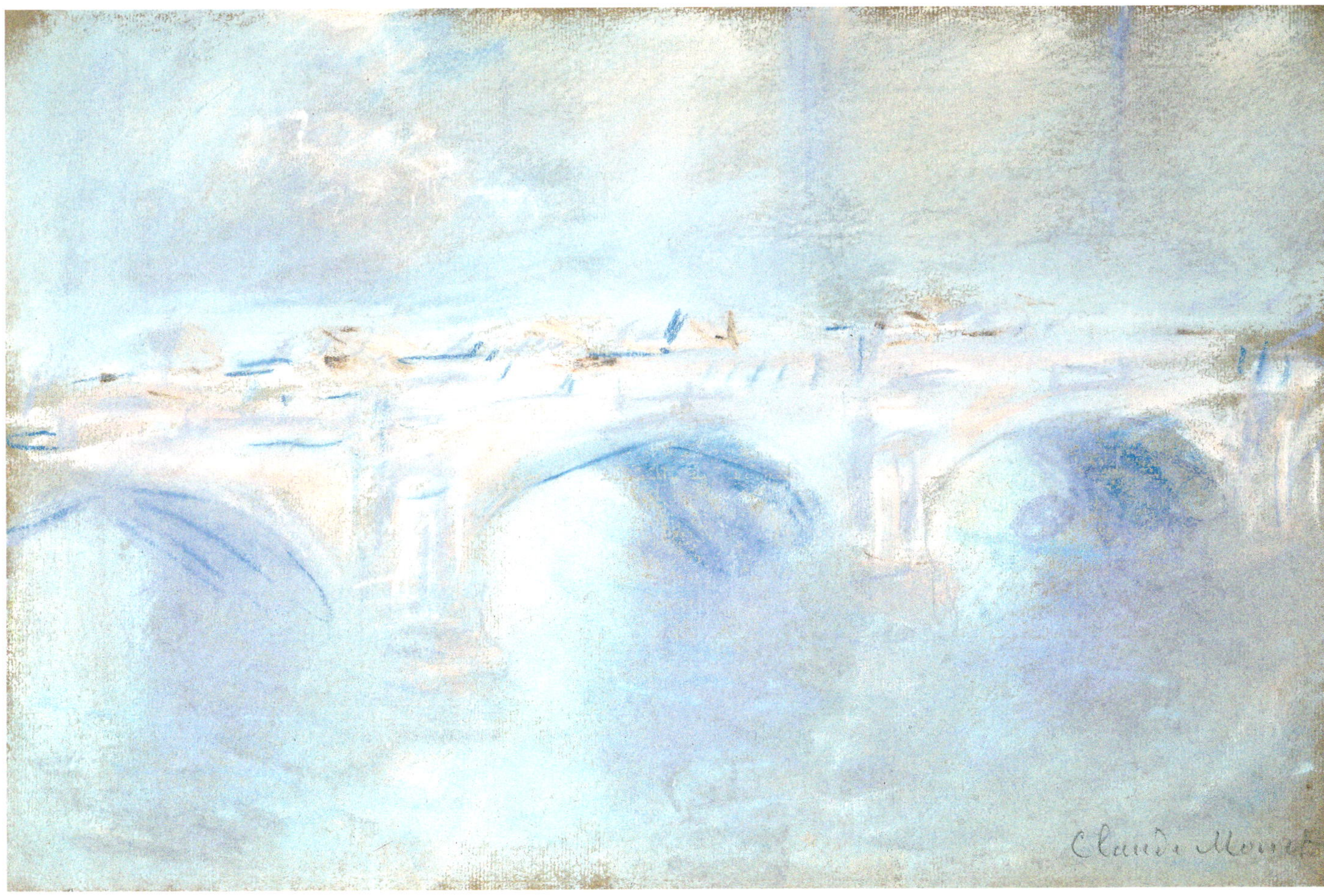

256
Waterloo Bridge, 1901. Pastel on beige laid paper, 311 x 485 mm. Musée d'Orsay, Paris [P100]

257
Waterloo Bridge, London, c. 1901. Pastel, 300 x 480 mm. Villa Flora, Winterthur, Switzerland [P109]

258
Waterloo Bridge, c. 1901. Pastel, 305 x 480 mm. Triton Foundation, The Netherlands [P101]

Unmistakable in the Indianapolis canvas is the linear character of Monet's brushwork, in which grids, streaks, curls, and spirals of paint suggest giant threads in a wild, multihued tapestry. These lines of color seem to have been the basic materials from which many—but not all—of Monet's London paintings were woven. Additional unfinished versions of this scene reveal a similarly anarchistic craft in action, while a number show a more liquid, broadly brushed approach.[41] Dates on several of the Charing Cross canvases indicate that Monet continued to develop them from 1899 until as late as 1904, leaving considerable latitude for creating the campaign that included the picture now in Indianapolis.[42] Whether it preceded or followed his pastel-making episode, the graphic nature of its facture inevitably brings to mind the sketches on paper of similar motifs. In *Waterloo Bridge* (fig. 256), for example, Monet's serpentine strokes of cobalt, pale violet, and white are similarly conspicuous, situating this vibrant image somewhere between the linear and the painterly.

Another relatively unembellished pastel of this kind, *Waterloo Bridge, Boats on the Thames* (see fig. 253), reveals even more of its origins, showing beneath its light application of color the dark chalk drawing of the bridge's structure and three boats. Monet appears to have begun a number of his London sheets, perhaps all of them, in this way, first drafting the major forms with relatively crisp lines, then spreading successive strokes of colored pastel as he developed his "effect." In most examples, the subsequent accumulation of powdery hues would be softened with his finger or with a stump, a cylinder of rolled paper kept by pastellists for this purpose. *Waterloo Bridge, London* (fig. 257) allows us to see several of these techniques in simultaneous operation, where emphatic strokes—some of them colored—have marked out the contours of bridge, boats, and distant chimneys. Over

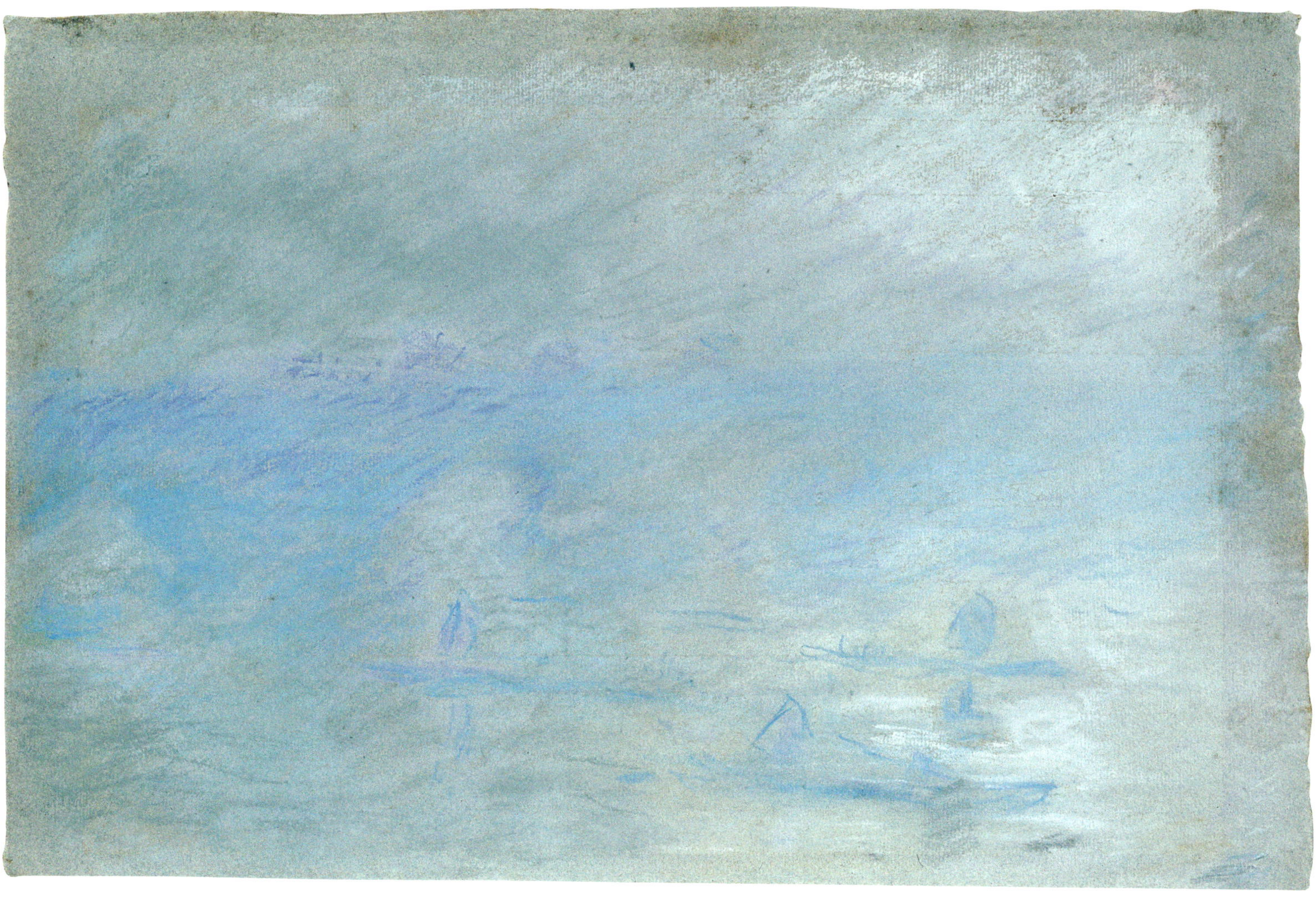

259
Waterloo Bridge, Fog, c. 1901. Pastel, 270 x 420 mm. Private collection [P103]

and around them, Monet has spread a thin veil of paler pastel, evoking the insubstantial effects of smoke or mist through his gentle manipulations. Another pastel of Waterloo Bridge (fig. 258) shows a similar process at a more advanced stage, where dense applications of pastel through much of the image conjure up haze in sky and water but also convey the density of light-caressed stonework. Significantly, much of the latter effect is achieved through drawn strokes of violet and pink pastel, which simultaneously define and embody their subject. These qualities are taken to even more sensuous extremes in *Waterloo Bridge, Fog* (fig. 259), which almost dissolves the gravity of its subject beneath a soft veil of tinted light. Most significant here is the introduction of the foreground boats, built entirely in lines of powder blue toward the end of the creative process. Beside these pastels, we are left in little doubt that the Indianapolis *Charing Cross Bridge* and associated works emerged from an analogous procedure in which colorful, exploratory brushstrokes would eventually be absorbed into a more consistent or continuous film of paint.

If his pastels of the visually delicate Charing Cross structure are appropriately vaporous, some of those representing the more historic Waterloo Bridge tend toward grandeur. Monet was clearly intrigued by these weighty stone pillars and their deep, shadowy arches, often spelling out their forms with care and noting slight variations in curvature as he changed his viewing position. But he was not oblivious to their practical purpose, using sharper strokes in one of his more detailed pastels to hint at the crowded thoroughfare passing overhead (see fig. 258). Typically choosing to represent

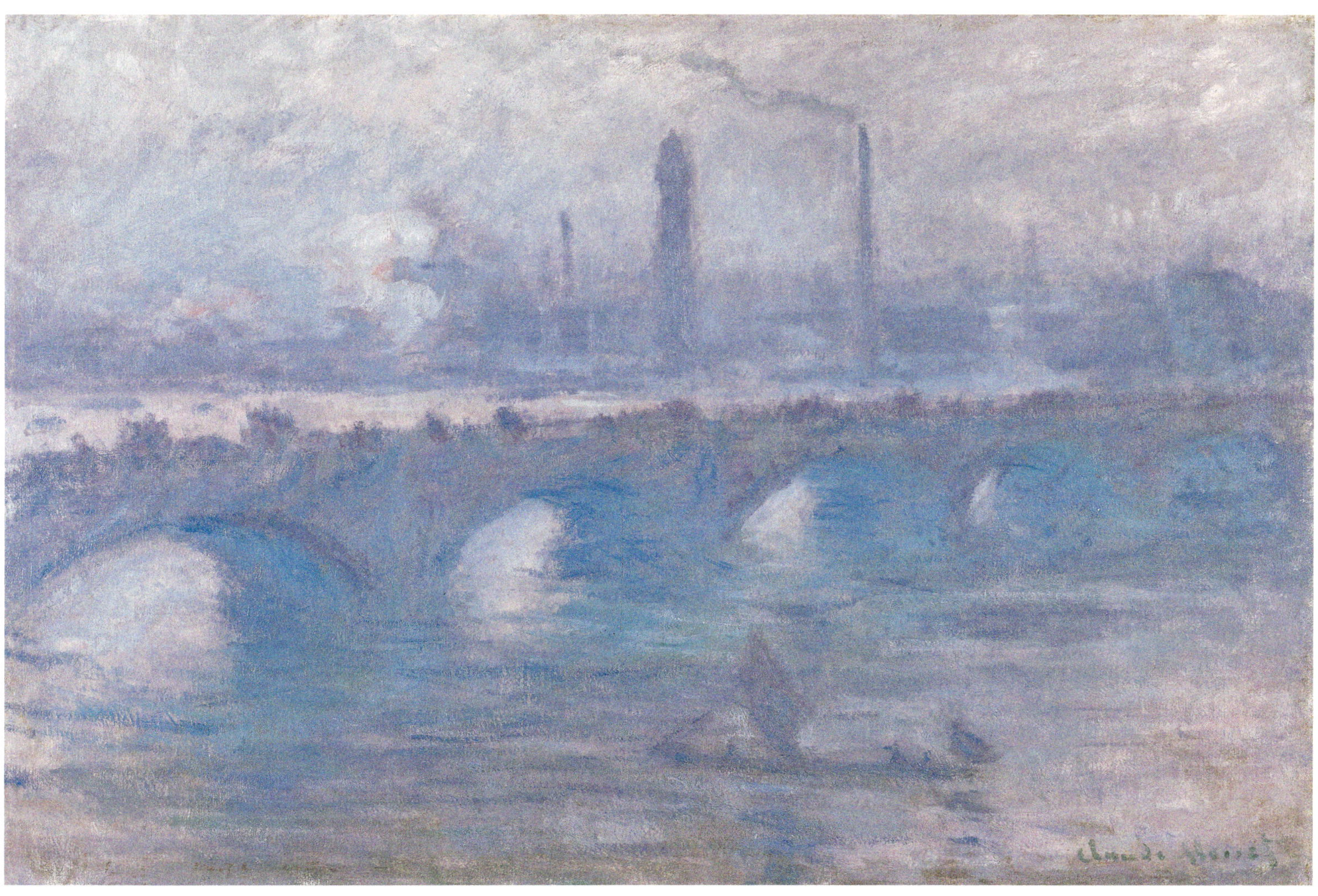

260
Waterloo Bridge, Morning Fog, 1901. Oil on canvas, 65.7 x 100.2 cm. Philadelphia Museum of Art. Bequest of Anne Thomson in memory of her father, Frank Thomson, and her mother, Mary Elizabeth Clarke Thomson, 1954 [W1559]

two or three complete spans in such a composition, rather than the four or five of his more expansive oil paintings, Monet similarly reduced the complexity of the wider cityscape when working on paper. In the background of his pastels of Waterloo Bridge, tall towers and smokestacks are vaguely discernible above the smog, just as the ghostly forms of the Parliament buildings hover behind Charing Cross Bridge in his parallel series. But neither of the pastel sequences approached the topographical exactitude of his most focused canvases, where distant warehouses and recognizable buildings, and even wavelets on the Thames and tiny figures on omnibuses, can be discerned. By this standard, all his London pastels are evocative rather than descriptive, as befits the character of the medium at hand. While it remains possible that the unsettled weather in late February 1901 largely determined the outcome, it is noticeable that all the works on paper incline toward mistiness and rarely aspire to precision.

In May 1904, the achievement of Monet's London oil paintings was further acknowledged with the purchase of *Waterloo Bridge, Morning Fog* (fig. 260) by Paul Durand-Ruel, who soon sold the picture to Mary Thomson of Philadelphia.[43] Matte in surface and muted in its pewter grays and soft blue-browns, this picture again seems to reflect the complex dialogue between paint and pastel that took place during his visits to London. Set apart from the more painstaking, documentary renderings on canvas of the same site, the gentle harmonies of the Philadelphia composition almost make us believe that they were stroked and smoothed with the hand. As in *Waterloo Bridge, Boats on the Thames* (see fig. 253), a traditional barge emerges from

261
James Abbott McNeill Whistler, *Evening, Little Waterloo Bridge*, 1896. Transfer lithograph in black with stumping on cream laid paper, 93 x 194 mm. Library of Congress Prints and Photographs Division, Washington, D.C.

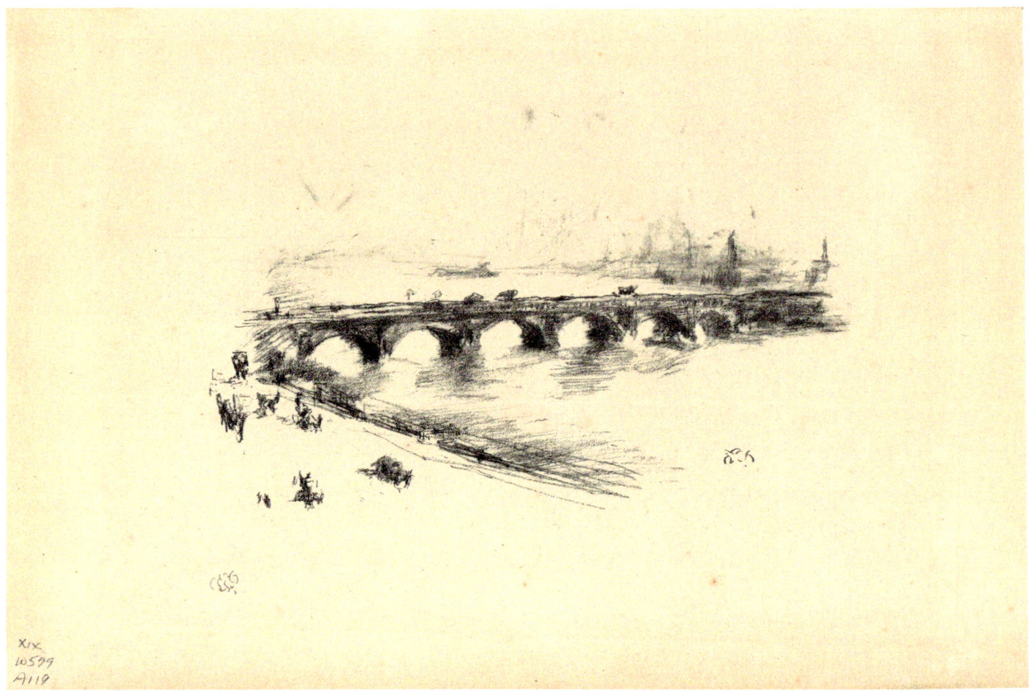

the rippling, murky waters, its eccentric sails recalling the earlier nocturnes of James Abbott McNeill Whistler. Monet had long admired the softly evocative drawings, prints, and paintings of Whistler and enjoyed a warm personal relationship with this "great artist," to use his own words.[44] In the London pastels, their mutual respect became even more explicit.

Over more than thirty years of friendship, Monet and Whistler promoted each other's art and acknowledged a close affinity in their taste and even in certain preferred techniques. In 1887, Monet suggested that Whistler should be invited to send fifty oils, watercolors, and pastels to Georges Petit's "International Exhibition" in Paris, a proposal followed by a similar opportunity for Monet to show in London.[45] Pastel had featured prominently in Whistler's output up to this time as a vehicle for both figure and landscape studies, though it would decline in prominence thereafter.[46] In 1891, Whistler sent Monet a pair of lithographs as a gift, exploiting their mutual friend Stephane Mallarmé as a courier.[47] When his wife became seriously ill five years later, the American artist preceded Monet by taking up temporary residence among the comforts of the Savoy, where a suite of evanescent watercolors and lithographs of the Thames gradually unfolded.[48] Executed in soft black crayon, the latter included several views toward the west and east of the hotel, and might almost be preparatory studies for Monet's later oil paintings of these sites. Though exquisitely finished, Whistler's *Evening, Little Waterloo Bridge* (fig. 261) effectively formed the kind of monochrome base on which dense layers of color would be superimposed in Monet's pastels. Having been encouraged by Monet and others to spend more time in France during these years, Whistler paradoxically missed two of Monet's visits to London, though the two men may have met during Monet's second painting campaign there in 1900.[49]

After completing his pastel sequences of the Thames bridges, there is no evidence that Monet turned to the medium again in later years. When a major exhibition of thirty-six London paintings was held at the Durand-Ruel gallery in Paris in May 1904, Monet followed his usual practice by excluding associated works on paper from the display.[50] Somewhat unexpectedly, however, one of the pastels — *Waterloo Bridge, Boats on the Thames* (see fig. 253) — carries the date 1902, while another is dated 1903, suggesting that he valued these studies sufficiently to refine and modify them alongside his oil paintings after

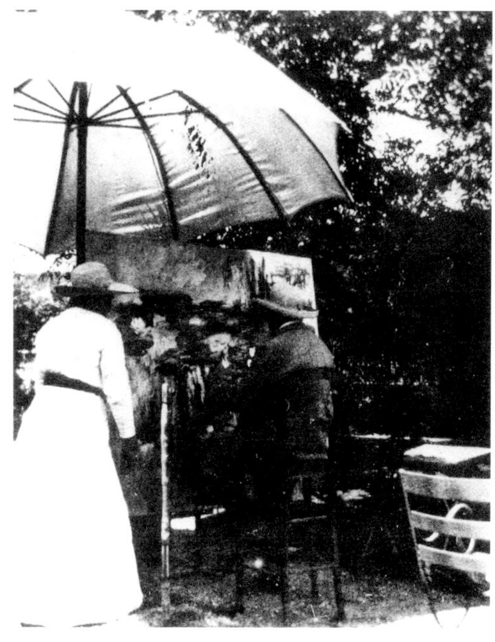

262
Monet working in his garden at Giverny, 1915

the return to Giverny.[51] In addition, Monet was willing for his pastel studies to be seen in public as complete, self-sufficient images. As we have noted, at least half the total number of London pastels left his studio before the artist's death, featuring among the collections of his friends and admirers, and in the holdings of several dealers in France and beyond.[52] A single example was exhibited in Switzerland in 1912 and others elsewhere in 1931 and 1935, but it was not until after the Second World War that the pastels slowly began to enter the canon of Monet's acknowledged achievements.[53]

Color and Drawing at Giverny

The reception of the London paintings was generally rapturous, spreading Monet's fame further across the seas and helping to define the character of late Impressionism for the new century. A prominent theme among the London critics was the primacy of color in the latest works, "these pyrotechnics of gold, of rose-pink, of rose-red, of rose dotted with red, of purple, of meadow green, of gilded or deep-blue green," as Gustave Kahn described them; "one could believe—for an instant—that this sight must be based on some principle of polychrome decoration rather than caused by an absolute obedience to nature," before adding that, on the contrary, the paintings were "meticulously crafted from precise notations."[54] Over the next two decades, Monet would pursue his love affair with nature's pyrotechnics into uncharted territory, where the prominence of motif and effect, of "precise notation" and decoration ebbed and flowed in his creative concerns. The garden he had created at Giverny was already an encapsulation of these themes, to be abandoned only once for a painting expedition of any substance, when he and Alice visited Whistler's beloved Venice in late 1908.[55] At Giverny, flowerbeds matured, wisteria slowly covered the Japanese bridge, and water lilies spread across the expanded and improved pond system. For the first time in his career, Monet's subject matter was on his doorstep and under his control as much as he could wish. His health was not as robust as before and the long walks with a sketchbook came to an end, with spacious and later purpose-built studios answering his every need. Secure in his income and his reputation, Monet could paint what he chose and in exactly the way it suited him.

In these novel working circumstances after the turn of the century, the role of preliminary sketches and other studies on paper was implicitly called into question. The exploratory function of drawing that had persisted since his youth was largely redundant, as was his need to investigate new series of related motifs; he was no longer expected to impress his peers or to cater to illustrated magazines; and the urge to address the human figure, which had flared again in paintings of his family in the 1880s and 1890s, was finally extinguished. Monet himself made few references to drawing in his late years, apart from offering some surprisingly conventional advice to beginners and declaring—rather misleadingly—to the Duc de Trévise, "I've never liked to separate drawing from color."[56] Ironically, this was the period of Monet's life when his working practices were best documented, mainly through the accounts of writers, celebrities, and others who visited his Giverny home. There was even a short filmed sequence of the artist dabbing at a canvas beside his pond, in a demonstrably staged performance

263

Water Lilies, c. 1914–19. Pencil, 235 x 315 mm. Sketchbook 6, fol. 8v. Musée Marmottan Monet, Paris [D347]

264

Water Lilies, Reflections of Willow Trees, 1916–19. Oil on canvas, 200 x 200 cm. Musée Marmottan Monet, Paris [W1862]

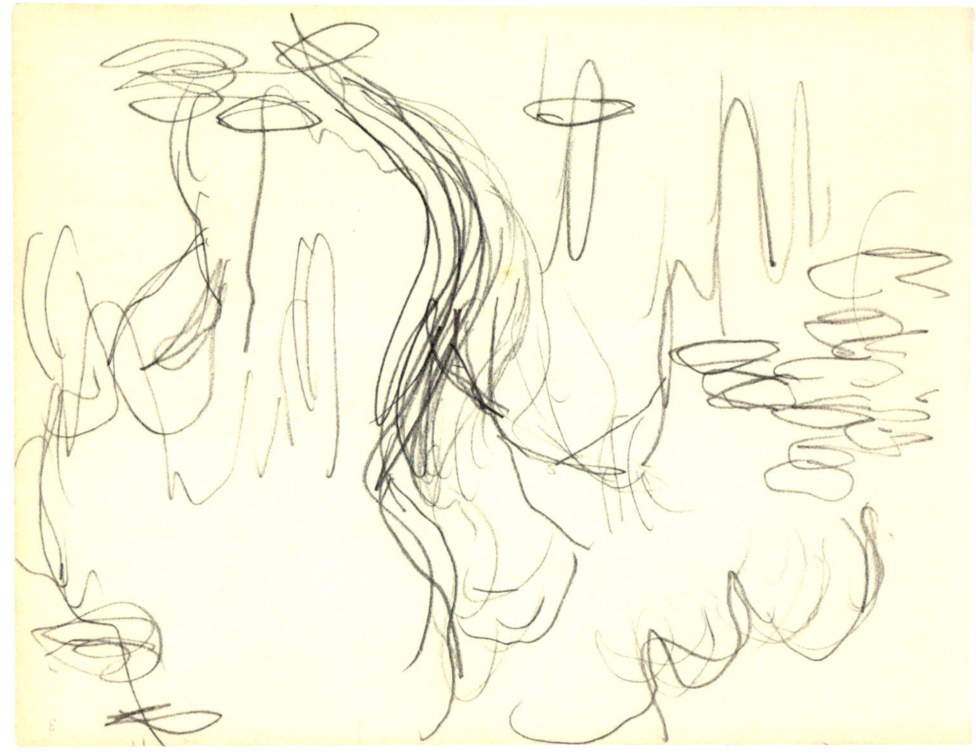

for the camera of Sacha Guitry, the eventual owner of one of Monet's London pastels.[57] Few if any of his guests, however, appear to have been invited to watch Monet paint in earnest, and there is much ambivalence about the precise manner in which he turned the garden subjects around him into works of art.

All of Monet's acquaintances seem to have agreed on at least one aspect of this new practice: the importance he attached to his specifically visual engagement with the Giverny garden. Above all, Arsène Alexandre noted, Monet wanted to have "his flower palette before him to look at all year round," while Kahn referred to "the series of water flowers, the so-called *nymphéas*, with an incredible variety of elusive nuances . . . yet the eye of the artist had seized them, and his palette had obeyed his eye."[58] To François Thiébault-Sisson, Monet explained that he always "shifted his vantage point" when making successive paintings of the same flowers and described some unexpected effects in the "mirror of water" that "went unnoticed by the untrained eye."[59] The stage between looking and painting, however, was less securely accounted for. Some of his earlier visitors fell back on stories from the time of the Grainstacks, Kahn asserting that "he sets up his easel outdoors" and worked on "a dozen or so canvases" at a time.[60] A commentator as shrewd as Roger Marx echoed this belief, reporting Monet's claim that this direct contact allowed him to paint "the impressions registered on my retina."[61] Alexandre was among the first to acknowledge that there were two modes in operation: "sometimes he works in the garden, exhilarating his eyesight and his imagination," he explained in 1901, but "sometimes, more often, he works in the large studio."[62] Nearly two decades later, however, when Jean Gimpel was shown the mural-size *Water Lilies*, the artist insisted that he had worked on such pictures in the open air. "One after another, I have them brought to me," Monet said, a ritual in part endorsed by photographs that show him working outdoors in 1915 (fig. 262).[63]

Still central to this testimony was the notion that Monet's later paintings grew out of an immediate interaction with nature, just as it was understood to have done throughout his previous career. In our own times, the complexities of this approach have been teased out through scholarly scrutiny of Monet's

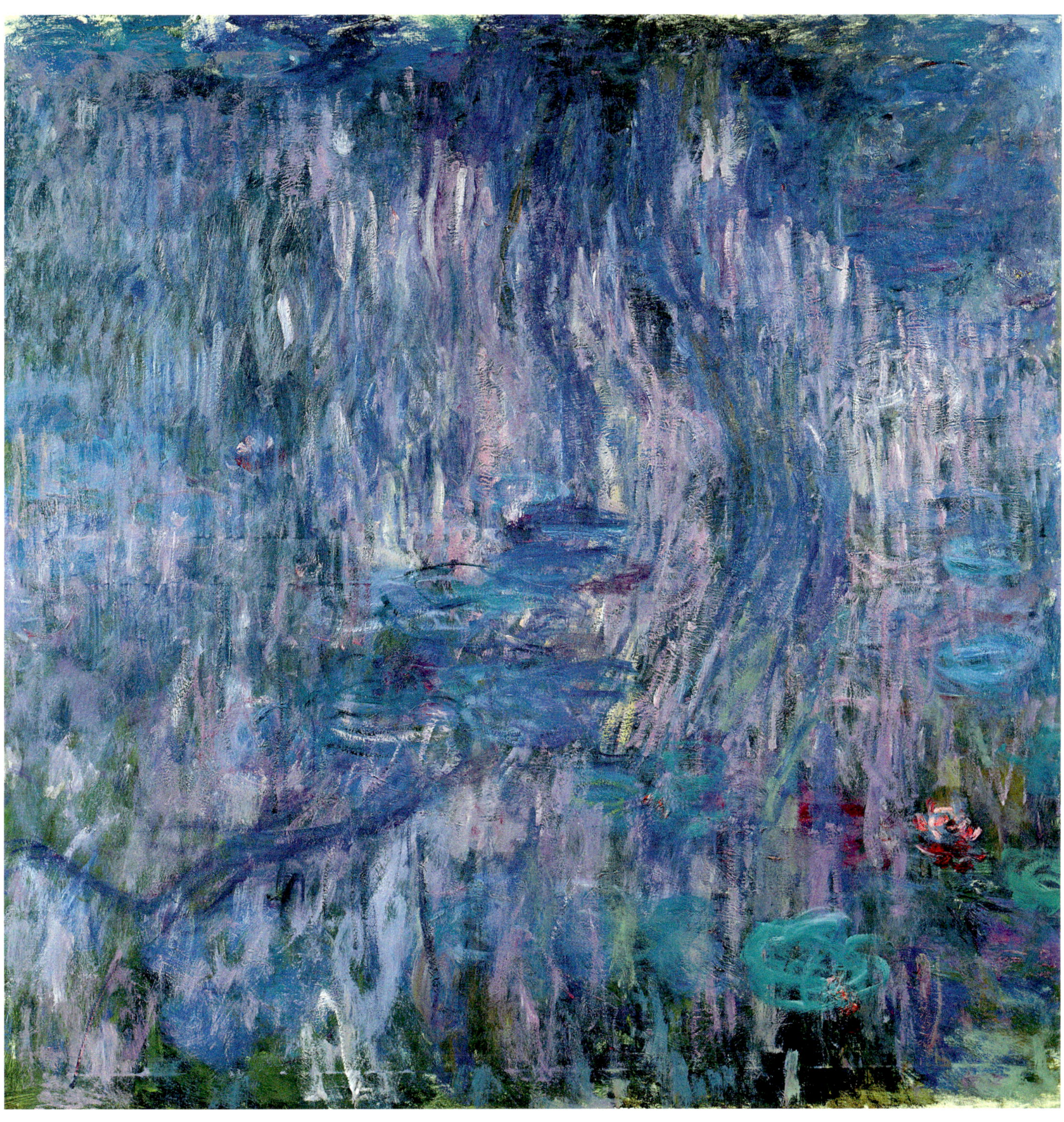

painting campaigns and of the works themselves, which has suggested that certain types of picture — such as the series canvases of the 1890s — were completed away from the motif that inspired them.[64] It has yet to be claimed, however, that Monet actually began any of these works at a distance from his subject and had thus broken the chain of direct experience and perhaps of authenticity. At Giverny, this issue took on a more acute significance, with both day-to-day implications and deeper challenges for understanding his later painting. With the source of his inspiration just a few steps from his easel, Monet could never be far from the

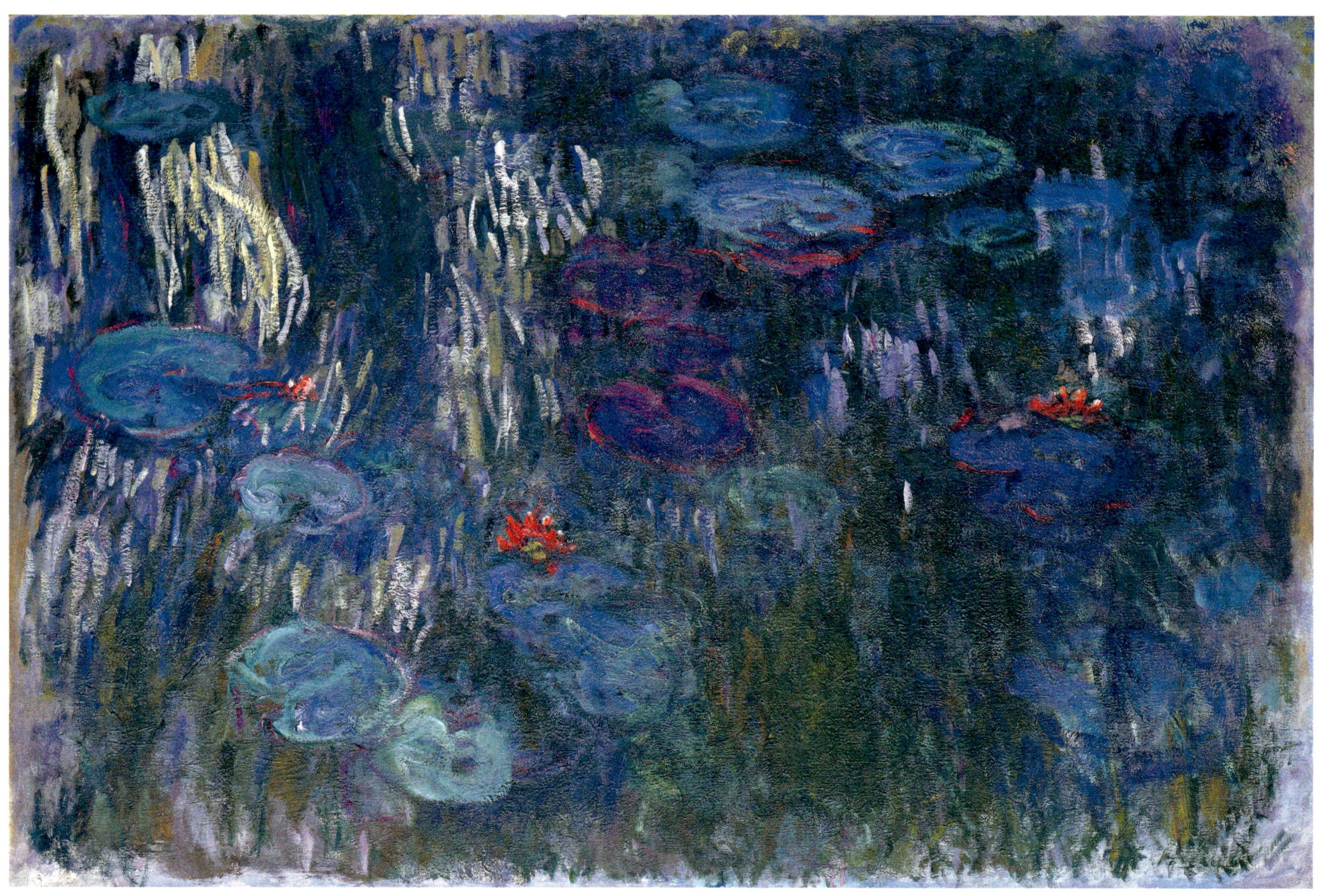

265
Water Lilies, c. 1918. Oil on canvas, 130.2 x 200.7 cm. The Metropolitan Museum of Art, New York. Gift of Louise Reinhardt Smith, 1983 [W1858]

"flower palette" that "exhilarated his eyesight" or the lush vistas and exotic sights of his Japanese footbridge, the winding pathways, and massed willow trees. Yet, increasingly, the substance of his art seemed elusive: Monet complained to Roger Marx about those who argued that he had "arrived at the ultimate degree of abstraction," insisting that when he made his paintings "one moment, one aspect of nature is all that is needed."[65]

Living face-to-face with his garden and its flowers, and painting them in spectacular color on canvas after canvas, the last activity we might expect from the seventy-year-old Claude Monet is drawing. For almost a century, the existence of around twenty-five studies on paper from this period has been either unknown or ignored, and even today it is habitually omitted from the story of the works that crown Monet's career. All the drawings in question relate to the *Water Lilies* and include both sketches of partial compositions and broad, horizontal designs for his most ambitious endeavors. Consistent with Monet's attitude toward much of his earlier graphic production, there are no records of him showing these drawings to his acquaintances or including them in exhibitions. By accident or design, however, they were never destroyed and have survived in two forms: a trio of studies on separate sheets of blue-green and gray laid paper, found among objects left by his son Michel to the Musée Marmottan Monet, and some twenty-two drawings in the pages of the artist's sketchbooks.[66]

The sketchbook drawings fall into three overlapping categories. The first includes a half-dozen single pages that appear to be drafts for individual canvases or discrete elements in a larger scheme.[67] The pencil study on folio 8

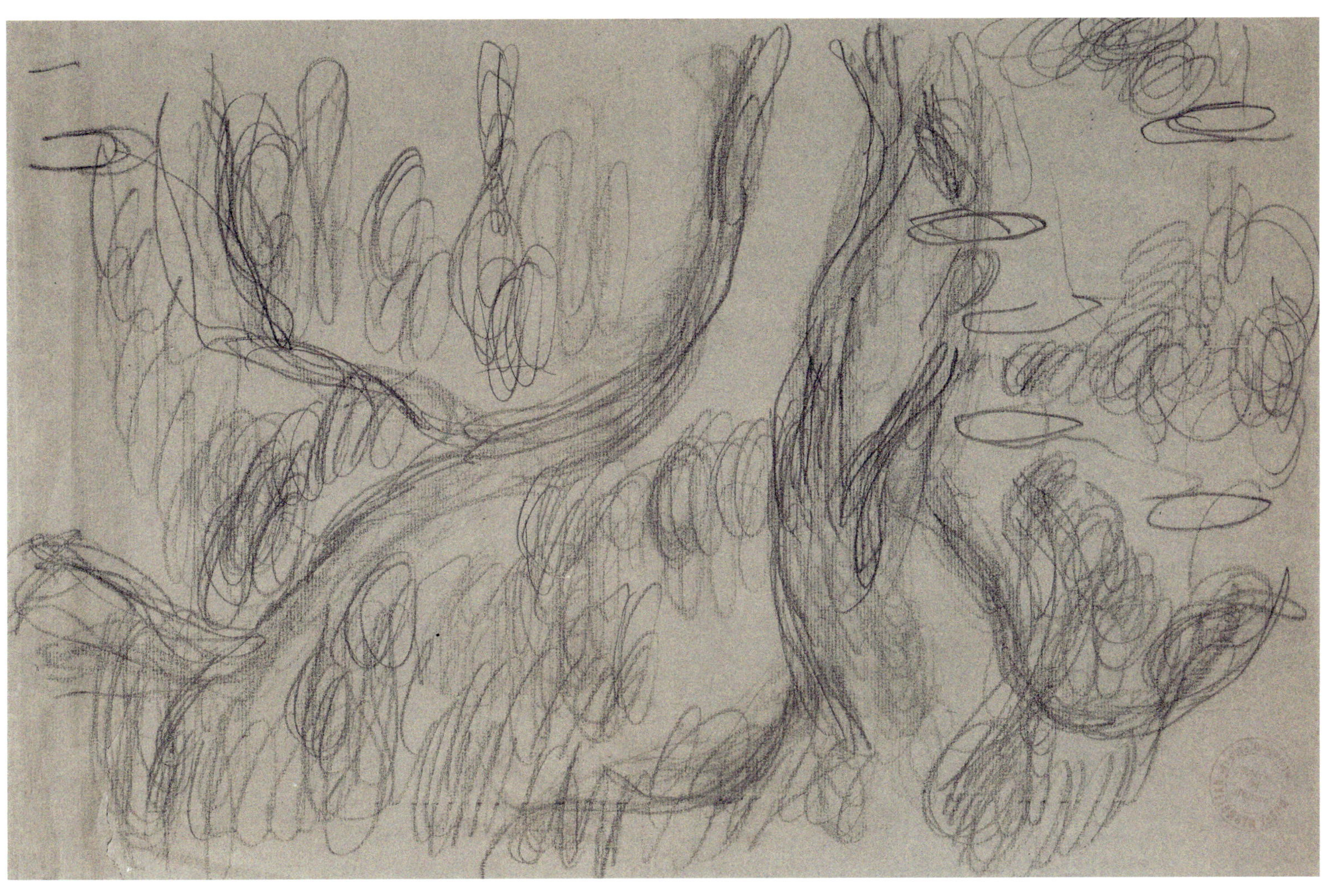

266
Reflections of Willows, c. 1918. Black crayon on blue-gray paper, 300 x 470 mm. Musée Marmottan Monet, Paris [D450]

verso of sketchbook 6 (fig. 263), for example, has a flourish of lines from top to bottom at its center that connects it with the mysteriously beautiful canvas in the Musée Marmottan, *Water Lilies, Reflections of Willow Trees* (fig. 264). Small oval forms in the same drawing emerge as Monet's graphic shorthand for lily pads, which also occur in the Marmottan canvas and in *Water Lilies*, a linked painting in the Metropolitan Museum (fig. 265). Other drawn studies in this group depict the trunks and branches of willow trees, and dense clusters of lily pads, all contributing in various ways to paintings of the same period without attaching themselves to an extant composition. Since many of the related paintings were modified over time in the artist's long, self-critical process of reworking, some drawings may also record earlier states of existing canvases. One of the independent drawings on tinted paper (fig. 266) has a motif of this kind, where a pattern of reflected branches and oval lily pads may have played a role in the emergence of *Water Lilies, Reflections of Willow Trees* and similar works.[68] While the fundamental rhythms remain, both the details and even the overall format of the drawing have been transformed in the evolution of the canvases.

Intriguingly, half the sketchbook drawings in this category include vertical or horizontal framing lines, like those applied to the pages Monet used when planning his paintings of the 1890s. Intended at that time as a step between drawing in front of the motif and designing a specific canvas, they were presumably used on the Giverny studies with a similar end in view. As with the Grainstack drawings, such sketches aspired to capture the characteristic form of a subject—now expressed by Monet

267

The Agapanthus, c. 1917. Oil on canvas, 200 x 150 cm. Musée Marmottan Monet, Paris [W1820]

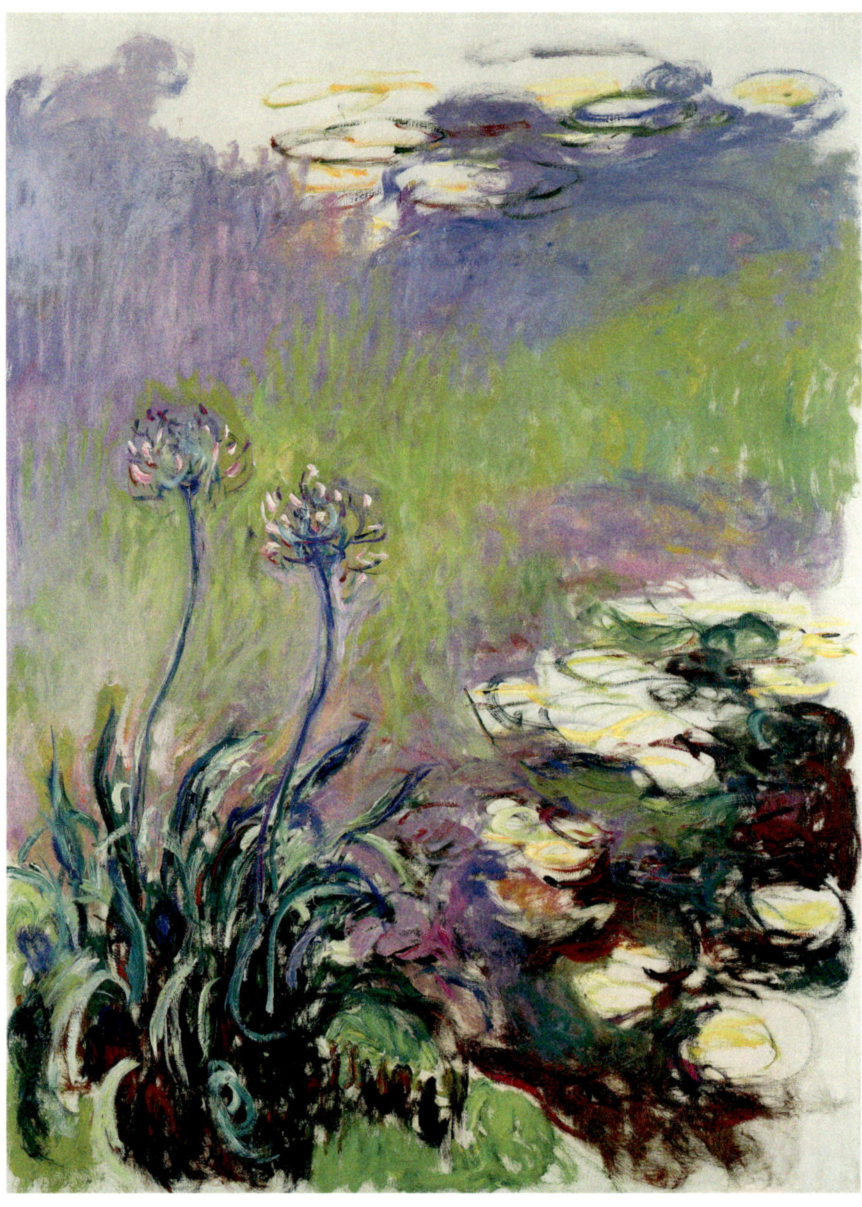

as the evidence of "one moment, one aspect of nature"—within the rectangle of a picture. In the substantial group of water-lily paintings that resulted, he translated some of these drawn designs into a suite of six large canvases, all two meters wide, a considerable advance in scale from the Grainstacks. In principle, these new pictures were neither too large nor too cumbersome to be worked on beside the pond at Giverny, where there were other hands to assist in moving canvases, easels, and necessary equipment. There is photographic and anecdotal evidence to endorse such activity, as well as frank testimony of its gradual decline. Initially, a combination of firsthand observation and direct painting, and sustained studio work throughout the seasons, seems to have prevailed, perhaps reignited by a small study in pencil and invigorated over time by visits to the water's edge. But as Monet's ambitions and confidence grew, and his canvases extended proportionately, the inconvenience of working outdoors must have become overwhelming. Once again, we can imagine his sketchbooks in their role as a conduit for information about the outside world.

Almost all the drawings in Monet's sketchbooks from this late Giverny period are concentrated on his pond and its flowers, rather than

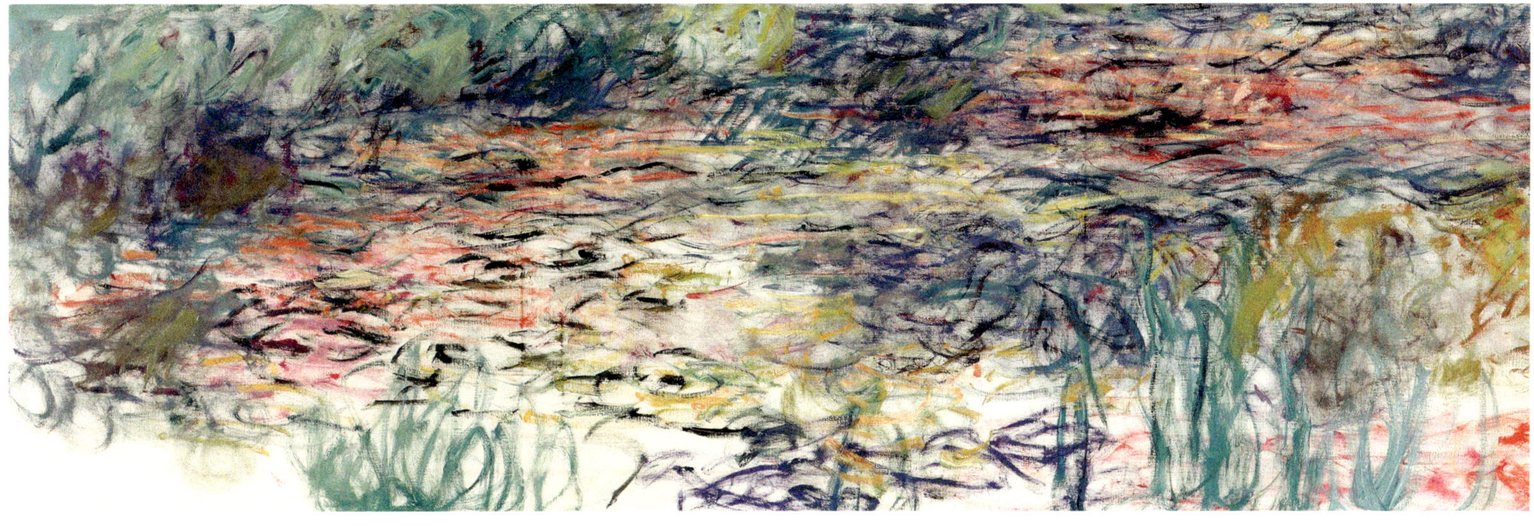

268
Water Lilies, 1917–19. Oil on canvas, 100 x 300 cm. Musée Marmottan Monet, Paris [W1902]

other motifs on the property. Unless drawing books have been lost, there were no studies on paper for the Japanese Bridge pictures, the avenues of blossoms, clumps of Hemerocallis, fiery willow trees, and tangled wisteria, though a solitary drawing of his house survives.[69] The logic of this pattern is not immediately clear, since many of these motifs have a specifically linear character that the more amorphous water-lily pictures lack. But as with Monet's London paintings, scrutiny of individual canvases—especially the less-finished examples that survive—helps to elucidate this issue. In the most direct sense, the Japanese Bridge pictures made at the turn of the century adhere to the same vertical-horizontal matrix as the Charing Cross Bridge series. As with the latter, the linear architecture of the Giverny footbridge scenes was almost certainly present in the works from the beginning. It is conspicuously visible in a lightly brushed version of the Japanese Bridge, made for a theatrical setting arranged by Sacha Guitry, which consists of little more than colored lines; this procedure is corroborated in other canvases of this same motif, where the brushwork is denser but the same approach prevails.[70]

Many later flower compositions also betray their linear origins, as in the Musée Marmottan's incomplete *The Agapanthus* (fig. 267), where Monet's brilliantly colored calligraphy is evident throughout. In passages of paint that have advanced further, a softening of his original design begins the transition into a more seamless, chromatic statement, recalling Monet's reported reluctance to "separate drawing from color." The most exotic survival of this kind is surely the dazzling work entitled *Water Lilies* (fig. 268), which resembles a mesh of agitated, brightly colored threads or slashes made with a brush. Suggestive of Jackson Pollock in its format and its wristy energy, and of Phillip Guston in the elusiveness of its image, this painting still defies expert analysis. Reproduced upside down, as it has been more than once, it can be compared with the wisteria series of around 1917, while in its more plausible orientation the brush marks re-form as a pond with marginal vegetation. It takes little effort, however, to trace similar gestural strokes of the brush beneath many more-refined works of this period, among them the wisteria paintings in a similar format.[71]

Many more densely encrusted canvases of similar pond subjects, such as the Metropolitan Museum of Art's *Water Lilies* (see fig. 265), preserve or even reintroduce their linearity at an advanced stage, in this case with white and yellow chalklike marks added over the saturated deep greens and purples that have preceded them. Conversely, it becomes increasingly easy to envisage the two remaining studies on paper (figs. 269 and 270) as stages in the conception of a comparable painting, with dense patterns of lines needing only the embodiment of color to give them resonant life. All of the separate components of

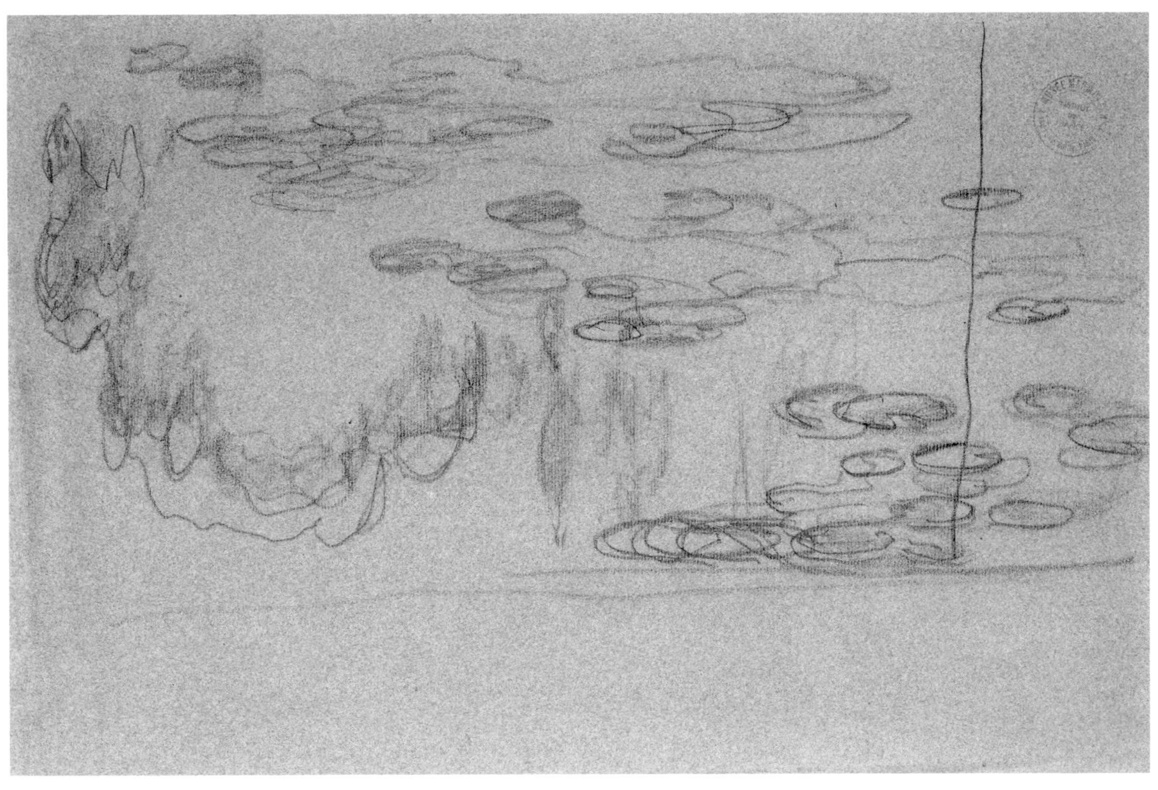

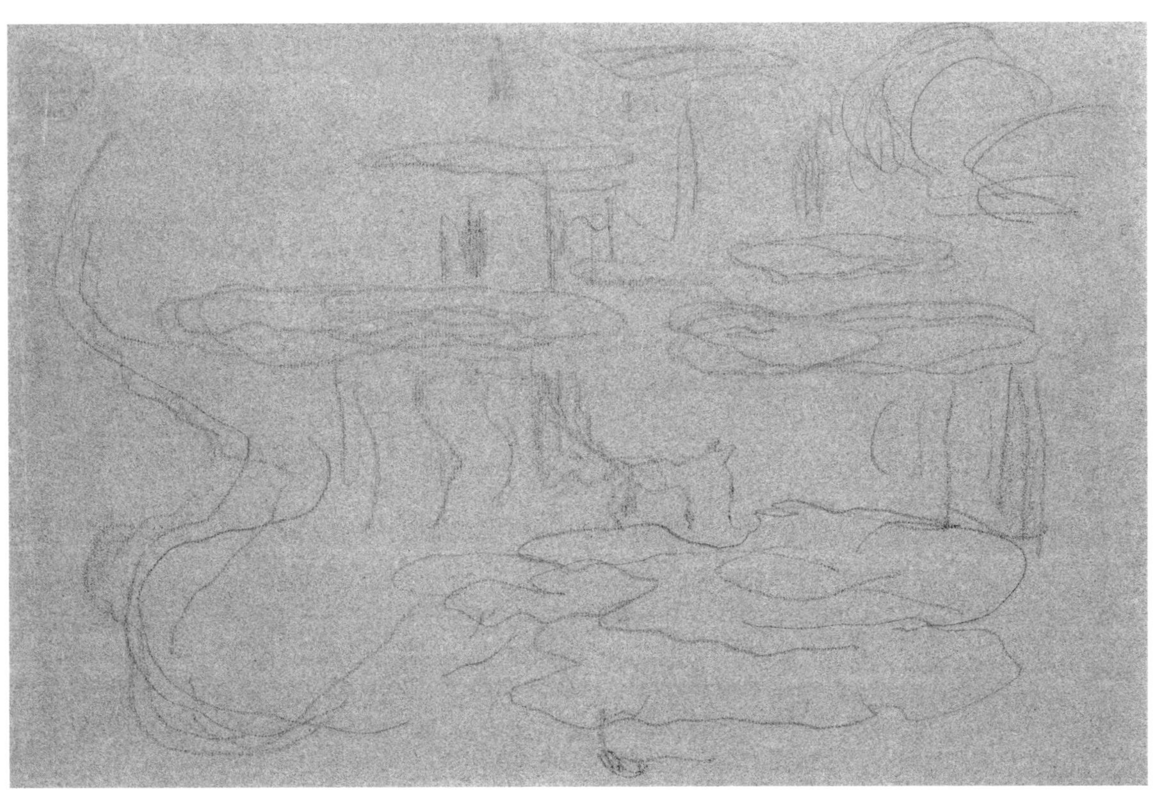

269
Water Lilies, c. 1918. Black crayon on blue-green paper, 315 x 475 mm. Musée Marmottan Monet, Paris [D448]

270
Water Lilies, c. 1918. Black crayon on blue-green paper, 315 x 475 mm. Musée Marmottan Monet, Paris [D449]

271
Water Lilies, 1916–19. Oil on canvas, 200 x 180 cm. Fondation Beyeler, Riehen/Basel [W1854]

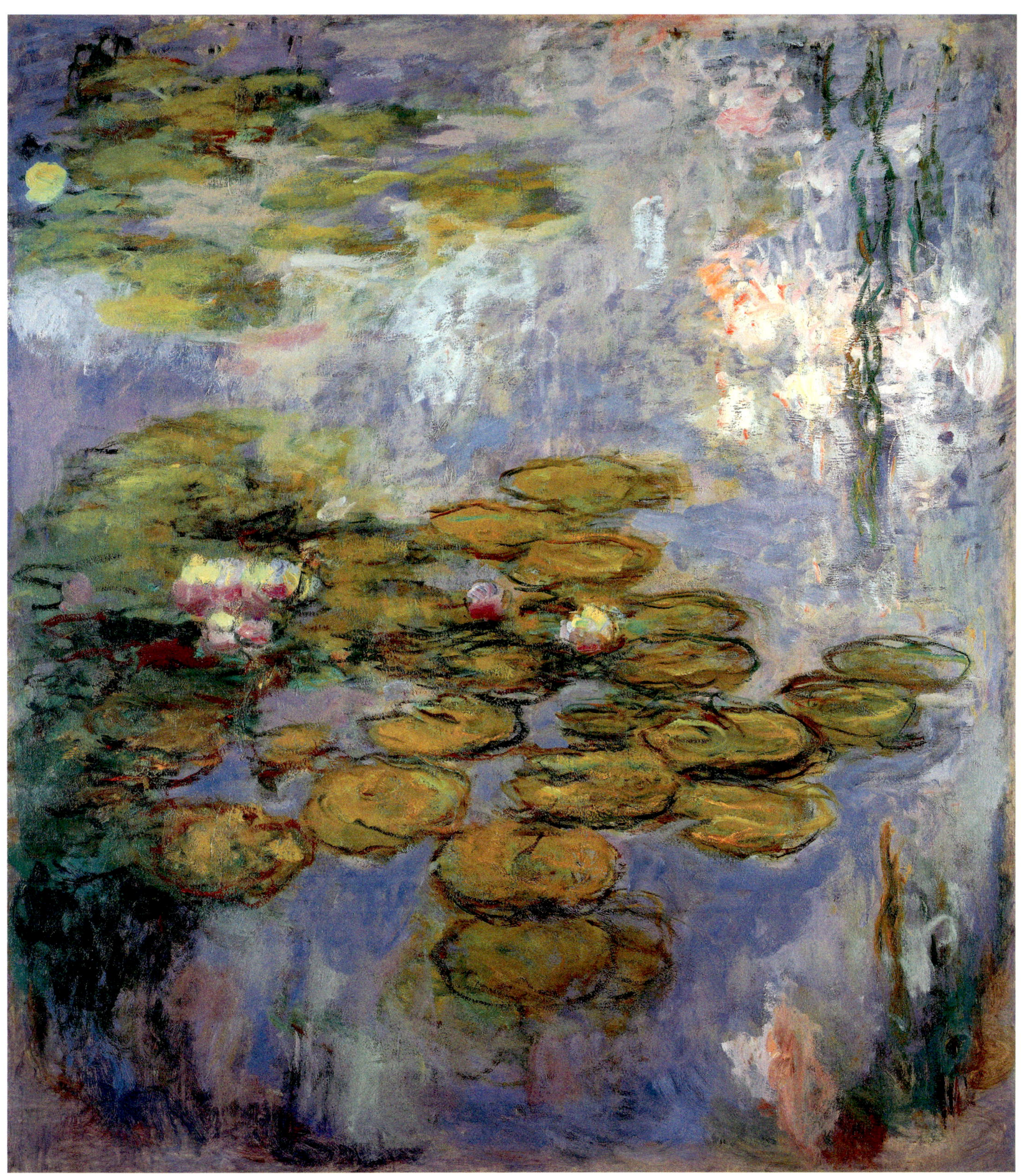

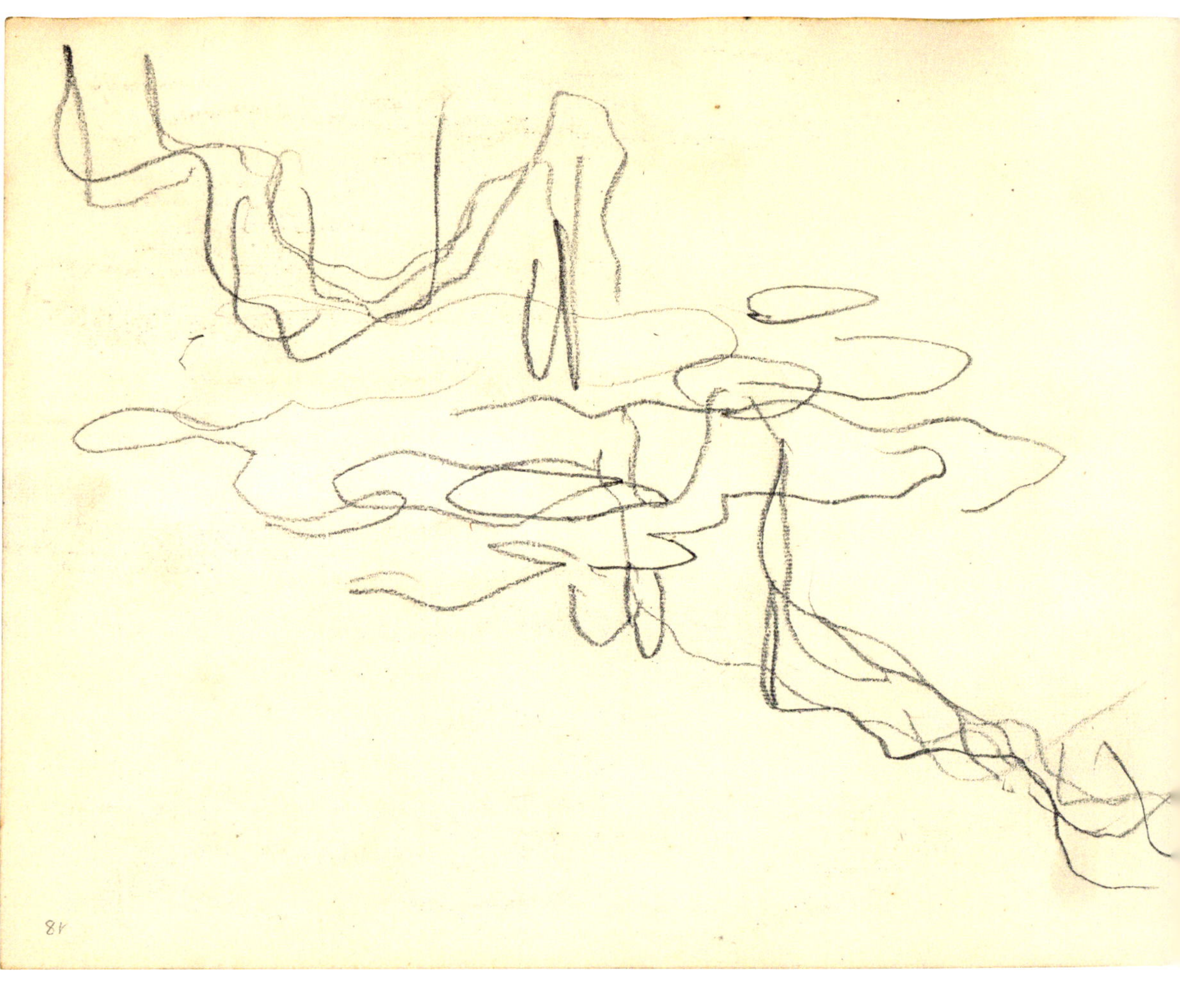

Water Lilies (fig. 271), for example, can be found in these two drawings, from the clusters of oval lily pads and the reflected clouds to the answering verticals of willow branches. Even the internal rhythms of the canvas, which swirl around its central area, are anticipated in the softened corners and curving forms of the pencil compositions.

When we return to the second group of sketchbook drawings, we discover a further suite of ten images that indicates similar connections with other types of late oil painting.[72] The drawings themselves are distinct from the earlier category in that each one now covers two facing pages of the book, offering miniature versions of the wider scenes on canvas. So convenient is the format and so close in proportion to certain of the frieze-like paintings that a more direct, causal link between the open sketchbooks and canvases might even be considered.[73] The pencil study on folios 17 and 18 of sketchbook 1 (fig. 272) exemplifies the pattern in question, creating a rectangle that is more than twice as wide as it is high—a format that haunts Monet's graphic career—with its lines and spaces continuous from left to right. In such audacious sketches, Monet seems to use line to stretch across the wide surface of his lily pond, while his imagination reaches toward canvases of a size unprecedented in his long working life. Less concerned with snatching the perceptions of a moment, these drawings look forward to a new vocabulary of painting that embraces expanses of shadowy water and flotillas of flowers, and ultimately to the *Grand Décorations* of the mid-1920s. The visual sweep of the drawings found more immediate expression in another cycle of two-meter-wide pictures, again with a shape that recalls the open sketchbook. *Water-Lily Pond* (fig. 273) has a strikingly similar dynamic to the drawing on folios 17 and 18, its lily pads seeming

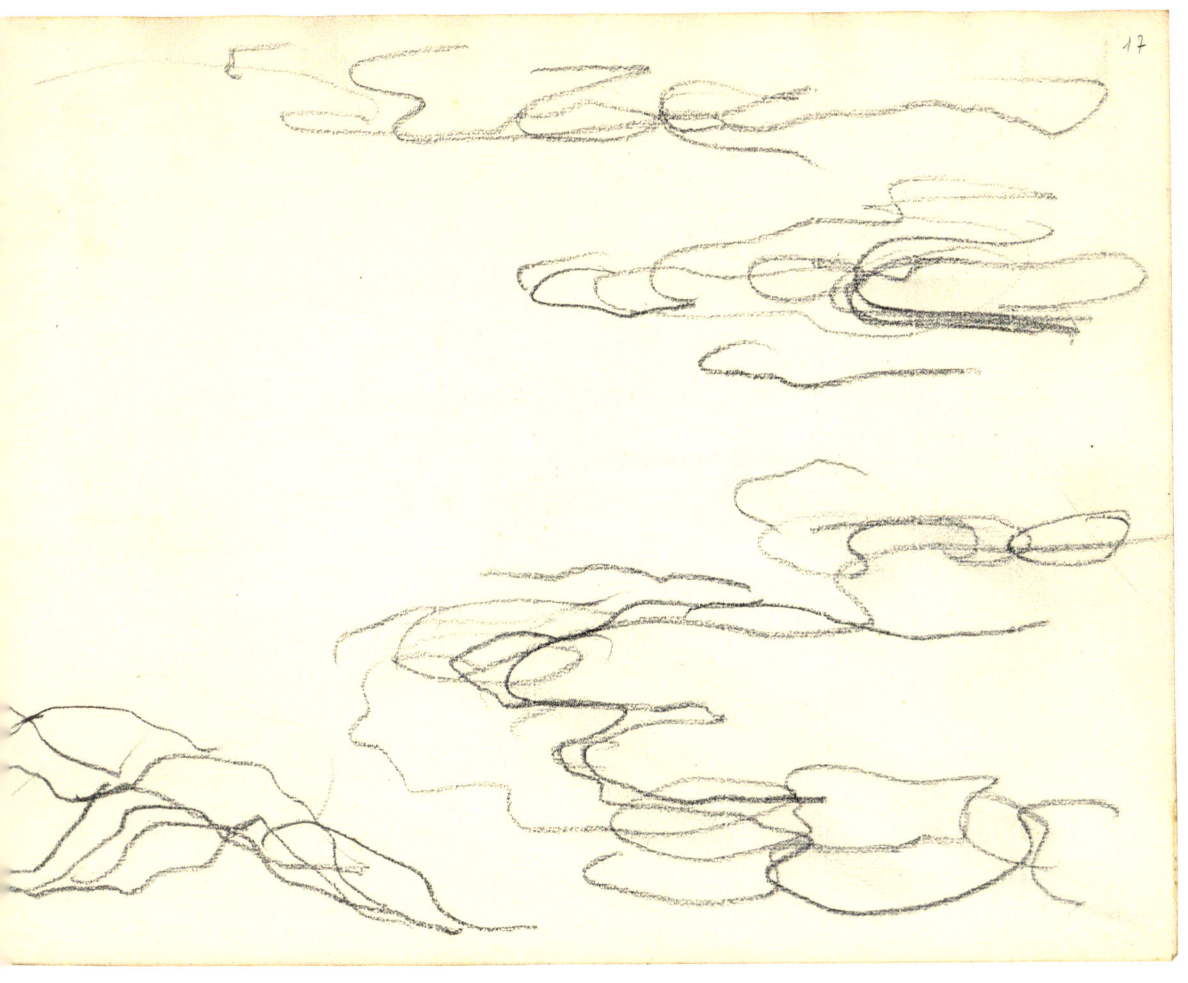

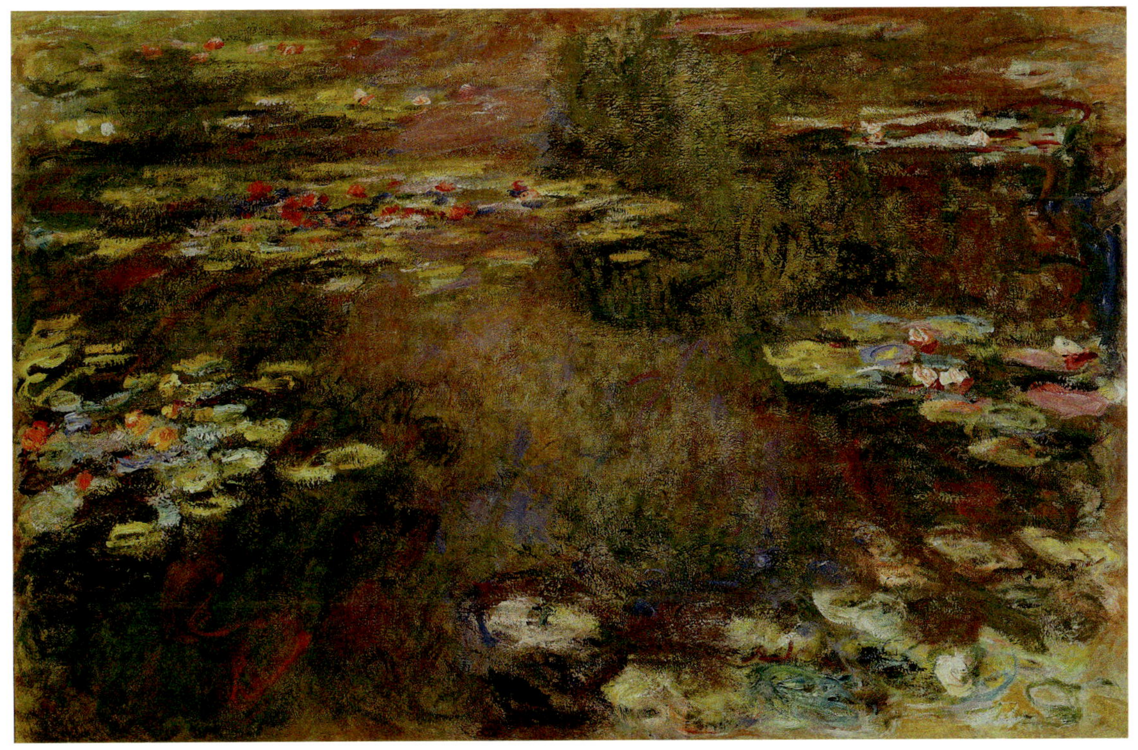

272

Water Lilies, c. 1914–19. Pencil, 255 x 680 mm (full spread). Sketchbook 1, fols. 17v and 18r. Musée Marmottan Monet, Paris [D120]

273

Water-Lily Pond, 1917–22. Oil on canvas, 130.2 x 201.9 cm. The Art Institute of Chicago. Gift of Mrs. Harvey Kaplan [W1889]

274
Monet painting the water lilies in his studio

275
Weeping Willow, c. 1914–19. Violet crayon, 255 x 680 mm (full spread). Sketchbook 1, fols. 21v and 22r. Musée Marmottan Monet, Paris [D123]

276
Water Lilies, c. 1914–19. Waxed crayon, 235 x 630 mm (full spread). Sketchbook 6, fols. 9v and 10r. Musée Marmottan Monet, Paris [D349]

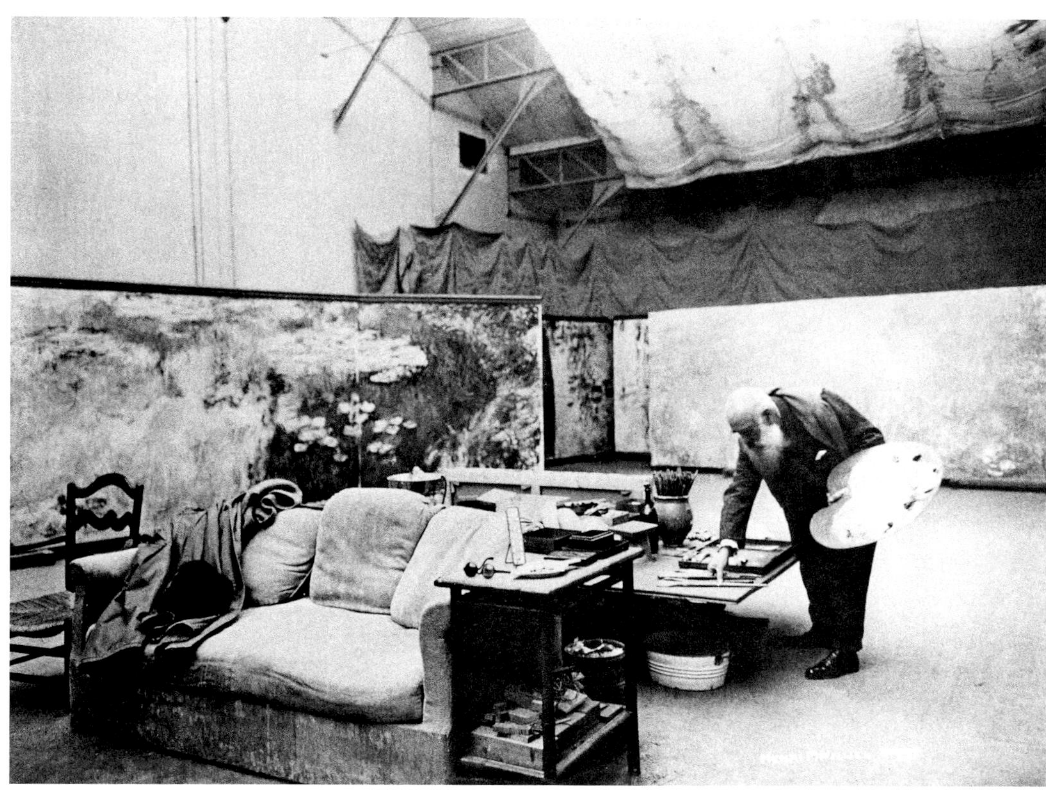

to float from lower right to upper left across a dark void. Other variants, all probably made around the time of the war, increase or decrease the number of discs of color and vary their clustering, while staying true to the spacious, diagonally oriented character of the first sketch.

If such canvases were executed entirely beside the water-lily pond, as some of Monet's admirers insisted, the need for the drawings becomes less clear. Perhaps these minimal sketches, too, were records of the *première pensée*, or the "one moment" that Monet argued was "all that is needed" to spark a new creation. The third type of sketchbook study, however, points us in a yet different direction, favoring self-conscious design for a sequence of as-yet barely imagined works, rather than intense accounts of local experience. The idea of a major cycle of mural-scale canvases seems to have emerged in Monet's mind before the outbreak of war in 1914, encouraged by his friend Georges Clemenceau. Gradually taking on a more monumental character, the project eventually expanded to fill the walls of part of the Orangerie, near the Louvre in central Paris. Living with deteriorating health and the threat of blindness, Monet struggled for more than a decade to complete the *Grand Décorations*. Some of the canvases produced in this process were preserved as separate works, measuring three, four, and even six meters from side to side and inevitably created from beginning to end in his large Giverny studio (fig. 274). The final works, removed from their stretchers and attached to the Orangerie's especially constructed curving walls, became even wider, though they had originated as smaller sections. It was conceivably in this context that Monet again used several double sketchbook pages to plan the overall rhythms of his imagery. Three of his designs have the extremely attenuated formats of the *Grand Décorations*, and may equally have served as first drafts for the wider scheme or even as explicatory diagrams for Monet and those around him.[74] Some of the components of the murals are vividly present, such as the massive tree trunks that punctuate the great spaces in the double sheet between folios 21 and 22 in sketchbook 1 (fig. 275). Other dynamic images include the motif of the reflected willow

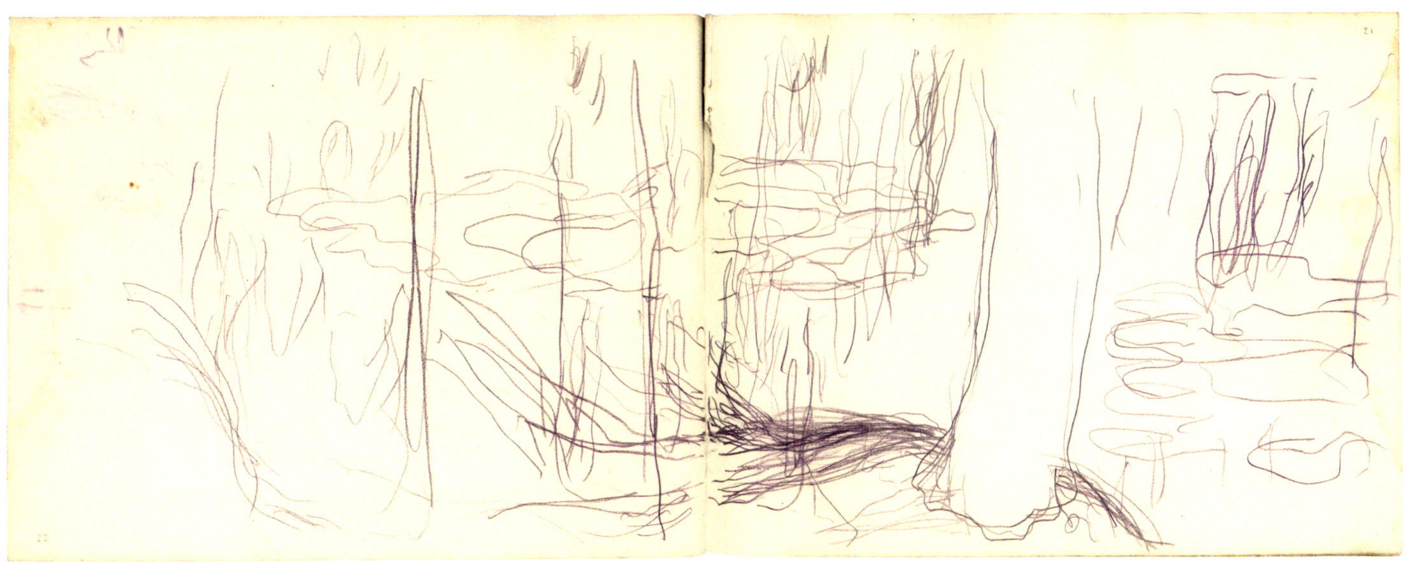

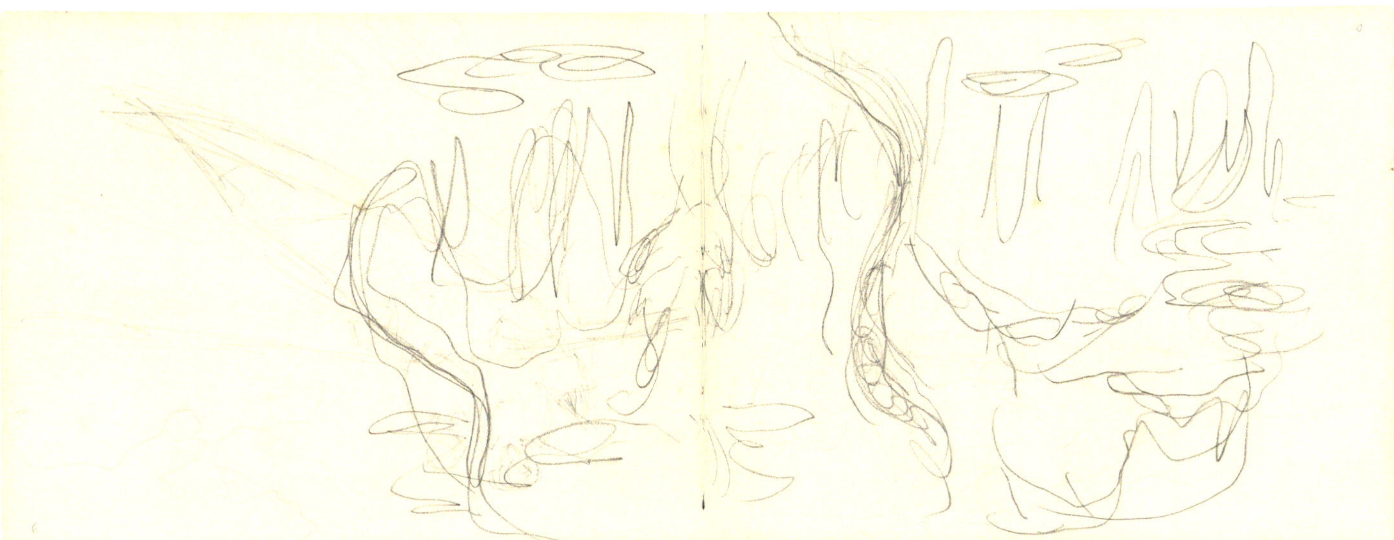

branches and the pale clouds surrounding them, rendered with little more than hasty lines and looping pencil strokes (fig. 276).

This conjunction of images in the same sketchbook from the years immediately prior to his death and almost every point in Monet's previous career can only be poignant. These humble books might be said to provide a conspectus, disordered but occasionally brilliant, not only of his life as a graphic artist but of the early eruption of his talent and of the visual convolutions of his maturity. Few stages of his artistic development are untouched by these lean, private studies, intended for his eyes only and for the practical functions of the studio. When added to the countless sheets described in the Beguin Billecocq Grand Journal, the pastel oeuvre that spans more than forty years of Monet's life, and the drawings made for lithography in the 1890s, they define a wide-ranging involvement with draftsmanship that bears comparison with the work of most of his contemporaries. That this involvement was never simple is now apparent, and the possibility that Monet himself denied, destroyed, camouflaged, and otherwise diverted attention from his use of drawing in a number of contexts — not excluding his most painterly late canvases — can no longer be doubted. It is equally inconceivable that future studies of Monet's art can proceed without taking account of these sketchbook pages and the curiously assorted sheets that accompany them.

APPENDIX The Thornley-Monet Portfolio

The prints reproduced here are from William Thornley's *20 Lithographies d'après Claude Monet* [*20 Lithographs after Claude Monet*] printed by Henry Belfond in an edition of twenty-five and published by J. Mancini, Paris, in 1894. The reproductions are from the unbound portfolio in the Jacques Doucet collection at the Bibliothèque de l'Institut National de l'Histoire de l'Art, Paris (fol. est. 83), the only known extant complete set. They are all transfer lithographs mounted on thick cream wove paper measuring 397 x 565 mm and bear the drystamp of Belfond and the stamped monogram of Thornley in red ink. In addition, the individual prints are signed in pencil by Monet (at lower left) and Thornley (at lower right). For more information on the identification of the Belfond drystamp, see Lugt 1956, p. 32, no. 225d.

The prints are listed chronologically according to the dates of the corresponding paintings that they reproduce. Wildenstein numbers for their corresponding paintings are provided in brackets. The captions indicate image sizes.

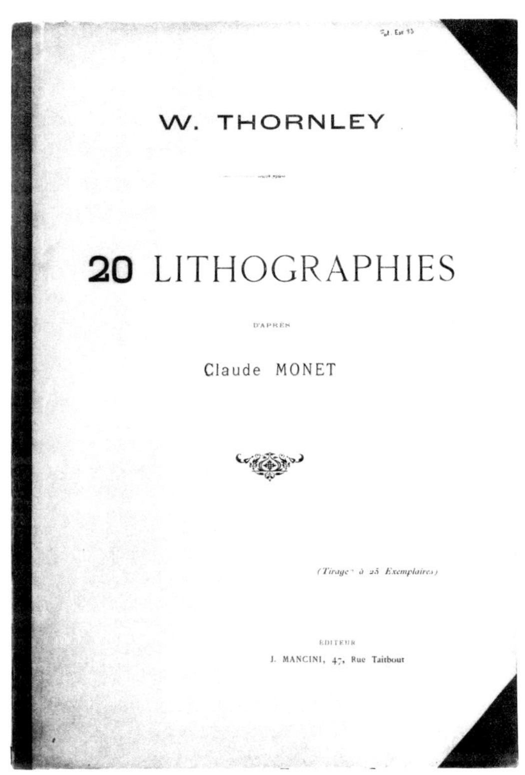

A0
Portfolio cover of *20 Lithographs after Claude Monet*
585 x 407 mm

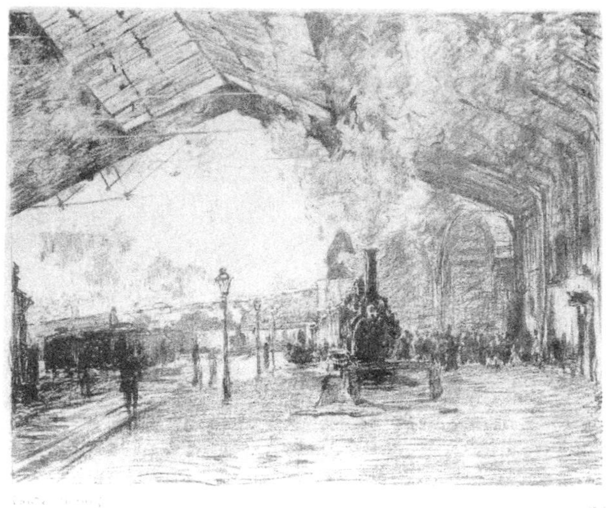

A1
Arrival of the Normandy Train, Gare Saint-Lazare
Transfer lithograph printed in warm gray on off-white chine appliqué, 212 x 260 mm
[W440]

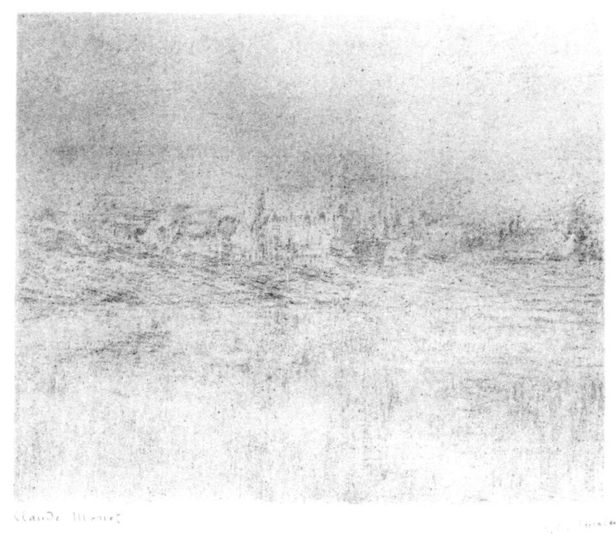

A2
Vétheuil in the Fog
Transfer lithograph printed in turquoise on off-white chine appliqué, 212 x 249 mm
[W518]

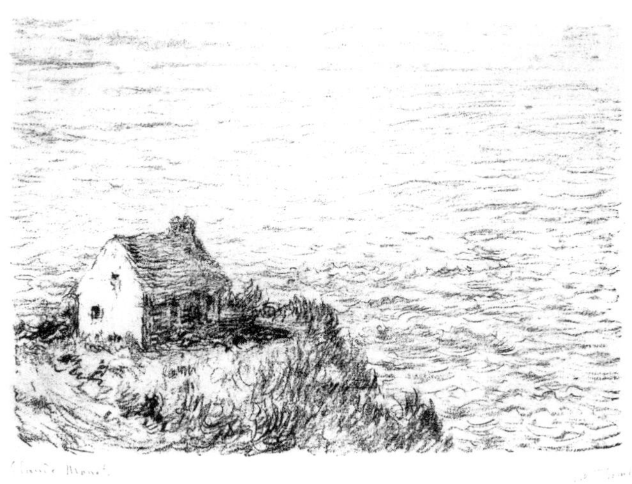

A3
The Customs House, Afternoon Effect
Transfer lithograph printed in green on off-white chine appliqué, 185 x 287 mm
[W737]

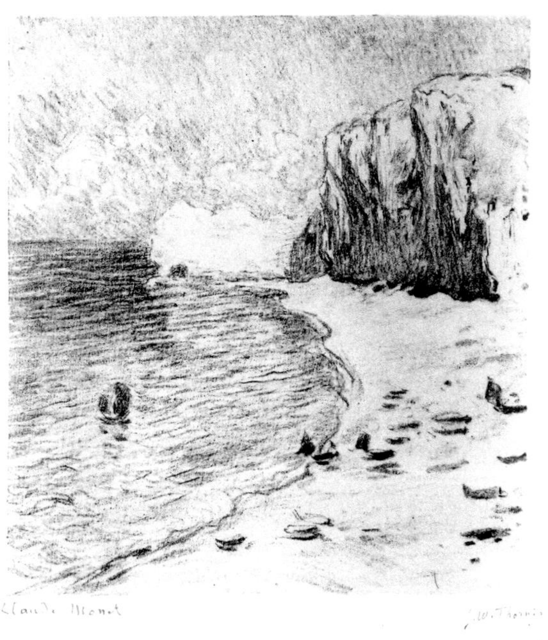

A4
The Beach and the Falaise d'Amont, Étretat
Transfer lithograph printed in reddish orange on off-white chine appliqué, 210 x 194 mm
[W1012]

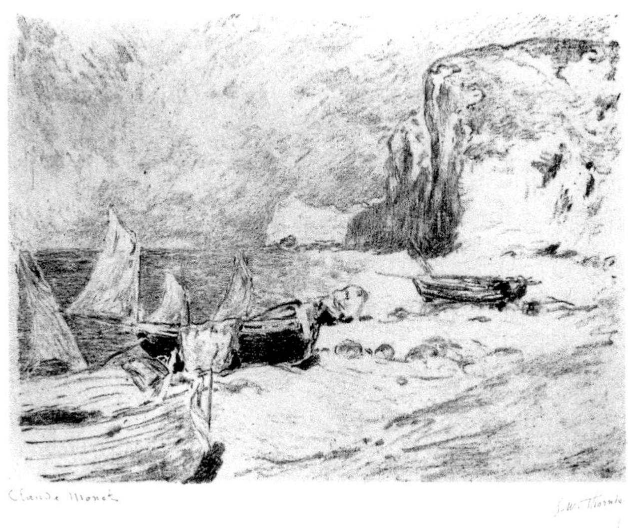

A5

Fishing Boats at Étretat
Transfer lithograph printed in brown on off-white chine appliqué, 184 x 252 mm
[W1013]

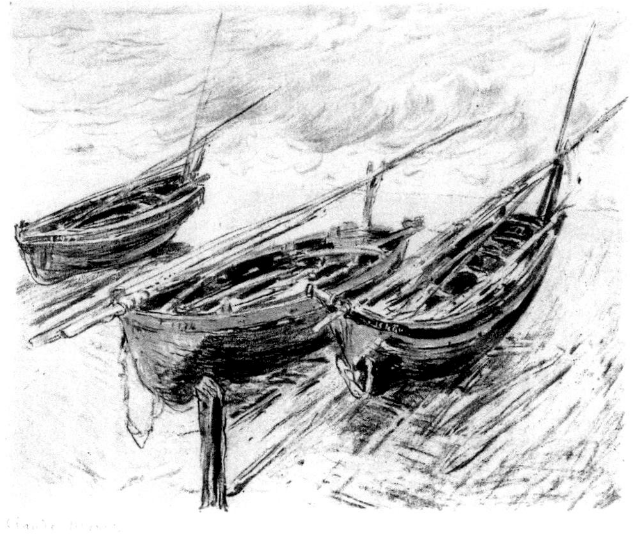

A6

Three Fishing Boats
Transfer lithograph printed in blue-gray (keystone), green, acidic yellow, and light pinkish beige on off-white chine appliqué, 210 x 265 mm
[W1029]

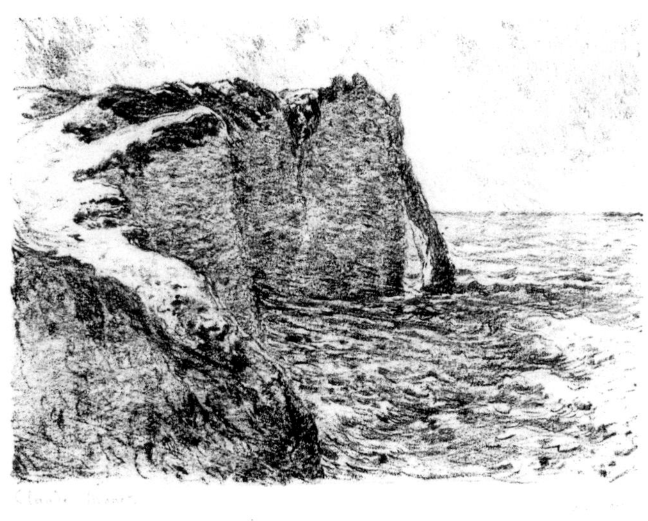

A7

The Cliff and the Porte d'Aval, Étretat
Transfer lithograph printed in greenish gray on off-white chine appliqué, 187 x 260 mm
[W1019]

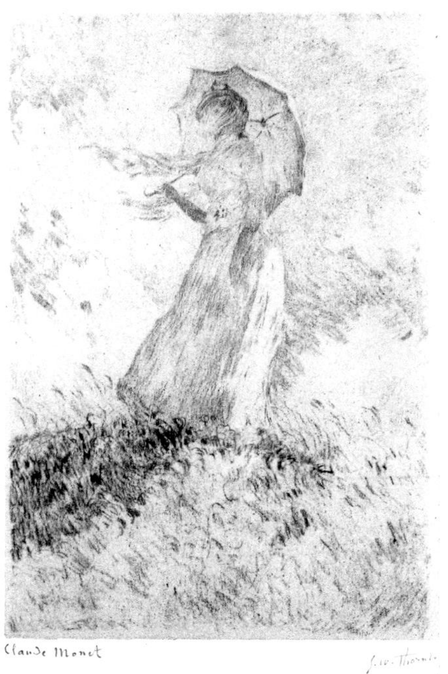

A8

Woman with a Parasol
Transfer lithograph printed in dull blue on off-white chine appliqué, 274 x 196 mm
[W1077]

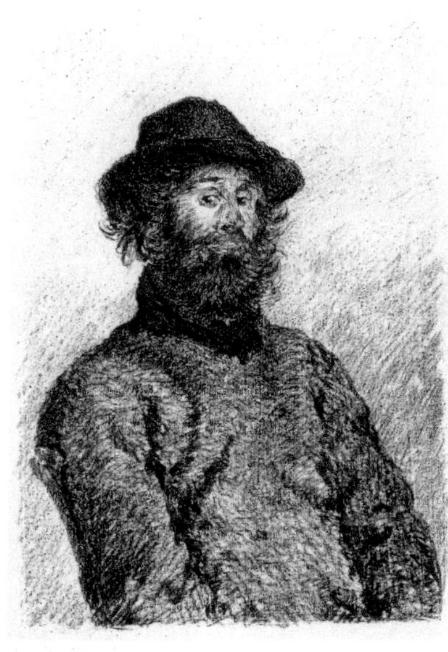

A9
Portrait of Poly
Transfer lithograph printed in dark gray on off-white chine appliqué, 223 x 164 mm
[W1122]

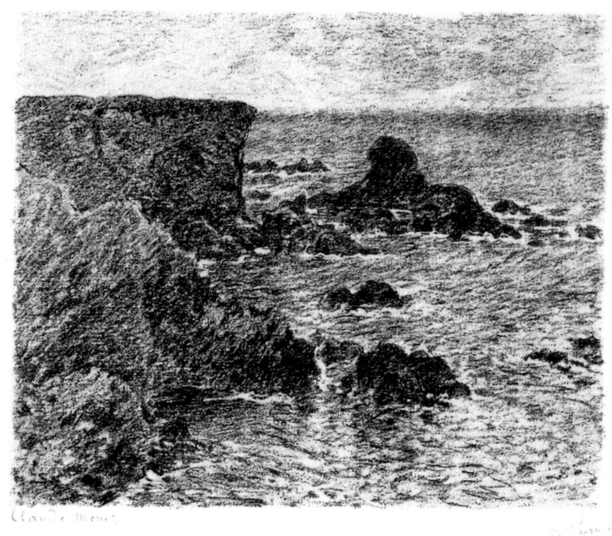

A10
Rocky Coast and the Lion Rock, Belle-Île
Transfer lithograph printed in warm gray on beige chine appliqué, 195 x 240 mm
[W1090]

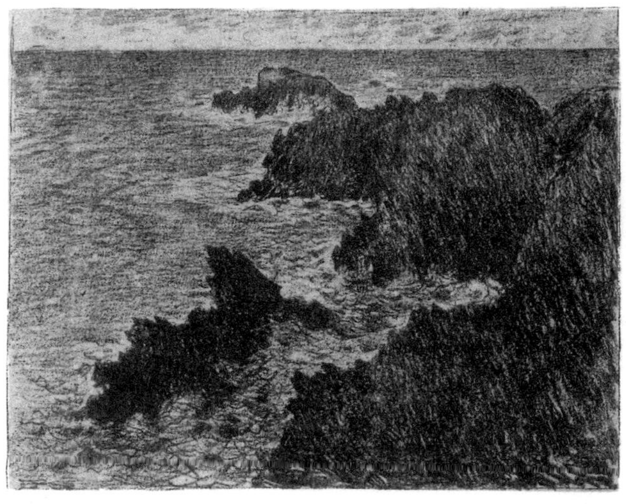

A11
The Côte Sauvage
Transfer lithograph printed in black on olive-toned chine appliqué, 210 x 277 mm
[W1100]

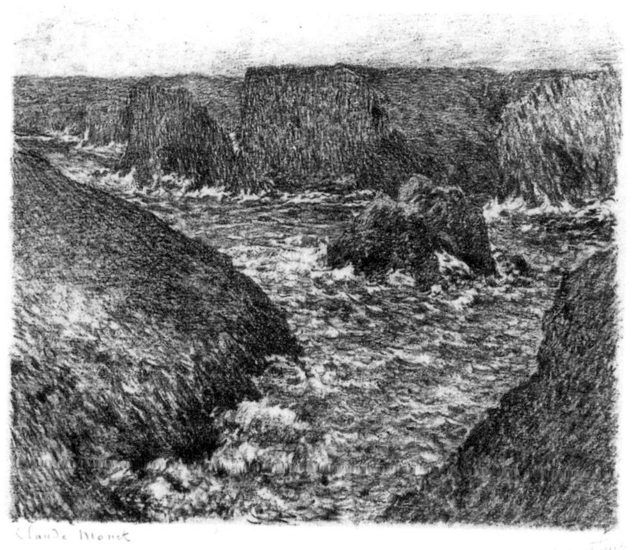

A12
Port-Domois at Belle-Île
Transfer lithograph printed in dark gray on off-white chine appliqué, 208 x 258 mm
[W1109]

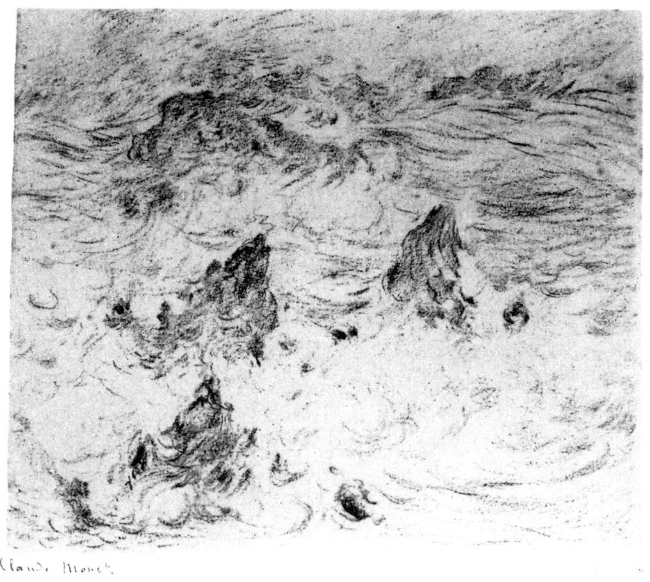

A13

Storm at Belle-Île

Transfer lithograph printed in green on off-white chine appliqué, 200 x 240 mm

[W1117]

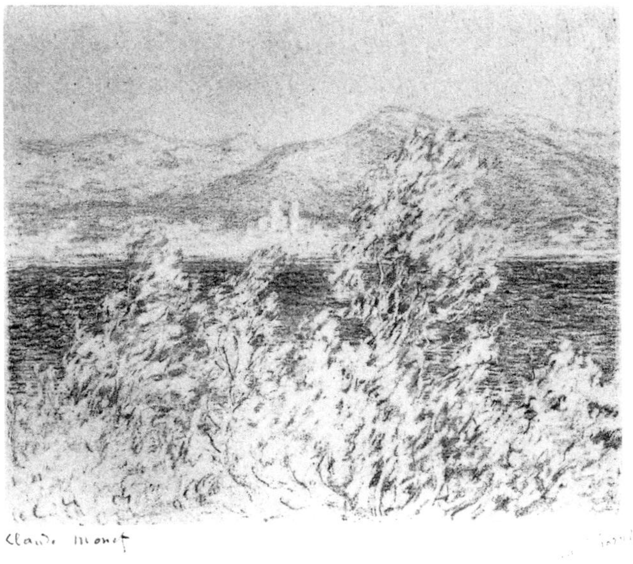

A14

View from the Cap d'Antibes

Transfer lithograph printed in bluish-gray on rose-toned chine appliqué, 145 x 178 mm

[W1174]

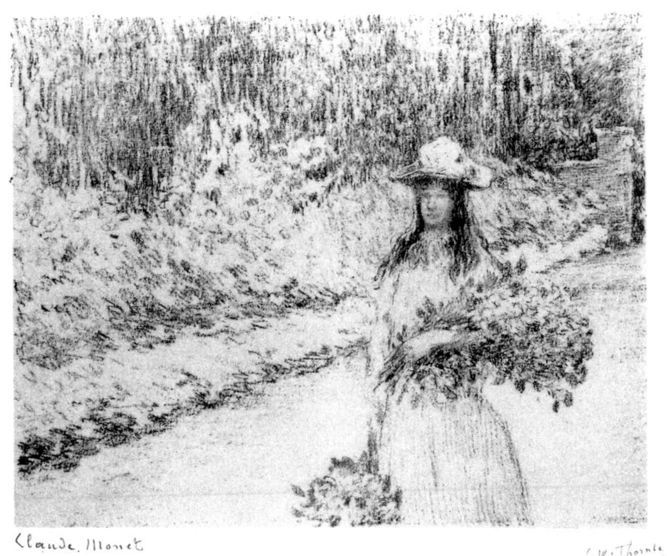

A15

Young Girl (Germaine Hoschedé) in the Garden at Giverny

Transfer lithograph printed in purple on off-white chine appliqué, 180 x 229 mm

[W1207]

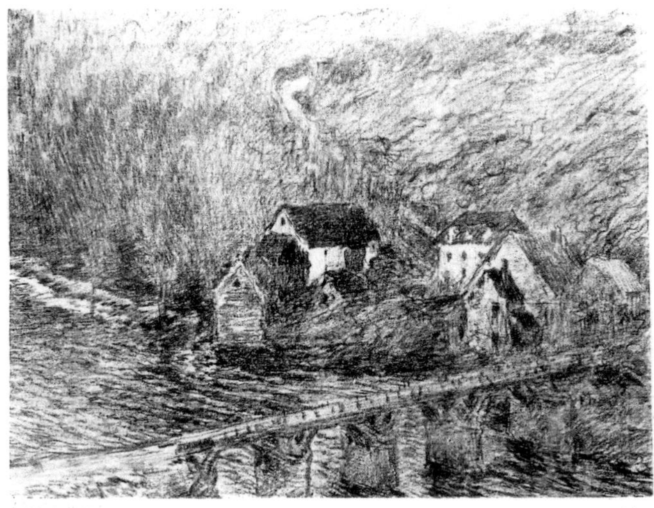

A16

The Bridge at Vervy

Transfer lithograph printed in greenish-gray on off-white chine appliqué, 212 x 291 mm

[W1234]

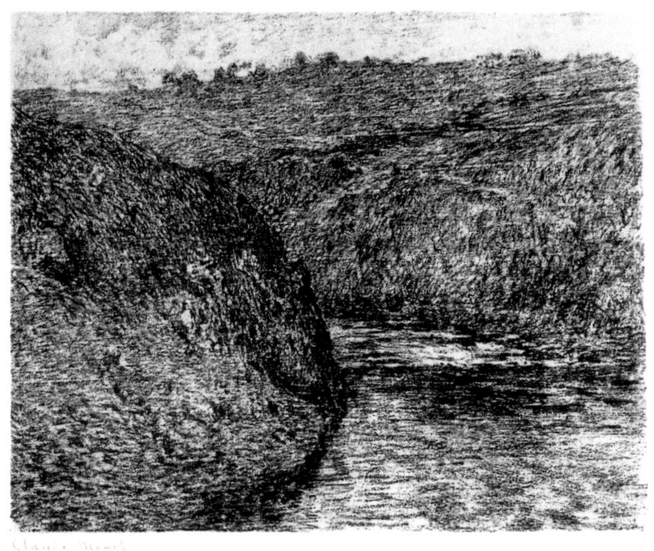

A17

The Creuse, Dark Weather
Transfer lithograph printed in greenish-gray on rose-toned chine appliqué, 204 x 257 mm
[W1224]

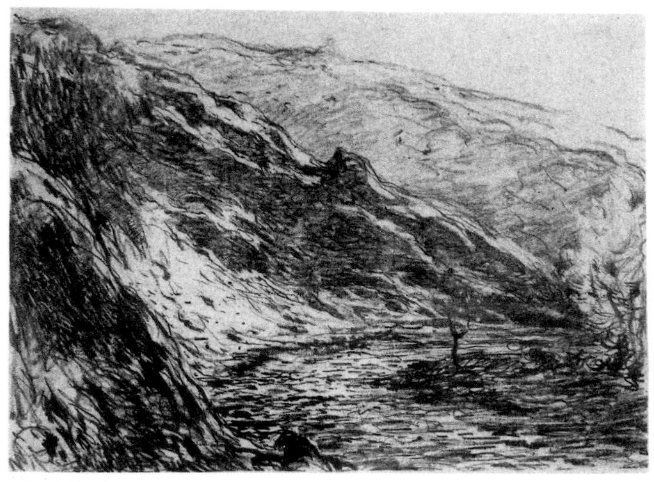

A18

Gorge of the Petite Cruese
Transfer lithograph printed in purplish-gray on olive-toned chine appliqué, 208 x 292 mm
[probably W1230]

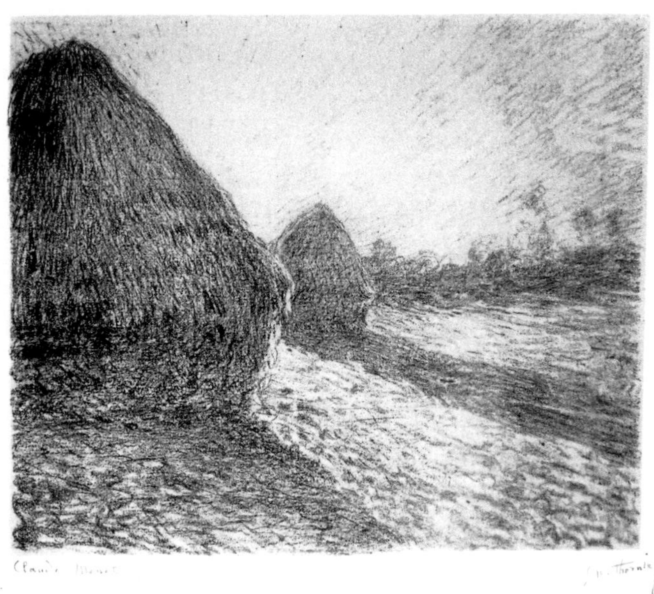

A19

Grainstacks, Last Sunrays
Transfer lithograph printed in orange on off-white chine appliqué, 217 x 262 mm
[W1272]

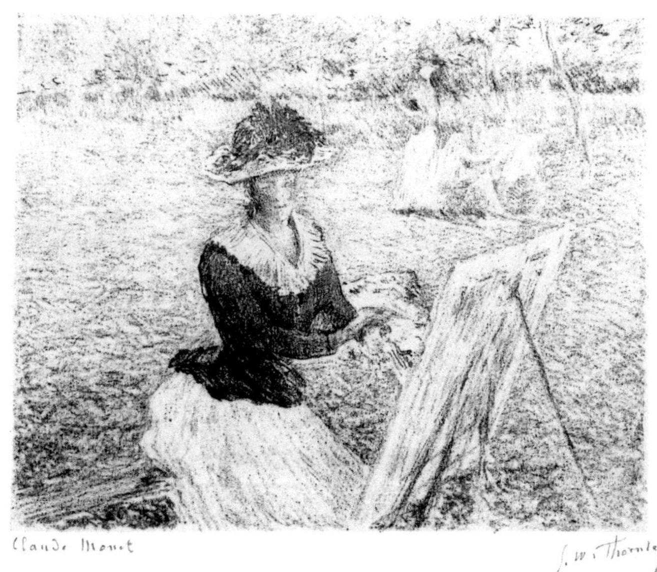

A20

Blanche Hoschedé Painting
Transfer lithograph printed in gray-black (keystone), green, and red on off-white chine appliqué, 160 x 200 mm
[W1330]

Notes

INTRODUCTION

1. Among the many citations that identify the subject of Monet's drawing, the following are characteristic: Daulte 1954, p. xv; Mount 1966, plate 5; and Wildenstein 1974–91, vol. 5, p. 131.
2. Mount 1966, plate 5; Cogniat 1967, p. 16.
3. See, for example, the drawings D443 and 446.
4. See "Note to the Reader," p. xi. Quotes taken from the Grand Journal throughout this catalogue derive from a typed transcription completed by Pierre-Olivier Caperan in 2005 and available in the library of the Sterling and Francine Clark Art Institute in Williamstown, Massachusetts.
5. Beguin Billecocq 2005, p. 148 [1858].
6. Ibid., p. 3 [1906].
7. Ibid.
8. Ibid., p. 291 [1881].
9. Venturi 1939, vol. 1, pp. 221–22; Claude Monet to Paul Durand-Ruel, 28 Apr. 1881, in Wildenstein 1974–91, vol. 1, p. 442, L215.
10. Beguin Billecocq 2005, p. 314 [1884].
11. Excerpts from this letter, which is in the Durand-Ruel Archives, Paris, were first published in Venturi 1939, vol. 1, p. 289; the complete text appears in Wildenstein 1974–91, vol. 2, p. 256, L529.
12. The original document was sold from the Camille Pissarro archives at Drouot, Paris, 21 Nov. 1975, no. 110, and is transcribed in Wildenstein 1974–91, vol. 2, p. 256, L532. Several other letters mention this trip; see Wildenstein 1974–91, vol. 2, p. 256, L531 and 533–35.
13. Beguin Billecocq 2005, p. 129 [1853].
14. Ibid., p. 294 [1882].
15. Claude Monet to Georges de Bellio, in Wildenstein 1974–91, vol. 2, p. 232, L386.
16. See Wildenstein 1974–91, vol. 5, p. 134, D451–59. Seven additional caricatures of the same type were recorded in the Billecocq collection; these are discussed in chapter 2.

CHAPTER ONE

Portrait of the Artist as a Young Draftsman

1. Théodore Duret, *Les peintres impressionnistes: Claude Monet, Sisley, C. Pisarro, Renoir, Berthe Morisot* (Paris: Librairie parisienne, 1878), translated in Stuckey 1985, p. 66.
2. Théodore Duret, *Le peintre Claude Monet* (Paris: La vie moderne, 1880), translated in Stuckey 1985, p. 72.
3. Émile Taboureux, "Claude Monet," *La vie moderne* 2 (12 June 1880), translated in Stuckey 1985, p. 91.
4. Philippe Burty, "The Landscapes of Claude Monet," *La République française*, 27 Mar. 1883, translated in Stuckey 1985, p. 98.
5. François Thiébault-Sisson, "Claude Monet: An Interview," *Le Temps*, 27 Nov. 1900, translated in Stuckey 1985, pp. 204–5.
6. Ibid., p. 205.
7. Elder 1924a, p. 15.
8. Gimpel 1966, p. 310, entry dated 11 Oct. 1920.
9. For instance, Fels 1929, pp. 7–16.
10. Tucker 1995, p. 5.
11. Ibid., p. 6.
12. Alphant 1993, p. 50, quoting Stendhal, *Mémoires d'un touriste* (1838).
13. Cahen 1900, pp. 16–27.
14. Jean-Aubry 1922, p. 171.
15. Wildenstein 1974–91, vol. 1, p. 6.
16. Ibid., vol. 1, p. 3, n. 11; vol. 5, p. 134.
17. Spate 1992a, p. 14; Alphant 1993, pp. 37, 155–57; Tucker 1995, p. 226, n. 2.
18. Beguin Billecocq 2005, p. 109 [1848].
19. Ibid., p. 124 [1852].
20. Ibid., p. 128 [1853].
21. Ibid.
22. Ibid., p. 129 [1853].
23. Ibid.
24. Ibid., p. 130 [1853].
25. Ibid., p. 129 [1853].
26. Ibid., p. 113 [1848].
27. Ibid., p. 131 [1853].
28. Alphant 1993, p. 52, cites Abbé A. Anthiaume, *Le Collège du Havre* (Le Havre: Havre-Éclair, 1905), vol. 2, p. 444, as giving 1 Apr. 1851 as the date of Oscar Monet's entry into the Collège du Havre.
29. Wildenstein 1996, vol. 1, p. 12.
30. Beguin Billecocq 2005, p. 136 [1855].
31. Ibid.
32. Ibid., pp. 139–40 [1856].
33. Wildenstein 1974–91, vol. 5, pp. 59–67, sketchbook 1, D1–28; sketchbook 2, D29–47.
34. Wildenstein specifies neither the auction venue, the identity of the consigner (Léon Monet?), nor the identity of the drawings' purchaser. Monet's 1895 dedication appears on D1.
35. Tucker 1995, p. 7.
36. Wildenstein 1974–91, vol. 5, p. 121.
37. Beguin Billecocq 2005, p. 141 [1856].
38. Ibid., p. 142 [1857].
39. Wildenstein 1974–91, vol. 5, pp. 68–78, D48–104.
40. Isaacson 1967. On the 1857 sketchbook, see pp. 25–30, 246–56.
41. Curiously, each of these specialists, Isaacson and Wildenstein, enjoyed a unique advantage over the other, and neither had access to the other's scholarship. The publication of Wildenstein's catalogue raisonné of the drawings postdated Isaacson's dissertation by twenty-four years, yet in compiling his authoritative tome, Wildenstein failed to notice his predecessor's important analysis. Isaacson's significant advantage over Wildenstein was that he had the opportunity to study the album before it was completely dispersed. Although Wildenstein could not study the original sketchbook in this way, he had an advantage over Isaacson in that he possessed a complete set of photographs of the individual pages commissioned at an unknown date by Michel Monet, including several sheets not seen by Isaacson.
42. Of Monet's later sketchbooks, the first drawings in sketchbooks 3 and 6 postdate those on subsequent folios; Monet's nonsequential use of his sketchbooks is discussed in chapter 7.
43. Isaacson 1967, pp. 26–28.

44. Beguin Billecocq 2005, p. 144 [1857].
45. Isaacson 1978, p. 25; Tucker 1995, p. 7.
46. Beguin Billecocq 2005, p. 144 [1857].
47. Ibid., p. 145 [1857].
48. Ibid., p. 146 [1857].
49. See Enfert 2003.
50. Ibid., p. 131.
51. Beguin Billecocq 2005, p. 144 [1857].
52. Ibid., p. 148 [1858].
53. Ibid.

CHAPTER TWO
Oscar Monet, Caricaturist

1. Gimpel 1966, p. 339.
2. D467, 470–77, 486, 500–504, 506–10, 513.
3. D451–66.
4. D478–80, 482–83.
5. The drawings mentioned by Gimpel were acquired in 1927–28 by the collector and former five-term mayor of Chicago Carter H. Harrison (1860–1953) from Henri I. Cottereau of Paris; D481, 490–92, 495–97, 499, 505, 515. Cottereau's source for at least one (D490, though presumably all) of the drawings was an individual named Alfred Dusseuil. Wildenstein learned from the Durand-Ruel Archives that Dusseil had left seven *portraits-charges* with the gallery that were returned to him on 14 Mar. 1927; Wildenstein 1974–91, vol. 5, p. 144. Harrison donated the drawings to the Art Institute of Chicago in 1933 (figs. 29, 31, 36, 41, 45).
6. The most informative published sources on Monet's caricatures are Walter 1976 and the section devoted to them in Wildenstein 1974–91, vol. 5, pp. 133–51, which provides biographical information on many of the sitters. See also Raymond Cogniat, "Les dessins de Claude Monet," in Lausanne 1993.
7. Baudelaire 1855, Baudelaire 1857a, Baudelaire 1857b.
8. Hannoosh 1992, p. 3.
9. See Hannoosh, chap. 4, "The Comic and Modernity," pp. 251–316.
10. Wildenstein catalogued 64 caricatures (D451–515) out of a total of 106 independent drawings by Monet.
11. Beguin Billecocq 2005, p. 129 [1853].
12. Baudelaire 1857b, p. 554f, translated in Hannoosh 1992, p. 146.
13. Compare the principal figure, for instance, with DR/LD 760 (DR = Daumier Register [www.daumier-register.org] and LD= Delteil 1997). Wildenstein explained that the stenciled inscription "PLICK" on this sheet was likely the "indiscrete intervention of a child," noting that it likely derived from the children's books *Les Malices de Plick et Plock* published from 1893 to 1904; Wildenstein 1974–91, vol. 5, p. 71.
14. Gamins: D61, 69; Zouaves: D57, 75.
15. The entire group consists of D451–69, of which all but the last three are directly traceable to the Billecocqs.
16. D451–59, Musée Marmottan Monet inventory numbers 5221–29. Of the remaining drawings, Wildenstein indicated that D460–66 and 468 were in private hands, D467 was left by Michel Monet to the Musée Marmottan in 1966 (inv. no. 5044), and D469 entered the collection of the Musée Rodin, Paris (inv. no. D7694) at an unknown date, possibly via Michel Monet.
17. Wildenstein notes drawings on the verso of D451, 452, 457, and 458.
18. D462.
19. See Gimpel 1966, p. 310, entry dated 11 Oct. 1920 and quoted in this volume on page 11, in which he reported that Monet's mother lavished praise on his copies of unspecified plaster models.
20. Drawing after Carjat: D499; after Hadol: D500, 501; after Nadar: D502–9. D470, a pastel on gray paper in the Musée Marmottan (inv. no. 5162), bears a signature and inscription in the artist's hand identifying the model as a plaster by "Cuquemelle," an obscure local artist in Le Havre who is known to have exhibited terra cottas; see Wildenstein 1974–91, vol. 5, p. 139.
21. A useful expression coined by Rodolphe Walter (see Walter 1976). Wildenstein picked up on this expression as well, referring to these drawings as *"témoignages d'un apprentissage clandestin"*; Wildenstein 1974–91, vol. 5, p. 146.
22. D504 after the *portrait-charge* by Nadar and Édouard Riou (1838–1900) published in *Journal amusant*, 22 Jan. 1859, p. 1 (reproduced in Walter 1976, p. 492, fig. 6); on Monet's performance in Scribe's play, see chap. 1, p. 18.
23. Before it was recognized as a copy of Carjat's *portrait-charge* of Uchard, Monet's drawing was thought to represent his drawing teacher, Jacques-François Ochard.
24. Monet made two additional copies of *portraits-charges* by Hadol published in the 23 May and 12 Sept. 1858 issues of the same journal (D500, 501).
25. Hemmings 1993, p. 206.
26. Wildenstein 1974–91, vol. 5, p. 148.
27. See Senici 2005, pp. 93–103.
28. On the *Panthéon Nadar*, see New York 1995. Before Monet's drawing was recognized as a copy from Nadar's *Panthéon*, Charles Merrill Mount (Mount 1966, p. 397) identified it as a portrait of Alfred Bruyas. Pierre Georgel (Georgel 1968) first recognized its connection with the Panthéon and identified the subject as Vacquerie.
29. D505–9.
30. François Thiébault-Sisson, "About Claude Monet," *Le Temps*, 29 Dec. 1926, translated in Stuckey 1985, p. 342.
31. The complete list of caricatures of dimensions roughly 320 by 240 millimeters comprises D466, 470–74, 499, 501–4, 506–9, 513. Monet's copy of *Auguste Vacquerie* after Nadar (D505) is on paper measuring 285 by 175 mm that is cropped within the drawing on the left side. D500, a portrait of *Frédéric Thomas* after Hadol, is drawn on paper measuring 340 by 250 mm.
32. Hervey 1847, p. 186.
33. Wildenstein 1974–91, vol. 5, p. 151.
34. Ibid., p. 150.
35. Thiébault-Sisson, *Le Temps*, 27 Nov. 1900, in Stuckey 1985, p. 205 (see chap. 1, n. 5).
36. *Registre des deliberations du conseil municipal du Havre, séance du 18 mai 1859*, fols. 157–62, quoted in Wildenstein 1974–91, vol. 1, p. 6.
37. Wildenstein 1974–91, vol. 5, p. 145.
38. Ibid., p. 144. Wildenstein speculates that the *Man Wearing a Small Hat* (D496) represents the son or grandson of Monsieur Lebas based on an inscription on the verso which reads "*Le Fieu* [Cauchois dialect for '*fils*'] *Le Bas*" ["Le Bas junior"]. Another drawing of an artisan that appears to be the pendant to this sheet (D497) may represent another employee in Lebas's shop.
39. D475–79, 481–83, 486–90, 515.
40. Wildenstein 1974–91, vol. 5, p. 141, identified Coësme's profession from an entry in the 1859 Le Havre business directory.
41. Ibid., p. 142. The portrait must postdate Manchon's 2 Dec. 1857 appointment as notary as recorded in the *Journal du Havre*, 4 Jan. 1858.
42. Inv. no. 952-3-9, D482.
43. Edwards 1943, p. 72

44. Wildenstein 1974–91, vol. 5, p. 151.
45. See Bouillon 1987, pp. 30–31, no. Aa11.
46. Adhémar and Lethève 1953, p. 573, no. 6.
47. It was published in Paris 1972, p. 29, no. 160 (inv. no. 5111).
48. It is commonly and erroneously stated that the newspaper *Diogène,* which included prints by both Monet and Manet in 1860, was published by Etienne Carjat; in fact, Carjat's publication of the same name ran only from 10 Aug. 1856 until 26 Apr. 1857; see Paris 1982, p. 101, no. 446. The later journal of this title was published between 10 Mar. 1860 and 17 Dec. 1863. Carjat was one of its contributors.
49. Louvet 1860, pp. 4–5.
50. D512.
51. On Laferrière, see Hemmings 1993, p. 11. According to Hemmings, "Laferrière's so-called 'feminine' vanity was almost proverbial at the time: Barbey d'Aurevilly began his series entitled *Les Vieilles Actrices* with a mordant hatchet-job on 'Mademoiselle Laferrière'"; Hemmings 1993, p. 275, n. 6.
52. Dolan 2000.
53. Claude Monet to Amand Gautier, 11 Aug. 1860, in Wildenstein 1974–91, vol. 1, p. 420, L5.

CHAPTER THREE

Encounters with Draftsmen, 1859–63

1. Claude Monet to Eugène Boudin, 19 May 1859, in Wildenstein 1974–91, vol. 1, p. 419, L1.
2. Jean-François Ochard (1800–1870), see Bénézit 1976, vol. 7, p. 771.
3. Delaborde 1870, p. 123; see also Holt 1966, pp. 35–36.
4. Previously unknown portraits are mentioned at several points in Beguin Billecocq 2005. See, for example, p. 144 [1857].
5. See Monet's references to Théodore Gudin (n. 6, below); "Vasseur" is presumably Louis Jean-Baptise Vasseur (dates unknown), in Rewald 1973, p. 39; and Charles Wissant, in Wildenstein 1996, vol. 1, p. 20.
6. Thiébault-Sisson, *Le Temps,* 27 Nov. 1900, in Stuckey 1985, p. 205 (see chap. 1, n. 5); Théodore Gudin had a long and productive career as painter of marine subjects; he painted several pictures of Le Havre, including two with the title *Entrance to the Port at Le Havre* (Musée Magnin, Dijon, and Musée Malraux, Le Havre).
7. His choice to approach Troyon is further evidence of Monet's aspiration toward landscape, but his selection of two still lifes for this interview remains puzzling.
8. Soullié 1900, p. viii.
9. "The Salon of 1859," in Baudelaire 1955, p. 275.
10. Ibid., pp. 276–68.
11. Beguin Billecocq 2005, p. 151 [1859]. This successful comic opera, set in Brittany, was also known also as *Dinorah, Le Pardon de Ploërmel.*
12. Ibid., p. 152 [1859].
13. Manoeuvre 1991, p. 182.
14. Elder 1924a, p. 16; Thiébault-Sisson, *Le Temps,* 27 Nov. 1900, in Stuckey 1985, p. 206 (see chap. 1, n. 5).
15. W1. Paul Tucker argues that *View from Ruelles* is too sophisticated to have been Monet's first painting; see Tucker 1995, p. 11.
16. Thénot 1856, p. 5.
17. Delaborde 1870, p. 123.
18. Ibid., p. 132.
19. Blanc's *L'histoire des peintres de toutes les écoles* was originally released in unbound sections and later gathered together into volumes. Cézanne and many other artists made use of the illustrations from these "part-works"; see Gowing 1988, pp. 12–13, 136–37.
20. Blanc 1867, p. 22.
21. For the date of their meeting, see Jean-Aubry 1922, p. 36, and Manoeuvre 1991, p. 183.
22. Some scattered anatomical studies in Boudin's sketchbooks in the Louvre suggest a brief acquaintance with this discipline.
23. Cahen 1900, p. 181, cited in Rewald 1973, p. 38.
24. Blanc 1867, p. 587.
25. See "Salon of 1859," in Baudelaire 1955, pp. 199–299, esp. pp. 280–82. Boudin's pastels were not included in this exhibition.
26. Ibid., p. 281. For Baudelaire's visit to Boudin, see Jean-Aubry 1922, p. 40.
27. "Salon of 1859," in Baudelaire 1955, p. 281.
28. Beguin Billecocq 2005, p. 155 [1859].
29. Claude Monet to Eugène Boudin, 20 Feb. 1860, in Wildenstein 1974–91, vol. 1, p. 419, L3.
30. See Johnson 1981–86, nos. 386, 360, and 408. Other exotic or African subjects were nos. 55, 114, 178, 195, 257, and 348.
31. Claude Monet to Eugène Boudin, 20 Feb. 1860 (see n. 29).
32. Beguin Billecocq 2005, p. 172 [1860].
33. Claude Monet to Eugène Boudin, 19 May 1859 (see n. 1). As teachers, François-Edouard Picot (another David pupil) and Léon Cogniet were both regarded as representatives of stricter times, while even the independent-minded Thomas Couture could be seen as a spent force; in his letter of 20 Feb. 1860 (see n. 29), the increasingly opinionated Monet remarked that "Couture has entirely given up painting. It's no great loss; he has several really bad pictures in this year's exhibition."
34. Ibid.
35. Pissarro 1980–91, vol. 1, p. 27.
36. Rewald 1939, pp. 20–21.
37. Venturi 1936, no. 100.
38. Claude Monet to Eugène Boudin, 21 Apr. 1860, in Wildenstein 1974–91, vol. 1, p. 420, L4.
39. Rewald 1973, p. 49; see also Brettell and Lloyd 1980, nos. 49c–64.
40. Beguin Billecocq 2005, p. 175 [1860].
41. Thiébault-Sisson, *Le Temps,* 27 Nov. 1900, in Stuckey 1985, p. 217 (see chap. 1, n. 5).
42. According to Wildenstein, P5 is inscribed on the verso "Yport, 1861, Claude Monet." The black crayon drawing, D410, is said to carry the same inscription on its cardboard backing, though it appears to belong with similar drawings from c. 1864; see chap. 4. The pastel P14 is also described as having the date 1861 on the verso. All these works are currently of unknown location.
43. The linked pastel P1 is rightly associated by Wildenstein with several sketchbook drawings of the 1850s: for the Sainte-Adresse pastel, P14, see n. 42.
44. See figs. 85 and 121.
45. Valéry 1989, p. 35.
46. Elder 1924a, p. 54.
47. Ornans 2004, p. 37. This publication fills out many aspects of the story of Gautier's early association with Monet. Some of Gautier's collaborations with Courbet are mentioned in Chu 1996, pp. 140, 163. For Monet's atheism and its importance for his art, see Edinburgh 2006.
48. Claude Monet to Eugène Boudin, 19 May 1859 (see n. 1) and 21 Apr. 1860 (see n. 38). The story of Daubigny is in Elder 1924a, p. 23.
49. Claude Monet to Amand Gautier, 11 Aug. 1860, in Wildenstein 1974–91, vol. 1, p. 420, L5.
50. For the dates of Monet's later caricatures, see chap. 2.
51. Geffroy 1924, p. 18. See also Wildenstein 1996, vol. 1, pp. 28–30.

52. Monet's caricature, which seems to have been made in Le Havre before he left for Paris, was copied from a figure by Nadar; see chap. 2. His memories of Pelloquet are cited in Geffroy 1924, p. 19, and Thiébault-Sisson, *Le Temps*, 29 Dec. 1926, in Stuckey 1985, p. 342 (see chap. 2, n. 30).
53. See Sensier 1881, pp. 101, 145, 158, 190.
54. Thiébault-Sisson, *Le Temps*, 27 Nov. 1900, in Stuckey 1985, p. 206 (see chap. 1, n. 5).
55. Thiébault-Sisson, *Le Temps*, 29 Dec. 1926, in Stuckey 1985, p. 342 (see chap 2, n. 30).
56. Thiébault-Sisson, *Le Temps*, 27 Nov. 1900, in Stuckey 1985. p. 206 (see chap. 1, n. 5); André Arnyvelde, "At Home with the Painter of Light," *Je Sais Tout*, 15 Jan. 1914, translated in Stuckey 1985, p. 271.
57. D28, 57, 75.
58. See n. 6: Gudin was an official artist to the Algerian campaign of 1830, exhibiting several of the resulting works at the Salon; his *Hurricane at the Roadsteads of Algiers, 7 Jan. 1831*, is in the Louvre.
59. Thiébault-Sisson, *Le Temps*, 29 Dec. 1926, in Stuckey 1985, p. 342 (see chap. 2, n. 30).
60. Thiébault-Sisson, *Le Temps*, 27 Nov. 1900, in Stuckey, pp. 206–7 (see chap. 1, n. 5).
61. Arnyvelde, *Je Sais Tout*, 15 Jan. 1914, in Stuckey 1985, p. 271 (see n. 56).
62. Gimpel 1966, p. 339, entry dated 12 June 1927.
63. Claude Monet to Gustave Geffroy, 8 May 1920, Wildenstein 1974–91, vol. 1, p. 405, L2348. A drawing with watercolor published in Seitz 1960, fig. 14, as a North African scene is now considered to be a depiction of Dieppe; see D406.
64. Beguin Billecocq 2005, pp. 178–79 [1861].
65. Ibid.
66. Ibid.
67. P84.
68. Elder 1924a, pp. 51–52; Gimpel 1966, pp. 152–53, entry dated 9 Oct. 1920.
69. Beguin Billecocq 2005, p. 184 [1862].
70. Ibid.
71. Ibid., p. 185.
72. Geffroy 1924, p. 32.
73. Thiébault-Sisson, *Le Temps*, 27 Nov. 1900, in Stuckey 1985, p. 207 (see chap. 1, n. 5).
74. In Thiébault-Sisson's 1924 interview, Monet relates that his father paid the necessary amount; in Wildenstein 1996, vol. 1, p. 40, reference is made to a letter from Monet's aunt, Marie-Jeanne Lecadre, indicating that she was responsible.
75. Toulemouche was married to a cousin of the Lecadres; see Wildenstein 1996, vol. 1, p. 42.
76. Toulemouche's advice is briefly reported in a number of reminiscences, including those of Arnyvelde, Elder, and Thiébault-Sisson.
77. Hauptman 1996, pp. 327, 335.
78. Elder 1924a, p. 20.
79. Hauptman 1996, p. 337; Albert Boime, "The Instruction of Charles Gleyre and the Evolution of Painting in the Nineteenth Century," in Wintherthur 1974, p. 102.
80. Quoted in Trévise, "Pilgrimage to Giverny," *La Revue de l'art ancien and moderne* 51 (Jan. and Feb. 1927), trans. Catherine J. Richards, in Stuckey 1985, p. 333; Clemenceau 1928, p. 36.
81. Beguin Billecocq 2005, p. 185 [1863].
82. Ibid.
83. Ibid.
84. Montpellier 1992, p. 155; March 1863 is specified as the date of their meeting.
85. Ibid., p. 156.
86. In Elder 1924a, p. 20, Monet claims to have precipitated the departure of the group; see also Thiébault-Sisson, *Le Temps*, 27 Nov. 1900, in Stuckey 1985, p. 208 (see chap 1. n. 5).
87. Ibid.
88. "Salon of 1859," in Baudelaire 1955, p. 275.
89. W51.

CHAPTER FOUR

Drawing and Painting, 1863–66

1. Claude Monet to Eugène Boudin, 19 May 1859 (see chap. 3, n. 1).
2. W11, 20.
3. W1, 5, 5a, 22, 23.
4. Williamstown 2000, p. 36.
5. Goupil 1882, p. 14.
6. W19, 65, 67, 63.
7. For detailed observations on *Luncheon on the Grass*, see the analysis later in this chapter.
8. Evidence for this date comes from *Le Bulletin de la vie artistique*, 15 Mar. 1921.
9. D7, 17, 19, 31, 42, 83.
10. This work is recorded as belonging to the collection of Michel Monet.
11. See, for example, D414, 404; P3.
12. The drawings and pastels of Troyon (see n. 16), and the sketchbooks of Boudin and Jongkind discussed in the present chapter, are cases in point to which Monet had already been exposed.
13. For example, D45, 61, 69, 70, 71.
14. P1 and P2.
15. Wadley 1991, p. 146.
16. Soullié 1900, pp. ix–x.
17. The work was *Les Graves de Villerville*; Hellebranth 1976, no. 597.
18. Musée du Louvre, RF 9119, recto.
19. Beguin Billecocq 2005, p. 180 [1861].
20. W17–19.
21. Claude Monet to Amand Gautier, 23 May 1863, in Wildenstein 1974–91, vol. 1, p. 420, L6.
22. Examples from 1856–60 include Fernier 1977–78, nos. 194–98, 243, 260, 266.
23. *The Spring Rut*, Fernier 1977–78, no. 279, is now in the Louvre.
24. For Courbet's drawings, see Fernier 1977–78, pp. 265–313.
25. Claude Monet to Frédéric Bazille, 15 July 1864, in Wildenstein 1974–91, vol. 1, p. 20, L8.
26. See, for example, Montpellier 1992, pp. 80, 83.
27. W42–44, 20, 22a and b, 38, 39.
28. For the most complete account of this establishment and its artists, see Williamstown 1976.
29. Ibid., nos. 38, 48, 97, 111, etc.
30. Beguin Billecocq 2005, p. 144 [1857].
31. Claude Monet to Eugène Boudin, late Oct.–early Nov. 1864, in Wildenstein 1974–91, vol. 1, p. 421, L13.
32. Claude Monet to Frédéric Bazille, 26 Aug. 1864, in ibid., vol. 1, pp. 420–21, L9.
33. The drawing is Louvre RF 22630; see also Honfleur 1996, nos. 50–54.
34. These pastels are largely undated but are widely considered to have been made from the mid-1850s into the following decade; see, for example, Manoeuvre 1991, nos. 6–8.
35. Hafting 1975, no. 307; see also nos. 281, 311.
36. The reference is on a sheet in the Louvre, RF 10872.30; the watercolor is Hafting 1975, no. 311. Monet's painting is W35.
37. Claude Monet to Frédéric Bazille, 14 July 1864 (see n. 25); Claude Monet to Frédéric Bazille, 14 Oct. 1864, in Wildenstein 1974–91, vol. 1, p. 421, L11.
38. Claude Monet to Frédéric Bazille, 14 July 1864 (see n. 25).
39. W24, 25, 28, 29, 30.
40. See, for example, Honfleur 1996, nos. 111, 113, 116.
41. P74.
42. Thiébault-Sisson, *Le Temps*, 27 Nov. 1900, in Stuckey 1985, p. 208 (see chap. 1, n. 5). In this account, Monet indicates that his meeting with Jongkind took place around the time he left Gleyre, which appears to have been in early 1863. In Hefting 1975, p. 346, the author asserts that the two artists met in 1862.

43. Elder 1924a, p. 16.
44. Claude Monet to Eugène Boudin, 20 Feb. 1860 (see chap. 3, n. 29). Thiébault-Sisson, *Le Temps*, 27 Nov. 1900, in Stuckey 1985, p. 208 (see chap. 1, n. 5).
45. Ibid., p. 217.
46. Goncourt 1956, vol. 2, p. 797; entry dated 4 May 1871.
47. In a letter to Gustave Geffroy, Monet regretted in later life that he had not used watercolor more, while referring to two studies of water lilies in the medium; Claude Monet to Gustave Geffroy, 8 May 1920 (see chap. 3, n. 63).
48. Paris 2003, p. 182.
49. See Marie-Pierre Salé, "Les albums de Jongkind," in Paris 2003.
50. This work is now in the collection of the Musée Marmottan Monet, Paris.
51. Recent x-rays show some changes to details of the boat and figures, for example, but suggest that such forms were defined and redefined with a brush. Several areas have been reworked, producing thicker layers of paint, and no drawn lines can be detected.
52. The most characteristic examples are D415–22; other works that may be linked to the set are D410, 411, 432, 433, and P10. None of these works are dated, but they seem to correspond most closely to the period 1864–66.
53. While some are currently unlocated, the following have been examined for this study at firsthand: D415–16, 421, 422, 433, P10.
54. Hefting 1975, no. 238. Other examples of this motif are found in Hefting 1975, nos. 226, 246, 248, 276, 361.
55. For Jongkind, see, for example, Hefting 1975, nos. 237–38, 246–48, 276; for Daubigny, see Hellebranth 1976, no. 593. It should also be noted that a few similarly angled compositions occur in Monet's early sketchbooks; see D81, 82, 96.
56. A narrative link between some of these works was first proposed by Daniel Wildenstein; see D417–421.
57. See the group of pastels associated with *After the Rain* (P48) in chap. 6.
58. Daubigny's drawings are linked through their narrative but were freely, almost wildly executed and bear no technical resemblance to Monet's crayon studies.
59. The *Voyage en bateau* etchings were published in 1861; see Delteil 1921.
60. See Melot 1996, pp. 49–51.
61. See Ornans 2004, p. 43.
62. Ibid., p. 40.
63. Claude Monet to Eugène Boudin, 19 May 1859 (see chap. 3, n. 1).
64. For this incident, see chap. 3, n. 48. In Fidell-Beaufort and Bailly-Herzberg 1975, p. 23, it is proposed that the painting in question was Daubigny's *Vendanges* of 1852.
65. *8 Gravures à l'eau forte* (Paris: Cadart, 1862).
66. In addition to the six prints, the set includes an etched title plate, which specifies that they were printed by Delâtre; see Delteil 1906, nos. 1–7.
67. Melot 1996, pp. 75–76.
68. Baudelaire 1862.
69. Melot 1996, pp. 72–73.
70. A comparable effect is found in another Jongkind plate in the series, no. 3, *The Wetnurse*, where a group of large trees and their shadows result in a similar contrast.
71. The second version is W34. The suggestion that both works were painted in 1866, rather than 1864, is put forward in New York 1994, pp. 425–26.
72. Hafting 1975, no. 268.
73. Jongkind's *Entrance to the Port of Honfleur* (Delteil 1906, no. 10), for example, an etching published separately in 1863, features an almost identical vessel in a larger Normandy harbor and somewhat further from the town. Comparable ships can be found in numerous works of this period, among them Hefting 1975, nos. 305, 335, 338, and 355.
74. Similar clouds appear, for example, in Jongkind's 1864 etching *Exit from the Port of Honfleur* (Delteil 1906, no. 11).
75. Other works of this kind that may be related to the larger set include D408, 410, 411; Boudin's drawing *Boats on the Beach* (Musée Eugène Boudin, Honfleur), offers a striking precedent for some of these works.
76. A tantalizing exception within the sequence, *Sainte-Adresse, Shipwrecked Sailboat* (P10), was partly developed in pastel, bridging the gap between Monet's extraordinary excursion into monochrome and his current work in other media.
77. Signed works are D410, 418, 419, 420, and 432.
78. Analysis by the conservation department at the Kimbell was unable to establish the presence of more extensive or substantial drawing beneath the paint. My thanks are due to Claire Barry and her colleagues for assistance in this inquiry.
79. Beguin Billecocq 2005, p. 197 [1864].
80. Claude Monet to Frédéric Bazille, c. 4 May 1865, in Wildenstein 1974–91, p. 422, L19.
81. Beguin Billecocq 2005, p. 201 [1865].
82. Claude Monet to Frédéric Bazille, c. 4 May 1865, in Wildenstein 1974–91, p. 422, L20.
83. "Gabrielle" is mentioned in L19 (see n. 80).
84. For detailed accounts of the making of this painting, see Isaacson 1972 and New York 1994, pp. 423–25.
85. See, for example, Chappuis 1973, nos. 69, 173, 171, 199.
86. Munich 2005, pp. 70–77.
87. W63.
88. W. Bürger, *Salons de W. Burger 1861 to 1868* (Paris: Librairie de Ve Jules Renouard, 1870), translated in Stuckey 1985, p. 35; the critic's real name was Théophile Thoré.
89. Beguin Billecocq 2005, p. 205 [1866].

CHAPTER FIVE
Monet's Pastels in Public

1. For a detailed account of Monet's involvement in the exhibition's inception, see Rewald 1973, pp. 309–18.
2. The original agreement was that each artist would submit up to two works, but this was not observed; see San Francisco 1986, p. 105.
3. Ibid., p. 106.
4. For the works exhibited, see Berson 1996, vol. 1, p. 6, and vol. 2, pp. 9–10.
5. Ibid., vol. 1, nos. 99–102. They were listed as three pairs of pastels, which were perhaps framed as pairs, and one single work. No titles or further details were given.
6. See, for example, the items listed in Paris 1874 as Morisot no. 109, Robert no. 160, Rouart no. 157, and Degas no. 60.
7. Léon de Lora mentioned "plusieurs croquis au pastel" in the three sentences he devoted to Monet's works; see Berson 1996, vol. 1, p. 27.
8. The pastels shown in 1874 are briefly referred to in House 1986, p. 228.
9. Bracquemond, for example, had exhibited a group of etchings in 1872; see Paris 1872, no. 1943. Manet showed his watercolor *Pulcinelle* two years later; see Paris 1874, no. 2357.
10. Claude Monet to Frédéric Bazille, 16 Oct. 1864, in Wildenstein 1974–91, vol. 1, p. 421, L12.
11. In the 1874 Salon catalogue, 1,852 paintings are listed. Works on paper are divided into

"Drawings," "Engraving," and "Lithography," totaling more than a thousand items; see Paris 1874.

12. Quoted in Reff 1968, p. 87.
13. Ward 1991, p. 603.
14. Ibid.
15. Thiébault-Sisson, *Le Temps*, 27 Nov. 1900, in Stuckey 1985, p. 217 (see chap. 1, n. 5).
16. Berson 1996, vol. 1, p. 4.
17. See the following in Berson 1996, vol. 1: Renoir's pastel is listed as no. 146 (p. 7); the responses to Morisot were from Sylvestre (p. 40), Carjat (p. 14), and Drumont (p. 21); the remark about the Degas is from Montifaud (p. 29).
18. For Morisot, see Paris 1872, no. 1142; for her submission to the 1873 Salon, see Washington 1987, p. 54. The pastel by Degas was Lemoisne 1946–49, no. 214.
19. See Lemoisne 1946–49, nos. 217–53 and New York 1993, chap. 4; in the latter, the possibility that these works were intended for exhibition, or were actually shown, is discussed on p. 86.
20. See the entries for these two works in Wildenstein 1974–91, vol. 5. Analysis of the approximately seventy-five pastels that appear to have been made before 1874 sheds some light on Monet's habits in releasing such works but is inconclusive in terms of the first Impressionist exhibition. The majority of pastels that were given away or sold by Monet in the earlier part of his career were signed by him, perhaps at the time they left his possession. His signature was always placed in a lower corner of the composition, as often on the right as on the left, and tended to take one of three forms. The simplest was his initials, rendered as "Cl. M"; the expanded form was "Cl. Monet"; and almost half the signed works of this period show his first Christian name followed by his surname, "Claude Monet." If we assume that the works exhibited in 1874 by this publicity-conscious young artist were signed in the latter manner, as were his five oil paintings, this narrows the field to some fifteen pastels. Only two of these works are dated, however, unlike all Monet's exhibited paintings. Both the pastels in question (P46 and 49) are simple inland scenes, raising the possibility that he used the medium in 1874 to publicly extend his pictorial repertoire.
21. See Wildenstein 1974–91, vol. 5, pp. 155–75. A significant number of works in pastel falsely attributed to Monet can be found in the collections of the Witt Library, Courtauld Institute of Art, London, and the Documentation of the Musée d'Orsay, Paris.
22. The portraits are P68, 70, 71.
23. Wildenstein 1974–91, vol. 5, p. 155.
24. See, for example, the entries for P14, 53, 65.
25. P13.
26. The pastel that belonged to Duranty, who died in 1880, is P27; his remark is in Berson 1996, vol. 1, p. 218.
27. Gachet's pastel was P17; Delage 1963 mentions two works in Chabrier's collection, while P1, 2, and 26 are all listed as belonging to the composer.
28. P26 carries the dedication "A l'ami Chabrier."
29. Faure is listed in Wildenstein 1974–91, vol. 5, as the owner of P5, 37, 77, 78, and 79; see also Distel 1990, chap. 6.
30. For details of this relationship, see chap. 6.
31. P29.
32. Claude Monet to Victor Chocquet, 4 Feb. 1876, in Wildenstein 1974–91, vol. 1, p. 430, L86; see also Distel 1990, p. 137.
33. P31.
34. P11, 80; both were sold at auction in Paris in March 1900.
35. This was presumably Shintaro Yamashita (1881–1966), a printmaker and painter who helped to introduce Post-Impressionist art to Japan. A memorial exhibition of his work was held at the Bridgestone Museum of Art in 1981.
36. The works in question and their histories are recorded by Wildenstein; see P32, 23, 4, 64, 66, respectively.
37. See P20, 33, 4, 95, respectively.
38. Those clearly catalogued as changing hands before 1926 are P84, 87, 94, 95, 99, 101, 105, 106, 108, while other possible candidates are less precisely documented.
39. P38; P65 was also given by the artist to a charitable auction.
40. See Wharton 1916, pp. 22–23; the drawing was D432.
41. P31.
42. P51.
43. P55, 56; Elder gave them to the Société des amis du Musée des Beaux-Arts de Nantes, which formally presented them to the museum in 1968.
44. P88.
45. Wildenstein indicates that the pastel, P4, was given to Mauclair by Marcel Bernheim.
46. P74; P81.
47. P20 was shown at the Ligue navale française in 1917 with one painting by the artist; Wildenstein also indicates that P31 may have been exhibited as part of the Gallatin Collection at the Metropolitan Museum of Art in 1924.
48. Duret, *Le peintre Claude Monet*, in Stuckey 1985, p. 72 (see chap. 1, n. 2).
49. Taboureux, *La vie moderne* 2 (12 June 1880), in Stuckey 1985, p. 90 (see chap. 1, n. 3).
50. Georges Jeanniot, "Notes on Art: Claude Monet," *La cravache parisienne*, 23 June 1888, trans. Catherine J. Richards, in Stuckey 1986, p. 129.
51. Blanc 1867, pp. 587–88.
52. Ibid., p. 586.
53. See New York 1993, pp. 88–89.
54. Blanc himself acknowledged the occasional large-scale achievements of pastellists such as Georges de La Tour and Joseph Vivien; see Blanc 1867, p. 587.
55. Etienne Carjat, "L'Exposition du boulevard des Capucines," *Le Patriote français*, 27 Apr. 1874, quoted in Berson 1996, vol. 1, pp. 14–15.
56. Castagnary, "Exposition du boulevard des Capucines: Les Impressionistes," *Le Siècle*, 29 Apr. 1874, quoted in ibid., p. 17.
57. Arthur Baignères, "Exposition de peinture par un groupe d'artistes, rue le Peletier, 11," *L'Echo universel*, 13 Apr. 1876, quoted in ibid., pp. 9, 55.
58. J. K. Huysmans, "L'Exposition des independents en 1880," in *L'Art moderne* (Paris: G. Charpentier, 1883), pp. 85–123, quoted in ibid., p. 292.
59. See New York 1997, no. 208; nos. 18–20; the pastel owned by Monet is *On the Beach* (fig. 107); the Degas pastel is Lemoisne 1946–49, no. 890.
60. Few of Millet's pastels were shown in his lifetime, though they were collected by individuals such as Emile Gavet and known before his death in 1875 to some fellow artists; see Williamstown 1999.
61. See ibid., p. 66.
62. Some minor exceptions are noted in Manoeuvre 1991, pp. 184–85.
63. Blanc 1867, p. 587.
64. Bataille and Wildenstein 1961, no. 417; the visit is described in Morisot 1986, pp. 20–22.
65. See Pissarro and Venturi 1939, nos. 1507–32.
66. Pissarro 1980–91, vol. 1, p. 79.
67. P48, 49, 57. A curiosity of Monet's pastel oeuvre that obliquely reflects its independent character is the fact that many such works were given as personal or charitable gifts. These ranged from pastels offered to Bazille and Duranty in his earlier years, and to Faure in the mid-

1880s, to a succession of works presented to acquaintances and to neighbors at Giverny after the turn of the century. Then, as now, artists are often pressed to part with their paintings or sculpture in such circumstances; not being a printmaker or prolific draftsman in his maturity, Monet clearly found it easier to offer his pastels, reduced-scale variants of his more well-known imagery, while protecting his primary oeuvre.

CHAPTER SIX
Monet's Pastels in Private

1. Several Étretat works, such as W832 and 833, depict the arch from close quarters but without showing the cliff beyond, while one early canvas (W258) offers a similar distant view but through a different rock arch.
2. Monet was looking in a roughly western direction and must therefore have been watching a setting sun.
3. The back of the framed picture carries various numbers and partial labels, including that of Adam Dupré, 19 rue Fontaine, a framer who was active in lower Montmartre from at least 1880 and framed many works for Degas.
4. The basic format recurs in works such as W522, 535, and 586 from the late 1870s, and a decade later in W1194–1202.
5. P48–51 and 54–56 are closely linked through composition and size; P36, 37, 39, and 40 have similar motifs but conform to a smaller format.
6. Both P48 and P49 are dated 1868, though there are no comparable works on canvas from this year; the date 1885 on P53 appears to be anomalous. In the entry for P48, Wildenstein suggests that the series may have been executed near Montvilliers, when Monet undertook the portrait of his patron, Mme Gaudibert (W121). He also notes that the canvas in question carries a charcoal drawing by Monet on the verso.
7. Unlike the later series paintings, of course, there is no evidence that Monet planned to exhibit this suite of pastels in public.
8. Claude Monet to Alice Hoschedé, 7 Feb. 1882, in Wildenstein 1974–91, vol. 2, p. 213, L235.
9. Claude Monet to Alice Hoschedé, 15 Feb. 1882, in Wildenstein 1974–91, vol. 2, p. 213–14, L242.
10. Beguin Billecocq 2005, p. 145 [1857]; for Faure, see chap. 5, as well as the discussion later in this chapter; for Maupassant, see Claude Monet to Alice Hoschedé, 15 Oct. 1885, in Wildenstein 1974–91, vol. 2, p. 262, L590.
11. Two scenes, P5 and P14, have their location inscribed in Monet's or another person's hand, but none have other titles written on them. A number of current titles, however, relate to works that Monet seems to have given or sold directly to their first owners in his earlier career; see, for example, P2, 5, 13, 21, 26, 29, and 32.
12. Three remarkable essays by Richard Brettell on the importance of Normandy for Impressionist painting, and for Monet's art and personal formation in particular, are in San Francisco 2006, pp. 15–49.
13. Examples of Monet's extreme attention to the details of local boat types can be found in the Wildenstein entries for such works as D20, 22–25, 51–55, 58–60, 102.
14. See n. 13 above and the Wildenstein entries for P25–27, 29.
15. P74, 65; other such works are P44–47, 65–67.
16. Beguin Billecocq 2005, p. 256 [1874].
17. Closely comparable features can be found in the riverbank, houses, and skyscapes of the Bougival scenes W150 and 151.
18. P72; for related paintings, see W709–12, 777–86, 791.
19. P74 and 75.
20. D44–45, 58, 69–71. The possibility that Monet used the sketchbook images when making the pastel, rather than drawing the figures from life, should be considered, as well as the implicit dating of *Study of Five Boys* close to 1857.
21. Monet may have chosen to reuse his earlier drawings of boys (see n. 20), as well as his two pastels, when making these paintings.
22. P5.
23. Beguin Billecocq 2005, p. 172 [1860].
24. Most of Monet's pastels appear to have been executed on laid paper of the "Ingres" type, evident in the distinctive parallel "chain" marks that are sometimes accentuated by strokes of chalky color. For the presence of "Michallet" watermarks in certain of his London pastels, see chap. 10.
25. The group of undated Sainte-Adresse pastels from these years includes P8–9, 11–15.
26. Beguin Billecocq 2005, p. 189 [1863].
27. Ibid., p. 197 [1864].
28. See P4–7, and n. 25 above.
29. This canvas is not dated or otherwise documented at the period, but its subject and handling have been widely accepted as appropriate to this year. Monet himself claimed in later life that the pastel that is now considered to relate to it, P34, was executed around 1862; see Claude Monet to J. Durand-Ruel, 15 Oct. 1907, in Wildenstein 1974–91, vol. 5, p. 291, pièce justificative no. 347.
30. Williamstown 2000, p. 100.
31. The complex surface of this pastel is difficult to read clearly, but Monet may have used a brush to drag or rub one color over another in areas of the sky. The use of water in pastel technique is unorthodox and not found elsewhere in Monet's oeuvre; it remains uncertain that it was followed here. Also atypical is the choice of black ink for the artist's initials (also used in P32), which seem to conform to the flourishing style of his earlier signed paintings.
32. The pattern of clouds and palette of colors in the upper part of Boudin's 1864 *Beach at Villerville* (National Gallery of Art, Washington) are remarkably close to Monet's pastel. This observation was made by Natasha Khandekar of the Museum of Fine Arts, Boston. See Khandekar 2005.
33. The following works are at least twice as wide as they are high: P4, 6, 7, 15, 20, 23, 28–32, 34, 36, 38, 40.
34. P30.
35. A closely comparable, though slightly smaller, pastel with similar proportions (P39) also shows a flat landscape with heaps of earth or manure in the foreground, here with a dramatic cloudscape dominating the sky. As with *After the Rain* (fig. 102) and its associated works, this pair seems to propose a modest serial relationship.
36. See Wharton 1916. Though it is not specified in Wharton's text, the implication is that the numerous works of art illustrated in *The Book of the Homeless* had been donated to this cause. P38 was subsequently owned by a member of the Bliss family in New York, who presented it to the Metropolitan Museum of Art.
37. In the catalogue entry for this work, W55a, Wildenstein suggests that the squat tower in the distance is that of the church at Chailly.
38. Harfleur is situated at the eastern edge of Le Havre and in the nineteenth century had an

unimpeded view across the Seine estuary and the sea beyond.

39. Chapus 1855, p. 183. This image is reproduced in Tucker 1982, p. 15, though not in the context of P63, where the author associates it more generally with Monet's identification with modernity.
40. Monet's visit is recorded in his letter to Frédéric Bazille, n.d., in Wildenstein 1974–91, vol. 1, p. 423, L29.
41. See Claude Monet to Frédéric Bazille, 29 June 1868, in ibid., vol. 1, p. 425, L40.
42. See Beguin Billecocq 2005, pp. 195, 197 [1864], 204 [1866], 213 [1868].
43. Ibid., p. 203 [1866].
44. Claude Monet to Frédéric Bazille, 25 June 1867, in Wildenstein 1974–91, vol. 1, pp. 423–24, L33; Claude Monet to Frédéric Bazille, 12 Aug. 1867, in ibid., vol. 1, p. 424, L37.
45. See P57 and 58; Wildenstein points out that, although P57 carries the artist's initials and the date 1868, it may have been made a decade later.
46. Claude Monet to Frédéric Bazille, Dec. 1868, in Wildenstein 1974–91, vol. 1, p. 425–26, L44.
47. Ibid.
48. Claude Monet to Arsène Houssaye, 2 June 1868, in ibid., vol. 1, p. 426, L49.
49. Claude Monet to Frédéric Bazille, 25 June 1867 (see n. 44).
50. W93, 91.
51. P8–9, P11–15; though listed with this group by Wildenstein, P10 seems much closer to the group of black-chalk drawings made in mid-1860s.
52. P14. Note that the pastel and associated paintings (W90 and 91) show the tip of a steeple, described by Wildenstein as that of the Church of Saint-Vincent, while P12 features a curious column that has not been identified at this site. P14 is inscribed on the back "Ste Adresse 1861, Claude Monet," either by another hand or by the artist in later life.
53. See Beguin Billecocq 2005, p. 145 [1857].
54. W22a and 22b.
55. Herbert 1994, chaps. 3, 4, and 6.
56. W22b.
57. The second drawing is inverted with respect to the first.
58. RF 16716 recto.
59. Claude Monet to Frédéric Bazille, Dec. 1868 (see n. 46).
60. P22, 18, 19–21.
61. P21, W127.
62. For Courbet's meeting with Monet and Camille, see Chu 1996, letter 66-25. Two paintings by Courbet of the northeastern aspect of the Étretat bay are dated 1866; see Fernier 1977–78, nos. 590, 593.
63. See ibid., nos. 718, 720, 721.
64. Gustave Courbet to his parents, Sept. (?) 1869, in Chu 1996, letter 69-7.
65. Several of these pastels carry the artist's signature; among them, P19 and 20 remained in Monet's collection, while P21 and 23 were sold, apparently in later years.
66. Tucker 1982, p. 10; Beguin Billecocq 2005, p. 249 [1872].
67. We are most grateful to Paul Tucker for bringing this work to our attention.
68. W150–52.
69. Beguin Billecocq 2005, p. 249 [1872].
70. Ibid.
71. Ibid.
72. Ibid., p. 267 [1877].
73. "Woodland," "fields," and "farms," for example, occur in P17, 38–39, 41–50, 64–67.
74. P65, P6. As Wildenstein explains, Monet himself challenged the inscribed date on the former.
75. See n. 73.
76. See n. 3; the picture remained in the artist's possession and was inherited by his son Michel.
77. The use of the foreground "screen," which becomes almost perversely unnegotiable in some cases, is especially common in the second half of this decade; good examples are W345-46, 408–10, 455–58, 490–91, and 519–21.
78. Edmond Drumont, "L'Exposition du boulevard des Capucines," *Le Petit Journal*, 19 Apr. 1872, quoted in Berson 1996, vol. 1, p. 21.
79. Castagnary, *Le Siècle*, 29 Apr. 1874, pp. 17, 18 (see chap. 5, n. 56).
80. Bernadille, "Chronique parisienne: L'Exposition des Impressionistes," *Le Français*, 13 Apr. 1877, quoted in Berson 1996, vol. 1, p. 130.
81. Duret, *Le peintre Claude Monet*, in Stuckey 1985, p. 71 (see chap. 1, n. 2).
82. W762; J. K. Huysmans, "L'Exposition des independents en 1880," quoted in Berson 1996, vol. 1, p. 86 (see chap. 5, n. 58); Gustave Geffroy, "Claude Monet," *La Justice*, 15 Mar. 1883, translated in Stuckey 1985, p. 96.
83. Ibid.
84. Ibid., pp. 96–97.
85. W68–81.
86. Two of these works, W74 and 75, are insistently rural and Norman, with no counterparts in the paintings of this decade, and may conceivably belong to an earlier period. W74 is discussed in chap. 4, in relation to Monet's documented stays at Saint-Siméon.
87. W968, but see also W965–67; the sketchbook studies are D295–307.
88. See Beguin Billecocq 2005, pp. 267 [1877], 269 [1878], 281 [1879].
89. Ibid., p. 148 [1858].
90. For the ages and identities of the depicted children, see the Wildenstein entry for P68.
91. A closely related photograph is in Wildenstein 1974–91, vol. 1, p. 101.
92. P70; W503, 504.
93. D110–15. See also Monet's later canvases of Blanche Hoschedé painting in the open air; W1131–32, 1149, 1330.
94. Claude Monet to Paul Durand-Ruel, 16 Sept. 1885, 2 Oct. 1885, and 8 Oct. 1885, in Wildenstein 1974–91, vol. 2, p. 261, L585–87.
95. P77–79.
96. Wildenstein specifies that W1018 was bought from Monet by Faure at Étretat; the second work was W1051.
97. P77; for a similar composition from a closer vantage point, see also P76.
98. The Delacroix of c. 1838 is now in the collection of the Musée Marmottan Monet, Paris.
99. Claude Monet to Alice Hoschedé, 1 Feb. 1883, in Wildenstein 1974–91, vol. 2, p. 223, L312.
100. In his catalogue entry for this work, Wildenstein suggests a connection with Monet's 1883 paintings of Étretat. The resemblance to such later works as W1014a and 1046, however, is arguably just as strong. It also seems less likely that Monet would have offered Faure a work from a previous visit.
101. To reach the site from which Monet painted this work, it is necessary to scramble down a steep cliff or make a short trip by boat; for Monet, encumbered with painting equipment, the latter seems to have been the preferred method. A reference to his use of a boat is in Claude Monet's letter to Alice Hoschedé, 21 Nov. 1885, in Wildenstein 1974–91, vol. 2, p. 267, L626.
102. See, for example, Lyell 1865, pp. 194–95.
103. Claude Monet to Alice Hoschedé, 29 Oct. 1885 and 6 Dec. 1885, in Wildenstein 1974–91, vol. 2, pp. 263–64 and 269, L603, 635.
104. Monet is here facing southwest and the sun is evidently setting.
105. Claude Monet to Paul Durand-Ruel, 28 Oct. 1885, in Wildenstein 1974–91, vol. 2, p. 263,

L601; Claude Monet to Alice Hoschedé, 24 Oct. 1885, in ibid., vol. 2, p. 263, L597.

106. Claude Monet to Alice Hoschedé, 13 Oct. 1885, in ibid., vol. 2, p. 262, L589.

107. For a forceful argument that Monet's view of Normandy in the 1880s, after the recent death of Camille, was "one of grief and loss," see San Francisco 2006, pp. 46–47.

108. For Monet's longstanding relationship with Whistler and admiration for his art, see chap. 10.

109. W1040–43.

110. Claude Monet to Alice Hoschedé, 21 Nov. 1885 (see n. 101).

111. W1039.

112. See the Wildenstein entries for W1039, P80.

113. Claude Monet to Alice Hoschedé, 12 Nov. 1885, in Wildenstein 1974–91, vol. 2, p. 266, L619.

CHAPTER SEVEN
Rough Drafts: The Sketchbook Drawings

1. Duret, *Le peintre Claude Monet*, in Stuckey 1985, p. 71 (see chap. 1, n. 2).
2. Musée Marmottan Monet inventory nos. 5128–35.
3. House 1986, pp. 228–30.
4. Wildenstein 1974–91, vol. 5, pp. 78–118, D105–404.
5. For example, sketchbook 1, which includes thirty-four extant folios, bears stubs of at least eighteen removed folios (one prior to folio 1; two between folios 10 and 11; one between folios 16 and 17; and fourteen between folios 20 and 21). Since folios 16 verso and 17 recto contain a single drawing of *Water Lilies* (D119), the page between them must have been removed by Monet prior to c. 1914.

   House 1986, pp. 228–29, speculated that the black-crayon drawing of *The Blue Boat,* formerly in the Armand Hammer collection (D442) and inscribed "Leaf from Monet's sk.book" may have originated in sketchbook 6, which contains five related studies (D335, 337, 341, 367, and 368). See also Baltimore 2004, pp. 130–31. Wildenstein also notes that D441, a black-crayon drawing of the Manneporte, may have been in the possession of Robinson. Interestingly, an accidental counterproof of this unfixed drawing appears on folio 18 verso of sketchbook 6, establishing that the sheet was at one time slipped in between folios 18 and 19. When it was removed, another counterproof was created on folio 19 recto (D358). There is no visible evidence that D441 was actually bound into the sketchbook, but the question remains open. We have been unable to locate the crayon drawing of the Manneporte.
6. See Manoeuvre and Rapetti 1987, pp. 4–5.
7. Marie-Pierre Salé, "Les albums de Jongkind, la 'machine à percevoir,'" in Paris 2003, pp. 181–201.
8. Renoir and Pirra 1971 reproduces an 1857 sketchbook containing sixty-two drawings; André 1955 reproduces in facsimile a pocket-sized sketchbook of twenty-five folios used by Renoir in Algeria and Italy in 1881–82. The contents of this *carnet* are discussed in Williamstown 2003. The locations of the 1857 and 1881–82 sketchbooks remain unknown; they were presumably dispersed.
9. Musée du Louvre, RF 5260 (217 x 293 mm, 50 fol.) and RF 5259 (240 x 345 mm, 68 fol.). Schulman 1995, pp. 264–309.
10. Musée du Louvre, RF 11169 (142 x 95 mm), the "Boulogne Sketchbook" of 1869. See de Leiris 1969, pp. 113–16.
11. Musée du Louvre, RF 11596. See Wildenstein 1959, pp. 57–60.
12. On Caillebotte's drawings, see Chardeau 1989. Loose sketchbook pages are illustrated on pp. 111–24.
13. Brettell and Lloyd 1980, pp. 57–58.
14. See Reff 1976. Reff discusses additional lost or dismembered sketchbooks in vol. 1, p. 2.
15. Rewald 1951; Chappuis 1973.
16. Philadelphia 1989, p. 8.
17. In Wildenstein 1996 (the edition in English released by Taschen), the painting entries cite related sketchbook drawings by Wildenstein number under bibliography.
18. Wildenstein 1974–91, vol. 5, p. 94. The catalogue entry on the painting does not cross-reference the sketchbook drawing; Wildenstein 1996, vol. 2, p. 293.
19. House 1986, p. 230, recognized that the presence of a study for D989–80 (fol. 32v, D377) in a sketchbook that was used no earlier than 1887–88 as evidence that the paintings in question, dated by Wildenstein to 1885, might be reassigned to c. 1888–90.
20. See n. 6 above—sketchbook 1 originally had at least fifty-two folios; stubs remain for eighteen removed pages.
21. A number of photographs of the sketchbooks in their pre-treatment state appear in Welton 1992, e.g., pp. 1, 8.
22. Information provided by Marianne Delafond of the Musée Marmottan Monet, Paris, written communication, 6 Oct. 2006.
23. London 1990, pp. 42–43. Callen 2000, pp. 104–5. On 19 May 1881, Monet wrote from Vétheuil to Durand-Ruel, asking him to remit 500 francs to MM. Vielle et Troisgros, "marchands de couleurs, 35, rue de Laval," an amount he had owed for some time; in Wildenstein 1974–91, vol. 1, p. 443, L217 and 221. The firm's stamp appears on the back of the canvas of *Vase of Flowers*, c. 1881–82 (W626), collection of the Courtauld Institute of Arts, London; the stamp is reproduced in London 1987, no. 12 (n.p.). On 18 Feb. 1884, Monet wrote to Durand-Ruel from Bordighera requesting another payment be sent to Troisgros; see Wildenstein 1974–91, vol. 2, p. 239, L423. On 25 Apr. 1901, Monet wrote from Giverny to Durand-Ruel, requesting that he send 800 francs to Mme Troisgros, 35 rue Victor Massé; Wildenstein 1974–91, vol. 4, p. 358, L1633.
24. Claude Monet to Alice Hoschedé, 27 and 29 Nov. 1885, in Wildenstein 1974–91, vol. 2, pp. 268–69, L631 and 634.
25. *Sky*, c. 1900–10, watercolor on white wove paper (accession no. 50.130.68).
26. The tan sheets are folios 31, 33, and 36; the blue-gray folios are 32, 34, and 35.
27. Sketchbook 1, fol. 1v (a scribble, not mentioned in Wildenstein), and D108, 109, 118, 123, and 124.
28. Sketchbook 6, fols. 9r–12v, D348–52.
29. House 1986, p. 229. Folio 31r (not in Wildenstein) contains additional touches of black crayon and pastel that do not resolve themselves into a recognizable composition. They are probably just test strokes.
30. Wildenstein 1974–91, vol. 5, p. 115. Monet forwards this same address in Sandvika in two letters in 1895: Claude Monet to Alice Hoschedé, from Christiania, 15 Feb. 1895, in Wildenstein 1974–91, vol. 3, p. 280, L1269, and Claude Monet to Paul Durand-Ruel, 9 Mar. 1895, in ibid., vol. 3, p. 283, L1280.
31. In a letter to P. Durand-Ruel, from Pourville, 23 Feb. 1882, in ibid., vol. 2, pp. 215–16, L249, Monet wrote of his difficulty

in compiling a list of works to exhibit. The list in the sketchbook appears on fol. 45v, and if it does relate to the forthcoming Impressionist exhibition, which opened to the public on 1 Mar., then it may date from the last week of Feb. 1882. The poor legibility is caused in part by staining of the paper. Among the decipherable entries are: (1) "bouquet soleil" [D628?]; (2) "effet d'inondation" [D642?]; (3) "vue prise à Grainval" [D655?]; (9) "les coquelicots" [D677?]; (10) "sentier dans les blés" [D676?]; (11) "paysage d'hiver, soleil couchant" [D576?]; (16) "Vetheuil (temps d'orage)"; (17) "[deux?] natures mortes" (D549 or 550?); (19) "Glaçons (Charpentier)" [D568?] (20) "les saules (Cahuzac)" [D611?]. The final number, 21, is blank. Monet exhibited thirty-five paintings in the seventh Impressionist exhibition.

32. A few of the more abstract drawings in the sketchbooks are so difficult to read that their correct viewing orientation is not clear. For instance, Wildenstein D196, fol. 26r of sketchbook 3, may be read either as a study of trees or their reflection in the water. Wildenstein based his tentative conclusion on the placement of the page number, but it appears more likely that the composition was in fact drawn in the opposite sense. Other drawings in this category are D175, 197, and 205.
33. As suggested by Wadley 1991, p. 158, "Perhaps, due to his failing sight, he was unaware of the first sketch; perhaps he knew and did not care."
34. Monet's drawings of the Gare Saint-Lazare are discussed in Washington 1998, pp. 108–23. See also Wadley 1991, pp. 154–55.
35. Sketchbook 1: fol. 23v, interior-*côté banlieue* (D125); Sketchbook 2: fol. 11r, exterior (D150); fol. 12r, exterior (D151); fol. 13r, exterior (D152); fols. 13v–14, interior-*côte grandes lignes*; fol. 15r, interior-*côte banlieue* (D154).
36. There are a number of other possible instances of children's handiwork in the sketchbooks; for instance, D139 and 157, sketchbook 1 inside cover (sketch of a house, not in Wildenstein), and sketchbook 2, fol. 24v (geometric sketch, perhaps of a figure, not in Wildenstein).
37. See a series of letters in Wildenstein 1974–91, vol. 4, pp. 337–38, L1434–35, 1437, 1445, 1452–62, 1465.
38. For example, Wildenstein identifies the boats in D184 with several paintings and pastels of Charing Cross and Waterloo Bridge and the Houses of Parliament (W1521, 1529, 1584, 1594, P86–88, 103–5). See entry on D184 in Wildenstein 1974–91, vol. 5, p. 90.
39. Fols. 40–43 (recto and verso) and fols. 44 and 45r (D324–31, 333).
40. Claude Monet to Alice Hoschedé, 24 Jan. 1884, translated in Kendall 1989, p. 108 (original in Wildenstein 1974–91, vol. 2, p. 233, L392).
41. Claude Monet to Alice Hoschedé, 7 Feb. 1882, translated in Kendall 1989, p. 100 (original in Wildenstein 1974–91, vol. 2, p. 213, L235).
42. Wildenstein mistakenly places D372 on fol. 30r; all four of the Bennecourt drawings are on the verso of fols. 29–32.
43. D140–149.
44. D268–72.
45. From an unspecified article by Émile Bergerat in *Journal Officiel*, 17 Apr. 1877, quoted in House 1986, p. 45.
46. House 1986, p. 230. Studies of young girls in a rowing boat: D335, 337, 341, 345, 346, 348, 368; poplars: D306, 355, 356, 370.
47. Wildenstein identified the following as studies for the National Gallery painting (W261): fols. 34v (D211), 35v (D213), 36r (D214), and 36v (D215).
48. A photograph by Gustave Le Gray taken from roughly the same vantage point in the collection of the Amsterdams Historisch Museum is reproduced in San Francisco 2006, p. 6.
49. Sketchbook 3: D178–79, 188–89, 191–95; sketchbook 5: D296.
50. D160, 162–71, 174. The sketches related to Rouen Cathedral are reproduced and discussed in Rouen 1994, pp. 92–95, no. 19.
51. Pissarro 1993, p. 94.
52. Sketchbook 1: D109, 116–17, 119–24; sketchbook 6: D347, 349–54, 357, 369, 379–80.
53. House 1986, p. 228, speculated that the eight Marmottan sketchbooks "may well have been the only such books he used" from the mid-1860s until the 1920s, discounting the possibility that additional *carnets* may have been lost. House believed that the lack of sketchbook drawings from Belle-Île and the Antibes indicated that "they were not indispensable to him in conceiving his landscapes, and that, particularly from the late 1880s onwards, he could normally visualize a motif for a painting without any preliminary jotting" (p. 230). In fact, more than 130 of the approximately 300 drawings in the Marmottan sketchbooks are datable from the late 1880s through the 1890s.
54. Claude Monet to Alice Hoschedé, 18 Jan. 1888, in Wildenstein 1974–91, vol. 3, p. 225, L809.

CHAPTER EIGHT
Drawing for the Mass Media

1. Unlike most of his contemporaries, Monet seems never to have undertaken drawn or painted copies of works by artists of the past whom he admired. Virtually all of his fellow Impressionists, for instance, registered to make copies in the galleries of the Louvre; see Reff 1964.
2. See Douglas Druick and Peter Zegers, "Degas and the Printed Image, 1856–1914," in Boston 1984, pp. xxxix–li.
3. Also known as "paniconographie" and "zincography." Adeline 1894, pp. 126–36. Antony Griffiths translated a significant portion of the relevant passages on gillotage in an addendum to Shapiro and Griffiths 1986.
4. Wildenstein's lament over the disappearance of the original drawing is based on a misunderstanding of the gillotage process; Wildenstein 1974–91, vol. 5, p. 150 (D511).
5. The transfer of the drawing to the zinc plate would have resulted in the reversal of the image. After etching and printing, the image would have been reversed a second time, so that the final printed image appears in the same orientation as the original drawing.
6. Paul Mantz, "The Salon of 1865," *Gazette des beaux-arts* 19, no. 1 (July 1865), translated in Stuckey 1985, p. 32.
7. Pigalle 1865b, p. 76.
8. Pigalle 1865a, pp. 37, 41.
9. From the essay "Peintres et aqua-fortistes," published anonymously in *Revue anecdotique*, Apr. 1862, and revised in *Le Boulevard*, 14 Sept. 1862, translated in Melot 1996, pp. 73–74. See May 1967, p. 39.
10. In his study of Monet's early paintings, Joel Isaacson compares Jongkind's and Monet's submissions to *L'Autographe au Salon de 1865* and concludes that the latter's drawing represented a brash departure even from Jongkind's drawing style; Isaacson 1967, pp. 76–77.
11. Gustave Caillebotte to Claude Monet, 10 Apr. 1879, in Berhaut 1994, p. 275, letter no. 17.

12. Edmond Renoir, *La vie moderne* 1 (10 Apr. 1879), quoted in Rewald 1945, p. 183.
13. Ibid.
14. Edmond Renoir, "Cinquième exposition de la vie moderne," *La vie moderne* 1, no. 11 (19 June 1879), pp. 174–75, reprinted in Venturi 1939, pp. 334–38.
15. Bergerat 1879, p. 402.
16. *La vie moderne* 1880a, p. 399.
17. Obreen 1879, p. 464.
18. Nadeau 1994, vol. 1, p. 117.
19. This difficulty applied when albumen or bitumen processes were used; see Harper 1893, p. 153.
20. Secretaire de la Redaction 1879, p. 239.
21. Champier 1879, p. 180.
22. Tout Paris, "Impressions of an Impressionist," *Le Gaulois*, 24 Jan. 1880, translated in Stuckey 1985, p. 69. Monet felt that this article was defamatory and tried unsuccessfully to counter it by submitting a rebuttal to *Le Gaulois*; see "The *Gaulois* Affair," Wildenstein 1974–91, vol. 1, pp. 107–8.
23. An insightful discussion of the circumstances surrounding this exhibition and its reception appears in Annette Dixon's essay "The Marketing of Monet: The Exhibition at *La vie moderne*," in Ann Arbor 1998, pp. 91–115.
24. Both are translated in Stuckey 1985. Duret's essay was republished in his book *Critique d'avant-garde*, 1885.
25. Duret, *Le peintre Claude Monet*, in Stuckey 1985, p. 72 (see chap. 1, n. 2).
26. Claude Monet to Émile Bergerat, Apr. 1880, in Wildenstein 1974–91, vol. 1, p. 439, L176. The content of the unlocated letter is summarized.
27. Ambroise Vollard, *En écoutant Cézanne, Degas, Renoir* (Paris: 1938), p. 190, translated in Rewald 1945, p. 186.
28. Camille Pissarro to Lucien Pissarro, 10 Feb. 1884, in Pissarro 1980–91, vol. 1, p. 282; translated in Melot 1996, p. 158.
29. *La vie moderne* 1880b, p. 400. The painting was entitled *Marine* in the exhibition catalogue and in the text on page 400; it is called *Paysage* in the caption below the print.
30. Ibid., p. 399.
31. Translated in Rewald 1945, p. 186; the original quote appears in Vollard 1938, p. 190.
32. Claude Monet to Georges Charpentier, 14 June 1880, in Wildenstein 1974–91, vol. 1, p. 439, L185.
33. Levine 1976, p. 52.
34. Claude Monet to Paul Durand-Ruel, 6 Mar. 1883, in Wildenstein 1974–91, vol. 2, p. 227, L337.
35. Claude Monet to Paul Durand-Ruel, 7 Mar. 1883, translated in Kendall 1989, p. 105 (partial translation; the rest is my translation from Wildenstein 1974–91, vol. 2, p. 227, L338).
36. W217.
37. Claude Monet to Paul Durand-Ruel, 15 Feb. 1883, in Wildenstein 1974–91, vol. 2, p. 226, L329.
38. See Pissarro 1990, pp. 8–9.
39. Claude Monet to Alice Hoschedé, 9 Apr. 1892, in Wildenstein 1974–91, vol. 1, p. 448, pièce justificatif no. 69. The painting sold at Drouot on 7 Apr. for 9200 francs; ibid., vol. 2, p. 208, W217.
40. See discussion in chap. 9, pp. 217–18.
41. De Lostalot 1883, p. 346.
42. A partially legible stamp on the verso of the Gillot board identifies the printing firm of A. Michelet, 76 rue de Rennes, Paris, as responsible for transferring Monet's drawing for printing in relief.
43. See Richard Shiff, "Monet and the Mark," in Rapetti 2002, pp. 164–69.
44. Fritz 1896, pp. 26–27.
45. *L'Art moderne* 1883, pp. 9 (ill.), 15–16.
46. *Portrait of Père Paul* (W744, no. 25 in the exhibition catalogue), *Walk on the Cliff at Pourville* (W758, no. 20), and *Low Tide at Pourville* (W776, no. 9).
47. W748.
48. We know that on 19 Mar. Monet sent a drawing by courier to Paris, presumably for one of the April articles either in the *Gazette des beaux-arts* or *L'Art moderne*; Claude Monet to Paul Durand-Ruel, 19 Mar. 1883, in Wildenstein 1974–91, vol. 2, p. 228, L340. The provenance of the smaller painting prior to 1919 is untraced. In that year, it was recorded as being in the collection of the Parisian art dealers Josse and Gaston Bernheim-Jeune. Régnier 1919, vol. 2, plate 89.
49. The dates and location are printed in *L'Art dans les deux mondes* 1891, p. 303.
50. Rambaud and Roddaz 1890, p. 2. See Assouline 2004, pp. 216–18.
51. Camille Pissarro to Lucien Pissarro, 2 Jan. 1891, in Pissarro 1972, p. 144.
52. Mirbeau 1891, pp. 183–85.
53. Geffroy 1891a.
54. W739.
55. Monet's letters to Mirbeau are published among his correspondence in Wildenstein; Mirbeau's letters to Monet appear in Mirbeau 1990.
56. Claude Monet to Paul Durand-Ruel, 3 Dec. 1890, in Wildenstein 1974–91, vol. 3, p. 259, L1082.
57. Claude Monet to Paul Durand-Ruel, 5 Dec. 1890, in ibid., vol. 3, p. 259, L1083.
58. Octave Mirbeau to Claude Monet, 7–10 Dec. 1890, in Mirbeau 1990, pp. 112–13, no. 48.
59. Claude Monet to Paul Durand-Ruel, 14 Dec. 1890, in Wildenstein 1974–91, vol. 3, p. 259, L1085.
60. Claude Monet to Paul Durand-Ruel, 21 Dec. 1890, in ibid., vol. 3, p. 259, L1088.
61. Ibid. The painting to which Monet referred is W843 (Yamagata Museum of Art, Yamagata, Japan).
62. Lemoisne 1946–49, vol. 2, no. 289.
63. Camille Pissarro to Lucien Pissarro, 2 Jan. 1891, in Pissarro 1972, p. 144.
64. Claude Monet to Paul Durand-Ruel, 4 Jan. 1891, in Wildenstein 1974–91, vol. 3, p. 260, L1093.
65. Claude Monet to Paul Durand-Ruel, 21 Jan. 1891, in Wildenstein 1974–91, vol. 3, p. 260, L1096.
66. Octave Mirbeau to Claude Monet, c. 10 Feb. 1891, in Mirbeau 1990, p. 119, no. 51.
67. Ibid.
68. Octave Mirbeau to Claude Monet, 7 Mar. 1891, in ibid., p. 123.
69. Octave Mirbeau, "Claude Monet," *L'Art dans les deux mondes* 16 (7 Mar. 1891), translated in Stuckey 1985, p. 158.
70. Mirbeau 1891, p. 184. Note that this passage is not included in the excerpt translated in Stuckey and cited n. 69.
71. W1100.
72. W1267. In addition to the drawing of *Grainstacks* in the collection of the National Museum of Western Art, Tokyo (D444) that was reproduced in *L'Art dans les deux mondes*, a second nearly identical version (D444bis) is in the Harry B. and Bessie K. Braude Memorial Collection, a promised gift to the Art Institute of Chicago. See Chicago 2006, pp. 134–35.
73. Octave Mirbeau, *L'Art dans les deux mondes* in Stuckey 1985, p. 160 (see n. 69; translation slightly modified; substituted "extrasensory" for "suprasensible").
74. Ibid.
75. W734.
76. W739, collection of the Fogg Art Museum, Harvard University Art Museums, Cambridge, Mass.
77. Claude Monet to James Abbott

McNeill Whistler, 2 Apr. 1891, in Wildenstein 1974–91, vol. 3, p. 261, L1103.

78. Geffroy 1891b.
79. Claude Monet to Gustave Geffroy, 29 June 1891, in Wildenstein 1974–91, vol. 5, p. 199, L2822 (1115c).
80. The painting (W540) appears on p. 89 with the caption "La Seine à Vétheuil, par Claude Monet / (Appartient à M. Durand-Ruel)."
81. Camille Pissarro to Lucien Pissarro, 14 July 1891, in Pissarro 1972, pp. 180–81.
82. Claude Monet to Paul Durand-Ruel, 17 July 1891, in Wildenstein 1974–91, vol. 3, p. 262, L1118.
83. Assouline 2004, p. 232. Around 1900, the drawing of the *Customs-Officer's Cabin near Pourville* hung in a corridor connecting the Durand-Ruel family's two apartments at 35–37 rue de Rome; Sotheby's 1993.
84. Gouliant 1927, p. 29.
85. E. B. S. 1893, pp. 242–44. *The Côte Sauvage* is illustrated on p. 242.
86. Ibid., p. 243.
87. Ibid., p. 244.
88. *The Côte Sauvage* was illustrated on p. 19, *Grainstacks* on p. 15.
89. *Woman with a Parasol* was illustrated on p. 14.
90. Tabarant 1921.
91. *Customs-Officer's Cabin near Pourville*, plate 24; *The Côte Sauvage*, plate 29; *Woman with a Parasol*, plate 31; *Grainstacks in Bright Sunlight*, plate 32. The *Customs-Officer's Cabin near Pourville* also appeared in Elder 1924b, plate 24.
92. Paris, Bernheim-Jeune, *Cl. Monet*, 15 Oct.–3 Nov. 1906.
93. Brussels, La Libre Esthéthique, *Salon jubilaire*, 1 Mar.–5 Apr. 1908. Durand-Ruel also lent three late Monet paintings to the exhibition (W1552, 1571, and 1632).
94. Liège, *Salon du dessin*, Nov.–Dec. 1909.
95. Paris, Bernheim-Jeune, *Cent aquarelles, pastels et dessins*, 3–21 Oct. 1922: *Grainstacks in Bright Sunlight*; Paris, Marcel Bernheim, untitled exhibition of pastels and drawings, Dec. 1923–Jan. 1924: *The Côte Sauvage* and *The Customs-Officer's Cabin near Pourville*.
96. Gimpel 1966, p. 339, entry dated 23 Sept. 1927.
97. Sotheby's 1993, lot 2 *(Woman with a Parasol)*, pp. 10–12, and lot 4 *(Customs-Officer's Cabin near Pourville)*, pp. 14–15.

CHAPTER NINE
Monet in Print

1. Wildenstein 1974–91, vol. 1, no. 5: *The Zaan at Zaandam* by Léon Gaucherel, W172 (1871); vol. 2, no. 81: *Apple Trees in Blossom* by Henri Émile Lefort, W201 (1872); vol. 3, no. 101: *Houses by the Zaan at Zaandam* by Léon Gaucherel, W185 (1871); vol. 3, no. 147: *A Windmill at Zaandam* by François Flameng, W171 (1871).
2. The etchings included *The Fisherman's House, Overcast Weather* (1882; W734) on p. 17; *Field of Tulips in Sassenheim near Haarlem* (1886; W1070) on p. 69; *Antibes Seen from the Salis Gardens* (1888; W1168) on p. 89; *Taking a Walk in Gray Weather* (1888; W1203) on p. 95; *Port-Domois* (1887, W1108) on p. 103; *Antibes* (1888, W1160) on p. 183; *Grainstacks at the End of the Summer, Morning Effect* (1891, W1266) on p. 249; and *The Church at Varengeville, Gray Weather* (1882; W725) on p. 257. Degas was unhappy with Lauzet's renderings of his own paintings in the same publication and went so far as to make replacements for two of them; see Douglas Druick and Peter Zegers, "Degas and the Printed Image, 1856–1914," in Boston 1984, pp. lviii–lix, 207–11. Monet and Lauzet struck up a friendship based in part on their mutual love of gardening. When Lauzet took ill and was unable to work, Monet was among the contributors of works of art to a sale organized by Silvestre for his benefit. Monet kept eight letters from Lauzet that were eventually handed down to his great-grandson Michel Cornebois and sold by him in the auction held at Artcurial, Paris, in 2006; see Artcurial 2006, lot 150.
3. Kahn 1904. Greux's etching *Houses of Parliament, Sunset* (coll. De M.P. van der Velde, Le Havre; W1603) appeared on a single sheet inserted between pp. 84 and 85 and Waltner's *Waterloo Bridge, Hazy Sun* (1903; W1591), between pp. 86 and 87.
4. Theodore Robinson, "Claude Monet," *The Century* 44 (Sept. 1892), pp. 696–701, reprinted in Baltimore 2004, pp. 212–17.
5. This letter, sent from New York on 22 Mar. 1892, is in the collection of the Getty Research Institute, no. 860757. An incomplete translation appears in Baltimore 2004, p. 204. For the original, see Wildenstein 1974–91, vol. 2, p. 293–94, pièce justificatif no. 93.
6. Three of Monet's paintings were reproduced in the article: *Springtime*, 1873 (W271, Collection William H. Fuller, New York, presently Metropolitan Museum of Art, New York); *Menton Seen from Cap Martin*, 1884 (W897, Collection James F. Sutton, presently Museum of Fine Arts, Boston); and *View of Bordighera*, 1884 (W853, Collection James F. Sutton).
7. Diary entry dated 8 Sept. 1892, transcribed in Baltimore 2004, p. 191.
8. Diary entry dated 14 Sept. 1892, transcribed in ibid. The Boston painting is W897.
9. See ibid., pp. 118–20, for the original photograph and drawing. Robinson's original cyanotype belongs to the Terra Foundation for the Arts (C1985.1.6) and his charcoal drawing dated 1890 is in the collection of Ann M. and Thomas W. Barwick.
10. Scribner's 1896, p. 125.
11. A series of Robinson's diary entries from 1895 transcribed in Baltimore 2004, p. 196, documents the circumstances surrounding the Jan. 1896 passage in *Scribner's Magazine*. On 19 Mar. he wrote, "Saw the A.A.A.—an early Monet—*Vue de Rouen* is delightful, '73 [*sic*]"; on 26 Apr. he attended the second evening of the sale, noting, "The lovely 'Vue de Rouen' [sold for] 2500"; on 13 July, he "Rec'd a proof—wood engraving—of Monet's 'Rouen' which seems to me to be very good"; on 1 Nov., he received "a letter from Jaccaci wanting me to write about Monet's 'Vue de Rouen' for the Jan. Scribner"; and on 7 Nov., another "letter from Jaccaci—thanking me for the screed on Monet's 'Vue de Rouen' and hoping I'll like his department—'The Field of Art'—in Scribner's."
12. Theodore Robinson to Claude Monet, 6 Feb. 1896, in the collection of the Getty Research Institute, translated in Baltimore 2004, p. 209. The original is transcribed in Wildenstein 1974–91, vol. 3, p. 300, pièce justificatif no. 123.
13. The portfolio is unmentioned in Wildenstein 1974–91. The only Monet scholar to have taken any notice of it is John House, who wrote in the appendix to House 1986, p. 228: "Monet was willing to sanction graphic copies of his paintings even when he had not drawn them himself; around 1890 he signed every copy of each lithograph in the limited edition of twenty-five copies of W. Thornley's *20 Lithographies d'après Claude Monet*; the effects obtained in Thornley's lithographs are not unlike those in

Monet's own drawings for *L'Art dans les deux mondes* in 1891."

14. In a letter from Arsène Alexandre to Claude Monet, 3 Dec. 1920, the writer made a reference to Marty, telling Monet that he recalled "your kindness when he formerly requested a lithograph from you for his enterprise so courageous but so little appreciated, *L'Estampe originale*"; Artcurial 2006, lot 5.
15. Claude Monet to unidentified recipient, 5 Dec. 1898, in Wildenstein 1974–91, vol. 3, p. 297, L1421. With contributions from twelve artists including Louis Anquetin, Théodore van Rysselbergh, Hermann-Paul, and Félix Valotton, the album was published in February 1899.
16. Gustave Geffroy to Claude Monet, 9 Apr. 1903, Artcurial 2006, lot 120; Claude Monet to Gustave Geffroy, 10 Apr. 1903, in Wildenstein 1974–91, vol. 4, p. 363, L1691.
17. Claude Monet to Gustave Geffroy, 3 Aug. 1903, in Wildenstein 1974–91, vol. 4, p. 364, L1696.
18. Gustave Geffroy to Claude Monet, 1 Aug. 1903, Artcurial 2006, lot 120.
19. Claude Monet to Gustave Geffroy, 1 Sept. 1903, in Wildenstein 1974–91, vol. 4, p. 364, L1697.
20. Thornley's birth certificate is reproduced in Osny 1994, inside front cover.
21. The Salon livret of 1878 identifies Thornley as a student of his father and M. Sirouy, and the livret of 1880 lists his teachers as Thornley *père*, MM. Sirouy, and Ciceri. In 1889 his teachers are given as "MM. Yon et E. Cicéri." Thornley's birth certificate identifies his father's profession as a professor.
22. The most important sources on this publication are Boston 1984; Bordeaux 1997, pp. 88–92.
23. Félix Fénéon, "Calendrier de Septembre 1888, Chez M. Van Gogh (Maison Boussod et Valadon, 17, boulevard Montmartre)," *La Revue indépendante*, Oct. 1888, p. 139, translated in Boston 1984, p. lviii (translation slightly modified).
24. Edgar Degas to William Thornley, 28 Apr. 1888, partial translation in Boston 1984, p. lviii. Degas 1945, pp. 146–57, letter 133.
25. Camille Pissarro to Lucien Pissarro, 14 Apr. 1898, in Pissarro 1980–91, vol. 4, p. 471, letter 1536.
26. Camille Pissarro to Lucien Pissarro, 24 Apr. 1898, in ibid., letter 1538.
27. Pissarro 1980–91 quotes a partial letter from Camille Pissarro to William Thornley dated 2 May 1898, in ibid., p. 472, n. 1.
28. Camille Pissarro to Lucien Pissarro, 29 Oct. 1889, in ibid., vol. 5, p. 48, letter 1667.
29. Lucien Pissarro to Camille Pissarro, c. 1 Nov. 1889, in Pissarro 1993, pp. 619–20.
30. Camille Pissarro to Lucien Pissarro, 3 Nov. 1889, in Pissarro 1980–91, vol. 5, p. 50, letter 1670.
31. Camille Pissarro to Lucien Pissarro, 24 Nov. 1899, in ibid., p. 53, letter 1673.
32. Camille Pissarro to Gustave Geffroy, 13 and 22 Apr. 1900, in ibid., pp. 80–81, letters 1702 and 1705.
33. Venturi 1939, vol. 1, p. 160.
34. The lithographs, all carried out in 1904–5, were published in Renoir 1919. Roger-Marx 1951, pp. 48–71, nos. 12–23.
35. Pissarro 1980–91, vol. 5, p. 213, letter 1870 (1902?), n. 1.
36. Camille Pissarro to Rodolphe Pissarro, 18 July 1903, in Pissarro 1980–91, vol. 5, p. 364, letter 2046.
37. Notice placed by Thornley in the journal *Progrès du Seine-et-Oise*, 31 Oct. 1908, transcribed in Osny 1994, p. 7.
38. Geffroy 1899, p. 1.
39. André Mellerio, "La lithographie originale en couleurs," translated by Margaret Needham in Cate and Hitchings 1978, p. 91.
40. James Abbott McNeill Whistler to Thomas R. Way, 12 Nov. 1893, in Stratis 1998, vol. 2, p. 68.
41. James Abbott McNeill Whistler to Thomas R. Way, 2 Nov. 1894, in ibid., p. 126.
42. Pat Gilmour, "Cher Monsieur Clot . . . Auguste Clot and his Role as a Colour Lithographer," in Gilmour 1988, p. 369, n. 13.
43. The entry in Lucas's address book no. 1 (collection of the Walters Art Gallery) reads "J. Mancini. Picture dealer . . . Beugniet's nephew"; Lucas 1979, vol. 1, p. 115 (in index). On the Beugniets, see Distel 1990, p. 35.
44. Camille Pissarro to Lucien Pissarro, 26 Jan. 1887, quoted in Distel 1990, p. 35, and Pissarro 1980–91, vol. 2, p. 124, letter 390.
45. On Brame, see Distel 1990, p. 36, and Yeide 1998. Yeide mistakenly places Brame senior's gallery on the rue Laffitte, when in fact it was his son Hector-Gustave Brame who relocated the gallery there after his father retired.
46. See Koyama-Richard 2001, p. 544, no. 731, bill for Alfred Stevens painting dated 16 Apr. 1891 from "H. Brame" to Hayashi, which gives Brame's address as 36 rue Taitbout. In the 1892 Bottins there were two Brames listed: "H. Brame" at 36 rue Taitbout, and "Hector Brame" at 22 rue Laffitte.
47. Lucas 1979, vol. 2, p. 789. Additional visits to Mancini's gallery are recorded on 26 May 1894 (vol. 2, p. 789), 25 May 1895 (vol. 2, p. 808), 18 May 1896 (vol. 2, p. 828), 6 Feb. 1897 (vol. 2, p. 841), 20 Apr. 1897 (vol. 2, p. 845), 7 July 1897 (vol. 2, p. 848), 20 Apr. 1899 (vol. 2, p. 875), and 25 Apr. 1899 (vol. 2, p. 876).
48. Annuaire 1905 and 1909.
49. Lemoisne, Brame, and Reff 1984, p. 136, no. 124. The provenance for a Degas pastel of the mid-1880s, *Les Danseuses roses*, indicates that the work passed at an unknown date from Georges Bernheim, Paris, to J. Mancini, Buenos Aires, and from Mancini to Sra A. L. de Zubigarreta, Buenos Aires.
50. House 1986, p. 228: "around 1890"; Bordeaux 1997, p. 92: "1898"; Swann 2000, lot 268: "c. 1908."
51. See Béraldi 1885–92, vol. 1, p. 7. In the introduction to his collector's guide, Béraldi offers his thanks to the printmakers who conveyed information regarding their oeuvres.
52. See Camille Pissarro to Henri Béraldi, 27 July 1889, in Pissarro 1980–91, vol. 2, pp. 280–85, letter 532.
53. See Wildenstein 1974–91, vol. 3, p. 255, L1047.
54. House 1986, p. 205.
55. Claude Monet to Georges de Bellio, 29 Apr. 1887, in Wildenstein 1974–91, vol. 3, p. 222, L786.
56. Clemenceau 1928, pp. 64–65, quoted in House 1986, p. 164.
57. Vincent van Gogh to Theo van Gogh, 5 May 1888, in Van Gogh 1958, vol. 2, p. 559, no. 482.
58. Claude Monet to Gustave Geffroy, 20 June 1888, translated in House 1986, p. 36.
59. Illustrated in Osny 1994, p. 3, collection Jean Claude Barrié.
60. The version of *Gorge of the Petit Creuse* (see fig. A18) reproduced by Thornley is uncertain. The lithograph is based either on W1230, 1231, or 1232. It appears closest to W1230, which was purchased by Monet from Durand-Ruel in Oct. 1890 and sold to a Boston collector the next year. The fact that the painting was in America during the period in which Thornley was engaged on the Monet portfolio suggests that he either worked from a photograph, or from one of the other versions, the early provenance of which are both unknown. The question remains unresolved.

61. Claude Monet to Paul Gallimard, 29 Jan. 1891, in Wildenstein 1974–91, vol. 5, p. 196, L2801 (1096b).
62. Claude Monet to "Hamman," 6–12 July 1891, in ibid., vol. 5, pp. 199–200, L2824 (1117b)–2827 (1117e).
63. Outside of the portfolio, Thornley executed an undated three-stone lithograph after another of Monet's Antibes paintings of 1888, W1181. Boussod and Valadon also acquired the painting in 1888. By 1891 it was with Durand-Ruel. An impression of the lithograph printed in orange, blue, and green is in the collection on display in the Espace William Thornley, Château de Grouchy, Osny, signed in pencil "G. W. Thornley" and inscribed "d'après Monet."
64. See Claude Monet to Alice Hoschedé, 17 Nov. 1886, in Wildenstein 1974–91, vol. 2, p. 289, L750.
65. Claude Monet to Alice Hoschedé, 6 Apr. 1889, in Wildenstein 1974–91, vol. 3, p. 243, L939.
66. See Tucker 1995, p. 37, figs. 46 and 46a, for two colored caricatures of *Camille, Woman in a Green Dress* and *The Port of Honfleur*, from *L'Epatoutfant*, 1868.
67. Quoted in House 1986, p. 133; from Rewald 1949, p. 101, journal entry dated 23 Aug. 1894.
68. Thornley executed a third three-color lithograph after *The Mediterranean, Mistral Wind* (W1181, dated 1888) but failed to include it in the portfolio. See n. 58 above.
69. RamBaud 1899, p. 255. These letters are unlocated.
70. Goupil, "Participations et Dépôts," fol. 270, accession number 90.III.1.138, Goupil Ledgers.
71. The letter of agreement has not been located; it is cited in two of the Goupil ledgers: Participations et Dépôts, fol. 270 (90.III.1.138), and Dépôts no. 2, fol. 96 (90.III.1.56).
72. The sales are tallied by year in the two Goupil ledgers: Participations et Dépôts, fol. 270 (90.III.1.138) and Dépôts no. 2, fols. 96, 127 (90.III.1.56).
73. André Mellerio, "La lithographie originale en couleurs," in Cate and Hitchings 1978, p. 80.
74. André Mellerio, "Exposition de la deuxième année de L'Album d'estampes originales; galerie Vollard, 6 rue Laffitte," in *L'Estampe et l'affiche*, vol. 2 (Jan. 1898): pp. 10–11, quoted in Gilmour 1988, p. 161.
75. In its first five years on the market, Thornley's *Quinze lithographies* after Degas sold only seventeen copies by Goupil; Bordeaux 1997, p. 92.
76. Claude Monet to Arsène Alexandre, 6 Dec. 1920, in Wildenstein 1974–91, vol. 4, p. 408, L2391.
77. Claude Monet to Georges Bernheim-Jeune, 20 Mar. 1921, in Wildenstein 1974–91, vol. 4, p. 409, L2415; Claude Monet to André Marty (*chez* Bernheim-Jeune), 20 Mar. 1921, in ibid., vol. 4, p. 409–10, L2416. Other letters concerned with the reproductions in Alexandre's forthcoming monograph are L2393, 2404, 2405, 2407, 2414, 2417, 2430, 2432; see also the letter from Alexandre to Monet dated 3 Dec. 1920, Artcurial 2006, lot 5.
78. Alexandre 1921, p. 94, plate 38 (W1272)
79. Geffroy 1922, p. 141: *The Red Kerchief, Portrait of Madame Monet* (W257); p. 193: *Group of Rocks at Port-Goulphar* (W1096; collection Geffroy); p. 289: *Weeping Willow and Water-Lily Pond* (W1867).
80. Claude Monet to Gustave Geffroy, 25 June 1922, in Wildenstein 1974–91, vol. 4, p. 415, L2500.
81. The following plates appeared trichromatic halftones, tipped into Elder 1924a: 16 (*The Seine at Argenteuil*, 1874, W325), 22 (*Winter on the Seine, Lavacourt*, 1879–80, W558), and 38 (*The Rio della Salute*, 1908, W1763).
82. Claude Monet to Arsène Alexandre, 6 Dec. 1920, in Wildenstein 1974–91, vol. 4, p. 408, L2391.

CHAPTER TEN
Lines of Color: Drawing in the Late Years

1. Georges Clemenceau, *Claude Monet* (Paris: Gallimard, 1929), translated in Stuckey 1985, p. 365.
2. Spate 1992b, p. 12.
3. See Munich 2002 and Riehen/Basel 2002. See also Romy Golan, "Organic Sensations: Monet's *Grand Décorations* and Mural Painting in France from 1927 to 1952," and Michael Leja," The Monet Revival and New York School Abstraction," both in Boston 1998.
4. Clement Greenberg, "The Later Monet," *Art News Annual* 55 (1956), cited in Leja, "The Monet Revival and New York School Abstraction," in Boston 1998, p. 102.
5. See chap. 5.
6. See, for example, London 1996 and New York 1977.
7. D361–62, 366, 374, 376, 378.
8. See W1237, 1230–32, 1218.
9. The sketchbook is the Musée Marmottan Monet, Paris, sketchbook 3.
10. D178–79, 188–89, 191, 192–95, 219; a further Grainstack drawing is in notebook 5, D296.
11. Certain of the drawings are referred to or reproduced, with minimal discussion, in House 1986, p. 230; and Boston 1989, p. 94.
12. See W993–95, 1073–74, 1362–64.
13. Some of the corresponding paintings are, respectively, W1074, 1284, 1276 and 1277, 1362–64.
14. The most specific link is between D192 and W1213–15.
15. Several letters from this period describe his work in the open air and the difficulties the weather was causing him; see, for example, Claude Monet to Gustave Geffroy, 21 July 1890, in Wildenstein 1974–91, vol. 3, p. 257, L1066; Claude Monet to Gustave Geffroy, 7 Oct. 1890, in ibid., vol. 3, p. 258, L1076; and Claude Monet to P. Durand-Ruel, 14 Dec. 1890, in ibid., vol. 3, p. 259, L1085. It is also widely accepted that time was spent on revision and "harmonization" of the series in the studio.
16. Boston 1989, pp. 88–92.
17. D296 is in a different sketchbook from the principal group and occurs among a sequence of sketches related to paintings of the mid-1880s; it seems closest to an early trio of grainstack scenes, such as W900.
18. One contemporary asserted that Monet "sketches his subjects in charcoal" before he started painting such a work, but offered no evidence; see William H. Fuller, *Claude Monet and His Paintings* (New York: 1899), in Stuckey 1985, p. 201.
19. Claude Monet to Alice Hoschedé, 12 Feb. 1892, in Wildenstein 1974–91, vol. 3, p. 263, L1132.
20. W1315.
21. W1316.
22. D355–56, 370; D381–403.
23. Claude Monet to Alice Monet, 3 Feb. 1895, in Wildenstein 1974–91, vol. 5, p. 279, L1265.
24. D381, 390, 394–95, 397–98, 402–3; W1406–18. See chap. 7.
25. D183.
26. Musée Marmottan Monet, Paris, sketchbook 8, D404.
27. Gustave Kahn, "The Claude Monet Exhibition," 32, no. 565 *Gazette des beaux-arts* (1 July 1904), translated in Stuckey 1985, p. 229.
28. Claude Monet to Alice Monet, 3 Feb. 1901, in Wildenstein

1974–91, vol. 4, p. 351, L1593, and Claude Monet to Alice Monet, 2 Mar. 1901, in ibid., p. 355, L1611.

29. Claude Monet to Alice Monet, 26 Jan. 1901, in ibid., p. 350, L1588.
30. Claude Monet to Alice Monet, 27 Jan. 1901, in ibid., p. 350, L1589.
31. Claude Monet to Alice Monet, 28 Jan. 1901, in ibid., pp. 350–51, L1590.
32. Claude Monet to Alice Monet, 1 Feb. 1901, in ibid., p. 351, L1591.
33. W1521.
34. A barely brushed-in canvas of *Charing Cross Bridge* (W1553) reveals how this underlying geometry was established at the inception of such a work, here in virtual monochrome.
35. W1590, 1583, 1577.
36. Gustave Geffroy, *Claude Monet, sa vie, son oeuvre* (1924; repr. Paris: Macula, 1980), translated in Stuckey 1985, p. 219.
37. The same mark is visible in P100.
38. See also P100, 107.
39. P84, P99, P105.
40. See chap. 5.
41. See, for instance, W1542, 1544.
42. W1521and 1552, for example, are dated 1899 and 1904, respectively.
43. See Wildenstein 1974–91 catalogue entry for W1559.
44. See London 2004, p. 29.
45. Ibid.
46. See Getscher 1991.
47. London 2004, p. 250.
48. For these events and some of the works in question, see ibid., pp. 179–88; MacDonald 1995, pp. 1471–72.
49. London 2004, pp. 32–33.
50. The complete list of exhibits is reproduced in Sieberling 1988, p. 93.
51. P94 and P105 are dated 1903 and 1902, respectively.
52. See chap. 5.
53. See P95; P105 and P100.
54. Kahn, *Gazette des beaux-arts* 32, no. 565 (1 July 1904), in Stuckey 1985, p. 226 (see n. 27).
55. Whistler had died in 1903.
56. Trévise, "Pilgrimage to Giverny," *La Revue de l'art ancient et moderne* 51 (Jan.–Feb. 1927), translated in Stuckey 1985, p. 333 (see chap. 3, n. 80).
57. The pastel was P99, and was perhaps given to Guitry as a result of their collaboration; a pastel of a rural subject, P66, was bought by Mme Guitry in 1912.
58. Arsène Alexandre, "Monet's Garden," *Le Figaro*, 9 Aug. 1901, translated in Stuckey 1985, p. 221; Kahn, "*Gazette des beaux-arts* 32, no. 565 (1 July 1904), in Stuckey 1985, p. 242 (see n. 27).
59. Thiébault-Sisson, "Claude Monet's Water Lilies," *La Revue de l'art ancient et moderne* (June 1927), translated in Stuckey 1985, p. 289.
60. Kahn, "*Gazette des beaux-arts* 32, no. 565 (1 July 1904), in Stuckey 1985, p. 242 (see n. 27).
61. Roger Marx, "M. Claude Monet's 'Water Lilies,'" *Gazette des beaux-arts* 1, no. 624 (June 1909), translated in Stuckey 1985, p. 267.
62. Alexandre, *Le Figaro*, 9 Aug. 1901, in Stuckey 1985, p. 222 (see n. 58).
63. Gimpel 1966, p. 60; two photographs reproduced in Guillaud 1983, pp. 224–25, show Monet painting water-lily canvases outdoors around 1915.
64. On the Grainstacks, see House 1986, pp. 183–91, 197–201; Boston 1989, pp. 186–87.
65. Marx, *Gazette des beaux-arts* 1, no. 624 (June 1909), in Stuckey 1985, p. 266 (see n. 61).
66. The provenance of the drawings is given in the Wildenstein catalogue entry for D448.
67. D118–19, 122, 347, 379–80.
68. See W1857–62, 1971.
69. D364; the distant house is seen beyond dense foliage.
70. W1669; see also 1668 and 1870.
71. W1903–10.
72. See D109, 116–17, 120–21, 349–52, 357.
73. It should be noted that Monet had never made sketchbook drawings across both full pages in the previous six decades of his career, nor made such wide paintings before the water-lily compositions. At the very least, the rapport between the opened sketchbooks and the frieze-like canvases offers a case of extreme sympathy between creative modes.
74. D124, 353, 354.

Works Cited

Exhibition catalogues are listed under the city of the organizing institution. Auction catalogues are listed under the name of the auction house.

Adeline 1894
Adliene, Jules. *Les Arts de reproduction vulgarisés.* Paris: Librairies-imprimeries réunies, 1894.

Adhémar and Lethève 1953
Adhémar, Jean, and Jacques Lethève. *Inventaire du fonds français après 1800.* Paris: Bibliothèque Nationale, 1953.

Alexandre 1921
Alexandre, Arsène. *Claude Monet.* Paris: Bernheim-Jeune, 1921.

Alphant 1993
Alphant, Marianne. *Claude Monet: Une vie dans le paysage.* Paris: Hazan, 1993.

André 1955
André, Albert. *Renoir, carnet de dessins: Renoir en Italie et en Algérie, 1881–1882.* Paris: Daniel Jacomet, 1955.

Ann Arbor 1998
Dixon, Annette, et al. *Monet at Vétheuil: The Turning Point.* Exh. cat. Ann Arbor: University of Michigan Museum of Art, 1998.

Annuaire 1905 and 1909
Annuaire —Almanach du commerce. Paris: Sociéte Didot-Bottin, 1905 and 1909.

Artcurial 2006
Artcurial, Paris. *Archives Claude Monet: Correspondence d'artiste.* Auction catalogue. Paris: Artcurial, 13 Dec. 2006.

Assouline 2004
Assouline, Pierre. *Discovering Impressionism: The Life of Paul Durand-Ruel.* Trans. Willard Wood and Anthony Roberts. New York: Vendome Press, 2004.

Baltimore 2004
Johnston, Sona, and Paul Hayes Tucker. *In Monet's Light: Theodore Robinson at Giverny.* Exh. cat. Baltimore: Baltimore Museum of Art; London: Philip Wilson, 2004.

Bataille and Wildenstein 1961
Bataille, Marie Louise, and Georges Wildenstein. *Berthe Morisot: Catalogue des peintures, pastels, et aquarelles.* Paris: Beaux-Arts, Éditions d'études et des documents, 1961.

Baudelaire 1855
Baudelaire, Charles. "De l'essence du rire et généralement du comique dans les arts plastiques." *Le Portefeuille*, 8 July 1855.

Baudelaire 1857a
Baudelaire, Charles. "Quelques caricaturistes français." *Le Présent*, 1 Oct. 1857.

Baudelaire 1857b
Baudelaire, Charles. "Quelques caricaturistes étrangers." *Le Présent*, 15 Oct. 1857.

Baudelaire 1862
Baudelaire, Charles. "Peintres et aquafortistes." *Revue anecdotique*, Apr. 1862.

Baudelaire 1955
Baudelaire, Charles. *The Mirror of Art: Critical Studies by Charles Baudelaire.* Trans. Jonathan Mayne. London: Phaidon Press, 1955.

Beguin Billecocq 2005
Beguin Billecocq, Théophile. "Le Grand Journal du Comte Beguin Billecocq: Ministre plénipotentiare (1825–1906): Chroniques d'une vie bien remplie." Ed. Prince Xavier Beguin Billecocq. Unpublished manuscript. Typescript by Pierre-Olivier Caperan on deposit at the Sterling and Francine Clark Art Institute, Williamstown, Mass.

Bénézit 1976
Bénézit, Emmanuel. *Dictionnaire critique et documentaire des peintres, sculpteurs, dessinateurs et graveurs de tous les temps et de tous let pays.* 10 vols. Paris: Gründ, 1976.

Béraldi 1885–92
Béraldi, Henri. *Les Graveurs du XIXe siècle: Guide de l'amateur d'estampes modernes.* 12 vols. Paris: L. Conquet, 1885–92.

Bergerat 1879
Bergerat, Emile. "Aux lecteurs et abonnés de la Vie Moderne." *La vie moderne* 1, no. 26 (4 Oct. 1879): 402–3.

Berhaut 1994
Berhaut, Marie. *Gustave Caillebotte: Catalogue raisonné des peintures et pastels.* 2nd ed. Paris: Wildenstein Institute, 1994.

Berson 1996
Berson, Ruth. *The New Painting: Impressionism 1874–1886.* 2 vols. San Francisco: Fine Arts Museums of San Francisco, 1996.

Blanc 1867
Blanc, Charles. *Grammaire des art du dessin: Architecture, sculpture, peinture.* Paris: J. Renouard, 1867.

Bordeaux 1997
Musée Goupil. *Degas, Boldini, Toulouse-Lautrec: Portraits inédits par Michel Manzi.* Exh. cat. Bordeaux: Musée Goupil, 1997.

Boston 1984
Museum of Fine Arts, Boston. *Edgar Degas: The Painter as Printmaker.* Exh. cat. Boston: Museum of Fine Arts, 1984.

Boston 1989
Tucker, Paul Hayes. *Monet in the '90s: The Series Paintings.* Exh. cat. New Haven and London: Yale University Press, 1989.

Boston 1998
Tucker, Paul Hayes, et al. *Monet in the 20th Century.* Exh. cat. New Haven and London: Yale University Press, 1998.

Bouillon 1987
Bouillon, Jean-Paul. *Félix Bracquemond: Le Réalisme Absolu, oeuvre gravé 1849–1859, catalogue raisonné.* Geneva: Skira, 1987.

Brettell and Lloyd 1980
Brettell, Richard, and Christopher Lloyd. *A Catalogue of the Drawings by Camille Pissarro in the Ashmolean Museum, Oxford.* Oxford: Clarendon Press; New York: Oxford University Press, 1980.

Cahen 1900
Cahen, Gustave B. *Eugène Boudin: Sa vie et son oeuvre.* Paris: Floury, 1900.

Callen 2000
Callen, Anthea. *The Art of Impressionism: Painting Technique and the Making of Modernity.* New Haven and London: Yale University Press, 2000.

Cate and Hitchings 1978
Cate, Phillip Dennis, and Sinclair Hitchings. *The Color Revolution: Color Lithography in France 1890–1900*. Santa Barbara: Peregrine Smith, 1978.

Champier 1879
Champier, Victor. "Chronique de l'année." *L'Année artistique* 2 (1879): 167–87.

Chappuis 1973
Chappuis, Adrien. *The Drawings of Paul Cézanne*. Greenwich: New York Graphic Society, 1973.

Chapus 1855
Chapus, Eugène. *Guides Itinéraires de Paris au Havre*. Paris: L. Hachette, 1855.

Chardeau 1989
Chardeau, Jean. *Les dessins de Caillebotte*. Paris: Editions Hermé, 1989.

Chicago 2006
McCullagh, Suzanne Folds, ed. *Drawings in Dialogue: Old Master Through Modern, The Harry B. and Bessie K. Braude Memorial Collection*. Exh. cat. Chicago: Art Institute of Chicago, distributed by Yale University Press, 2006.

Chu 1996
Chu, Petra ten-Doesschate. *Correspondance de Gustave Courbet*. Paris: Flammarion, 1996.

Clemenceau 1928
Clemenceau, Georges. *Claude Monet: Les nymphéas*. Paris: Plon, 1928.

Cogniat 1967
Cogniat, Raymond. *The Century of the Impressionists*. Trans. Graham Snell. New York: Crown Publishers, 1967.

Daulte 1954
Daulte, François. *Le dessin français de Manet à Cézanne*. Lausanne: Spes, 1954.

Degas 1945
Degas, Edgar. *Letters*. Ed. Marcel Guérin. Trans. Marguerite Kay. Oxford: B. Cassirer; New York: Studio Publications, 1945.

Delaborde 1870
Delaborde, Henri. *Ingres: Sa vie, ses travaux, sa doctrine*. Paris: H. Plon, 1870.

Delage 1963
Delage, Roger. "Chabrier et ses amis les Impressionistes." *L'Oeil* (Dec. 1963): 18.

De Lostalot 1883
Lostalot, Albert de. "Exposition des oeuvres de M. Claude Monet." *Gazette des beaux-arts* 27 (Apr. 1883): 342–48.

Delteil 1906
Delteil, Loys. *J. F. Millet, Th. Rousseau, Jules Dupré, J. Barthold Jongkind*. Paris: Published by the author, 1906.

Delteil 1921
Delteil, Loys. *Charles François Daubigny*. Paris: Published by the author, 1921.

Delteil 1997
Delteil, Loys. *Delacroix, the Graphic Work: A Catalogue Raisonné*. Trans. and rev. ed. by Susan Strauber. San Francisco: Alan Wolfsy Fine Arts, 1997.

Distel 1990
Distel, Anne. *Impressionism: The First Collectors*. Trans. Barbara Perroud-Benson. New York: Abrams, 1990.

Dolan 2000
Dolan, Therese. "Manet's Portrait-Charge of Emile Olivier." *Print Quarterly* 17, no. 1 (Mar. 2000): 17–26.

Duret 1885
Duret, Théodore. *Critique d'avant-garde*. Paris: G. Charpentier, 1885.

E. B. S. 1893
E. B. S. "Some Sketches by Claude Monet and Eugène Boudin." *The Studio* 1, no. 6 (Sept. 1893): 242–44.

Edinburgh 2006
Fowle, Frances, ed. *Monet and the French Landscape: Vétheuil and Normandy*. Exh. cat. Edinburgh: National Galleries of Scotland, 2006.

Edwards 1943
Edwards, Hugh. "The Caricatures of Claude Monet." *Bulletin of the Art Institute of Chicago* 37, no. 5 (Sept.–Oct. 1943): 71–72.

Elder 1924a
Elder, Marc [Marçel Tendron]. *A Giverny, chez Claude Monet*. Paris: Bernheim-Jeune, 1924.

Elder 1924b
Elder, Marc [Marçel Tendron]. "Claude Monet au travail." *Bulletin de la vie artistique* 5, no. 18 (15 Sept. 1924): 416–18.

Enfert 2003
Enfert, Renaud d'. *L'Enseignement du dessin en France, Figure humaine et dessin géometrique (1750–1850)*. Paris: Belin, 2003.

Fels 1929
Fels, Marthe de. *La Vie de Claude Monet*. Paris: Gallimard, 1929.

Fernier 1977–78
Fernier, Robert. *La vie et l'oeuvre de Gustave Courbet: Catalogue raisonné*. 2 vols. Geneva: Fondation Wildenstein; Lausanne: Bibliothèque des arts, 1977–78.

Fidell-Beaufort and Bailly-Herzberg 1975
Fidell-Beaufort, Madeleine, and Janine Bailly-Herzberg. *Daubigny*. Paris: Geoffroy-Dechaume, 1975.

Fritz 1896
Fritz, Georg. *Photo-Lithography*. Trans. E. J. Wall. New York: G. Gennert, 1896.

Geffroy 1899
Geffroy, Gustave. "L'Art d'aujourd'hui: W. Thornley." *Le Journal* 8 (15 June 1899): 1.

Geffroy 1891a
Geffroy, Gustave. "Exposition Claude Monet, Galeries Durand-Ruel." *L'Art dans les deux mondes* 25 (9 May 1891): 297–98.

Geffroy 1891b
Geffroy, Gustave. "James McNeill Whistler." *L'Art dans les deux mondes* 2, no. 6 (27 June 1891): 63–65.

Geffroy 1922
Geffroy, Gustave. *Claude Monet, sa vie, son temps, son oeuvre*. Paris: G. Crès et Cie., 1922.

Geffroy 1924
Geffroy, Gustave. *Claude Monet, sa vie, son oeuvre*. Paris: G. Crès & Cie, 1924.

Georgel 1968
Georgel, Pierre. "Monet, Bruyas, Vacquerie et le *Panthéon Nadar*." *Gazette des beaux-arts* 72, no. 1199 (Dec. 1968): 331–34.

Getscher 1991
Getscher, Robert H. *James Abbott McNeill Whistler—Pastels*. New York: G. Braziller, 1991.

Gilmour 1988
Gilmour, Pat, ed. *Lasting Impressions: Lithography as Art*. Philadelphia: University of Pennsylvania Press, 1988.

Gimpel 1966
Gimpel, René. *Diary of an Art Dealer*. Trans. John Rosenberg. New York: Farrar, Straus, and Giroux, 1966.

Goncourt 1956
Goncourt, Edmond de, and Jules de Goncourt. *Journal: Mémoires de la vie littéraire*. 4 vols. Paris: Fasquelle, 1956.

Gouliant 1927
Gouliant, Jean-Gabriel. "La Technique de Claude Monet." *L'Art vivant* 3, no. 49 (1 Jan. 1927): 28–29.

Goupil 1882
Goupil, Frédéric-Auguste-Antoine. *Traité de paysage mis à la portée de tous*. Paris: Le Bailly, 1882.

Goupil Ledgers
Goupil Ledgers. Archives of the Musée Goupil, Bordeaux. "Participations et Dépôts," fol. 270 (90.III.1.138) and "Dépôts no. 2," fols. 96 and 127 (90.III.1.58).

Gowing 1988
Gowing, Lawrence. *Cézanne: The Early Years, 1859–1872*. Ed. Mary-Anne Stevens. London: Royal Academy of Arts, 1988.

Guillaud 1983
Guillaud, Maurice. *Claude Monet at the Time of Giverny*. Paris: Centre Culturel du Marais, 1983.

Hannoosh 1992
Hannoosh, Michele. *Baudelaire and Caricature: From the Comic to an Art of Modernity*. University Park: Pennsylvania State University Press, 1992.

Harper 1893
Harper, C. G. "Pen Drawing for Reproduction—Comparative Processes." *The Studio* 4 (July 1893): 152–55.

Hauptman 1996
Hauptman, William. *Chalres Gleyre, 1806–1874*. 2 vols. Princeton, N.J.: Princeton University Press; Basel, Switzerland: Swiss Institute for Art Research, 1996.

Hefting 1975
Hefting, Victorine. *Jongkind: Sa vie, son oeuvre, son époque*. Paris: Arts et métiers graphiques, 1975.

Hellebranth 1976
Hellebranth, Robert. *Charles-François Daubigny: 1817–1878*. Morges: Matutue, 1976.

Hemmings 1993
Hemmings, Frederic William John. *The Theatre Industry in Nineteenth-Century France*. Cambridge: Cambridge University Press, 1993.

Herbert 1994
Herbert, Robert L. *Monet on the Normandy Coast: Tourism and Painting, 1867–1886*. New Haven and London: Yale University Press, 1994.

Hervey 1847
Hervey, Charles. *The Theatres of Paris*. Rev. ed. Paris: Galignani; London: John Mitchell, 1847.

Holt 1966
Holt, Elizabeth Bosye Gilmore. *From the Classicists to the Impressionists: A Documentary History of Art and Architecture in the 19th Century*. Garden City, N.Y.: Anchor Books, 1966.

Honfleur 1996
Bergeret-Gourbin, Anne-Marie, et al. *Eugène Boudin: Peintures et dessins*. Exh. cat. Honfleur: Société des amis du Musée Eugène Boudin; Paris: Somogy, 1996.

House 1986
House, John. *Monet: Nature into Art*. New Haven and London: Yale University Press, 1986.

Isaacson 1967
Isaacson, Joel. "The Early Paintings of Claude Monet." Ph.D. diss., University of California, Berkeley, 1967.

Isaacson 1972
Isaacson, Joel. *Monet: Le dejeuner sur l'herbe*. London: Allen Lane the Penguin Press, 1972.

Isaacson 1978
Isaacson, Joel. *Claude Monet: Observation and Reflection*. Oxford: Phaidon, 1978.

Jean-Aubry 1922
Jean-Aubry, Georges. *Eugène Boudin d'après des documents inédits, l'homme et l'oeuvre*. Paris: Bernheim-Jeune, 1922.

Johnson 1981–86
Johnson, Lee. *The Paintings of Eugène Delacroix: A Critical Catalogue*. 6 vols. Oxford: Clarendon Press, 1981–86.

Kahn 1904
Kahn, Gustave. "L'Exposition Claude Monet." *Gazette des beaux-arts* 32 (July 1904): 82–88.

Kendall 1989
Kendall, Richard. *Monet by Himself: Paintings, Drawings, Pastels, Letters*. London: Macdonald Orbis, 1989.

Khandekar 2005
Khandekar, Natasha. "Eugène Boudin." *Plein Air Magazine* 11, no. 5 (May 2005): 42–47.

Koyama-Richard 2001
Koyama-Richard, Brigitte, et al. *Correspondance addressée à Hayashi Tadamasa*. Tokyo: Kokusho Kankokai, 2001.

L'Art dans les deux mondes 1891
Advertisement for a Monet exhibition at Durand-Ruel Gallery. *L'Art dans les deux mondes* 25 (9 May 1891): 303.

L'Art moderne 1883
"A travers l'art." *L'Art moderne* 2, no. 5 (Apr. 1883): 9–16.

Lausanne 1993
Fondation de l'Hermitage. *Claude Monet et ses amis: Oeuvres choisies du Musée Marmottan et de collections privées*. Exh. cat. Lausanne: Bibliothèque des arts, 1993.

La vie moderne 1880a
"Les dessins du numéro." *La vie moderne* 2, no. 25 (19 June 1880): 399.

La vie moderne 1880b
"Notre Exposition Claude Monet." *La vie moderne* 2, no. 25 (19 June 1880): 400.

de Leiris 1969
de Leiris, Alain. *The Drawings of Edouard Manet*. Berkeley and Los Angeles: University of California Press, 1969.

Lemoisne 1946–49
Lemoisne, Paul André. *Degas et son oeuvre*. 4 vols. Paris: P. Brame and C. M. de Hauke, 1946–49.

Lemoisne, Brame, and Reff 1984
Lemoisne, Paul-André, Philippe Brame, and Theodore Reff. *Degas et son oeuvre: A Supplement*. New York: Garland Publishers, 1984.

Levine 1976
Levine, Steven. *Monet and His Critics*. New York: Garland Publishers, 1976.

London 1987
Courtauld Institute Galleries. *Impressionist and Post-Impressionist Masterpieces: The Courtauld Collection*. Exh. cat. New Haven and London: Yale University Press, 1987.

London 1990
Bomford, David, et al. *Art in the Making: Impressionism*. Exh. cat. London: National Gallery of Art in association with Yale University Press, 1990.

London 1996
Kendall, Richard. *Degas Beyond Impressionism*. Exh. cat. London: National Gallery Publications, 1996.

London 2004
Lochnan, Katharine, et al. *Turner, Whistler, Monet*. Exh. cat. London: Tate Publishing in association with the Art Gallery of Ontario, 2004.

Louvet 1860
Louvet, Alfred. "Laferrière." *Diogène* 1, no. 3 (24 Mar. 1860): 4–5.

Lucas 1979
Lucas, George. *The Diary of George A. Lucas: An American Art Agent in Paris, 1857–1909*. Transcribed by Lilian M. C. Randall. 2 vols. Princeton, N.J.: Princeton University Press, 1979.

Lugt 1956
Lugt, Frits. *Les marques de collections de dessins et d'estampes . . . Supplément*. The Hague: Martinus Nijhoff, 1956.

Lyell 1865
Lyell, Charles. *The Elements of Geology*. London: J. Murray, 1865.

MacDonald 1995
MacDonald, Margaret F. *James McNeill Whistler: Drawings, Pastels, and Watercolors: A Catalogue Raisonné*. New Haven and London: Yale University Press, 1995.

Manoeuvre and Rapetti 1987
Manoeuvre, Laurent, and Rodolphe Rapetti. *Eugène Boudin dessins inédits: Les Dossiers du Musée d'Orsay*. Paris: Editions de la Réunion des musées nationaux, 1987.

Manoeuvre 1991
Manoeuvre, Laurent. *Eugène Boudin: Dessins*. Arcueil: Anthèse, 1991.

May 1967
May, Gita. *Diderot et Baudelaire, critiques d'art*. Geneva: Droz, 1967.

Melot 1996
Melot, Michel. *The Impressionist Print*. New Haven and London: Yale University Press, 1996.

Mirbeau 1891
Mirbeau, Octave. "Claude Monet." *L'Art dans les deux mondes* 16 (7 Mar. 1891): 183–85.

Mirbeau 1990
Mirbeau, Octave. *Correspondance avec Claude Monet*. Ed. Pierre Michel and Jean-François Nivet. Tusson, Charente: Du Lérot, 1990.

Montpellier 1992
Jourdan, Aleth. *Frédéric Bazille: Prophet of Impressionism*. Exh. cat. Trans. John Goodman. Montpellier: Musée Fabre; Paris: Editions de la Réunion des musées nationaux; Brooklyn: The Brooklyn Museum, 1992.

Morisot 1986
Morisot, Berthe. *Berthe Morisot: The Correspondence with Her Family and Her Friends*. Ed. Denis Rouart. Trans. Betty W. Hubbard. Introduction and notes by Kathleen Adler and Tamar Garb. London: Camden, 1986.

Mount 1966
Mount, Charles Merrill. *Monet: A Biography*. New York: Simon and Schuster, 1966.

Munich 2002
Sagner-Düchting, Karin, ed. *Monet and Modernism*. Exh. cat. Trans. John William Gabriel. Munich and New York: Prestel, 2001.

Munich 2005
Hansen, Dorothee, and Wulf Herzogenrath. *Monet und Camille: Frauenportraits in Impressionismus*. Exh. cat. Munich: Hirmer, 2005.

Nadeau 1994
Nadeau, Luis. *Encyclopedia of Printing, Photographic, and Photomechanical Processes*. 2 vols. Fredericton, New Brunswick: Atelier Luis Nadeau, 1994.

New York 1977
Rubin, James, et al. *Cézanne: The Late Work*. Exh. cat. New York: Museum of Modern Art, 1977.

New York 1993
Kendall, Richard. *Degas Landscapes*. Exh. cat. New Haven and London: Yale University Press in association with the Metropolitan Museum of Art, New York, and the Museum of Fine Arts, Houston, 1993.

New York 1994
Tinterow, Gary, and Henri Loyrette. *Origins of Impressionism*. Exh. cat. New York: Metropolitan Museum of Art, 1994.

New York 1995
Hambourg, Maria Morris, Françoise Heilbrun, and Philippe Néagu. *Nadar*. Exh. cat. New York: Metropolitan Museum of Art, 1995.

New York 1997
Ives, Colta, et al. *The Private Collection of Edgar Degas: A Summary Catalogue*. Exh. cat. New York: Metropolitan Museum of Art, 1997.

Obreen 1879
Obreen, O. "La Vie Moderne à L'Etranger: Extrait du Nieuwe Rotterdamsche Courant, 6 Octobre 1879." *La vie moderne* 1, no. 29 (25 Oct. 1879): 464.

Ornans 2004
Nessler, Marie-Chantal. *Amand Gautier, 1825–1894: Un amitié à la Courbet*. Exh. cat. Ornans: Musée Courbet, 2004.

Osny 1994
Espace William Thornley. *William Thornley Retrospective*. Exh. cat. Osny: Espace William Thornley, 1994.

Paris 1872
Explication des ouvrages de peinture, sculpture, architecture, gravure et lithographie des artistes vivants. Paris: Imprimerie nationale, 1872.

Paris 1874
Explication des ouvrages de peinture, sculpture, architecture, gravure et lithographie des artistes vivants. Paris: Imprimerie nationale, 1874.

Paris 1972
Daulte, François, Claude Richebé, and Raymond Cogniat. *Monet et ses amis, le legs Michel Monet, nouveaux enrichissements*. Exh. cat. Paris: Musée Marmottan, 1972.

Paris 1982
Musée Carnavalet. *Etienne Carjat, 1828-1906: Photographe*. Exh. cat. Paris: Musée Carnavalet, 1982.

Paris 2003
Gache-Patin, Sylvie, John Sillevis, and Götz Czymmek. *Jongkind, 1819–1891*. Exh. cat. Paris: Réunion des musées nationaux, 2003.

Philadelphia 1989
Reff, Theodore, and Innis Howe Shoemaker. *Paul Cézanne, Two Sketchbooks: The Gift of Mr. and Mrs. Walter H. Annenberg to the Philadelphia Museum of Art*. Exh. cat. Philadelphia: Philadelphia Museum of Art, 1989.

Pigalle 1865a
Pigalle. "Jongkind." *L'Autographe au Salon* 5 (27 May 1865): 37, 41.

Pigalle 1865b
Pigalle. "Monet." *L'Autographe au Salon* 9 (24 June 1865): 76.

Pissarro 1972
Pissarro, Camille. *Camille Pissarro: Letters to His Son Lucien*. 3rd rev. ed. Ed. John Rewald. Mamaronack, N.Y.: P. P. Appel, 1972.

Pissarro 1980–91
Pissarro, Camille. *Correspondance de Camille Pissarro*. Ed. Janine Bailly-Herzberg. 5 vols. [Vol. 1: *1865–1885*. Vol. 2: *1886–1890*. Vol. 3: *1891–1894*. Vol. 4: *1895–1898*. Vol. 5: *1899–1903*.] Paris: Presses universitaires de France, 1980.

Pissarro 1990
Pissarro, Joachim. *Monet's Cathedral, Rouen 1892–1894*. New York: Knopf, distributed by Random House, 1990.

Pissarro 1993
Pissarro, Lucien. *The Letters of Lucien to Camille Pissarro, 1883–1903*. Ed. Anne Thorold. Cambridge and New York: Cambridge University Press, 1993.

Pissarro and Venturi 1939
Pissarro, Ludovico, and Lionello Venturi. *Camille Pissarro: Son art, son oeuvre*. Paris: P. Rosenberg, 1939.

RamBaud 1899
RamBaud, Yveling (pseud.). *Silhouettes d'artistes: Avec portraits dessinés par eux-mêmes*. Paris: Société française d'éditions d'art, 1899.

Rambaud and Roddaz 1890
Rambaud, Yveling (pseud.), and Camille de Roddaz. "Notre programme." *L'Art dans les deux mondes* no. 1 (22 Nov. 1890): 2.

Rapetti 2002
Rodolphe Rapetti, ed. *Monet: Atti del convegno*. Conegliano: Linea d'ombra libri, 2002.

Reff 1964
Reff, Theodore. "Copyists in the Louvre, 1850-1870." *Art Bulletin* 46, no. 4 (Dec. 1964): 552–59.

Reff 1968
Reff, Theodore. "Some Unpublished Letters of Degas." *Art Bulletin* 50, no. 1 (Mar. 1968): 87–93.

Reff 1976
Reff, Theodore. *The Notebooks of Edgar Degas*. 2 vols. Oxford: Clarendon Press, 1976.

Régnier 1919
Régnier, Henri de. *L'Art moderne et quelques aspects de l'art d'autrefois: Cent-soixante-treize planches d'après la collection privée de MM. J. & G. Bernheim-Jeune*. 2 vols. Paris: Bernheim-Jeune, 1919.

Renoir and Pirra 1971
Renoir, Paul, and Stefano Pirra. *125 dessins inédits de Pierre-Auguste Renoir*. Turin: Arte pinacoteca, 1971.

Rewald 1939
Rewald, John. *Paul Cézanne: A Biography*. Trans. Margaret H. Liebman. New York: Simon and Schuster, 1939.

Rewald 1945
Rewald, John. "Auguste Renoir and His Brother." *Gazette des beaux-arts* 27 (Mar. 1945): 171–88.

Rewald 1949
Rewald, John. "Extraits du Journal inédit de Paul Signac." *Gazette des beaux-arts* 36 (1949): 97–128.

Rewald 1951
Rewald, John. *Carnets de dessins: Cézanne*. Paris: Quatre Chemins Éditart, 1951.

Rewald 1973
Rewald, John. *The History of Impressionism*. New York: Museum of Modern Art, 1973.

Riehen/Basel 2002
Fondation Beyeler. *Claude Monet—Up to Digital Impressionism*. Exh. cat. Munich and New York: Prestel, 2002.

Roger-Marx 1951
Roger-Marx, Claude. *Les Lithographies de Renoir*. Monte-Carlo: André Sauret, 1951.

Rouen 1994
Musée des Beaux-Arts. *Rouen, les Cathédrales de Monet*. Exh. cat. Rouen: Ville de Rouen; Paris: Réunion des musées nationaux, 1994.

San Francisco 1986
Moffett, Charles S. *The New Painting: Impressionism, 1874–1886*. Exh. cat. Geneva: R. Burton, in association with the Fine Arts Museums of San Francisco, 1986.

San Francisco 2006
Brettell, Richard, David Steel, and Lynn Federle Orr. *Monet in Normandy*. Exh. cat. New York: Rizzoli International Publications, 2006.

Schulman 1995
Schulman, Michel. *Frédéric Bazille, 1841–1870, Catalogue raisonné: Peintures, dessins, pastels, aquarelles; sa vie, son oeuvre, sa correspondence*. Paris: Éditions de l'amateur, 1995.

Scribner's 1896
"Claude Monet." *Scribner's Magazine* 19, no. 1 (Jan. 1896): 125.

Secretaire de la Redaction 1879
Le Secretaire de la Redaction. "Notre Exposition: Les dessins de La Vie moderne.—Première série." *La vie moderne* 1, no. 15 (17 July 1879): 239.

Seitz 1960
Seitz, William Chapin. *Claude Monet*. New York: Abrams, 1960.

Senici 2005
Senici, Emanuele. *Landscape and Gender in Italian Opera: The Alpine Virgin from Bellini to Puccini*. Cambridge: Cambridge University Press, 2005.

Sensier 1881
Sensier, Alfred. *Jean-François Millet: Peasant and Painter*. Trans. Helena De Kay. London: Macmillan, 1881.

Shapiro and Griffiths 1986
Shapiro, Barbara Stern, and Antony Griffiths. "Manet as Printmaker." *Print Quarterly* 3, no. 2 (1986): 147–48.

Sieberling 1988
Sieberling, Grace. *Monet in London*. Seattle and London: University of Washington Press, 1988.

Sotheby's 1993
Sotheby's, London. *Impressionist Paintings, Drawings and Sculpture from the Collection of Marie-Louise Durand-Ruel*. Auction catalogue. London: Sotheby's, 22 June 1993.

Soullié 1900
Soullié, Louis. *Peintures, pastels, aquarelles, dessins de Constant Troyon relevés dans les catalogues de ventes de 1833 à 1900*. Paris: L. Soullié, 1900.

Spate 1992a
Spate, Virginia. *Claude Monet: Life and Work*. New York: Rizzoli, 1992.

Spate 1992b
Spate, Virginia. *The Colour of Time: Claude Monet*. London: Thames and Hudson, 1992.

Stratis 1998
Stratis, Harriet K., ed. *The Lithographs of James McNeill Whistler*. Chicago: Art Institute of Chicago in association with the Arie and Ida Crown Memorial, 1998.

Stuckey 1985
Stuckey, Charles F., ed. *Monet: A Retrospective*. New York: Hugh Lauter Levin Associates, Inc., 1985.

Swann 2000
Swann Galleries. *Works of Art on Paper*. Auction catalogue. New York: Swann Galleries, 11 May 2000.

Tabarant 1921
Tabarant, Adolphe. "Les peintres à la campagne." *Bulletin de la Vie* 2 (1 Sept. 1921): 460–64.

Thénot 1856
Thénot, Jean Pierre. *Le Pastel mis a la portée de toutes les intelligences*. Paris: Alphonse Giraux and Co., 1856.

Tucker 1982
Tucker, Paul Hayes. *Monet at Argenteuil*. New Haven and London: Yale University Press, 1982.

Tucker 1995
Tucker, Paul Hayes. *Claude Monet: Life and Art*. New Haven and London: Yale University Press, 1995.

Valéry 1989
Valéry, Paul. *Degas, Manet, Morisot*. Trans. David Paul. Princeton, N.J.: Princeton University Press, 1989.

Van Gogh 1958
Gogh, Vincent van. *The Complete Letters of Vincent Van Gogh*. 3 vols. London: Thames and Hudson, 1958.

Venturi 1936
Venturi, Lionello. *Cézanne: Son art, son oeuvre*. 2 vols. Paris: P. Rosenberg, 1936.

Venturi 1939
Venturi, Lionello. *Les Archives de l'impressionisme*. 2 vols. Paris and New York: Durand-Ruel, 1939.

Vollard 1938
Vollard, Ambroise. *En écoutant Cézanne, Degas, Renoir*. Paris, 1938.

Wadley 1991
Wadley, Nicholas. *Impressionist and Post-Impressionist Drawing*. London: Laurence King, 1991.

Walter 1976
Walter, Rodolphe. "Claude Monet as a Caricaturist: A Clandestine Apprenticeship." Trans. Eric Young. *Apollo* 103, no. 172 (June 1976): 488–93.

Ward 1991
Ward, Martha. "Impressionist Installations and Private Exhibitions." *Art Bulletin* 73, no. 4 (Dec. 1991): 599–622.

Washington 1987
Stuckey, Charles, and William Scott. *Berthe Morisot: Impressionist*. Exh. cat. New York: Hudson Hills, 1987.

Washington 1998
Wilson-Bareau, Juliet. *Manet, Monet, and the Gare Saint-Lazare*. Exh. cat. Washington, D.C.: National Gallery of Art; New Haven and London: Yale University Press, 1998.

Welton 1992
Welton, Jude. *Eyewitness Guides: Monet*. London: Dorling Kindersley, 1992.

Wharton 1916
Wharton, Edith. *The Book of the Homeless*. New York: Scribner's, 1916.

Wildenstein 1959
Wildenstein, Georges. "Un carnet de dessins de Sisley au Musée du Louvre." *Gazette des beaux-arts* 53, no. 1 (Jan. 1959): 57–60.

Wildenstein 1974–91
Wildenstein, Daniel. *Claude Monet: Biographie et catalogue raisonné*. 5 vols. [Vol. 1: *1840–81, peintures*. Vol. 2: *1882–86, peintures*. Vol. 3: *1887–98, peintures*. Vol. 4.: *1899–1926, peintures*. Vol. 5: *Supplément aux peintures, dessins, pastels, index*.] Lausanne and Paris: La Bibliothèque des arts, 1974–91.

Wildenstein 1996
Wildenstein, Daniel. *Monet, or, The Triumph of Impressionism*. 4 vols. [Rev. ed. of *Claude Monet: Biographie et catalogue raisonné*, in English, French, and German. Vol. 1: *Triumph of Impressionism*. Vol. 2: *Catalogue raisonné, nos. 1–968*. Vol. 3: *Catalogue raisonné, nos. 969–1595*. Vol. 4: *Catalogue raisonné, nos. 1596–983*.] Cologne: Taschen, 1996.

Williamstown 1976
Cunningham, Charles Crehore. *Jongkind and the Pre-Impressionists: Painters of the École Saint-Siméon*. Exh. cat. Williamstown, Mass.: Sterling and Francine Clark Art Institute, 1976.

Williamstown 1999
Murphy, Alexandra R., et al. *Jean-François Millet: Drawn into the Light*. Exh. cat. New Haven and London: Yale University Press, 1999.

Williamstown 2000
Brettell, Richard R. *Impression: Painting Quickly in France, 1860–1890*. Exh. cat. New Haven: Yale University Press in association with the Sterling and Francine Clark Art Institute, 2000.

Williamstown 2003
Benjamin, Roger. *Renoir and Algeria*. Exh. cat. New Haven and London: Yale University Press in association with the Sterling and Francine Clark Art Institute, 2003.

Wintherthur 1974
Kunstmuseum Wintherthur. *Charles Gleyre ou les illusions perdues*. Exh. cat. Zurich: Schweizerisches Institut für Kunstwissenschaft, 1974.

Yeide 1998
Yeide, Nancy. "Hector Brame: An Art Dealer in Nineteenth-Century Paris." *Apollo* 147, no. 433 (Mar. 1998): 40–47.

Exhibition Checklist

All works are by Claude Monet unless otherwise indicated.

DRAWINGS

The Old "Le Pollet" Quarter of Dieppe, 1856–57
Graphite and watercolor on scratch-board, 134 x 219 mm
Museum of Fine Arts, Boston. Gift of Elizabeth K. Davis
Fig. 10 | D406

Alley of Trees, Gournay, 1857
Pencil, 307 x 228 mm
The World Children's Art Museum, Okazaki, Japan
Fig. 14 | D84

Bather Wearing a Hat, 1857
Pencil on buff paper, 309 x 230 mm
Private collection
Fig. 21 | D63
Williamstown only

Cliff at Sainte-Adresse, 1857
Pencil and white chalk on gray paper, 228 x 307 mm
The World Children's Art Museum, Okazaki, Japan
Fig. 16 | D96

Tree Trunks at La Mare au Clerc, 1857
Pencil, approx. 310 x 220 mm
Musée Eugène Boudin, Honfleur
Fig. 15 | D90

Water Mill on the Lézarde at Épouville, 1857
Pencil on warm gray paper, 228 x 307 mm
The World Children's Art Museum, Okazaki, Japan
Fig. 13 | D83

Dandy with a Cigar, c. 1857
Pencil heightened with gouache on gray paper, 240 x 160 mm
Musée Marmottan Monet, Paris
Fig. 27 | D457
Williamstown only

The Painter with a Pointed Hat, c. 1857
Watercolor and pencil with white gouache on beige paper, 312 x 242 mm
Private collection
Fig. 28 | D466

Young Man with a Monocle, c. 1857
Pencil heightened with gouache on beige paper, 240 x 160 mm
Musée Marmottan Monet, Paris
Fig. 26 | D451
Williamstown only

Caricature of Adolphe-Victor Coësme, 1858
Charcoal heightened with white chalk on blue laid paper (discolored to gray), 620 x 390 mm
Private collection
Fig. 39 | D478

AFTER NADAR (FÉLIX TOURNACHON)
Caricature of Adolphe Dennery, c. 1858
Black crayon, 320 x 240 mm
Musée Marmottan Monet, Paris
Fig. 30 | D503
Williamstown only

Caricature of Félix (Alexandre Ursule Cellérier), c. 1858
Pencil, 310 x 237 mm
Musée Marmottan Monet, Paris
Fig. 33 | D513
Williamstown only

Caricature of Grandfather Lebas, c. 1858–59
Pencil, 241 x 146 mm
Private collection
Fig. 38 | D493

Caricature of Henri Cassinelli ("Rufus Croutinelli"), c. 1858
Graphite on tan wove paper, laid down on commercially prepared tan wove card, 130 x 84 mm
The Art Institute of Chicago. Mr. and Mrs. Carter H. Harrison Collection
Fig. 36 | D495

Caricature of Jules Didier, "Butterfly Man," c. 1858
Charcoal heightened with white chalk on blue laid paper (discolored to gray), 616 x 436 mm
The Art Institute of Chicago. Mr. and Mrs. Carter H. Harrison Collection
Fig. 45 | D515

Caricature of Léon Manchon, c. 1858
Charcoal with stumping heightened with white chalk on blue laid paper (discolored to gray), 612 x 452 mm
The Art Institute of Chicago. Mr. and Mrs. Carter H. Harrison Collection
Fig. 41 | D481

Caricature of a Man with a Snuff Box, c. 1858
Charcoal heightened with white chalk on blue laid paper (discolored to gray), 588 x 330 mm
Sterling and Francine Clark Art Institute, Williamstown, Massachusetts
Fig. 40 | D488

AFTER ETIENNE CARJAT
Caricature of Mario Uchard, c. 1858
Graphite on tan wove paper, 320 x 243 mm
The Art Institute of Chicago. Mr. and Mrs. Carter H. Harrison Collection
Fig. 29 | D499

Caricature of Young Woman at the Piano, c. 1858
Black crayon heightened with white chalk, 320 x 240 mm
Musée Marmottan Monet, Paris
Fig. 37 | D472
Williamstown only

AFTER NADAR (FÉLIX TOURNACHON)
Caricature of Auguste Vacquerie, c. 1859
Graphite on tan wove paper, laid down on commercially prepared cream wove card, 283 x 175 mm
The Art Institute of Chicago. Mr. and Mrs. Carter H. Harrison Collection
Fig. 31 | D505

Little Theatrical Pantheon, c. 1859
Pencil heightened with gouache, 340 x 470 mm
Musée Marmottan Monet, Paris
Fig. 34 | D510
Williamstown only

Study of Cows, c. 1863
Black crayon, 240 x 470 mm
Collection of Faruk A. Alatan
Fig. 67 | D413

Boats on the Beach in Normandy [recto and verso], c. 1864
Black chalk on off-white laid paper, 135 x 305 mm
Private collection, courtesy of Elrick-Manley Fine Art, Inc.
Figs. 85 and 121 | D433

Cliffs and Sea, Sainte-Adresse, c. 1864
Black chalk on off-white laid paper, 206 x 314 mm
The Art Institute of Chicago. Clarence Buckingham Collection (1987.56)
Fig. 78 | D421

Coast of Lower Normandy, c. 1864
Black chalk on off-white laid paper, 180 x 300 mm
Private collection
Fig. 84 | D416

The Coast of Normandy Viewed from Sainte-Adresse, c. 1864
Black chalk on off-white laid paper, 175 x 308 mm
Fine Arts Museums of San Francisco. Memorial Gift from Dr. T. Edward and Tullah Hanley, Bradford, Pennsylvania
Fig. 77 | D419

Houses by the Sea, c. 1864
Black chalk on off-white laid paper, 246 x 334 mm
The Museum of Modern Art, New York. Gift of Mr. and Mrs. Marion Joseph Lebworth
Fig. 81 | D422

The Port at Touques, c. 1864
Black chalk on off-white laid paper, 210 x 330 mm
Sterling and Francine Clark Art Institute, Williamstown, Massachusetts
Fig. 83 | D415

Mouth of the Seine at Honfleur, 1865
Pen and ink, 245 x 360 mm
Private collection, courtesy of Brame and Lorenceau, Paris
Fig. 180 | D423

Figure of a Woman (Camille), c. 1865
Black chalk on off-white laid paper, 472 x 315 mm
Family of Richard S. Davis, courtesy of Stiebel, Ltd.
Fig. 90 | D424

The Luncheon on the Grass, c. 1865
Black chalk on blue-gray laid paper, 305 x 468 mm
National Gallery of Art, Washington, D.C. Collection of Mr. and Mrs. Paul Mellon
Fig. 88 | not in Wildenstein

The Two Anglers, 1883
Black crayon and scratchwork on Gillot paper, 256 x 344 mm
The Fogg Art Museum, Harvard University Art Museums, Cambridge. Bequest of Meta and Paul J. Sachs, 1965
Fig. 193 | D435

View of Rouen, 1883
Black crayon and scratchwork on Gillot paper, 313 x 475 mm
Sterling and Francine Clark Art Institute, Williamstown, Massachusetts
Fig. 189 | D434

Portrait of a Woman, c. 1890–95
Red chalks with stumping, 285 x 210 mm
Private collection
Fig. 1 | D447
Williamstown only

The Côte Sauvage, 1891
Black crayon, 234 x 315 mm
National Museum of Western Art, Tokyo
Fig. 198 | D443
London only

Grainstacks, 1891
Black crayon, 233 x 292 mm
National Museum of Western Art, Tokyo
Fig. 203 | D444
London only

Reflections of Willows, c. 1918
Black crayon on blue-gray paper, 300 x 470 mm
Musée Marmottan Monet, Paris
Fig. 266 | D450
Williamstown only

Water Lilies, c. 1918
Black crayon on blue-green paper, 315 x 475 mm
Musée Marmottan Monet, Paris
Fig. 269 | D448
Williamstown only

Water Lilies, c. 1918
Black crayon on blue-green paper, 315 x 475 mm
Musée Marmottan Monet, Paris
Fig. 270 | D449
Williamstown only

PASTELS

Yport and the Falaise d'Aval, c. 1861
Pastel, 185 x 395 mm
Private collection
Fig. 59 | P4

View of the Sea at Sunset, c. 1862–64
Pastel, 153 x 400 mm
Museum of Fine Arts, Boston. Bequest of William P. Blake in memory of his sister, Anne Dehon Blake
Fig. 111 | P34
Williamstown only

Study of Five Boys, c. 1864
Black chalk and pastel on buff paper, 140 x 250 mm
Museum Boijmans Van Beuningen, Rotterdam. Koenigs Collection
Fig. 108 | P2

Broad Landscape, c. 1864–66
Pastel, 174 x 359 mm
Museum of Fine Arts, Boston. Bequest of William P. Blake in memory of his sister, Anne Dehon Blake
Fig. 113 | P32
Williamstown only

Landscape with Houses, c. 1864–66
Pastel on beige paper, 219 x 425 mm
The Metropolitan Museum of Art. Bequest of Susan Dwight Bliss, 1966
Fig. 114 | P38

Study of Sailboats and Harbor, c. 1864–68
Pastel, 480 x 320 mm
Private collection
Fig. 105 | P25

The Seine Estuary, c. 1864–70
Pastel on paper laid down on canvas, 251 x 375 mm
Private collection
Fig. 116 | P63

Caloges and Boat at Étretat, c. 1865–70
Pastel, 207 x 405 mm
Israel Museum Collection, Jerusalem. Gift of Abraham M. Adler, New York, to America-Israel Cultural Foundation, 1971
Fig. 124 | P23
London only

Cat Sleeping on a Bed, c. 1865–70
Pastel, 110 x 210 mm
Private collection, courtesy of Jill Newhouse and Neffe de-Gandt Fine Art, London
Fig. 118 | P60

Nightfall, c. 1865–70
Pastel on gray paper, 212 x 379 mm
Musée des Beaux-Arts de Nantes. Gift of the Société des amis du Musée des Beaux-Arts de Nantes, 1968
Fig. 103 | P55

Sainte-Adresse, View across the Estuary, c. 1865–70
Pastel, 216 x 279 mm
Private collection
Fig. 119 | P12

Three Cows in a Pasture, c. 1865–70
Pastel, 320 x 250 mm
Private collection
Fig. 106 | P47

Twilight, c. 1865–70
Pastel on gray paper, 189 x 311 mm
Musée des Beaux-Arts de Nantes. Gift of the Société des amis du Musée des Beaux-Arts de Nantes, 1968
Fig. 104 | P56

Fruit Trees, c. 1865–75
Pastel, 225 x 292 mm
Private collection, courtesy of Galerie Jan Krugier & Cie., Geneva
Fig. 73 | P75

After the Rain, 1868
Pastel, 179 x 295 mm
Private collection
Fig. 102 | P48

Bank of the Seine, c. 1869
Pastel on tan paper, 245 x 425 mm
Private collection
Fig. 127 | not in Wildenstein
Williamstown only

Étretat, the Cap d'Antifer, c. 1885
Pastel, 270 x 346 mm
Private collection
Fig. 139 | P80

Étretat, the Manneporte at Low Tide, c. 1885
Pastel on beige paper, 230 x 330 mm
Private collection, London
Fig. 101 | P79
London only

Étretat, the Needle Rock and Porte d'Aval, c. 1885
Pastel on tan paper, 400 x 235 mm
Private collection
Fig. 138 | P78

The Road and the House, c. 1885
Pastel, 210 x 292 mm
Private collection
Fig. 131 | P42

Charing Cross Bridge, c. 1901
Pastel, 310 x 485 mm
Triton Foundation, The Netherlands
Fig. 251 | P84

Charing Cross Bridge, London, c. 1901
Pastel, 300 x 470 mm
Private collection
Fig. 252 | P83
Williamstown only

Waterloo Bridge, c. 1901
Pastel, 305 x 480 mm
Triton Foundation, The Netherlands
Fig. 258 | P101

Waterloo Bridge, Fog, c. 1901
Pastel, 270 x 420 mm
Private collection
Fig. 259 | P103

Waterloo Bridge, London, c. 1901
Pastel, 310 x 480 mm
Villa Flora, Winterthur, Switzerland
Fig. 257 | P109
London only

Waterloo Bridge, Boats on the Thames, 1902
Pastel on blue-gray paper, 310 x 480 mm
Private collection
Fig. 253 | P105

PAINTINGS

Farmyard in Normandy, 1863
Oil on canvas, 65 x 80 cm
Musée d'Orsay, Paris. Bequest of M. and Mme Raymond Koechlin, 1931
Fig. 66 | W16

Towing a Boat, Honfleur, 1864
Oil on canvas, 55.2 x 82.1 cm
Memorial Art Gallery of the University of Rochester. Gift of Marie C. and Joseph C. Wilson
Fig. 110 | W37

Rue de la Bavole, Honfleur, c. 1864
Oil on canvas, 55.9 x 61 cm
Museum of Fine Arts, Boston. Bequest of John T. Spaulding
Fig. 82 | W33

Grainstacks near Chailly at Sunrise, 1865
Oil on canvas, 30.2 x 60.3 cm
San Diego Museum of Art (Museum Purchase)
Fig. 115 | W55a
London only

Bazille and Camille (Study for "Luncheon on the Grass"), c. 1865
Oil on canvas, 93.5 x 69.5 cm
National Gallery of Art, Washington, D.C. Ailsa Mellon Bruce Collection
Fig. 89 | W61

Seascape: Storm, c. 1866–67
Oil on canvas, 48.7 x 64.7 cm
Sterling and Francine Clark Art Institute, Williamstown, Massachusetts
Fig. 75 | W86

View of Rouen, 1872
Oil on canvas, 54 x 73 cm
Private collection, courtesy of Pyms Gallery, London
Fig. 188 | W217

The Two Anglers, 1882
Oil on canvas, 38 x 52.5 cm
Private collection
Fig. 192 | W749
Williamstown only

The Cliff and the Porte d'Aval, Étretat, 1885
Oil on canvas, 65 x 92 cm
Bequest of Marie Dabek, Paris, to the State of Israel in Memory of Jack and Mimi Dabek. On permanent loan to The Israel Museum, Jerusalem, from the Administrator General of the State of Israel
Fig. 225 | W1019
London only

The Cliffs at Étretat, 1885
Oil on canvas, 64.9 x 81.1 cm
Sterling and Francine Clark Art Institute, Williamstown, Massachusetts
Fig. 134 | W1034

The Côte Sauvage, the Cliffs of Belle-Île, 1886
Oil on canvas, 65 x 81.5 cm
Musée d'Orsay, Paris. Bequest of Gustave Caillebotte, 1894
Fig. 197 | W1100
Williamstown only

Three Fishing Boats, 1886
Oil on canvas, 73 x 92.5 cm
Szépművészeti Múzeum, Budapest
Fig. 235 | W1029
London only

Rouen Cathedral, Façade, 1894
Oil on canvas, 106.3 x 73.7 cm
Sterling and Francine Clark Art Institute, Williamstown, Massachusetts. Acquired in memory of Anne Strang Baxter
Fig. 248 | W1358
Williamstown only

Charing Cross Bridge, c. 1900
Oil on canvas, 66 x 92.7 cm
Indianapolis Museum of Art. Gift of Several Friends of the Museum
Fig. 255 | W1530

Waterloo Bridge, Morning Fog, 1901
Oil on canvas, 65.7 x 100.2 cm
Philadelphia Museum of Art. Bequest of Anne Thomson in memory of her father, Frank Thomson, and her mother, Mary Elizabeth Clarke Thomson, 1954
Fig. 260 | W1559

Water Lilies, 1916–19
Oil on canvas, 200 x 180 cm
Fondation Beyeler, Riehen/Basel
Fig. 271 | W1854

Water Lilies, c. 1918
Oil on canvas, 130.2 x 200.7 cm
The Metropolitan Museum of Art, New York. Gift of Louise Reinhardt Smith, 1983
Fig. 265 | W1858

Lion Rock, Rocks at Belle-Île, 1886
Oil on canvas, 65.7 x 81.8 cm
Des Moines Art Center. Purchased with funds from the Coffin Fine Arts Trust; Nathan Emory Coffin Collection of the Des Moines Art Center
W1090
London only

PRINTS

Caricature of Louis Fortuné Adolphe Laferrière, 1860
Gillotage, 385 x 280 mm
Musée Carnavalet-Histoire de Paris
Fig. 48 | D511

A. BELLOGUET,
AFTER CLAUDE MONET
Mouth of the Seine at Honfleur, 1865
Gillotage, 165 x 280 mm. From *L'Autographe au Salon de 1865* 9 (24 June 1865), p. 76
Sterling and Francine Clark Art Institute, Williamstown, Massachusetts
Fig. 181

AFTER CLAUDE MONET
The Cabin at Sainte-Adresse, 1880
Gillotage, 145 x 191 mm. From *La vie moderne* 2 (19 June 1880), p. 400
W.E.B. Du Bois Library, University of Massachusetts Amherst
Fig. 185 | D436

AFTER CLAUDE MONET
View of Rouen, 1883
Gillotage, 135 x 205 mm. From *Gazette des beaux-arts* 27, no. 4 (1 Apr. 1883), p. 345
Sterling and Francine Clark Art Institute, Williamstown, Massachusetts
Fig. 190

AFTER CLAUDE MONET
The Two Anglers, 1883
Gillotage, 167 x 234 mm
The Fogg Art Museum, Harvard University Art Museums, Cambridge, Massachusetts. Drawing Department Fund for Special Acquisitions
Fig. 194

AFTER CLAUDE MONET
The Côte Sauvage, 1891
Gillotage, 249 x 309 mm. From *L'Art dans les deux mondes* 1 (7 Mar. 1891), p. 181
Sterling and Francine Clark Art Institute, Williamstown, Massachusetts
Fig. 199

AFTER CLAUDE MONET
The Côte Sauvage, 1893
Gillotage, 154 x 204 mm. From *The Studio* 1 (1893), p. 242
Sterling and Francine Clark Art Institute, Williamstown, Massachusetts
Fig. 200

WILLIAM THORNLEY,
AFTER CLAUDE MONET
Arrival of the Normandy Train, Gare Saint-Lazare, c. 1894
Transfer lithograph printed in warm gray on off-white chine appliqué, 212 x 260 mm
Bibliothèque de l'Institut National de l'Histoire de l'Art, Paris. Collections Jacques Doucet
Figs. 223 and A1
London only

WILLIAM THORNLEY,
AFTER CLAUDE MONET
The Beach and the Falaise d'Amont, Étretat, c. 1894
Transfer lithograph printed in reddish-orange on off-white chine appliqué, 210 x 194 mm
Collection of Dr. Morton and Tobia Mower
Williamstown only

WILLIAM THORNLEY,
AFTER CLAUDE MONET
Blanche Hoschedé Painting, c. 1894
Transfer lithograph printed in gray-black, green, and red on off-white chine appliqué, 160 x 200 mm
Bibliothèque de l'Institut National de l'Histoire de l'Art, Paris. Collections Jacques Doucet
Figs. 237 and A20
Williamstown only

WILLIAM THORNLEY,
AFTER CLAUDE MONET
The Cliff and the Porte d'Aval, Étretat, c. 1894
Transfer lithograph printed in greenish-gray on off-white chine appliqué, 187 x 260 mm
Bibliothèque de l'Institut National de l'Histoire de l'Art, Paris. Collections Jacques Doucet
Fig. A7
Williamstown only

WILLIAM THORNLEY,
AFTER CLAUDE MONET
The Cliff and the Porte d'Aval, Étretat, c. 1894
Transfer lithograph printed in greenish-gray on off-white chine appliqué, 187 x 260 mm
Collection of Dr. Morton and Tobia Mower
Fig. 226
London only

WILLIAM THORNLEY,
AFTER CLAUDE MONET
The Côte Sauvage, c. 1894
Transfer lithograph printed in black on olive-toned chine appliqué, 210 x 277 mm
Bibliothèque de l'Institut National de l'Histoire de l'Art, Paris. Collections Jacques Doucet
Figs. 202 and A11
Williamstown only

WILLIAM THORNLEY,
AFTER CLAUDE MONET
The Côte Sauvage c. 1894
Transfer lithograph printed in black on blue-toned chine appliqué, 210 x 277 mm
Collection of Dr. Morton and Tobia Mower
Fig. 201

WILLIAM THORNLEY,
AFTER CLAUDE MONET
The Creuse, Dark Weather, c. 1894
Transfer lithograph printed in greenish-gray on rose-toned chine appliqué, 204 x 257 mm
Bibliothèque de l'Institut National de l'Histoire de l'Art, Paris. Collections Jacques Doucet
Fig. A17
Williamstown only

WILLIAM THORNLEY,
AFTER CLAUDE MONET
The Creuse, Dark Weather, c. 1894
Transfer lithograph printed in dark blue on off-white chine appliqué, 204 x 257 mm
Collection of Dr. Morton and Tobia Mower
London only
Fig. 233

WILLIAM THORNLEY,
AFTER CLAUDE MONET
Fishing Boats at Étretat, c. 1895
Transfer lithograph printed in reddish-brown on grayish blue chine appliqué, 184 x 252 mm
Sterling and Francine Clark Art Institute, Williamstown, Massachusetts

WILLIAM THORNLEY,
AFTER CLAUDE MONET
Gorge of the Petite Cruese, c. 1894
Transfer lithograph printed in purplish-gray on olive-toned chine appliqué, 208 x 292 mm
Bibliothèque de l'Institut National de l'Histoire de l'Art, Paris. Collections Jacques Doucet
Fig. A18
London only

WILLIAM THORNLEY,
AFTER CLAUDE MONET
Gorge of the Petite Creuse, c. 1894
Transfer lithograph printed on blue-toned chine appliqué, 208 x 292 mm
Collection of Dr. Morton and Tobia Mower
Fig. 234

WILLIAM THORNLEY,
AFTER CLAUDE MONET
Grainstacks, Last Sunrays, c. 1894
Transfer lithograph printed in orange on off-white chine appliqué, 217 x 262 mm
Bibliothèque de l'Institut National de l'Histoire de l'Art, Paris. Collections Jacques Doucet
Fig. A19
Williamstown only

WILLIAM THORNLEY,
AFTER CLAUDE MONET
Grainstacks, Last Sunrays, c. 1894
Transfer lithograph with scraping printed in orange on off-white chine appliqué, 217 x 262 mm
Collection of Dr. Morton and Tobia Mower
Fig. 229
London only

WILLIAM THORNLEY,
AFTER CLAUDE MONET
Portrait of Poly, c. 1894
Transfer lithograph with scraping printed in dark gray on off-white chine appliqué, 223 x 164 mm
Collection of Dr. Morton and Tobia Mower
Fig. 232

WILLIAM THORNLEY,
AFTER CLAUDE MONET
Rocky Coast and the Lion Rock, Belle-Île, c. 1894
Transfer lithograph printed in warm gray on beige chine appliqué, 195 x 240 mm
Bibliothèque de l'Institut National de l'Histoire de l'Art, Paris. Collections Jacques Doucet
Figs. 227 and A10
London only

WILLIAM THORNLEY,
AFTER CLAUDE MONET
Rocky Coast and the Lion Rock, Belle-Île, c. 1894
Transfer lithograph printed in warm gray on off-white chine appliqué, 195 x 240 mm
Collection of Dr. Morton and Tobia Mower
Williamstown only

WILLIAM THORNLEY,
AFTER CLAUDE MONET
Three Fishing Boats, c. 1894
Transfer lithograph printed in blue gray (keystone), green, acidic yellow, and light pinkish beige on off-white chine appliqué, 210 x 265 mm
Bibliothèque de l'Institut National de l'Histoire de l'Art, Paris. Collections Jacques Doucet
Figs. 236 and A6
London only

WILLIAM THORNLEY,
AFTER CLAUDE MONET
View from the Cap d'Antibes, c. 1894
Transfer lithograph printed in bluish-gray on rose-toned chine appliqué, 145 x 178 mm
Bibliothèque de l'Institut National de l'Histoire de l'Art, Paris. Collections Jacques Doucet
Fig. A14
Williamstown only

WILLIAM THORNLEY,
AFTER CLAUDE MONET
View from the Cap d'Antibes, c. 1894
Transfer lithograph printed in green on off-white chine appliqué, 145 x 178 mm
Collection of Dr. Morton and Tobia Mower
London only

WILLIAM THORNLEY,
AFTER CLAUDE MONET
Woman with a Parasol, c. 1894
Transfer lithograph printed in dull blue on off-white chine appliqué, 274 x 196 mm
Bibliothèque de l'Institut National de l'Histoire de l'Art, Paris. Collections Jacques Doucet
Figs. 228 and A8
London only

NADAR (FÉLIX TOURNACHON)
Panthéon Nadar, 1854
Lithograph, 819 x 1,149 mm (sheet)
The Metropolitan Museum of Art, New York. A. Hyatt Mayor Purchase Fund, Marjorie Phelps Starr Bequest, 1993
Fig. 32

SKETCHBOOKS

Marmottan Sketchbook 1, c. 1865–1919
Sketchbook, cover: 263 x 352 mm; sheet: 255 x 340 mm
Musée Marmottan Monet, Paris
D105–39 (Marmottan inv. 5128)
Williamstown only

Marmottan Sketchbook 3, c. 1887–1900
Sketchbook, cover: 120 x 186 mm; sheet: 110 x 180 mm
Musée Marmottan Monet, Paris
D160–222 (Marmottan inv. 5134)
Williamstown only

Marmottan Sketchbook 4, c. 1881–85
Sketchbook, cover: 120 x 200 mm; sheet: 110 x 195 mm
Musée Marmottan Monet, Paris
D223–74 (Marmottan inv. 5131)
Williamstown only

Marmottan Sketchbook 6, c. 1886–1925
Sketchbook, cover: 242 x 322 mm; sheet: 234 x 315 mm
Musée Marmottan Monet, Paris
D334–80 (Marmottan inv. 5129)
Williamstown only

Index

Photography Credits

Permission to reproduce illustrations is provided by courtesy of the owners listed in the captions. The map on p. xii was adapted from John Murray, *A Handbook for Travellers in France: Alsace and Lorraine* (London: J. Murray, 1873). Additional photography credits are as follows:

Archives Charmet / The Bridgeman Art Library: fig. 195
Archives départementales des Yvelines, Montigny-le-Bretonneux, France: fig. 164
© Archives Durand-Ruel, Paris: fig. 238
Archives Wildenstein Institute, Paris: figs. 11–12, 19–20, 25, 35, 56, 186
© The Art Institute of Chicago: figs. 29, 31, 36, 41, 45, 78, 146, 273 (photo by Michael Tropea)
Artothek: fig. 123 (photo by Ursula Edelmann)
Courtesy of Dr. Xavier Beguin Billecocq: figs. 3–6, 17, 18
Service Photographique, Bibliothèque de l'INHA: figs. 202, 222–25, 227–28, 234, 236–37, A0–A20
Bibliothèque nationale de France, Paris: figs. 49, 92
The Bridgeman Art Library: figs. 2, 112
CamerArts, Inc., New York: fig. 1
Courtesy of Christie's Images, Inc.: figs. 67, 95
© 2006 The Detroit Institute of Arts: fig. 54
Courtesy of Elrick-Manley Fine Art, Inc.: figs. 85, 121
Courtesy of Richard L. Feigen & Co., New York: fig. 252
© 2006 Fine Arts Museums of San Francisco: figs. 43, 77
Brad Flowers: fig. 131
Paul Foster: fig. 105
Courtesy of Galerie Brame & Lorenceau, Paris: fig. 180
Courtesy of Galerie Jan Krugier & Cie., Geneva: fig. 73
Giraudon, Paris / The Bridgeman Art Library: figs. 26–27, 30, 33–34, 37, 46–47, 57, 61, 63, 87, 94, 107, 125–26, 129, 132–33, 135, 140–45, 147–58, 161–63, 165–75, 177–78, 184, 205, 242–44, 246–47, 249, 250, 263–64, 266–70, 272, 275–76
© President and Fellows of Harvard College (Harvard University Art Museums Photographic Services): figs. 193–94
Luiz Hossaka: fig. 58
Courtesy of Iris and B. Gerald Cantor Center for Visual Arts, Stanford University: fig. 127
© The Israel Museum, Jerusalem: fig. 124 (photo by David Harris)
Courtesy of Lefevre Fine Art Ltd., London: fig. 138
© Mairie de Bordeaux: figs. 218 (photo by B. Fontanel); 239 (photo by Lysiane Gauthier)
Marunuma Art Park, Tokyo: fig. 52
© The Metropolitan Museum of Art, New York: figs. 32, 76, 114, 137, 265
Musée Eugène Boudin, Honfleur: figs. 15, 23
Musée Fabre, Montpellier: fig. 65 (photo Frédéric Jaulmes)
© Photothèque des musées de la ville de Paris: fig. 48 (photo by Briant Remi)
© Musées de la Ville de Rouen: fig. 42 (photo by Catherine Lancien and Carole Loisel)
© 2006 Museum Associates / Los Angeles County Museum of Art: fig. 86
© 2007 Museum of Fine Arts, Boston: figs. 10, 70, 82, 111, 113, 130, 159
© The Museum of Modern Art, New York / Licensced by SCALA / Art Resource, New York: fig. 81
© The National Gallery, London: fig. 176
© 2006 Board of Trustees, National Gallery of Art, Washington, D.C.: figs. 22, 88–89
The National Museum of Western Art, Tokyo: figs. 198, 203
Courtesy of Christian Neffe: fig. 139
The New York Public Library: fig. 44
© The Norton Simon Foundation: fig. 179
Courtesy of Martha Parrish: fig. 119
Stephen Petegorsky: fig. 128
Courtesy of Pyms Gallery, London: fig. 188
Réunion de Musées Nationaux / Art Resource, New York: figs. 62, 68, 93, 256 (photo by Gérard Blot); 53, 71, 100, 136 (photo by Michèle Bellot); 98 (photo by Bulloz); 74 (photo by Thiérry Le Mage); 55, 197 (photo by Hervé Lewandowski); 51 (photo by René-Gabriel Ojéda); 66, 69, 72, 109, 122
SCALA / Art Resource, New York: fig. 91
Courtesy of Sotheby's Picture Library, London: figs. 96, 206
© Sterling and Francine Clark Art Institute, Williamstown, Massachusetts: figs. 2, 7–9, 21, 50, 60, 64, 75, 79, 80, 83–84, 97, 117, 134, 181–82, 187, 189, 190, 196, 199–201, 204, 207–14, 217, 219–21, 226, 229–30, 232–33, 240–41, 248 (photo by Michael Agee)
Courtesy Stiebel, Ltd., London: fig. 90
© Szépmüvészeti Múzeum, Budapest: fig. 235
James Via: fig. 110
Courtesy of Villa Flora, Winterthur, Switzerland: fig. 257
© Ville de Nantes, Musée des Beaux-Arts: figs. 103–4 (photo by A. Guillard)
Roger Viollet, Paris / The Bridgeman Art Library: figs. 231, 274
Courtesy of Waddington Galleries, London: fig. 101
W. E. B. DuBois Library, University of Massachusetts, Amherst: fig. 185 (photo by Michael Agee)
Courtesy of Wildenstein & Co., Inc.: figs. 28, 38–40, 59, 102, 106, 116, 192, 253
Williams College, Sawyer Library, Williamstown, Massachusetts: figs. 191, 215–16 (photo by Michael Agee)
© Worcester Art Museum, Worcester, Massachusetts: fig. 99
© The World Children's Art Museum, Okazaki, Japan: figs. 13–14, 16

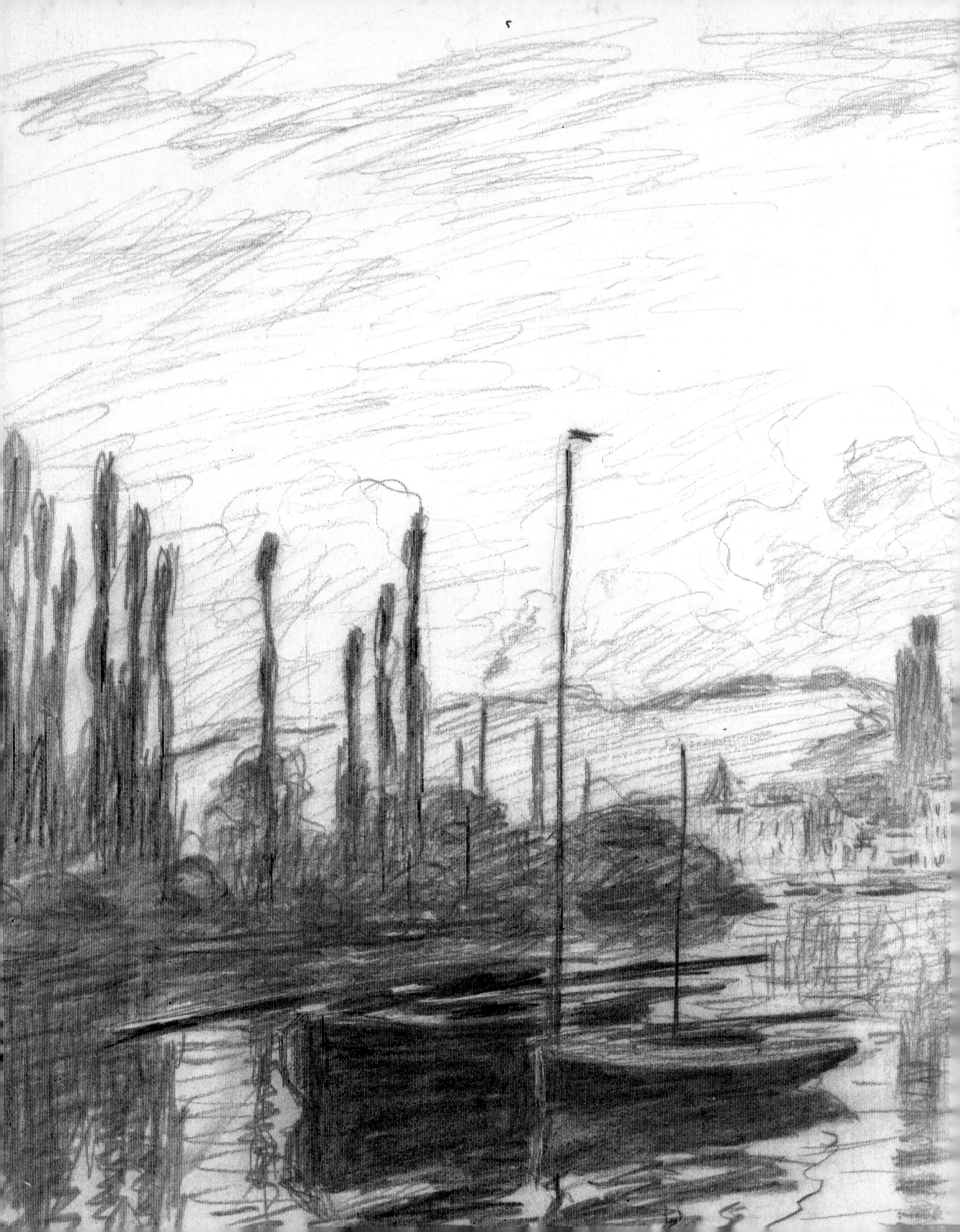

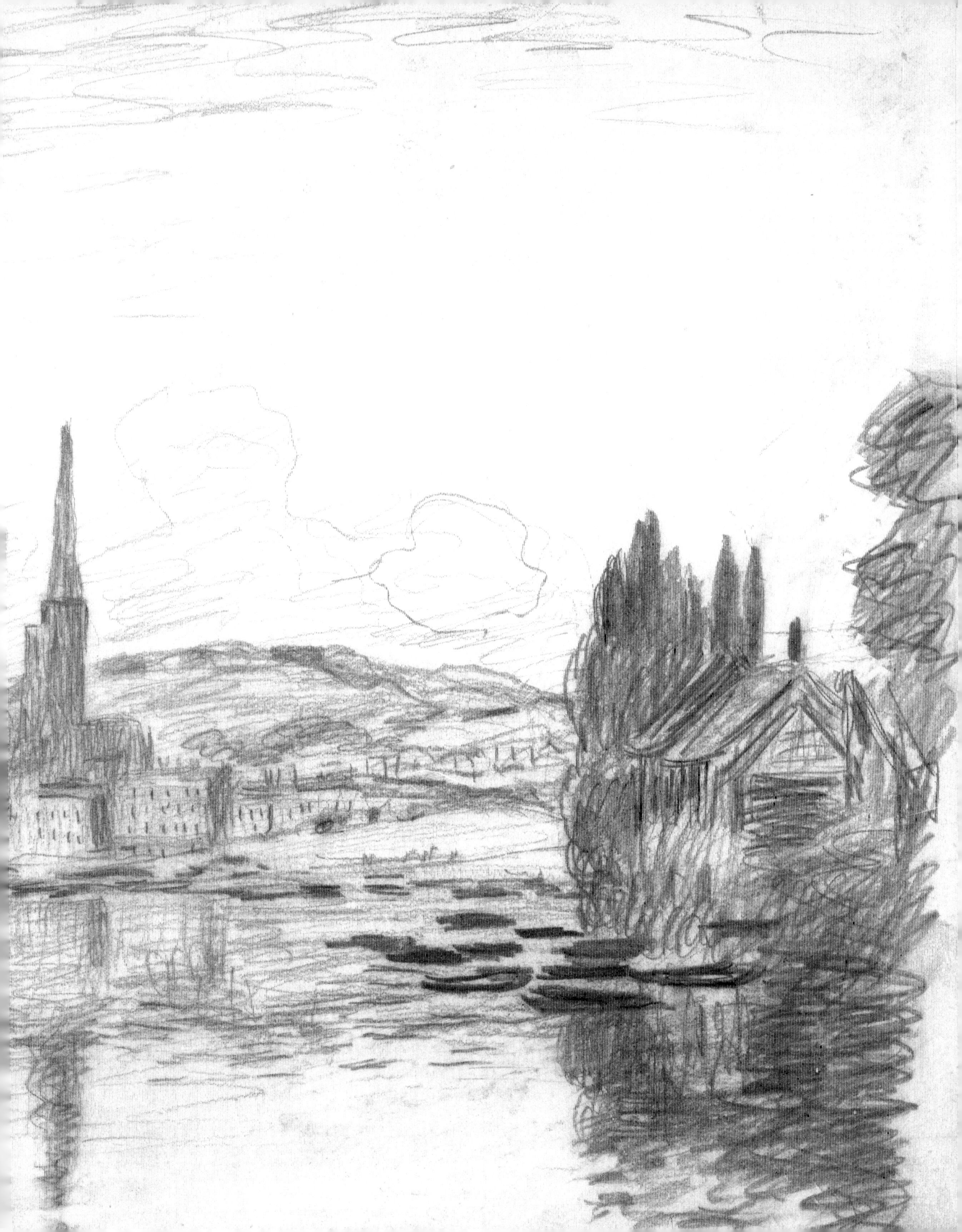